Oregon

COMMUNITY TREASURES

by William Faubion

a part of the Morgan & Chase Treasure Series
www.treasuresof.com

 MORGAN & CHASE PUBLISHING INC.

Published by:
Morgan & Chase Publishing, Inc.
531 Parsons Drive, Medford, Oregon 97501
(888) 557-9328
www.treasuresof.com

Printed by:
Taylor Specialty Books - Dallas TX

First edition 2006

ISBN: 1-933989-04-1

**THE
TREASURE
SERIES**

*I gratefully acknowledge the contributions
of the many people involved in the writing and production of this book.
Their tireless dedication to this endeavor has been inspirational.*
—Damon Neal, *Publisher*

Managing Editor:
David Smigelski

Senior Story Editor:
Mary Beth Lee

Senior Writer:
Gregory Scott

Proof Editors:
Avery Brown and Robyn Sutherland

Graphic Design:
C.S. Rowan, Jesse Gifford, Tamara Cornett, Jacob Kristof, Michael Frye

Photo Coordinators:
Wendy Gay and Donna Lindley

Website:
Casey Faubion, Molly Bermea, Ben Ford

Morgan & Chase Home Team
Cindy Tilley Faubion, Anita Fronek, Emily Wilkie, Cari Qualls, Anne Boydston,
Virginia Arias, Danielle Barkley, Shauna O'Callahan, Clarice Rodriguez, Terrie West

Contributing Writers:
Dusty Alexander, Jeff Clark, Amber Dusk, Larry George, Robert B. Goldberg,
Paul Hadella, Jenny Harris, Catherine Hartwell-Wire, Jan Maddron, Maggie McClellen,
Mickie McCormic, Chris McCrellis-Mitchell, Kevin Monk, Candy Schrodek, Susan Vaughn, Todd Wels

Special Recognition to:
Nancy McClain, Jolee Moody, Robert Mutch, Judy Stallcop, Mike Stallcop, Jennifer Strange, Kimberley Wallan

This book is dedicated to our pioneer families.
*They gave us life, helped shape our work ethic
and taught us how to be honest, productive members of the community.*

With special thanks to the loving memory of
*Mildred G. Tilley, George B. Tilley, A.J. Faubion, Jenny Faubion Welch,
Edith Worthington Carter, A.B. Carter and Eva Thornburgh.*

Thank you also to
*Ida P. Tilley, Shirley Faubion Saunders,
Ruth Carter and Everett Thornburgh.*

How to use this book

Oregon Community Treasures is divided into eight main sections covering The Oregon Coast, Portland Metro, Columbia Gorge/Mt. Hood, Willamette Valley, Umpqua Valley, Southern Oregon, Central Oregon and Eastern Oregon. The Coast is broken into three subsections detailing the north, central and south coast. The Portland Metropolitan area is broken into five geographic sections, including one for Vancouver, Washington.

As you page through each section, you'll note that the cities within each region are presented alphabetically. We've included a short description of each city, including a selected list of nearby parks, attractions and events.

In the index, cities and Treasures are listed alphabetically.

We have provided contact information for each Treasure in the book, because these are places and businesses we have personally visited, and which we encourage you to visit on your travels through Oregon.

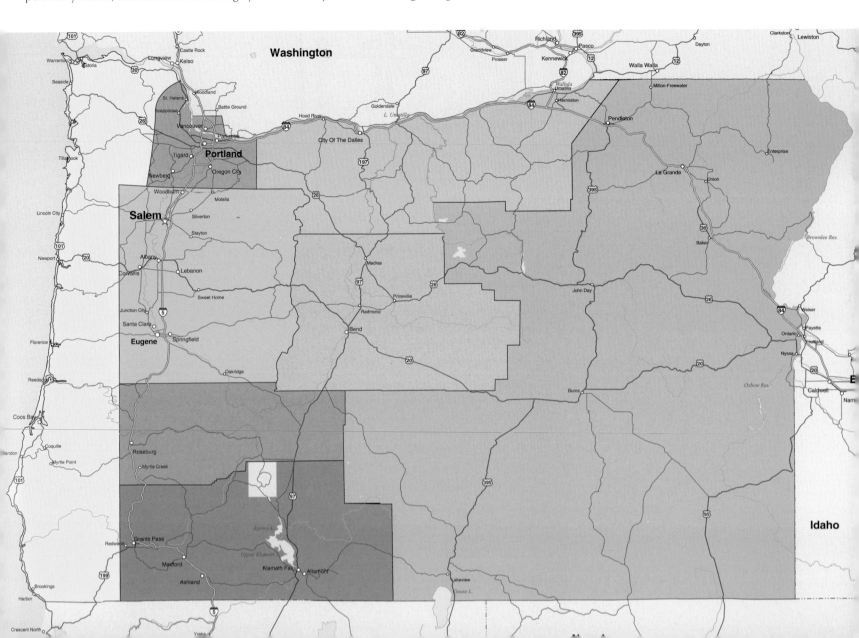

Free Treasure Dollars!

The businesses featured in *Oregon Community Treasures*, as well as those in all the Treasure Series books, can be found on **www.TreasuresOf.com**.

Look for those Treasures with **"Treasure Dollar Participant"** next to their name. These Treasures have chosen to offer something special in exchange for one of our Treasure Dollars. The offers may be substantial; anything from a free night's stay to a free meal or gift. Many offers are worth $100 or more, and you can cash in just by giving them a free coin.

To get your three FREE Treasure Dollars,
please send your name, address, and receipt for this book to:

Morgan & Chase Publishing
Treasure Dollar Division
PO Box 1148
Medford, OR 97501-0232

Happy travels from the staff at Morgan & Chase Publishing.

Forward

Welcome to *Oregon Community Treasures*. This book is intended as a resource that can guide you to some of the best places in the great state of Oregon.

Oregon is virtually unmatched in what it has to offer both residents and visitors. It is a state of great economic, cultural, historical, climatic and geographical diversity. It boasts Pacific Ocean beaches, towering volcanos, deserts, rain forests, lakes, rivers and hotsprings. It features more micro-climates than most countries.

Oregon is a state of immense agricultural importance. From oysters, salmon and crabs to flowers, fruit and wine grapes, Oregon is a literal cornucopia. It is internationally known as an incubator for progressive social and political thought. It is a global center for the arts. It is a sports and outdoors paradise.

Oregon is also home to some of the most energetic and independent people you'll ever meet.

From Astoria to Hells Canyon, from the ocean beaches to the high desert, we traveled every corner of Oregon while compiling this book. We spent time along the California border. We kayaked the Columbia River between Oregon and Washington. We ate and shopped and slept in Portland, Eugene, Pendleton and Bend. We thrifted in Sisters. We took wine tours in the Dundee Hills and Umpqua Valley. We marveled at the Native America petroglyphs in the Columbia River Gorge and visited the tribal museum on the Warm Springs Reservation. We saw glass blowers, potters and painters in action. We got our hair cut in Prineville, visited spas in Ashland, and talked to literally thousands of small-business people about their products, their services and their vision.

You are holding the result of our efforts in your hands. Oregon Community Treasures is a 600-page compilation of the best places in Oregon to eat, shop, play, explore, learn and relax. We did the legwork. All you have to do now is enjoy.

—David Smigelski

View of the Northern Coast with Haystack Rock in the distance

North Coast

PLACES TO GO

- Astoria Aquatic Center
  1997 Marine Drive
  (503) 325-7027

- Astoria Column Criegee Circle
  (503) 325-4530

- Columbia River Maritime Museum
  1792 Marine Drive
  (503) 325-2323

- Flavel House
  444 8th Street
  (503) 325-2203

- Fort Stevens State Park
  100 Peter Iredale Road, Hammond

- Fort Clatsop National Memorial
  Fort Clatsop Road

- Heritage Museum
  1618 Exchange Street
  (503) 325-2203

- Uppertown Firefighter's Museum
  Astoria Children's Museum
  2968 Marine Drive
  (503) 325-2203

THINGS TO DO

April
- Crab & Seafood Festival
  (800) 875-6807

June
- Scandinavia Midsummer Festival
  www.astoriascanfest.com

July
- FinnFest USA
  (888) 374-FINN (3466)

- Buoy 10 Brew Fest
  (800) 875-6807

August
- Clatsop County Fair
  (503) 325-4500

- Astoria Regatta
  (800) 875-6807

November
- Arts Night Out Gallery Walk
  (503) 325-0759

December
- Starving Artist Art Faire
  (503) 458-6250

ASTORIA

History lives in Astoria, the very first American settlement west of the Rocky Mountains. As a result, the town offers numerous attractions and activities. The Lewis and Clark Expedition spent the winter of 1805 to 1806 at Fort Clatsop, just southwest of modern Astoria. The town's true foundation, however, came in 1811, when John Jacob Astor's Pacific Fur Company established it as a trading post and named it after the company's owner. In later years, its economy centered on fishing, fish canning and lumber. Today, tourism, a growing art scene and light manufacturing are the main economic activities. Astoria is a regular port of call for cruise ships. Its fine old houses have also made it a popular spot to film movies.

Astoria Sealion Caves
Photo by Jolee Moody

Columbia River Maritime Museum

ATTRACTIONS:

Best exhibits of the Columbia

The Columbia River Maritime Museum offers a rich panorama of history, danger and bravery. Its exhibits record the constant vigilance demanded by life on the Columbia, one of the most consistently hazardous marine environments in the world. The museum's interpretation of a 44-foot Coast Guard lifeboat in the midst of a daring rescue is one of the best displays of its kind in the country. Another exhibit shows what it is like to live in Astoria during the height of salmon fishing. The museum's interactive exhibits are set against the backdrop of today's Columbia River, seen through the museum's picture windows. With six galleries, the great hall and the Lightship Columbia, the museum makes a wealth of historical and natural history materials available. All told, the museum has 30,000 objects, 15,000 photographs and a 7,000-volume research library. Executive Director Jerry Ostermiller has brought together a top-notch educational staff that works with more than 10,000 children every summer. The Columbia River Maritime Museum, the official maritime museum of the state of Oregon, celebrated its 40th anniversary with a $6 million remodeling and expansion in 2002.

1792 Marine Drive, Astoria OR
(503) 325-2323
www.crmm.org

Photo By Michael Mathers

Clatsop County Historical Society

Best source of local history

For more than 50 years, the Clatsop County Historical Society has taken great care to protect and exhibit fine examples of life a century ago. Clatsop County historians preserve and present the area's deep and varied history in three museums and a historic house. In the Heritage Museum, in a former city hall, you can see exhibits on natural history, early industries and ordinary life. One recent exhibit presented the Clatsops and other Native peoples. Another depicted the saloons and brothels once found in Astoria. The Uppertown Firefighter's Museum and the Children's Museum are located in an historic building that was once a brewery and later a firehouse. On the first floor, you can find hand-drawn, horse-drawn and motorized fire engines dating from 1879 to 1963 and many photos from that era. On the second floor, the hands-on Children's Museum offers activities for the whole family. Also, view the luxurious elegance of the George Flavel House, a Queen Anne-style residence built between 1884 and 1886. Here you can enjoy beautiful workmanship, stunning architecture and park-like gardens. The Clatsop County Historical Society holds several annual events to celebrate the rich history of this beautiful area. These include the Mother's Day Tea and Scones, the Historic Homes Tour, Old Timers' Talks and the Victorian Crafts Children's Festival. Be sure to stop by one of these events on your next trip to Astoria.

1618 Exchange Street, Astoria OR
(503) 325-2203 (Historical Society)
(503) 325-8395 (Heritage Museum)
2968 Marine Drive, Astoria OR
(503) 325-0920 (Firefighter's Museum)
(503) 325-8669 (Children's Museum)
441 8th Street, Astoria OR (George Flavel House)
www.clatsophistoricalsociety.org
www.ears.net/museum (Children's Museum)

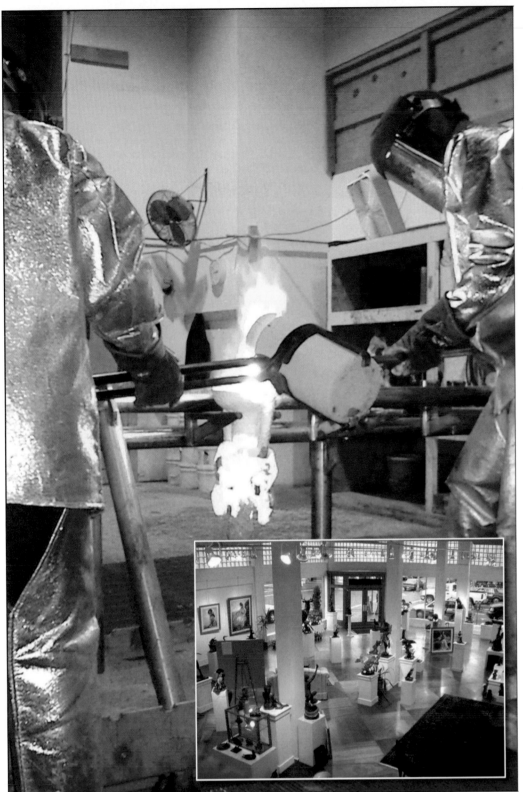

Valley Bronze of Oregon
GALLERIES: *Best metal artisans*

Excellence is the essence of Valley Bronze of Oregon. From its modest headquarters in Joseph in the heart of Northeast Oregon's isolated Wallowa Valley, Valley Bronze has established itself as one of the nation's best fine art and ornamental foundries and specialized metal fabrication services. The 24-year-old company achieved wide acclaim and recognition for its high-quality work and performance on projects such as the National World War II Memorial in Washington, D.C., for which it received a Star Award for excellence in 2005, and for casting and fabricating bas relief bronze cathedral doors for Our Lady of the Lourdes in Spokane. Highly visible monuments, such as the longhorn bulls that adorn Houston's Reliant Stadium, the Freedom Horses that grace the George Bush presidential library and remnants of the Berlin Wall in Germany were all cast, assembled and installed by Valley Bronze artisans. In 2006, the foundry created and installed bronze frames and metal and protective glass display cases for the original Declaration of Independence, Bill of Rights, and Constitution in the National Archives Building. The foundry works in all metals, including stainless and silver. They accept a full range of casting projects, including small editions, monuments, ornamental metal, and investment cast parts for antique airplane and marine hardware. The company expanded its ornamental metal fabrication services following its work on the cathedral doors and the National World War II Memorial, and has increased its capacity for specialized metal fabrication. For fine art enthusiasts, Valley Bronze's elegant showrooms located in Joseph and Astoria feature sculptures by a variety of artists, many of whose works are cast at the foundry, and paintings and prints by nationally and internationally known artists.

(Astoria Gallery)
1198 Commercial Street, Astoria OR
(503) 325-3076 or (800) 559-2118
(Joseph Gallery)
18 S Main Street, Joseph OR
(541) 432-7445
(Foundry)
307 W Alder Street, Joseph OR
(541) 432-7551
www.valleybronze.com

Josephson's Smokehouse

MARKETS: *Best seafood market*

Linda and Mike Josephson and their specialty seafood market embody a four-generation tradition of perseverance, dedication and honesty. From the beginning in 1920, the fish have been free of preservatives, dyes and additives. Josephson's Smokehouse uses only top grade seafood, natural ingredients and natural Alderwood. The smokehouse works with some of the top chefs in the United States to develop the very best cured, marinated, and smoked seafood products. Some of the most popular selections are wine maple-smoked salmon, smoked halibut and salmon jerky. Cold-smoked Chinook Salmon can be ordered in the traditional or lox styles. Josephson's has been featured in an endless series of articles in such publications as *Esquire, Woman's Day, House Beautiful* and *The New York Times*, as well as on national radio shows. The Josephson family combines time-honored techniques with the best of modern processing methods. To achieve the consistent quality and fine flavor that is the hallmark of Josephson's products, the fish are prepared daily in small batches. Josephson's ships worldwide and you can order their items through their website or toll-free phone number. When you visit this historic smokehouse to pick up some excellent seafood, you can also learn all about the traditional smoking processes while you sample the tasty products.

106 Marine Drive, Astoria OR
(503) 323-2190 or (800) 772-3474
www.josephsons.com

Astoria-Megler Bridge Over The Columbia River

Silver Salmon Grille

 *Best seafood dinners*

The Silver Salmon Grille specializes in fresh Northwest cuisine and also offers more than 190 wine selections, many of which are regional. *Wine Spectator* magazine has recognized the Silver Salmon for its exceptional wine list. The dining room, decorated with colorful salmon murals and rich wood accents, is warm and inviting. Owners Laurie and Jeff Martin have reinvented this 80-year-old Astoria restaurant as an attraction for local folks and visitors alike. Everything is impressive here, from the 120-year-old Scottish cherry wood bar in the saloon to the fabulous cuisine. As you would expect, salmon takes center stage here. Silver Salmon Supreme, stuffed with crab, shrimp, fresh herbs and smoked Gouda cheese; Herb Parmesan-Encrusted Salmon; and the moist House Smoked Salmon fillet are just a few of the options. You can also try the tropical prawn salad, pan-fried Pacific oysters, or choose among the many local seafood specialties. Vegetarian meals are available, as well as an excellent array of steaks, desserts, appetizers and beverages. The restaurant has banquet rooms and a catering service. For an artistic dining experience that is sure to please everyone's tastes, try the Silver Salmon Grille.

1105 Commercial Street, Astoria OR
(503) 338-6640
www.silversalmongrille.com

T. Paul's Urban Café

 *Most eclectic eatery*

Located on the North Coast in the heart of Astoria, T. Paul's Urban Café has been a hit with locals and visitors since it opened in February of 2000. The restaurant has been an important part of the revitalization of Astoria's downtown. Co-owners Teona Dawson and her uncle Paul Flues have created a hip, easygoing atmosphere that draws people from all over Oregon and Washington. The back room is a relaxing area with saltwater fish tanks that will enchant both you and the kids. The menu is eclectic and includes fresh seafood, pasta and vegetarian dishes. Try the Caribbean jerk quesadilla or the towering turkey sandwich. The taco salad has been called the best anywhere. Fridays and Saturdays are for meat-lovers, with prime rib, lamb and thick pork ribs. T. Paul's also features regional wines and microbrews served with soft live music. As the restaurant's motto says, eat well, laugh often, and love much at T. Paul's Urban Café.

1119 Commercial Street, Astoria OR
(503) 338-5133

CANNON BEACH

Nine miles of wide, walkable beach await visitors to Cannon Beach. The scenic beauty of the sea stacks offshore and headlands onshore make your stroll on the sand particularly delightful. The city is planned for strolling, and many visitors take advantage of this to visit bookstores, shops and bistros. In 1846, the U.S. Navy schooner *Shark* sank off the coast, and a large piece of deck with a cannon attached washed up on the beach, giving the town its name. Haystack Rock, at 235 feet high, is one of the largest coastal monoliths in the world. The tide pools around the rock contain starfish, crabs, anemones and many other creatures. Several bird species nest on the rock, such as the colorful Tufted Puffin. The sound of the shorebirds at sunset is an experience you will remember.

PLACES TO GO

- Arcadia Beach State Recreational Site
  U.S. Highway 101

- Ecola State Park
  Ecola Park Road

- Hug Point State Recreational Site
  U.S. Highway 101

- Oswald West State Park
  U.S. Highway 101

- *Tolovana Beach State Recreational Site*
  U.S. Highway 101

THINGS TO DO

April
- Earth, Wind & Sea Kite Festival
  (800) 547-6100

June
- Sand Castle Day
  (503)436-2623 ext. 3

November
- Stormy Weather Arts Festival
  (503) 436-2623 ext. 3

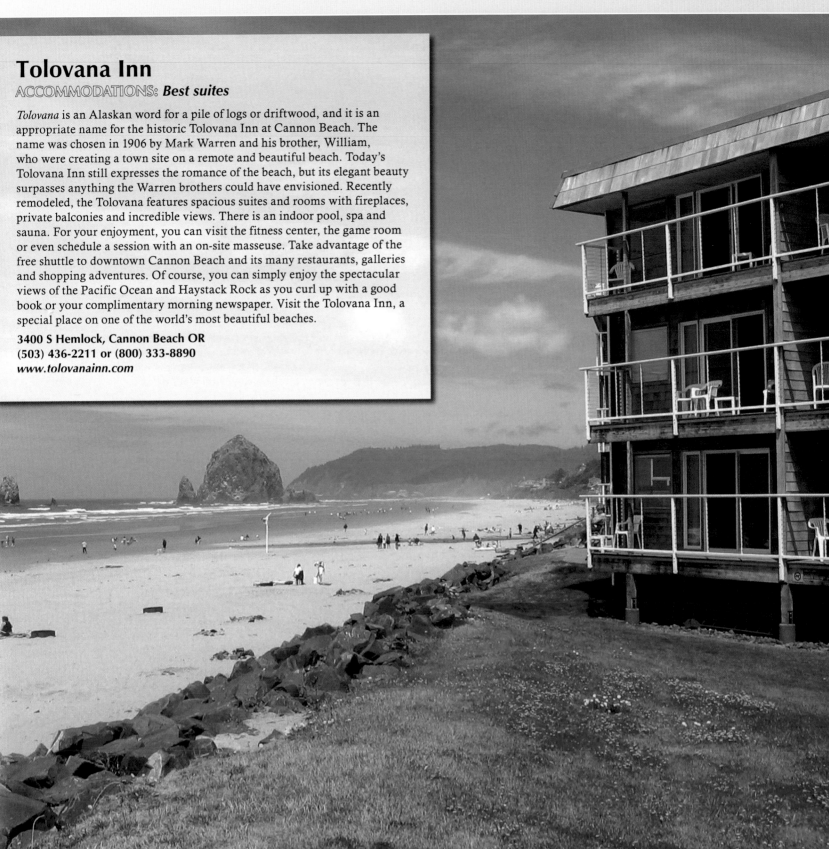

Tolovana Inn

ACCOMMODATIONS: *Best suites*

Tolovana is an Alaskan word for a pile of logs or driftwood, and it is an appropriate name for the historic Tolovana Inn at Cannon Beach. The name was chosen in 1906 by Mark Warren and his brother, William, who were creating a town site on a remote and beautiful beach. Today's Tolovana Inn still expresses the romance of the beach, but its elegant beauty surpasses anything the Warren brothers could have envisioned. Recently remodeled, the Tolovana features spacious suites and rooms with fireplaces, private balconies and incredible views. There is an indoor pool, spa and sauna. For your enjoyment, you can visit the fitness center, the game room or even schedule a session with an on-site masseuse. Take advantage of the free shuttle to downtown Cannon Beach and its many restaurants, galleries and shopping adventures. Of course, you can simply enjoy the spectacular views of the Pacific Ocean and Haystack Rock as you curl up with a good book or your complimentary morning newspaper. Visit the Tolovana Inn, a special place on one of the world's most beautiful beaches.

3400 S Hemlock, Cannon Beach OR
(503) 436-2211 or (800) 333-8890
www.tolovanainn.com

The Jeffrey Hull Gallery
GALLERIES: *Showcase of NW watercolorist*

The Jeffrey Hull Gallery, located on Sandpiper Square in the heart of downtown Cannon Beach, features the work of Jeffrey Hull. Jeffrey began painting more than 30 years ago. Though primarily self-taught, he studied under three Northwest watercolorists. Jeffrey is known for his ability to capture the beauty and moods of the places where water joins land. He controls the difficult medium of watercolor, often in very large paintings. Recently after many years of working exclusively in watercolor, Jeff returned to painting in oil, as well. He is rarely found far from the ocean's edge, the source of his inspiration. His deep love for the area is clearly seen in his original paintings and prints. At the gallery, which opened in 1987, you can see Jeffrey's representational work in watercolors, oils and giclée and lithograph prints. Jeffrey's paintings inspire a peaceful, relaxed mood. His work will remind you of the Pacific Northwest's gorgeous coastline for years to come. Take home a piece of art, and a piece of the Oregon Coast, when you visit the Jeffrey Hull Gallery.

172 N Hemlock Street, Cannon Beach OR
(503) 436-2600 or (888) 436-2606
www.hullgallery.com

Geppetto's Toy Shoppe
SHOPPING: *Best toy shoppe*

Geppetto's Toy Shoppe is an invitation for all ages to play. Visitors to Geppetto's discover puzzles and games, toy cars and trains, puppets and dolls, blocks and educational toys. For adventures on the beach, Geppetto's carries sand castle molds, sand pails, outdoor adventure kits, magnifying glasses and bubble blowing accessories. German clocks made in the Black Forest and fascinating cuckoo clocks will entertain everyone. Coastal Cannon Beach is famous for its annual sand castle contest, which brings people of all ages from miles around to create artwork in the sand. Children are more than welcom. Some help the artists or simply watch them work. Make this adventure a part of your summer plans, and join in the fun with castle-building supplies and toys from Geppetto's Toy Shoppe. Cheryl Johnson owns and manages the hands-on store, and her husband and four children will be there to assist you.

200 N Hemlock, Cannon Beach OR
(503) 436-2467

SEASIDE

Three miles of powder-soft beach and two miles of manicured, ocean front boardwalk make Seaside a popular tourist town. Downtown streets are lined with greenery and flowers. The Seaside Civic and Convention Center hosts a spectrum of events, conferences and functions in one of the finest facilities on the West Coast. The Lewis and Clark Expedition reached the Pacific Ocean at this spot. Ben Holladay, a pioneer Oregon railroad builder, founded Seaside as a summer resort in the early 1870s when he constructed the Seaside House, a luxury hotel for which the city was named.

PLACES TO GO

- Delray Beach State Recreational Area
  U.S. Highway 101,

- The Salt Works
  Lewis and Clark Way and S Promenade

- Seaside Historical Society Museum
  570 Necanicum Drive (503) 738-7065

- Sunset Beach State Recreational Area
  Sunset Beach Road, Sunset Beach

THINGS TO DO

July
- BikeFest
  Seaside Convention Center
  (503) 738-6614

Camp 18

ATTRACTIONS: *Best logging exhibits*

Gordon Smith's dream of building the biggest log cabin anyone had ever seen became a reality with Camp 18, home of the Old Time Logging Museum, Restaurant and Gift Shop. Gordon began construction in the early 1970s. The late Maurie Clark was the riggin' boss because of his knowledge of the timber industry. Together they located and restored pieces of old logging equipment. All of the timber used in the building came from the local area and Gordon logged it himself. It was hauled in, hand-peeled and draw-knifed with the help of his family and friends. The massive structure has a 25-ton, 85-foot ridgepole surrounded by cedar and fir beams, and two 500-pound, handcarved fir front doors. The two fireplaces were built using 50 tons of local rock. Gordon grew up in the area and has been in the logging business all his life. He is a kind, down-to-earth host who regales visitors with tales of logging history as they tour the museum. The grounds are covered with steam shovels, cranes, cabooses and other logging equipment. The restaurant features huge servings. The menu includes a smorgasbord of Oregon Coast specialties such as razor clams, salmon and oysters. Try an omelet or the three-berry cobbler. The cinnamon bun is famous. Wash all this down with a micro-brew. Be sure to check out Camp 18, located at milepost 18 on Hwy 26, on your next trip to the north coast.

**Mile Post 18, Highway 26, Elsie OR
(503) 755-1818 or (800) 874-1810
(restaurant)
(503) 755-2476 or (800) 874-1810
(gift shop)**

Razor Clam diggers on Sunset Beach

Bell Buoy of Seaside

MARKETS:

Best seafood market

A 50-year tradition, Bell Buoy of Seaside offers the freshest seafood from the Pacific Northwest. You can get almost anything here that is in season. Razor clams are a major specialty. Bell Buoy also cans its own seafood. Staff members are very friendly and can give you great tips on how to prepare your fish. This famous fish market has now branched out to provide locals and tourists alike some of the best-tasting seafood dining anywhere. Owners and brothers Terry and Jon Hartill have opened the Buoy's Best Fish House right next door to the seafood market. You can be sure you are eating some of the freshest ocean delicacies available when you dine there. The fish and chips, the shrimp and crab cocktails, and the clam chowder are among the favorites from the menu. Jon and Terry oversee the day-to-day operation of both businesses, and you can be certain that quality assurance, customer satisfaction and the freshest products possible are their first priority. If you are dreaming of seafood, but are far from Seaside, you can contact Bell Buoy through its website.

1800 S Roosevelt Drive, Seaside OR
(503) 738-2722 or (800) 529-2722
www.bellbuoyofseaside.com

PLACES TO GO

- Cape Lookout State Park
  13000 Whiskey Creek Road

- Cape Meares State Scenic Viewpoint
  Cape Meares Loop

- Latimer Quilt and Textile Center
  2105 Wilson River Loop Road
  (503) 842-8622

- Munson Creek State Natural Site
  Munson Creek Road, E of Highway 101 S

- Oceanside Beach State Recreation Site
  Pacific Avenue NW, Oceanside

- Tillamook Air Museum
  6030 Hangar Road
  (503) 842-1130

- Tillamook Cheese Visitor's Center
  4175 Highway 101 N
  (503) 815-1300

- Tillamook County Pioneer Museum
  2106 2nd Street
  (503) 842-4553

THINGS TO DO

February
- Birding & Blues Festival
  Pacific City (503) 965-7242

March
- Taste of Tillamook
  Fairgrounds (503) 842-2236

May
- Farm Fest
  Fairgrounds (503) 842-6036

June
- Wine, Cheese & All That Jazz
  Rockaway Beach (503) 355-8108

- Tillamook June Dairy Festival
  Downtown (503) 842-7525

- Tillamook County Rodeo
  Fairgrounds (503) 842-5855

August
- Tillamook Moonlight Madness
  Downtown (503) 842-7940

- Tillamook County Fair
  Fairgrounds (503) 842-2272

September
- Moograss Bluegrass Festival
  Fairgrounds www.moograss.com

TILLAMOOK

Tillamook is famous for dairy farms. The cows that supply the Tillamook County Creamery Association graze on the farmland surrounding the city. The result is cheese, particularly cheddar; gourmet ice cream and yogurt; and of course milk. Millions of people visit the Tillamook cheese factory each year. Tillamook is one of the largest towns in the North Oregon coast region and is straight west of Metro Portland. Therefore, even though it is a few miles inland, it is an ideal base for exploring the coast.

Best Western Inn & Suites Tillamook

ACCOMMODATIONS: *Best suites hotel*

The Best Western Inn & Suites Tillamook lies in the picturesque land of trees, breeze and cheese. The hotel is located just off Highway 101, immediately north of downtown Tillamook. Guests enjoy a complimentary Continental breakfast. The rooms are large and comfortable. Every room offers a refrigerator and microwave. A pool and hot tub will help you relax after a long day on the gorgeous Oregon beaches. Within close walking distance, you will find exciting attractions, great dining opportunities and friendly townspeople. The hotel is just south of the famous Tillamook Cheese Factory, one of the Oregon Coast's biggest visitor attractions. For a comfortable, relaxing stay at one of the most conveniently located hotels in Tillamook, the Best Western Inn & Suites Tillamook will add to your enjoyment of the Oregon Coast.

1722 Makinster Road, Tillamook OR
(503) 842-7599 or (800) 299-4817

Tillamook Air Museum
ATTRACTIONS: *Top flight museum*

One of the top aircraft collections in the United States is two miles south of Tillamook. You cannot miss it—it is located in a World War II blimp hangar more than 15 stories high and longer than six football fields. The hangar, which was built in 1942, houses an exceptional collection of more than 35 vintage aircraft, most of which are quite rare. Children enjoy trying their flying skills in the flight simulators, and everyone has fun learning the history of these amazing planes. In the gift shop, you can find a wide range of books, videos and models to relive your experience when you get home. When hunger strikes, head over to the Air Base Café for a meal in the museum's classic and spacious diner. A nice selection of burgers, sandwiches, soups and plate dishes are available. The museum is open every day of the year except Thanksgiving and Christmas.

6030 Hangar Road, Tillamook OR
(503) 842-1130
www.tillamookair.com

Tillamook Cheese
ATTRACTIONS: *Best dairy*

The Tillamook Cheese Visitor's Center is one of the most popular tourist destinations in Oregon, with nearly one million visitors yearly. The famous Tillamook-brand cheese is produced by a farmer-owned cooperative formally known as the Tillamook County Creamery Association. When founded in 1909, the co-op had 10 members. It now has almost 150. The Visitor's Center features a fascinating self-guided tour. You can begin with historical displays, then examine a milking machine. Videos explain how cheese and ice cream are made, how the Cheddar Master system works and much more. You can view the cheese-making room and packaging departments through observation windows. There are interactive kiosks for the kids and kids at heart, and of course free cheese sampling. For your sweet tooth, the center has ice cream and fudge counters. For sit-down meals, try the Farmhouse Café. A gift shop carries cheese, Northwest gourmet food and other gifts. Visit the Tillamook Cheese Visitors Center and see why Tillamook is a favorite with cheese lovers everywhere.

4175 Highway 101 N, Tillamook OR
(503) 815-1300
www.tillamookcheese.com/VisitorsCenter

La Tea Da
Tea Room & Gift Shoppe
BAKERIES, COFFEE & TEA: *Best tea room*

La Tea Da Tea Room & Gift Shoppe was created for the enjoyment of friends, tea and other lovely things. Owners and best friends Terry Mizée and Suzanne Petty envisioned a place where friends could unwind and treat themselves to special delicacies. A wide variety of fine teas, sumptuous desserts, delicate sandwiches and soups is only part of the La Tea Da experience. This is a place to go when you want to leave the worries of the world behind. La Tea Da cooks with fresh Tillamook dairy products and Ocean Spray cranberries grown on the Mizée farm. You can enjoy La Tea Da High Tea, the Governor's Tea, the Villager's Lunch or several other choices. The Scamp's Tea is designed for children 10 and under. The gift shop will entice you with unique gift ideas as well as home décor. La Tea Da is available for private parties. For a delightful escape where you will feel like royalty, visit La Tea Da.

904 Main Street, Tillamook OR
(503) 842-5447
www.lateada-tearoom.com

Florence Kite Surfer
Photo by Nancy McClain

Central Coast

DEPOE BAY

Depoe Bay bills itself both as the world's smallest navigable harbor and the whale watching capital of the world. Small harbor, big whales. A resident pod of grey whales makes its home here 10 months of the year. The town itself is a fairy tale fishing village brimming with shops and restaurants. A huge sea wall runs the length of the downtown area allowing visitors to shop or dine with a continuous view of the ocean.

PLACES TO GO

- Boiler Bay State Scenic Viewpoint
  U.S. Highway 101

- Rocky Creek State Scenic Viewpoint
  U.S. Highway 101

- Whale Watching Center
  U.S. Highway 101

THINGS TO DO

April
- Wooden Boat Show,
  Crab Feed & Ducky Derby
  (877) 485-8348

May
- Memorial Day Fleet of Flowers
  (877) 485-8348

September
- Indian-Style Salmon Bake
  (877) 485-8348

- Sunday in the Park
  (877) 485-8348

Depoe Bay
Photo by rockdoggydog

Depoe Bay Candy Shoppe

FUN FOODS:
Best candy shoppe

You can find more than 63 flavors of fresh saltwater taffy at the Depoe Bay Candy Shoppe. At this store, the taffy is made with a special recipe, right in the shop. Owner Terri-Anne Thalman encourages visitors to put a piece in their pocket when they first arrive. As you walk around the shop, it will warm in your pocket, and in time you can enjoy its full flavor. Terri-Anne truly loves children. You can see that in the way she lets children pick their pieces of taffy for themselves. Terri-Anne's German family candy-making shop has everything you could possibly want, and then a few extra delicious surprises. You will find goodies that are made right in the shop's kitchens, including hand-dipped chocolates, jawbreakers, cotton candy and fresh licorice. Caramel corn is made fresh daily. There is also a full line of sugar-free candies, old-fashioned candies, Jelly Bellies, caramel apples, suckers, divinity, fudge and more. Be sure to visit Terri-Anne at the Depoe Bay Candy Shoppe to satisfy your sweet tooth.

**102 SE Highway 101,
Depoe Bay OR**
(541) 765-2727

Dancing Coyote and Art on the Edge Galleries

GALLERIES: *Best galleries*

In Depoe Bay, two neighboring art galleries face the highway. Dancing Coyote and Art on the Edge galleries are innovative venues for fine art and contemporary crafts. The galleries feature creations by more than 150 nationally known artists specializing in art glass, bronze sculpture, metal sculpture, jewelry, ceramics and pottery. Dancing Coyote has displayed the work of jewelry maker David Freeland, whose creations are Native American inspired, yet contemporary in appeal. Other recent exhibitors include metal artist James A. Amann, who creates unique functional craftworks. Scott and Laura Curry have shown beautiful hand-blown and cast glass. At Art on the Edge you will find many large glass pieces. Recent examples include James Alloway's jellyfish lamps and chandeliers that incorporate up to 50 pieces of blown glass, and Jeff and Heather Thompson's Glass Temple. Dancing Coyote owners Lenore Preston and Christopher Callahan emphasize that their shop is "where the human hand works in harmony with the beauty of nature." Lenore is an interior custom decorator and Christopher is an artist and lighting consultant, so this gallery space is one of the most breathtaking you will ever see.

**34 NE Highway 101, Depoe Bay OR
(Dancing Coyote)   541) 765-3366
50 NE Highway 101, Depoe Bay OR
(Art on the Edge)   (541) 765-7797**
www.oregoncoast101.com/coyote.html

Lookout Gift Shop
SHOPPING: *Best gift shop*

The Lookout Gift Shop is located on Cape Foulweather, a rugged and scenic spot that was named by Captain Cook. During World War II, the lookout on this site was used by the Coast Guard to watch for enemy ships and submarines. Today, the lookout is a gift shop perched on a promontory 500 feet above the ocean. Crashing surf, sea birds on rocks, sea lions in the sun and whales are just a few of the sights that you can enjoy from its windows. If you can pull your eyes away from the view, you will find yourself surrounded by quality gifts. Owner Katherine Peyton has filled this Oregon historic spot with intriguing and traditional Oregon Coast gift items, including Pendleton Woolen Mills products, Oregon Myrtlewood creations, sculptures, hand-blown glass floats, hats, clothing items and more. The shop has meteorites and collectible rocks. Katherine also has a special treasure chest filled with time-honored grab bags. Visiting this treasure chest year after year has become a fun tradition for many families. Be sure to stop by the Lookout Gift Shop on your next trip to the Oregon Coast for a breathtaking view and a beautiful gift collection.

4905 Otter Crest Loop, Depoe Bay OR
(541) 765-2270
www.lookoutgiftshop.com

FLORENCE

Florence is a top retirement choice on the central Oregon coast. Florence is a playground destination, where lush green forests meet the ocean's edge along one of America's most beautiful and dramatic coastlines. Florence is just across the Siuslaw River from the Oregon Dunes National Recreation Area, which stretches all the way south to Coos Bay and provides a host of outdoor activities. Other nearby attractions include Sea Lion Caves, Heceta Head Lighthouse, Siltcoos Lake, casinos and outlet malls.

PLACES TO GO

- Carl G. Washburne Memorial State Park
  U.S. Highway 101

- Darlingtonia State Natural Site
  U.S. Highway 101

- Heceta Head Lighthouse Scenic Viewpoint
  U.S. Highway 101

- Jessie M. Honeyman Memorial State Park
  U.S. Highway 101

- Muriel O. Ponsler Memorial
  State Scenic Viewpoint
  U.S. Highway 101

- Oregon Dunes National Recreation Area
  U.S. Highway 101

- Sea Lion Caves
  91560 Highway 101 N (541) 547-3111

THINGS TO DO

March
- Home & Garden Show
  Events Center (541) 997-1994

May
- Rhododendron Festival
  (541) 997-3128

July
- Independence Day Celebration
  (541) 997-3128

September
- Florence Fall Festival: Chowder,
  Blues and Brews
  Events Center (541) 997-3128

October
- Humane Society Chocolate & Wine Gala
  (541) 997-4277

Historic Highway 101 Bridge in Florence
Photo by David Smigelski

Sea Lion Caves
ATTRACTIONS: *World's largest sea cave*

For an amazing family adventure, come to the world's largest sea cave on the beautiful Oregon Coast. This cavern began forming around 25 million years ago. It is as high as a 12-story building and stretches the length of a football field. It is the habitat for a herd of 200 Stellar sea lions and a variety of seabirds, including the rare Pigeon Guillemot. You can also see spectacular Heceta Head lighthouse from this viewpoint. From April to mid-July, the sea lions birth and raise their young on rock ledges just outside the cave. During the breeding season, bull seals fight for territory on the rocky ledges just outside the cave. Only the largest and strongest bulls maintain harems. The rest, called bachelor bulls, are driven away to live elsewhere until the season is over. Sea lions pups are about four feet long at birth and weigh from 40 to 50 pounds. They remain with their mothers well over a year. Stellar sea lions have a life span that can reach 20 years. They love bottom fish such as skate, small sharks, squid and rock fish. When you have finished viewing these magnificent creatures, stop at one of the best gifts shops on the Oregon Coast. For an unforgettable memory, visit Oregon's Sea Lion Caves.

91560 Highway 101, Florence OR   (541) 547-3111   *www.sealioncaves.com*

BJ's Ice Cream
FUN FOODS: *Best ice cream*

Ice cream is good any day, especially if it is old-fashioned, homemade ice cream. BJ's Ice Cream is one of Oregon's greatest ice cream parlors. Its homemade old-fashioned ice cream has been served for more than four generations. People throughout Oregon have spread the word about BJ's, which has more than 50 flavors of ice cream, including 23 sugar-free flavors and 30 non-fat frozen yogurts. In addition to ice cream, the shop has 36 varieties of cheesecake, 132 flavors of saltwater taffy, a full espresso bar, assorted pastries and chocolate candies. To top it all off, BJ's also has homemade butter and cream fudge. BJ's Ice Cream is an excellent choice if you crave old-fashioned goodness.

2930 Highway 101, Florence OR
1441 Bay Street, Florence OR
(541) 997-7286

GLENEDEN BEACH

Gleneden Beach is a coastal resort area
that boasts the world-famous Salishan
Spa & Golf Resort. You can also visit the
Gleneden Beach State Recreation Site, a soft
sand beach flanked by crumbling orange
sandstone bluffs. Those really are seal
heads peering at you from the surf. Wetsuit-
clad surfers often catch waves here in the
mornings. As you hike to the right along the
beach, the horizon is dominated by the dark
green cape of Cascade Head.

PLACES TO GO

- Fogarty Creek State Recreation Area
  U.S. Highway 101
- Gleneden Beach State Recreation Site
  U.S. Highway 101

Salishan Spa & Golf Resort

ACCOMMODATIONS: *Best golf resort*

Salishan Spa & Golf Resort is situated on 750 gorgeous wooded acres along scenic Highway 101. This destination resort is one of the most beautiful locations you will ever visit, and a recent multi-million dollar renovation has enhanced its splendor and refinement. Golf pro Peter Jacobson created Salishan's 18-hole championship golf course. Peter may be Oregon's best known professional golfer. The resort offers a practice green, driving range and pro shop. Professional instruction is available. The spa and resort were designed

to reflect the earthy elegance of the Pacific Northwest. The Sun Room Restaurant features all-day dining and serves award-winning northwest cuisine. There is a lounge and a wine cellar, and full-service catering is available for your special event. The restaurant provides 24-hour room service. The 205 guest rooms and suites feature gas fireplaces and step-out balconies or decks with views. Amenities include a fitness center, pool, saunas and a hot tub. You can schedule an in-room fireside massage. There are three indoor tennis courts and one outdoor court. You have easy beach access, hiking trails and convenient shopping. Travel & Leisure magazine has named Salishan Spa & Golf Resort one of the 500 best hotels in the world. Condé Nast lists it as one of the best places to stay in the world. The resort has received the AAA Four Diamond award and the Award of Excellence from Wine Spectator magazine. Visit Salishan Spa & Resort for an experience you will never forget.

7760 Highway 101 N, Gleneden Beach OR
(541) 764-2371 or (800) 452-2300
www.salishan.com

Le Domaine

HOME: *Best home and kitchen store*

Penny Lewman, owner of Le Domaine, has creatively made use of her floor space by adding a second business to her shop. On one side of her store you will find Le Domaine, and on the other, Hot Pots. Le Domaine has distinctive linens and accessories, bath accessories, curtains, furniture, lamps and more. This is a must-see shop for home and bath. The store carries silk goods from Dreamsacks, Peacock Alley bedroom furnishings, and items from Petunia Pickle Bottom. Penny can assist you in making selections that will reflect your personality while making your home a stylish oasis. On the other side of the store, Hot Pots has every kind of cooking implement you can imagine, along with the highest quality cookware, excellent cookbooks and small kitchen appliances designed to make your life easier.

Penny is very knowledgeable about the products she carries in this shop and she is always willing to give advice about which item is best suited to your needs. Hot Pots also stocks gourmet food. No matter which side of the store is your favorite, you are sure to find something you will love.

7755 Highway 101, Gleneden Beach OR
Hot Pots (541) 764-2000
Le Domaine (541) 764-3833

LINCOLN CITY

Lincoln City is located along seven miles of sandy beaches on the Central Oregon Coast. Nestled between the 680-acre scenic Devils Lake and the Pacific Ocean, it is a major tourist destination. Lincoln City hosts multiple kite festivals and bills itself as the kite capital of the world. The city was created after a vote in 1964 to unite the cities of Oceanlake, Delake and Taft with the unincorporated communities of Cutler City and Nelscott. These were all adjacent communities along U.S. Highway 101, Lincoln City's main street. In 1995, the Confederated Tribes of Siletz opened Chinook Winds Casino on a site overlooking the Pacific Ocean, thus providing an additional tourist draw.

PLACES TO GO

- Connie Hansen Garden Conservatory
  1931 NW 33rd Street (541) 994-6338

- Devils Lake State Recreation Area
  NE U.S. 101 and NE 6th Drive

- D River State Recreation Site
  SW U.S. 101 and SE 1st Street

- Neskowin Beach State Recreation Site
  U.S. Highway 101, Neskowin

- North Lincoln County Historical Museum
  4907 SW U.S. 101 (541) 996-6614

- Roads End State Recreation Site
  NW Logan Road

THINGS TO DO

June
- Cascade Head Music Festival
  St. Peter the Fisherman Lutheran Church
  (877) 994-5333

- Summer Kite Festival
  (800) 452-2151

- Festival of Gardens
  Connie Hansen Garden (541) 994-6338

September-October
- Plein Air Art Fest
  Taft District (800) 452-2151

October
- Fall Kite Festival
  (800) 452-2151

Inn at Spanish Head

ACCOMMODATIONS: *Best seaside hotel*

Featuring one of the most exquisite ocean views in the Pacific Northwest, the Inn at Spanish Head is the ideal place to escape for a romantic weekend or fantastic family adventure. Guests have unlimited use of the outdoor heated pool, exercise room, enclosed spa and saunas. The Inn is built into a cliff and stands on one of the most breathtaking beaches on the coast. Every room at the inn has an unobstructed ocean view through the floor-to-ceiling windows. Nearby recreational opportunities include hiking, golf and deep-sea fishing. Nature lovers can participate in whale watching, tidepooling and bird watching. Agates are found in droves up and down the beach on both sides of the Inn. On the 10th floor of the hotel, you will find Fathoms, a restaurant and bar where you can experience a sumptuous breakfast, lunch or dinner while watching the waves. If you are planning an event, the Inn's staff can help whether you want a beach barbecue, a bonfire or a formal wedding reception. Experience true luxury by visiting the Inn at Spanish Head Resort Hotel.

4009 SW Highway 101, Lincoln City OR
(541) 996-2161 or (800) 452-8127
www.spanishhead.com

Chinook Winds Casino

ATTRACTIONS: *Best casino resort*

Owned and operated by the Confederated Tribes of the Siletz Indians, Chinook Winds Casino Resort is a lively place to enjoy the Oregon Coast. The casino, which opened in 1995, is one of the most complete recreation destinations in the Pacific Northwest. Chinook Winds features many free family-friendly outdoor events, as well as a Las Vegas-style casino with more than 1,200 slot machines, Keno, bingo, poker, blackjack and craps. The casino books many headliner acts and sponsors cultural events. You have a stunning view of the Pacific Ocean from three dining room options: casual fine dining, a buffet or deli-style fare. For the parents of younger children, the Play Palace Childcare Center offers a four-hour break from family responsibilities. The casino is beautifully decorated in a traditional style that pays homage to the indigenous people of the area. In the spirit of the tribe, Chinook Winds regularly gives back to the community with programs that enhance the lives of the people of the region. Open 24 hours a day, seven days a week, the Chinook Winds Casino is a great place to enjoy Oregon's natural beauty while adding a bit of excitement to your life.

1777 NW 44th Street, Lincoln City OR
(541) 996-5766 or (888) CHINOOK (244-6665)

Mossy Creek Pottery
GALLERIES: *Best pottery gallery*

The picturesque setting of Mossy Creek Pottery, next to the lush Siletz Bay Wildlife Refuge, is enough to inspire anyone. This pottery studio and showroom, founded in 1972, is tucked in among lush trees, willowy vegetation and a beautiful garden. Dan Wheeler, a potter for more than 20 years, works on-site as the resident artist along with his wife Susan, a fused-glass artist. Mossy Creek Pottery features the works of more than 40 of the finest potters from the Pacific Northwest. The pieces are done in porcelain, stoneware and raku. The wide variety includes both functional and decorative items. You can find dinnerware, serving pieces, lamps, platters and vases in a large number of glazes and colors. Mossy Creek Pottery is one stop on the coast that you will never forget.

**483 Immonen Road, Gleneden Beach OR
(541) 996-2415**
www.mossycreekpottery.com

Bay House Restaurant

RESTAURANTS & CAFÉS: *Best seafood*

The only thing that could possibly be better than the food at the Bay House Restaurant is the view. The restaurant features an amazing panoramic view of the Siletz Bay, complete with dramatic sunsets. Owner Leslie Dressel and her family have operated this Lincoln City landmark for decades, and the Bay House Restaurant's reputation is unsurpassed in the Northwest. The Salem *Statesman Journal* says, "The Bay House is four-star (our highest rating) all the way." Chef Jesse Otero uses only the freshest ingredients from local organic farmers, coastal fisherman and wild forest foragers. He has a particular weakness for European cheeses and other delicacies, and strives to create dishes that taste delicious when paired with a wonderful wine. (The Bay House is a recipient of *Wine Spectator's* Award of Excellence for its wine list.) Probably the most famous item at this establishment is the fresh dungeness crab cocktail, which will melt in your mouth. The dessert list includes homemade ice cream served with a delicate lace cookie and warm chocolate and caramel sauce, or hazelnut crepes with lemon cream. The Bay House also features a full selection of after-dinner ports, liqueurs, dessert wines and single-malt scotches. For a memorable dining experience, do not miss the Bay House Restaurant.

5911 SW Highway 101, Lincoln City OR
(541) 996-3222
www.bayhouserestaurant.com

Blackfish Café

RESTAURANTS & CAFÉS: *Best casual dining*

Chef Rob Pounding could open a restaurant 90 miles down a dirt road and his loyal customers would still gladly make the commute. Fortunately, Rob's restaurant, the Blackfish Café, is conveniently located right on Highway 101 in Lincoln City. He and his wife have been in the food industry for many years and they are still as excited about it as when they first began. Blackfish Café is casual, but the food is as uptown as you can get. Fresh seafood is Rob's calling card, and his salads and desserts are wonderful, too. He is licensed to buy fish and shellfish directly from area fishermen, and he purchases the bulk of his vegetables and herbs from area market gardeners. Everything from the coffee to the wine is selected for its full, rich flavor. The service is unparalleled and the staff is friendly and helpful. Additionally, Rob and his staff give back to the community in many ways, including hunger relief efforts and sponsoring Taft High School's cooking class all the way through winning a national competition. In 2001, *Northwest Palate Magazine* readers voted the Blackfish Café the best new restaurant in Oregon outside Portland, and *Lincoln City Newsguard* readers named it the best restaurant on the beach. Rob has won many gold and silver medals in culinary competitions, including the IKA Hoga in Germany, known as the Culinary Olympics. Don't miss the Blackfish Café in beautiful coastal Lincoln City.

2733 NW Highway 101, Lincoln City OR
(541) 996-1007 *www.blackfishcafe.com*

PLACES TO GO

- Agate Beach State Recreation Site
  U.S. Highway 101

- Alsea Bay Historic Interpretive Center
  U.S. Highway 101, Waldport

- Beverly Beach State Park
  U.S. Highway 101

- Hatfield Marine Science Center
  2030 S Marine Science Drive
  (541) 867-0100

- Nye Beach
  Downtown

- Ona Beach State Park
  U.S. Highway 101

- Oregon Coast Aquarium
  2820 SE Ferry Slip Road
  (541) 867-FISH (3474)

- Seal Rock State Recreation Site
  U.S. Highway 101

- South Beach State Park
  U.S. Highway 101

- Yaquina Bay State Recreation Site and
  Lighthouse
  U.S. Highway 101

THINGS TO DO

May
- Newport Jazz Festival
  Elks Lodge 541-265-2105

June
- Beachcomber Days Festival
  Waldport (541) 563-2133

June-July
- Ernest Bloch Music Festival
  Performing Arts Center (800) 262-7844

July
- Newport Clambake and Seafood Barbeque
  Nye Beach (866) 592-5556

- Lincoln County Fair & Rodeo
  Fairgrounds (541) 265-6237

August
- Port of Toledo Wooden Boat Show
  Toledo (541) 336-5207

November
- Oyster Cloyster Festival
  Oregon Coast Aquarium (541) 867-3474

NEWPORT

Newport began in 1855, when the first settlers came and discovered oysters. The word soon got out. Officially, though, Newport was founded on July 4, 1866 and not long after became a popular travel destination. This is fairly amazing, considering the first road into town was built only in 1927. Newport steadily grew into what it is today—a thriving fishing harbor, commercial center and tourist destination. Newport is a fun place to visit, but much of the fun is educational, too. The Oregon Coast Aquarium ranks among the top 10 aquariums in the nation. At Oregon State University's Mark O. Hatfield Marine Science Center, visitors can explore the geology of the ocean floor, find out about coastal hazards such as tsunamis, and learn the results of the latest whale research. Kids can touch a live octopus. The Yaquina Head Interpretive Center teaches more than 500,000 annual visitors about the Head's unique environment and the famous lighthouse.

Embarcadero Resort Hotel

ACCOMMODATIONS: *Best resort*

Overlooking Yaquina Bay, the Embarcadero Resort Hotel & Marina is one of the most famous places to stay along the Oregon coast. All rooms face the water and have private balconies. Are you a boater? The Embarcadero supplies guests with a private crab dock, and guests can use the hotel's nearby crab cooker for free. If you'd rather someone else do the cooking, visit the on-site restaurant for breakfast, lunch or dinner. The restaurant has a fantastic Sunday champagne brunch. You can order great hot or cold sandwiches or seafood and pasta dishes for lunch. There are a variety of excellent dinner plates. You can dine outside on your private balcony and watch the sunset over the bay. Take advantage of the Embarcadero's marina and arrive on your boat or yacht to spend the night, pick up supplies or enjoy the town. On the bay front, you can ride your bike, run or go for a stroll. Be sure to check in to the Embarcadero Resort Hotel on your next trip to the beautiful Oregon coast.

999 SE Bay Boulevard, Newport OR
(541) 265-8521 or (800) 547-4779
www.embarcadero-resort.com

Marine Discovery Tours
ATTRACTIONS: *Best boat excursions*

Marine Discovery Tours is the official cruise company of the Oregon Coast Aquarium in Newport. Owners Fran and Don Mathews and their well trained, friendly staff of naturalists invite you to board the 65-foot *Discovery* for a fun and informative Sea Life Cruise. You can pull crab pots or navigate from the wheelhouse. Look for a school of salmon or the blow of a gray whale, and check out plankton you have just collected on video screens. If you would rather "kick it up a notch," as Fran laughingly puts it, take a ride on the *Oregon Rocket*, Don's solution to his midlife crisis. At 27 feet and with seating for 16, it is the largest inflatable boat on the coast. Put on an all-weather suit and goggles, and then enjoy the search for sea life, scenery and above all speed. Fran and Don explain that their family-owned business is based on a love story.

A marine journalist and a Bering Sea crabber met, married and fished the rugged Pacific waters from the Gulf of Alaska to the Oregon Coast. When the children, Brendan and Caitie, arrived, they decided to trade their footloose fishing days for a life on the shore. In 1994, they launched a company that blended all of their loves together—their passion for exploring and sharing the marine environment, for boating, and for family togetherness. Contact Marine Discovery Tours to reserve your coastal adventure today.

345 SW Bay Boulevard, Newport OR
(541) 265-6200 or (800) 903-BOAT (2628)
www.marinediscovery.com

Sylvia Beach Hotel

ACCOMMODATIONS: *Best hotel*

The Sylvia Beach Hotel is a book lover's dream. At this oceanfront bed and breakfast you are free from noisy televisions or telephones. You will find a relaxing, tranquil refuge from the outside world where you can sit beside a crackling fire overlooking the astonishingly beautiful Nye Beach. The Sylvia Beach has dedicated its rooms to such literary luminaries as Emily Dickinson, Mark Twain, Agatha Christie, Dr. Seuss, Oscar Wilde, Jane Austen, Tennessee Williams, Alice Walker, Gertrude Stein and Ernest Hemingway. In all, 20 of the rooms have been decorated to fit the personality of a famous author. With your room comes a complimentary breakfast. The hotel is famous for its family-style, five-course dinners. Owners Sally Ford and Goody Gable came up with the theme of the Sylvia Beach Hotel. Sally and Goody grew up in the same neighborhood and have been lifelong friends. They have made it their mission in life to give others a refuge from the hectic pace of life in the 21st century. One of the best views at the Sylvia Beach Hotel is from the top floor, which houses the hotel's library, fireplace and gift shop. Stay at the Sylvia Beach Hotel and you will find out why it is a favorite haven for word lovers. Be sure to book your stay well in advance, because this is one of Oregon's most sought-after accommodations.

267 NW Cliff Street, Newport OR
(541) 265-5428 or (888) 795-8422
www.sylviabeachhotel.com

Oregon Coast Aquarium
ATTRACTIONS: *Best coastal aquarium*

The Oregon Coast Aquarium offers one of the most unforgettable experiences you can have while you are in the Pacific Northwest. The aquarium is a private, nonprofit educational facility that introduces people to Oregon's unique coastal resources in a fun and interactive way. The aquarium first came into the international spotlight when it became the temporary home of Keiko, the killer whale who starred in the movie Free Willy. You will not want to miss the daily Keeper Talks, scheduled animal feedings which provide excellent photo opportunities. The multitude of exhibits includes a 200-foot, transparent underwater tunnel that takes you through three separate ocean habitats. Indoor galleries exhibit sandy shores, rocky shores and coastal waters. The aquarium regularly rotates interactive and display exhibits, so you can enjoy a completely new experience whenever you return. The Oregon Coast Aquarium offers a long list of annual programs for children and adults, such as the Family Sleepover. The aquarium is dedicated to providing excellent care for animals, a great experience for visitors and a better future for all living things. Visit the Oregon Coast Aquarium and discover how awe-inspiring the sea and its creatures can be.

2820 SE Ferry Slip Road, Newport OR
(541) 867-3474
www.aquarium.org

FACETS Gem & Mineral Gallery

SHOPPING: *Best gems and minerals*

If you are looking for a piece of fine jewelry, a gift for someone special, or a beautiful home accent, FACETS Gem & Mineral Gallery in Newport is the place to go. *Driving The Pacific Coast* magazine has noted its "large selection of shells, gemstones, mineral specimens, jewelry and various gift items, which are tastefully displayed." Established in 1987, FACETS has an impressive array of treasures that the owners have designed or personally selected for their unique qualities from different regions of the world. You can find exotic gems, plus fossils and rocks that are millions of years old. The shop also carries books, maps, rock-polishing equipment and supplies for the creative craftsman. Owner and gemologist Richard Petrovic boasts more than 30 years of experience in designing, creating, repairing and appraising fine jewelry. Since the late 1970s, Richard and his wife, Kay, have personally mined and collected gems and minerals in six states as hobbyists. Together they have more than 50 years of expertise in the lapidary field and the jewelry industry. Let FACETS Gem & Mineral Gallery, with its friendly and informative staff, help you select that perfect gem on your next trip to the Oregon coast.

1125 SW Coast Hwy. 101, Newport OR
(541) 256-6330 or (888) 4-FACETS (432-2387)
www.4facets.com

The Flying Dutchman Winery

WINERIES: *Best winery*

Situated at one of the most breathtaking ocean views in the Pacific Northwest, the Flying Dutchman Winery is a treasure in every sense of the word. Owned by the Cutler family, it is the only working winery on the Oregon Coast. The Cutlers have worked diligently to create award-winning wines. Richard purchases fresh-picked grapes from the Willamette, Umpqua and Rogue valleys. He immediately returns them to the Flying Dutchman Winery for processing, even if he arrives at 3 am. The winery crushes only 16 tons of grapes each year, so the wines are available only at the winery or through the website. The winery picnic area is ideal for small functions and is becoming a popular place for musical events, wedding receptions and the like. A gift shop has clothing, posters and wine accessories. See JoAnn's 1934 Dodge truck, converted into an ice cream and espresso shop. For a view you are sure to remember and wine you will never forget, visit the Flying Dutchman Winery.

915 1st Street, Otter Rock OR
(541) 765-2553
www.dutchmanwinery.com

PLACES TO GO

- Beachside State Recreational Site
  U.S. Highway 101

- Cape Perpetua Visitors Center & Theater
  U.S. Highway 101
  (541) 547-3289

- Governor Patterson Memorial State
  Recreation Site
  U.S. Highway 101

- Neptune State Scenic Viewpoint
  U.S. Highway 101

- Smelt Sands State Recreation Site
  U.S. Highway 101

- Stonefield Beach State Recreation Site
  U.S. Highway 101

- Yachats Ocean Road State Natural Site
  U.S. Highway 101 and Yachats Ocean Road

- Yachats State Recreation Area
  U.S. Highway 101 and 2nd Street

THINGS TO DO

May
- Spring Arts & Crafts Fair
  Yachats Commons
  (541) 547-4738

July
- Yachats Music Festival
  Presbyterian Church
  (510) 601-7919

- Yachats Coastal Garden Tour
  (541) 547-3338

October
- Yachats Village Mushroom Fest
  (800) 929-0477

November
- Harvest and Holidays Arts & Crafts Fair
  Yachats Commons
  (541) 547-4738

- Yachats Celtic Music Festival
  Yachats Commons
  (541) 547-3000

YACHATS

Yachats is pronounced Yah-hawts. The name comes from the Siletz language, and means at the foot of the mountain. In fact, the Coastal Range comes unusually close to the shore here. This charming little village is ideal for rest, relaxation and renewal. Be sure to visit the Cape Perpetua Scenic Area, which includes a visitor's center and the Cape Perpetua Overlook, the highest point on the Oregon Coast.

Neptune Beach, Yachats
Photo courtesy of C.S. and Jessica Rowan

The Adobe Resort

ACCOMMODATIONS: *Best resort*

The Adobe Resort has been bringing people back to Yachats for many years, as it is the quintessential ocean-side resort. Along with breathtaking views from the comfortable, oversized rooms, the resort offers delectable seaside food in one of the best restaurants in Oregon. When you are ready to relax, you will find a spacious indoor pool with a sauna and hot tub and a wonderful staff who take care of your every need. The key word at the Adobe Resort is pampering. Upon arrival, you will see the open gateway and then the lush green rolling lawns. Inside is a wonderful gift shop with everything from souvenirs and essentials to incredible works of art. Once you take your first look at the ocean view from any of the Adobe's windows, you'll know you have just found a little bit of heaven on earth. The restaurant is overseen by one of the state's greatest chefs, famous for his seafood creations. Try his gingerbread cakes or any of the delightful omelets. Favorites from the lunch menu are fried oysters or the Adobe's renowned razor clams. Dinner is an especially memorable experience—try baked Yaquina oysters or the Adobe baked crab pot. No matter what you choose, it will be accompanied by a gorgeous sunset. To set the mood, an expansive wine list features the best Northwest wines, as well as selections from all over the world. The Adobe Resort is very popular, so call well in advance to reserve your room.

1555 Highway 101, Yachats OR
(541) 547-3141 or (800) 522-3623
www.adoberesort.com

The Fireside
ACCOMMODATIONS: *Best pet friendly hotel*

Attention animal lovers: If you can't bear to travel without your four-legged companion, The Fireside motel is for you. At the Fireside, your pets are offered a Bone Appétit Pet Package that includes a water bowl, edible treats and toys. The Fireside is not just for pet owners, however. The motel is immediately next to miles of walking trails, crashing surf, beautiful views of the coast and surrounding attractions which bring people back year after year. For many families, staying at The Fireside is a tradition. Before you leave, do not forget to visit the gift shop for many unique items from local artists, a great selection of pet gifts and many other possibilities.

1881 Highway 101 N, Yachats OR
(541) 547-3636 or (800) 336-3573
www.firesidemotel.com

Overleaf Lodge

ACCOMMODATIONS: *Best luxury hotel*

Overleaf Lodge is one of the most luxurious places to stay along the Oregon Coast. Welcoming and friendly staff members accommodate your wishes and ensure that your visit is comfortable, relaxing and stress-free. All accommodations at the lodge are oceanfront and have spectacular views. All are spacious. Room types range from Whale Watcher rooms with two queen beds and window seats to the lavish two-room Sunset Suites with fireplaces, kitchenettes, whirlpool baths and either a balcony or a patio. Even the mid-range rooms may come with a fireplace, a kitchenette, a whirlpool bath or a balcony. You can easily find a combination of amenities to suit your needs. In the morning enjoy a delicious complimentary breakfast. Be kind to your body and take advantage of the rejuvenating massage and the exercise room. Overleaf Lodge is now constructing a 3,000-square-foot spa with ocean views. You can try the meandering level trails along the breathtaking rugged shoreline. The trails are great for speed walks or meditative strolls. Stop at the Overleaf Lodge, where you can refresh your outlook, rekindle your relationships or rejuvenate your spirit.

280 Overleaf Lodge Lane, Yachats OR
(541) 547-4880 or (800) 338-0507
www.overleaflodge.com

Whaleshead Beach
Photo by David Smigelski

South Coast

BANDON

Like many coastal Oregon cities, Bandon once lived by fishing and timber, but now earns most of its living through tourism. Cranberry growing is also important. The beach here, strewn with massive rock formations called sea stacks, is one of the most spectacular on earth and a must-see. Downtown Bandon-by-the-Sea, as it is also known locally, is filled with art shops and fine restaurants specializing in seafood. What makes Bandon famous throughout the world, however, is golf. Publications such as *Golf Magazine, Golf Digest* and *Golfweek* regularly mark the three courses at the Bandon Dunes Golf Resort among the world's very best. Further, because Bandon Dunes is a resort rather than a club, play is open to anyone. The popularity of the links is such that Bandon has had to upgrade its general aviation airport to handle the increased traffic. Bandon Dunes is a walk-only experience and employs more than 300 caddies. As you might guess, the resort's impact on the local economy is as beneficial as its impact on the game of golf itself.

PLACES TO GO

- Bandon State Natural Area
  Beach Loop Road

- Bullards Beach State Park
  S: Ocean Drive SW N: Park Road

- Coquille River Museum
  270 Fillmore Avenue
  (541) 347-2164

- Face Rock State Scenic Viewpoint
  Beach Loop Road

THINGS TO DO

May
- Wine and Food Festival
  City Park (541) 347-9616

September
- Cranberry Festival
  (541) 347-9616

December
- Celebration of Lights
  (541) 347-9616

Bandon Harbor
Photo by David Smigelski

Sunset Oceanfront Lodging

ACCOMMODATIONS: *Best beachside accommodations*

One of Bandon's best and most highly acclaimed hotels, Sunset Oceanfront Lodging is beautifully situated on high ground overlooking two miles of sandy beach. From the hotel, guests can view majestic sea stacks such as the famous Face Rock. All guests enjoy beach access. You can watch spectacular sunsets, explore tide pools and sea caves, and discover fascinating inter-tidal life such as the rare sun stars. Other pursuits include crabbing, kayaking and hiking. Bryan and Jeff Longland, fourth generation family owners, work diligently to keep their visitors comfortable and satisfied, and many come back year after year. The 71-unit complex offers a variety of accommodations. The newest are 18 ocean-view studios, each with a gas fireplace, refrigerator and microwave, Internet access and a deck or patio. The three-story oceanfront Vern Brown Addition has 21 modern rooms with private balconies. Some rooms have kitchenettes or fireplaces. Eight beach houses offer privacy in a variety of configurations. The six original oceanfront rooms are pet-friendly, as are the rustic rooms. These include 14 ocean-view rooms and a few economy rooms with no view. The complex includes Lord Bennett's Restaurant and Lounge. For an unobstructed view of the Pacific in all its glory, Sunset Oceanfront Lodging is the place to stay.

1865 Beach Loop Drive, Bandon OR
(541) 347-2453 or (800) 842-2407
www.sunsetlodging.us

West Coast Game Park

ATTRACTIONS: *Best wildlife park*

The West Coast Game Park is America's largest wild animal petting park, the original walk-through safari. For more than 38 years, Mary and Bob Tenney have dedicated themselves to the park and to the relationship between humans and wildlife. The West Coast Game Park has more than 450 animals. The 75 different species from around the world include great cats such as lions, tigers, snow leopards, black panthers, cougars and lynx. North America provides bears, bison and elk. From the Old World come chimps, camels and zebras. You may even meet an animal you did not know existed. This hands-on experience has been lovingly created by the Tenneys and their exceptional staff of animal keepers. When they show you an animal, they tell you about when the animal was born, how it was raised and how rare it is. You can pet the creature as long as it is pet-friendly. You will want to remember your visit, so be sure to stop at the gift shop for representations of the beautiful animals in the park. A walk through the West Coast Game Park is something the entire family will remember for a lifetime.

46914 Highway 101 S, Bandon OR
(541) 347-3016
www.gameparksafari.com

Bandon Glass Art Studio

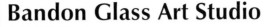

GALLERIES: *Best glass art*

Since its opening in 1997, Bandon Glass Art Studio and Gallery has become one of the most popular stops for Bandon visitors. The glass-blowing process is fascinating. At the studio, you can watch owners Aro and Dutch Schulze create glasswork right before your eyes. You can also wander through the gallery and admire the Schulze's stunning collection of artwork. Aro and Dutch purchase some of the work from other glass blowers they have met over the years and whose work they admire. About half of the work in the gallery is created on the premises by Dutch or Aro and their crew. Since they sell this work directly and show it in their own gallery, they enjoy great freedom of expression. This freedom gives many of the pieces a unique, sometimes quirky character. Some of the Schulze's most famous works include Aro's coral reef paperweights, and Dutch's large blown glass vases and his cast glass sculpture. Visit Bandon Glass Art Studio and Gallery and let the glasswork stir your imagination.

240 Highway 101, Bandon OR
(541) 347-4723
www.bandonglassart.com

Timeless Accents

HOME: *Best home décor*

At the Bandon Mercantile Company, you can enjoy a free cup of coffee while you survey the beautiful accessories for the home. Naturally, the store has a wide variety of gourmet coffee and coffee appliances. The shop stocks a full line of kitchen gadgets and the latest in household cookware. The beautiful home accessories include baskets, potpourri, rugs, and items made from copper or stone. You can find quality natural style clothing and jackets that make wonderful gifts. Bed and bath essentials are also on hand. A feline proprietor wanders wherever he pleases in both the gift shop and the cozy town of Bandon. Ed and Beth Wood, the great people who own the Bandon Mercantile Company, also own Timeless Accents. Located in a separate building on the same site, Timeless Accents sells furniture for the office and home. You may meet the cat here, too. Whichever store you visit, you are warmly welcomed by Ed, Beth

or the cat, and their staff will be more than happy to help you select an item that meets your needs. Old-fashioned service, affordable prices, and unique products make The Bandon Mercantile a store for everyone. Be sure to stop and explore it on your next trip through Bandon.

198 2nd Street SE, Bandon OR
(541) 347-8274
www.bandonmercantile.com

Bandon Dunes Golf Resort

RECREATION: *Best golf resort*

At Bandon Dunes Golf Resort you will find three distinctly different courses built on a beautiful stretch of sand dunes perched 100 feet above the Pacific Ocean. The Bandon Dunes and Pacific Dunes courses run along a bluff overlooking 23 miles of sweeping, undisturbed shoreline. It can be said that these two courses, as well as the newest addition, Bandon Trails, were discovered rather than built. The game of golf was born in Scotland on rugged, wind-swept land like this. Altogether, 54 golf holes lie amidst the coastal forest, dunes and gorse. Bandon Dunes is on the list of America's Top 50 golf courses. Private and group golf lessons are available and knowledgeable caddies are always ready to assist you. The Gallery Restaurant provides Pacific Northwest cuisine. The Tufted Puffin Lounge has a full menu and is open until the wee hours of the night. The Bunker Bar provides a light menu along with a pool table or you can visit McKee's Pub, a traditional Scottish-style gathering place that serves pub fare, microbrews and single malt scotches. Bandon Dunes offers more than 150 comfortable, luxurious suites and rooms, many of which have dramatic views of the course. The new Grove Cottages are designed specifically for a foursome of golfers, with four private rooms and a shared parlor and patio. To experience golf as it was meant to be, come to Bandon Dunes Golf Resort.

57744 Round Lake Drive, Bandon OR
(541) 347-5959
www.bandondunesgolf.com

Big Wheel General Store
SHOPPING: *Best fudge*

If you love fudge, then the Big Wheel General Store is the place for you. This is the home of the fudge factory, where you can choose from more than 24 mouth-watering flavors of cream and butter fudge. Try the Cranberry Walnut. Inside the building, once a feed and farm store, you find a delightful, old-fashioned candy shop that carries 16 flavors of Umpqua ice cream and all kinds of hard-to-find nostalgic candy. The Big Wheel is also filled to the brim with gifts, such as Myrtlewood creations, local jams and jellies, food products, antiques and novelty items. Oregon-made Just Ducky sweatshirts are pre-washed, pre-shrunk and come in a variety of designs. The store features a free driftwood museum and an art gallery. While the driftwood is not for sale, you can purchase artwork ranging from intarsia inlaid mosaics to metal-and-wood sculptures to watercolors. Come down and visit the Big Wheel General Store, across from the crabbing docks on the waterfront.

130 Baltimore Avenue SE, Bandon OR
(541) 347-3719
www.bandonbythesea.com/bigwheel.htm

Woods of the West
SHOPPING: *Best carved wood gifts*

Just off of Highway 101, nestled in the pristine coastal woods, you can find Woods of the West. This Oregon treasure is worth a visit. Created by Tom Olive, Woods of the West features lovingly crafted gifts that are imaginative, inspiring, sometimes humorous and always works of art. You can find cutting boards, bowls, treasure boxes, jewelry and clocks. Woods of the West does laser engraving and makes special order key chains while you watch.

Hobby wood and lumber are available. Tom loves to give tours to show the process of turning raw Myrtlewood into beautiful keepsakes. A live Myrtlewood tree grows outside the shop, so visitors can see where their beautiful products originate. The Woods of the West is a perfect place for the entire family to enjoy.

47611 Highway 101 S,
Bandon OR
(541) 347-9915

BROOKINGS

The Brookings area includes the city of Brookings and the community of Harbor. The port, called the Port of Brookings-Harbor, is a great base for recreational and commercial fishing. Brookings-Harbor is the warmest spot on the Oregon Coast, partly because it is almost in California, but mostly because of favorable wind currents. As a result of the mild climate, this is one of the nation's most important flower-growing regions. The 12-mile stretch between Brookings and the Smith River in California provides almost every lily bulb sold in North America. You can see some of the local flowers at Azalea Park. The azalea bushes were here long before European settlers arrived. As an historical note, the forest above Brookings was the target of the only Japanese pilot to bomb the U.S. mainland during World War II. Damage was negligible. Twenty year later, the city invited the pilot back for a celebration.

PLACES TO GO

- Alfred A. Loeb State Park
  N Bank Chetco River Road

- Azalea Park
  N Bank Chetco River Road

- Crissey Field State Recreation Site
  U.S. Highway 101

- Harris Beach State Park
  U.S. Highway 101

- McVay Rock State Recreation Site
  Oceanview Drive

- Winchuck State Recreation Site
  U.S. Highway 101

THINGS TO DO

May
- Azalea Festival
  (800) 535-9469

July
- Southern Oregon Kite Festival
  Port of Brookings Harbor (541) 469-2218

August
- Brookings Harbor Festival of the Arts
  Port (541) 469-7120

Harris Beach
Photo by Donna K Lindley

Best Western Beachfront Inn

ACCOMMODATIONS:
Best beach hotel

Sunset from the Beachfront Inn
Photo by Nancy McClain

Wake up and open your balcony door to hear the majestic Pacific Ocean whisper and roar. See the waves rush to meet the sand and inhale the refreshing salt breeze. The Best Western Beach Front Inn is the only oceanfront hotel in Brookings. It is only a few feet from the beautiful, sandy beach, one of the warmest in Oregon. Every one of the 78 guestrooms at the Beach Front Inn overlooks the ocean. Suites are available, including Jacuzzi suites with an ocean-view whirlpool. Some rooms have kitchenettes or special designs for handicapped persons. Amenities include a heated pool, a large outdoor spa and a great sundeck. This is the perfect place for a romantic evening for two or a revitalizing weekend for the entire family. For business or social gatherings, meeting rooms are available. The staff is friendly and makes every effort to make your stay memorable. While in the Brookings area, you can enjoy beachcombing and tide pools, schedule a deep-sea fishing trip, or simply watch the ever changing moods of the ocean. Just six miles from the California border, Brookings is Oregon's gateway to the most scenic coast on the continent. There is no better way to begin or end your tour than to stay at the Best Western Beach Front Inn.

16008 Boat Basin Road, Brookings OR
(541) 469-7779
www.bestwesternoregon.com

Oh My Goodness Candy

FUN FOODS: *Best old-time candy*

Oh My Goodness Candies specializes in hard-to-find old-fashioned candies. Take a step back into your childhood as you drift down the aisles of this picture-perfect candy and gift shop. Oh My Goodness Candy stocks old favorites like Walnettos BB Bats, Boston Baked Beans, Root Beer Barrels and many, many more. In addition to candy, Oh My Goodness also offers a large selection of plush toys and gifts for all occasions. The gifts include an extensive selection of Austrian crystals. Oh My Goodness strives to help you with your gift giving needs. The staff's motto is Being Sweet To You Is Our Business, and that's exactly how they are. Pay Oh My Goodness Candies a visit and pick up something for someone special, or for yourself.

16350 Lower Harbor Road, Suite 204, Harbor OR
(541) 469-6600 or (877) 469-6600
www.ohmygoodness.net

At Home by the Sea

HOME: *Best home decor*

At Home by the Sea specializes in home décor, beautiful accessories and gifts for the home and garden. Beach Babies, with goods for infants, is on the same premises. Co-owner Hazel Barry is a professionally trained designer and her thoughtfully planned shop is proof of her talent. Inside you can find items for bed, bath, baby and home that look, feel and smell wonderful. The shop has several theme rooms, such as The Powder Room, which features boudoir and bath goods. At Home by the Sea carries the Hedges line of quality dried and preserved floral arrangements. Also on hand are Shamiana bedding and panels. You can find books, furniture, art and lamps. The aroma of scented candles will cause you to linger as you search through the treasures that fill this shop. Hazel is always ready to assist you with those hard-to-buy-for friends and relatives, and will wrap your selection for you. Downstairs, on the alley, you will find a great dress shop called Sea Weeds, which features natural, comfortable clothing in a wonderful garden setting, complete with a fireplace and seating. Hazel and Jim Barry own both shops, plus a home décor and antiques store in Medford called Veranda. Hazel and Jim and their wonderful staff invite you to At Home by the Sea and Sea Weeds.

519 Chetco Avenue, Brookings OR
(541) 412-3220 (At Home by the Sea)
(541) 469-2826 (Sea Weeds)

Great American Smokehouse & Seafood

MARKETS: *Best clam chowder*

Nancy and Lee Myers raised their children on a fishing boat. When they finally moved ashore they decided to use their expertise to sell fresh fish. Later, they began smoking and canning, as well. Now, decades later, the Myers have top-rated products and a restaurant that serves the freshest and most delectable fish. Food taster David Rosengarten tasted 200 cans of tuna from around the world and picked the Great American Deluxe Albacore Tuna as the best. As is done at other boutique canneries, the tuna is cooked in the can in its own juices, without added water or oil. The Great American tuna, however, stands out from the others by the way it melts in your mouth. Another best-selling signature product is the Indian-Style Smoked Salmon Jerky. Part of the success of this family owned and operated business is the Myers' attention to detail. The fish market lacks the common fishy odor because fresh fish has very little odor, and cleanliness is the rule at the Smokehouse. At the restaurant, you can sample snow crab legs, lobster, albacore or a seafood combo plate. No matter what you choose, you will savor each and every bite. The Myers also have a gift shop where you can buy all your favorites to take home or send as gifts. When you are in Brookings, the Great American Smokehouse & Seafood is an essential stop for anyone who loves great food.

15657 Highway 101 S, Harbor OR
(541) 469-6903 or (800) 828-FISH (3474)
www.smokehouse-salmon.com

Sporthaven Beach

Salmon Run Golf

RECREATION: *Most beautiful golf course*

A day spent outdoors on a beautiful golf course can make you feel like you are on top of the world, and there is no golf course more beautiful than Salmon Run in Brookings. This 18-hole championship golf course is located on America's Wild River Coast. Once you have been here, you will come back time and time again. When you are here, you can find an abundance of wildlife at every turn while you play on one of the most thoughtfully designed courses in the Pacific Northwest. Eighteen unique holes, including nine elevated tees, test your skills and challenge your mind. While on the course you will notice Jack's Creek—which is where the salmon run every season. Check out the incredible water view from Salmon Run's signature Hole 4, the Lombard Street Hole. Salmon Run is recommended by Mike McAllister of *Sports Illustrated*. Stay-and-play packages are available through Portside Suites and the Chetco River Inn. With a pro shop and Bogey's Restaurant, all of your needs will be easily met while you are at Salmon Run Golf.

99040 S Bank Chetco River Road, Brookings OR
(541) 469-4888
www.salmonrun.net

Candle Garden

SHOPPING: *Best candles*

One of the most wonderful things about life is that you never know what new experiences are waiting for you just around the corner. A visit to the Candle Garden is one of those treats that will spark your creative side. At the Candle Garden, artist and owner Kathy Ramsay creates German-style candles while you watch. If you wish, Kathy can make a candle to your exact specifications as you look on. The Candle Garden offers an intriguing selection of candles that have already been made, some carved in the shape of a lighthouse. If you are planning a wedding or special event, Kathy can design centerpiece candles that will enhance any décor. The shop also carries plants and other gifts. Kathy's husband is a vintage car enthusiast and an artist in his own right, and he designs the shirts featuring vintage cars that you will find at the Candle Garden. Be sure to stop by this unique shop on your next trip through Brookings.

16350 Lower Harbor Road, Brookings OR
(541) 469-9255

Brandy Peak Distillery

SHOPPING: *Best brandies*

One of only a handful of wood-burning distilleries still in operation in the United States, Brandy Peak Distillery is truly a unique operation. At Brandy Peak Distillery, the fire is always on as the Nowlin family creates some of the finest brandies on the West Coast. R. L. Nowlin, president of Brandy Peak Distillery, had the dream "to capture the varietal characteristics of fruit as brandy." With his son David, he opened the distillery to meet that challenge. Brandy Peak Distillery makes award-winning pear and grape brandies, grappas, *eaux de vie* and blackberry liqueurs. The first production run of brandies was in 1994. By 1997, the Aged Pear Brandy was able to win double gold at the San Francisco International Wine Competition. You are invited to come to this scenic sylvan setting and watch the age-old art of brandy making. Tasting rooms for spirits are rare in the United States, but Brandy Peak has one and these expert brandy-makers will let you sample some of the fruits of their labor. To take a tour or to simply visit the tasting room and gift shop, visit Brandy Peak Distillery.

18526 Tetley Road, Brookings OR
(541) 469-0194
www.brandypeak.com

CHARLESTON

Charleston, at the ocean entrance to Coos Bay, is the area's commercial and sport fishing center. The Charleston Marina Complex provides moorage for commercial and pleasure boats and can accommodate more than 550 vessels. Seafood processing and other marine activities are important. Charleston is the site of the Oregon Institute of Marine Biology and the South Slough National Estuarine Research Reserve, a 4,770-acre reserve along the Coos Bay Estuary. It was the first such reserve created in the United States.

PLACES TO GO

- Cape Argo State Park
  Cape Argo Highway

- Seven Devils State Recreation Site
  Seven Devils Road

- Shore Acres State Park
  Cape Argo Highway

- Sunset Bay State Park
  Cape Argo Highway

THINGS TO DO

February
- Charleston Crab Feed
  Old Charleston Elementary School
  (541) 888-4875

March
- Southcoast Clambake Jazz Festival
  (541) 888-4386

April
- Bonsai Day
  Shore Acres State Park
  (541) 756-5401

- Charleston Oyster Feed
  Oregon Institute of Marine Biology
  (541) 888-6871

May
- Mother's Day Rhododendron Sunday
  Shore Acres State Park
  (541) 756-5401

August
- Charleston Seafood Festival
  Small Marina (541) 888-4875

Photo by Larry Osborne

Chuck's Seafood

MARKETS: *Best seafood*

The best place in Charleston to raise your omega-3 intake has to be Chuck's Seafood. Since 1953, Chuck's Seafood has made some of the finest seafood products imaginable. Owners Jack and Dee Dee Hampel offer delicacies caught by local fishermen, fresh, smoked or canned. Chuck's oysters, from its own farm, are raised in estuaries near Charleston and are some of the best you will ever taste. Chuck's sells them live in the shell, shucked, freshly smoked or canned. Visitors rave about the smoked albacore and smoked salmon. The Oregon dungeness crab is another great choice. Chuck's is also a full-blown gourmet food shop with goods such as Black Lava Sea Salt, local honey and special sashimi sauces. The friendly staff at Chuck's can custom-design a Myrtlewood gift basket filled with the items of your choice. They can tell you how to prepare your fresh fish, and they are more than happy to suggest the right item if you are not sure which delicacy to give as a gift. Chuck's gift packs and samplers are freshly prepared, hand packed and processed to keep their natural flavor. The products are free from artificial ingredients. Smoked selections are prepared over Alderwood coals. Stop by Chuck's Seafood whenever you pass through Charleston. You will be glad you did.

91135 Boat Basin Drive, Charleston OR
(541) 888-5525
www.chuckseafoods.com

Betty Kay Charters

RECREATION: *Best fishing charters*

Join captains Bill Whitmer and Kathi Johnson for fun and adventure on your next fishing trip. Betty Kay Charters will go all out to help you get your fish. Your safety is key, but most of all your hosts want you to have fun. The five-hour rock fish expedition is the most popular. You see the beautiful Oregon coastline while fishing near shore in 60 to 200 feet of water. Your trip takes you over kelp pads, reefs and pinnacles that are rich habitat for rock fish. You will catch blue rock fish, black rock fish, cabazon or a half-dozen other rock fish types, and you may catch ling cod. Limits are regularly caught. Nothing can beat the taste and flavor of fresh Oregon ocean-caught fish. Other trips take you after salmon, tuna or halibut. You can also enjoy an eco-tour, bay cruise or whale-watching jaunt. All gear is supplied for fishing trips. The Betty Kay is a 50-foot twin-engine vessel with restroom facilities. Coffee is available at all times. All you need is warm clothing and a snack. Back on land, Betty Kay Charters has a great gift shop where you can purchase a treat for later. Captain Bill and Captain Kathi truly care about giving you the best fishing adventure possible, so when you visit Charleston, be sure to come to Betty Kay Charters.

7788 Albacore Avenue, Charleston OR
(541) 888-9021
www.bettykaycharters.com

COOS BAY

The largest city in Coos County, Coos Bay is the commercial center of Oregon's south coast, with growing retail, service and professional sectors. The city's rejuvenated downtown area, adjacent to the Coos Bay Boardwalk, provides an attractive commercial area for residents and visitors alike. Coos Bay was established in the 1850s and incorporated in 1874. The town was then known as Marshfield, but in 1944 residents voted to change its name to Coos Bay. The area continues to be a major seafood harvesting and processing center, and the Port of Coos Bay is one of the country's leading shipping centers. Newer items now being manufactured here are precision tools, sports equipment and specialty sound systems.

PLACES TO GO

- Coos Art Museum
  235 Anderson Avenue
  (541) 267-3901

- Coos Bay Boardwalk
  Downtown

THINGS TO DO

March
- Southcoast Clambake Jazz Festival
  (541) 888-4386

April
- Home Show
  (541) 297-3319

May
- Historic Walking Tour of Coos Bay
  (541) 269-9388

- Memorial Day Parade and Ceremony
  (541) 888-6354

July
- 4th of July Celebration
  (541) 269-8918

August
- Blackberry Arts Festival
  (541) 266-9706

September
- Bay Area Fun Festival
  (541) 267-5008

- South Coast Rock & Gem Fest
  (541) 267-5008

Benetti's Italian Restaurant
RESTAURANTS & CAFÉS: *Best Italian food*

Bring your family or friends to Joe Benetti's fabulous restaurant overlooking beautiful Coos Bay. Benetti's is widely known in Coos Bay for its excellent cuisine and nightly seafood specials. The chicken fettuccine is out of this world. The veggie lasagna and the cannelloni are both excellent. Try the gnocchi, an Italian potato pasta tossed with your choice of marinara, meat, pesto or garlic parmesan sauce. Benetti's has a varied menu and offers smaller portions for seniors and children. All meals are served with soup, salad and delicious garlic bread. To accommodate varying dining environments, Benetti's seats families downstairs and reserves the upper level for adults. Benetti's provides banquet facilities for large groups and celebrations. Though his restaurant has kept Joe very busy, he has politics in his blood. He served on the Coos Bay City Council for 12 years, and has been mayor of the city for two terms. Come to Benetti's, a superb restaurant where you can enjoy a lovely meal served by a friendly staff while gazing at the bay.

260 S Broadway, Coos Bay OR
(541) 267-6066
www.benettis.com

GOLD BEACH

Gold Beach is a seaside town and it is a river town, where the wild and scenic Rogue River meets the Pacific Ocean. It is a forest town and a mountain town. The Coast Ranges are a mile high 15 miles inland. The town's name comes from the gold discovered on the Rogue River beach in 1853. Gold Beach is a center for arts and crafts, ocean charters, river exploration and fishing of all sorts. The Rogue River is widely known for its prolific salmon and steelhead. The Rogue Reef is home to a massive stellar sea lion rookery, and also provides some of the best bottom fishing on the entire coast.

PLACES TO GO

- Geisel Monument State Heritage Site
  U.S. Highway 101

- Otter Point State Recreation Site
  U.S. Highway 101

- Cape Sebastian State Scenic Corridor
  U.S. Highway 101

THINGS TO DO

February
- Sweethearts Day Crab Crack
  (541) 247-0923

May
- Seafood, Art and Wine Festival
  (541) 247-0923

July
- Party at the Port and Fireworks
  (541) 247-0923

- Curry County Fair
  (541) 247-4541

August
- Indian Creek BBQ
  Indian Creek Hatchery
  (541) 247-0396

October
- Hathaway Jones Tall Tales Festival
  (541) 247-0923

- Wild Rivers Coast Home and Leisure Show
  (541) 247-4541

Gold Beach bridge over the Rogue River

Indian Creek Resort
ACCOMMODATIONS: *Best cabins*

Imagine yourself sitting in a cozy little cabin overlooking the magnificent Rogue River. Sooner or later you are bound to see river otters frolicking in the water, deer grazing along the riverbank and salmon jumping after low-flying insects. This is what you will find at Indian Creek Resort. The resort has homey, picturesque cabins for rent, or you can even buy one to ensure you will always have an oasis away from the hustle and bustle of everyday life. The fishing is great. Indian Creek Resort is also an RV park that offers more than just a space to stay. You can take advantage of hot showers and a laundry, cable TV and public phones. A grocery store, restaurant and lounge are available. Whether you are in a cabin or your own RV, you will feel you have found home, especially when you soak in a heavenly hot tub. The resort is only a half mile from the Pacific Ocean, but that is just far enough to protect you from the high winds. Owners Scott and Karen Knox invite you to check in to Indian Creek Resort for a stay like no other.

94680 Jerry's Flat Road, Gold Beach OR
(541) 247-7704 or (800) 537-7704

Turtle Rock RV Resort
ACCOMMODATIONS: *Best RV resort*

Your hosts Julian and Kachina Starr invite you to Turtle Rock RV Resort. The resort is right outside of Gold Beach but feels miles from civilization. Choose a sunny RV site by Hunter Creek or a forested tent site surrounded by emerald-leafed trees. Pacific beaches dotted with dramatic rock formations are a few steps away. You have unrestricted access to a 14-mile stretch of beach suitable for long seaside walks, agate and driftwood gathering, sunset viewing and experiencing the awe of the sea. In the summer, you can pick wild blackberries and smell the scent of mint underfoot. If you do not have an RV, stay in the rental cottages. These accommodations provide the luxury you would find in a five-star hotel, surrounded by exquisite landscaping and natural beauty. Each one-bedroom cottage has a full kitchen, large deck with a hot tub and barbecue, and a sleeping loft for the kids. If you find yourself wishing you could stay forever, you can purchase a cabin of your own. However you visit, you will want to keep coming back to the Turtle Rock RV Resort.

28788 Hunter Creek Loop, Gold Beach OR
(541) 247-9203 or (800) 353-9754
www.turtlerockresorts.com

Ireland's Rustic Lodges

ACCOMMODATIONS:
Best beachside lodges

The Gold Beach Inn and Ireland's Rustic Lodges are on the sand in the heart of Gold Beach, where the surf is high and the majestic Rogue River flows into the sea. The two oceanfront lodgings are side by side. From either, private beach paths lead to a viewing deck and the ever-changing ocean. You can stroll, gather driftwood and watch for seals or whales. In the other direction, you can easily walk through gardens to restaurants, bookstores and art galleries in charming Gold Beach. Enjoy the friendliness and calm that only a small Oregon coastal town can offer. The ocean and river support fishing, crabbing and jet boat rides. Other local activities include golfing and horseback riding. Ireland's Rustic Lodges offers private beach cabins and vacation homes built with beautiful knotty pine. All cabins have fireplaces. The Gold Beach Inn is a four-story hotel; all third- and fourth-story rooms have oceanview balconies. Both the rustic lodges and the full-service inn provide stunning ocean views and breathtaking sunsets. For even more relaxation, two large ocean-front spas are opening soon. RV fans can stay at Ireland's Ocean RV Park on the water at the south end of town, still within walking distance of everything in Gold Beach. The RV park has a lighthouse tower to view the sunsets or even wandering deer. To truly experience the Oregon Coast, stop at the Gold Beach Inn and Ireland's Rustic Lodges.

**29346 Ellensburg Avenue,
Gold Beach OR**
(541) 247-7718 or (877) 447-3526
www.goldbeachinn.com
www.irelandsrusticlodges.com

Photo by Larry Osborne

Jerry's Rogue Jets
ATTRACTIONS: *Best excursions*

There are very few places in the United States where you can see the lay of the land exactly as the first pioneers did. You can view one of those extraordinary areas by booking a trip with Jerry's Rogue Jets. Family-owned and operated, Jerry's Rogue Jets was the first company to take jet propulsion boats up the Rogue River. The boats are a completely safe and comfortable way to ride, and each boat pilot has years of experience on the river. The pilots share with you the interesting history of the Rogue and point out geological anomalies as they come into view. They are expert at spotting wildlife and will point out the animals. Each pilot has a deep love and respect for the river that shines through as they describe a world many people never get to see. You can take the 64-mile scenic trip, the 80-mile whitewater trip or the 104-mile whitewater trip. Each one is more exciting, informative and exhilarating than the last. There is an on-site museum with exhibits on the rich history of the Rogue River canyon, as well as a gift shop. Visit Jerry's Rogue Jets on the water at the Port of Gold Beach for an experience you will never forget.

192 Port of Gold Beach Road, Gold Beach OR
(541) 247-4571 or (800) 451-3645 *www.roguejets.com*

LAKESIDE

Tenmile Lakes is one of Oregon's largest and most popular recreation lakes. Fishing is superb year round. You can catch large-mouth bass, trout and bluegill. Tenmile Creek, which feeds into the ocean, provides great steelhead fishing in the spring and fall. The lake is also perfect for watercraft sports. William M. Tugman State Park is on Eel Lake immediately north of Lakeside. Eel Lake is also a great spot for fishing. The sand dunes of the Oregon Dunes National Recreation Area are as close as they could possibly be—they are directly across U.S. Highway 101 from Lakeside. Clamming, crabbing and fishing are other ocean activities only minutes away.

PLACES TO GO

- Oregon Dunes National Recreation Area
  U.S. Highway 101
- William M. Tugman State Park
  U.S. Highway 101

THINGS TO DO

July
- Cardboard Boat Races
  Tenmile Lakes Docks
  (541) 759-2801

September
- Labor Day Regatta
  S Tenmile Lake
  (541) 756-3201

Tenmile Lake

Lakeshore Lodge and RV Park
ACCOMMODATIONS: *Best place to stay*

The Lakeshore Lodge and RV Park is the perfect spot for your weekend getaway. It is on Ten Mile Lake, the third-largest lake in Oregon and one of the top bass-fishing lakes in the state. The lake is also a haven for yellow perch, trout and bluegills. The picturesque Lakeshore Lodge offers lakefront dining. House specialties include fresh Winchester Bay oysters, prime rib and Diane's Own chicken-fried steak. The lodge has a lounge complete with shuffleboard and pool tables. There is a great dock where you can teach the younger family members to fish. Within minutes of the lodge are dune buggy rentals, camping areas, beach-combing areas and good fishing spots. With live music and dancing most weekends, this resort is an ideal place for a romantic weekend. Guests can wake up in the morning to the sunrise over a pristine lake. All rooms have a lake view and private patio or balcony. The RV Park has accommodations for those who love to take their home with them. The songs of birds and friendly smiles of the locals are more than enough to keep you coming back year after year.

290 S 8th Street, Winchester Bay OR
(541) 759-3161 or (800) 759-3951
www.lakeshorelodgeor.com

NORTH BEND

North Bend's name reflects its location at the north bend of the Coos Bay channel. In the town's early years, timber baron Asa Simpson built large sawmills and shipyards. Another prominent early figure was Vern Gorst, whose land, water and air service provided the embryo of United Airlines. Today, North Bend is home to a U.S. Coast Guard air station and the North Bend Municipal Airport, which provides commercial passenger service and general aviation facilities. Pony Village Mall in North Bend is the largest enclosed mall on the Oregon coast. You can find many antique stores and other unique shops throughout the downtown area.

THINGS TO DO

March
• Southcoast Clambake Jazz Festival
  (541) 888-4386

April
• Southcoast Woodcarvers Show & Sale
  North Bend Community Center
  (541) 348 2371

• North Bend Powwow
  North Bend Middle School
  (541) 756-2521, ext. 260

• Oregon Coast Gourmet Fest
  Pony Village Mall
  (541) 756-0433

May
• Gold Coast Chorus Barbershop
  Harmony Show
  Little Theater (541) 237-7892

June
• Bay Area Lumberjack Competition
  The Mill Casino
  (541) 672-0757

July
• North Bend July Jubilee
  (541) 756-4613

September
• Dahlia Show
  Pony Village Mall
  (541) 759-4309

Shore Acres State Park

The Mill Casino & Hotel
ATTRACTIONS: *Best place to stay and play*

Casino action, a great hotel and fine dining make the Mill Casino & Hotel a perfect getaway. The hotel and casino are owned by the Coquille Indian Tribe. All facilities are open 24 hours a day. When you enter the casino, the rustic Northwest décor and the beautiful stone fireplace tell you that you are someplace special. The casino has more than 500 slot machines, a bingo pavilion and weekly blackjack tournaments. Live music every night ranges from jazz and rhythm and blues to adult contemporary. Nationally known acts are frequent headliners. The hotel contains 112 luxurious rooms, including bay-view corner suites with Jacuzzi tubs. The hotel is one of the best in the area, and draws guests who simply want a comfortable place to spend the night as well as gaming enthusiasts. Whether you come for the casino, the hotel or both, you should join the free Millionaire's Club, which provides discounts. Dining choices include the Waterfront Plank House Restaurant, the 24-hour Timbers Café, the Hook Tender Saloon and seafood at the amazing Saw Blade Buffet. The casino provides complimentary valet parking and free shuttles to and from other area hotels. A nearby RV park is available to those who prefer to bring their home with them. The Mill Casino & Hotel creates nearly 500 jobs for the local economy and helps support the tribe's other community activities. Visit the Mill Casino & Hotel, where even the view is a winner.

3201 Tremont Avenue, North Bend OR
(541) 756-8800 or (800) 953-4800
www.themillcasino.com

Pancake Mill Restaurant
RESTAURANTS & CAFÉS: *Best pancakes*

Owners Beverly Rice and Gary Goodson welcome you to try any of the delectable breakfast and lunch treats served daily at the Pancake Mill Restaurant. You can order a slice of freshly baked pie or a three-egg omelet made with real cream and cheddar cheese. The pancake breakfast comes with buttermilk, buckwheat, potato, cornmeal or Swedish pancakes. The homey environment is ideal for the family. Beverly and Gary also offer light meals, vegetarian dishes, and entrees low in fat and sodium. If you feel like lunch, you can choose one of the Pancake Mill's specialties, such as the croissant Monte Cristo with turkey, ham and cheese, or the three-bean vegetarian chili with cornbread. With 24-hour notice you can order from 16 different types of pies that your family and friends are sure to love. The Pancake Mill also provides affordable catering for special events. Be sure to stop by the Pancake Mill Restaurant.

2390 Tremont Street, North Bend OR
(541) 756-2751
www.pancakemill.com

Myrtlewood Factory
SHOPPING: *Best gifts*

The Myrtlewood Factory in North Bend is the oldest and largest enterprise of its type in the state. You can take a tour of this working factory to see the entire process by which a piece of a Myrtlewood becomes a one-of-a-kind treasure. The Myrtlewood Factory carries items for every room in your home. Every part of the tree is used. Branches become walking sticks, leaves are used for cooking, flowers become perfume and the wood becomes functional, decorative and stunning household items. From serving spoons and plates to bowls and napkin holders, your dinner table can be set with Myrtlewood. At the Myrtlewood Factory you can special-order furnishings or pick up chests, trunks and tables ready made. Check out the warm and rich flooring options. Myrtlewood exhibits a wide variety of colors and patterns—no two patterns are the same. Minerals drawn up from the soil color the wood. Stress during the growth of the tree causes the figurations. Many grain patterns appear in myrtle, including burls, tiger-stripe, fiddleback, quilt, inkline and flame grain. Inspired by the beauty of this versatile wood? The factory carries slabs, boards and lumber. If you do not find the exact gift item you are looking for, let the staff members know. They can custom-craft a piece and ship it anywhere.

68794 Hauser Depot Road,
North Bend OR
(541) 756-2220 or (877) 755-2220
www.myrtlewoodfactory.com

PISTOL RIVER

Pistol River was the site of the Rogue River Indian War, a fierce and decisive battle between Indians and settlers in 1856. Its name reflects those days. The coast at Pistol River State Park is marked by dunes. Ocean windsurfing is so good that national championships have been held here three years in a row. Also on the coast is the Pistol River estuary, 230 acres with a watershed of about 106 square miles. You can hike towards the miniature dunes between the estuary to the left and jumbled flotsam and brush to the right. Cross the dunes to the beach, and explore as far as you like. South of Pistol River, U.S. Highway 101 courses through the Samuel H. Boardman State Scenic Corridor, 12 miles of forested, rugged, steep coastline interrupted by small sand beaches. You can admire the 300-year-old sitka spruce trees and gaze at the amazing Arch Rock and Natural Bridges.

PLACES TO GO

- Pistol River State Park
  U.S. Highway 101

- Samuel H. Boardman
  State Scenic Corridor
  U.S. Highway 101

Photo by Jolee Moody

Hawk's Rest Ranch

ACCOMMODATIONS: *Best place to stay*

Hawk's Rest Ranch brings fantasy to life. Here, you can ride a beautiful horse across a sandy beach while waves crash against the shore. The ranch offers trail rides on a pioneer homestead past a quiet stream on the forest edge, where you can spot many species of plants and wildlife. This 200-acre ranch is located in the historic Pistol River Valley on the Southern Oregon Coast. Named for the abundant red-tailed hawks soaring overhead, Hawk's Rest Ranch is surrounded by the Siskiyou Mountains to the east and the rocky shores of the Pacific Ocean to the west. Almost a mile inland, much of the ranch is protected from the coastal winds and fog that hug the coastline. For more than 100 years, the Walker family has lived and worked the ranch. Russ Walker, the current owner, has turned the family heritage into a working horse ranch. Horses are available both for the beginning rider and the more experienced equestrian. The ranch has pony rides for children under five, trail riding for beginning and advanced riders, and even offers rides in the family's handcrafted oak surrey. A historic one-room schoolhouse serves as a gift shop, museum and postal station. For an unforgettable riding experience, visit Hawk's Rest Ranch.

94727 N Bank Road, Pistol River OR
(541) 247-6423
www.siskiyouwest.com/hawk's_rest_ranch.htm

Portland Metro

CITY OF PORTLAND

Big city excitement and small town charm make Portland, the City of Roses, a favorite destination. Portland is located in a magnificent setting between the Columbia and Willamette Rivers. Mount Hood looms in the distance. Portland's galleries, museums and theater can keep you busy for weeks. Its lush green parks are perfect for a picnic or an afternoon stroll. It's neighborhoods are diverse, self-contained, well planned and interesting. For a city its size, Portland is easy to navigate. The City is divided into four quadrants that meet where Burnside Street crosses the Willamette River. Everything east of the river is east, everything west is west. Everything north of Burnside is north, everything south is south. Thus, streets and avenues have a quadrant designation—NW, SW, NE or SE depending on their relation to Burnside and the Willamette. The Portland street-numbering system extends well out into the suburbs. You can travel around the wider region using metro Portland's award-winning mass transit system, one of the most extensive and advanced in the country. It includes an historic trolley and the MAX, a light rail rapid transit line. Rides are free within a downtown zone. The entire city of Portland was built with walking and bicycling in mind. The short blocks, combined with public art, fountains and bridges offer opportunities for contemplation for the casual stroller. Bicycling magazines routinely rate Portland as the most bicycle friendly city in the country, with clearly marked bicycle lanes on most city streets. Nightlife in Portland is excellent and varied. It includes the world-class performances of the Oregon Symphony. See art up close at the First Thursday art gallery walks in the Pearl District or last Thursdays in the Alberta Arts District. The Portland Rose Festival in early June is Portland's largest event. The Portland waterfront turns into a carnival for a week as military ships moor alongside Waterfront Park. Portland is famous for its microbrews. Local enthusiasts claim the city has more breweries than any other on earth. Portland is the home of the Trail Blazers basketball team. Unsurpassed livability makes Portland a city to visit and remember.

photo by Stuart Seeger

photo by Stuart Seeger

PLACES TO GO

- Governor Tom McCall Waterfront Park
  750 SW Front Avenue

- Hoyt Arboretum
  4000 SW Fairview Boulevard
  (503) 228-8733

- International Rose Test Garden
  400 SW Kingston Avenue
  (503) 823-3636

- Oregon History Center
  1200 SW Park Avenue
  (503) 222-1741

- Oregon Maritime Museum
  Foot of SW Pine Street
  (503) 224-7724

- Oregon Museum of Science and Industry
  1945 SE Water Avenue
  (503) 797-4000

- Oregon Vietnam Veterans Memorial
  4000 SW Canyon Road

- Oregon Zoo
  4001 SW Canyon Road
  (503) 220-2781

- Portland Art Museum
  1219 SW Park Avenue
  (503) 226-2811

- Portland Children's Museum
  4015 SW Canyon Road
  (503) 223-6500

- Portland Classical Chinese Garden
  NW 3rd Avenue and Everett Street
  (503) 228-8131

- Portland Institute for Contemporary Art
  219 NW 12th Avenue
  (503) 242-1419

- Portland Japanese Garden
  611 SW Kingston Avenue
  (503) 223-1321

- Powell's City of Books
  1005 W Burnside Street
  (800) 878-7323

- Washington Park
  4501 SW Canyon Court

- World Forestry Center
  4033 SW Canyon Road
  (503) 228-1367

THINGS TO DO

January-February

- Chinese New Year Celebration
  Portland Classical Chinese Garden
  (503) 228-8131

- Chinese New Year Cultural Fair
  Oregon Convention Center
  (503) 771-9560

February

- Oregon Seafood & Wine Festival
  Convention Center
  (360) 210-5275

- Portland International Film Festival
  (503) 221-1156

- ChocolateFest
  World Forestry Center
  (503) 228-1367

March

- St. Patrick's Day Celebration
  Holy Rosary Church
  (503) 286-4812

April

- Quilt Show
  University Place
  (503) 643-1067

- Spring Beer & Wine Fest
  Convention Center
  (503) 246-4503

- Wordstock (book fair)
  Convention Center
  (503) 546-1013

May

- Ceramic Showcase
  Convention Center
  (503) 222-0533

- Cinco de Mayo Fiesta
  Governor Tom McCall Waterfront Park
  (503) 232-7550

- Portland Indie Wine Festival
  Urban Wine Works (503) 961-2205

- Norwegian Constitution Day
  Norse Hall (503) 236-3401

- Woodfest
  World Forestry Center
  (503) 228-1367

May-June

- MythFest: Art, Theatre, Ancient Tales
  (503) 295-4997

Photo by Larry Osborne

June
- Portland Rose Festival
  (503) 224-4400

- Portland Pride Festival and Parade
  Riverfront Park
  (503) 295-9788

June-July
- Waterfront Blues Festival
  Waterfront Park (503) 282-0555

July
- Bastille Day Celebration
  Carafe Restaurant (503) 223-8388

- Yoshida's Sand in the City
  (sand sculpture competition)
  Pioneer Courthouse Square
  (503) 736-3200

- Portland International Piano Festival
  World Forestry Center (503) 228-1388

- Festival of Cheese
  Hilton Hotel (503) 583-3783

- Carifest (Caribbean celebration)
  Portland State University
  (503) 358-9254

- Oregon Brewers Festival
  Waterfront Park (503) 778-5917

August
- Senior Prom (senior citizens)
  Pioneer Courthouse Square
  (503) 223-1613

- The Bite of Oregon
  Waterfront Park (503) 248-0600

- Festa Italiana
  Pioneer Courthouse Square
  (503) 223-1613

September
- Time Based Art Festival
  (503) 242-1419

- Salmon Nation Block Party
  Ecotrust Building (503) 227-6225

September-October
- Under the Autumn Moon (Moon Festival)
  Old Town Chinatown (503) 823-3294

December
- Portland Holiday Ale Festival
  Pioneer Courthouse Square
  (503) 252-9899

- Champagne Ball
  Hilton Hotel (503) 224-8499

Portland Farmers Market

ATTRACTIONS: *Best farmers market*

The community activists who created the Portland Farmers Market in 1992 set out to bring the best of the country to the heart of the city. Today, local farmers connect directly with consumers through four market sites in downtown Portland. Products for sale go beyond fruits and vegetables to include flowers, baked goods, cheese and meat, and almost anything else that can be grown or processed locally. Vendors and their products go through careful screenings. The markets provide public education on regional farming, gardening and food preparation through cooking demonstrations and classes. Customers sample unusual fruits and vegetables at Taste the Place tasting stations, and hunger relief organizations have access to produce at the end of each market day. The flagship market at Portland State University attracts a crowd each Saturday beginning in April. Downtown workers look forward to the midday market on Wednesdays in Shemanski Park, beginning in May. A newer Thursday evening market at Ecotrust in the Pearl district features 35 vendor stalls, chef demonstrations and a popular June berry festival. The newest venue is the Eastbank market, organized by the Buckman neighborhood. Families and neighbors enjoy strolling out Thursday evenings to buy fresh produce and dinner while listening to local musicians. The nonprofit Portland Farmers Market relies on sponsors, fundraising, vendor fees and countless hours of volunteer time. For a weekly festival celebrating the fresh foods of the region, visit the Portland Farmers Market.

**Portland State University, between SW Harrison Street and SW Montgomery
SW Park Avenue Shemanski Park, between SW Salmon Street and Main Street
Pearl District, NW 10th Avenue between Irving Street and Johnson Street
Eastbank, SE Salmon Street and 20th Avenue**
(503) 241-0032
www.portlandfarmersmarket.org

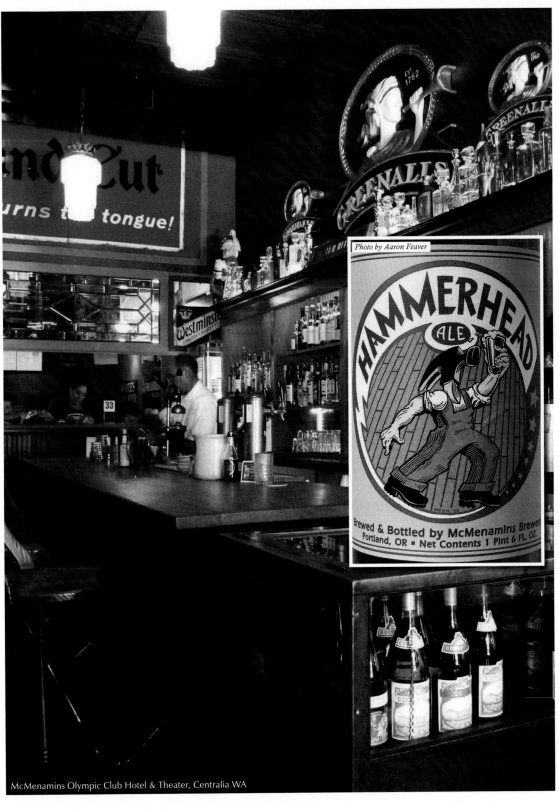

Photo by Aaron Feaver

HAMMERHEAD ALE

Brewed & Bottled by McMenamins Brewery
Portland, OR ▪ Net Contents 1 Pint 6 FL. OZ.

McMenamins Olympic Club Hotel & Theater, Centralia WA

McMenamins

ATTRACTIONS:

Best string of unique businesses in the Northwest

In Portland you can stop just about anyone and ask them about a McMenamins. Watch their eyes light up as they point you in the direction of the closest one. McMenamins is the name behind more than 50 destination pubs, microbreweries and hotel spots all over Oregon and Washington. With fun and entertaining atmospheres that are kid and adult friendly you will find that many folks have been to at least one and most have a bona fide favorite. (Ours would be a toss-up between Edgefield, Kennedy School and The Crystal Ballroom). Started in 1974 by the McMenamin brothers as a philosophical pursuit of fun, funky and friendly gathering spots for good food and good beer, the concept has found a captivated audience and a region of devoted fans. Now providing neighborhood pubs, movie houses, microbreweries, hotels, bus tours, music venues and ballrooms, there seems to be no end to the magic created by these two truly inspired entrepreneurs. Each location is entirely unique unto itself, yet retains historical preservation, artistic diversity, musical style and a neighborhood allegiance that is unsurpassed. Consider visiting one each week and you'll be busy all year. Some of the fabulous sights you'll see on your journey through their Kingdom of Fun are the 360-degree view from Hotel Oregon's Rooftop Bar, the floating dance floor at the Crystal Ballroom, the Kennedy School's Detention Bar, the Mission Theater Pub, Edgefield in Troutdale, and the Old St. Francis School in Bend. There is so much more to these locations than we can cover here that you will just have to see them in person to appreciate the full experience.

Headquarters
1624 NW Glisan, Portland OR
(503) 223-0109
www.mcmenamins.com

Oregon Zoo

ATTRACTIONS: *Oldest zoo west of the Mississippi*

More than a million visitors come to the Oregon Zoo each year to view rare and exotic animals and learn about the zoo's residents through fun events and exciting educational opportunities. The creative staff of the Oregon Zoo has put together something for everyone. Of course the main attraction is the animals. You will find yourself coming back again and again to get to know them. There is even a petting zoo for the young and young at heart, and no visit is complete without a ride on the Washington Park and Zoo Railway. You will always find something wonderful to see and do at the Oregon Zoo. The Zoo's Cascade Grill Restaurant has a spacious dining room with a high, open-beam ceiling arching over cozy wooden booths. Its carpet and metalwork chandeliers are commissioned art pieces reflecting the great Northwest. When the sun is out the large outdoor deck is the place to be. You can look out over alpine rocks and hear the sounds of exotic animals while you eat a wonderful meal. The Restaurant also has a banquet area for large groups and events. Cascade Outfitters, the Zoo's gift shop, is a treat for the discriminating shopper looking for unique and eco-friendly animal-related gifts. Each purchase helps the zoo fund its conservation programs and environmental education efforts. No zoo admission is necessary to shop in this attractive store. The Oregon Zoo is located five minutes west of downtown Portland.

4001 SW Canyon Road, Portland OR
(503) 226-1561
www.oregonzoo.com

World Forestry Center
ATTRACTIONS: *Best interactive exhibits*

The World Forestry Center in Portland's Washington Park is a five-acre campus that includes the Center's Discovery Museum. The museum gives you a hands-on, interactive experience that teaches about the forests and trees of the Pacific Northwest and the world. Exhibits are designed to show visitors how we interact with the forests and their importance in our lives. The Dynamic Forest provides both an underground *root crawl* experience and a canopy walk through the upper branches. While the simulated smoke jumping and whitewater rafting exhibits demonstrate how people work and play in the forest. Upstairs, you can take a journey through some exotic places in the world and learn of boreal, sub-tropical, temperate, and tropical forests as well as explore temporary exhibits about art, culture and history. Since 1971, the World Forestry Center has been providing an exciting and educational experience for adults and children alike. The Museum's history traces back to the Lewis and Clark Centennial American Pacific Exposition and Oriental Fair held in Portland in 1905. Civic leaders first named it the Western Forestry Center, a non-profit educational institution that would later be renamed the World Forestry Center to reflect its international mission. The World Forestry Center's Discovery Museum is housed in a massive wooden building commanding magnificent hilltop views across the park and the city beyond. The building is considered a masterpiece of Cascadian style architecture. The World Forestry Center campus also has two other beautiful wooden buildings which can be rented out for social functions and business meetings.

Washington Park, Portland OR
(503) 228-1367
www.worldforestry.org

Portland Children's Museum
ATTRACTIONS: *Best children's museum*

This lively, entertaining and totally captivating enterprise is now called the Portland Children's Museum 2nd Generation, or CM2 for short. The new name came with a move from cramped quarters to a spacious new location close to the Oregon Zoo. CM2 has been serving Oregon since 1949 and is the sixth oldest children's museum in the United States. Their mission is to foster creative behavior in people, especially children. CM2 serves approximately 250,000 children and parents per year. Go to the colorful Website to see a full schedule of children's favorite activities. They have areas for dress-up, water play and music-making, as well as regularly scheduled story times. They have an interactive Animal and Animal Homes exhibit, a puppet theater, a hands-on clay studio and the Wonder Corner where they can draw plants and rocks, using microscopes. The newsletter *CM2 and You!* tells members all about their activities and with a wealth of benefits for membership at a wide variety of levels, joining CM2 is an investment that every family will profit from. CM2 has pointers in their newsletters that help parents, like how to support imagination and literacy in the home. Volunteers play a critical part at CM2 by playing with the kids, building exhibits, sewing costumes and props, doing art with children, reading stories and many other activities. Individuals, service organizations and corporate groups are all invited get involved at Portland Children's Museum 2nd Generation.

4015 SW Canyon Road, Portland OR
(503) 223-6500
www.portlandcm2.org

NE Portland

Mt. Hood over Portland International Airport
Photo by David Smigelski

NE PORTLAND

Northeast Portland is an unpretentious, arty quarter with an extensive mix of residential neighborhoods, art districts, shopping and large scale attractions, such as Portland International Airport and the Rose Quarter, home to the Rose Garden Arena and the Memorial Coliseum. The NBA Trail Blazers play here, as do the Winter Hawks of the Western Hockey League and the Lumberjax of the National Lacrosse League. Lloyd Center, a huge shopping and office complex, is also in the neighborhood, as is the Oregon Convention Center and a large collection of fine hotels. NE neighborhoods include Irvington, with its fine old architecture, the Alberta Arts District, which features Last Thursday art walks, Concordia, home of McMenamin's Kennedy School, and the Hollywood District.

PLACES TO GO

- Columbia Park
  7651 N Chautauqua Boulevard

- East Delta Park
  N Martin Luther King Jr. Boulevard

- The Grotto (botanical garden)
  NE 85th Avenue and NE Sandy Boulevard

- The Kennedy School
  5736 NE 33rd Avenue

THINGS TO DO

April-May
- Historic Irvington Home Tour
  (503) 288-9234

May
- Alberta Art Hop
  NE Alberta Street (503) 236-6132

June
- Champ Car Grand Prix
  (503) 821-4344

July
- America's Largest Antique
  and Collectibles Show
  Expo Center (503) 736-5200

August
- Lowrider Tour
  Expo Center (503) 736-5200

Furever Pets

ANIMALS & PETS:
Best local pet supply store

At Furever Pets, customers are thought of as guests. That's because store owner Symon Lee's roots are in Singapore, where customers are respected and valued. As you enter this brightly painted store, you'll not only get a cheerful greeting, but you'll find it well organized, too. Furever Pets carries top quality pet toys, treats and nutritional products primarily for dogs and cats, but there's also a selection for birds and rabbits. Furever Pets is very active in the community by sponsoring a little league team and working with various animal shelters through support and donations. Once a month, Symon offers a pet for adoption from differing shelters. He feels it's important to increase the awareness of adoption over purchasing pets from breeders and pet stores. Symon and his knowledgeable staff do their best to assist pet owners in selecting the right product for their pet. Seminars, lectures and ongoing learning opportunities are scheduled on a regular basis. Furever Pets was an immediate success when first opened three years ago and it continues to grow and develop a loyal clientele. In addition to toys and treats you'll find 12 to 15 brands of select pet food that cannot be purchased in grocery stores. There's even a selection of bones and raw or fresh frozen meats. Stop in and visit this wonderful store. It feels good just to be there even if you don't have a pet.

**1902 NE Broadway,
Portland OR
(503) 282-4225**

Les Schwab

AUTO: *If they can't guarantee it, they won't sell it*

The birth of the Les Schwab Tire Company occurred in January of 1952, when Les Schwab purchased a small OK Rubber Welders tire store in Prineville. With a $3,500 investment and a strong desire to own his own business, Les increased the sales of his store from $32,000 to $150,000 in the first year. Les had a strong determination to provide a business opportunity for people who could not afford to go into business for themselves. As the company continued to grow, Les came up with what is known as the supermarket tire store concept. His goal was to have his warehouse in his showroom so that customers could walk through the racks of tires and pick out the actual tires that would go on their vehicle. He also stocked more than one brand of tire in each size to give customers a choice. Today, the Les Schwab Tire Company is one of the largest independent tire companies in the United States. Les is the first to say the success of the Les Schwab Tire Company has been made possible by wonderful customers who are the most important people in the business. Nothing happens at Les Schwab until a customer leads the way by choosing new tires, a wheel alignment or any of the other services they offer. Les Schwab is proud to feature neat clean stores, supermarket selection, convenient credit, sudden service, and a written warranty you don't pay extra for. Les's slogan is, "If we can't guarantee it, we won't sell it!" Come into one of the 385 Les Schwab stores today.

www.lesschwab.com

Tires LES SCHWAB

Star Motors

AUTO: *Best place for Mercedes-Benz owners*

Gunther Hirschmann had many years of experience working on Mercedes-Benz automobiles prior to opening his own shop in 1993. He understands that these exceptional vehicles are best serviced in exceptional surroundings. Star Motors is just such a place. The reception area is sparkling clean, fresh-smelling, light and airy. There is a window to the back bays where you can watch skilled technicians performing expert work in a nearly spotless environment. The owners specialize in all things mechanical for your Mercedes. They provide top-notch routine maintenance and the highest quality, most reliable work on the engine, transmission or undercarriage. They are eminently qualified to take care of the new vehicles being produced by Mercedes-Benz, as well as the classic models. With the skyrocketing cost of fuel, Star Motors knows how important it is to keep your car in its best possible condition. They will happily provide courtesy ride service to your home or office while giving your Mercedes the attention it deserves. For all your maintenance and repair needs, call on Star Motors.

19215 SW Teton Avenue, Tualatin OR
(503) 691-9826

Lukas Auto Paint and Repair

AUTO: *An Oregon success story*

Four generations of the Lukas-Carlson family has served the auto painting and repair needs of Portland. Alex Lukas, a blacksmith by trade, started the shop with his son, Melvin, in 1936. After 45 years, Mel decided to retire and close the business, whereby his daughter, Laurie, stepped up. She was informed by many of her competitors that "Women don't belong in this business," but she didn't listen. Laurie successfully owned and operated Lukas Auto Paint and Repair for 25 years. She recently sold it to her son J.R., but remains fully involved with marketing. Today, J.R. continues the family tradition of absolute integrity, top-notch customer service, expert collision repair, painting and detailing. The entire staff is certified. Lukas provides the most modern equipment to bring your vehicle to pre-collision condition. They will work with you and your

insurance company, and every repair receives a lifetime warranty for as long as you own your vehicle. The Elders in Action organization deems Lukas "elder friendly." Lukas was named Body Shop of the Year by a national jury of its peers and Laurie was honored by the S.B.A. as the Small Business Person of the Year for the state of Oregon. You can place your damaged vehicle in the hands of Lukas Auto Paint and Repair, a trusted community favorite for 70 years.

1722 E Burnside, Portland OR
(503) 235-5671

Si's Auto Body

AUTO: *Bodywork you can count on*

In a small northeast Portland neighborhood, Si's Auto Body opened, in 1972, to serve the community. Kraig Weninger bought the shop and, with his 35 years of experience in the field, is dedicated to continuing the tradition of providing the best service to his customers. Kraig and his staff of certified I-CAR and ASE (Automotive Service Excellence) technicians concentrate solely on auto body collision repair and painting. Their efforts result in superlative restoration of your vehicle. Working with the latest technology, the experts at Si's can fix anything, from the smallest door ding to major damage. They will deal directly with either you or your insurance company, whichever you wish. Estimates are free, as is the drop-off service provided while your vehicle is being repaired. For Kraig and his crew, Satisfaction Guaranteed is more than mere words. It is both the mission and the motto of Si's Auto Body.

6708 NE Glisan, Portland OR
(503) 254-8531

Kadel's Auto Body
AUTO: *Best auto body*

In 1954, Kadel's Auto Body began as a one-man shop in downtown Tigard. There are now 13 shops located throughout Oregon, Washington and Idaho. Walk into any of their clean and friendly locations and you will be welcomed by people who know their business, ready to take care of your auto body needs. Repairing more than 20,000 vehicles every year, Kadel's offers the best in customer service and gives lifetime guarantees on all their work. At Kadel's, they understand that auto body repair can be unexpected and, at times, costly. They will expertly assess the damage and make sure you know all your options, so that you can make the best decision about your car. The employees are experts in their field, receiving on-going training to keep up with changes in the industry. They repair any vehicle from the smallest import to massive SUVs. Kadel's provides the skill, patience, and state-of-the-art technology to get your repair done right. Kadel's and its staff appreciate the communities they serve, and they support youth activities and charities with their time and money. For all your auto body repairs, come to Kadel's, a community favorite for more than 50 years.

9350 SW Tigard Street, Tigard OR
(503) 598-1159
www.kadels.com

Turquoise Learning Tree
BUSINESS: *Safe and fun learning*

Since 1996, Rob and Carolina Peterson have been fulfilling a vision. They have been building a network of Learning Tree Day Schools to provide fun for kids and peace of mind for parents. Leaders in affordable childcare, Learning Trees offer a safe and supportive environment for children from six weeks to 12 years of age. Sparing no expense, they provide the best furniture, supplies, toys and food for children. Main meals are delicious, well balanced and hot. There are pre-school, kindergarten and summer camp programs. The teachers are highly qualified and receive on-going training. All are certified in CPR and first aid and have attended the Oregon Child Care Basics program. The emphasis of the schools is on treating children with respect, encouraging self esteem and helping with social and emotional development. Caring, sharing, conflict-resolution and good sportsmanship skills are all part of the lessons. There are reading programs, arts and crafts, swimming lessons and plenty of healthful outdoor activity. If you are looking for the best care for your child in an environment that supports healthy child development, you can count on Learning Tree Day Schools.

15135 SW Beard Road, Beaverton OR
(503) 590-8409
www.learningtreeschools.com

ReMax Equity Group
BUSINESS: *Hometown real estate experts*

When you purchase or sell your home with ReMax Equity Group, you are working with the number one real estate company in the state of Oregon and the ninth-fastest growing real estate company in the country. Founded in 1984, the Equity Group has held this number one ranking in Oregon every year since 1994. Their sales in 2004 reached $5.3 billion, utilizing more than 1,200 professionals in 19 locations in the Portland Metro Area. They also serve clients in the Salem and Bend areas. As they say, "we've got you covered," with sales professionals and brokers averaging more than 13 years in the real estate field. With more than 80-percent of their business from referrals and repeat customers, you can rest assured they are providing the best in service. Equity Group has a full service relocation department. Almost all of their relocation services are free of charge. There is a convenient local contact in Portland. Whether you need local or national relocation services, they have the staff to satisfy your needs. Connected with the community they serve, in 2004 they donated more than $92,000 to 25 local charities through the Equity Group Foundation. Much of this is due to the hard-working people at Equity Group serving as leaders, participating in their communities and devoting time and money to the local charities. Giving back to the community is one of their missions. When selecting your realtor, consider ReMax Equity Group, The Hometown Experts with a World of Experience.

8405 SW Nimbus Avenue, Suite C, Beaverton OR
(503) 670-3000
www.equitygroup.com

Foxfire Teas

BAKERIES, COFFEE & TEA: *Best tea room*

Foxfire Teas in Portland is a fun and relaxing modern tea bar, serving organic teas, locally made pastries and tasty sandwiches. The engaging owners of this pleasant venue are Quinn and Katherine Losselyong, who started Foxfire Teas because of their passion for tea and interest in entertaining. Quinn and Katherine designed much of the Foxfire décor, including the fireplace, sculptures and tables. Foxfire specializes in bulk, loose-leaf teas stored in special tins where customers can easily make their personal selections. Tea choices are broad, with selections covering all major tea categories, including green, black, herbal, oolong and white teas. Although tea is the mainstay drink here, guests can also choose tea lattes, coffee, hot chocolate or an elixir tonic, plus fresh pastries to accompany their refreshments. Order your teas to go, or stay and soak up Foxfire's inviting space. Large overstuffed chairs and a living room setting encourage relaxation, while a children's area with chalkboard, coloring table, toys and books allows parents to sip their tea while watching their children. With free, wireless Internet access, you can peruse the web over a rejuvenating cup of tea. Visit Foxfire Teas and experience the joys of tea and the easygoing charm of this delightful teahouse.

4605 NE Fremont Street, #102, Portland OR
(503) 288-6869
www.foxfireteas.com

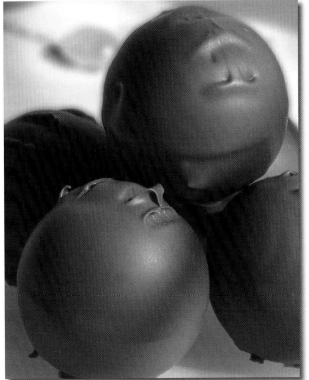

Moonstruck Chocolate Co.

FUN FOODS: *Best chocolate*

No matter where you are in Portland, chances are you are close to a Moonstruck Chocolate Café. These cafés are easy-going settings for drinking chocolate and espresso drinks and sampling Moonstruck Chocolate Company's handcrafted artisan chocolates, made fresh in Portland. The chocolates, which take up to three days to produce, are miniature works of art. Moonstruck uses the finest cocoa beans in the world and blends in fresh ingredients, many from the Pacific Northwest. The company's superior raw materials and exacting techniques have led to an endless series of awards and media mentions. The chocolate is regularly included in the gift baskets given to celebrities at the Academy and Emmy Awards. Moonstruck has been featured in *O Magazine* and on the Food Network. The chocolates are carried by fine chocolate retailers and grocers nationwide, as well as through the company's website. Moonstruck Chocolate Cafés are popping up in other states. The whimsical atmosphere, a line of irresistible truffles, and beverages such as Chocolate Chai and Brown Cow are just a few of the many attractions awaiting the chocolate connoisseur. Stop by a Moonstruck Chocolate Café and sample their chocolate perfection. It will alter the entire course of your day.

608 SW Alder Street, Portland OR (503) 241-0955
526 NW 23rd Avenue, Portland OR (503) 542-3400
45 S State Street, Lake Oswego OR (503) 697-7097
11705 SW Beaverton-Hillsdale Highway, Beaverton OR (503) 352-0835
(800) 557-MOON (6666) Moonstruck corporate office
www.moonstruckchocolate.com

Terra-Sol Landscaping

HOME: *Best landscaping*

During a summer job on Hayden Island, David Zimmerman developed an affinity for working outdoors in landscaping, construction and design. He continued to gain experience working for a design-landscape company. After earning a degree in Landscape Architecture, he started his own business, Terra-Sol Landscaping. Along with his experienced and professional staff, David serves the greater Portland metropolitan area. Working within any budget, they will strive to create the outdoor space of your dreams. They can build retaining walls, patios, garden paths and steps. Water features are also a specialty, including ponds, fountains, bubble rocks and waterfalls. Garden lovers enjoy working with David in creating their special garden spaces. Terra-Sol, meaning Earth-Sun, has provided landscaping for several homes at the annual Street of Dreams. In addition to landscaping, Terra-Sol is a long-time sponsor of Little League in the community. They are well known and well respected. You can trust your next outdoor project to Terra-Sol Landscaping, a community favorite since 1977.

(503) 691-6105
www.terrasollandscaping.com

Broadway Floral Home & Garden

GARDENS, PLANTS & FLOWERS: *At the same location for 76 years*

The pleasure of shopping, the thrill of discovery and the joy of giving are all found at Broadway Floral Home & Garden. Doug and Janice Fick are third-generation family owners who have been operating the store since 1970. Located near 17th Avenue in the Lloyd District, Broadway Floral has been in the same location for 76 years. Founded at the turn of the century, they were originally called Canby Floral. At this time, they supplied plants and flowers to other florists. In 1928, they became a retail flower shop. Just after WWII ended they erected a greenhouse, one of the few left in Portland. Although they don't use it for growing plants anymore, you will find

it filled with home décor, gifts and, of course, plants and flowers. Broadway Floral has a very knowledgeable staff that is always eager and willing to help you. Doug and Janice focus their business on beautifying people's lives through nature. Broadway Floral is well known for being a European Florist. They have a wide variety of cut flowers incorporated into hand-tied bouquets or arrangements. They also carry unique jewelry. As much as possible, they use seasonal local growers with sustainably harvested products. Visit Broadway Floral Home & Garden for a great selection of quality bouquets and gifts.

1638 NE Broadway, Portland OR
(503) 288-5537 *www.broadwayfloral.com*

Oregon Rainforest Company

GARDENS, PLANTS & FLOWERS: *Best hydroponics supplies*

Across the globe many intrepid gardeners have begun to grow things hydroponically, thinking they are utilizing revolutionary new tactics. However, the Aztecs, Babylonians and ancient Egyptians all used a form of hydroponics to grow vegetable crops. At Oregon Rainforest Company you can learn how to use this ages-old technique to grow healthy, delicious fruits and vegetables along with flora of all kinds. Owners Josh and Lynsey Serpa, along with their two young daughters, are passionate about creating a healthier, safer world for future generations. They are exceptionally knowledgeable about alternative energy sources and offer many of the needed supplies at Oregon Rainforest Company. Here you can find a wide range of indoor gardening materials, which represent 80-percent of the business, along with a great selection of books, clothes and seeds. If you're not familiar with the mechanics of hydroponics, the Serpa's are happy to give you an in-store, crash course on hydroponics, and will assist you in creating a starter kit including seeds, germination trays, oasis cubes and proper lighting. According to Lynsey, "Plants grow faster with hydro than in soil, so you get to come home and see how it's grown." You don't need a fancy greenhouse to cultivate hydroponically grown goods; you can do it on the kitchen table with proper lighting. Visit today and learn more about hydroponics and sustainability at Oregon Rainforest Company.

19949 E Burnside Street, Portland OR
(503) 826-1414 *www.oregonhydro.com*

Skin Deep Beyond

HEALTH & BEAUTY: *Best day spa*

Cindy Ogden took her degree from the Esthetics Institute in Portland, added her amazing energy and persistence, and built her business from the ground up. Open since 2000, customer satisfaction has spread the word and Skin Deep & Beyond is now known as the best day spa in Tualatin. With extra-clean treatment rooms, candles and soothing music, you will relax knowing you are receiving the best of care. Using the finest products and technology, Cindy and her expert staff provide facials and proven facial enhancements, nail care, waxing and body wraps. The licensed massage therapists perform a variety of techniques, including Swedish, deep-tissue and pregnancy massage. Treat yourself to any of the spa packages offered or have one customized just for you. Cindy and her associates are committed to providing you with a totally satisfying and personalized spa experience. For a personalized spa package for yourself or a loved one, come into Skin Deep & Beyond, where exceptional results are guaranteed.

8373 SW Warm Springs Street, Tualatin OR
(503) 692-2888
www.skindeepandbeyond.com

Massage on the Go

HEALTH & BEAUTY: *Most versatile massage*

Mary Dalton, Owner

Does anything feel better than a great massage? Are you dreaming of one right now? Massage on the Go will come straight to your door, whether at home, the office, a hotel, or a special event. You won't have to wait for an appointment, fit it into your busy schedule, or fight traffic to get relief. Mary Dalton and her staff of fully accredited spa and massage specialists provide a wide range of relaxing and therapeutic treatments. They are skilled in hand and foot reflexology, water therapy, Shiatsu, deep-tissue and classic Swedish massage, as well as Reiki energy healing and techniques for relief of myopathy pain. If you want a facial or body wrap, those are part of the service, as well. In addition to the mobile service, you may want to visit their conveniently located spa, where you can check out the Bio-Photonic Scanner, one of only 15 in Oregon. The scanner allows the technicians to determine the types of supplements to suggest for increasing antioxidants for better health at the cellular level. From the inside out, Massage on the Go is a center for healing and wellness.

8879 SW Center Street, Tigard OR
(503) 620-0724

Pennington Massage Clinic

HEALTH & BEAUTY: *Dedicated to helping people build muscles*

Todd and Pam Pennington of Pennington Massage Clinic believe that if you take care of your body now, it will take care of you later. The clinic, which opened in 1992, is dedicated to helping people reduce tension in the muscles in order to increase functionality. Todd and Pam are Oregon Licensed Massage Therapists, and Nationally Certified Medical Massage Therapists. They listen to client concerns and work to bring balance and functionality. Todd and Pam use Medical Massage tests to determine muscles that are weak and in spasm. They also use many different techniques to release tension and manual therapy techniques that assist in injury recovery. By using recognized medical tests to determine problem muscles and to test improvement, it is easier to recognize progress. Todd and Pam's goal is to bring harmony to the body by balancing the musculature and building proper function and support for tendons, ligaments and bones. In many cases even chronic muscle pain is reduced when the muscle tension is released. While some clients self refer, much of Todd and Pam's work is medically prescribed, and the process is a cooperation between doctor, patient and massage therapist. To get started on your way to greater health and well-being, call the Pennington Massage Clinic for an appointment.

10175 SW Barbur Boulevard, Suite 210, Portland OR
(502) 244-4427
LMT #3833 (Todd) and #8027 (Pam)
www.penningtonmassage.com

Northwest Personal Training and Fitness Education

HEALTH & BEAUTY: *Best personal fitness team*

Helping people change their lives in positive ways is what drives Alex and Sherri McMillan, owners of Northwest Personal Training and Fitness Education. Their passion in their business is to assist people in their efforts to look and feel better. They offer highly skilled trainers who are motivated to help clients get results. Alex and Sherri have extensive backgrounds in the fitness industry, and they have used their expertise to create a remarkable place for clients to enjoy a community-oriented workout setting. "We only hire amazing people," explains Sherri. The energetic and warm reception you will experience when you step through the door shows that commitment to customer service. As a training studio, Northwest Personal Training and Fitness Education is distinctly different from a standard fitness gym, because the focus is on the individual's experience. Both Alex and Sherri have been invited to consult and speak with others in the industry around the world to discuss their operating model. With spa services also available, the company offers a complete package for prospective customers seeking to change their lives. Come by to see the impact that the dedication of these two remarkable people is having on the lives of their clients. They are making a difference in the Portland fitness community.

2714 NE Broadway, Portland OR
(503) 287-0655
www.NWPersonalTraining.com

Goodnight Room

HOME: *Best room décor for youngsters*

The Goodnight Room is a one-stop shop for anyone outfitting a child's room. Owner Ann Adrian focuses on room décor, furniture and bedding for chuildren and teens. This colorful and welcoming store has an interesting layout, with simulated rooms of various colors set up and furnished to convey the many options available. The store exudes fun, with areas such as the Construction Zone, the Land of Make Believe, and a working Little Engine That Could train. With experienced designers in-house and custom services available, the Goodnight Room offers a personal relationship with customers. Ann's husband, Jeff Scott, manages the operations end of the business with a sure and steady hand. Ann and her staff believe it is an honor to serve families, and that feeling shows in their work. Take time to visit the Goodnight Room when your family needs furnishings. It is an out-of-the-ordinary children's store.

1517 NE Broadway, Portland OR
(503) 281-5516
Brideport Village
7283 SW Bridgeport Road, Tigard OR
(503) 684-9510
www.goodnightroom.com

Kitchens & More Northwest

HOME: *Best cabinetry*

Fine cabinetry offers much more than a place to put your things, it enhances a home's beauty and utility and defines your home's décor. At Kitchens & More Northwest in Hillsboro, you'll find the best service and craftsmanship in the industry plus a wide range of style options and wood species. Since opening Kitchens & More Northwest in 1989, owners Drew and Val Tolmie and their talented crew have been working with individual homeowners and area builders to style custom-made specialty cabinets for every room in your house. When you enlist the services of Kitchens & More Northwest, you can expect expert guidance in designing the perfect kitchen, office, entertainment

center or bathroom, plus durable finishes and high quality hardware that assure your lasting satisfaction. The Kitchens & More showroom is bound to stir up your dreams with almost a dozen cabinet displays and a wall exhibiting door styles, color selections, knobs and pulls. Area builders have chosen the prize-winning work of the Kitchens & More Northwest team to appear for the past 16 years in the Street of Dreams project, a display of cutting-edge style options for today's finest homes. "We believe fine cabinetry is the heart of a home," says Drew. When you are ready to experience the beauty and practicality of custom cabinetry, turn to the experts at Kitchens & More Northwest. They will use their expertise and state-of-the-art equipment to build a lasting heart into your home.

460 SW Armco, Hillsboro OR (503) 648-0499
http://kitchensandmorenw.com

Portland Closet Company

HOME: *Best closet company*

Even the roomiest closet can become a black hole of lost shoes and clothing. Portland Closet Company has the solution. This company enhances the lives of its clients by designing and installing superior organizing systems. Portland Closet offers complimentary in home design consultation, professional installation by experienced carpenters and spotless clean up. You can visit their large, airy showroom in Portland's Pearl District to get a taste of their custom work. In addition to designing superior walk-in and reach-in closets, the company has solutions for offices, pantries and garages. Portland Closet carries Tilt-Away wall beds in twin, double and queen styles that can double the functional size of a room. Closet systems and cabinetry use melamine or real wood veneers for a handsome, durable finish. You can also find brightly colored shelves and drawers for children's closets. Founded in 1985, this local, family-owned business has earned a reputation for exceptional design, service and installation. The staff members strive to work within your budget and on schedule. They respect your ideas, add their expertise, and turn your dreams into reality. They want your experience with them to be so delightful that you will be eager to recommend them to your friends. Visit Portland Closet Company and see what a difference beautifully organized storage can make in your life.

1120 NW 14th Avenue, Portland OR
(503) 274-0942 or (800) 600-5654
www.portlandcloset.com

Lile North American

HOME: *Best North American Van Lines interstate agent*

Established in 1959, Lile has safely moved people, businesses and products throughout the Pacific Northwest and far beyond. It is a second-generation family company that is certified by the Women's Business Enterprise National Council as a 100 percent woman-owned business. Lile is active in the community, working with Northwest Medical Teams and the Oregon Food Bank. While it has grown to include six branches in Washington and three in Oregon, Lile remains committed to its founding principle of providing claim-free, reliably delivered, customer-focused moving and storage services. Ranking as one of NorthAmerican Van Lines' top U.S. agents, Lile earned their Quality Excellence Award for the last two years and was named its top booker of military business. In addition to its national and international relocation capabilities, Lile offers sophisticated on-line logistics services, including an interactive international rate-quote system, and order-entry and shipment tracking. Lile's Warehousing & Distribution division reliably meets its service commitments to customers. For all your moving and storage needs at home and abroad, you can count on Lile.

19480 SW 118th Avenue, Tualatin OR
(503) 691-3500
www.lile.net

West-Meyer Fence

HOME: *Best fence company*

Lance and Jennifer West and Ron Meyer combined their skills and formed West-Meyer Fence in 1997. Lance learned the trade from his father, Jennifer is a talented designer, and Ron has extensive fence-construction experience. Together they will take you through the bid process, design your project, and work within your budget to meet your fencing needs. West-Meyer provides fencing to residential, commercial and industrial customers, and they work with the top names in the home-construction trades. They can handle any request and they work with a wide range of materials. From ornamental iron, glass railings, concrete and stone to vinyl, wood and chain link, they will build the perfect fence for you. West-Meyer takes pride in their craftsmanship. Tour the Street of Dreams and you will find many examples of their fine work. For everything from security fencing to a beautiful enclosure for your home, call on West-Meyer Fence.

712 N Columbia Boulevard, Portland OR
(503) 978-1830

Tri-County Temp Control

HOME: *Best HVAC*

In 1987, Alan Sanchez founded Tri-County Temp Control, determined that the company would grow and prosper by delivering superior customer service. Referrals from satisfied customers have consistently proven him right. With a crew of more than 70, Tri-County has a long and distinguished track record throughout the metro Portland area. Tri-County has installed thousands of retro-fit and new-construction HVAC systems, earning its status as the name you can trust. Their work is well represented on the Street of Dreams and greatly respected by homeowners, businesses and contractors throughout the area. Tri-County can assess your home or office space,

then design and install the system that best meets your needs. When you visit their massive showroom, you will be greeted by friendly people with expert knowledge of their business. Every effort is made to provide products primarily manufactured in the USA. In addition, the company is committed to environmentally friendly products and procedures. For all your heating, air-conditioning and indoor air-quality needs call on Tri-County Temp Control. You will become a customer for life.

13150 S Clackamas River Drive, Oregon City OR
(503) 557-2220

Sunset Heating & Cooling

HOME: *Custom systems by the experts*

Originally established as Sunset Fuel in 1922, this company began as a fuel delivery business. At first, they delivered sawdust from a local lumber yard. As times and technology changed, they moved from sawdust to wood to coal to heating oil. Today, the name has been changed to Sunset Heating & Cooling to reflect the refocus on furnaces, air conditioning, heat pumps and indoor air quality products. Sunset has been a Carrier dealer since 1958 and has been designated a Factory Authorized Dealer. This means that Sunset has well trained and certified technicians and salespeople, as well as being in the top five percent of Carrier's dealers nationwide. This also means that all Carrier products installed by Sunset come with a 100-percent customer satisfaction

guarantee backed by Carrier. Sunset's comfort specialists evaluate your site, listen to your needs and goals to customize the right system for your home. Estimates are free. From system design to installation and service, Sunset's highly trained staff will work to ensure your total satisfaction. If you ever do need service, Sunset's service department is there for you 24 hours a day. For the highest quality products and customer service, you can't go wrong at Sunset Heating & Cooling.

0607 SW Idaho Street, Portland OR
(503) 234-0611

Pro-Tech Cleaning Services

HOME: *Best carpet cleaning*

Chris Boston is on the job at every job ensuring that your needs are met with the best service, products and prices. Pro-Tech Cleaning Services is certified in commercial and residential carpet cleaning, dyeing and repair, as well as care of oriental rugs, textile and leather upholstery, and tile, stone and wood floors. As the array of choices in fabrics and surfacing materials grows, the crew at Pro-Tech learns the latest procedures and chemistry, employing the most up-to-date techniques and equipment. Chris and his staff pursue on-going education through trade shows, seminars and classes. Committed to each and every customer, Pro-Tech has established and maintained an excellent reputation. Real estate agents recommend Pro-Tech to their sellers and buyers. Elders in

Action has certified them as an Elder-Friendly Business for their fair practices, ethical and respectful treatment and their extra efforts in meeting special needs. Pro-Tech does not believe in surprises. You will receive a free estimate for your job and they provide a written complaint policy to ensure your complete satisfaction. Their motto is, The Most Thorough Cleaning Ever, Or It's Free. For all your floor and upholstery cleaning needs, call Pro-Tech Cleaning Services.

12150 Camden Lane, Beaverton OR
(503) 975-7577
www.protechcleaning.com

Nu-Art LLC

HOME: *Best green building products*

A unique company in Portland specializes in providing "green products" for use during the construction process. Nu-Art owners Marc Stumpf and Wade Martin know they are doing something special and even those outside the industry can recognize that sustainable product solutions are the wave of the future in construction. Nu-Art offers an assortment of environmentally friendly products and services to meet the residential and commercial needs of West Coast contractors. Nu-Art specializes in a wide selection of alternative and recycled-content materials that prevent the need for harvesting natural stone. One of these products, Slatescape, is a

man-made product with the feel and look of natural stone that weighs 40-percent less than stone. Richlite is a paper-based countertop material that is created with environmentally sustainable resources, including some recycled fibers, yet is long-lasting and durable. See how and why designers and architects are responding to the responsible ethic of the Pacific Northwest by visiting this cutting-edge company next time you are in Portland.

8454 N Interstate Place, Portland OR
(503) 452-7642
www.greensurfaces.com

Mergenthaler Transfer & Storage

HOME: *A fleet based on integrity*

Art and Nick Mergenthaler opened for business in Helena, Montana in 1934. Back then, their 1933 Dodge half-ton truck was hauling 100-pound bags of flour, sugar, potatoes, and other goods for local grocers. The 1950s brought transporting construction supplies for dam building and a contract to haul mail for the U.S. Postal Service. Mergenthaler grew steadily, and when Art died in 1972, his four sons took over the business, expanding it to an interstate operation. Now owned and operated by two of Art's grandsons, the company is still growing by leaps and bounds. Though they have fleets of modern vehicles and massive storage facilities, this community favorite has never forgotten its core principle of building open, honest, and ethical relationships with the people it serves. The more than 285 employees are proud of the history and reputation of their company and are able and ready to provide you with personalized, local, professional service. To meet your transportation and storage needs, call Mergenthaler.

7895 SW Hunziker Road, Tigard OR
(800) 547-0795
www.mergenthaler.net

The Heights at Columbia Knoll

LIFESTYLE DESTINATIONS:
Best retirement community

Located next to The Grotto, with a view of Mount Saint Helens, The Heights at Columbia Knoll is a visionary senior retirement community. The first thing most people notice is how much heart is evident in the attention to detail and caring. This senior retirement community is dedicated to serving a population that is typically underserved. The management and staff make a special effort to go that extra mile to provide a quality life for seniors. The Heights is income-based, with moderate prices. Residents enjoy many services, such as housekeeping, a movie theater, beauty salon, private dining room, concierge and many other amenities. The people involved are very passionate about the facility. The fact that it is located on the site of the former Shriners Children's Hospital is significant. The Shriners was shut down 18 years ago. To preserve the memory of the old hospital, the keystone that was above the doorway of the hospital now enjoys prominence embedded in the stonework of the fireplace. Furthermore, the original copper entryway is now in the outdoor courtyard and 65 of the original plants, such as the camellia bushes, were saved from the original landscaping. With 208 units for seniors, The Heights has a sophisticated security system. You will find raised beds in the courtyards, so residents may enjoy gardening if they wish. For more information, check out the website or call The Heights at Columbia Knoll.

8320 NE Sandy Boulevard, Portland OR

(503) 203-1094

www.TheHeightsatCK.com

Oregon Baptist Retirement Homes

LIFESTYLE DESTINATIONS:
Highest quality senior community

Since 1944, Oregon Baptist Retirement Homes (OBRH) has lived by its motto, Seniors Our Concerns, Christ Our Motivation. The mission of Oregon Baptist Retirement Homes is to provide a continuum of services for senior adults, encouraging lifelong personal growth for the residents, their families, staff and the surrounding community. Located on a beautiful six-acre campus in a quiet neighborhood near medical services, shopping and banking, the Independent Living and Assisted Living apartments offer six levels of care as appropriate to the individual resident. OBRH is Medicaid licensed. Three delicious daily meals with many entrée choices, transportation to appointments and events, and plenty of on-site activities are provided by the dedicated staff, many of whom have served for more than 20 years. Seasonal gardening on the spacious grounds is a favorite pastime, and everyone is welcome to attend and participate in church services held on the campus. You are invited to come for a tour or stop by and share a meal. Just call the friendly staff to arrange your visit to Oregon Baptist Retirement Homes.

1825 NE 108th Avenue, Portland OR
(503) 255-7160
www.obrh.org

Westside Dance & Gymnastics Academy

RECREATION: *Leader in dance and gymnastics*

The mission of Westside Dance & Gymnastics Academy is to provide a safe, fun and positive environment, promote creativity and fitness, and inspire students to achieve their goals. Owner Mellanie Heniff is a long-time student of dance and gymnastics. She offers classes for all age groups, encouraging whole families to participate. The 12,000-square-foot facility provides the best USA Gymnastics-certified equipment. Private lessons are available for all gymnasts. Mellanie believes dance helps children develop self-confidence, flexibility, a sense of rhythm and coordination. She and her staff encourage values of good sportsmanship, self-discipline, respect and accountability. The academy is open seven days a week, has a pro shop and offers Summer camp programs in dance, theater, cheerleading and gymnastics. Their academic pre-school and after-school care programs enable you to find a program that will work for you and your family. For an exciting alternative in a safe and welcoming atmosphere, Westside Dance & Gymnastics Academy is a leader in education, dance and gymnastics.

11632 SW Pacific Highway, Tigard OR
(503) 639-5388
www.westsideacademy.com

Bridges Café and Catering

RESTAURANTS & CAFÉS:
Best neighborhood café

For more than five years, Tom and Laura have been in the business of serving people delicious food and friendly service at Bridge's Café and Catering. They have made a name for themselves for their memorable breakfasts, and their restaurant is a wonderful place to linger and see friends while enjoying homemade soups and baked goods. Tom and Laura's dream was to create a second kitchen for the neighborhood, providing the kind of food you would lovingly prepare at home. The breakfasts are made fresh, with seasonal, locally grown organic ingredients. The establishment is open for lunch, as well. In addition, Bridge's Café provides topnotch catering for events and special occasions. To complement their delectable menu, the café completes your satisfying meal away from home by providing great service, courtesy of their fun and friendly staff. With the down-home atmosphere that welcomes you when you walk in the door, all you need to do is arrive hungry. The staff at Bridge's Cafe and Catering will make sure you leave satisfied.

2716 NE Martin Luther King Jr. Boulevard, Portland OR
(503) 288-4169

Chameleon Restaurant and Bar

RESTAURANTS & CAFÉS:
Best fine dining

"Asian-inspired fine dining with an eclectic European flair" is the best way to describe Pat Jeung's Chameleon Restaurant and Bar. As you enter, the cozy romantic environment and warm soft lighting compel you to drop everything and relax. As Pat puts it, Chameleon offers fine dining without attitude, demonstrating that he and his staff recognize they can offer stellar cuisine without the pretension so commonly associated with top-notch fare. Using organic produce and free-range meat as much as possible, Pat demonstrates his dedication to quality in every food item he offers. Music, usually that of European-styled vocalists, is used intentionally to enhance the intimate dining experience. The restaurant is available for special events and Chameleon is often the site of fundraisers and charity dinners. The lovely, large patio is used extensively in the summer. With signature dishes such as rack of lamb with rosemary sauce, and butternut squash ravioli calling to you, make a date to rendezvous with Chameleon Restauranty and dine in the comfortable elegance of Pat's place.

2000 NE 40th, Portland OR
(503) 460-2682
www.chameleonpdx.com

Photos by RyanPhotoStudio.com

Colosso

RESTAURANTS & CAFÉS: *Best tapas*

Broadway's lone tapas bar, Colosso, will entice you with quality cuisine, innovative specialty drinks and a flirtatious environment. Colosso features tapas, small plates of gourmet fare, along with a comprehensive selection of Spanish wines and signature, made-to-order cocktails with freshly squeezed juices. Plates of prawns, calamari with capers or assorted marinated olives encourage light dining. A house specialty that consistently gets rave reviews is sautéed mushrooms with Madeira wine and lemon thyme served on grilled garlic bread. Owner Julie Colosso buys food locally as much as possible. By doing this, she not only supports the local economy, but ensures the freshness and high quality of the menu selections and spices up the menu with seasonal fare. Colosso's atmosphere is intimate, hip and ever-so-stylish. Patrons come for the late night dining, the chance to experience the sensual tone of the tapas bar, to see and to be seen in this Portland hot spot. Although there is no dancing, Colosso hosts music with a live disc jockey on the weekends, attracting a wide demographic of customers. Julie supports the community by hanging local artwork and rotating it monthly. Colosso has been called one of the sexiest joints in town and is available to host fund-raising or other charitable events. On your next trip to Portland, be sure to visit Colosso. where full-service fare continues into the late night hours.

1932 NE Broadway Street, Portland OR
(503) 288-3333

Trade Roots

SHOPPING: *Best boutique*

Walk in the door of Trade Roots in Portland, and the world's colorful folk art spreads before you in all its dazzling diversity. You'll find the latest styles of jewelry, accessories and clothing, often with an ethnic flair. Many of the artists behind the folk art live a little better than they once did thanks to fair trade and the awareness of business owners Katy Keys and Tamara Patrick. This 16-year-old import store seeks to make a difference by purchasing, when possible, from ethical wholesalers and artisans who make a fair wage and have good working conditions. Katy and Tamara not only admire the work they sell, they feel a strong desire to see that the artisans and the consumer all benefit from the transaction. This eclectic shop is a world bazaar where delicate cutwork clothing from Indonesia might sit next to a carved yak bone necklace from Nepal or a hand-carved box from El Salvador. Trade Roots carries many gifts appropriate for any time of year, including Mexico's Day of the Dead. Visit Trade Roots whenever you need a gift for a friend, but don't be surprised if you walk away with a few things for yourself.

1831 NE Broadway, Portland OR
(503) 281-5335
www.traderootsinc.com

GRESHAM

With almost 100,000 people, Gresham is the population center of eastern Multnomah County. This city, the fourth largest in the state, lies between the big-city hustle of Portland to the west and the solitude of the countryside to the east. The Portland urban growth boundary runs along Gresham's east side, guaranteeing easy access to sylvan relaxation. Gresham's design emphasizes livability, with bike paths, landscaped sidewalks and many different kinds of housing. Two MAX light rail stations provide rapid transit to Portland. Gresham Station, next to the MAX rail line, features more than 50 shops and restaurants in a unique village setting. The Gresham Farmers Market features locally grown produce, flowers, entertainment and local artists. Gresham is home of the annual Mt. Hood Jazz Festival.

PLACES TO GO

- Blue Lake Regional Park
  20500 NE Marine Drive, Fairview

- Chinook Landing Marine Park
  22300 NE Marine Drive

- Dabney State Recreation Area
  Historic Columbia River Highway

- Main City Park
  219 S Main Avenue

- Oxbow Regional Park
  SE Gordan Creek Road

THINGS TO DO

July
- The Portland Highland Games
  (503) 293-8501

August
- Mt. Hood Jazz Festival
  www.mthoodjazz.com

September
- Teddy Bear Parade
  (503) 665-1131

October
- Salmon Festival
  Oxbow Park
  (503) 797-1850

Priestley & Sons Moving

BUSINESS: *Most helpful movers*

More than 75 years ago, Carroll H. Priestley founded his company to meet the moving and hauling needs of a growing Portland. Today, Teresa Priestley, Chris Brown and Jeff Brown continue the family tradition of excellent, personalized customer service. Originally haulers of groceries and firewood, Priestley & Sons Moving has grown and changed with the times. They provide a fleet of the most modern moving trucks and up-to-date professional moving equipment to ensure that your move, be it large or small, is smooth and trouble-free. One of the oldest, continuously running moving companies in the state of Oregon, Priestley & Sons Moving offers heated, secure warehouses. This community favorite believes in supporting the local economy, employing more than 25 people and allowing no outsourcing of labor. Committed to its community, Priestley & Sons provides service to the Assistance League of Oregon and pays special attention to the residents of the numerous retirement homes in the area. For outstanding service with your moving and storage requirements, call on Priestley & Sons Moving. They've been keeping this area moving since 1929.

2255 NW Birdsdale Avenue, Gresham OR
(503) 661-7920
Portland (503) 232-3332
SW Washington (800) 700-7920
http://priestleymoving.com

TROUTDALE

Troutdale grew up around a pretty, historic downtown and the pristine Sandy River. The city has long been the gateway into metro Portland from the east. The railway came through in 1882. The Columbia River Highway was constructed in 1916, and the Multnomah County section was the first paved highway in the Pacific Northwest. Today, 40 miles of the original road are open as the Historic Columbia River Highway. The 24 westernmost miles starting in Troutdale provide access to dozens of hiking trails, Crown Point Vista House, and numerous waterfalls, such as Multnomah Falls. The Troutdale Airport serves as a base for scenic aerial tours of the Columbia River Gorge. Troutdale is the location of a crown jewel in the local McMenamins brewpub chain, the 38-acre Edgefield resort. The town is also known for the Columbia Gorge Premium Outlets, a collection of 45 name-brand outlet stores

PLACES TO GO

- The Barn Museum
  726 E Historic Columbia River Highway

- Harlow House Museum
  726 E Columbia River Highway

- Historical Society Museum
  104 SE Kibling Street

- Lewis and Clark State Recreation Site
  I-84 exit 18

- McMenamins Edgefield (resort)
  2126 SW Halsey Street

THINGS TO DO

July
- SummerFest
  (503) 669-7473

- Bite & Bluegrass Festival
  biteandbluegrass.troutdale-oregon.com

August
- Troutdale Cruise-In
  (503) 669-7473

September
- Antique Street Fair
  (503) 674-6820

- Harvest Faire
  (503) 669-7473

Bridge over
Sandy River
Photo by Jeff Muceus

Columbia Gorge Salon & Spa

HEALTH & BEAUTY: *Best salon spa*

Columbia Gorge Salon & Spa in historic downtown Troutdale offers three floors of services devoted to beauty and relaxation. Plan an entire day of pampering or combine spa and salon services with visits to neighboring boutiques, antique shops and galleries. The pampering begins from the moment you walk into the refurbished brick building with its wood beam ceilings and hand-painted walls. For the next few hours, the cell phones are off and the focus is on you with 23 congenial and well trained employees to cater to your every need. Spa packages group popular choices together, or you can choose your own set of treatments. Pedicures and manicures will leave your feet ready to dance and your hands like satin, while massage therapy is customized to decrease stress and relieve muscle tension. Among the many skin care treatments are customized facials, including toning for your eyes and microdermabrasion, a non-invasive skin resurfacing that reduces the appearance of fine lines, enlarged pores and scars. Body treatments are equally appealing and encourage relaxation, cellulite reduction and skin glowing with good health. Bridal parties can seek special occasion hair and make-up consultations. Your hair will receive equal attention to detail with coloring and cuts prepared to bring out your best features. Columbia Gorge sells quality products to keep you feeling and looking your best between visits, plus specialty items like Oregon's Canyon Creek scented candles. Reservations help, but the spa can often make last-minute arrangements. Visit Columbia Gorge Salon & Spa and prepare to revitalize.

205 E Historic Columbia River Highway, Troutdale OR
(503) 491-1336

Celebrate Me Home

HOME: *Best home décor*

Celebrate Me Home in the Sandy River town of Troutdale carries a mix of furnishings that are sure to turn any house into a home. Owner Mary Greenslade has created an environment that is both welcoming and inspiring with many vignettes to showcase everything from rustic to more traditional styles with brands like Lane, Stanley and Lee. Whether you need furnishings for a den, a living room or a child's bedroom, chances are Celebrate Me Home has an idea for you. The entire three floors are devoted to comfortable furnishings and a comfortable shopping experience. Sip coffee from the in-house espresso bar while you check out the new merchandise that regularly appears in the showrooms. Rustic with a Twist is the theme for a casual selection of fine pieces that complement the relaxed and natural lifestyles of the Pacific Northwest. The store even features appropriate Born shoes to match the easy elegance of this style. Art, Ink, Letters features a thoughtful collection of furniture and accessories for home and professional offices, including sophisticated stationery. The store's Design Studio is the place to turn for advice on furnishings and window treatments. Their experienced design team can help you balance your vision with your budget and make appropriate choices that create the look you crave. Celebrate Me Home takes a team approach to style with 20 talented staff members to answer your questions. Find the inspiration you need to enhance your personal spaces at Celebrate Me Home.

319 E Historic Columbia River Highway, Troutdale OR
(503) 618-9394
www.iinet.com/~cmh/index.html

Hawthorne Bridge at Night

SE Portland Metro

SOUTHEAST PORTLAND

Southeast Portland stretches from the warehouses by the Willamette River south to Reed College and the city of Milwaukie, and east to Gresham. SE Portland contains dozens of great neighborhoods, which in true Portland style are served by well-organized neighborhood associations. Some areas, especially Hawthorne and Sellwood, have a countercultural flavor. Southeast Portland harbors a large number of excellent restaurants. On the Willamette across from downtown is the Oregon Museum of Science and Industry, better known as OMSI, with its Omnimax theater. A paved path leads north from OMSI to the newly minted Eastbank Esplanade, a 1.5-mile walkway that runs between the Hawthorn and Steel Bridges and provides some of the best views of downtown Portland. Southeast Portland also features Mt. Tabor Park and Powell Butte Nature Park, both of which contain extinct volcanoes.

PLACES TO GO

- Elk Rock Island
  Willamette River off SE Sparrow Street

- Laurelhurst Park
  SE 39th Avenue and Stark Street

- Leach Botanical Garden
  6704 SE 122nd Avenue
  (503) 823-9503

- Mount Tabor Park
  6350 SE Yamhill Street

- Powell Butte Nature Park
  16160 SE Powell Boulevard

- Sellwood Riverfront/Oaks Pioneer Parks
  SE Spokane Street

- Westmoreland Park
  SE McLoughlin and Bybee Boulevards

- Woodstock Park
  SE 47th Avenue and Steele Street

THINGS TO DO

September
- Muddy Boot Organic Festival
  St. Philp Neri Church (503) 764-7525

Sellwood Bridge
Photo by Norman Eder

Oregon Museum of Science & Industry

ATTRACTIONS:
World-class attraction

If you're visiting Oregon, one of the most important places you can go is the Oregon Museum of Science and Industry, better known as OMSI. Located in the heart of Portland, this 219,000-square-foot building has the largest science outreach education program in the United States. It also has more popular exhibits that have been featured throughout North America and Europe than any other institution. OMSI evolved from a donated house in 1955 to a hand-built brick building constructed by volunteers in 1957. It found its home on a donated 18-acre site along the east bank of the Willamette River. The facility was completed in 1994, and now entertains one million visitors a year. OMSI has dedicated a significant portion of its space to teaching children science and math in stimulating and fun ways, from its Science Playground where young children can learn activities through playing games and inspecting the resident reptiles and critters, to the Physics, Chemistry, Laser and Holography Labs equipped for teens and young adults. But OMSI isn't just a great place to bring young ones, with its exclusive state-of-the-art 330-seat dome screen OMNIMAX Theatre and 200-seat planetarium. OMSI has a place for everyone interested in creative experiences. If exploring becomes too demanding, there's always the Science Café by the river for a peaceful place to unwind before jumping back into the adventures. With hundreds of different activities for the young and old, both residents and travelers, OMSI is a priority for anyone who loves discovery.

1945 SE Water Avenue, Portland OR
(800) 955-OMSI (955-6674)
www.omsi.edu

Les Schwab

AUTO: *If they can't guarantee it, they won't sell it*

The birth of the Les Schwab Tire Company occurred in January of 1952, when Les Schwab purchased a small OK Rubber Welders tire store in Prineville. With a $3,500 investment and a strong desire to own his own business, Les increased the sales of his store from $32,000 to $150,000 in the first year. Les had a strong determination to provide a business opportunity for people who could not afford to go into business for themselves. As the company continued to grow, Les came up with what is known as the supermarket tire store concept. His goal was to have his warehouse in his showroom so that customers could walk through the racks of tires and pick out the actual tires that would go on their vehicle. He also stocked more than one brand of tire in each size to give customers a choice. Today, the Les Schwab Tire Company is one of the largest independent tire companies in the United States. Les is the first to say the success of the Les Schwab Tire Company has been made possible by wonderful customers who are the most important people in the business. Nothing happens in the Les Schwab Tire Company until a customer leads the way by choosing new tires, a wheel alignment or any of the other services they offer. Les Schwab is proud to feature neat clean stores, supermarket selection, convenient credit, sudden service, and a written warranty you don't pay extra for. Les's slogan is, "If we can't guarantee it, we won't sell it!" Come into one of the 385 Les Schwab stores today.

www.lesschwab.com

Tires LES SCHWAB

Avanti Auto Body

AUTO: *Doing business with a conscience since 1978*

Quality is more than just a word at Avanti Auto Body. Automotive painting and refinishing are truly an art, and Avanti's artists and superior craftsmen can expertly restore your slightly dented or even nearly totaled vehicle to pre-crash condition. The professionals at Avanti Auto Body are I-CAR and ASE-certified and are able to combine the latest techniques and the highest quality materials with their expert eye to create showroom-quality finishes. In addition to auto repair and refinishing, Avanti specializes in restoring classic cars, as well as painting and repairing commercial vehicles. Owner Janet Shore was named 2004 Business Woman of the Year by the National Republican Congressional Committee and is committed to the motto, Doing Business with a Conscience since 1978. She and her staff give generously to their community. The Waverly Children's Home, Special Olympics, American Diabetes Association, Perry Center, and Oregon Food Bank are just some of the organizations that have been helped by Avanti's generosity. Janet is proud of her staff and they look forward to providing you with timely, expert repair and refinishing that will put you safely back on the road.

2922 SE 82nd Avenue, Portland OR
(503) 777-3303

Bradshaw's Service Center

AUTO: *Quality auto repair since 1938*

Gene Bradshaw established his auto repair business in 1938. It is still in the same location, and is enjoying its nearly seven-decade reputation as a community favorite. Owner Kenneth Glasgow started working at Bradshaw's in 1969. In 1987, he bought the business, opened a second location and more than doubled the staff. Take your domestic or foreign vehicles to the shop and receive the best of care for all things mechanical. At Bradshaw's Transmission Annex, they specialize in the care of transmissions, clutches and differentials. All of their technicians are ASE certified, and all are capable of handling the most modern and high-tech systems and amenities. Their combined 150 years of experience ensures that your job will be done right the first time and will exceed your expectations every time. Their longevity and customer loyalty attest to the fact that they always live up to the slogan, Get an Honest Repair, at a Competitive Price. Say goodbye to your car troubles at Bradshaw's Service Center.

1025 SE Hawthorne Boulevard, Portland OR
(503) 235-4156
Bradshaw's Transmission Annex
909 SE 12th Avenue, Portland OR
(503) 233-9934
www.bradauto.com

Star Motors

AUTO: *Best place for Mercedes-Benz owners*

Gunther Hirschmann had many years of experience working on Mercedes-Benz automobiles prior to opening his own shop in 1993. He understands that these exceptional vehicles are best serviced in exceptional surroundings. Star Motors is just such a place. The reception area is sparkling clean, fresh-smelling, light and airy. There is a window to the back bays where you can watch skilled technicians performing expert work in a nearly spotless environment. The owners specialize in all things mechanical for your Mercedes. They provide top-notch routine maintenance and the highest quality, most reliable work on the engine, transmission, or undercarriage. They are eminently qualified to take care of the new vehicles being produced by Mercedes-Benz, as well as the classic models. With the skyrocketing cost of fuel, Star Motors knows how important it is to keep your car in its best possible condition. They will happily provide courtesy ride service to your home or office while giving your Mercedes the attention it deserves. For all your maintenance and repair needs, call on Star Motors.

Serving Greater Portland/Vancouver
19215 SW Teton Avenue, Tualatin OR
(503) 691-9826

Willamette River runs through SE Portland

Lukas Auto Paint and Repair

AUTO: *An Oregon success story*

Four generations of the Lukas-Carlson family has served the auto painting and repair needs of Portland. Alex Lukas, a blacksmith by trade, started the shop with his son, Melvin, in 1936. After 45 years, Mel decided to retire and close the business, whereby his daughter, Laurie, stepped up. She was informed by many of her competitors that "Women don't belong in this business," but she didn't listen. Laurie successfully owned and operated Lukas Auto Paint and Repair for 25 years and recently sold it to her son J.R., but remains fully involved with marketing. Today, J.R. continues the family tradition of absolute integrity, top-notch customer service, expert collision repair, painting and detailing. The entire staff is certified. Lukas provides the most modern equipment to bring your vehicle to pre-collision condition. They will work with you and your insurance company, and every repair receives a lifetime warranty for as long as you own your vehicle. The Elders in Action organization deems Lukas "elder friendly." Lukas was named Body Shop of the Year by a national jury of its peers and Laurie was honored by the S.B.A. as the Small Business Person of the Year for the state of Oregon. You can place your damaged vehicle in the hands of Lukas Auto Paint and Repair, a trusted community favorite for 70 years.

1722 E Burnside, Portland OR (503) 235-5671

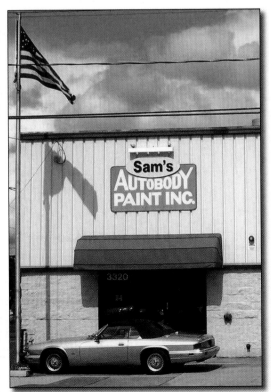

Sam's Auto Body & Paint Inc.

AUTO: *Great auto body repair*

Sam's Auto Body & Paint, Inc. has been providing top quality auto body and paintwork on luxury automobiles, specializing in Jaguars and Mercedes, since 1980. Owner and founder Sam Park and his crew of 10 mechanics eagerly tackle even the most daunting automobile repairs. With state-of-the-art equipment, Sam's works with Portland's leading Jaguar dealers and is the only certified auto body shop in Oregon that can perform service on their aluminum frames. Sam's affords each customer the highest degree of courtesy and respect. A former president of the Metro Portland Lion's Club, Sam is an active member of Portland's Korean community, volunteering his time with Holt Adoption Service. For all your luxury automobile service and repair needs, visit Sam's Auto Body & Paint.

3320 SE 50th Avenue, Portland OR (503) 771-3131

Kadel's Auto Body

AUTO:

In business for more than 50 years

In 1954, Kadel's Auto Body began as a one-man shop in downtown Tigard. There are now 13 shops located throughout Oregon, Washington and Idaho. Walk into any of their clean and friendly locations and you will be welcomed by people who know their business and are ready to take care of your auto body needs. Repairing more than 20,000 vehicles every year, Kadel's offers the best in customer service and gives lifetime guarantees on all their work. At Kadel's, they understand that auto body repair can be unexpected and, at times, costly. They will expertly assess the damage and make sure you know all your options, so that you can make the best decision about your car. The employees are experts in their field, receiving on-going training to keep up with changes in the industry. They repair any vehicle, from the smallest import to massive SUVs. Kadel's provides the skill, the patience, and state-of-the-art technology to get your repair done right. Kadel's and its staff appreciate the communities they serve, and they support youth activities and charities with their time and money. Come to Kadel's for all your auto body needs. They've been a community favorite for over 50 years.

9350 SW Tigard Street, Tigard OR (503) 598-1159
www.kadels.com

Lents Body Shop

AUTO: *An Eco-logical and Gold Class repair shop*

Since 1968, Lents Body Shop has pursued one mission: to provide professional, factory-quality auto body, paint and collision repairs in a state-of-the-art facility. Lents works with all insurance companies to return your vehicle safely to the road in the shortest time possible and make you comfortable in the process. Owner Randy Dagel has built a business that has earned top recognition as a Gold Class facility by II-CAR (Inter-Industry Conference on Auto Collision Repairs). Gold Class shops are always expanding their ongoing education and technical training to stay on the cutting edge of auto repair. Lents Body Shop is a PPG Automotive "Certified First" repair facility. Inspected yearly by a representative of Underwriters Laboratories, it meets the most stringent facility, equipment, personal warranty and customer satisfaction requirements. Certified First shops also receive the Good Housekeeping seal of approval for their lifetime paint performance guarantee. Lents leads in protecting the environment, too. Under a pollution prevention outreach program, Lents Body Shop is a Certified Eco-Logical Automotive Business, meeting strict requirements set by the Oregon Department of Environmental Quality, the City of Portland and the Metro Open Spaces program. For first-class auto rebuilding, collision repair and painting on foreign and domestic automobiles, rely on the friendly service at Lents Body Shop.

9038 SE Foster Road, Portland OR
(503) 774-7497
www.lentsbodyshop.com

JaCiva's

BAKERIES, COFFEE & TEA: *Best gourmet bakery*

People who have frequently traveled the highway to Mount Hood may remember Heidi's Swiss Village Bakery, a fine pastry shop run by Jack and Iva Elmer. In 1986, Jack and Iva created a new pastry shop in SE Portland. JaCiva's, which combines their two names, is one of Oregon's finest producers of exquisite European chocolate, truffles, candies, tortes, wedding cakes, pastries and surprises. Would you like to get your business logo sculpted in chocolate? This is the place to get it done. In addition to their bakery, Jack and Iva's creations may be found at elegant Portland hotels, fine restaurants, high-end supermarkets and many other fine locations in the metropolitan area. JaCiva's has received many awards over the years, including the United States Pastry Alliance Gold Medal and the Austin Family Business Award. Jack Elmer understands that making great chocolates is an art. When you stop by, you'll discover that the family-oriented atmosphere is the best place to enjoy a treat, be it a piece of chocolate or a magnificent wedding cake. You can get cakes for any special occasion, or choose from the full line of European pastries and tortes. Try a different confection each time you come in and when you've tried everything, start over again.

4733 SE Hawthorne Avenue, Portland OR
(866) 522-4827 (JACIVAS) or (503) 234-8115
www.jacivas.com

Turquoise Learning Tree

BUSINESS: *Safe and fun learning*

Since 1996, Rob and Carolina Peterson have been fulfilling a vision. They have been building a network of Learning Tree Day Schools to provide fun for kids and peace of mind for parents. Leaders in affordable childcare, Learning Tree offers a safe and supportive environment for children from six weeks to 12 years of age. Sparing no expense, they provide the best furniture, supplies, toys and food for children. Main meals are delicious, well-balanced and hot. There are pre-school, kindergarten and summer camp programs. The teachers are highly qualified and receive on-going training. All are certified in CPR and first aid and have attended the Oregon Child Care Basics program. The emphasis of the schools is on treating children with respect, encouraging self esteem and helping with social and emotional development. Caring, sharing, conflict-resolution and good sportsmanship skills are all part of the lessons. There are reading programs, arts and crafts, swimming lessons and plenty of healthy outdoor activity. If you are looking for the best care for your child in an environment that supports healthy child development, you can count on Learning Tree Day Schools.

15135 SW Beard Road, Beaverton OR
(503) 590-8409
www.learningtreeschools.com

ReMax Equity Group

BUSINESS: *Hometown real estate experts*

When you purchase or sell your home with ReMax Equity Group, you are working with the number one real estate company in the State of Oregon and the ninth fastest growing real estate company in the country. Founded in 1984, the Equity Group has held this number one ranking in Oregon every year since 1994. Their sales in 2004 reached $5.3 billion, utilizing over 1200 professionals in 19 locations in the Portland Metro Area. They also serve clients in the Salem and Bend areas of Oregon. As they say, "we've got you covered," with sales professionals and brokers averaging more than 13 years in the real estate field. With over 80% of their business from referrals and repeat customers, you can rest assured that they are truly providing the best in service. Equity Group has a full service relocation department. Almost all of their relocation services are free of charge. There is a convenient local contact in Portland. Whether you need local or national relocation services, they have the staff to satisfy your needs. Connected with the community they serve, in 2004 they donated over $92,000 to 25 local charities through the Equity Group Foundation. Much of this is due to the hard-working people at Equity Group serving as leaders, participating in their communities and devoting time and money to the local charities. Giving back to the community is one of their missions. Remember, when selecting your realtor choose ReMax Equity Group, The Hometown Experts with a World of Experience.

8405 SW Nimbus Avenue, Suite C, Beaverton OR
(503) 670-3000
www.equitygroup.com

Lile North American

BUSINESS: *Best North American Van Lines interstate agent*

Established in 1959, Lile has safely moved people, businesses and products throughout the Pacific Northwest and far beyond. It is a second-generation family company that is certified by the Women's Business Enterprise National Council as a 100 percent woman-owned business. Lile is active in the community, working with Northwest Medical Teams and the Oregon Food Bank. While it has grown to include six branches in Washington and three in Oregon, Lile remains committed to its founding principle of providing claim-free, reliably delivered, customer-focused moving and storage services. Ranking as one of NorthAmerican Van Lines' top U.S. agents, Lile earned their Quality Excellence Award for the last two years and was named its top booker of military business. In addition to its national and international relocation capabilities, Lile offers sophisticated on-line logistics services, including an interactive international rate-quote system, and order-entry and shipment tracking. Lile's Warehousing & Distribution division reliably meets its service commitments to customers. For all your moving and storage needs at home and abroad, you can count on Lile.

19480 SW 118th Avenue, Tualatin OR
(503) 691-3500
www.lile.net

Gold Leaf Restoration

BUSINESS: *Best restoration work*

Nancy Thorn became interested in Medieval crafts while earning an art degree at Portland State University in the early 1970s. That interest blossomed into a long and fulfilling career. Nancy, owner of Gold Leaf Restoration, is an accomplished gilder, applying thin layers of 23K gold, brass, and other metals to objects. Nancy specializes in the ancient technique of water gilding. This method of leafing involves adhering gold or silver to wood or composition surfaces and burnishing the metal to a high polish. Nancy also uses oil gilding, an extremely durable technique ideal for outdoor use. In restoration, she preserves the integrity of the piece by matching the existing finish, rather than replacing it. Gilding techniques were obscure outside of the trade, but Nancy taught herself from 13th century translations of crafts books, then went on to apprentice with two master gilders in Boston and Connecticut before returning to Portland to open her restoration business in 1980. Over the years, she's gilded countless frames for old paintings, furniture, clocks, harps, chandeliers and sculptures. She makes closed corner picture frames for historic paintings, and she's added spark to sculptures on eight Royal Caribbean Cruise Line ships. She also gilded the Joan of Arc statue in NE Portland. Gold Leaf Restoration specializes in architectural gilding, restoration and fabrication. Some of Nancy's most important restoration work has been residential work for private Portland collectors. Next time you need to put a golden glow on an object in your life, visit Gold Leaf Restoration for glittering success.

544 SE Oak Street, Portland OR
(503) 236-2260
www.goldleafdesign.net

Priestley & Sons

BUSINESS: *Most helpful movers*

More than 75 years ago, Carroll H. Priestley founded his company to meet the moving and hauling needs of a growing Portland. Today, Teresa Priestley, Chris Brown and Jeff Brown continue the family tradition of excellent, personalized customer service. Originally haulers of groceries and firewood, Priestley & Sons Moving has grown and changed with the times. They provide a fleet of the most modern moving trucks and up-to-date professional moving equipment to ensure that your move, be it large or small, is smooth and trouble-free. One of the oldest, continuously running moving companies in the state of Oregon, Priestley & Sons Moving offers heated, secure warehouses. This community favorite believes in supporting the local economy, employing more than 25 people and allowing no outsourcing of labor. Committed to its community, Priestley & Sons provides service to the Assistance League of Oregon and pays special attention to the residents of the numerous retirement homes in the area. For outstanding service with your moving and storage requirements, call on Priestley & Sons Moving. They've been keeping this area moving since 1929.

Portland (503) 232-3332
2255 NW Birdsdale Avenue, Gresham OR (503) 661-7920
SW Washington (800) 700-7920
http://priestleymoving.com

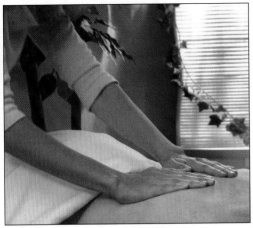

Skin Deep Beyond

HEALTH & BEAUTY: *Best day spa*

Cindy Ogden took her degree from the Esthetics Institute in Portland, added her amazing energy and persistence, and built her business from the ground up. Open since 2000, customer satisfaction has spread the word and Skin Deep & Beyond is now known as the best day spa in Tualatin. With extra-clean treatment rooms, candles, and soothing music, you will relax knowing you are receiving the best of care. Using the finest products and technology, Cindy and her expert staff provide facials and proven facial enhancements, nail care, waxing and body wraps. The licensed massage therapists perform a variety of techniques, including Swedish, deep-tissue and pregnancy massage. Treat yourself to any of the spa packages offered or have one customized just for you. Cindy and her associates are committed to providing you with a totally satisfying and personalized spa experience. For a personalized spa package for yourself or a loved one, come into Skin Deep & Beyond, where exceptional results are guaranteed.

Serving Metro Portland/Vancouver
8373 SW Warm Springs Street, Tualatin OR
(503) 692-2888
www.skindeepandbeyond.com

Massage on the Go

HEALTH & BEAUTY: *Most versatile massage*

Does anything feel better than a great massage? Are you dreaming of one right now? Massage on the Go will come straight to your door, whether at home, the office, a hotel, or a special event. You

won't have to wait for an appointment, fit it into your busy schedule, or fight traffic to get relief. Mary Dalton and her staff of fully accredited spa and massage specialists provide a wide range of relaxing and therapeutic treatments. They are skilled in hand and foot reflexology, water therapy, Shiatsu, deep-tissue and classic Swedish massage, as well as Reiki energy healing and techniques for relief of myopathy pain. If you want a facial or body wrap, those are part of the service, as well. In addition to the mobile service, you may also want to visit their conveniently located spa where you can check out the Bio-Photonic Scanner, one of only 15 in Oregon. The scanner allows the technicians to determine the types of supplements to suggest for increasing antioxidants for better health at the cellular level. From the inside out, Massage on the Go is truly a center for healing and wellness.

Serving Metro Portland
8879 SW Center Street, Tigard OR
(503) 620-0724

Mary Dalton, owner

Pennington Massage Clinic

HEALTH & BEAUTY: *Dedicated to helping people build muscles*

Todd and Pam Pennington of Pennington Massage Clinic believe that if you take care of your body now, it will take care of you later. The clinic, which opened in 1992, is dedicated to helping people reduce tension in the muscles in order to increase functionality. Todd and Pam are Oregon Licensed Massage Therapists, and Nationally Certified Medical Massage Therapists. They listen to client concerns and work to bring balance and functionality. Todd and Pam use Medical Massage tests to determine muscles that are weak and in spasm. They also use many different techniques to release tension and manual therapy techniques that assist in injury recovery. By using recognized medical tests to determine problem muscles and to test improvement, it is easier to recognize progress. Todd and Pam's goal is to bring harmony to the body by balancing the musculature and building proper function and support for tendons, ligaments and bones. In many cases even chronic muscle pain is reduced when the muscle tension is released. While some clients self refer, much of Todd and Pam's work is medically prescribed, and the process is a cooperation between doctor, patient and massage therapist. To get started on your way to greater health and well-being, call the Pennington Massage Clinic for an appointment.

10175 SW Barbur Boulevard, Suite 210, Portland OR
(502) 244-4427
LMT #3833 (Todd) and #8027 (Pam)
www.penningtonmassage.com

Oregon College of Oriental Medicine

HEALTH & BEAUTY:
Best school of Eastern healing arts

The Oregon College of Oriental Medicine in Portland has been offering an extraordinary educational experience since it opened its doors in 1983. As a recognized national leader, the college upholds high standards for its students, who follow a four-year academic program in acupuncture and Oriental medicine leading to a master's degree. A two-year post-graduate program for licensed acupuncturists leads to a doctorate, the first of its kind in the country. Students are required to cultivate their own health and well-being using the principles they learn in this program. The college also conducts clinical research and is the first alternative medicine college in the country to receive funding from the National Institutes of Health. Its Acupuncture & Herbal Clinic treats about 1,500 patients a month with acupuncture, Chinese herbs and various massages intended to regulate the body's organs and recover the use of tendons, bones and joints. Still other components of healing taught here include practices to cultivate the heart and mind, like taiji quan and qigong, ancient healing systems that involve slow movements, postures and meditation. The staff, under the leadership of President Michael Gaeta, strives to make OCOM the best destination for an education in Oriental medicine and to redefine health care in the U.S. through its partnerships with other medical institutions. If the study and use of Oriental Medicine is your goal, visit Oregon College of Oriental Medicine, where high standards and compassion are integral parts of the college community.

10525 SE Cherry Blossom, Portland OR
(503) 253-3443
www.ocom.edu

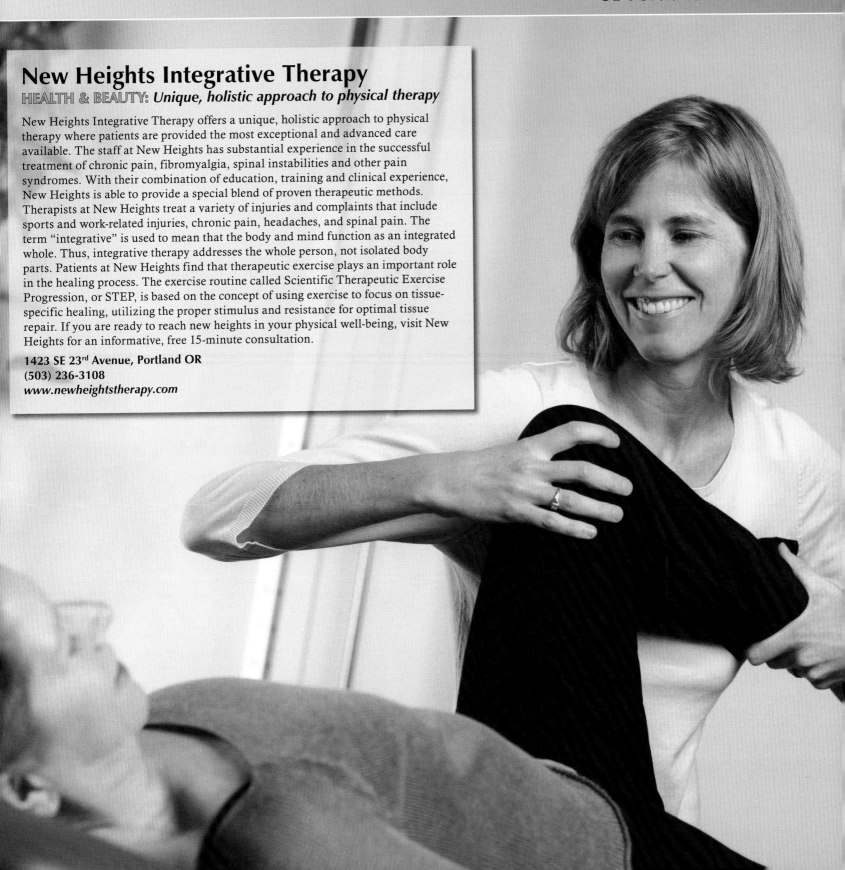

New Heights Integrative Therapy

HEALTH & BEAUTY: *Unique, holistic approach to physical therapy*

New Heights Integrative Therapy offers a unique, holistic approach to physical therapy where patients are provided the most exceptional and advanced care available. The staff at New Heights has substantial experience in the successful treatment of chronic pain, fibromyalgia, spinal instabilities and other pain syndromes. With their combination of education, training and clinical experience, New Heights is able to provide a special blend of proven therapeutic methods. Therapists at New Heights treat a variety of injuries and complaints that include sports and work-related injuries, chronic pain, headaches, and spinal pain. The term "integrative" is used to mean that the body and mind function as an integrated whole. Thus, integrative therapy addresses the whole person, not isolated body parts. Patients at New Heights find that therapeutic exercise plays an important role in the healing process. The exercise routine called Scientific Therapeutic Exercise Progression, or STEP, is based on the concept of using exercise to focus on tissue-specific healing, utilizing the proper stimulus and resistance for optimal tissue repair. If you are ready to reach new heights in your physical well-being, visit New Heights for an informative, free 15-minute consultation.

1423 SE 23rd Avenue, Portland OR
(503) 236-3108
www.newheightstherapy.com

Yoga Union
HEALTH & BEAUTY: *Best yoga training*

There is a good reason Portland's *Willamette Week* newspaper named Yoga Union as the Best Yoga Studio in town, and that reason is excellence. When owner Julie Wagner started the studio six years ago, she envisioned a friendly, community-oriented place where people of all skill levels could share her passion for yoga. The highly trained, dedicated, longtime instructors at Yoga Union create a personalized experience for their students with classes that offer lots of individual guidance and encouragement. The variety of classes allows students to explore many yoga styles and find a style that meets their needs. Classes include Hot Yoga, which is conducted in a heated room and benefits muscle relaxation and toxin release. You'll find yoga for children and Prenatal and Postnatal Yoga for new moms. Pilates classes offer another avenue to strength and flexibility, and a massage service allows students to relax further following their sessions. Whether you are curious about yoga or are highly experienced, Yoga Union has a program to fit you. Call or drop by Yoga Union Community Wellness Center for a visit, and take that first step toward a healthier you.

2043 SE 50th Avenue, Portland OR
(503) 235-YOGA (9642)
www.yogaunioncwc.com

Olena's European Spa & Salon
HEALTH & BEAUTY: *Best European salon spa*

Olena's European Spa & Salon in Portland is a unique spa that provides excellent service and great results. Here you can escape from reality to a world of complete European serenity for a truly relaxing experience. Since 2003, owner Olena Trone's salon has earned a reputation as a highly desirable, full-service day spa. Olena comes with 15 years of training in Russia, the Ukraine, Paris and the U.S. Olena is able to utilize the latest technology and finest products to relax and rejuvenate her customers. The salon offers European facials, detoxifying deep hydrating wraps, Swedish massage and a variety of other luscious body treatments. Olena's also offers hair salon services and wonderful pedicures and manicures for men and women. Try some of Olena's signature services, such as the unique caviar facial, vitamin response facial, alpha-clear anti-pigmentation treatment, air brush spray tanning, French silky smooth body treatment and many other stimulating body treatments. Hydrotherapy, Finland sauna and many spa packages are offered, especially for couples. Gift certificates make wonderful presents. A visit to Olena's ensures that you will leave feeling rested, pampered and ready to visit again.

8101 SE Cornwell Street, Portland OR
(503) 775-0900 *www.olenasdayspa.com*

Bamboo Lifestyles

HOME:
Best sustainable products

Bamboo and internationally sustainable products are the central theme to Bamboo Lifestyles. Owner Robbé Hardenette has created a wonderful boutique filled with products from all over the world. Here you'll find a selection of goods made from bamboo, jute, riverweed and acacia. There's also a selection of premium bamboo flooring. Robbé's life is centered on sustainable principles and educating the public about being socially responsible for our environment. He achieves this through the avenue of his retail store. All goods in the store are harvested in such a way as to sustain the environment or are fair trade items. Local artists and craftsmen are also represented and supported by the store. Organic smoothies, juices, snacks and teas are served in the store, as well. Every second Friday he hosts a popular and entertaining evening program called Uprooted. It's fashioned after *The Tonight Show* and is open to all. Its purpose is to provide knowledge on sustainable principles. You're invited in to browse around Bamboo Lifestyles, an environmentally responsible store.

**3321 SE Hawthorne, Portland OR
(503) 227-7521**

Sunset Heating & Cooling

HOME:
Custom systems by the experts

Originally established as Sunset Fuel in 1922, this company began as a fuel delivery business. At first, they delivered sawdust from a local lumber yard. As times and technology changed, they moved from sawdust to wood to coal to heating oil. Today, the name has been changed to Sunset Heating & Cooling to reflect the refocus on furnaces, air conditioning, heat pumps and indoor air quality products. Sunset has been a Carrier dealer since 1958 and has been designated a Factory Authorized Dealer. This means that Sunset has well-trained and certified technicians and salespeople, as well as being in the top five percent of Carrier's dealers nationwide. This also means that all Carrier products installed by Sunset come with 100-percent Customer Satisfaction Guarantee backed by Carrier. Sunset's comfort specialists evaluate your site, listen to your needs, and customize the right system for your home. Estimates are free. From system design to installation and service, Sunset's highly trained staff will work to ensure your total satisfaction. If you ever need service, Sunset's service department is there for you 24 hours a day. For the highest quality products and superior customer service, you can't go wrong at Sunset Heating & Cooling.

Serving Metro Portland
0607 SW Idaho Street, Portland OR
(503) 234-0611

West-Meyer Fence

HOME: *Best fence company*

Lance and Jennifer West and Ron Meyer combined their skills and formed West-Meyer Fence in 1997. Lance learned the trade from his father, Jennifer is a talented designer, and Ron has extensive fence-construction experience. Together they will take you through the bid process, design your project, and work within your budget to meet all of your fencing needs. West-Meyer provides the best fencing to residential, commercial, and industrial customers, and they work with the top names in the home-construction trades. They can handle any request and they work with a wide range of materials. From ornamental iron, glass railings, concrete, and stone to vinyl, wood, and chain link, they will build the perfect fence for you. West-Meyer takes pride in their craftsmanship and the professionalism of their staff. Take a tour of annual the Street of Dreams and you will find many examples of their fine work. For everything from security fencing to a beautiful enclosure for your home, call on the reliable and experienced professionals at West-Meyer Fence.

712 N Columbia Boulevard,
Portland OR
(503) 978-1830

Portland Closet Company

HOME: *Best closet company*

Even the roomiest closet can become a black hole of lost shoes and clothing. Portland Closet Company has the solution. This company enhances the lives of its clients by designing and installing superior organizing systems. Portland Closet offers complimentary in-home design consultation, professional installation by experienced carpenters, and spotless clean up. You can visit their large, airy showroom in Portland's Pearl District to get a taste of their custom work. In addition to designing superior walk-in and reach-in closets, the company has solutions for offices,

pantries and garages. Portland Closet carries Tilt-Away wall beds in twin, double and queen styles that can double the functional size of a room. Closet systems and cabinetry use melamine or real wood veneers for a handsome, durable finish. You can also find brightly colored shelves and drawers for children's closets. Founded in 1985, this local, family-owned business has earned a reputation for exceptional design, service and installation. The staff members strive to work within your budget and on schedule. They respect your ideas, add their expertise, and turn your dreams into reality. They want your experience with them to be so delightful that you will be eager to recommend them to your friends. Visit Portland Closet Company and see what a difference beautifully organized storage can make in your life.

Serving Metro Portland
1120 NW 14th Avenue, Portland OR
(503) 274-0942 or (800) 600-5654
www.portlandcloset.com

Environmental Building Supplies
HOME: *Best green home supplies*

In 1992, Environmental Building Supplies opened with a pioneering vision of homes that are healthy for people and our world. The Portland store, now housed in a 14,000 square foot former factory, stands at the epicenter of today's sustainable building movement. A 5,000-square-foot satellite store is in Bend, Oregon's fastest-growing city. The top-selling product is Marmoleum, a flooring made from natural linseed oil that comes in a full spectrum of beautiful colors. Unlike petroleum-based vinyl flooring, the color and pattern go all the way through, so it wears for up to 30 years and biodegrades harmlessly. Environmental Building Supplies performs extensive research before bringing a product into the showroom, always mindful of the different and even conflicting values consumers balance when deciding what to use in their home. The result is a carefully curated, beautifully presented selection of local products, such as Madrone flooring sourced from cooperatively managed forests, efficient products, like RAIS wood-burning stoves, and innovative natural products that are easier to use, such as itch-free insulation made from recycled blue jeans. Environmental Building Supplies stocks FSC-certified lumber and plywood, in addition to several lines of low toxic, no-VOC paints, American Clay Plaster, and a broad selection of books on topics ranging from straw bale construction to color theory. The store installs wool carpet, flooring, countertops and photovoltaic systems that generate electricity from the sun. The staff is committed to helping you find the best product for your values. Stop by and see what's new in Portland or Bend.

819 SE Taylor Street, Portland OR
(503) 222-3881
50 SW Bond Street, Suite 4, Bend OR
www.ecohaus.com

The Joinery

HOME: *Best home decorating*

Building tomorrow's antiques today has been the motto of The Joinery for 23 years. Each piece of hardwood furniture is masterfully constructed using Old World construction techniques and tools like chisels and hand planes, as well as modern machinery. Their heirloom furniture is both aesthetically pleasing and well constructed by skilled craftsmen who proudly sign and date each piece. More than 75 percent of what they build is made from certified sustainable wood. There is a solid commitment to the environment at The Joinery, and they are proud to have been one of the first builders of furniture in the Pacific Northwest using wood that's certified according to the strict guidelines of the Forest Stewardship Council. Their lumber is harvested from the well managed Pennsylvania Forest owned by The Collins Companies. Owner Marc Gaudin states, "Every step, every employee is important. We try to excel at it all, start to finish." Environmental stewardship is important at The Joinery. Their entire 20,000-square-foot facility uses 100-percent clean wind power. The facility features an expansive 7,000-square-foot showroom that features a viewing platform so you can watch their craftsmen creating furniture they like to call functional art. Each piece is made to order so they work closely with their customers to produce exactly what the customer wants. Stop in at The Joinery and you'll find that they'll do whatever it takes to create a treasured heirloom just for you.

4804 SE Woodstock, Portland OR
(503) 788-8547
www.thejoinery.com

Stanton Furniture

HOME: *Largest selection of unfinished furniture*

For more than 45 years, Stanton Furniture has been selling solid wood furniture to the Portland area. You won't find any particleboard in either of their two locations, only the fresh smell of solid woods. These family-owned stores are rooted in this community and have a strong reputation built on selling only quality unfinished and finished furniture. They have the state's largest selection of unfinished furniture, and have a piece that would look good in any room in your house. These are stores to take your time exploring. There is so much variety to be found, don't be surprised if you end up spending an entire afternoon just browsing. Internet users can visit Stanton's website for a partial catalogue of their various offerings, as well as tips on how to stain and protect your new unfinished purchases. Stanton Furniture knows how to make your house look and feel more like home. Visit their showroom for great ideas.

10800 SE 82ⁿᵈ Avenue, Portland OR
(503) 654-5282
10175 SW Beaverton-Hillsdale Highway,
Beaverton OR
(503) 644-7333
www.stantonfurniture.com

Kitchens & More Northwest

HOME: *Best cabinetry*

Fine cabinetry offers much more than a place to put your things. Cabinets enhance a home's beauty and utility and help define your home's décor. At Kitchens & More Northwest in Hillsboro, you'll find the best service and craftsmanship in the industry plus a wide range of style options and wood species. Since opening Kitchens & More Northwest in 1989, owners Drew and Val Tolmie and their talented crew have been working with individual homeowners and area builders to style custom-made specialty cabinets for every room in your house. When you enlist the services of Kitchens & More, you can expect expert guidance in designing the perfect kitchen, office, entertainment center or bathroom, plus durable finishes and high quality hardware that assure your lasting satisfaction. The Kitchens & More Northwest showroom is bound to stir up your dreams with almost a dozen cabinet displays and a wall exhibiting door styles, color selections, knobs and pulls. Area builders have chosen the prize-winning work of the Kitchens & More Northwest team to appear for the past 16 years in the prestigious Street of Dreams project, a display of cutting-edge style options for today's finest homes. "We believe fine cabinetry is the heart of a home," says Drew. When you are ready to experience the beauty and practicality of custom cabinetry, turn to the experts at Kitchens & More Northwest. They will use their expertise and state-of-the-art equipment to build a lasting heart into your home.

460 SW Armco, Hillsboro OR
(503) 648-0499
http://kitchensandmorenw.com

Mergenthaler Transfer & Storage
HOME: *A fleet based on integrity*

Art and Nick Mergenthaler opened for business in Helena, Montana in 1934. Back then, their 1933 Dodge half-ton truck was hauling 100-pound bags of flour, sugar, potatoes, and other goods for local grocers. The 1950s brought transporting construction supplies for dam building and a contract to haul mail for the U.S. Postal Service. Mergenthaler grew steadily, and when Art died in 1972, his four sons took over the business, expanding it to an interstate operation. Now owned and operated by two of Art's grandsons, the company is still growing by leaps and bounds. Though they have fleets of modern vehicles and massive storage facilities, this community favorite has never forgotten its core principle of building open, honest, and ethical relationships with the people it serves. The more than 285 employees are proud of the history and reputation of their company and are able and ready to provide you with personalized, local, professional service. To meet your transportation and storage needs, call Mergenthaler.

7895 SW Hunziker Road, Tigard OR
(800) 547-0795 *www.mergenthaler.net*

Pro-Tech Cleaning Services
HOME: *Best carpet cleaning*

Chris Boston is on the job at every job ensuring that your needs are met with the best service, products and prices. Pro-Tech Cleaning Services is certified in commercial and residential carpet cleaning, dyeing and repair, as well as care of Oriental rugs, textile and leather upholstery, and tile, stone and wood floors. As the array of choices in fabrics and surfacing materials grows, the crew at Pro-Tech learns the latest procedures and chemistry, employing the most up-to-date techniques and equipment. Chris and his staff pursue on-going education through trade shows, seminars and classes. Committed to each and every customer, Pro-Tech has established and maintained an excellent reputation. Real estate agents recommend Pro-Tech to their sellers and buyers. Elders in Action has certified them as an Elder-Friendly Business for their fair practices, ethical and respectful treatment and their extra efforts in meeting special needs. Pro-Tech does not believe in surprises. You will receive a free estimate for your job and they provide a written complaint policy to ensure your complete satisfaction. Their motto is, The most thorough cleaning ever, or it's free. For all your floor and upholstery cleaning needs, call Pro-Tech Cleaning Services.

12150 Camden Lane, Beaverton OR
(503) 975-7577 *www.protechcleaning.com*

Skullers on the Willamette River in Sellwood
Photo by Stu Seeger

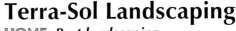

Terra-Sol Landscaping

HOME: *Best landscaping*

During a summer job on Hayden Island, David Zimmerman developed an affinity for working outdoors in landscaping, construction and design. He continued to gain experience working for a design-landscape company. After earning a degree in Landscape Architecture, he started his own business, Terra-Sol Landscaping. Along with his experienced and professional staff, David serves the greater Portland metropolitan area. Working within any budget, they will strive to create the outdoor space of your dreams. They can build retaining walls, patios, garden paths and steps. Water features are also a specialty, including ponds, fountains, bubble rocks and waterfalls. Garden lovers enjoy working with David in creating their special garden spaces. Terra-Sol, meaning Earth-Sun, has provided landscaping for several homes at the annual Street of Dreams. In addition to landscaping, Terra-Sol is a long-time sponsor of Little League in the community. They are well known and well respected. You can trust your next outdoor project to Terra-Sol Landscaping, a community favorite since 1977.

Serving Metro Portland
(503) 691-6105
www.terrasollandscaping.com

Premier Home Care

LIFESTYLE DESTINATIONS:
Best adult foster care

In a quiet neighborhood near Powell Butte Park is the immaculate foster-care home of Angela Iuga. Angela offers attentive and loving assistance to clients at all levels of care. The lovely home is wheelchair accessible, has in-room cable television and phone lines, and boasts a sunny deck with a beautiful view of Mount Hood. Angela provides medication management, assistance for activities of daily living, schedule coordination, transportation, security, and general oversight. All housekeeping, including laundry, is provided for the residents. An accomplished cook, Angela serves delicious and nutritious home-style meals and can accommodate special dietary requirements. Her home is available for temporary illness and adult day care, as well as for long-term and hospice care. Clients and their families discover friendship, gentleness and excellent service here, and you can read their many notes of gratitude in Angela's album. You can place your trust in the caring and capable hands at Premier Home Care.

4108 SE Lee Anna Way, Portland OR
(503) 492-1124
www.premieradultcare.com

Bike N' Hike

RECREATION: *One of the nation's Top 100 Bicycle Retailers*

Since 1971, Bike N' Hike has been serving Portland's bike community. Started by Al and Dorothy French, the business specializes in all areas of cycling, offering a wide range of bikes, parts and accessories, and full-service repairs. Bike N' Hike takes special care to fit and size bikes according to the rider. In addition to bike sales and service, they also rent skis, snowshoes and snowboards. They proudly sponsor three bike teams, BMX, Beaverton Bicycle Club and Presto Velo, and are one of the largest Giant Bicycle dealers in Oregon. With stores in Albany, Beaverton, Hillsboro, Milwaukie and Corvallis, Bike N' Hike is the source for all of your biking needs.

400 SE Grand Avenue, Portland OR
(503) 736-1074
www.bikenhike.com

Westside Dance & Gymnastics Academy

RECREATION: *Leader in dance and gymnastics*

The mission of Westside Dance & Gymnastics Academy is to provide a safe, fun and positive environment, promote creativity and fitness, and inspire students to achieve their goals. Owner Mellanie Heniff is a long-time student of dance and gymnastics. She offers classes for all age groups, encouraging whole families to participate. The 12,000-square-foot facility provides the best USA Gymnastics-certified equipment. Private lessons are available for all gymnasts. Mellanie believes dance helps children develop self-confidence, flexibility, a sense of rhythm and coordination. She and her staff encourage values of good sportsmanship, self-discipline, respect and accountability. The academy is open seven days a week, has a pro shop and offers summer camp programs in dance, theater, cheerleading and gymnastics. Their academic pre-school and after-school care programs enable you to find a program that will work for you and your family. For an exciting alternative in a safe and welcoming atmosphere, Westside Dance & Gymnastics Academy is a leader in education, dance and gymnastics.

11632 SW Pacific Highway, Tigard OR
(503) 639-5388 *www.westsideacademy.com*

The Portland Music Company

SHOPPING: *Everything for the musician*

Portland musicians have been shopping at Portland Music Company for more than 75 years, and it continues to set the standard by which musical instrument and sheet music stores are measured. It all began in 1927 when saxophonist and entrepreneur Bob Christiansen opened his first store. Known then as The Saxophone Shop, it occupied the downtown corner of Fourth and Morrison. The music business was jumping until the market crash in 1929 brought an abrupt end to the saxophone craze. Bob had to adapt and he did so by expanding his selection to carry everything musical. With expansion came an appropriate new name: Portland Music Company. Always an innovator, Bob became Oregon's Music Man. He was the first to offer band rentals to the region's school children. As a way to encourage school music, Bob and his staff criss-crossed the state in a caravan of converted hearses giving free evening concerts in schoolhouses. Returning the next day, he would find a music director and rent the community a whole band's worth of instruments. For 50 years, Bob and his wife, Violet, grew the company, finally passing it on to current owner Mark Taylor. The company has five locations, each with its own personality and selection. School rentals are still offered, of course, but lessons, repairs, guitars, drums, keyboards, amps, sheet music, and recording gear are also available. At Portland Music Company, everything is for musicians and the music they make.

531 SE Martin Luther King Boulevard, Portland OR   (503) 226-3719
2502 NE Broadway, Portland OR   (503) 228-8437
12334 SE Division, Portland OR   (503) 760-6881
10075 SW Beaverton-Hillsdale Highway, Portland OR   (503) 641-5505
www.portlandmusiccompany.com

Cascade Cigar and Tobacco Company

SHOPPING: *Best cigar store*

Cigar lovers can enjoy their indulgence in the company of other aficionados at Cascade Cigar and Tobacco Company. This popular purveyor of hundreds of classic cigar brands opened its doors in Milwaukie in 1992 and moved to its location on 82nd Avenue in 1998. A second location has been opened on 6th Avenue in Portland. The original store is home to a 1,000-square-foot walk-in humidor that holds the largest selection of cigars in the city. Additionally, Cascade Cigar provides a large selection of roll-your-own supplies, including tobacco, tubes, ashtrays and rolling machines. Look for 60 different pipe tobacco blends and a gorgeous array of quality pipes. At Cascade Cigar's smoking room, the Cascade Taproom, cigar and fine tobacco lovers can gather with like-minded individuals while watching a game on the taproom's television, playing chess or cards or chatting with friends. The Cascade Taproom serves a variety of microbrews along with domestic and imports on tap and a choice selection of wines, ports and sodas. If you find a wine, beer or port that you are especially fond of, the taproom can pack up a bottle or a six-pack for you to take home along with your favorite cigar or tobacco blend. The shop hosts numerous wine and microbrew tasting events throughout the year, and lighting up your favorite stogie is never frowned upon. Grab a friend and head to Cascade Cigar and Tobacco Company.

9691 SE 82nd Avenue, Portland OR
(503) 775-5885 or (800) 593-4123
5185 SW 6th Avenue, Portland OR
(503) 790-9045

CoCo & Toulouse Go Shopping
SHOPPING: *Best boutique*

Fun and Fine Gifts for Girls of all Ages is the slogan for Southeast Portland's compellingly named boutique, CoCo and Toulouse Go Shopping. With a delightful selection of gifts available in Jo Ellen Newton's store, there is almost always something new and fresh every time you stop by. A cheerful, whimsical environment beckons, and visitors are quick to realize this is a welcoming place. Some customers stop by just for the pick-me-up that the fun décor and upbeat music provide, while the vast selection of unique and special gifts creates a feast for the senses and an immediate lift to the mood. As a neighborhood store owner, Jo Ellen feels it's important for her shop to serve as a haven from the world outside. Her loyal customers clearly agree. Many repeat customers travel from other states to shop her store. Jo Ellen invites you to come in and enjoy the shopping sanctuary she has created in the heart of Sellwood. Enjoy the fantastic colors, aromas and textures that make CoCo and Toulouse Go Shopping such a pleasurable place to visit.

7080 SE 16th Street, Portland OR
(503) 236-5999

Village Merchants
SHOPPING:
Best mall alternative

Reduce. Reuse. Recycle. At Village Merchants, recycling is their game. Started by Marcee Meijer in 1998, this consignment shop carries everything from furniture and art, to clothing and jewelry. Voted the Best Mall-Alternative in Portland, it operates in much the same way an old-fashioned trading post did. Believing there is no reason to buy new if you don't have to, the store buys, sells, trades and consigns quality items for those downsizing, combining, redecorating or simplifying their lives. Stop by Village Merchants to find the practical and beautiful at affordable prices.

3360 SE Division Street,
Portland OR
(503) 234-6343

Hip Chicks Do Wine

WINERIES: *Funky warehouse turned winery*

Found amongst the artistic dwellings and industrial factories near Reed College is an unexpected winery, Hip Chicks Do Wine. A unique urban micro winery designed with the Gen X crowd in mind, Hip Chicks Do Wine is also a boutique winery that handcrafts their wine in very small batches with grapes from several Oregon Appellations. They believe that this is the key to their wines with full, well rounded fruit flavors. Producing only around 2,500 cases annually, this small winery produces truly inspired wines while experimenting with new processes each year. They use a half-ton basket press to gently extract the best quality juices from fruity full-bodied Pinot Noirs, Chardonnays, Reislings, Gewurtzraminers and Merlots. Special treatment of the different grapes in small bins, French oak barrels or stainless steel tubs according to what is best for that particular wine style is only possible due to the small batches created here. These wines are intended to be enjoyed when purchased, without any need to cellar. Tasting room hours are Tuesday through Sunday from 11 am until 6 pm. Wines offered include Shardoneaux, Vin Nombril, Pinot Noir and Riot Girl Rose. Check out their apparel, gifts and accessories while you're there, you may find another souvenir of this adventure.

**4510 SE 23rd Avenue, Portland OR
(503) 753-6374**
www.hipchicksdowine.com

CANBY

Canby is separated from its larger urban neighbors by a beautiful stretch of farmland, rolling hills and fields. Entering Canby from the north brings visitors past the beautiful Willamette River. Hart's Reptile World Zoo in Canby has gained a national reputation. Surrounded by four golf courses and clubs, Canby is a great town for golfers. You can cross the Willamette River on the Canby Ferry, one of three ferries still in operation on the Willamette River. Fruit, vegetable and flower stands abound seasonally in some of the finest farmland in Oregon.

PLACES TO GO

- Canby Depot Museum
  888 NE 4th Avenue
  (503) 266-6712

- The Canby Ferry
  N Holly Street
  (503) 650-3030

- Molalla River State Park
  N Holly Street

- Phoenix & Holly Railroad
  at the Flower Farmer
  N Holly Street
  (503) 266-3581

THINGS TO DO

June
- Canby Wine & Art Festival
  Fairgrounds
  (503) 266-1136

July
- General Canby Days
  www.generalcanbydays.org

August
- Clackamas County Fair
  Fairgrounds
  (503) 266-1136

- Swan Island Dahlia Festival
  (503) 266-7711

September
- St. Joseph's Grape Stomping Festival
  (503) 651-3190

Canby Dahlia Festival, 2006
Photo by Jeff Muceus

St. Josef's Winery
WINERIES: *Best natural wines*

St. Josef's Winery is located in the heart of the Willamette Valley, just 25 minutes south of Portland and neighboring the National Historic District town of Aurora. Owner and Winemaker Josef emigrated from Europe and started producing wines here in 1978, making St. Josef's one of Oregon's wine pioneers. Today, St. Josef's is still family owned and operated. The St. Josef's Winery proudly produces award-winning Pinot Noir, Gewürztraminer, Pinot Gris, Cabernet Sauvignon and White Riesling. Besides the primary label, St Josef's second generation has developed the international medal-winning KB Merlot and Kitara Pinot Noir. Come out and enjoy the charming European flavor and hospitality of the Tasting Room and the four-tiered picnic grounds. After a visit to St Josef's you will take pleasure in what the Oregon wine industry is all about: hard-working, fun-loving people who put their name and reputation in every bottle. St. Josef's is located on Barlow Road just south of Highway 99E. Visitors are welcome Thursdays through Sundays, from March through December in the Tasting Room and the tiered picnic areas. Don't miss the annual Grape Stomping in September and St. Josef's Day in March.

28836 S Barlow Road, Canby OR
(503) 651-3190
http://stjosefs.tripod.com

GLADSTONE

Gladstone is at the confluence of the Clackamas and Willamette rivers. Meldrum Bar, just downstream from the confluence, is one of the hottest fishing spots in the state for migrating chinook and steelhead. Indians once traded, settled disputes and conducted marriages under the Pow-Wow Maple in Gladstone. The Indians operated a ferry across the Clackamas. When European settlers arrived, they replaced the ferry with a bridge. The town itself was founded by Harvey Cross, who laid out the streets and named it after the famous British prime minister. From 1895, Gladstone was home to the Willamette Valley Chautauqua, a park and auditorium that made the town an entertainment center for the entire region. Railroad and street cars brought people from Portland and other places for concerts, ball games and revival meetings. Popular attractions included band leader John Phillip Sousa, preacher Billy Sunday and orator William Jennings Bryan. Today, the old Chautauqua property is the Gladstone Park Seventh Day Adventist Camp. Most of Gladstone is residential, but the town is a good place to shop for a car, as dealerships of all makes line State Route 99E from Gladstone up towards Milwaukie.

PLACES TO GO

• Max Paterson Park
  E Exeter Street

• Meldrum Bar City Park
  Meldrum Bar Park Road

THINGS TO DO

August
• Chautauqua Festival
  Max Paterson Park
  (503) 656-5225, ext. 4

Willamette River near Gladstone
photo by pdxjeff

DSC Designworks, Inc.
BUSINESS: *Best interior design*

Is your home stuck in the 1960s, the '80s, or some other decade you'd like to leave behind? If you have been thinking about an update, or if you are looking for a way to make your home a truer expression of yourself, DSC Designworks can help. Dale and Barbara Crittenden opened their design and remodeling business in 1993, specializing in custom cabinetry, woodwork and furnishings. The original business was so successful they expanded it and now offer interior design and new construction services, as well. DSC will work directly with you or your designer to create the custom home you desire. Dale's training at the Temple University School of Art in Pennsylvania, paired with his years of experience, enable him to make every project a complete success. He is known for his ability to incorporate the taste and sense of style of his clients into the home of their dreams. For creative ideas and high-quality solutions for your home, call DSC Designworks.

630 E 1st Avenue, Gladstone OR
(503) 650-7950

MILWAUKIE

Milwaukie, the City of Dogwoods, has been named as one of the 50 Best Places to Raise a Family. Access to the Willamette River is available at the Jefferson Street boat ramp and at Elk Rock Island. Swimming and other water fun is offered in the state-of-the-art North Clackamas Aquatics Park, which has a wave pool, lap and diving pools, kiddie pool and spa. Milwaukie High School hosts a nationally known Living History Day that invites veterans to campus to celebrate their service. The Milwaukie area is also the home of an authentic World War II B17G bomber. Gasoline station owner Art Lacey bought it and flew it to Troutdale Airport in 1947 to serve as an advertisement for the station. Trucking the plane from Troutdale to Milwaukie was an astounding feat. Today, the Lacey family runs a restaurant at the site called The Bomber. Milwaukie is the birthplace of the Bing cherry and the home of Dark Horse Comics.

PLACES TO GO

- Aquatic Park
  7300 SE Harmony Road

- The Bomber Restaurant
  13515 SE McLoughlin Boulevard

- North Clackamas Park/Milwaukie Center
  5440 SE Kellogg Creek Drive

THINGS TO DO

March
- Airing of the Quilts (quilt show)
  Milwaukie Center
  (503) 653-8100

July
- Milwaukie River Fest
  Jefferson Street boat ramp
  (503) 654-2493

September
- Fall into Art
  North Clackamas Park
  (503) 653-8100

Flowering Dogwood
Photo by Eric Milot

Stevens Marine in Milwaukie
RECREATION: *Serious boating pleasure*

Stevens Marine opened its doors in Milwaukie to better serve Portland-area boaters on the eastside of the Willamette River. The original location was opened in 1986. Thanks to a loyal and growing customer base, they moved to their current location at 18023 SE Addie Road, in Milwaukie, one block east of McLoughlin Boulevard. Stevens Marine's Milwaukie store is a state-of-the-art marine retail and service operation boasting a huge indoor showroom capable of exhibiting 30 boats indoors with a total building size of 17,000 square feet set on 1.5 acres. There are more than 100 new and used boats for sale at any time with a complete outboard and inboard service shop, in-house marine canvas and top shop, over-the-counter parts sales, a complete selection of accessories and an outstanding staff of boating professionals. Stevens Marine's Milwaukie location is proud to carry some of the top names in boating, including Alumaweld, Bluewater and Smoker Craft boats, as well as Mercury outboard motors. You'll also find a unique brand of financing dubbed Full Spectrum Financing, a Stevens Marine exclusive that makes owning a new or used boat or outboard easier than ever. Page Stevens' service and customer legacy is clearly reflected in how business is conducted, and the customers are treated superbly at all Stevens Marine locations, where serious boating pleasure is the order of every day. Stevens Marine is open six days a week and closed on Sundays.

18023 SE Addie Road, Milwaukie OR
(503) 652-1444 or (800) 576-7371
www.stevensmarine.com

OREGON CITY

Oregon City was once the most important city in the Pacific Northwest. Dr. John McLoughlin established it in 1829 while he was factor of the Hudson's Bay Company at Fort Vancouver. McLaughlin was able to take advantage of the power of Willamette Falls on the Willamette River for a lumber mill. McLaughlin retired to Oregon City in 1846. During the 1840s and 1850s the city was the end of the Oregon Trail, the destination for those wanting to file land claims after traveling the trail. Oregon City was the capital of Oregon Territory from its establishment in 1848 until 1851, and it rivaled Portland for early supremacy. Oregon City contains many well preserved historical buildings, including Ermatinger House and McLoughlin's Georgian home, now a National Historic Site under the Vancouver National Historic Reserve. Several other museums record the history of the town, including the Museum of the Oregon Territory and the End of the Oregon Trail Interpretive Center.

PLACES TO GO

- Carnegie Center (for the arts)
  606 John Adams Street (503) 723-9661

- End of the Oregon Trail Interpretive Center
  1726 Washington Street (503) 657-9336

- Ermatinger House
  619 W 6th Street (503) 557-9199

- Haggart Astronomical Observatory
  Inskeep Center, Clackamas CC

- McLaughlin House
  713 Center Street (503) 656-5146

- Museum of the Oregon Territory
  211 Tumwater Drive (503) 655-5574

THINGS TO DO

June
- Eel Festival
  (800) 424-3002

July
- First City Arts Faire
  (503) 313-0024

Photo by Zach Casper

Tri-County Temp Control
HOME: *Best HVAC*

In 1987, Alan Sanchez founded Tri-County Temp Control, determined that the company would grow and prosper by delivering superior customer service. Referrals from satisfied customers have consistently proven him right. With a crew of more than 70, Tri-County has a long and distinguished track record throughout the metro Portland area. Tri-County has installed thousands of retro-fit and new-construction HVAC systems, earning its status as the name you can trust. Their work is well represented on the Street of Dreams and greatly respected by homeowners, businesses and contractors throughout the area. Tri-County can assess your home or office space, then design and install the system that best meets your needs. When you visit their massive showroom, you will be greeted by friendly people with expert knowledge of their business. Every effort is made to provide products primarily manufactured in the USA. In addition, the company is committed to environmentally friendly products and procedures. For all your heating, air-conditioning and indoor air-quality needs, call on Tri-County Temp Control. You will become a customer for life.

13150 S Clackamas River Drive, Oregon City OR
(503) 557-2220

SANDY

Sandy is on the Mt. Hood Highway (U.S. 26) between Portland and Mt. Hood. Residents enjoy a mild climate, clean air and beautiful scenic views in a country setting. Sandy has all the advantages of small-town living, yet it is possible to reach the urban amenities of downtown Portland in 45 minutes. If you'd rather not drive, the city of Sandy operates a free bus to Gresham, where passengers can connect to the MAX rapid transit system into Portland.

PLACES TO GO

- Bonnie Lure State Recreation Area
  Dowty Road, Eagle Creek

- Jonsrud Viewpoint
  SE Bluff Road

- Meinig Memorial Park
  Meinig Avenue

- Milo McIver State Park
  S Springwater Road, Estacada

- Philip Foster Farm National Historic Site
  29912 SE Hwy. 211, Eagle Creek
  (503) 637-6324

- Roslyn Lake Park
  SE Ten Eyck Road

THINGS TO DO

July
- Sandy Mountain Festival
  Meinig Memorial Park
  (503) 668-5900

- Fly-In & Cruise-In
  McKinnon's Airport
  (503) 723-3734

September
- Sandy Oktoberfest
  (503) 251-2668

December
- Sandy Chamber Holiday Festival
  (503) 668-4006

Affordable Tree Service

HOME: *Arborist provides complete service*

Affordable Tree Service had already been a community favorite for some 30 years when Troy Curtis bought it in the mid 1990s. Troy is a true outdoorsman who enjoys "helping nature to give us beauty." An arborist and tree climber from way back, Troy has expanded the business to include disease diagnosis and removal, as well as hazard assessment and mitigation. Troy understands and will take care of all necessary permitting procedures. With more than 30 years of experience, Troy can help you evaluate your landscape and set goals. From fine ornamental pruning and care of hedges to planting of trees and shrubs, Troy can assist you in designing a progressive landscaping plan that can be budgeted for and carried out over any number of months or years. He will provide you the best information on correct placement of plants and trees to accommodate their size at maturity and give you the care tips that will provide for the greatest health and longevity of your landscape. For Troy, the job is not over until you are happy: it is 100-percent guaranteed. Call Affordable Tree Service to enhance the beauty of your natural surroundings.

37280 SE Trubel Road, Sandy OR
(503) 668-7638

SW Portland Metro

SW PORTLAND

Portland has a downtown other cities dream about. It's not like other downtowns, full of office workers in the daytime, a concrete desert at night. Downtown Portland is alive, pedestrian friendly and clean. Southwest Portland includes both downtown, Washington Park and Old Town. Central downtown offers famous department stores, great hotels and high-end restaurants of all types. Downtown and some adjacent areas are in the Fareless Square, where public transit is free. The MAX light rail system connects downtown with Hillsboro, North Portland, the airport and Gresham. The Portland Streetcar, which begins in the Northwest Nob Hill and Pearl districts, continues on through downtown past the Main Library and the Portland Art Museum to Portland State University, Tom McCall Waterfront Park and the new South Waterfront high-rises. West of downtown is Washington Park, home of marvelous attractions that include the zoo and the Japanese Garden. The view of downtown from the Japanese Garden is among the most spectacular in town and is emblematic of Portland. The MAX station at the park is America's deepest underground station.

PLACES TO GO

- Gabriel Park
  SW 45th Avenue and Vermont Street

- Tryon Creek State Natural Area
  SW Terwilliger Boulevard

- Alpenrose Dairy and Dairyville
  6149 SW Shattuck Road

THINGS TO DO

January
- Mochitsuki (Oregon Nikkei Legacy Center)
  Performing Arts Center (971) 226-3571

July
- Alpenrose Challenge (bicycle race)
  www.alpenrosechallenge.com

August
- Multnomah Days
  (503) 869-1632

Japanese Gardens

The Benson Hotel

ACCOMMODATIONS:
A Portland landmark for nine decades

A visit to Portland must include a stop at the venerable Benson Hotel, listed on the National Register of Historic Places. A landmark for nine decades and a tribute to its founder and designer, this stately 287-room hotel retains the opulence for which it is world-famous. A.E. Doyle's architectural talent, combined with Simon Benson's tenacity, business savvy and impeccable taste, lives on as the foundation of an American classic. Guests often stand in awe of the palatial lobby featuring Austrian-crystal chandeliers, Circassian walnut walls, columns and Italian marble floors. Lounging by the lobby fireplace during winter months often leads to celebrity sightings. Twenty-four-hour room service, the acclaimed Les Clef D'Or Concierge Services, and the most chivalrous and polite doormen add to the Benson's reputation for excellence. Modern luxury is on display in the Grand Suite with a baby grand piano, fireplace and Jacuzzi, and it continues through each of the panoramic view penthouses and Junior Suites. Deserving of unending AAA Four Diamond ratings, all guest room amenities include two phone lines and dataport, plush terry cloth bathrobes, honor bar, iron and ironing board, and hair dryer. Guests also enjoy a comfortable chair and ottoman, armoire with television, games and movies. Décor throughout is a traditional style with velvet throw pillows on the beds, taupe-and-black checkered window treatments, brass lamps and a writing desk. Elegant décor and soft lighting create an intimate dining ambience for hotel guests and locals alike at the London Grill, a well-known fixture in the Northwest's restaurant scene.

309 SW Broadway, Portland OR
(888) 523-6766
www.bensonhotel.com

Britannia at Terwilliger Vista

ACCOMMODATIONS: *Most elegant bed & breakfast*

With five luxurious rooms, the Britannia at Terwilliger Vista offers a refuge in the heart of Portland. The grounds of this 1940s-era Georgian Colonial home are meticulously landscaped into terraced lawns. A quiet hideaway, The Britannia bed and breakfast is a quiet hideaway located just minutes from downtown. Hosts Irene and Carl Keyes have chosen appealing themes for the rooms. The Garden Retreat, perfect for the romantic, includes a full wall of window seats in the midst of a garden setting, plus a canopy bed and a large bath with a whirlpool tub. Rooms come outfitted with robes, firewood and bubble bath. The Gold Room captures the style of the 1940s with large, bay window views of the back gardens and an Art Deco-style tiled bath and shower. Up to three people can stay in the spacious Burgundy Rose Suite, with its down featherbed, extra large Art Deco-style bathroom and view of the Willamette Valley. If you're in the mood for a Victorian weekend, take the Blue Room, with its wicker furniture, Victorian wallpapers and bay windows overlooking the terraced gardens. On sunny mornings, guests can take breakfast out to the back patio under the maple tree. Wonderful hikes are just minutes away. For a retreat from the city while still in the city, reserve a room at the Britannia at Terwilliger Vista.

515 SW Westwood Drive, Portland OR
(503) 244-0602 or (888) 244-0602
www.terwilligervista.com

Hotel Vintage Plaza

ACCOMMODATIONS: *Most romantic hotel*

Built in 1894 and listed on the National Register of Historic Places, the Hotel Vintage Plaza is a charming European-style hotel featuring urban luxury and elegance. All 1,007 guest rooms are named for and dedicated to Oregon wineries and vineyards. Lodging options include deluxe guest rooms, hospitality suites and starlight rooms with conservatory-style windows. You can enjoy townhouse suites or garden suites with outdoor hot tubs. All rooms feature fully stocked honor bars and refrigerators, a complimentary shoe-shine kit and newspapers. You will enjoy 24-hour room service, two multi-line speaker phones with data ports and valet parking. Most guest rooms have two-person jetted soaking tubs. The hotel has more than 5,000 square feet of unique, flexible meeting and banquet space, including a wine cellar that can accommodate up to 80 people for dinner. The meeting space can be divided into eight separate meeting rooms and can comfortably accommodate groups of 10 to 275 people. Catering is provided by the nationally recognized Pazzo Ristorante. The cozy Fireside Lobby offers complimentary Starbucks coffee and tea each morning, plus evening wine tasting. The hotel also offers an onsite fitness center. The Hotel Vintage Plaza has everything to make your stay complete.

422 SW Broadway, Portland OR
(503) 228-1212 or (800) 243-0555
www.vintageplaza.com

Hilton Portland & Executive Tower

ACCOMMODATIONS:
Best executive hotel

The Hilton Portland & Executive Tower stands in the bustling heart of Portland's financial and entertainment districts, just blocks from the city's best restaurants. Whether you're a business or vacation traveler, this central location and the many luxuries you expect from the Hilton name will make your stay in this dynamic city a pure pleasure. Rooms here feature large windows, two-line phones and high-speed Internet access. You'll find desks, movies and video games, plus the Hilton's renowned Suite Dream beds and luxurious bath products. Guestrooms offer views of the city, mountains or river. Dining at the Hilton offers the distinct pleasure of choices for every mood and appetite. Consider the Northwest cuisine and panoramic views from the 23rd-floor Alexander's, or casual dining in the lobby's Bistro 921. Porto Terra Tuscan Grill & Bar offers Italian specialties, award-winning wines and specialty cocktails and martinis. With full concierge services, an athletic club and two indoor pools, Hilton Portland is prepared to meet every need of the business or pleasure traveler. The two towers of the Hilton Portland offer 40,000 square feet of flexible meeting, banquet and exhibit space, as well as 782 impeccable guestrooms. General Manager Tracy Marks and his professional staff will make your visit comfortable and memorable. Nearby attractions include the Portland Art Museum, Oregon Zoo and Classical Chinese Garden. For an exquisite stay in the heart of Portland, visit the Hilton Portland & Executive Tower.

921 SW 6th Avenue, Portland OR
(503) 226-1611 or (503) 944-1072
www.portland.hilton.com

RiverPlace Hotel
ACCOMMODATIONS: *Best waterfront hotel*

A landmark presence on the waterfront, RiverPlace Hotel is a premier upscale hotel on the banks of the Willamette River. RiverPlace is a haven of warmth and tranquility, serenely removed from the noise of the city, yet only a few blocks from the heart of downtown. The hotel's staff provides a comfortable, inviting refuge where you'll be treated with a level of care not often experienced. RiverPlace has exciting news for visitors, a $4 million renovation has just been completed. The new lobby welcomes guests with a warm ambience of Northwest craftsman-style detailing, a comfortable lobby library and a complimentary full service business center complete with high-speed Internet access. The Hotel offers a variety of accommodations from oversized deluxe guest rooms to FirePlace Suites with beautiful views and RiverFront Residential Suites, which are the finest riverfront accommodations in the Northwest. Each room and suite features the new FeatherBorne Bed, the finest in sleep comfort, a DVD player and personal refrigerator. As part of the renovation, a new restaurant and bar called Three Degrees was opened. "Meet, Greet, Eat" is the philosophy of Portland's newest riverview restaurant and bar. The menu features many Northwest favorites prepared with the finest fresh, local ingredients. A unique feature of the bar is the outside deck that offers a wonderful river view, teak rocking chairs and heat lamps for year round use. The RiverPlace has earned AAA's 4 Diamond rating for 19 consecutive years. With the recent renovations, RiverPlace will continue to be considered one of the finest hotels in the Northwest.

1510 SW Harbor Way, Portland OR
(503) 228-3233 or (800) 227-1333
www.riverplacehotel.com

The Mark Spencer Hotel
ACCOMMODATIONS: *Best hospitality*

A beloved landmark in Portland's Theater District, The Mark Spencer Hotel has been providing its guests with Continental style, old-fashioned courtesy, and hospitality since 1907. Visiting performers still make The Mark Spencer their home away from home, just as they have in decades past. A visitor to the city couldn't do any better. Originally called the Nortonia, the twin six-story buildings were renamed The Mark Spencer in 1966, and the Hotel is now owned by a Portland family. The Hotel maintains its commitment to elegance and customer satisfaction. Eighteen different floor plans characterize the 102 rooms, presenting an exceptional variety of choices. Guests receive a free Continental breakfast, and The Mark Spencer serves tea every afternoon from 3 pm to 6 pm in the library. You will find cable television, voicemail, data ports, high-speed wireless access, and fully-equipped kitchens in the rooms. The Mark Spencer features the best of the past and the present. Friendly staff will be glad to help you find interesting new places to visit nearby, or you can simply kick back and relax in the rooftop garden area. The Mark Spencer is just a few minutes' walk from the Pearl District's galleries, Powell's City of Books, PGE Park, and the thriving nightlife of downtown Portland. Meeting room services for conferences, seminars and receptions are available.

409 SW 11th Avenue, Portland OR
(800) 548-3934
www.markspencer.com

The Portland Music Company
ARTS & CRAFTS: *Everything for the musician*

Portland musicians have been shopping at Portland Music Company for more than 75 years, and it continues to set the standard by which musical instrument and sheet music stores are measured. It all began in 1927 when saxophonist and entrepreneur Bob Christiansen opened his first store. Known then as The Saxophone Shop, it occupied the downtown corner of Fourth and Morrison. The music business was jumping until the market crash in 1929 that brought an abrupt end to the saxophone craze. Bob had to adapt and he did so by expanding his selection to carry everything musical. With the expansion came an appropriate new name: Portland Music Company. Always an innovator, Bob became Oregon's Music Man. He was the first to offer band rentals to the region's school children. As a way to encourage school music, Bob and his staff criss-crossed the state in a caravan of converted hearses giving free evening concerts in schoolhouses. Returning the next day, he would find a music director and rent the community a whole band's worth of instruments. For 50 years, Bob and his wife, Violet, grew the company, finally passing it on to current owner Mark Taylor. Today, the company has five locations, each with its own personality and selection. School rentals are still offered, of course, but lessons, repairs, guitars, drums, keyboards, amps, sheet music, and recording gear are also available. At Portland Music Company, everything is for musicians and the music they make.

531 SE Martin Luther King Boulevard, Portland OR   (503) 226-3719
2502 NE Broadway, Portland OR   (503) 228-8437
12334 SE Division, Portland OR   (503) 760-6881
10075 SW Beaverton-Hillsdale Highway, Portland OR   (503) 641-5505
www.portlandmusiccompany.com

Oregon Historical Society
ATTRACTIONS: *Best history museum*

The Oregon Historical Society opened its first office and museum in Portland City Hall and began development of a regional research library and collection of historical artifacts. In 1917 OHS moved into Portland's Public Auditorium, and in 1966, moved again to its current location at the corner of SW Jefferson and Park in downtown Portland. OHS has published the Oregon Historical Quarterly continuously since 1900. More than 150 books on Oregon history, politics and culture, as well as biographies, field guides and exhibit catalogs, have also been published by OHS since 1929. The OHS artifacts collection comprises more than 85,000 items, and the Research Library contains one of the country's most extensive collections of state history materials. The Library's photographic archives include more than 2.5 million images from pre-statehood to the present day. OHS also sponsors Education Programs. The Oregon Historical Society Museum is open seven days a week. Visit them to enjoy world-class exhibits offering a glimpse into the history of the Pacific Northwest.

1200 SW Park Avenue, Portland OR
(503) 222-1741
www.ohs.org

Les Schwab

AUTO: *If they can't guarantee it, they won't sell it*

The birth of the Les Schwab Tire Company occurred in January of 1952, when Les Schwab purchased a small OK Rubber Welders tire store in Prineville. With a $3,500 investment and a strong desire to own his own business, Les increased the sales of his store from $32,000 to $150,000 in the first year. Les had a strong determination to provide a business opportunity for people who could not afford to go into business for themselves. As the company grew, Les came up with what is known as the supermarket tire store concept. His goal was to have his warehouse in his showroom so customers could walk through the racks of tires and pick out the actual tires that would go on their vehicle. He also stocked more than one brand of tire in each size to give customers a choice. Today, the Les Schwab Tire Company is one of the largest independent tire companies in the United States. Les is the first to say the success of the Les Schwab Tire Company has been made possible by wonderful customers who are the most important people in the business. Nothing happens at Les Schwab until a customer leads the way by choosing new tires, a wheel alignment or any of the other services they offer. Les Schwab is proud to feature neat clean stores, supermarket selection, convenient credit, sudden service, and a written warranty you don't pay extra for. Les's slogan is, "If we can't guarantee it, we won't sell it!" Visit one of the 385 Les Schwab stores soon.

www.lesschwab.com

Burnside Firestone Tire & Service

AUTO: *Complete auto care*

Burnside Firestone Tire & Service has been in this location for more than 75 years. In the past, the store offered all manner of goods, including appliances, toys, bicycles, gas and even outboard motors. Today the emphasis is on the Firestone Complete Auto Care Service concept of offering premium automotive service and tires. Manager Lewis L. Hess and the ASE and Firestone-certified team provide most manufacturers' scheduled maintenance services along with most auto repairs. Import and domestic vehicles are welcomed and any work not available by this team can be sublet out to other select business in the area. This way you don't have to shop around, saving

you valuable time. With a variety of on-demand services and tires in stock, you may decide to wait while your vehicle is being serviced. Make yourself comfortable in the lounge area where you will find free coffee, satellite television and wireless Internet. The Burnside Firestone Team is committed to every detail, and to your complete safety and satisfaction. Bring your car and concerns to Burnside Firestone Tire & Service.

815 W Burnside, Portland OR
(503) 228-9268
www.bfmastercare.com

Lukas Auto Paint and Repair

AUTO: *An Oregon success story*

Four generations of the Lukas-Carlson family has served the auto painting and repair needs of Portland. Alex Lukas, a blacksmith by trade, started the shop with his son, Melvin, in 1936. After 45 years, Mel decided to retire and close the business, whereby his daughter, Laurie, stepped up. She was informed by many of her competitors that "Women don't belong in this business," but she didn't listen. Laurie successfully owned and operated Lukas Auto Paint and Repair for 25 years. She recently sold it to her son J.R., but remains fully involved with marketing. Today, J.R. continues the family tradition of absolute integrity, top-notch customer service, expert collision repair, painting and detailing. The entire staff is certified. Lukas provides the most modern equipment to bring your vehicle to pre-collision condition. They will work with you and your

insurance company, and every repair receives a lifetime warranty for as long as you own your vehicle. The Elders in Action organization deems Lukas "elder friendly." Lukas was named Body Shop of the Year by a national jury of its peers and Laurie was honored by the S.B.A. as the Small Business Person of the Year for the state of Oregon. You can place your damaged vehicle in the hands of Lukas Auto Paint and Repair, a trusted community favorite for 70 years.

1722 E Burnside, Portland OR
(503) 235-5671

Kobos Coffee Company

BAKERIES, COFFEE & TEA:
Best coffee and tea supplies

When David and Susan Kobos opened Kobos Coffee Company in Portland in 1973, their goal was to bring to the Pacific Northwest the same distinctive and aromatic coffees, teas and spices they had found readily available in New York City, where they first met. In those early years David did all of the roasting himself, which is where he learned there is no substitute for high quality arabica beans, perfectly roasted and sold at the peak of flavor. Over the past three decades David and Susan have developed lasting relationships with the world's most renowned growers and brokers, which allows them to bring you some of the most extraordinary coffees in the world. In conjunction with their fine coffees and coffee blends, such as the Black and White and popular Bistro Blend, Kobos offers a distinguished collection of hand-selected teas from around the globe that have been carefully blended to provide distinctive and thoroughly delicious brews, including such blends as Black Current, Seattle Spice and Japan's Sencha Spider Leg. Kobos Coffee Company provides a complete line of espresso and standard brewing equipment, along with coffee condiments, accessories and coffee training for vendors. Enjoy your own exceptional coffee experience with a visit to the Kobos Coffee Company, where great taste is revered.

2355 NW Vaughn Street, Portland OR
(503) 222-2181
200 SW Market Street, Portland OR
(503) 221-0418 or (800) 557-5226
www.koboscoffee.com

St. Honore Boulangerie

BAKERIES, COFFEE & TEA:
Best French bakery

Who would expect to find an authentic French neighborhood bakery and café in the heart of northwest Portland? Probably very few, but that is exactly what St. Honore Boulangerie provides. With an inviting and friendly ambience, it has become a gathering place for friends and community seeking a gourmet experience. Owners Dominique and Stephanie Geulin have created a menu that reflects Dominique's heritage growing up in his family's bakery in Normandy, France. He attended different schools to perfect his knowledge of authentic French baking and was awarded the distinction of Meilleur Ouvrier de France, a title awarded once every four years to artisans who work to preserve French culture. Genuine French cuisine and style is the goal of this neighborhood eatery. As patrons settle in for their visit, it is easy to see that the Geulins have achieved their purpose. Everything from the imported clay firebrick to the stone grain mill captures the spirit of France. Offering seasonal items for many holidays, St. Honore's four bakers create highlights for each time of year, including their delectable handcrafted chocolate truffles. Regardless of what you choose to enjoy while visiting this little piece of France, you can rest assured it will be an authentic, fresh-tasting delight.

2335 NW Thurman, Portland OR
(503) 445-4342
www.sthonorebakery.com

Priestley & Sons Moving
BUSINESS: *Most helpful movers*

More than 75 years ago, Carroll H. Priestley founded his company to meet the moving and hauling needs of a growing Portland. Today, Teresa Priestley, Chris Brown and Jeff Brown continue the family tradition of excellent, personalized customer service. Originally haulers of groceries and firewood, Priestley & Sons Moving has grown and changed with the times. They provide a fleet of the most modern moving trucks and up-to-date professional moving equipment to ensure that your move, be it large or small, is smooth and trouble-free. One of the oldest, continuously running moving companies in the state of Oregon, Priestley & Sons Moving offers heated, secure warehouses. This community favorite believes in supporting the local economy, employing more than 25 people and allowing no outsourcing of labor. Committed to its community, Priestley &

Sons provides service to the Assistance League of Oregon and pays special attention to the residents of the numerous retirement homes in the area. For outstanding service with your moving and storage requirements, call on Priestley & Sons Moving. They've been keeping this area moving since 1929.

**2255 NW Birdsdale Avenue, Gresham OR
(503) 661-7920
Portland (503) 232-3332
Southwest Washington (800) 700-7920**
http://priestleymoving.com

John Helmer Haberdasher
FASHION: *Best haberdashery in the Pacific Northwest*

If you're drawn to classic clothing and unique accessories for men, look no further than John Helmer Haberdasher. Third-generation proprietor John Helmer III welcomes you to peruse one of the largest selections of hats and caps in the Pacific Northwest. You'll discover European berets, Greek fisherman caps, tweed driving caps, Humphrey Bogart fur felt fedoras, Panama hats and English-style derbies. Every nook and cranny of the store boasts not-often-found treasures like sock garters, spats, braces, monogrammed handkerchiefs, ascot ties, silk scarves and walking sticks. Whatever you need for the final touch of class to your wardrobe, you'll find it at John Helmer Haberdasher. Since 1921, they have provided their customers with quality clothing, including Southwick suits and sport coats, custom-made shirts, Robert Talbott neckwear, Alden shoes, Pendleton sportswear and Alan Paine sweaters. John Helmer Haberdasher searches the world for traditional clothing, hats and accessories for the well dressed man. Visit John Helmer Haberdasher and find something for that special gift. Chances are you'll also find something for yourself. The store is located in downtown Portland, on the corner of SW Broadway and Salmon.

**969 SW Broadway, Portland OR
(503) 223-4976 or (866) 855-4976**
www.johnhelmer.com

Johnny Sole
FASHION: *Best boots*

For seven years, John and Gretchen Plummer have been providing shoes and boots for an urban lifestyle at Johnny Sole. They specialize in 21st century, business-friendly shoes that marry unique styling with comfort. Their clerks will help but never hassle you. Brands include Blundstone, Frye and Steve Madden. Shoes are just a part of this store's offerings. When you peruse the stock at Johnny Sole, you'll be exploring a bi-level department store that brings footwear to a whole new level. On the lower level, women will find sexy boots and kitten heels, while men discover looks that can take them to work or dinner. Upstairs, look for goods to satisfy the rest of you, including designer jeans with silk screen patterns, cotton t-shirts, belts and bags. Johnny Sole can complete your look with jewelry and hats. Many of the store's accessories come from local artisans. For the ultimate in cool, try Johnny's killer sunglasses. To discover your own style, come to the style mavens at Johnny Sole. Regardless of the pressures you and your feet face each day, your feet will find comfort and style here.

**815 SW Alder Street, Portland OR
(503) 228-5844 or (503) 225-1241**
www.johnnysole.net

Clogs-N-More
FASHION: *Best clog selection*

When someone mentions clogs as a type of footwear, you may get a mental picture of a classic Dutch wooden shoe. Some clogs are still made with wooden soles, but many now make use of manufactured materials to provide the same support as wood with a greater amount of cushion. Clogs-N-More offers one of the largest selections of clogs to be found in the Pacific Northwest. What makes clogs so special? Owner Ahmed Abraibesh says, "The clog is healthier than any other shoe." There are medical practitioners who support his claim. Many of Ahmed's customers are shopping for clogs on their doctor's recommendation. Because of their construction and support, clogs are good for the knees, back and feet. The bottom line is that clogs are incredibly comfortable and that's what makes them so popular with people who are on their feet all day. Name brands such as Bastad, Merrell, Joseph Seibel and Dansko can all be found at Clogs-N-More. There are five locations in the greater Portland metropolitan area, including Clogs-N-More Kids, offering quality children's shoes at affordable prices. If you have questions about the different styles, don't hesitate to ask. The knowledgeable staff enjoys educating customers about the clogs they sell. If you think clogs all look the same, you are in for a pleasant surprise. As the popularity of clogs has grown, a greater variety of fashionable styles and colors have become available. Visit Clogs-N-More. Your feet will thank you.

717 SW Alder Street, Portland OR
(503) 279-9358 or (888) 302-clog (2564)
3439 SE Hawthorne, Portland OR
(503) 232-7007
The Streets of Tanasbourne Mall,
Portland OR
(503) 690-4577
2006 NE Broadway, Portland OR
(503) 288-9909
www.clogsnmore.com

Mt. Rainier and Mt. St. Helens over Portland
Photo by Katie Baxter

Portland Outdoor Store

FASHION: *Best Western clothing*

Some things are better left firmly alone. That's the philosophy at Portland Outdoor Store, which has carried some of the same clothing lines for 90 years. The store has changed little since it was established in 1914. It clings successfully to the true Western look with traditional styling and fabrics. You won't find new synthetic fabrics at this store, where most clothing is made of cotton or wool, and top lines like Pendleton, Woolrich and Filson prevail.

At Portland Outdoor Store you can still find wool plaid coats and the Tin jackets long preferred by lumbermen in the field. Tin is a cotton fabric treated with a paraffin coating for waterproofing. Cowboy shirts have real front and back yokes and pearl buttons, and boots come from traditional manufacturers like Fry, Dan Post and Lucchese. Look for Levi's, cowboy hats and bandanas. You'll even find a no-commission saddle-selling service with about 100 used saddles for sale at any given time. President Bradley Popick keeps a close eye on the availability of traditional Western wear. He stocks vintage Western smile pocket shirts with embroidered pockets that end in triangles, and hopes HBarC will start making the popular style again in the near future. Join the many lovers of classic Western wear who beat a path to Portland Outdoor Store each year. The store is the largest urban Western wear outfitter on the West Coast and a destination worth your time and effort.

304 SW 3rd Avenue, Portland OR
(503) 222-1051

Oregon Brewers Festival

FESTIVALS: *Best beer celebration*

On the last full week of July, Portland welcomes more than 50,000 beer lovers to the Oregon Brewers Festival, held at Tom McCall Waterfront Park on the west bank of the Willamette River. This grassroots festival began in 1988 as a way to expose the public to microbrews at a time when the craft brewing industry was just getting started. Much has changed in the world of craft brewing, but the festival's purpose remains the same: to provide an opportunity to sample and learn about a variety of craft-beer styles. The festival showcases 72 of the finest beers the industry has to offer. There are more than 20 different styles to taste, from hoppy pale ales to rich porters, from chocolatey stouts to refreshing pilsners. Always expect a few eclectic styles to be thrown into the mix. Live music plays throughout the four-day affair. An educational tent provides a variety of industry exhibits, including exhibits on hop growers, national beer writers and home brewers. Craft vendors present their wares, and food booths offer light meals. A root beer garden presents complimentary soda to minors and designated drivers. Admission is free, but purchase of a souvenir mug is required for consuming beer. Patrons obtain beer by buying tokens. One token provides a taste, and four tokens yields a full mug. Visit the Oregon Brewers Festival for a true Beervana experience.

Tom McCall Waterfront Park
1020 SW Naito Parkway, Portland OR
(503) 778-5917
www.oregonbrewfest.com

River West Chiropractic Clinic

HEALTH & BEAUTY: *Best chiropractic clinic*

When Dr. Dean Clark was running track at Tigard High School, standard medicine could do little to relieve his sports-related injuries. His search for help brought him to a chiropractcor. The connection eventually determined his life's work as a chiropractor and his strong interest in sports-related injuries. Dr. Clark continued to run track throughout college, eventually becoming a track coach at Oregon State and later at Stanford University. He received his Doctor of Chiropractic from Western States Chiropractic and went on to become a Certified Chiropractic Sports Physician in 1995. He works with athletes at many local high schools and George Fox University. He was the chiropractor for the 2000 U.S. Olympic Track and Field team in Sydney, Australia, where he used Computerized Thermal Imaging (CTI) to detect injuries to muscles and nerves not easily detected by standard X-ray, CT scans or MRIs. It is the only technology in the Northwest of this type. By using methods such as these, he can find the origin of the problem, thereby helping to resolve the condition much quicker. Dr. Clark has at his disposal a wide variety of techniques that help athletes perform in the face of injury. He has helped hundreds of people dealing with sports-related injuries. Besides chiropractic manipulation, reflexology and massage, Dr. Clark employs a Photonic Stimulator. This device is a painless infrared light that penetrates the skin, improves nerve function and promotes circulation. The effects bring temporary and long-lasting pain relief. For state-of-the-art solutions to your pain, visit Dr. Dean Clark at River West Chiropractic Clinic.

6105 SW Macadam Avenue, Portland OR
(503) 244-3389
www.drdeanclark.com

Pennington Massage Clinic

HEALTH & BEAUTY: *Dedicated to helping people build muscles*

Todd and Pam Pennington of Pennington Massage Clinic believe that if you take care of your body now, it will take care of you later. The clinic, which opened in 1992, is dedicated to helping people reduce tension in the muscles in order to increase functionality. Todd and Pam are Oregon Licensed Massage Therapists, and Nationally Certified Medical Massage Therapists. They listen to client concerns and work to bring balance and functionality. Todd and Pam use Medical Massage tests to determine muscles that are weak and in spasm. They also use many different techniques to release tension and manual therapy techniques that assist in injury recovery. By using recognized medical tests to determine problem muscles and to test improvement, it is easier to recognize progress. Todd and Pam's goal is to bring harmony to the body by balancing the musculature and building proper function and support for tendons, ligaments and bones. In many cases even chronic muscle pain is reduced when the muscle tension is released. While some clients self refer, much of Todd and Pam's work is medically prescribed, and the process is a cooperation between doctor, patient and massage therapist. To get started on your way to greater health and well-being, call the Pennington Massage Clinic for an appointment.

10175 SW Barbur Boulevard, Suite 210, Portland OR
(502) 244-4427
LMT #3833 (Todd) and #8027 (Pam)
www.penningtonmassage.com

Mountain Park Health Clinic

HEALTH & BEAUTY:
Best naturopathic clinic

At Mountain Park Health Clinic, doctors Kenneth Rifkin and John K. Monagle are naturopathic physicians who employ a range of natural and traditional approaches to treat the whole person. To determine the underlying cause of illness and support and stimulate the healing power of nature, the clinicians use botanical medicine, Chinese medicine, homeopathy and clinical nutrition. They provide counseling, physical medicine, acupuncture and physical therapy. Their primary areas of focus include women's health issues, menopause and intestinal and bowel disease. Other specialties range from the treatment of migraines and allergies to the care of sprains, strains and sports-related injuries. Blending naturopathy with conventional diagnosis and treatment, the doctors are qualified to perform lab tests, X-rays, minor surgery and other procedures. Dr. Rifkin, also an acupuncturist, has been in practice for 23 years. The Mountain Park Health Clinic accepts insurance reimbursement. For your own good, make an appointment at Mountain Park Health Clinic.

11030 SW Capitol Highway, #100, Portland OR
(503) 892-8788

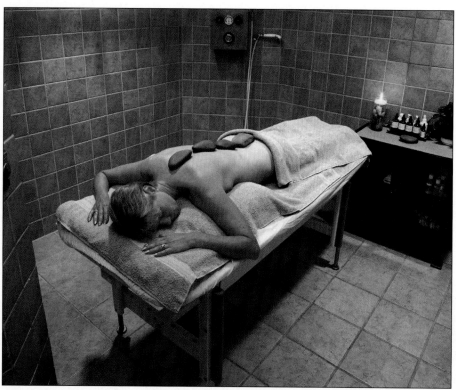

Rejuvenation Day Spa

HEALTH & BEAUTY: *Best day spa in Portland*

Rejuvenation Day Spa in Portland is one of the premier spas in the Northwest. Since 1999, owners Diana Governalé and Shari Jacobson have sought to provide a sanctuary of harmony and healing; a place where both men and women can escape to rejuvenate physically, mentally, emotionally and spiritually. At Rejuvenation, the air and water are vigorously purified, and all the plants, herbs and minerals used in the treatments are as natural and curative as possible. With treatments ranging from the spa's signature Aromatherapy Facial to the Tangerine Dream exfoliating skin treatment, as well as holistic body wraps and hot stone therapy, Rejuvenation provides the latest in self-renewal. Their studio offers numerous yoga and Pilates classes, and frequent workshops are held that emphasize a holistic approach to well-being. Whether you visit the spa, or buy a gift certificate for a deserving someone in your life, rest assured that Rejuvenation Day Spa will leave you with a newfound feeling of serenity.

6333 SW Macadam Avenue, Suite 105, Portland OR
(503) 293-5699
www.rejuvenationdayspa.com

Reynolds Optical Company

HEALTH & BEAUTY: *Best place for glasses*

Reynolds Optical Downtown

Find a terrific pair of glasses that lets you see perfectly and is ideally suited to your personal taste and lifestyle at Reynolds Optical Company, where people have been finding glasses they love for nearly a century. Reynolds Optical first opened in downtown Portland in 1910. Over the decades Reynolds has built a reputation of excellence based on exemplary, hands-on customer service and distinctive, quality eyewear. Company representatives travel to the best international shows to select fabulous lines that will be showcased at the three Reynolds Optical locations. Each of the stores has been carefully designed to suit its neighborhood, and each offers a welcoming, relaxed atmosphere that invites you to take your time and find what works for you. At Reynolds Optical you can choose from glasses by renowned designers, such as Francis Klein, Prada, Gucci and Mykita, or find an original design from In House, Reynolds' own frame and optics maker and maker of the Aero line. Beyond frames, In House crafts lenses for all three locations, guaranteeing you quality combined with a fast turn-around time. Reynolds Optical further prides itself on giving back to the community by offering vision benefits to local businesses that otherwise might not be able to provide vision care to their employees. Whether you need a quick fix or brand new glasses, trust your vision care needs to the friendly experts at Reynolds Optical.

800 SW Alder, Portland OR
(503) 442-4285
3535 SE Hawthorne Boulevard, Portland, OR
(503) 232-3222
625 NW 23rd Avenue, Portland OR
(503) 221-6539
www.inhouseeyewear.com

Intelligent Design
HOME: *Best specialty furniture*

If you like design, if you like furniture, or if you just want to visit a cool place, Intelligent Design is it. There may be no other place in America quite like it. If you have been to Starbucks, you have seen their work. Intelligent Design has also supported Disney, Nike and the Seattle Library. Old Navy is now remodeling with concepts from Intelligent Design. With the opening of an Intelligent Design retail outlet in Portland, homeowners can now take advantage of this wealth of design expertise. Intelligent Design stocks products from some of the best home furnishings manufacturers in the world, with names such as Fritz Hansen, Casa Milano, Arper and Moooi, to cite but a few. Prices begin in the midrange, and a large selection of pre-owned office furniture is also available. Whether it is wood furnishings from Germany, modern design from all over Europe or custom designs and colors, Intelligent Design can do it all. Portland is a hotbed for designers because of Nike, Adidas, Columbia Sportswear and other businesses that require design work. Under President William Fritts, Intelligent Design has been able to tap into the local design talent to create a destination place you will want to visit.

537 SW 12th Avenue, Portland OR
(503) 228-8825
www.idcollection.net

Sunset Heating & Cooling

HOME:
Custom systems by the experts

Originally established as Sunset Fuel in 1922, this company began as a fuel delivery business. At first, they delivered sawdust from a local lumber yard. As times and technology changed, they moved from sawdust to wood to coal to heating oil. Today, the name has been changed to Sunset Heating & Cooling to reflect the refocus on furnaces, air conditioning, heat pumps and indoor air quality products. Sunset has been a Carrier dealer since 1958 and has been designated a Factory Authorized Dealer. This means that Sunset has well trained and certified technicians and salespeople, as well as being in the top five percent of Carrier's dealers nationwide. This also means that all Carrier products installed by Sunset come with a 100-percent customer satisfaction guarantee backed by Carrier. Sunset's comfort specialists evaluate your site, listen to your needs and goals to customize the right system for your home. Estimates are free. From system design to installation and service, Sunset's highly trained staff will work to ensure your total satisfaction. If you ever do need service, Sunset's service department is there for you 24 hours a day. For the highest quality products and customer service, you can't go wrong at Sunset Heating & Cooling.

0607 SW Idaho Street, Portland OR
(503) 234-0611

West-Meyer Fence

HOME: *Best fence company*

Lance and Jennifer West and Ron Meyer combined their skills and formed West-Meyer Fence in 1997. Lance learned the trade from his father, Jennifer is a talented designer, and Ron has extensive fence-construction experience. Together they will take you through the bid process, design your project, and work within your budget to meet your fencing needs. West-Meyer provides fencing to residential, commercial and industrial customers, and they work with the top names in the home-construction trades. They can handle any request and they work with a wide range of

materials. From ornamental iron, glass railings, concrete and stone to vinyl, wood and chain link, they will build the perfect fence for you. West-Meyer takes pride in their craftsmanship. Tour the Street of Dreams and you will find many examples of their fine work. For everything from security fencing to a beautiful enclosure for your home, call on West-Meyer Fence.

712 N Columbia Boulevard, Portland OR
(503) 978-1830

Tri-County Temp Control

HOME: *Best HVAC*

In 1987, Alan Sanchez founded Tri-County Temp Control, determined that the company would grow and prosper by delivering superior customer service. Referrals from satisfied customers have consistently proven him right. With a crew of more than 70, Tri-County has a long and distinguished track record throughout the metro Portland area. Tri-County has installed thousands of retro-fit and new-construction HVAC systems, earning its status as the name you can trust.

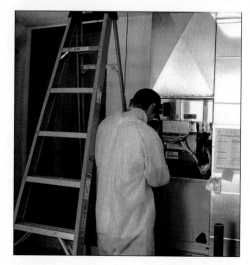

Their work is well represented on the Street of Dreams and greatly respected by homeowners, businesses and contractors throughout the area. Tri-County can assess your home or office space, then design and install the system that best meets your needs. When you visit their massive showroom, you will be greeted by friendly people with expert knowledge of their business. Every effort is made to provide products primarily manufactured in the USA. In addition, the company is committed to environmentally friendly products and procedures. For all your heating, air-conditioning and indoor air-quality needs call on Tri-County Temp Control. You will become a customer for life.

13150 S Clackamas River Drive, Oregon City OR
(503) 557-2220

Portland Closet Company

HOME: *Best closet company*

Even the roomiest closet can become a black hole of lost shoes and clothing. Portland Closet Company has the solution. This company enhances the lives of its clients by designing and installing superior organizing systems. Portland Closet offers complimentary in home design consultation, professional installation by experienced carpenters and spotless clean up. You can visit their large, airy showroom in Portland's Pearl District to get a taste of their custom work. In addition to designing superior walk-in and reach-in closets, the company has solutions for offices, pantries and garages. Portland Closet carries Tilt-Away wall beds in twin, double and queen styles that can double the functional size of a room. Closet systems and cabinetry use melamine or real wood veneers for a handsome, durable finish. You can also find brightly colored shelves and drawers for children's closets. Founded in 1985, this local, family-owned business has earned a reputation for exceptional design, service and installation. The staff members strive to work within your budget and on schedule. They respect your ideas, add their expertise, and turn your dreams into reality. They want your experience with them to be so delightful that you will be eager to recommend them to your friends. Visit Portland Closet Company and see what a difference beautifully organized storage can make in your life.

1120 NW 14th Avenue, Portland OR
(503) 274-0942 or (800) 600-5654
www.portlandcloset.com

Kitchens & More Northwest

HOME: *Best cabinetry*

Fine cabinetry offers much more than a place to put your things, it enhances a home's beauty and utility and defines your home's décor. At Kitchens & More Northwest in Hillsboro, you'll find the best service and craftsmanship in the industry plus a wide range of style options and wood species. Since opening Kitchens & More Northwest in 1989, owners Drew and Val Tolmie and their talented crew have been working with individual homeowners and area builders to style custom-made specialty cabinets for every room in your house. When you enlist the services of Kitchens & More Northwest, you can expect expert guidance in designing the perfect kitchen, office, entertainment center or bathroom, plus durable finishes and high quality hardware that assure your lasting satisfaction. The Kitchens & More showroom is bound to stir up your dreams with almost a dozen cabinet displays and a wall exhibiting door styles, color selections, knobs and pulls. Area builders have chosen the prize-winning work of the Kitchens & More Northwest team to appear for the past 16 years in the Street of Dreams project, a display of cutting-edge style options for today's finest homes. "We believe fine cabinetry is the heart of a home," says Drew. When you are ready to experience the beauty and practicality of custom cabinetry, turn to the experts at Kitchens & More Northwest. They will use their expertise and state-of-the-art equipment to build a lasting heart into your home.

460 SW Armco, Hillsboro OR (503) 648-0499
http://kitchensandmorenw.com

Terra-Sol Landscaping

HOME: *Best landscaping*

During a summer job on Hayden Island, David Zimmerman developed an affinity for working outdoors in landscaping, construction and design. He continued to gain experience working for a design-landscape company. After earning a degree in Landscape Architecture, he started his own business, Terra-Sol Landscaping. Along with his experienced and professional staff, David serves the greater Portland metropolitan area. Working within any budget, they will strive to create the outdoor space of your dreams. They can build retaining walls, patios, garden paths and steps. Water features are also a specialty, including ponds, fountains, bubble rocks and waterfalls. Garden lovers enjoy working with David in creating their special garden spaces. Terra-Sol, meaning Earth-Sun, has provided landscaping for several homes at the annual Street of Dreams. In addition to landscaping, Terra-Sol is a long-time sponsor of Little League in the community. They are well known and well respected. You can trust your next outdoor project to Terra-Sol Landscaping, a community favorite since 1977.

(503) 691-6105
www.terrasollandscaping.com

Martinottis' Café and Deli
MARKETS: *Best Italian deli*

In 1978, Armond Martinotti decided to open a pasticceria, or Italian deli, much like the one his family owned on the Italian Riviera. Martinottis' Café and Deli would be a place where the whole family could work and share the goodness of Italian food. In the pursuit of excellence, Dixie Martinotti, Armond's wife and partner, attended and graduated from Marcella Hazan's School of Classic Italian Cooking in Venice. (Marcella Hazan is a famous Italian chef and food writer.) Today, son Frank Martinotti takes a leading role in the enterprise. In addition to Italian food, Martinottis' is famous for wine, and its wine cellar has been called the best and most extensive on the West Coast. Some bottles date back to the 1930s. Although Martinottis' features Italian products, its wine cellar contains elite wines from every country. Nor have Oregon's superior Pinot Noir and Pinot Gris been neglected. In addition to the deli and wine business, Martinottis' offers catering that can range from a few sandwiches to a sit-down dinner for 500. If you like real Italian food or wish to pick up wine of the highest quality, Martinottis' is the place to go.

404 SW 10th Avenue, Portland OR
(503) 224-9028
http://martinottis.citysearch.com

Friends of Tryon Creek
PARKS: *Best SW trail system*

To escape the hustle and bustle of the city, take a stroll through Tryon Creek State Park's nature trails. Explore the fantastic scenery at this lush green oasis just minutes from downtown. The 645-acre Tryon Creek State Natural Area is open to cyclists, horseback riders, hikers, joggers and tourists year round, although occasional closures may occur due to weather. Many different trails are available for all ability levels, including the Trillium Trail, which is fully accessible to those with mobility-related concerns. The park is full of history. Located in Tryon Creek Canyon, the area was logged in the 1880s by Oregon Iron Company to help provide energy to the Lake Oswego area. Now that the forest has been regrown, there are numerous tree species to enjoy, including red alder, Douglas fir, big leaf maple and western red cedar. In addition, more then 50 species of birds and many mammals make their home in the park. Youth camps are available seasonally, and school tours are offered. Tryon Creek is unique in that it contains a steelhead trout run, one of the few urban creeks to still do so. The Friends of Tryon Creek State Park operate a nature store and hold special events. Take a break from city life and commune with nature at Tryon Creek.

Off Interstate 5, Terwilliger Boulevard, Portland OR
(503) 636-9886

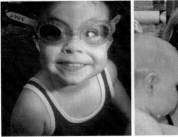

Children of the Sea
RECREATION: *Best swim school*

Children of the Sea, or Keiki Kai in Hawaiian, was founded in the early 1980s by owner Lynne Zavrski. She began her career teaching swimming in city and county pools in and around Oahu. It was there she began to develop her individually paced teaching philosophy that has become the Water Safe Program of Children of the Sea. In 1996, Lynne brought her knowledge and methods to the mainland and in Portland founded and built a state-of-the-art facility for Children of the Sea. Beginning with the basic premise that children progress at their own speed, highly qualified instructors are trained to emphasize, with gentle and patient encouragement, the latest in aquatic techniques. At Children of the Sea, the staff believes that each child can learn to love and respect the water. Their teaching approach is designed to build awareness and self-confidence in the water. The staff takes pride in teaching the uniquely innovative water-safe program. Through stimulation, positive reinforcement, patience and practice, students learn new skills while having fun. Sign up today. There is always a session in progress. You can be pro-rated for the days that you may have missed prior to signing up. Children of the Sea is a place where the pool is your classroom and learning is fun.

10170 SW Nimbus Avenue, Suite H-7, Portland OR
(503) 620-5970
www.childrenofthesea.com

Fernando's Hideaway
RESTAURANTS & CAFÉS: *Best Spanish cuisine*

Fernando's Hideaway, located in the historic Yamhill district of downtown Portland, has offered authentic Spanish cuisine, wine and dancing for more than a decade. In 2001, Fernando Moreno, the restaurant's founder, turned the establishment over to Neverstill Enterprises and managers Lorrie Reierson and Lane Karavaic. Fernando's Hideaway has built its reputation on authentic Mediterranean and Spanish-style tapas, salads, entrées and paellas. Chef Dwayne Edwards combines local, organic and native ingredients to create modern as well as traditional Spanish dishes. Chef Edwards coordinates his menus with Fernando's wine steward to heighten the overall dining experience. Fernando's award-winning wine list focuses on the wines of Spain, making it one of the finest and most extensive lists in the Northwest. Attentive, professional and knowledgeable staff members guide guests through the menus, pointing out highlights and wine pairings. Fernando's has hosted many weddings and parties in its private dining rooms and serves countless anniversaries and special occasions each year. The dining room is romantic and intimate, and the tapas bar is casual yet upscale. A late night dance club features the dances of Spain and Latin America on Thursday, Friday and Saturday. Fernando's offers free salsa lessons those evenings. Fernando's is community oriented and supports local businesses, schools and charities. Experience the food, wine and dance of Spain at Fernando's Hideaway.

824 SW 1st Avenue, Portland OR
(503) 248-4709 *www.fernandosportland.com*

Photo by John Ecklund

Huber's

RESTAURANTS & CAFÉS: *Best roast turkey in Oregon*

Founded in 1879, Huber's is Portland's oldest restaurant and one of its best. You can get a variety of fare at Huber's, but the restaurant is famous for roast turkey. Jim Louie, a Chinese immigrant who began cooking turkeys in 1891, said, "A young fellow, he cook 100 turkeys and know nothing… cook 50,000 turkeys, he knows something about it." In those days, Huber's was a saloon that served Portland's business elite. Frank Huber ceremoniously prepared drinks at the bar while Jim sliced turkey for the sandwiches handed out free with the booze. Jim took over when Frank died in 1912, and when Prohibition arrived, Jim converted the saloon into a restaurant. Huber's is now owned by the third generation of the Louie family—David, Lucille and James. Beyond roast turkey, consider the sugar-glazed ham, a recipe that dates back more than a century. The menu also includes seafood, red meats and pasta. Huber's coleslaw, served with all sandwiches, is a tradition. Customers who normally avoid coleslaw praise this version. Another renowned treat is Flaming Spanish Coffee, made tableside with Triple Sec, 151-proof rum, Kahlua and whipped cream. Servers amaze the guests as the liquor dances three feet into the glass. Huber's décor is utterly traditional, with huge mahogany booths and a stained glass skylight. Every brass fixture and wooden molding gleams as if just polished. Huber's is open for lunch and dinner.

For wonderful food and a slice of history, Huber's is the place.

411 SW 3rd Avenue, Portland OR
(503) 228-5686 *www.hubers.com*

Jake's Famous Crawfish

RESTAURANTS & CAFÉS: *A tradition for generations*

A downtown Portland landmark for more than a century, Jake's Famous Crawfish has its name in lights on its historical marquee. When you follow this sign, you will find yourself enjoying one of the top 10 seafood restaurants in the nation, a place that must not be missed on a trip to the city. Established in 1892, and run by renowned restaurant owners McCormick & Schmick's, a full menu from Jake's can be found on their website. The Restaurant features more than 30 varieties of fresh fish and seafood, which is flown in daily, in the true Northwest tradition of product, taste and presentation. In *Willamette Week's* Best Restaurants issue, they complimented not only the food, but also the "friendly, knowledgeable staff," always an essential part of a great restaurant experience. At Jake's, you will have a wealth of fine food to choose from: Salmon Roasted on a Cedar Plank, Oregon Dungeness Crab, Chinook Salmon Stuffed with Crab, great pasta, poultry dishes and an outstanding selection of prime steaks. Jake's has been voted the Best Seafood Restaurant by *CitySearch.com*. They are also justly proud of their very popular bar. Jake's Famous Crawfish is remarkably simple and undeniably satisfying.

401 SW 12th Avenue, Portland OR
(888) 344-6861 or (503) 226-1419
www.JakesFamousCrawfish.com

McCormick & Schmick's Seafood Restaurants

RESTAURANTS & CAFÉS:
Best seafood dynasty

This is the restaurant that was so acclaimed it led to a collection of great eateries all across the country. You will find the original McCormick & Schmick's Seafood Restaurant in Portland's Henry Failing Building, built in 1886. The setting is full of history, and the ambience is just one of the reasons why this is such a popular gathering spot for locals and a terrific find for tourists. From the striped awning outside to the gleaming rows of glasses and bottles behind the bar, a trip to McCormick & Schmick's is a gratifying experience for all the senses. The *Oregonian* described it in 2000, "A crisply attired, highly professional wait staff and an abundance of oak and brass contribute to the timeless aura, while the top of the menu proclaims what's up-to-the-minute here… the freshest fish and seafood from around the world." The keystone of McCormick & Schmick's success is wonderful seafood and service. Menus are printed every day, reflecting the best food available at that particular time, and including up to 100 freshly prepared items. The original restaurant, located at 1st and Oak Streets, is renowned for its very popular and lively bar.

235 SW First Avenue, Portland OR
(503) 224-7522 or (888) 344-6861
309 SW Montgomery, Portland OR
(503) 220-1865
9945 SW Beaverton-Hillsdale Hwy,
Beaverton OR
(503) 643-1322
17015 SW 72nd Avenue, Tigard OR
(503) 684-5490
www.mccormickandschmicks.com

Original Pancake House
RESTAURANTS & CAFÉS: *Best breakfast*

Les Highet and Erma Hueneke founded the Original Pancake House in 1953. Since then it has become a second- and third-generation family business with more than 100 franchises from coast to coast, and the very first restaurant in Portland is still going strong. Drawing upon years of experience in the culinary field and their matchless working knowledge of national and ethnic pancake recipes, the Original Pancake House has been able to offer a unique and original menu that has gained national acclaim. Their pancake recipes demand only the finest ingredients, including the purest butter and 36-percent whipping cream, fresh eggs, hard-wheat unbleached flour, and the restaurant's own sourdough starter. The batters and sauces are made fresh in each restaurant's kitchen. But there are more than pancakes at the Original Pancake House. Their unique omelets are rolled in a skillet and then oven baked for a light, moist delicacy. Their gourmet crepes include the Cherry Kijafa, a blend of tart cherries and sweet Danish cherry wine. Their signature coffee is blended, roasted and ground just for them. It is their pleasure is to serve you the finest food with pleasant and courteous service. The Original Pancake House has locations in Salem, Bend and Eugene.

8601 SW 24th Avenue, Portland OR
(503) 246-9007
www.originalpancakehouse.com

Seasons & Regions Seafood Grill
RESTAURANTS & CAFÉS:
Fresh seafood grill

Start with fresh seafood, transform it into world-class cuisine and serve it in a relaxed dining atmosphere with a smile. This is the approach that has made Seasons & Regions Seafood Grill a smash hit since it opened five years ago. Offering an extensive specials menu that features seafood items currently in season, Seasons & Regions is open for lunch and dinner seven days a week and for breakfast on the weekends. Enjoy favorites such as the San Francisco hangtown fry, consisting of fried oysters scrambled with eggs, bacon and other fresh ingredients, or the huge halibut burrito packed with pepper jack cheese, salsa and chipotle black beans. The dinner menu takes you from Alaskan chinook salmon to Louisiana jambalaya or three-shrimp etouffee. Sample the soup du jour and a decadent dessert. All items are prepared in the Seasons & Regions kitchen. They even smoke their own salmon. You can sign up on the Seasons & Regions website to receive email notification of the menu specials and the latest soup creations by inter-galactic soup Jedi and owner Greg Schwab. If you prefer to eat at home, all items on the menu are available to go. Be sure to ask about the curlers and fuzzy slippers pick-up window. Stop by Seasons & Regions Seafood Grill and treat yourself to a delicious meal.

6660 SW Capitol Highway, Portland OR
(503) 244-6400
www.seasonsandregions.com

Raccoon Lodge & Brew Pub
RESTAURANTS & CAFÉS:
Best brewpub

From its décor, you might think the Raccoon Lodge & Brew Pub is a hunting lodge. The moose head mounted over the stone fireplace ought to be a dead giveaway. In reality, the Raccoon Lodge is a restaurant and brewery. Here, you can lunch or dine on upscale comfort food, enjoy great beer and talk with a friend. Owner Art Larrance certainly knows his microbrews. In 1986, he founded Portland Brewing Company with two pals. Art is also the director of the Oregon Brewers Festival, which he started in 1987. "But I'm not really on the brewing side of things," he says. "I'm more on the drinking side." In fact, the Raccoon's brew master and chief imagineer is Ron Gansberg, who uses a 10-barrel brewing system to produce ales ranging from Ring Tail Pale Ale to Black Snout Stout. Ron is particularly pleased with the well balanced Blond Bock, though the India Pale Ale is the best seller. You can use these brews to wash down a sandwich, burger or fish and chips. You can fill up on more than a dozen entrées, including meatloaf, jambalaya or Black Tie Pasta with chicken. Everyone raves about the deep-fried potatoes, which come with dipping sauces such as barbecue, ranch or Raspberry Habanero. In good weather, enjoy the beer garden. Raccoon Lodge got its name from the raccoons that live in the garden fir trees. Join your furry friends at Raccoon Lodge & Brew Pub, one of the best spots in town.

7424 SW Beaverton Hillsdale Highway, Portland OR
(503) 296-0110
www.raclodge.com

Photo © Fink's Luggage & Repair Company

Fink's Luggage & Repair Company
SHOPPING: *Best luggage store*

If you are looking for the highest quality travel products, Fink's Luggage will meet your needs. From luggage and briefcases to wallets and handbags, Fink's offers a wide range of products to accommodate your travels. In addition to superb products, they also have one of the most highly regarded repair centers on the West Coast. In today's busy traveling world, your luggage and bags may not be handled with the care you desire, so let Fink's help you. They specialize in the tough repairs to luggage, from hardside crack and dent repair to shell and lining replacements. They can also take care of problems with zippers, locks, frame alignment and sticking problems. No problem is too small for Fink's, for they will repair handbags as well, and can provide leather reconditioning for any item, even your favorite leather jacket. Fink's Luggage prides themselves on customer service, and can fix many items that other repair shops may consider unrepairable, with an amazingly fast turn around. Owner Alex Fink and founder Harry Fink have worked hard to establish quality customer service, while offering a vast array of brands and styles. They say "We've got a handle on your baggage," and they truly do. Wherever your travels take you, let Fink's services help you to make it more enjoyable.

517 SW 12th Avenue, Portland OR   (503) 222-6086
1336 NE Orenco Station Parkway, Hillsboro OR   (503) 547-8532
www.finksluggage.com

Portland State University Bookstore
SHOPPING: *Best college bookstore*

The school that is now Portland State University was born just after World War II, with a different name and in a different place. Returning veterans seeking college education prevailed upon the state legislature to create Vanport College, but when the campus disappeared along with the rest of Vanport during the Memorial Day Flood of 1948, the college was moved to downtown Portland. Portland State College was granted university status in 1969. The PSU Bookstore has had many locations, as well, since it was formed as a student cooperative at Vanport. You will find the Bookstore now at the PSU Urban Center, where it serves both PSU students and the public. Like other visitors, you may be surprised to find such a wide selection of best sellers, travel books, cookbooks, art supplies and children's books. The PSU Bookstore's mission is to serve everyone in the Portland area and it does a great job. The Bookstore offers special benefits to Co-op members, including 10-percent savings on all books except textbooks. Students from all universities are entitled to a 10-percent discount on some items if they show student ID. Fans of the PSU Vikings know that the PSU Bookstore is the first stop for the best selection of official Viking apparel, souvenirs and gifts.

1715 SW Fifth Avenue, Portland OR
(503) 226-2631
www.psubookstore.com

University of Oregon Book Store & The Duck Shop of Portland

SHOPPING: *Best store for Ducks fans*

If you venture downtown near the beautiful Willamette River in Portland you will find a unique retail store full of wonderful collegiate sportswear, books and gifts. Entering the Duck Shop is like going back in time. Located in a historic building full of old city charm, you will see murals adorning the walls capturing collegiate life from the early days of the University of Oregon until the present. The Duck Shop is inviting, elegantly merchandised and it has something for everyone and every pocketbook. Whether you are a Duck fan or just a visitor, the staff is eager to share their pride in their University and Portland. The University of Oregon opened the Portland Duck Shop in 1989 to serve the Portland area alumni and friends of the University, giving them a way to connect with the campus 110 miles south in Eugene. From the very beginning the Duck Shop has been a success and has helped the University expand its presence in Portland by offering students classes and seminars taught by UO faculty. Whether you are searching for car accesories, athletic equipment or ladies fashions, come to the The Duck Shop of Portland. See the website for other locations and information.

734 SW Second Avenue, Portland OR
(503) 725-3057
www.uobookstore.com

Oregon Wines on Broadway

SHOPPING: *Best wine shop*

At Oregon Wines on Broadway you can sample Portland's best selection of Pacific Northwest wines. If you are too busy to visit the wine country, you can come in and try the Northwest's best by the taste, the glass or the bottle. They have Tastings on the first and third Thursday of each month from 5 to 8 pm, featuring a different wine maker each time. They usually pour new releases. The tasting includes food and three wines for $12. A schedule of the wine makers who will be there is posted on Oregon Wines on Broadway's website. They offer membership in their Northwest Wine Collector's Club, which offers Pinot Noirs of Oregon's Willamette Valley, Washington's Red Mountain Cabernets, and Walla Walla's incredible Merlots, Syrahs and blends. When you join, you receive two or three bottles of these magnificent wines delivered to your home each month. With your shipment you'll receive winemaker's notes and information about the wines. Oregon Wines on Broadway ships nationally, offers local wine delivery, as well as custom gift baskets, and has travel boxes for airplane carry-on to help you bring home the locally grown and produced wines. Their website has a full list of the wines they have at any particular time. Oregon Wines on Broadway has an impressive inventory listed on this convenient site. Enjoy browsing their website, but come in for their terrific wine tastings to get the full experience.

515 SW Broadway, Portland OR
(503) 228-4655
www.oregonwinesonbroadway.com

ALOHA

Aloha is an unincorporated community in Washington County, located between Hillsboro and Beaverton. Its name is similar to the Hawaiian word, aloha, although the place name is pronounced uh-lo-huh rather than ah-lo-hah. Aloha is considered by its residents to have one of the few remaining markets for affordable yet desirable homes in the Portland metro area. It is a good place for working families to live due to its proximity to a number of major Intel campuses and the Nike world headquarters. The Intel Aloha Campus is right in Aloha itself. The MAX light rail line runs along Aloha's northern boundary. The Jenkins Estate, south of town, is owned by the Tualatin Hills Park and Recreation District. Aloha is home to roughly 46,500 people.

PLACES TO GO

• Jenkins Estate
8005 SW Grabhorn Road
(503) 629-6355

THINGS TO DO

February
• Chocolate Fantasy at the Jenkins Estate
(503) 642-3855

April
• Tualatin Valley Chapter Spring Rhododendron Show
Jenkins Estate
(503) 629-6355

May
• Quilt Festival at the Jenkins Estate
(503) 642-3855

August
• Summer Anniversary Concert
Jenkins Estate
(503) 629-6355

B.J. Rex Construction

HOME:

Most dependable contractor

Owner Ben Witkowski established his business to join the forces of the best and most experienced local talents in the building, design and remodeling trades. Dustin Stetson, Candi Lindley, and a team of top-notch, hand-picked subcontractors are central to the mix that allows B.J. Rex to offer diverse services from excavation, masonry, and concrete work to custom kitchen and bath design, renovations, additions, and remodels. Experienced in historical renovation as well as repair of fire and water damage, B.J. Rex is well versed in "green" building materials and practices, too. The design team will provide you with complete sets of drawings for your project to help prevent costly errors or misunderstandings and save you time and money. The company also has financial programs available, including limited warranties and short-term financing, to get your project underway and provide additional security. Experienced on-site project managers ensure that your job goes smoothly, on schedule, on budget, and to specifications. B.J. Rex Construction today for comprehensive, dependable contracting services.

6485 SW 201st Avenue, Aloha OR
(503) 349-5069

BEAVERTON

Beaverton offers a variety of family activities and amenities, including the region's largest farmers market, a new library, 25 miles of bike paths and 30 miles of hiking trails. Residents enjoy an award-winning parks district, high-achieving schools and a community-oriented government. With 86,000 people, Beaverton is the fifth largest city in the state and the largest in Washington County. Global companies such as Nike and Tektronix support the local economy. Beaverton is the home of the Open Source Development Labs and IBM's Linux Technology Center. Beaverton is home to the Oregon Graduate Institute School of Science and Engineering, part of Oregon Health and Sciences University. The MAX light rail system runs through the north part of town, stopping at the Beaverton Transit Center and other stations. Beginning in 2008, a new commuter rail line will run south from the Transit Center to Washington Square, Tigard, Tualatin and Wilsonville.

PLACES TO GO

- Bethany Lake Park
  Neakahnie Drive and 185th Avenues

- Greenway Park
  Parkway Loop

- Tualatin Hills Nature Park
  15655 SW Millikan Boulevard

THINGS TO DO

March
- Celebration of Creativity (art show)
  (503) 644-2073

April
- Hearing Voices Storytelling Festival
  (503) 846-3235

July
- Old Town Beaverton Festival
  (503) 646-7136

September
- Festival Japan
  (503) 552-8811

- Oktoberfest
  (503) 643-5345

- Beaverton Celebration Parade
  (503) 526-2243

ReMax Equity Group
BUSINESS: *Hometown real estate experts*

When you purchase or sell your home with ReMax Equity Group, you are working with the number one real estate company in the state of Oregon and the ninth-fastest growing real estate company in the country. Founded in 1984, the Equity Group has held this number one ranking in Oregon every year since 1994. Their sales in 2004 reached $5.3 billion, utilizing more than 1,200 professionals in 19 locations in the Portland Metro Area. They also serve clients in the Salem and Bend areas. As they say, "we've got you covered," with sales professionals and brokers averaging more than 13 years in the real estate field. With more than 80-percent of their business from referrals and repeat customers, you can rest assured they are providing the best in service. Equity Group has a full service relocation department. Almost all of their relocation services are free of charge. There is a convenient local contact in Portland. Whether you need local or national relocation services, they have the staff to satisfy your needs. Connected with the community they serve, in 2004 they donated more than $92,000 to 25 local charities through the Equity Group Foundation. Much of this is due to the hard-working people at Equity Group serving as leaders, participating in their communities and devoting time and money to the local charities. Giving back to the community is one of their missions. When selecting your realtor, consider ReMax Equity Group, The Hometown Experts with a World of Experience.

8405 SW Nimbus Avenue, Suite C, Beaverton OR
(503) 670-3000
www.equitygroup.com

Turquoise Learning Tree
BUSINESS: *Safe and fun learning*

Since 1996, Rob and Carolina Peterson have been fulfilling a vision. They have been building a network of Learning Tree Day Schools to provide fun for kids and peace of mind for parents. Leaders in affordable childcare, Learning Trees offer a safe and supportive environment for children from six weeks to 12 years of age. Sparing no expense, they provide the best furniture, supplies, toys and food for children. Main meals are delicious, well balanced and hot. There are pre-school, kindergarten and summer camp programs. The teachers are highly qualified and receive on-going training. All are certified in CPR and first aid and have attended the Oregon Child Care Basics program. The emphasis of the schools is on treating children with respect, encouraging self esteem and helping with social and emotional development. Caring, sharing, conflict-resolution and good sportsmanship skills are all part of the lessons. There are reading programs, arts and crafts, swimming lessons and plenty of healthful outdoor activity. If you are looking for the best care for your child in an environment that supports healthy child development, you can count on Learning Tree Day Schools.

15135 SW Beard Road, Beaverton OR
(503) 590-8409 *www.learningtreeschools.com*

Caring Heart Health & Home Services

HEALTH & BEAUTY: *Best home care*

The moment you meet Dixie Hofer and Alexia Keck, you feel warmth and caring for other people emanate from these two home health professionals. Dixie and Alexia bring decades of experience and competence to their work. Dixie is the mother of three boys and has 30 years of experience in the nursing field. Alexia is the mother of four children and also has a 30-year history in medicine. Their in-home care service, Caring Heart Health & Home Services, provides respite for as little as one hour or up to 24-hour care. By going to people's homes, they deliver the personal care that is so important to people in need. With their staff of more than 100 caregivers, they live up to their motto: Experienced Service with a Caring Touch. All of their caregivers are supervised by a registered nurse who is available 24 hours a day. Caring Heart accepts long-term care insurance clients, as well as private pay. For no charge, they have a nurse supervisor do an initial assessment of client needs, as well as follow-up nurse supervisor visits every 30 to 60 days. With office locations in Beaverton and Gresham, Caring Heart is available to assist you 24 hours a day, 365 days a year. Take a break and give Caring Heart Health & Home Services a call.

7380 SW 163rd place, Beaverton, OR
(503) 848-7069
www.caringheartinc.com

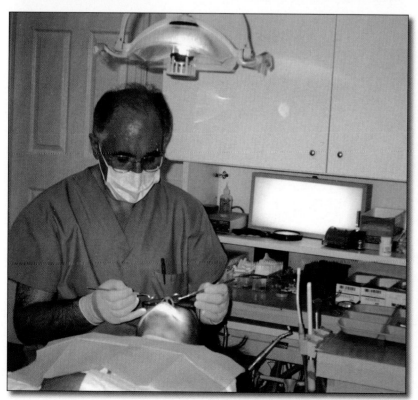

Beaverton Family Dentistry

HEALTH & BEAUTY:

A Beaverton community favorite

Settle into the comfortable chair, start the movie of your choice, then relax and enjoy your next dental appointment. Owned by Tony Moghimian, DDS, Beaverton Family Dentistry is a general practice. They perform all dental procedures, including teeth whitening, fillings, root canal, crown and bridge, partial, dentures and cosmetic dentistry. Dr. Moghimian's compassion, expertise and good humor combine with state-of-the-art dental equipment to give you excellent treatment and a positive experience. He is a member of the American Dental Association and the Oregon Dental Association. A community favorite, Beaverton Family Dentistry is a member of the Raleigh West Neighborhood Association. It is also among the leaders in the Beaverton area addressing wise energy use by local businesses. For all your dental needs, you and your family will receive the best of care at Beaverton Family Dentistry.

10950 SW Beaverton-Hillsdale Highway, Beaverton OR
(503) 641-1100

All Seasons Deck & Fence
HOME: *Best decks and fencing*

Mark Eickhoff spun off All Seasons Deck & Fence from a division of Eickhoff Construction, Inc. With 25 years in the field, he has the know-how to meet your deck and fencing needs and has earned a reputation for outstanding customer service. Thumbing their noses at Oregon's often inclement weather, Mark and his top-notch staff will complete your job in sun, rain, sleet or snow. They will meet with you, listen to your ideas for your deck, fence, or arbor trellis and they will work to complete your job within days of your final go-ahead. All Seasons is accustomed to working with builders and developers and can ensure expert work performed around their schedules and yours. With our more-hectic lifestyles and greater population density, homeowners are increasingly interested in no-maintenance yards, preferring decking and trellis work to define outdoor living space. All Seasons works with the best materials such as cedar, redwood and Douglas fir. From new construction to upgrading existing installations, they can handle steep and challenging lots and complex patterns and designs. For your "just right" deck, fence or trellis, call on All Seasons. They are Big Enough to Handle the Job, Small Enough to Care.

2235 SW 194th Avenue, Beaverton OR
(503) 348-4331

Garoken Energy Company
HOME: *Best residential HVAC service*

If you are fishing for the best in residential heating, ventilating and air conditioning (HVAC) service, you have found the right company. Garoken Energy Company, celebrating their 25th year in business, is owned and operated by Donna Jordan, an avid fisherwoman who has appeared on the cover of *Fishing Magazine* with her husband Bob. Donna has been the driving force behind Garoken Energy, handling all the sales for this residential heating and air conditioning company. Garoken offers repair service on all major brands of HVAC equipment. As a Lennox Premier Dealer™ Garoken is committed to high standards of service and customer satisfaction. You can always get the most up-to-date equipment. A new and popular line of products is the Healthy Climate® indoor air quality systems, all of which have earned the Good Housekeeping Seal. For all your home comfort needs, call Donna at Garoken Energy Company, or stop by the office where you will be greeted by her 13-year-old Shih-Tzu, Buffy, and the hospitable staff of Garoken Energy Company.

3565 SW 182nd Avenue, Beaverton OR
(503) 848-3838

Homecove Merchants-Caldera Spas
HOME: *Best spas*

A long soak in a hot tub is one of life's most relaxing experiences. The benefits, however, exceed mere pleasure. Spa jets provide the type of hydrotherapy massage that is so helpful for painful muscles and joints. Sink into your spa and you will immediately feel mental and emotional relaxation, greatly reducing your level of stress. A spa is also a great place to spend quality time with family or friends. Homecove is a full-service dealer for the renowned Caldera spas and hot tubs. Rated Best of Class by *poolandspa.com* and a Quality Buy by *Pool and Spa Living* magazine, Caldera is one of the most trusted brands in the industry. Homecove brings the comfort, performance and style of these fine spas to your home. They provide full delivery and set-up services and they specialize in water-balance products, accessories and spa covers to make maintaining your spa simple. Homecove Merchants also offers gazebos in all sizes and styles, along with fiber-optic lighting designs to make your spa and yard glow. Come in and let Homecove help you find the relaxation you seek.

10205 SW Beaverton-Hillsdale Highway, Beaverton OR
(503) 626-1527 or (800) 650-2683
www.calderaspas.com

Stanton Furniture
HOME: *Best unfinished furniture*

For more than 45 years, Stanton Furniture has been selling solid wood furniture to the Portland area. You won't find any particleboard in either of their two locations, only the fresh smell of solid woods. These family-owned stores are rooted in this community and have a strong reputation built on selling quality unfinished and finished furniture. They have the state's largest selection of unfinished furniture, and have a piece that would look good in every room in your house. These are stores to take your time exploring. There is so much variety to be found, don't be surprised if you end up spending an entire afternoon just browsing. Internet users can visit Stanton's website for a partial catalogue of their various offerings, as well as tips on how to stain and protect your new unfinished purchases. Stanton Furniture knows how to make your house look and feel more like home. Come see their showroom for great ideas.

10800 SE 82nd Avenue, Portland OR
(503) 654-5282
10175 SW Beaverton-Hillsdale Highway, Beaverton OR
(503) 644-7333
www.stantonfurniture.com

Pro-Tech Cleaning Services

HOME: *Best carpet cleaning*

Chris Boston is on the job at every job ensuring that your needs are met with the best service, products and prices. Pro-Tech Cleaning Services is certified in commercial and residential carpet cleaning, dyeing and repair, as well as care of oriental rugs, textile and leather upholstery, and tile, stone and wood floors. As the array of choices in fabrics and surfacing materials grows, the crew at Pro-Tech learns the latest procedures and chemistry, employing the most up-to-date techniques and equipment. Chris and his staff pursue on-going education through trade shows, seminars and classes. Committed to each and every customer, Pro-Tech has established and maintained an excellent reputation. Real estate agents recommend Pro-Tech to their sellers and buyers. Elders in Action has certified them as an Elder-Friendly Business for their fair practices, ethical and respectful treatment and their extra efforts in meeting special needs. Pro-Tech does not believe in surprises. You will receive a free estimate for your job and they provide a written complaint policy to ensure your complete satisfaction. Their motto is, The Most Thorough Cleaning Ever, Or It's Free. For all your floor and upholstery cleaning needs, call Pro-Tech Cleaning Services.

12150 Camden Lane, Beaverton OR
(503) 975-7577
www.protechcleaning.com

Cooper Mountain Vineyards

WINERIES: *Best organic winery*

Cooper Mountain Vineyards rests along the gentle slopes of an ancient volcano west of Beaverton. With four vineyard sites covering 123 acres, the Winery produces just over 15,000 cases of premium wine annually. It is within these vineyard sites that Cooper Mountain retains an increasingly important distinction among vintners. Under the direction of owner and visionary Dr. Robert Gross, these vineyards are certified organic and biodynamic. For the lay person, this simply means that the use of chemical pesticides and fertilizers have been eliminated in favor of herb and mineral preparations. For the connoisseur, this means wines of distinction, wines that reflect their unique terroir. When you sample Cooper Mountain's wines you are supporting a new direction in fine wine, one that has gone from the fringes of alternative farming to mainstream consciousness. These practices utilize compost preparations that include yarrow, chamomile, nettle, oak bark, dandelion and a host of other natural compounds all brought together in recipes developed to enhance the soil and improve the natural ecosystem. Still controversial, biodynamic viticulture is gaining acceptance industry wide, in part due to the early efforts of Cooper Mountain Vineyards and their sensational wines. The Tasting Room is open afternoons every day, but is closed in January and on major holidays. Wines offered include Pinot Noir, Chardonnay, Pinot Gris and Pinot Blanc. Special reserves and premium blends are also available.

9480 SW Grabhorn Road, Beaverton OR
(503) 649-0027
www.coopermountainwine.com

DAYTON

Dayton lies in the heart of the Yamhill County wine country. A commercial ferry began crossing the Yamhill River at Dayton in 1844. Andrew Smith and Joel Palmer founded the town in the winter of 1848-49. Dayton was named for Smith's former hometown of Dayton, Ohio. Palmer, who later served as superintendent of Indian affairs for Oregon, built a flour mill. The Federal government opened the Dayton post office in 1851. A Dayton landmark is the Grand Ronde blockhouse in the northwest corner of the City Park. This structure was built by settlers in the Grand Ronde Valley in 1855 and 1856. In 1856, Federal troops established Fort Yamhill there, but the fort was abandoned as a military post in the 1860s, and the blockhouse was moved to Grand Ronde Agency. Grand Ronde Agency was abandoned as well, and the blockhouse fell into disrepair. John G. Lewis of Dayton secured permission to move the logs to Dayton in 1911. The structure was rebuilt and dedicated to Palmer. Joel Palmer House is both a historic site and a fine restaurant.

PLACES TO GO

- Dayton Block House
  3rd and Main Streets

- Yamhill Landing Park
  SE Neck Road

THINGS TO DO

July
- Old Timer's Weekend
  (503) 864-2221

August
- Lafayette Heritage Days
  Lafayette
  (503) 864-2451

Domaine Serene
WINERIES: *Best Pinot Noir*

Atop the prestigious Dundee hills of Oregon sit the Domaine Serene vineyards, where the red volcanic soil and ideal climate combine to create a place to grow world renowned Pinot Noir and Chardonnay grapes. "Pinot Noir knows everything that happens to it–and it remembers," says Grace Evenstad. She and her husband, Ken, have been proprietors of Domaine Serene for 14 years. Ken designed a state-of-the-art, gravity flow winemaking facility where Tony Rynder, winemaker, creates award-winning wines. In fact, in June 2004 at a blind tasting of Domaine Serene wines against the world's most expensive and celebrated Burgundy producer, Domaine de la Romanee-Conti, Domaine Serene ranked first and second in vintages from 1998, 1999 and 2000. Ratings were on aroma, taste and preference. The Domaine Serene wines, priced at $75 per bottle, ranked first and second against wines priced to $595. July 2004 *Wines & Spirits Magazine* named Domaine Serene Estate Winery of the Year in their annual buying guide which was released in October 2004. This is the winery's second consecutive year to receive this prestigious award, which places them among the 100 top wineries of the world. All of the fruit is estate-grown with an insistence on extremely low yields to maximize the quality. Domaine Serene's vineyards are sustainably farmed without the use of chemical insecticides. The Tasting Room is open on Saturdays only, tours are conducted by appointment.

6555 NE Hilltop Lane, Dayton OR
(503) 864-4600
www.domaineserene.com

DUNDEE

The small city of Dundee, outside of Newberg, is a destination for wine connoisseurs from around the world. Dundee is nestled between the Red Hills of Dundee and the Willamette River. Its major industries are wine production and hazelnut processing. In the 1970s, it was discovered that the Red Hills of Dundee had a soil composition similar to that of the Bordeaux region in France. Today, there are 25 wineries in the immediate area. Before the wine grapes arrived, Dundee was famous for prunes. In 1881, the Oregonian Railway built a depot and hotel and named the area the Dundee Junction. Dundee was incorporated in 1895, at which time the city fathers proceeded to prohibit profane language and disorderly conduct, restrict the sale of spirituous liquors, and prohibit hogs from running at large within the corporate limits. Only two persons were ever confined in the town jail, which was sold for scrap in 1936 for $17. The Dundee Women's Club, founded in 1913 and open to all Dundee women, is one of the oldest continuously operating clubs in the state.

THINGS TO DO

August
• Annual Party in the Park
  (503) 554-9025

Vinyard between Dundee and Newberg
Photo by Stuart Seeger

Photo © Jason Tomczak

Argyle Winery

WINERIES: *Leading the quality revolution in Oregon*

Handcrafted fine wines are the promise and the purpose of the Argyle Winery. *Fodor's* travel editors recently named Oregon's Willamette Valley America's top romantic destination, and the Dundee area, in the heart of Yamhill County, has been praised by both *Gourmet* and *Travel & Leisure* for its charms. Argyle's Tasting Room, located in an old hazelnut plant, is right in the heart of Dundee on Highway 99. Boasting beautiful gardens, they are open from 11 am to 5 pm daily, year round. The friendly tasting room staff will be happy to give travel recommendations as they pour Argyle wines for your pleasure. (It is also reported that there's a tasting room ghost, a unique remnant from this 1880s building's long and colorful history.) All grapes for Argyle wines are hand-harvested into small baskets and transported to the winery. Argyle farms three vineyards. The 120-acre Knudsen Vineyard, first planted in the early 1970s, the Stoller Vineyard, planted in 1995, and the Lone Star Vineyard, 15 miles south of Argyle's Winery in Dundee. Texan Rollin Soles, with a reputation as one of America's most talented winemakers, co-founded Argyle Winery in 1987. Come and visit this top winery that is leading the quality revolution in Oregon.

691 Highway 99W, Dundee OR
(888) 427-4953
www.argylewinery.com

Duck Pond Cellars

WINERIES:

High quality at every step

Beautiful landscaping lines the driveway to the Duck Pond Cellars tasting room. Meticulously landscaped grounds surround the outdoor patio where you may sip wine and enjoy a picnic beside the pond. Duck Pond Cellars, the largest family-owned winery in Oregon, was founded in 1993 by Doug and Joann Fries. They, their children and families extend their expertise and warm hospitality toward every guest's enjoyment. At each step, from tending the soil to distributing worldwide, members of the family have given their all to ensure that Duck Pond wines deliver the highest possible quality for their price. With distribution to 45 states and six foreign nations, the Duck Pond label from Oregon is getting well deserved attention. Chardonnay is the number one seller, followed by Pinot Noir. Enjoy these and many other wines in the Tasting Room, where the warm, friendly and knowledgeable staff help to make your wine tasting experience memorable.

Join the wine club for even more wine tasting opportunities in your own home and a tasting room discount at the Cellars.

Both complimentary and nominally priced tastings and tours are available daily May through October. Open hours change in November through April. Duck Pond Cellars is closed for Thanksgiving, Christmas, New Year's Day and Easter. Groups from two to 40 people are welcome on informative tours for everyone from novices to wine connoisseurs. Many people just stop by for tasting, but Duck Pond Cellars can also accommodate groups, clubs, families and bus tours just out enjoying the countryside.

23145 Highway 99W, Dundee OR
(800) 437-3213 or (503) 538-3199
www.duckpondcellars.com

Erath Vineyards
WINERIES:
Willamette Valley wine pioneer

Dick Erath started his wine career as a home winemaker in San Francisco, falling in love with Pinot Noir when he tasted some old French Burgundies. That was 37 years ago, and he is now one of the original wine pioneers of Oregon. You can visit Erath Vineyards and see the stunning setting of his award-winning winery. You can also read about Erath's passion for wine in *The Boys Up North-Dick Erath and the Early Oregon Winemakers* by Paul Pintarich, published by The Wyatt Group, a recounting of the early days of Pinot Noir in Oregon. (You can purchase it on the very helpful and informative Erath website). In the 1960s, Erath traveled up and down the West Coast in search of an ideal place to grow Pinot Noir. Determined to make elegant, food-friendly Pinot Noir, he finally found what he was looking for in the then-unproven northern Willamette Valley. He made extensive studies of the soil and climate, and was convinced that this was the place where he could make his dream of world-class, affordable Pinot Noir a reality. In 1969 he planted a vineyard in Yamhill County and in 1972 he produced his first Pinot Noir and Riesling wines. Today, Erath produces around 40,000 cases of wine per year of Pinot Noir, Pinot Gris, Pinot Blanc and smaller amounts of Riesling, Gewürztraminer and Dolcetto. Erath's cellar-quality wines, produced in extremely limited quantities of 100 to 500 cases each, rank with some of the finest Pinot Noirs in the world. They are bottled only when they display the hallmarks of their pedigree and terroir. Dick Erath invites you to come and see Erath's 115 acres of grapes first-hand, in the Dundee Hills of Oregon's Willamette Valley. Taste for yourself what makes his wines distinctive.

9409 NE Worden Hill Road, Dundee OR
(503) 538-3318 or (800) 539-9463
www.erath.com

LAKE OSWEGO

Lake Oswego boasts the most expensive housing market in Oregon. The town began as an iron production center, with the first blast furnace on the West Coast. Smelting started in 1867 and reached peak production in 1890. As the iron industry declined, residential housing took off. Developer Paul Murphy founded Oswego Lake Country Club in the 1920s, and he encouraged noted architects to design fine homes during the 1930s and 1940s. In subsequent years, development around the lake accelerated. The Lake Oswego Corporation, a non-profit organization, manages all matters regarding the 403-acre Oswego Lake and its architecturally stunning 694 lakefront properties. This artificial lake is navigable, and on a weekend, many small boats may be found plying its waters. There is a dock at the east end of the lake, where boaters can dock, disembark and go to a nearby movie theater or restaurant. The city maintains 573 acres of parks and open spaces. The 24 developed parks include a swim park, a water sports center on the Willamette River and many tennis courts. A fun excursion is the Willamette Shore Trolley, which runs between Lake Oswego and a stop in Portland south of downtown next to the Spaghetti Factory.

PLACES TO GO

- Lakewood Center for the Arts
  368 S State Street (503) 636-1060

- Willamette Shore Trolley
  600 SW Bancroft Street, Portland
  N State Street and A Avenue, Lake Oswego

THINGS TO DO

June
- Lake Oswego Festival of the Arts
  (503) 636 1060

July
- Taste of Lake Oswego
  www.tasteofoswego.com

September
- Boones Ferry Days
  (503) 635-5100

Kiln Man Jaro

ARTS & CRAFTS: *Best place to create your own pottery designs*

At Kiln Man Jaro, lively conversation fills the air as laughter and brilliant color mingle during the creation of original pottery pieces. Owner Lyn Golden has created an atmosphere where anyone from a novice to a professional artist can create a beautiful gift or keepsake. Kiln Man Jaro is the perfect place to host parties for adults and kids. The fired pieces of pottery make perfect gifts or pieces for auction. Because of the approachable nature of painting your own pottery, it is an appropriate activity for office parties or team-building exercises, school field trips and wedding showers. Kiln Man Jaro offers wine and food at their painting parties. They can accommodate up to 50 people. In addition to their spectacular parties, drop-ins are welcome at the shop. They consider themselves part of the community, and that sense of community is only furthered when strangers are immersed in a non-threatening creative atmosphere where friendly discourse is sparked by shared joy. When that inevitable question of what to do arises, stop by Kiln Man Jaro and create something memorable.

41 B Avenue, Lake Oswego OR
(503) 636-4940
www.kilnmanjaro.com

The Hasson Company
BUSINESS: *Fourth highest sales volume*

Mike Hasson started his company in 1983, with the goal of becoming the top-selling and best independent real estate brokerage in the Metro area. Today, the Hasson Company boasts the fourth highest sales volume per agent in the country. The company has expanded as far as Bend and Vancouver, Washington. Hasson selects brokers for their experience, business philosophy, production and professional references. More than 250 associates in eight offices average $6.5 million in annual sales. These agents know the area, know the market, and know real estate. Their customers say their honesty, integrity and hard work stand out. Complementing the residential real estate side of the business, The Hasson Company provides relocation services, including their own publication, *Introducing Portland*, a CD with neighborhood and school information, and materials from the Portland Oregon Visitors Association and Chambers of Commerce. The Hasson Company sponsors the Children's Theater in Portland and many local Chamber of Commerce events. Whether you are relocating to the area, selling your home, or looking to buy, put yourself in the expert hands of The Hasson Company.

4500 Kruse Way, Suite 170 Lake Oswego OR
(503) 636-4000
www.country-real-estate.com

John L. Scott Real Estate
BUSINESS: *Third generation in business*

John L. Scott Real Estate was founded in 1931 in downtown Seattle and is currently led by third-generation chairman and CEO, J. Lennox Scott. With more than 56,000 closed transactions last year, John L. Scott grossed more than $13 billion in sales volume, making it one of the largest and most successful regional real estate companies in the nation. John L. Scott has 126 offices and more than 4,000 sales associates located throughout Washington, Oregon and Idaho, including 19 in the Portland metropolitan market. Using the latest technology, John L. Scott offers instant marketing, information and transaction processes, while maintaining the highest professional standards. J. Lennox Scott states, "we endeavor to enhance the home ownership experience through the perfect balance of tradition and innovation." In its commitment to service, the John L. Scott Foundation raises millions of dollars for medical care for children. Doernbecher Children's Hospital, Seattle Children's Hospital and Boise's St. Luke's Children's Hospital are among 18 such institutions benefiting from the generous volunteer work and donations of John L. Scott's staff. A community favorite for more than 70 years, John L. Scott is proud to be part of the rich history of the Pacific Northwest. To find a John L. Scott office near you visit their website.

www.johnlscott.com

Keller Williams Realty

BUSINESS: *Portland native*

Keller Williams Realty's Joanie Montgomery is a Portland native who has worked in real estate for nearly 10 years. She applies her thorough knowledge of real estate and her well honed communications and negotiating skills to serve the metropolitan area. Joanie specializes in southwest Portland, where she lives. Buying a house is likely the largest investment most people will make. Acutely aware of potential pitfalls, Joanie attends to every detail to save her clients money, fend off problems and ensure a successful and timely completion of the transaction. And she doesn't stop there. She maintains contact, providing referrals to the many fine local businesses that offer services to new home owners, and keeps clients informed of real estate trends and ways to enhance the value of their home. More than 90 percent of Joanie's new business comes from client referrals. Appreciated for her compassion and great sense of humor, Joanie's clients say she is patient, involved, interested, hardworking and fun to work with. Let Joanie Montgomery go above and beyond the call of duty to make your real estate transaction a pleasant, successful experience. Call or visit her at Keller Williams Realty.

4035 Douglas Way, Lake Oswego OR
(503) 789-7575

Anna's Bridal Boutique & Bridal Bliss

SHOPPING: *Best bridal boutique*

If you are planning a wedding or other special event, you will surely want to make a visit to Anna's Bridal Boutique. This beautiful shop not only has an extensive inventory of bridal wear and accessories, but also offers Bridal Bliss, an in-house event planning service specializing in, but not limited to, weddings. Anna's Bridal Boutique features gowns from simple to elegant, in every size, price range and color. From custom designs in beautiful fabrics to exclusive lines like Melissa Sweet, Wearkstatt, Vera Wang, Caroline Herrera and Janell Berte, you will be amazed at the selection. Anna's Bridal Boutique carries sample lines of dresses for the whole wedding party and provides in-house alterations. Their full-service event coordination includes planning, budgeting, locating vendors and all the countless details any important event requires. The service is a creative resource for the developing of agendas and themes, choosing sites and attire and arranging for a photographer. They can also provide professional catering, entertainment and much, much more. Because Anna's has researched and developed relationships with vendors, special rates are passed on to the customer as part of the service. If you've begun to plan for that special day, schedule a complimentary consultation to see how stress-free it can be to plan for a memorable event.

17050 SW Pilkington, #210, Lake Oswego OR
(503) 636-1474
www.annasbridal.com

Newberg farm and pond
Photo by Stuart Seeger

NEWBERG

Newberg is conveniently close to Portland, but it retains a distinct identity because it is buffered from the metropolis by a greenbelt of rural forests and farmlands. The Chehalem Mountains surrounding the community and the broad Willamette River create a natural bowl, providing a special sense of place that Newberg citizens cherish. With about 20,000 inhabitants, Newberg is an anchor of the Oregon wine country. Newberg is home to George Fox University, a school that combines a strong Christian emphasis with top-flight academic standards. Nearby Champoeg, a state park and a ghost town, is where Oregon's provisional government was established in 1843. Many early Newberg settlers were members of the Friends Church, better known as the Quakers. They founded what is now George Fox University as Pacific Academy in 1885. Herbert Hoover lived in Newberg as a boy.

PLACES TO GO

- Champoeg State Heritage Area
  8239 Champoeg Road NE

- Chehalem Skate Park
  1201 S Blaine Street (503) 538-7454

- Ewing Young Historical Park
  1089 S Blaine Street

- Hoover-Minthorn House Museum
  115 S River Street (503) 538-6629

THINGS TO DO

May
- Memorial Weekend in the Wine Country
  (503) 646-2985

July
- St. Paul Rodeo
  (503) 633-2011

- Newberg's Old-Fashioned Festival
  (503) 538-9455

September
- Pioneer Farmstead Day
  (503) 678-1251 ext. 221

November
- Wine Country Thanksgiving
  (503) 646-2985

Steve's Auto Service

AUTO: *Best auto service*

In 2001, the corner of Hancock Street and Meridian Way in Newberg gained a new look with the completion of a modern, state-of-the-art auto center. At Steve's Auto Center, Steve Drew and his team of ASE (Automotive Service Excellence) certified mechanics will treat your vehicle like it is their own. The fast-growing city of Newberg has always retained a special sense of place, thanks to its strategic location between the Chehalem Mountains and the Willamette River. Citizens here are proud of their town and retain a relaxed and friendly approach to business in the face of change. Steve's Auto Service fits right in to the traditional Newberg lifestyle. When you do business with Steve Drew and his team, you get not only the assurance you are dealing with an elite group of professionals, but a code of ethics that guarantees first-class workmanship, materials recommended by manufacturers and recommendations you can trust. Steve's Auto Service is living proof that small town friendliness and values can sit side-by-side with technological marvels. Next time your vehicle needs service or repair, bring it to Steve's Auto Service and experience Steve's personal sense of quality and down-home pride.

112 N Meridian Way, Newberg OR
(503) 554-1778

Adelsheim Vineyard & Winery

WINERIES: *One of Oregon's founding wineries*

Adelsheim Vineyard is one of Oregon's founding wineries, having produced top-quality wines for almost 30 years in the north Willamette Valley. Founders David and Ginny Adelsheim planted their first grapes in 1972. The plantings have since grown from the original 15 acres to 175 acres at eight separate sites, all on the southern slopes of the Chehalem Mountains. The Adelsheim approach in the vineyard focuses on sustainability and perfect timing. In the winery, they favor a hands-off method to ensure that all the flavors achieved by growing grapes in Oregon's cool climate end up in the bottle. Adelsheim Vineyard is widely known for its exceptional Pinot Noir, Pinot Gris and Chardonnay. These wines can be found at fine wine merchants and in the best restaurants throughout North America. Harder to find are the limited-production single-vineyard Pinot Noirs and a line of white wines from rare varieties, whimsically called "wacky whites." The surest way to purchase these is by visiting the beautiful, understated winery. Tastings and tours are offered from 11 am to 4 pm three days a week in winter, six days a week in summer. Serious fans of the acclaimed single-vineyard Pinot Noirs join the winery's Club Noir, so as not to miss out on any of these full-flavored, rich-textured wines. Club members receive quarterly shipments of two, four or six bottles and are invited to take part in private club events.

16800 NE Calkins Lane, Newberg OR
(503) 538-3652
www.adelsheim.com

TIGARD

Incorporated in 1961 and home to 47,000 people, Tigard is a clean, livable city. While primarily residential, Tigard also provides shopping opportunities such as those at Washington Square, one of Metro Portland's largest and most attractive malls. Once called Tigardville, the community is named after Wilson Tigard, head of an early pioneer family. Before the Oregon Electric Railway arrived in 1910, Tigardville was a small commercial center serving the local farmers, many of whom were immigrants from Germany. Thereafter, the railroad shortened the town's name, and population growth accelerated. The city features 10 historic structures that represent the architectural styles of yesteryear. These include the John Tigard House, built by Wilson Tigard's eldest son and an example of early frame construction. Beginning in 2008, a new commuter rail line will run south from the Beaverton Transit Center to Washington Square, Tigard, Tualatin and Wilsonville. The line will connect to the MAX light rail rapid transit system at Beaverton.

PLACES TO GO

- Cook Park
  17005 SW 92nd Avenue

- John Tigard House
  10310 SW Canterbury Lane

- Summerlake Park
  11450 SW Winterlake Drive

THINGS TO DO

June
- Tigard Festival of Balloons
  Cook Park
  (503) 612-8213

September

- Tigard Blast
  Downtown
  (503) 866-1658

Kadel's Auto Body

AUTO: *Best auto body*

In 1954, Kadel's Auto Body began as a one-man shop in downtown Tigard. There are now 13 shops located throughout Oregon, Washington and Idaho. Walk into any of their clean and friendly locations and you will be welcomed by people who know their business, ready to take care of your auto body needs. Repairing more than 20,000 vehicles every year, Kadel's offers the best in customer service and gives lifetime guarantees on all their work. At Kadel's, they understand that auto body repair can be unexpected and, at times, costly. They will expertly assess the damage and make sure you know all your options, so that you can make the best decision about your car. The employees are experts in their field, receiving on-going training to keep up with changes in the industry. They repair any vehicle from the smallest import to massive SUVs. Kadel's provides the skill, patience, and state-of-the-art technology to get your repair done right. Kadel's and its staff appreciate the communities they serve, and they support youth activities and charities with their time and money. For all your auto body repairs, come to Kadel's, a community favorite for more than 50 years.

9350 SW Tigard Street, Tigard OR
(503) 598-1159
www.kadels.com

Tigard Learning Center

BUSINESS: *Where learning is fun*

Jeff and Lavonne Boyer started the Tigard Learning Center in 1999 in order to provide a

Montessori learning environment for local children. They are committed to giving each child the best possible educational beginning, laying the foundation for life-long learning. With a hands-on approach, they encourage the development of motor skills, phonics, math understanding, reading and writing. The children learn to identify colors, shapes, letters, sounds and textures. With daily snacks, activities and monthly themes, the children enjoy learning and interacting with other children. They may attend part-time or full-time and there is flexibility in scheduling. The Boyers offer junior pre-school, pre-school, kindergarten, elementary aftercare and summer school in a trusted, warm and welcoming atmosphere. As the Boyers say, Tigard Learning Center is where learning is fun, and it's the perfect kind of place for children to be.

14361 SW Pacific Highway, Tigard OR
(503) 603-0593

Mergenthaler Transfer & Storage

HOME: *A fleet based on integrity*

Art and Nick Mergenthaler opened for business in Helena, Montana in 1934. Back then, their 1933 Dodge half-ton truck was hauling 100-pound bags of flour, sugar, potatoes, and other goods for local grocers. The 1950s brought transporting construction supplies for dam building and a contract to haul mail for the U.S. Postal Service. Mergenthaler grew steadily, and when Art died in 1972, his four sons took over the business, expanding it to an interstate operation. Now owned and operated by two of Art's grandsons, the company is still growing by leaps and bounds. Though they have fleets of modern vehicles and massive storage facilities, this community favorite has never forgotten its core principle of building open, honest, and ethical relationships with the people it serves. The more than 285 employees are proud of the history and reputation of their company and are able and ready to provide you with personalized, local, professional service. To meet your transportation and storage needs, call Mergenthaler.

7895 SW Hunziker Road, Tigard OR
(800) 547-0795
www.mergenthaler.net

Massage on the Go
HEALTH & BEAUTY: *Most versatile massage*

Does anything feel better than a great massage? Are you dreaming of one right now? Massage on the Go will come straight to your door, whether at home, the office, a hotel, or a special event. You won't have to wait for an appointment, fit it into your busy schedule, or fight traffic to get relief. Mary Dalton and her staff of fully accredited spa and massage specialists provide a wide range of relaxing and therapeutic treatments. They are skilled in hand and foot reflexology, water therapy, Shiatsu, deep-tissue and classic Swedish massage, as well as Reiki energy healing and techniques for relief of myopathy pain. If you want a facial or body wrap, those are part of the service, as well. In addition to the mobile service, you may want to visit their conveniently located spa, where you can check out the Bio-Photonic Scanner, one of only 15 in Oregon. The scanner allows the technicians to determine the types of supplements to suggest for increasing antioxidants for better health at the cellular level. From the inside out, Massage on the Go is a center for healing and wellness.

8879 SW Center Street, Tigard OR
(503) 620-0724

Goodnight Room
HOME: *Best room décor for youngsters*

The Goodnight Room is a one-stop shop for anyone outfitting a child's room. Owner Ann Adrian focuses on room décor, furniture and bedding for chuildren and teens. This colorful and welcoming store has an interesting layout, with simulated rooms of various colors set up and furnished to convey the many options available. The store exudes fun, with areas such as the Construction Zone, the Land of Make Believe, and a working Little Engine That Could train. With experienced designers in-house and custom services available, the Goodnight Room offers a personal relationship with customers. Ann's husband, Jeff Scott, manages the operations end of the business with a sure and steady hand. Ann and her staff believe it is an honor to serve families, and that feeling shows in their work. Take time to visit the Goodnight Room when your family needs furnishings. It is an out-of-the-ordinary children's store.

1517 NE Broadway, Portland OR
(503) 281-5516
Brideport Village
7283 SW Bridgeport Road, Tigard OR
(503) 684-9510
www.goodnightroom.com

Westside Dance & Gymnastics Academy

RECREATION: *Leader in dance and gymnastics*

The mission of Westside Dance & Gymnastics Academy is to provide a safe, fun and positive environment, promote creativity and fitness, and inspire students to achieve their goals. Owner Mellanie Heniff is a long-time student of dance and gymnastics. She offers classes for all age groups, encouraging whole families to participate. The 12,000-square-foot facility provides the best USA Gymnastics-certified equipment. Private lessons are available for all gymnasts. Mellanie believes dance helps children develop self-confidence, flexibility, a sense of rhythm and coordination. She and her staff encourage values of good sportsmanship, self-discipline, respect and accountability. The academy is open seven days a week, has a pro shop and offers summer camp programs in dance, theater, cheerleading and gymnastics. Their academic pre-school and after-school care programs enable you to find a program that will work for you and your family. For an exciting alternative in a safe and welcoming atmosphere, Westside Dance & Gymnastics Academy is a leader in education, dance and gymnastics.

11632 SW Pacific Highway, Tigard OR
(503) 639-5388
www.westsideacademy.com

Stevens Marine

RECREATION: *Home of affordable boating*

Stevens Marine, Inc. began in a small service shop in Lake Oswego, where Page Stevens repaired outboard motors and earned an enviable reputation as both a mechanic and a customer service specialist. Now, 35 years later, Stevens Marine has grown to be one of the largest and most complete boat dealerships in the Northwest. Offering Alumaweld, Bluewater and Smoker Craft boats and Mercury outboards, Stevens Marine features the top brands—all built in Oregon—along with a full service outboard and engine shop. In addition, they offer used boat and outboard sales, custom rigging services, in-house top and marine canvas shop, custom fabrication and boat repair. Besides having an expert staff, Stevens Marine also has a full service parts and accessories department. Stevens Marine provides a full range of tailored financing options designed to make boat purchasing easier and more affordable. Stevens Marine's Tigard location, just south of Portland, is a model facility that houses dozens of fully-rigged boat packages for your shopping convenience, with hundreds of outboards in stock ready for immediate delivery. You're invited to stop by Stevens Marine, the home of affordable boating, and sample their distinctive brand of hospitality that has placed them as the number one boat dealer in Oregon.

9180 SW Burnham Street, Tigard OR
(503) 620-7023 or (800) 225-7023
www.stevensmarine.com

TUALATIN

Tualatin contains more than 200 acres of parks and greenways. Tualatin Commons, located downtown, includes a pedestrian promenade around a three-acre lake, public plazas and an interactive fountain. The city holds concerts here in the summer. Community Park, the city's largest park, is on the Tualatin River. It includes an award-winning skatepark along with many other services. Tualatin boasts an Artwalk, a self-guided tour of the city's public art. It is made up of four loops with interconnected trails. Map kiosks help visitors find their way and interpretive signs explain the many different kinds of art on display. Features range from sculptures to murals to a mastodon skeleton. Tualatin's Heritage Tree Program provides for the protection and planting of trees. Each year, the city chooses up to five trees for their size, species or historic value and adds them to Tualatin's list of Heritage Trees. A map of these trees is available from the Tualatin Chamber of Commerce. The Bridgeport Village Shopping Center in Tualatin offers a shopping, dining and entertainment experience unlike any other in the Pacific Northwest.

PLACES TO GO

- Tualatin Commons
  8325 SW Nyberg Street

- Community Park
  8515 SW Tualatin Road

THINGS TO DO

June
- Tualatin River Discovery Days
  (503) 620-7507

July
- Artsplash
  (503) 691-3062

August
- Tualatin Crawfish Festival
  (503) 692-0780

November
- Tualatin Riverkeepers Fall Fest
  (503) 620-7507

Tualatin River

Century Hotel
ACCOMMODATIONS:
Best executive hotel

The Century Hotel is located on the south shore of Tualatin's serene Lake of the Commons. Designed as an executive hotel for the 21st century, you will find more than a home away from home here. Each of their 70 rooms is equipped with in-room coffee and coffee maker, personal microwave and refrigerator, iron and ironing board, and hairdryer. Guests can expect attentive friendly service, a complimentary full hot breakfast selection, and a complimentary newspaper each day. Take advantage of their indoor swimming pool, hot tub and Universal Gym exercise room, or select the private deluxe spa room with Jacuzzi tub. Relaxing views are available from rooms or while enjoying a meal at Hayden's Lakefront Bar and Grill. With menu selections specially prepared by executive chef Mark Bernetich, you will find options that vary from deep Southern flavors to Italian, Southwestern, Asian and, of course, Great Northwestern. For a sample of the chef's unique menu try the Drunken Spicy Shrimp appetizer, the rich Northwest chowder of razor clams, Dungeness crab and smoked salmon, Charlie's Chop Saltimbocca Double Cut Pork Chop with maple glaze and candied pecans, and for dessert try the Panna Cotta Baked Cream with berry compote. Stroll the nearby parks and shopping districts or take advantage of special guest privileges at nearby golf and athletic clubs.

8185 SW Tualatin-Sherwood Road, Tualatin OR
(503) 692-3600 or (800) 240-9494
www.thecenturyhotel.com

Star Motors

AUTO: *Best place for Mercedes-Benz owners*

Gunther Hirschmann had many years of experience working on Mercedes-Benz automobiles prior to opening his own shop in 1993. He understands that these exceptional vehicles are best serviced in exceptional surroundings. Star Motors is just such a place. The reception area is sparkling clean, fresh-smelling, light and airy. There is a window to the back bays where you can watch skilled technicians performing expert work in a nearly spotless environment. The owners specialize in all things mechanical for your Mercedes. They provide top-notch routine maintenance and the highest quality, most reliable work on the engine, transmission or undercarriage. They are eminently qualified to take care of the new vehicles being produced by Mercedes-Benz as well as the classic models. With the skyrocketing cost of fuel, Star Motors knows how important it is to keep your car in its best possible condition. They will happily provide courtesy ride service to your home or office while giving your Mercedes the attention it deserves. For all your maintenance and repair needs, call on Star Motors.

19215 SW Teton Avenue, Tualatin OR
(503) 691-9826

Tualatin Auto Body

AUTO: *Best auto body shop*

At the Tualatin Auto Body and So-Cal NW Speed Shop, owners Davis and Alexandra Carney want you to know that quality is never an accident. Auto repair and painting are the mainstay of their business, but they also sell parts and accessories, and build and repair hot rods and classic cars. Excellent customer service and extraordinary repairs take place in their 40,000 square feet of workspace. David and Alexandra are dedicated to working with each customer as an individual. If your vehicle has been in an accident, it will be repaired to factory specifications. If a part has to be pulled during repairs, a computerized frame-measuring system ensures that the frame or unibody is returned to the manufacturer's specifications. Their highly skilled technicians use only the highest-quality equipment, parts and materials. They pride themselves on their emphasis on excellence, evident in their auto body work as well as their sponsorship and support of services in the community. This combination of service and community involvement has brought them national recognition and has made them a community favorite. At Tualatin Auto Body, they look forward to working with you to provide a level of service and professionalism that you are sure to appreciate.

19705 SW Teton Avenue, Tualatin OR
(503) 692-1579
www.tualatinautobody.com

The Garden Corner

GARDENS, PLANTS & FLOWERS: *Best hanging baskets*

Have you ever wondered where those beautiful downtown Lake Oswego hanging flower baskets come from? The answer is the Garden Corner. This shop specializes in planting and preparing lovely baskets, but it also carries plenty of nursery stock, pots and fountains. Knowledgeable staff members help you find exactly the right plant for your garden and send you home with a humorous, instructional CD on how to maintain the plants you have purchased. Good humor is the key to the Garden Corner's business. Staff members make gardening fun, relaxing and rewarding without taking themselves too seriously. Owner and chief laborer Jonn Karsseboom notes that the Garden Corner was founded for "fun with a tad bit of lunacy." All kidding aside, Jonn and his people have created a gardener's paradise. The grounds are beautiful, the plants are healthy and the selection of water fountains is the best around. The shop stocks extras that range from comfy washable gloves to cushy waterproof boots. Tell the staff members what your interests are and they will come up with a variety of new ideas. Whether you are drawn to pots and planters or beds and borders, the Garden Corner will share the secrets to get you growing.

21550 SW 108th Avenue, Tualatin OR
(503) 885-1934

The Flowering Jade
GARDENS, PLANTS & FLOWERS:
Best floral arrangements

Since Gary Shigeno opened The Flowering Jade in 1982, he's been dedicated to providing the best in floral arrangements and customer service in the area. The shop offers the healthiest plants and the finest bouquets in a variety of styles and price ranges. At The Flowering Jade they know the language of flowers and can custom design your gift to give expression to what you may find difficult to say. To send well-wishes, celebrate an anniversary, or just because, Gary and his staff can provide you with the perfect arrangement. For weddings, they will work closely with you to ensure that your vision is beautifully realized. Whether ordering over the phone, on the website, or in person, you can trust that your arrangements will be customized to your wishes. For quality, variety, service and professional attention to every detail, you can satisfy all your floral needs with The Flowering Jade.

8101 SW Nyberg Road, Tualatin OR
(503) 692-0340
www.floweringjade.com

Skin Deep Beyond
HEALTH & BEAUTY: *Best day spa*

Cindy Ogden took her degree from the Esthetics Institute in Portland, added her amazing energy and persistence, and built her business from the ground up. Open since 2000, customer satisfaction has spread the word and Skin Deep & Beyond is now known as the best day spa in Tualatin. With extra-clean treatment rooms, candles and soothing music, you will relax knowing you are receiving the best of care. Using the finest products and technology, Cindy and her expert staff provide facials and proven facial enhancements, nail care, waxing and body wraps. The licensed massage therapists perform a variety of techniques, including Swedish, deep-tissue and pregnancy massage. Treat yourself to any of the spa packages offered or have one customized just for you. Cindy and her associates are committed to providing you with a totally satisfying and personalized spa experience. For a personalized spa package for yourself or a loved one, come into Skin Deep & Beyond, where exceptional results are guaranteed.

8373 SW Warm Springs Street, Tualatin OR
(503) 692-2888
www.skindeepandbeyond.com

Lile North American
HOME: *Best North American Van Lines interstate agent*

Established in 1959, Lile has safely moved people, businesses and products throughout the Pacific Northwest and far beyond. It is a second-generation family company that is certified by the Women's Business Enterprise National Council as a 100 percent woman-owned business. Lile is active in the community, working with Northwest Medical Teams and the Oregon Food Bank. While it has grown to include six branches in Washington and three in Oregon, Lile remains committed to its founding principle of providing claim-free, reliably delivered, customer-focused moving and storage services. Ranking as one of NorthAmerican Van Lines' top U.S. agents, Lile earned their Quality Excellence Award for the last two years and was named its top booker of military business. In addition to its national and international relocation capabilities, Lile offers sophisticated on-line logistics services, including an interactive international rate-quote system, and order-entry and shipment tracking. Lile's Warehousing & Distribution division reliably meets its service commitments to customers. For all your moving and storage needs at home and abroad, you can count on Lile.

19480 SW 118th Avenue, Tualatin OR
(503) 691-3500
www.lile.net

WILSONVILLE

Wilsonville is a gateway from Metro Portland to the wine country. The city is the headquarters of Mentor Graphics, which makes software to design integrated circuits. It is also home to Hollywood Video and InFocus multimedia projectors. Nike and Xerox are important employers. Wilsonville's Town Center includes a large interactive waterfall and wading pool, a pavilion, play structures and benches for enjoying warm summer days. The Oregon Korean War Veterans Memorial, located in the park, is a sweeping expanse of Carnelian granite containing the names of Oregon servicemen killed in the Korean War. Three ribbons running parallel to the monument represent major battle lines of the war. Beginning in 2008, a new commuter rail line will run south from the Beaverton Transit Center to Washington Square, Tigard, Tualatin and Wilsonville. The line will connect to the MAX light rail rapid transit system at Beaverton.

PLACES TO GO

- Champoeg State Heritage Area
  8239 Champoeg Road NE
- Memorial Park
  8100 SW Wilsonville Road
- Molalla River State Park
  N Holly Street
- Town Center Park
  29250 SW Parkway Court

THINGS TO DO

June
- Art on the Town
  Town Center Park
  (503) 682-3314

August
- Wilsonville Celebration Days
  Town Center Park
  www.funinthepark.info

September
- Wilsonville Community Fall Food Fest
  (503) 682-0411

Oregon Korean War Memorial

Avamere Assisted Living

LIFESTYLE DESTINATIONS:
Best assisted living

Avamere Assisted Living started with a single nursing home in Hillsboro in 1995. In just a decade, it has grown into one of the Northwest's largest senior care and housing services. Avamere is a resident-centered agency, dedicated to enhancing the life of every person it serves. Taking the lead in the industry, Avamere works with Portland Community College to develop curricula for health care workers. Avamere's own staff has one of the lowest turnover rates in the field and they are committed to providing every resident with a full, well-cared-for life. A broad range of services is available, including 22 skilled nursing facilities, residential care facilities, Alzheimer's and dementia care, home care, contract rehabilitation services and the luxurious Cottage Living community. Food committees at each facility meet with the chef to plan excellent menus. Vans are available to transport residents, and several times a year residents of the various facilities get together to share games, dancing, sports and an all-around good time. For yourself or for a loved one, Avamere provides an enriching environment at all levels of care.

**25117 SW Parkway, Suite F,
Wilsonville OR**
(503) 783-2470
or (877) AVAMERE (282-6373)
www.avamere.com

Fremont Bridge over the Willamette River
photo by amis2004

NW Portland Metro

NW PORTLAND

Northwest Portland has to be the most culturally hip section of a culturally hip city. Close to downtown, and you can access NW by the Portland Streetcar or on foot. We list many of its varied attractions under the Downtown Portland heading in this book. The NW neighborhood begins west of the Willamette River in Chinatown, home to restaurants, groceries and the Classical Chinese Garden. To the west, at Burnside Street on the Streetcar line, is Powell's City of Books, the largest independent bookstore in the world. Moving north with the Streetcar, you enter the Pearl District, a former warehouse and brewery zone now filled with art galleries, upscale restaurants and condominiums. Children play in the fountain at the new Jamison Park. The Streetcar then turns west and heads for the Northwest neighborhood, also known as Nob Hill. This and the Pearl District are two of Portland's most fashionable neighborhoods. Nob Hill's 24th Avenue is lined with an amazing collection of boutiques, coffeehouses and restaurants. The street scene is hopping. Further west, the northern end of the West Hills, containing Portland's ritziest subdivisions, forms a natural boundary to the city. Beyond the hills to the northwest is the immense Forest Park. With 5,100 wooded acres, it is the largest forested natural area within city limits in the United States.

PLACES TO GO

- Audubon Society of Portland (bookstore, sanctuary and trails)
  5151 NW Cornell Road (503) 292-9453

- Forest Park
  NW 29th Avenue & Upshur Street

- Pittock Mansion
  3229 NW Pittock Drive (503) 823-3624

- Sauvie Island

- Wallace Park
  2550 NW Raleigh Street

THINGS TO DO

June
- Berry Jam Festival
  Sauvie Island (503) 621-3489

Photo by amis2004

Photo by bandita

Forest Park

ATTRACTIONS: *Best city park*

With its massive tree canopy and substantial undergrowth, Portland's Forest Park provides a hushed and peaceful environment. The park stretches for nearly eight miles along the northeast slope of the Tualatin Mountains, overlooking the Willamette River. A recent inventory found 62 mammal species and 112 types of birds, but in fact there are surely more. In the spring, hillsides sparkle with trilliums amidst the sword ferns. Hundreds of other flowers and shrubs bloom during the year. Hikers, bicyclists and others enjoy the forest atmosphere. A 30-mile-long Wildwood Trail crosses the park from Hoyt Arboretum to Newberry Road. The Stone House, built in the mid-1930s by the Works Progress Administration, is a favorite spot to rest along the trail. In all, the park has more than 70 miles of interconnecting trails and lanes. Almost from the earliest European settlement, civic leaders dreamt of turning this area into a great park. The first of these visionaries was the Rev. Thomas Lamb Eliot, whose persistence led to the formation of the Municipal Park Commission in 1899. The Commission asked the famous landscape firm, Olmsted Brothers, to prepare a park study in 1903. The firm's recommendations included the development of a park with a wild, woodland character. Various setbacks, including rumors of oil, delayed the formation of the park until 1948. Forest Park now includes more than 5,100 acres (about eight square miles) making it the largest forested natural area within city limits in the United States.

NW 29th Avenue and Upshur Street to Newberry Road
www.friendsofforestpark.org

Pittock Mansion

ATTRACTIONS: *Former home of Portland's Rose Festival founders*

Open to the public since 1965, Portland's Pittock Mansion is a community landmark. Completed in 1914, Pittock Mansion was home to Portland pioneers Henry and Georgiana Pittock from 1914 to 1919. The Mansion was designed by architect Edward Foulkes and incorporated Turkish, English and French designs, but Oregon craftsmen and artisans used Northwest materials to build it. The grand staircase is a magnificent structure. Home to the Pittock family until 1958, the Pittock Mansion Estate was purchased by the City of Portland in 1964 and restored over a 15-month period. A nexus that unites all of Portland's community in a volunteering effort to preserve history, Pittock Mansion invites you to share a unique piece of Portland's past. Situated 1,000 feet above downtown, the Mansion is nestled on 46 acres. It's the perfect place to spread your picnic blanket and enjoy an exclusive view of the city while savoring the scents of one of the most famous gardens in Oregon's history.

3229 NW Pittock Drive, Portland OR   (503) 823-3624   *www.pittockmansion.com*

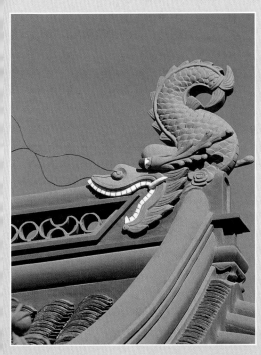

Portland Classical Chinese Garden
ATTRACTIONS: *A year round wonder*

In the midst of Portland's urban Northwest streets there is a walled haven, a city block of peace and grace. The Portland Classical Chinese Garden was created to nurture and inspire its visitors. Architects and artisans came from Portland's sister city in China, Suzhou. They built breathtaking effects and symbolic meaning into every part of the garden. Home to hundreds of rare and unusual plants, the garden incorporates serpentine walkways, a bridged lake, and open colonnades as elements in a balanced and harmonious design. Seven pavilions offer places to sit and enjoy the views. The beautifully designed paths made of pebble mosaics take you along walkways that provide cover on more than 85 percent of the garden, creating a truly all-seasons retreat. The very names of the buildings evoke the culture the garden brings. Names like Moon-Locking Pavilion, Tower of Cosmic Reflections and Reflections in Clear Ripples. Portland Classical Chinese Garden is a cultural heritage destination, unique in the United States. The garden is an authentic Ming Dynasty scholar's garden, reflecting the mood and elegance of a Chinese dynasty that ended 360 years ago and epitomized the height of cultural achievement. As well as beauty and peace in the midst of city life, the garden offers programs that encourage us to appreciate authentic Chinese traditions. The staff at the garden is proud of the wide and lively range of events, classes, programs and concerts. The Portland Classical Chinese Garden is open daily, except for Thanksgiving, Christmas and New Year's Day.

NW 3rd and Everett Streets, Portland OR
(503) 228-8131
www.portlandchinesegarden.org

Noah's Arf

ANIMALS & PETS: *Best pet daycare*

When Kris Price decided to open a pet-care facility, she wanted to create something unlike anything anyone had ever experienced. With Noah's Arf she has certainly done it. Noah's Arf is a 24-hour, full-service facility for dogs and cats. Services include overnight boarding and daycare, as well as in-home visits to walk, feed and cuddle your pet while you're away. If a clean animal is what you need, Noah's has both self-serve bathing and complete grooming services available. Your pet will enjoy a huge, safe and fun environment for playing, along with plenty of love and attention from well trained staff members. The employees can administer medications, handle special needs pets, and take care of any concerns you may have. Noah's Arf also has a gift shop, evening obedience classes and specially planned canine parties. Kris and her professional staff obviously love animals just as much as you do. Be careful, though, your pets might have such a terrific time at Noah's Arf you won't be able to convince them to come home.

1306 NW 18th Avenue, Portland OR
(503) 223-6624
www.noahsarf.com

The Pearl Retriever
ANIMALS & PETS: *Best canine supply store*

Tucked away behind the Modern Confectionery Lofts on Northwest 13th in Portland is the Pearl Retriever, a charming shop dedicated to man's best friend. Owner Andrea Schneider and her best friend and partner Ellie, a golden retriever, opened this popular shop in October 2005 and have quickly become a favored resource for all things canine. When visitors first arrive they can expect a double dose of warm welcomes from exuberant Ellie and the equally friendly Andrea, both of whom are dedicated to providing you and your four-footed pals with the best service and products in the Willamette Valley. The Pearl Retriever carries a wide range of excellent merchandise, including WackyWalkr stress-free ergonomic leashes and Monty dog beds. The Pearl Retriever is also the only dog store in the nation to carry Alora Ambiance and other luxury products that will have your pooch smelling anything but doggy. You can also indulge your dog with a special treat from the Biscuit Bar, where scrumptious canine goodies are always on the menu. The Pearl Retriever is so pet-friendly they even have a special potty patio available that was designed by Doggy Duty, so you never have to worry about leaving in a hurry. Andrea and Ellie are also supportive of their community and have pledged to donate 10 percent of their profits after 5 pm on the first Thursday of the month to Dove Lewis Pet Emergency Hospital. Treat yourself and your dog to something special at the Pearl Retriever.

526 NW 13th Avenue, Portland OR
(503) 295-6960
www.pearlretriever.com

Lint
ARTS & CRAFTS: *Best yarn and knitting store*

Lint is not your typical yarn and knitting shop. Lint has done for knitting what the Swiss did for clocks. Melissa Chakmakian studied weaving at the Art Institute of Chicago and became a card-carrying member of the knitting elite after working at shops in Chicago and Los Angeles. Realizing the exciting future of this new filament fad, Melissa transported knit-mania to Portland, where her family lives, and opened Lint in 2003. If you're not a knitter when you come into the store, once you see the beautiful walls filled with exquisite yarns, needles and tools, you'll be ready to learn. Melissa has carefully chosen a gorgeous selection of fine and distinctive yarns to suit any taste, including brands like Rowan, Blue Sky Alpacas and Brown Sheep. She keeps an extensive selection of books, tools and patterns on hand that focus on fresh, modern designs and current knitting techniques. You can knit in her comfortable sitting area or browse through yarns and patterns. Melissa is proud to have some of Portland's best knitting teachers offering classes at Lint, and she hosts a popular Tuesday Knit Knight, where knitters of all levels are invited to share projects, techniques and a glass of wine among friends. Come and discover the many satisfactions to be found in the gentle art of knitting at Lint, open daily for your convenience.

1700 NW Marshall Street, Portland OR
(503) 226-8500
www.lintinc.com

Les Schwab

AUTO: *If they can't guarantee it, they won't sell it*

The birth of the Les Schwab Tire Company occurred in January of 1952, when Les Schwab purchased a small OK Rubber Welders tire store in Prineville. With a $3,500 investment and a strong desire to own his own business, Les increased the sales of his store from $32,000 to $150,000 in the first year. Les had a strong determination to provide a business opportunity for people who could not afford to go into business for themselves. As the company continued to grow, Les came up with what is known as the supermarket tire store concept. His goal was to have his warehouse in his showroom so that customers could walk through the racks of tires and pick out the actual tires that would go on their vehicle. He also stocked more than one brand of tire in each size to give customers a choice. Today, the Les Schwab Tire Company is one of the largest independent tire companies in the United States. Les is the first to say the success of the Les Schwab Tire Company has been made possible by wonderful customers who are the most important people in the business. Nothing happens in the Les Schwab Tire Company until a customer leads the way by choosing new tires, a wheel alignment or any of the other services they offer. Les Schwab is proud to feature neat clean stores, supermarket selection, convenient credit, sudden service, and a written warranty you don't pay extra for. Les's slogan is, "If we can't guarantee it, we won't sell it!" Come into one of the 385 Les Schwab stores today.

www.lesschwab.com

Star Motors

AUTO: *Best place for Mercedes-Benz owners*

Gunther Hirschmann had many years of experience working on Mercedes-Benz automobiles prior to opening his own shop in 1993. He understands that these exceptional vehicles are best serviced in exceptional surroundings. Star Motors is just such a place. The reception area is sparkling clean, fresh-smelling, light and airy. There is a window to the back bays where you can watch skilled technicians performing expert work in a nearly spotless environment. The owners specialize in all things mechanical for your Mercedes. They provide top-notch routine maintenance and the highest quality, most reliable work on the engine, transmission, or undercarriage. They are eminently qualified to take care of the new vehicles being produced by Mercedes-Benz as well as the classic models. With the skyrocketing cost of fuel, Star Motors knows how important it is to keep your car in its best possible condition. They will happily provide courtesy ride service to your home or office while giving your Mercedes the attention it deserves. For all your maintenance and repair needs, call on Star Motors.

Serving Greater Portland/Vancouver
19215 SW Teton Avenue, Tualatin OR
(503) 691-9826

Lukas Auto Paint and Repair

AUTO: *An Oregon success story*

Four generations of the Lukas-Carlson family has served the auto painting and repair needs of Portland. Alex Lukas, a blacksmith by trade, started the shop with his son, Melvin, in 1936. After 45 years, Mel decided to retire and close the business, whereby his daughter, Laurie, stepped up. She was informed by many of her competitors that "Women don't belong in this business," but she didn't listen. Laurie successfully owned and operated Lukas Auto Paint and Repair for 25 years and recently sold it to her son J.R., but remains fully involved with marketing. Today, J.R. continues the family tradition of absolute integrity, top-notch customer service, expert collision repair, painting and detailing. The entire staff is certified. Lukas provides the most modern equipment to bring your vehicle to pre-collision condition. They will work with you and your insurance company, and every repair receives a lifetime warranty for as

long as you own your vehicle. The Elders in Action organization deems Lukas "elder friendly." Lukas was named Body Shop of the Year by a national jury of its peers and Laurie was honored by the S.B.A. as the Small Business Person of the Year for the state of Oregon. You can place your damaged vehicle in the hands of Lukas Auto Paint and Repair, a trusted community favorite for 70 years.

1722 E Burnside, Portland OR
(503) 235-5671

Kadel's Auto Body

AUTO:
In business for more than 50 years

In 1954, Kadel's Auto Body began as a one-man shop in downtown Tigard. There are now 13 shops located throughout Oregon, Washington and Idaho. Walk into any of their clean and friendly locations and you will be welcomed by people who know their business and are ready to take care of your auto body needs. Repairing more than 20,000 vehicles every year, Kadel's offers the best in customer service and gives lifetime guarantees on all their work. At Kadel's, they understand that auto body repair can be unexpected and, at times, costly. They will expertly assess the damage and make sure you know all your options, so that you can make the best decision about your car. The employees are experts in their field, receiving on-going training to keep up with changes in the industry. They repair any vehicle, from the smallest import to massive SUVs. Kadel's provides the skill, the patience, and state-of-the-art technology to get your repair done right. Kadel's and its staff appreciate the communities they serve, and they support youth activities and charities with their time and money. Come to Kadel's for all your auto body needs. They've been a community favorite for over 50 years.

9350 SW Tigard Street, Tigard OR
(503) 598-1159
www.kadels.com

Priestley & Sons
BUSINESS: *Most helpful movers*

More than 75 years ago, Carroll H. Priestley founded his company to meet the moving and hauling needs of a growing Portland. Today, Teresa Priestley, Chris Brown and Jeff Brown continue the family tradition of excellent, personalized customer service. Originally haulers of groceries and firewood, Priestley & Sons Moving has grown and changed with the times. They provide a fleet of the most modern moving trucks and up-to-date professional moving equipment to ensure that your move, be it large or small, is smooth and trouble-free. One of the oldest, continuously running moving companies in the state of Oregon, Priestley & Sons Moving offers heated, secure warehouses. This community favorite believes in supporting the local economy, employing more than 25 people and allowing no outsourcing of labor. Committed to its community, Priestley & Sons provides service to the Assistance League of Oregon and pays special attention to the residents of the numerous retirement homes in the area. For outstanding service with your moving and storage requirements, call on Priestley & Sons Moving. They've been keeping this area moving since 1929.

Portland (503) 232-3332
2255 NW Birdsdale Avenue, Gresham OR
(503) 661-7920
SW Washington
(800) 700-7920
http://priestleymoving.com

Turquoise Learning Tree
BUSINESS: *Safe and fun learning*

Since 1996, Rob and Carolina Peterson have been fulfilling a vision. They have been building a network of Learning Tree Day Schools to provide fun for kids and peace of mind for parents. Leaders in affordable childcare, Learning Trees offer a safe and supportive environment for children from six weeks to 12 years of age. Sparing no expense, they provide the best furniture, supplies, toys and food for children. Main meals are delicious, well-balanced and hot. There are pre-school, kindergarten and summer camp programs. The teachers are highly qualified and receive on-going training. All are certified in CPR and first aid and have attended the Oregon Child Care Basics program. The emphasis of the schools is on treating children with respect, encouraging self esteem and helping with social and emotional development. Caring, sharing, conflict-resolution and good sportsmanship skills are all part of the lessons. There are reading programs, arts and crafts, swimming lessons and plenty of healthy outdoor activity. If you are looking for the best care for your child in an environment that supports healthy child development, you can count on Learning Tree Day Schools.

15135 SW Beard Road, Beaverton OR
(503) 590-8409
www.learningtreeschools.com

ReMax Equity Group
BUSINESS: *Hometown real estate experts*

When you purchase or sell your home with ReMax Equity Group, you are working with the number one real estate company in the State of Oregon and the ninth fastest growing real estate company in the country. Founded in 1984, the Equity Group has held this number one ranking in Oregon every year since 1994. Their sales in 2004 reached $5.3 billion, utilizing more than 1,200 professionals in 19 locations in the Portland Metro Area. They also serve clients in the Salem and Bend areas of Oregon. As they say, "we've got you covered," with sales professionals and brokers averaging more than 13 years in the real estate field. With more than 80 percent of their business from referrals and repeat customers, you can rest assured they are providing the best in service. Equity Group has a full service relocation department. Almost all of their relocation services are free of charge. There is a convenient local contact in Portland. Whether you need local or national relocation services, they have the staff to satisfy your needs. Connected with the community they serve, in 2004 they donated $92,000 to 25 local charities through the Equity Group Foundation. Much of this is due to the hard-working people at Equity Group serving as leaders, participating in their communities and devoting time and money to the local charities. Giving back to the community is one of their missions. Remember, when selecting your realtor consider ReMax Equity Group, The Hometown Experts with a World of Experience.

8405 SW Nimbus Avenue, Suite C, Beaverton OR
(503) 670-3000
www.equitygroup.com

Mio Gelato

FUN FOODS: *Best gelato in town*

Travel from Oregon to the streets of Italy with a visit to one of Portland's three Mio Gelato shops. Gelato is an Italian ice cream that is denser and richer than regular ice cream, but surprisingly has less fat than most premium ice creams. Owner and popular gelato artisan Bob Lightman oversees the creation of all of the extraordinary gelatos made fresh at his shops. In addition to its famous gelato, Mio Gelato is known for its drinks, including coffee. *USA Today* has named it one of the 10 best places in the United States for gourmet hot chocolate. The shop sells cioccolato caldo, an authentic Italian-style hot chocolate with a rich flavor and thick texture like gelato. Mio Gelato has come to the attention of both *Bon Appétit* and *Sunset* magazines. If you are looking for more than dessert, be sure to stop by for fresh, grilled-to-order panini sandwiches and traditional homemade soups that are simmered for hours. Bob is passionate about quality and uses ingredients that are natural, fresh and local. Visit Mio Gelato and join the Portland gelato craze.

25 NW 11th Avenue, Portland OR
(503) 226-8002
1517 NE Brazee Street, Portland OR
(503) 288-4800
838 NW Kearney Avenue, Portland OR
(503) 241-9300

Saint Cupcake

FUN FOODS: *Best cupcakes*

Saint Cupcake, a little bakery in northwest Portland, is almost an all-cupcake bakery. Owned and operated by Jami and Matthew Curl, Saint Cupcake didn't start out offering only cupcakes. At first the bakery carried a wide array of goods, but the demand for cupcakes and cinnamon rolls left little time to bake other products. Now, for most of the year, the Curls bake and dispense only these two bakery items, with the whimsy and good humor shown by the slogan, Saint Cupcake Loves You. Jami and Matthew do believe that a fruit pie can rival a cupcake, so when fruit season begins, they roll up their sleeves and work overtime to bake pies, too. Once you've tasted these little treasures, it's easy to understand why the demand for cupcakes by Saint Cupcake is so high. Many of the recipes belonged to Jami's Grandma Dot. The Curls bake daily, using the highest quality ingredients. They offer so many flavors of cupcakes that it is hard for most people to name a favorite, but the toasted coconut cream cupcake is the top seller. The Southern belle of the bakery, Red Velvet, is a buttermilk cake with a hint of cocoa, a great red color and loads of yummy icing. As the patron saint of sweet, it's no wonder that Saint Cupcake loves to celebrate and helps out so many weddings and parties. Check the Saint Cupcake website for daily specials, then stop in for some truly luscious little cakes.

407 NW 17th Avenue, Portland OR
(503) 473-8760
www.saintcupcake.com

Judith Arnell Jewelers

FASHION: *Best jewelers*

It's only right that Judith Arnell Jewelers in Portland's Pearl District should have the look and feel of an art gallery, because, in essence, that is what it is. Judith Arnell has been working in the diamond and jewelry business for more than 30 years with stores in Chicago and Portland. She buys only the finest Assher-cut diamonds, known for their brilliance, and carries loose diamonds, her own designs and those from the collections of some of the finest jewelry designers in the country. She also carries a collection of antique diamond jewelry. Customers are encouraged to take their time strolling around this large store, where every piece is a work of art. Among the exclusive pieces here are Philip Stein watches, including the diamond-studded Teslar® series, which not only look and perform magnificently, but bring a sense of well-being to their wearer by increasing the body's electromagnetic field. Judith Arnell also features the luxury jewelry of the Daniel K line, including Daniel Koren's coveted bridal and classic collections, known as pieces women long to wear. Judith has been designing jewelry since her teens and believes that each piece of jewelry should embody creative genius, masterful craftsmanship and be a solid investment, in other words, a piece of art. She is one of the founders of the Women's Jewelers Association, Midwest chapter, and an active member of the American Gem Society. She invites you to "find your diamond in the Pearl" with a visit to Judith Arnell Jewelers.

320 NW 10th Avenue, Portland OR
(503) 227-3437 or (800) 205-9951
www.juditharnelljewelers.com

Quintana Galleries

GALLERIES: *Best selection of indigenous art*

The Quintana Galleries in Portland carries the finest representation of Native American art in the Portland region. They have been in business for 33 years, developing a world-class selection of art from the wide range of Native cultures of the Northwest Coast, Alaska, the Southwest and Mexico. Pioneers in the Portland art community, Rose and Cecil Quintana recently moved from their landmark location downtown to the 9th Avenue Art Corridor in the Pearl District. Their expertise is highly sought. Research, consultation and appraisal of Native American arts are important parts of their business. It is important to them to share their knowledge, welcoming students as well as collectors to their gallery. They have been active with Native communities as well as the arts community, and you can often find special events, such as live carving demonstrations, in the Gallery. With one of the most striking websites to be seen, the Quintanas have made a virtual gallery of art objects available online. You can view masks, totems, rattles and other wood carvings, argillite and prints. Other areas cover kachinas, baskets, beadwork and pottery. While their website is worth visiting, nothing can compare with seeing these art objects in person. Visit Quintana Galleries and see some of the finest indigenous art in the world.

120 NW 9th Avenue, Portland OR
(503) 223-1729 or (800) 321-1729
www.quintanagalleries.com

Skin Deep Beyond

HEALTH & BEAUTY: *Best day spa*

Cindy Ogden took her degree from the Esthetics Institute in Portland, added her amazing energy and persistence, and built her business from the ground up. Open since 2000, customer satisfaction has spread the word and Skin Deep & Beyond is now known as the best day spa in Tualatin. With extra-clean treatment rooms, candles, and soothing music, you will completely relax knowing that you are receiving the best of care. Using the finest products and technology, Cindy and her expert staff provide facials and proven facial enhancements, nail care, waxing and body wraps. The licensed massage therapists perform a variety of techniques, including Swedish, deep-tissue, and pregnancy massage. Treat yourself to any of the spa packages offered or have one customized just for you. Cindy and her associates are committed to providing you with a totally satisfying and personalized spa experience. For a personalized spa package for yourself or a loved one, come into Skin Deep & Beyond, where exceptional results are guaranteed.

8373 SW Warm Springs Street, Tualatin OR
(503) 692-2888
www.skindeepandbeyond.com

Massage on the Go

HEALTH & BEAUTY:
Most versatile massage

Mary Dalton, Owner

Does anything feel better than a great massage? Are you dreaming of one right now? Massage on the Go will come straight to your door, whether at home, the office, a hotel, or a special event. You won't have to wait for an appointment, fit it into your busy schedule, or fight traffic to get relief. Mary Dalton and her staff of fully accredited spa and massage specialists provide a wide range of relaxing and therapeutic treatments. They are skilled in hand and foot reflexology, water therapy, Shiatsu, deep-tissue and classic Swedish massage, as well as Reiki energy healing and techniques for relief of myopathy pain. If you want a facial or body wrap, those are part of the service, as well. In addition to the mobile service, you may also want to visit their conveniently located spa where you can check out the Bio-Photonic Scanner, one of only 15 in Oregon. The scanner allows the technicians to determine the types of supplements to suggest for increasing antioxidants for better health at the cellular level. From the inside out, Massage on the Go is truly a center for healing and wellness.

Serving Metro Portland
8879 SW Center Street, Tigard OR
(503) 620-0724

Ogle
Art For Your Eyes

HEALTH & BEAUTY: *Best glasses*

What do you get when an artist marries an optometrist? The answer is a fabulously innovative and edgy new idea, a high-end eyewear studio cum avant-garde art gallery called Ogle Art for Your Eyes. Stunning is the only word for this unique new venue that features exclusive eyewear and full service eye care, together with unconventional international and local art. Valentina Barroso Graziano, an artist trained at the School of the Art Institute of Chicago, is the curator for Ogle's art gallery, while her husband, Dr. Jeremy Graziano, O.D., focuses on eye exams and artistic eyewear. Set in a beautifully restored 1914 space on the edge of the Pearl district, you will find exclusive eyewear from designers like Oliver Peoples, Anne et Valentin and Face a Face displayed throughout the gallery alongside the artwork. While Jeremy is checking on the health of his patient's eyes, Valentina will expertly steer you through the many beautiful choices for either your walls or your face. This extraordinary gallery changes exhibitions monthly, providing a setting for artists who work in many different media, from painting and sculpture to video installations. You will see up-and-coming local artists as well as established international names. If you crave the unusual and the daring, in a top-quality professional setting, the choice is Ogle. Whether it is art for the eyes or eyes for the art, it is a winning combination.

310 NW Broadway, Portland OR
(503) 227-4333
www.ogleinc.com

Kombucha Wonder Drink Co.

HEALTH & BEAUTY: *Best tonic*

The wonder drink of the new millennium is a Himalayan tonic that's thousands of years old. Kombucha Wonder Drink strives to bring this naturally fermented tea to every consumer who is willing to take the plunge into wellness. The founder of Kombucha Wonder Drink, Stephen Lee, who has 30 years' experience in the tea industry, discovered the drink while on a tea trip to Russia. The recipe came from his Russian business partner's mother. Legends say it's the fountain of youth. Some say it's a drink so strong it gives soldiers on the battlefield energy. Known to be high in antioxidants, immune system enhancers and natural detoxifiers, Kombucha is a crisp and effervescent beverage with health-giving benefits that has been astounding cultures throughout Eurasia for 5,000 years. Today, word of the drink spreads through friends. Whether you're seeking a fountain of youth, a natural drink that strengthens the body or a taste of the old way of sitting with friends over a relaxing beverage, Kombucha Wonder Drink can deliver what you seek. The company's vintage Airstream, called the Wonderstream, is traveling the country bringing the drink to upscale grocery stores, restaurants and spas. When the Wonderstream comes to your neighborhood, stop under its awning to hear the story and enjoy the sparkling, ancient drink known as Kombucha Wonder Drink.

1410 NW Johnson Street, Portland OR
(503) 224-7331 or (877) 224-7331
www.wonderdrink.com

Pennington Massage Clinic

HEALTH & BEAUTY: *Dedicated to helping people build muscles*

Todd and Pam Pennington of Pennington Massage Clinic believe that if you take care of your body now, it will take care of you later. The clinic, which opened in 1992, is dedicated to helping people reduce tension in the muscles in order to increase functionality. Todd and Pam are Oregon Licensed Massage Therapists, and Nationally Certified Medical Massage Therapists. They listen to client concerns and work to bring balance and functionality. Todd and Pam use Medical Massage tests to determine muscles that are weak and in spasm. They also use many different techniques to release tension and manual therapy techniques that assist in injury recovery. By using recognized medical tests to determine problem muscles and to test improvement, it is easier to recognize progress. Todd and Pam's goal is to bring harmony to the body by balancing the musculature and

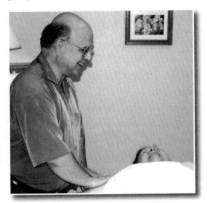

building proper function and support for tendons, ligaments and bones. In many cases even chronic muscle pain is reduced when the muscle tension is released. While some clients self refer, much of Todd and Pam's work is medically prescribed, and the process is a cooperation between doctor, patient and massage therapist. To get started on your way to greater health and well-being, call the Pennington Massage Clinic for an appointment.

10175 SW Barbur Boulevard, Suite 210, Portland OR
(502) 244-4427
LMT #3833 (Todd) and #8027 (Pam)
www.penningtonmassage.com

Mergenthaler Transfer & Storage

HOME: *A fleet based on integrity*

Art and Nick Mergenthaler opened for business in Helena, Montana in 1934. Back then, their 1933 Dodge half-ton truck was hauling 100-pound bags of flour, sugar, potatoes, and other goods for local grocers. The 1950s brought transporting construction supplies for dam building and a contract to haul mail for the U.S. Postal Service. Mergenthaler grew steadily, and when Art died in 1972, his four sons took over the business, expanding it to an interstate operation. Now owned and operated by two of Art's grandsons, the company is still growing by leaps and bounds. Though they have fleets of modern vehicles and massive storage facilities, this community favorite has never forgotten its core principle of building open, honest, and ethical relationships with the people it serves. The more than 285 employees are proud of the history and reputation of their company and are able and ready to provide you with personalized, local, professional service. To meet your transportation and storage needs, call Mergenthaler.

7895 SW Hunziker Road, Tigard OR
(800) 547-0795
www.mergenthaler.net

Pro-Tech Cleaning Services

HOME: *Best carpet cleaning*

Chris Boston is on the job at every job ensuring that your needs are met with the best service, products and prices. Pro-Tech Cleaning Services is certified in commercial and residential carpet cleaning, dyeing and repair, as well as care of oriental rugs, textile and leather upholstery, and tile, stone and wood floors. As the array of choices in fabrics and surfacing materials grows, the crew at Pro-Tech learns the latest procedures and chemistry, employing the most up-to-date techniques and equipment. Chris and his staff pursue on-going education through trade shows, seminars and classes. Committed to each and every customer, Pro-Tech has established and maintained an excellent reputation. Real estate agents recommend Pro-Tech to their sellers and buyers. Elders in Action has certified them as an Elder-Friendly Business for their fair practices, ethical and respectful treatment and their extra efforts in meeting special needs. Pro-Tech does not believe in surprises. You will receive a free estimate for your job and they provide a written complaint policy to ensure your complete satisfaction. Their motto is, The most thorough cleaning ever, or it's free. For all your floor and upholstery cleaning needs, call Pro-Tech Cleaning Services.

12150 Camden Lane, Beaverton OR
(503) 975-7577
www.protechcleaning.com

West-Meyer Fence
HOME: *Best fence company*

Lance and Jennifer West and Ron Meyer combined their skills and formed West-Meyer Fence in 1997. Lance learned the trade from his father, Jennifer is a talented designer, and Ron has extensive fence-construction experience. Together they will take you through the bid process, design your project, and work within your budget to meet all of your fencing needs. West-Meyer provides the best fencing to residential, commercial, and industrial customers, and they work with the top names in the home-construction trades. They can handle any request and they work with a wide range of materials. From ornamental iron, glass railings, concrete, and stone to vinyl, wood, and chain link, they will build the perfect fence for you. West-Meyer takes pride in their craftsmanship and the professionalism of their staff. Take a tour of annual the Street of Dreams and you will find many examples of their fine work. For everything from security fencing to a beautiful enclosure for your home, call on the reliable and experienced professionals at West-Meyer Fence.

**712 N Columbia Boulevard,
Portland OR
(503) 978-1830**

Lile North American
HOME: *Best North American Van Lines interstate agent*

Established in 1959, Lile has safely moved people, businesses and products throughout the Pacific Northwest and far beyond. It is a second-generation family company that is certified by the Women's Business Enterprise National Council as a 100 percent woman-owned business. Lile is active in the community, working with Northwest Medical Teams and the Oregon Food Bank. While it has grown to include six branches in Washington and three in Oregon, Lile remains committed to its founding principle of providing claim-free, reliably delivered, customer-focused moving and storage services. Ranking as one of NorthAmerican Van Lines' top U.S. agents, Lile earned their Quality Excellence Award for the last two years and was named its top booker of military business. In addition to its national and international relocation capabilities, Lile offers sophisticated on-line logistics services, including an interactive international rate-quote system, and order-entry and shipment tracking. Lile's Warehousing & Distribution division reliably meets its service commitments to customers. For all your moving and storage needs at home and abroad, you can count on Lile.

**19480 SW 118th Avenue, Tualatin OR
(503) 691-3500
*www.lile.net***

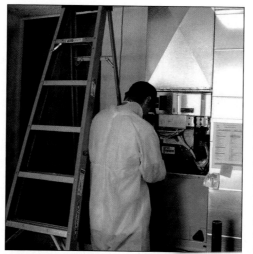

Tri-County Temp Control
HOME: *Best HVAC*

In 1987, Alan Sanchez founded Tri-County Temp Control, determined that the company would grow and prosper by delivering superior customer service. Referrals from satisfied customers have consistently proven him right. With a crew of more than 70, Tri-County has a long and distinguished track record throughout the Metro Portland area. Tri-County has installed thousands of retro-fit and new-construction HVAC systems, earning its status as the name you can trust. Their work is well represented on the Street of Dreams and greatly respected by homeowners, businesses and contractors throughout the area. Tri-County can assess your home or office space, then design and install the system that best meets your needs. When you visit their massive showroom, you will be greeted by friendly people with expert knowledge of their business. Every effort is made to provide products primarily manufactured in the US. In addition, the company is committed to environmentally friendly products and procedures. For all your heating, air-conditioning and indoor air-quality needs call on Tri-County Temp Control. You will become a customer for life.

**13150 S Clackamas River Drive, Oregon City OR
(503) 557-2220**

Pearl Hardware

HOME: *Best hardware store*

Putting your customers first is what good service is all about, and when a business gives quality care and attention, it creates the kind of loyalty that's made Pearl Hardware a neighborhood fixture since 1950. Ken McQuestion, Sr. started this family-owned business more than 50 years ago, and now his daughter and her husband, Sherry and Duane Cook, are carrying on the tradition of an old-fashioned neighborhood hardware store, the kind where every customer is known by their first name. Duane and his friendly staff pride themselves on having the knowledge and expertise to guide you through any home improvement project. Not only that, but Pearl Hardware has kept up with the times and boasts an ever expanding, diversified inventory in its three locations. Always attentive to the changing needs of its customers, Pearl now carries an extensive selection of housewares, cooking utensils, barbecues and gardening supplies. You can find absolutely everything you need at Pearl, without the bother and bustle of a mega home store. The prices are reasonable, and the staff has the time and is actually happy to answer your questions. Though he's retired now, people still remember getting that kind of help from Ken. They come back now because of it, and because his family has carried on in his footsteps. Good service equals good memories, and good memories will keep you coming back to Pearl Hardware.

1621 NW Glisan Street, Portland OR
(503) 228-5135
www.pearlhardware.com

Portland Closet Company
HOME: *Best closet company*

Even the roomiest closet can become a black hole of lost shoes and clothing. Portland Closet Company has the solution. This company enhances the lives of its clients by designing and installing superior organizing systems. Portland Closet offers complimentary in-home design consultation, professional installation by experienced carpenters, and spotless clean up. You can visit their large, airy showroom in Portland's Pearl District to get a taste of their custom work. In addition to designing superior walk-in and reach-in closets, the company has solutions for offices, pantries and garages. Portland Closet carries Tilt-Away wall beds in twin, double and queen styles that can double the functional size of a room. Closet systems and cabinetry use melamine or real wood veneers for a handsome, durable finish. You can also find brightly colored shelves and drawers for children's closets. Founded in 1985, this local, family-owned business has earned a reputation for exceptional design, service and installation. The staff members strive to work within your budget and on schedule. They respect your ideas, add their expertise, and turn your dreams into reality. They want your experience with them to be so delightful that you will be eager to recommend them to your friends. Visit Portland Closet Company and see what a difference beautifully organized storage can make in your life.

Serving Metro Portland
1120 NW 14th Avenue, Portland OR
(503) 274-0942 or (800) 600-5654
www.portlandcloset.com

Sunset Heating & Cooling
HOME: *Custom systems by the experts*

Originally established as Sunset Fuel in 1922, this company began as a fuel delivery business. At first, they delivered sawdust from a local lumber yard. As times and technology changed, they moved from sawdust to wood to coal to heating oil. Today, the name has been changed to Sunset Heating & Cooling to reflect the refocus on furnaces, air conditioning, heat pumps and indoor air quality products. Sunset has been a Carrier dealer since 1958 and has been designated a Factory Authorized Dealer. This means that Sunset has well-trained and certified technicians and salespeople, as well as being in the top five percent of Carrier's dealers nationwide. This also means that all Carrier products installed by Sunset come with 100-percent Customer Satisfaction Guarantee backed by Carrier. Sunset's comfort specialists evaluate your site, listen to your needs, and customize the right system for your home. Estimates are free. From system design to installation and service, Sunset's highly trained staff will work to ensure your total satisfaction. If you ever need service, Sunset's service department is there for you 24 hours a day. For the highest quality products and superior customer service, you can't go wrong at Sunset Heating & Cooling.

Serving Metro Portland
0607 SW Idaho Street, Portland OR
(503) 234-0611

Madison Millinger
HOME: *Best handmade rugs*

Located in Portland's Pearl District, Madison Millinger provides the best handmade rugs from all over the world. Each rug is personally hand selected by owner Christiane Millinger. "I have to like it," she says. Born in Austria, she received her schooling in the textile sciences. Her 17-year career has been well spent by doing something that requires passion, artistic sensitivity and extraordinary knowledge. Christiane says, "Rugs talk for themselves. They are a history without words." Quality, knowledge and variety help the staff at Madison Millinger accomplish their goal of finding you the perfect rug that will complement your lifestyle now and for many years to come. They can help guide you through their vast selection of fine hand-woven contemporary, traditional or tribal art rugs. They can even help you with custom options or an antique rug search. They are dedicated to fair trade and guarantee their rugs come from sources committed to fair labor practices. Proud to be a part of the current renaissance in the Asian and Mid-East rug industry, they carry rugs of extraordinary handmade beauty and quality not seen since the early days of the last century. Stop in and explore Madison Millinger, where they guarantee their extensive selection of rugs will excite your senses and invigorate your soul.

1307 NW Glisan Street, Portland OR
(503) 274-4440
www.madisonmillinger.com

Terra-Sol Landscaping
HOME: *Best landscaping*

During a summer job on Hayden Island, David Zimmerman developed an affinity for working outdoors in landscaping, construction and design. He continued to gain experience working for a design-landscape company. After earning a degree in Landscape Architecture, he started his own business, Terra-Sol Landscaping. Along with his experienced and professional staff, David serves the greater Portland metropolitan area. Working within any budget, they will strive to create the outdoor space of your dreams. They can build retaining walls, patios, garden paths and steps. Water features are also a specialty, including ponds, fountains, bubble rocks and waterfalls. Garden lovers enjoy working with David in creating their special garden spaces. Terra-Sol, meaning Earth-Sun, has provided landscaping for several homes at the annual Street of Dreams. In addition to landscaping, Terra-Sol is a long-time sponsor of Little League in the community. They are well known and well respected. You can trust your next outdoor project to Terra-Sol Landscaping, a community favorite since 1977.

Serving Metro Portland
(503) 691-6105
www.terrasollandscaping.com

Westside Dance & Gymnastics Academy
RECREATION:
Leader in dance and gymnastics

The mission of Westside Dance & Gymnastics Academy is to provide a safe, fun and positive environment, promote creativity and fitness, and inspire students to achieve their goals. Owner Mellanie Heniff is a long-time student of dance and gymnastics. She offers classes for all age groups, encouraging whole families to participate. The 12,000-square-foot facility provides the best USA Gymnastics-certified equipment. Private lessons are available for all gymnasts. Mellanie believes dance helps children develop self-confidence, flexibility, a sense of rhythm and coordination. She and her staff encourage values of good sportsmanship, self-discipline, respect and accountability. The academy is open seven days a week, has a pro shop and offers summer camp programs in dance, theater, cheerleading and gymnastics. Their academic pre-school and after-school care programs enable you to find a program that will work for you and your family. For an exciting alternative in a safe and welcoming atmosphere, Westside Dance & Gymnastics Academy is a leader in education, dance and gymnastics.

Serving Metro Portland
11632 SW Pacific Highway, Tigard OR
(503) 639-5388
www.westsideacademy.com

Henry's 12th Street Tavern
RESTAURANTS & CAFÉS: *Best tavern in the Pearl*

The former Blitz-Weinhard Brewery in northwest Portland's Brewery Blocks is now home to Henry's 12th Street Tavern. Henry's is a unique 14,500-square-foot restaurant and bar named in honor of Henry Weinhard. Henry's pays tribute to the original brewery by offering 100 varieties of beer and hard cider on tap. The cavernous brick interior with 24-foot ceilings is home to such state-of-the-art innovations as a built-in frozen drink rail in the bar that keeps poured drinks from getting warm. Flat-screen and plasma TV screens are set up throughout the bar, but Henry's is much more than a bar. The extensive menu offers great food, beginning with appetizers like Crispy Salt and Pepper Calamari and Gorgonzola Fries. Fresh seafood from the Pacific Northwest highlights the entrees, with specialties such as Cumin-dusted Pacific Swordfish. This Tavern appears to be split into two categories: half flashy bar, half upscale restaurant. Henry's is a Portland hot spot. As with other Pacific Coast Restaurants locations, Henry's features a Happy Hour specialties menu from 3 pm to 6 pm daily, with many selections under five dollars. On the upper level of Henry's are more special treats, including seven custom, regulation-sized billiards tables and another full-service bar. Whether you're shooting a round or relaxing in one of the overstuffed leather club chairs, Henry's 12th Street Tavern is the perfect place to relax after a meal.

10 NW 12th Avenue, Portland OR
503) 227-5320
www.henrystavern.com

Via Delizia
RESTAURANTS & CAFÉS: *Best dessert house and café*

Via Delizia means "Street of Delights," and it is well on its way to becoming Portland's premier dessert house and café. Chris and Karen Lawless opened their doors in the newly minted north end of Portland's Pearl District in 2004. Offered are Euro-style breakfast, lunch and light-dinner menus seven days a week, but it's their legendary pastry chef, Daniel Jasso, who propels their dessert menu into the stratosphere. Every dessert is an artistic creation reflecting the personality of Chef Jasso and the vision of the owners. It's hard to resist a dark velvety chocolate cake in the form of a volcano, or creamy golden cheesecake in a sweeping cylinder. Then there's the Chocoholic, a delectable assemblage of fudgy chocolate circles, cones and squares, straight out of the 1939 World's Fair. No Italian dessert house is complete without gelato. Via Delizia has 200-plus flavors, offered 24 at a time, to tempt your palate. One of their first customers, a native Italian visiting a friend in Portland, said he frequently traveled two hours to enjoy the finest pistachio gelato in Italy. Thinking no gelateria could top his Italian find, he found his new favorite at Via Delizia. Hearing that, Chris and Karen Lawless knew they had captured the essence of Italy. Discover what savvy Portlanders already know with a visit to Via Delizia.

1105 NW Marshall Street, Portland OR
(503) 225-9300
www.viadelizia.com

Duck Duck Goose

SHOPPING:
Best young children's clothing

For beautiful children's clothing that is the height of fashion, trendy yet tasteful and exquisite beyond compare, Portland's Duck Duck Goose offers the finest in children's attire. This boutique carries adorable merchandise for play and special occasions in sizes ranging from newborn to 14. They offer the finest European and domestic lines and the kind of customer service that busy parents have come to trust. Look for specialized clothing suitable for christenings, weddings and communions. The matching boy and girl outfits for siblings will be favorites in your photo album long after your tots outgrow them. Duck Duck Goose solves the dilemma of finding creative clothing for boys. Owners Tavia Dechant and Debby Hilgedick pay close attention to every detail in the shop, from customer service to displays. They hand select the store's merchandise and look for clothing that follows the trends while remaining tasteful and age-appropriate. The fashions represent the finest brands in the industry, including Catimini, Petite Bateau and Floriane. A customer review on *Citysearch* observed that Duck Duck Goose is "single-handedly raising the cuteness level of Portland's children." This is the store to visit if you want children's clothing that reaches out and pulls at your heartstrings. You might find pajamas embroidered with French sayings or a t-shirt that spells out Mommy's Little Girl in pink rhinestones. The store has many loyal customers who rely on Duck Duck Goose to outfit their children. For clothes, accessories and gifts that capture the special joys and activities of young children, visit Duck Duck Goose.

517 NW 23rd Avenue, Portland OR
(503) 916-0636

CORNELIUS

Cornelius is a small quiet town with stately pioneer homes and abundant parks. Vineyards surround the town. Local farms grow blueberries and, above all, hazelnuts. Oregon accounts for almost all of American hazelnut production and Cornelius is the center of the hazelnut industry. Cornelius is one of many western communities that owe their life to a railroad. In 1871, entrepreneur Ben Holladay ran a railroad into the Tualatin Valley west of Portland. The existing communities of Forest Grove and Hillsboro denied Holladay free right-of-way, so he ran his tracks through Free Orchards, a farmland area. Colonel Thomas R. Cornelius built a warehouse and store at Free Orchards, and then a creamery and two sawmills. Later, he helped build the first church and school. Now an important farm center, Free Orchards incorporated in 1893 and re-named itself after its founder. Today, Cornelius and neighboring Forest Grove, home of Pacific University, are twin cities.

PLACES TO GO

- Harleman Park
  S 10th Avenue and S Heather Street

- Henry Hagg Lake (county park)
  SW Scoggins Valley Road

- Lincoln Park
  Main Street, Forest Grove

- Pacific University Museum
  2043 College Way (503) 357-6151

- Valley Art Association
  2022 Main Street (503) 357-3703

THINGS TO DO

January
- Annual Crab & Steak Feed
  Cornelius Elementary (503) 357-3840

April
- Luau Wahi Kupaianaha
  Pacific University (503) 352-2107

June
- Arts & Flowers
  New Leaf Greenhouse (503) 357-3703

September
- Forest Grove Founder's Day Corn Roast
  Pacific University (503) 357-3006

Young hazelnuts ripening on the tree

Hazelnut Growers of Oregon

FUN FOODS: *Cooperative effort provides the best hazelnuts*

At Hazelnut Growers of Oregon, their only business is hazelnuts, an expertise that we can all benefit from as we enjoy the wide and luscious selection of hazelnut products they offer. Ninety-nine percent of all hazelnuts grown in the United States come from the rich soil of the Willamette Valley. They explain this as the result of the region's gentle climate and abundant rainfall, which produces larger nuts with an exquisite flavor and freshness. These hazelnuts are widely considered to be the best in the world. You can visit their website to get the facts about the sweetest hazelnuts in the world. Just a few of the things you will find on the Oregon Orchard site are wonderful recipes for appetizers, breads, pasta, salads, sauces, desserts, and beef or fish and other main courses. They make it easy to shop online for seasoned nuts, toffee-coated nuts, dry roasted nuts, and more. You'll also find a selection of gift tins, from the Hazelnut Six Pack O'Cans to their Hazelnut Happiness. You can also visit their outlet store in Cornelius, which was established in 1995. The Hazelnut Growers of Oregon ship from this store to customers all over the world. This is the only hazelnut cooperative in the United States. Founded in 1984, Hazelnut Growers of Oregon has more than 150 growers and more than 10,000 acres. They have a strong commitment to their customers and employees and, as a cooperative, profits are distributed to its grower members. When you think of hazelnuts, think of the specialists at the Hazelnut Growers of Oregon.

195 N 26th Avenue, Cornelius OR
(800) 923-NUTS (6887)
www.oregonorchard.com

PLACES TO GO

- Jackson Bottom Wetland Preserve
  2600 SW Hillsboro Highway

- Noble Woods Park
  475 SW 231st Avenue and 23480 W Baseline Road

- Rice NW Museum of Rocks and Minerals
  26385 NW Groveland Drive
  (503) 647-2418

- Rood Bridge Park
  4000 SE Rood Bridge Road

- Shute Park Aquatic and Recreation Center
  953 SE Maple Street
  (503) 681-6127

- Walters Cultural Arts Center
  527 E Main Street
  (503) 615-3485

- Washington County Historical Society & Museum
  17677 NW Springville Road, Portland
  (503) 645-5353

THINGS TO DO

February
- Westside Home Show
  Fairgrounds (503) 640-1360

March
- Murphy's St. Patrick's Day Parade
  (503) 640-1124

April
- Hearing Voices Storytelling Festival
  (503) 846-3235

May
- Draft Horse Plowing Exhibition
  Portland Community College, Rock Creek
  (503) 645-5353

July
- July 4th Parade
  www.hillsbororotary.org/parade

- Berry Festival
  Smith Berry Barn
  (503) 628-2172

- Oregon International Airshow
  Hillsboro Airport (503) 629-0706

- Washington County Fair
  Fair Complex
  (503) 648-1416

HILLSBORO

Fast-growing Hillsboro is the county seat of Washington County. The downtown blends old and new buildings. The historic Washington County Courthouse, with its stately sequoia trees, is across the street from the modern Civic Center, which incorporates environmentally friendly construction and design. The Hillsboro Saturday Farmers' Market is held May through October on the streets around the Courthouse and Civic Center. Hillsboro's largest shopping district, which runs along 185th Avenue on the east edge of the city, includes the Tanasbourne district just south of Sunset Highway. Hillsboro is the center of Oregon's high-tech Silicon Forest. Intel's largest site is in Hillsboro, and Intel is the largest local employer. Sun Microsystems High-End Operations is headquartered in Hillsboro. Other high-tech companies include Japanese firms such as Fujitsu, Epson, and NEC. Park-like high tech campuses blend in with the countryside. The Hatfield Government Center in Hillsboro is the western terminus of the MAX Blue Line, part of the Portland metropolitan area's light-rail rapid transit system. Developers took advantage of MAX to create the pedestrian-oriented community of Orenco Station within Hillsboro. Orenco Station was called the Best Planned Community of 1999 by the National Association of Home Builders and was named Best New 'Burb by Sunset magazine in 2006. Hillsboro Airport provides general aviation services and puts on a famous air show.

Oregon International Air Show

EVENTS: *Best air show*

For young and old, few things are more thrilling than an air show, and the Oregon International Air Show at Hillsboro, held one weekend each July, is among the best. Flame-driven metal sculptures execute spectacular maneuvers above your head. The roar of the engines can send chills down your spine. You might avoid driving your car as close to another car as these planes fly next to each other. The precision of the pilots and their trust in one another is amazing. F-16 and F-18 demonstration teams are among the most spectacular events, but the air show offers much else. You can see vintage planes, experimental aircraft and model planes. The U.S. Army Golden Knights Parachute Team performs frequent choreographed drops. The Air Force Reserve Smoke-n-Thunder Jet Car pulls 4.5Gs at takeoff and accelerates to 11Gs before coming to a stop at the end of the runway. The show opens with a free kids event on Saturday morning. The MAX Blue Line makes it easy to get to the air show; the airport is a convenient walk from the nearest station. The Hillsboro air show dates to 1928, when Dr. E.H. Smith organized Hillsboro's first air circus, as the shows were then called. Some of the best pilots in the Northwest participated. Hundreds of spectators went on airplane rides. About 10,000 people, more than three times the population of Hillsboro, saw the show. Most watched it from outside the airport grounds, however, and the show's promoters lost a bundle.

**Hillsboro Airport,
3355 NE Cornell Road, Hillsboro OR
(503) 629-0706**
www.oregonairshow.com

Longbottom Coffee & Tea

BAKERIES, COFFEE & TEA:
Handcrafted blends of regional coffee

The Longbottom Coffeehouse and Roasting Factory in Hillsboro is more than your average coffee stop. Michael Baccellieri has crafted a warmly designed outlet for his coffee roasting perfection. This extensive factory makes hand-crafted blends of prized regional coffees from 100-percent Arabica beans. They can handle coffee bean orders from 1.5 ounces to one million pounds. Even though you are at a fully functioning factory, the Café is relaxed and cheerful, a far cry from the hustle and bustle one might expect. Longbottom offers more than coffee. They provide excellent teas, along with full cases of hot pastries, muffins and scones that are freshly baked each morning. They offer traditional hot breakfasts, as well. Check them out for lunch any day, but especially on Thursdays and Fridays when they create their succulent signature Traeger Smokehouse Barbecue and offer Slow Smoked Ribs, chicken, roast beef and sirloin. Their use of fresh local ingredients takes their meals up another notch. The enjoyable atmosphere, excellent coffee, friendly service and free wireless Internet access make this a great place to enhance your day.

4893 NW 235th Avenue, Hillsboro OR
(503) 648-1271
www.longbottomcoffee.com

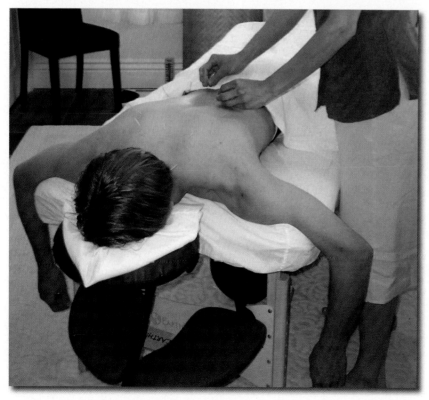

Hillsboro Acupuncture Center

HEALTH & BEAUTY: *Best holistic medicine*

When you enter the Hillsboro Acupuncture Center, you enter a quiet and restful environment conducive to healing. Mark Leberg is a registered nurse who works in intensive care and trauma units. He also has a masters degree in Oriental Medicine and practices Taiwanese acupuncture. This complete medical system is used to treat pain and enhance wellness. Employing acupuncture, Chinese herbs, Oriental massage, and a thorough knowledge of nutrition and exercise, Mark treats the whole person. He understands that each individual is more than a physical complaint and that emotions, environment, and lifestyle must all be taken into consideration when he develops a treatment plan for his patients. His work has successfully addressed addictions and stress, as well as respiratory, digestive, gynecological, cardiovascular, and autoimmune conditions. Balancing his thorough knowledge of Western medicine with his understanding of the ancient modalities of the Orient, Mark Leberg can bring holistic healing and balance to your life.

2251-A NE Cornell Road Hillsboro OR
(503) 640-5123

Kitchens & More Northwest
HOME: *Best cabinetry*

Fine cabinetry offers much more than a place to put your things. Cabinets enhance a home's beauty and utility and help define your home's décor. At Kitchens & More Northwest in Hillsboro, you'll find the best service and craftsmanship in the industry plus a wide range of style options and wood species. Since opening Kitchens & More Northwest in 1989, owners Drew and Val Tolmie and their talented crew have been working with individual homeowners and area builders to style custom-made specialty cabinets for every room in your house. When you enlist the services of Kitchens & More, you can expect expert guidance in designing the perfect kitchen, office, entertainment center or bathroom, plus durable finishes and high quality hardware that assure your lasting satisfaction. The Kitchens & More Northwest showroom is bound to stir up your dreams with almost a dozen cabinet displays and a wall exhibiting door styles, color selections, knobs and pulls. Area builders have chosen the prize-winning work of the Kitchens & More Northwest team to appear for the past 16 years in the prestigious Street of Dreams project, a display of cutting-edge style options for today's finest homes. "We believe fine cabinetry is the heart of a home," says Drew. When you are ready to experience the beauty and practicality of custom cabinetry, turn to the experts at Kitchens & More Northwest. They will use their expertise and state-of-the-art equipment to build a lasting heart into your home.

460 SW Armco, Hillsboro OR
(503) 648-0499
http://kitchensandmorenw.com

Oak Knoll Winery
WINERIES: *Best area winery*

From milking parlor to main wine cellar, the Oak Knoll Winery facility has changed dramatically from its early days as a dairy. The Oak Knoll Winery story began in 1970, when Ronald and Marjorie Vuylsteke founded the first winery in Washington County. Both native Oregonians, Ron was an electronics engineer in the early 1960s when a bumper crop of blackberries at the family home led to a gallon of outstanding blackberry wine, and the family winemaking heritage was born. The Oak Knoll Winery is a family-owned and operated business, with Marjorie and the children being involved since the very first crush. They did everything from unloading flatbed trucks filled with berries to hand labeling the bottles. Today, all five of the Vuylsteke sons and a nephew have followed in Ron and Marj's footsteps, and have become knowledgeable wine professionals in their own right. The longevity of Oak Knoll Winery can be attributed to its having produced some of the finest wines anywhere. A wine connoisseur from the *Wine Advocate* commented on the high quality of their Pinot Noirs and Chardonnays. Oak Knoll also produces a delightful, Burgundian-balanced Chardonnay; a slightly sweet, Spatlese-styled Riesling; and a native-American varietal, Niagara. Besides a sterling reputation for fine dry table wines, Oak Knoll is a premier producer of superior quality Raspberry wine with their perfectly balanced Frambrosia. This specialty dessert wine is the only fruit wine still made at Oak Knoll. Nearly one pound of fruit is used for each half bottle, and it is sought after by fine wine shops and restaurants.

29700 SW Burkhalter Road, Hillsboro OR
(503) 648-8198 or (800) 625-5665
www.oakknollwinery.com

NORTH PLAINS

North Plains, a charming rural town near the foothills of the Coastal range, is surrounded by miles of picturesque farmland, creeks and forests. Called the City to the Sunset, North Plains is on the Sunset Highway, the major thoroughfare from Portland to the Oregon Coast. With a population of 1,700 (not including pets and horses), North Plains is great for families. Each year, the town sponsors the popular Elephant Garlic Festival. A year-round draw is Horning's Hideout, a private park that offers picnicking, fishing and camping, and hosts many Portland-area weddings.

PLACES TO GO

- Horning's Hideout
  21277 NW Brunswick Canyon Road
  (503) 647-2920

THINGS TO DO

June
- Strawberry Festival
  Dixie Mountain Grange
  (503) 647-2207

August
- Elephant Garlic Festival
  Jesse Mays Community Center
  (503) 647-2619

- Northwest String Summit
  Horning's Hideout
  (503) 647-2129

October
- Pumpkin Patch and Corn Maze
  Lake View Farms
  (503) 647-2336

November-December
- Loch Lolly Christmas Forest
  (503) 647-2619

Pumpkin Ridge Golf Club

RECREATION: *Best golf club*

Pumpkin Ridge Golf Club first opened its doors in 1992 and has since built a reputation for excellence based upon its magnificent courses, stunning views and superior services. In 1996, Tiger Woods won his third consecutive U.S. Amateur title here. Since then, Pumpkin Ridge's side-by-side courses, designed by Robert Cupp, have proved a difficult yet fair test for two U.S. Women's Opens and both the boys' and girls' U.S. Junior Amateur Championships, held simultaneously on the two courses. The Pumpkin Ridge Golf Club encompasses 350 rolling acres of scenic farmland 20 miles west of downtown Portland. With views of the Coast and Cascade mountain ranges, as well as the Tualatin Hills, this popular course is the ideal place to enjoy a great game of golf while feasting your eyes on some of the state's most serene vistas. Pumpkin Ridge offers a well designed and expansive 17-acre practice facility along with a full menu of instructional programs which are taught by some of the top PGA Professionals in America, including Jerry Mowlds, the golf club's PGA Director of Instruction, named in *Golf* magazine's prestigious list of America's Top 100 Teachers. Pumpkin Ridge members and guests enjoy two luxurious clubhouses, fine dining and personalized services by an attentive staff. Enjoy the peace, challenge and beauty on the two adjoining courses of the Pumpkin Ridge Golf Club.

12930 NW Old Pumpkin Ridge Road, North Plains OR
(503) 860-4653 or (888) 594-GOLF
www.pumpkinridge.com

Portland Metro-Vancouver

VANCOUVER

When the Lewis and Clark expedition camped at Vancouver in 1806, Lewis wrote that it was "the only desired situation for settlement west of the Rocky Mountains." That observation may have been a bit hard on the rest of the Oregon Country, but it certainly is true that Vancouver was a great place to settle.

PLACES TO GO

- Clark County Historical Museum
  1511 Main Street
  (360) 993-5679

- Fort Vancouver National Historic Site
  612 E Reserve Street
  (360) 696-7655

- General Oliver Otis Howard House
  750 Anderson Street
  (360) 992-1820

- George C. Marshall House
  1301 Officers Row
  (360) 693-3103

- Pearson Air Museum
  1115 E 5th Street
  (360) 694-7026

- Ulysses S. Grant House
  1101 Officers Row
  (360) 694-5252

- Esther Short Park
  800 Columbia Street

- Marine Park
  SE Marine Park Way and Columbia Way

- Old Apple Tree Park
  112 Columbia Way

- Salmon Creek Park/Klineline Pond
  1112 NE 117th Street

- Vancouver Lake Park
  6801 NW Lower River Road

- Waterfront Park
  115 Columbia Way

- Water Works Park
  Fourth Plain and Ft. Vancouver Way

Salmon Run Bell Tower in Esther Shore Park
Photo Courtesy of SW Washington Convention and Visitors Bureau

Columbia River Renaissance Trail
Photo courtesy of SW Washington Convention and Visitors Bureau

THINGS TO DO

June
- The Family Fair
  Esther Short Park
  (360) 695-1325

July
- Fort Vancouver Rodeo
  Clark County Saddle Club
  (360) 896-6654

- Fourth of July fireworks
  Fort Vancouver
  (360) 816-6200

August
- The Taste of Vancouver
  Esther Short Park www.
  thetasteofvancouver.com

- Vancouver Wine & Jazz Festival
  Esther Short Park
  (503) 224-8499

September
- Vancouver Sausage Festival
  St. Joseph School
  (360) 696-4407

October
- Old Apple Tree Festival
  Old Apple Tree Park
  (360) 619-1108

December
- Skyview Jazz Festival
  Skyview High School
  (360) 695-3565

Vancouver National Historic Reserve

ATTRACTIONS:

Best historical monument

Fort Vancouver and its associated sites form the most important historic monument in the Northwest. Fort Vancouver was the main regional supply depot for the western part of North America in the early 1900s and was known as the New York of the West. The Vancouver sites, known collectively as the Vancouver National Historic Reserve, include Fort Vancouver, the Vancouver Barracks and the Pearson Field aviation site. Millions of archaeological artifacts lie under the ground, left by American Indians, Hudson Bay Company employees and their families, U.S. Army soldiers and their families and others who once lived or passed through here. You can join more than a dozen different tours at the reserve. Park rangers offer guided tours of the reconstructed fort daily. Attend living history demonstrations in the kitchen, blacksmith shop, period garden and elsewhere. Several tours teach visitors about the science of archeology or let them view some of the 1.5 million artifacts found at the site. Rangers introduce children to the past through Kids Digs and the Counting House Exhibit. The Vancouver Barracks, on the ridge above the fort, were a major Army center for a century. Many officers who later gained fame were stationed at Vancouver early in their careers, including George McClelland, Ulysses Grant and George Marshall. Even today, units of the U.S. Army Reserve are based in parts of the barracks. Neighboring Pearson Field is one of the oldest airports on the West Coast. Here, you can visit the Pearson Air Museum at the Jack Murdock Aviation Center. Other attractions managed by the reserve include the Columbia River Waterfront Park, the Water Resources Education Center and even the McLoughlin House in Oregon City, Oregon. You can easily spend a day enjoying the past at Vancouver National Historic Reserve.

612 E Reserve Street, Vancouver WA
(360) 696-7655
www.nps.gov/fova

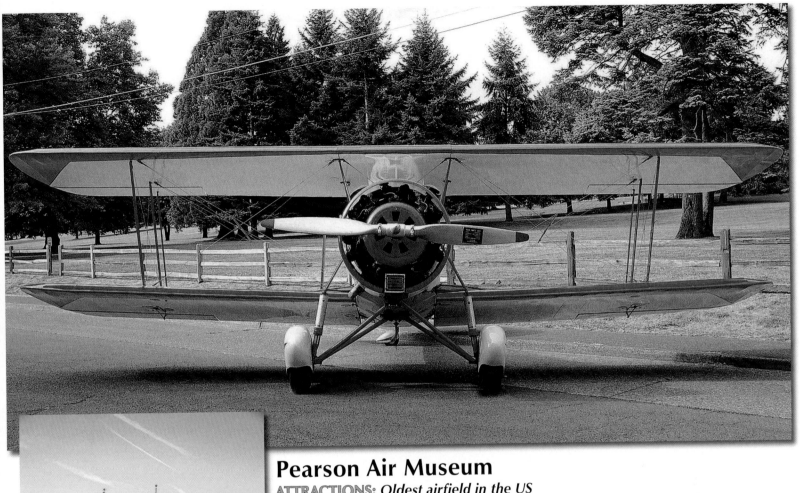

Pearson Air Museum
ATTRACTIONS: *Oldest airfield in the US*

Pearson Air Museum is at historic Pearson Field, the oldest continuously-operating airfield in the United States and part of Vancouver's National Historic Reserve. The museum sports a small collection of well-restored aircraft housed in the country's second-oldest wooden aircraft hangar. A 1913 Voisin III is one of the oldest aircraft on display. The museum offers a hands-on learning center where kids of all ages can learn about aerodynamics. A theater shows aviation films on demand. Visitors can tour the maintenance shop, where volunteer mechanics restore antique aircraft. In the summer, the museum hosts Cruz-in the Runway, a weekly fly-in event that features classic aircraft plus pre-1974 cars. The current museum is the first step in a project to recreate the Army Air Corps field that existed in the 1920s and 1930s. The field was originally the polo grounds of the Vancouver Barracks. In 1912, Silas Christofferson flew the first airplane to land here. He launched his Curtis-type pusher aircraft from the roof of the Multnomah Hotel in Portland. A replica of this plane is in the museum. Pearson Field really took off during World War I, when the Army used the site to mill wood for airplanes. The Army put up a building for the mill in 1918. In 1921, this became the field's airplane hangar. It housed Italian prisoners of war during World War II. Browse through the exhibits and displays at Pearson Air Museum and discover the pioneering days of aviation in the Pacific Northwest.

1115 E 5th Street, Vancouver WA
(360) 694-7026
www.pearsonairmuseum.org

Photos courtesy of Southwest Washington Convention & Visitors Bureau

Heathman Lodge
ACCOMMODATIONS: *Best lodge in Vancouver*

The Heathman Lodge is an Alpine-style lodge filled with the art and charm of the Pacific Northwest. General manager Brett Wilkerson describes it as an unexpected urban retreat that offers travelers and visitors from the Portland/Vancouver area a blend of "heart-felt service, business amenities, and rustic mountain lodge comfort." The Lodge itself is an impressive work of rustic architecture built by craftsmen out of wood from Northwest forests. As you walk into the lobby, you'll see shining stone floors, gleaming wood and wonderful handwoven blankets. The Heathman Lodge website has an intriguing feature that allows a virtual visitor to stand in the lobby or several other locations and slowly turn in a full circle, seeing the full scope of the furnishings. Hudson's Restaurant features Iron Chef winner Mark Hosack preparing handcrafted American food in the rustic setting. From the hand-carved newel posts in the lobby with their representations of the Raven and a powerful North Coast Indian figure to the custom-made furniture throughout, you will find many treasures of the region at the Heathman Lodge. What you will also find are 121 spacious guest rooms, 21 signature suites, a business level, indoor pool, whirlpool, sauna and fitness center, excellent communications amenities, including data ports, and private dining rooms that can seat up to 300, along with service that can't be matched.

7801 NE Greenwood Drive, Vancouver WA
(360) 254-3100 or (888) 475-3100
www.heathmanlodge.com

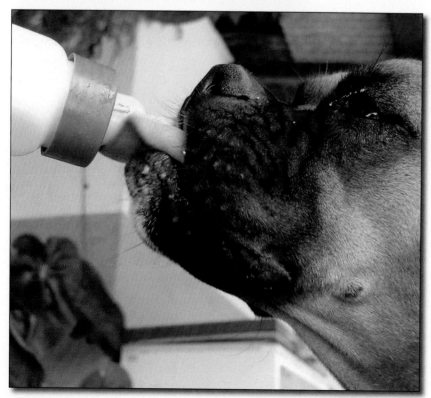

Cascade Park Animal Hospital
ANIMALS & PETS: *Best animal care*

In 1991 Dr. Maurine Fritch purchased her small animal clinic in Vancouver, Washington. Since then she has forged her practice into one of the foremost veterinary hospitals in Portland's greater metropolitan area. Her bright, new facility accommodates the continuum of veterinary care, providing healthy pet maintenance, rehabilitation, surgery, and a full range of dental services. Cascade Park Animal Hospital has developed its Animal Rehabilitation and Fitness division into a cutting edge facility that includes underwater treadmills, a swimming pool, therapeutic ultrasound, and other state of the art equipment to provide the highest quality rehabilitative veterinary medicine. Dr. Fritch is working with the Evergreen School District to develop a program for school children interested in veterinary medicine. She, her associate Dr. Tracy Thompson, and the hospital staff are committed to providing the best care for your pets, treating them as they would their own animals. They strive daily to uphold their mission statement: "Cascade Park Animal Hospital is dedicated to quality service, an excellent standard of care, and continual education of staff and clients. All patients and clients are treated as family, with empathy and integrity." Call or visit today and let Cascade Park Animal Hospital take excellent care of your pets.

16820 SE McGillivray Boulevard, Vancouver WA
(360) 892-2122

Les Schwab

AUTO: *If they can't guarantee it, they won't sell it*

The birth of the Les Schwab Tire Company occurred in January of 1952, when Les Schwab purchased a small OK Rubber Welders tire store in Prineville. With a $3,500 investment and a strong desire to own his own business, Les increased the sales of his store from $32,000 to $150,000 in the first year. Les had a strong determination to provide a business opportunity for people who could not afford to go into business for themselves. As the company continued to grow, Les came up with what is known as the supermarket tire store concept. His goal was to have his warehouse in his showroom so that customers could walk through the racks of tires and pick out the actual tires that would go on their vehicle. He also stocked more than one brand of tire in each size to give customers a choice. Today, the Les Schwab Tire Company is one of the largest independent tire companies in the United States. Les is the first to say the success of the Les Schwab Tire Company has been made possible by wonderful customers who are the most important people in the business. Nothing happens in the Les Schwab Tire Company until a customer leads the way by choosing new tires, a wheel alignment or any of the other services they offer. Les Schwab is proud to feature neat clean stores, supermarket selection, convenient credit, sudden service, and a written warranty you don't pay extra for. Les's slogan is, "If we can't guarantee it, we won't sell it!" Come into one of the 385 Les Schwab stores today.

www.lesschwab.com

Tires LES SCHWAB

Star Motors

AUTO: *Best place for Mercedes-Benz owners*

Gunther Hirschmann had many years of experience working on Mercedes-Benz automobiles prior to opening his own shop in 1993. He understands that these exceptional vehicles are best serviced in exceptional surroundings. Star Motors is just such a place. The reception area is sparkling clean, fresh-smelling, light and airy. There is a window to the back bays where you can watch skilled technicians performing expert work in a nearly spotless environment. The owners specialize in all things mechanical for your Mercedes. They provide top-notch routine maintenance and the highest quality, most reliable work on the engine, transmission, or undercarriage. They are eminently qualified to take care of the new vehicles being produced by Mercedes-Benz as well as the classic models. With the skyrocketing cost of fuel, Star Motors knows how important it is to keep your car in its best possible condition. They will happily provide courtesy ride service to your home or office while giving your Mercedes the attention it deserves. For all your maintenance and repair needs, call on Star Motors.

Serving Greater Portland/Vancouver
19215 SW Teton Avenue, Tualatin OR
(503) 691-9826

Lukas Auto Paint and Repair

AUTO: *An Oregon success story*

Four generations of the Lukas-Carlson family has served the auto painting and repair needs of Portland. Alex Lukas, a blacksmith by trade, started the shop with his son, Melvin, in 1936. After 45 years, Mel decided to retire and close the business whereby his daughter, Laurie, stepped up. She was informed by many of her competitors that "Women don't belong in this business," but didn't accept the word *no* as an answer. Laurie successfully owned and operated Lukas Auto Paint and Repair for 25 years and recently sold it to her son J.R., but remains fully involved with marketing. Today, J.R. continues the family tradition of absolute integrity, top-notch customer service, expert collision repair, painting and detailing. The entire staff is certified. Lukas provides the most modern equipment to bring your vehicle to pre-collision condition. They will work with you and your insurance company, and every repair receives

a lifetime warranty for as long as you own your vehicle. The Elders in Action organization deems Lukas "elder friendly." Lukas was named Body Shop of the Year by a national jury of its peers and Laurie was honored by the S.B.A. as the Small Business Person of the Year for the state of Oregon. You can place your damaged vehicle in the hands of Lukas Auto Paint and Repair, a trusted community favorite for 70 years.

1722 E Burnside, Portland OR
(503) 235-5671
Lukas@lukasauto.com

Kadel's Auto Body

AUTO: *In business for more than 50 years*

In 1954, Kadel's Auto Body began as a one-man shop in downtown Tigard. There are now 13 shops located throughout Oregon, Washington and Idaho. Walk into any of their clean and friendly locations and you will be welcomed by people who know their business, ready to take care of your auto body needs. Repairing more than 20,000 vehicles every year, Kadel's offers the best in customer service and gives lifetime guarantees on all their work. At Kadel's, they understand that auto body repair can be unexpected and, at times, costly. They will expertly assess the damage and make sure you know all your options, so that you can make the best decision about your car. The employees are experts in their field, receiving on-going training to keep up with changes in the

industry. They repair any vehicle from the smallest import to massive SUVs. Kadel's provides the skill, the patience, and state-of-the-art technology to get your repair done right. Kadel's and its staff appreciate the communities they serve, and they support youth activities and charities with their time and money. For all your auto body repairs, come to Kadel's, a community favorite for more than 50 years.

9350 SW Tigard Street, Tigard OR
(503) 598-1159
www.kadels.com

Priestley & Sons Moving

BUSINESS: *Most helpful movers*

More than 75 years ago, Carroll H. Priestley founded his company to meet the moving and hauling needs of a growing Portland. Today, Teresa Priestley, Chris Brown and Jeff Brown continue the family tradition of excellent, personalized customer service. Originally haulers of groceries and firewood, Priestley & Sons Moving has grown and changed with the times. They provide a fleet of the most modern moving trucks and up-to-date professional moving equipment to ensure that your move, be it large or small, is smooth and trouble-free. One of the oldest, continuously running moving companies in the state of Oregon, Priestley & Sons Moving also offers heated, secure warehouses. This Community Favorite believes in supporting the local economy, employing more than 25 people and allowing no outsourcing of labor. Committed to its community, Priestley & Sons provides service to the Assistance League of Oregon and pays special attention to the

residents of the numerous retirement homes in the area. For outstanding service with your moving and storage requirements, call on Priestley & Sons Moving. They've been keeping this area moving since 1929.

Serving Greater Portland/Vancouver
Portland (503) 232-3332
2255 NW Birdsdale Avenue, Gresham OR
(503) 661-7920
Southwest Washington
(800) 700-7920
http://priestleymoving.com

ReMax Equity Group

BUSINESS: *Hometown real estate experts*

When you purchase or sell your home with ReMax Equity Group, you are working with the number one real estate company in the State of Oregon and the ninth fastest growing real estate company in the country. Founded in 1984, the Equity Group has held this number one ranking in Oregon every year since 1994. Their sales in 2004 reached $5.3 billion, utilizing over 1200 professionals in 19 locations in the Portland Metro Area. They also serve clients in the Salem and Bend areas of Oregon. As they say, "we've got you covered," with sales professionals and brokers averaging more than 13 years in the real estate field. With over 80% of their business from referrals and repeat customers, you can rest assured that they are truly providing the best in service. Equity Group has a full service relocation department. Almost all of their relocation services are free of charge. There is a convenient local contact in Portland. Whether you need local or national relocation services, they have the staff to satisfy your needs. Connected with the community they serve, in 2004 they donated over $92,000 to 25 local charities through the Equity Group Foundation. Much of this is due to the hard-working people at Equity Group serving as leaders, participating in their communities and devoting time and money to the local charities. Giving back to the community is one of their missions. Remember, when selecting your realtor choose ReMax Equity Group, The Hometown Experts with a World of Experience.

Serving Greater Portland/Vancouver
8405 SW Nimbus Avenue, Suite C, Beaverton OR
(503) 670-3000
www.equitygroup.com

A-1 Integrity Window Cleaning

BUSINESS:
Window cleaning professionals

"Clean windows are good for the soul." With those words, four gentlemen combined years of experience in their individual window-cleaning companies to form A-1 Integrity Window Cleaning. The merging of these community favorites makes A-1 tops in the field of residential, commercial and particularly challenging high-rise window cleaning. In this business, safety comes first. A-1 provides their expert staff with the very latest and safest equipment, including belts, nylon or fiberglass ropes and self-leveling ladders. Water-fed poles deliver de-ionized water to even the hardest-to-reach windows in tight spaces and inclines. For inside work, the staff wears protective booties over their shoes to protect floor coverings Residential customers can receive estimates over the phone or A-1 will go to the home and prepare a bid at no cost. Count on A-1 Integrity Window Cleaning to brighten your life.

P.O. Box 820368, Vancouver WA
(360) 254-3554 or (503) 254-3554
www.a1integrity.com

Blue Bird Moving and Storage

BUSINESS: *Most flexible movers*

Family owned and operated Blue Bird Moving and Storage promises that, "You have just found the flexibility and expertise to solve your current relocation challenges." Since 1928, Blue Bird has exemplified versatility and willingness to go the extra mile. Blue Bird uses state-of-the-art computers and an electronic dispatch system, along with old-fashioned customer service to do every job well. President Wade McLaren and his 53-member staff will see that Blue Bird, a recipient of Washington State's Best Small Business Award several times, handles your job with ease. Blue Bird represents a happy combination of professional values and community spirit as a sponsor of local activities such as girls' softball, YWCA, YMCA, Friends of the Carpenter, Susan G. Komen Breast Cancer Foundation, and many others. Give them a call any time you have a storage or moving need.

2500 E Fifth Street, Vancouver WA
(800) 632-6344

Turquoise Learning Tree

BUSINESS: *Safe and fun learning*

Since 1996, Rob and Carolina Peterson have been fulfilling a vision. They have been building a network of Learning Tree Day Schools to provide fun for kids and peace of mind for parents. Leaders in affordable childcare, Learning Trees offer a safe and supportive environment for children from six weeks to 12 years of age. Sparing no expense, they provide the best furniture, supplies, toys and food for children. Main meals are delicious, well-balanced and hot. There are pre-school, kindergarten and summer camp programs. The teachers are highly qualified and receive on-going training. All are certified in CPR and first aid and have attended the Oregon Child Care Basics program. The emphasis of the schools is on treating children with respect, encouraging self esteem and helping with social and emotional development. Caring, sharing, conflict-resolution and good sportsmanship skills are all part of the lessons. There are reading programs, arts and crafts, swimming lessons and plenty of healthy outdoor activity. If you are looking for the best care for your child in an environment that supports healthy child development, you can count on Learning Tree Day Schools.

15135 SW Beard Road, Beaverton OR
(503) 590-8409
www.learningtreeschools.com

Skin Deep Beyond

HEALTH & BEAUTY: *Best day spa*

Cindy Ogden took her degree from the Esthetics Institute in Portland, added her amazing energy and persistence, and built her business from the ground up. Open since 2000, customer satisfaction has spread the word and Skin Deep & Beyond is now known as the best day spa in Tualatin. With extra-clean treatment rooms, candles, and soothing music, you will completely relax knowing that you are receiving the best of care. Using the finest products and technology, Cindy and her expert staff provide facials and proven facial enhancements, nail care, waxing and body wraps. The licensed massage therapists perform a variety of techniques, including Swedish, deep-tissue, and pregnancy massage. Treat yourself to any of the spa packages offered or have one customized just for you. Cindy and her associates are committed to providing you with a totally satisfying and personalized spa experience. For a personalized spa package for yourself or a loved one, come into Skin Deep & Beyond, where exceptional results are guaranteed.

8373 SW Warm Springs Street, Tualatin OR
(503) 692-2888
www.skindeepandbeyond.com

Pennington Massage Clinic

HEALTH & BEAUTY:
Dedicated to helping people build muscles

Todd and Pam Pennington of Pennington Massage Clinic believe that if you take care of your body now, it will take care of you later. The clinic, which opened in 1992, is dedicated to helping people reduce tension in the muscles in order to increase functionality. Todd and Pam are Oregon Licensed Massage Therapists, LMT #3833 (Todd) and #8027 (Pam), and Nationally Certified Medical Massage Therapists, NCMMT #1150 (Todd) and #1149 (Pam). They listen to client concerns and work to bring balance and functionality. Todd and Pam use Medical Massage tests to determine muscles that are weak and in spasm. They also use many different techniques to release tension and manual therapy techniques that assist in injury recovery. By using recognized medical tests to determine problem muscles and to test improvement, it is easier to recognize progress. Todd and Pam's goal is to bring harmony to the body by balancing the musculature and building proper function and support for tendons, ligaments and bones. In many cases even chronic muscle pain is reduced when the muscle tension is released. For more information on their techniques, see the website. While some clients self refer, much of Todd and Pam's work is medically prescribed and the process is a cooperation between doctor, patient and massage therapist. To get started on your way to greater health and well-being, call the Pennington Massage Clinic for an appointment.

10175 SW Barbur Boulevard, Suite 210, Portland OR
(502) 244-4427
www.penningtonmassage.com

Northwest Personal Training and Fitness Education

HEALTH & BEAUTY: *Best personal trainers*

Helping people change their lives in positive ways is what drives Alex and Sherri McMillan, owners of Northwest Personal Training and Fitness Education. Their passion in their business is to assist people in their efforts to look and feel better and they offer highly skilled trainers who are motivated to help clients get results. Alex and Sherri have extensive backgrounds in the fitness industry and they have used their expertise to create a remarkable place for clients to enjoy a community-oriented workout setting. "We only hire amazing people" explains Sherri, and the energetic and warm reception you will experience when you step through the door shows that commitment to customer service. As a training studio, Northwest Personal Training and Fitness Education is distinctively different from a standard fitness gym because the focus is on the individual client's experience. Both Alex and Sherri have been invited to consult and speak with others in the industry around the world to discuss their operating model. With spa services available too, the company offers a complete package for prospective customers seeking to change their lives. Come by to see the impact that the dedication of these two remarkable people is having on the lives of their current clients. You will see first-hand the difference they are already making in the Portland fitness community.

2714 NE Broadway, Portland OR
(503) 287-0655
www.NWPersonalTraining.com

Massage on the Go

HEALTH & BEAUTY:
Most versatile massage

Does anything feel better than a great massage? Are you dreaming of one right now? Massage on the Go will come straight to your door, whether at home, the office, a hotel, or a special event. You won't have to wait for an appointment, fit it into your busy schedule, or fight traffic to get relief. Mary Dalton and her staff of fully accredited spa and massage specialists provide a wide range of relaxing and therapeutic treatments. They are skilled in hand and foot reflexology, water therapy, Shiatsu, deep-tissue and classic Swedish massage, as well as Reiki energy healing and techniques for relief of myopathy pain. If you want a facial or body wrap, those are part of the service, as well. In addition to the mobile service, you may also want to visit their conveniently located spa where you can check out the Bio-Photonic Scanner, one of only 15 in Oregon. The scanner allows the technicians to determine the types of supplements to suggest for increasing antioxidants for better health at the cellular level. From the inside out, Massage on the Go is truly a center for healing and wellness.

8879 SW Center Street, Tigard OR
(503) 620-0724

Pro-Tech Cleaning Services

HOME: *Best carpet cleaning*

Chris Boston is on the job at every job ensuring that your needs are met with the best service, products and prices. Pro-Tech Cleaning Services is certified in commercial and residential carpet cleaning, dyeing and repair, as well as care of oriental rugs, textile and leather upholstery, and tile, stone and wood floors. As the array of choices in fabrics and surfacing materials grows, the crew at Pro-Tech learns the latest procedures and chemistry, employing the most up-to-date techniques and equipment. Chris and his staff pursue on-going education through trade shows, seminars and classes. Committed to each and every customer, Pro-Tech has established and maintained an excellent reputation. Real estate agents recommend Pro-Tech to their sellers and buyers. Elders in Action has certified them as an Elder-Friendly Business for their fair practices, ethical and respectful treatment and their extra efforts in meeting special needs. Pro-Tech does not believe in surprises. You will receive a free estimate for your job and they provide a written complaint policy to ensure your complete satisfaction. Their motto is, The most thorough cleaning ever, or it's free. For all your floor and upholstery cleaning needs, call Pro-Tech Cleaning Services.

12150 Camden Lane, Beaverton OR
(503) 975-7577
www.protechcleaning.com

Kitchens & More Northwest

HOME: *Best kitchen cabinets*

Fine cabinetry offers much more than a place to put your things, it enhances a home's beauty and utility and defines your home's décor. At Kitchens and More Northwest in Hillsboro, you'll find the best service and craftsmanship in the industry plus a wide range of style options and wood species. Since opening Kitchens and More Northwest in 1989, owners Drew and Val Tolmie and their talented crew have been working with individual homeowners and area builders to

style custom-made specialty cabinets for every room in your house. When you enlist the services of Kitchens and More Northwest, you can expect expert guidance in designing the perfect kitchen, office, entertainment center or bathroom, plus durable finishes and high quality hardware that assure your lasting satisfaction. The Kitchens and More Northwest showroom is bound to stir up your dreams with almost a dozen cabinet displays and a wall exhibiting door styles, color selections, knobs and pulls. Area builders have chosen the prize-winning work of the Kitchens and More Northwest team to appear for the past 16 years in the prestigious Street of Dreams project, a display of cutting-edge style options for today's finest homes. "We believe fine cabinetry is the heart of a home," says Drew. When you are ready to experience the beauty and practicality of custom cabinetry, turn to the experts at Kitchens and More Northwest. They will use their expertise and state-of-the-art equipment to build a lasting heart into your home.

P.O. Box 721 Hillsboro, OR
(503) 648-0499

Mergenthaler Transfer & Storage

HOME:
A fleet based on integrity

Art and Nick Mergenthaler opened for business in Helena, Montana in 1934. Back then, their 1933 Dodge half-ton truck was hauling 100-pound bags of flour, sugar, potatoes, and other goods for local grocers. The 1950s brought transporting construction supplies for dam building and a contract to haul mail for the U.S. Postal Service. Mergenthaler grew steadily, and when Art died in 1972, his four sons took over the business, expanding it to an interstate operation. Now owned and operated by two of Art's grandsons, the company is still growing by leaps and bounds. Though they have fleets of modern vehicles and massive storage facilities, this community favorite has never forgotten its core principle of building open, honest, and ethical relationships with the people it serves. The more than 285 employees are proud of the history and reputation of their company and are able and ready to provide you with personalized, local, professional service. To meet your transportation and storage needs, call Mergenthaler.

7895 SW Hunziker Road, Tigard OR
(800) 547-0795
www.mergenthaler.net

Lile North American

HOME: *Best North American Van Lines interstate agent*

Established in 1959, Lile has safely moved people, businesses and products throughout the Pacific Northwest and far beyond. It is a second-generation family company that is certified by the Women's Business Enterprise National Council as a 100 percent woman-owned business. Lile is active in the community, working with Northwest Medical teams and the Oregon Food Bank. While it has grown to include six branches in Washington and three in Oregon, Lile remains committed to its founding principle of providing claim-free, reliably delivered, customer-focused moving and storage services. Ranking as one of NorthAmerican Van Lines' top U.S. agents, Lile earned their Quality Excellence Award for the last two years and was named its top booker of military business. In addition to its national and international relocation capabilities, Lile offers sophisticated on-line logistics services, including an interactive international rate-quote system, and order-entry and shipment tracking. Lile's Warehousing & Distribution division reliably meets its service commitments to customers. For all your moving and storage needs at home and abroad, you can count on Lile.

19480 SW 118th Avenue, Tualatin OR
(503) 691-3500 *www.lile.net*

Tri-County Temp Control

HOME: *Best HVAC*

In 1987, Alan Sanchez founded Tri-County Temp Control, determined that the company would grow and prosper by delivering superior customer service. Referrals from satisfied customers have consistently proven him right. With a crew of more than 70, Tri-County has a long and distinguished track record throughout the metro Portland area. Tri-County has installed thousands of retro-fit and new-construction HVAC systems, earning its status as the name you can trust. Their work is well represented on the Street of Dreams and greatly respected by homeowners,

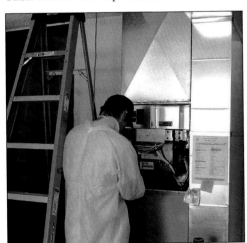

businesses and contractors throughout the area. Tri-County can assess your home or office space, then design and install the system that best meets your needs. When you visit their massive showroom, you will be greeted by friendly people with expert knowledge of their business. Every effort is made to provide products primarily manufactured in the USA. In addition, the company is committed to environmentally friendly products and procedures. For all your heating, air-conditioning and indoor air-quality needs call on Tri-County Temp Control. You will become a customer for life.

13150 S Clackamas River Drive, Oregon City OR
(503) 557-2220

West-Meyer Fence

HOME: *Best fence company*

Lance and Jennifer West and Ron Meyer combined their skills and formed West-Meyer Fence in 1997. Lance learned the trade from his father, Jennifer is a talented designer, and Ron has extensive fence-construction experience. Together they will take you through the bid process, design your project, and work within your budget to meet your fencing needs. West-Meyer provides fencing to residential, commercial, and industrial customers and they work with the top names in the home-construction trades. They can handle any request and they work with a wide range of materials. From ornamental iron, glass railings, concrete, and stone to vinyl, wood, and chain link, they will build the perfect fence for you. West-Meyer takes pride in the craftsmanship of their staff. Take a tour of the Street of Dreams and you will find many examples of their fine work. For everything from security fencing to a beautiful enclosure for your home, call on West-Meyer Fence.

712 N Columbia Boulevard, Portland OR
(503) 978-1830

Terra-Sol Landscaping
HOME: *Best landscaping*

During a summer job on Hayden Island, David Zimmerman developed an affinity for working outdoors in landscaping, construction and design. He continued to gain experience working for a design-landscape company. After earning a degree in Landscape Architecture, he started his own business, Terra-Sol Landscaping. Along with his experienced and professional staff, David serves the greater Portland metropolitan area. Working within any budget, they will strive to create the outdoor space of your dreams. They can build retaining walls, patios, garden paths and steps. Water features are also a specialty, including ponds, fountains, bubble rocks and waterfalls. Garden lovers enjoy working with David in creating their special garden spaces. Terra-Sol, meaning Earth-Sun, has provided landscaping for several homes at the annual Street of Dreams. In addition to landscaping, Terra-Sol is a long-time sponsor of Little League in the community. They are well known and well respected. You can trust your next outdoor project to Terra-Sol Landscaping, a community favorite since 1977.

Serving Metro Portland/Vancouver
(503) 691-6105
www.terrasollandscaping.com

Portland Closet Company
HOME: *Best closet company*

Even the roomiest closet can become a black hole of lost shoes and clothing. Portland Closet Company has the solution. This company enhances the lives of its clients by designing and installing superior organizing systems. Portland Closet offers complimentary in home design consultation, professional installation by experienced carpenters and spotless clean up. You can visit their large, airy showroom in Portland's Pearl District to get a taste of their custom work. In addition to designing superior walk-in and reach-in closets, the company has solutions for offices, pantries and garages. Portland Closet carries Tilt-Away wall beds in twin, double and queen styles that can double the functional size of a room. Closet systems and cabinetry use melamine or real wood veneers for a handsome, durable finish. You can also find brightly colored shelves and drawers for children's closets. Founded in 1985, this local, family-owned business has earned a reputation for exceptional design, service and installation. The staff members strive to work within your budget and on schedule. They respect your ideas, add their expertise, and turn your dreams into reality. They want your experience with them to be so delightful that you will be eager to recommend them to your friends. Visit Portland Closet Company and see what a difference beautifully organized storage can make in your life.

Serving Vancouver/Portland Metro
1120 NW 14th Avenue, Portland OR
(503) 274-0942 or (800) 600-5654
www.portlandcloset.com

Westside Dance & Gymnastics Academy
RECREATION: *Leader in dance and gymnastics*

The mission of Westside Dance & Gymnastics Academy is to provide a safe, fun and positive environment, promote creativity and fitness, and inspire students to achieve their goals. Owner Mellanie Heniff is a long-time student of dance and gymnastics. She offers classes for all age groups, encouraging whole families to participate. The 12,000-square-foot facility provides the best USA Gymnastics-certified equipment. Private lessons are available for all gymnasts. Mellanie believes dance helps children develop self-confidence, flexibility, a sense of rhythm and coordination. She and her staff encourage values of good sportsmanship, self-discipline, respect and accountability. The academy is open seven days a week, has a pro shop and offers Summer camp programs in dance, theater, cheerleading and gymnastics. Their academic pre-school and after-school care programs enable you to find a program that will work for you and your family. For an exciting alternative in a safe and welcoming atmosphere, Westside Dance & Gymnastics Academy is a leader in education, dance and gymnastics.

11632 SW Pacific Highway, Tigard OR
(503) 639-5388
www.westsideacademy.com

The Bedford

LIFESTYLE DESTINATIONS: *Best independent living in Vancouver*

Since 1998, the Bedford has been giving seniors seeking a retirement residence in the Vancouver area a superior choice. The Bedford offers several roomy floor plans with full kitchens, full-sized washers and dryers, walk-in closets and cozy fireplaces. The secure environment and beautiful grounds assure your comfort and safety, and several comfortable transportation options promise your continued independence. Residents can enjoy the company of friends and neighbors while dining on nutritious, chef-prepared meals. The Bedford provides a range of activities to assure an active retirement lifestyle. Take advantage of an exercise room, an indoor heated pool and spa, plus a library, hair salon, billiards room and lounge with a large-screen television. There's always a game, movie or class awaiting your participation. The Bedford is conveniently located near hospitals, shopping and a golf course. On a clear day, some of the apartments feature views of Mount Hood and east Portland. Managers live on-site and provide round-the-clock service. Holiday Retirement Corporation owns and manages this stunning property, along with gracious retirement living centers across Canada, the United States and Great Britain. With all that experience, you can be assured this corporation provides the kind of gracious retirement living today's seniors demand. Print out the coupon on the Bedford website for a free lunch and tour of this prestigious independent living community.

13303 SE McGillivray Boulevard, Vancouver WA
(360) 891-6898 or (800) 322-0999
www.the-bedford.com

Pasta Cucina

RESTAURANTS & CAFÉS: *Best Italian food*

When you are looking for delicious and reasonably priced Italian food, look no further than Pasta Cucina. Pasta Cucina is the perfect place for authentic homemade dishes served in a home-like setting where children are always welcome. A customer favorite dish, Tortellini Rosé, is made from cheese-filled tortellini tossed with sun-dried tomatoes and served in a rosé sauce. Another favorite entrée is a boneless breast of chicken wrapped with Italian bacon and topped with mozzarella and Gorgonzola cheeses. Choose from a good selection of sumptuous salads in addition to a variety of appetizers and desserts. The house wine is Luna di Luna Merlot. Beer and wine are also available. Owners Jason Lawson and Dawn and Brandon Clark established Pasta Cucina in the same location more than five years ago. In addition to the restaurant, they offer catering services. For an authentic taste of Italy, be sure to stop in at Pasta Cucina.

212 NE 164th Avenue, Vancouver WA
(360) 882-5122

Woodburn Tulip Festival

Willamette Valley

AMITY

Amity is Pinot Noir country. To the east of town lies the Eola-Amity Hills district American Viticultural Area. Pioneer Ahio Watt founded the town in 1849. The Amity Church dates to 18 46 and is one of the oldest Protestant churches west of the Rockies. Amity received its name after an agreement on the site for a school, which had been the subject of a fierce fight. Today, the Amity public schools put on an annual Daffodil Festival with walks and drives to see the daffodils, wineries and other local attractions. The festival includes a daffodil show with prizes and an art exhibit. The school serves snacks and a hearty lunch.

PLACES TO GO

- Maude Williams State Park
  Wallace Road NW

THINGS TO DO

March
- Daffodil Festival
  Amity Elementary School
  (503) 835-2181

July
- Pancake Breakfast
  Amity Women's Club
  (503) 835-0400

Brigittine Monastery

FUN FOODS: *Best fudge*

The Brigittine Monks of the Willamette Valley have been skillfully preparing and selling delicious high quality fudges and truffles since the early 1980s. A fully self-supporting monastery, they quietly produce gourmet confections utilizing only the best and freshest ingredients to create delicious packages of pure luxury. Highly acclaimed in gourmet periodicals and top-ranked news programs, the chocolate fudges and truffles of the Brigittine are renowned. During a visit to their year round gift shop in a serene section of the Willamette Valley, you will enjoy an unhurried and peaceful shopping experience where quality and service are the rule rather than the exception. At the Brigittine Monastery you will find Chocolate Fudge Royale available with or without nuts, in chocolate, amaretto, pecan praline and chocolate cherry nut options. The Truffles Royale are available in chocolate, cherry chocolate amaretto, chocolate cherry, chocolate mint, chocolate maple, chocolate raspberry, chocolate butter rum, and milk chocolate. The Monks use pure chocolate, fresh dairy butter, real cream, the freshest nuts and real flavors. Visit the Brigittine Monastery for great chocolate and an uplifting experience.

23300 Walker Lane, Amity OR
(503) 835-8080
www.brigittine.org

Kristin Hill Winery
WINERIES: *Winery sparkles with good taste*

Located in the heart of the Yamhill County wine country, one mile north of Amity, you will find a truly unique winery owned and operated by the warm and friendly Linda and Eric Aberg. The lovely late 1800s home accented by an absolutely stunning Camperdown Elm Tree, which is thought to be at least as old as the home, lets you know that you have arrived. Giant Sequoias, Ponderosa pines and Port Orford cedars flank the property and provide interest to the grounds. Bring along a picnic lunch, find a complementary sparkling wine to match, and enjoy a restful meal in their constantly blooming garden with 20 acres of vineyard views. Sparkling wines are their specialty with their first vintage in 1990. Jennifer Falls, a blend of Pinot Noir and Chardonnay, is their signature wine. Jordan's Joy is an inspired salmon colored Pinot Noir. The cranberry colored, cherry-sweetened Fizzy Lizzie is wonderfully unique and all are worth trying. Seek out the Generic Eric Blush, Spice is Nice Gewurztraminer, Pinot Gris, Chardonnay, Pinot Noir, Muller Thurgau and Port red wines.

3330 SE Amity Dayton Highway,
Amity OR
(503) 835-0850

Amity Vineyards

WINERIES:

A winery of distinction

Oregon is renowned for pioneers, and Amity Vineyards is a pioneer in the expanding world of Willamette Valley wine. An Oregon Winery of Distinction, it has been at the forefront of building Oregon's reputation as a premier producer of Pinot noir. Wine authority Robert Parker declared Amity's Pinot noir to be one of the best he ever tasted. It was the first winery in the United States to produce a true Gamay noir, from authentic cuttings from Beaujolais, France. Amity also produces Pinot blanc, dry and sweet Gewürztraminer and Riesling, as well as a premium white blend, Crown Jewel Reserve, and a traditional dry Rose, Ravenous Rose. Owner and winemaker Myron Redford also created ECO•WINE®, a sulfite-free Pinot noir made from organically grown grapes. It was a great challenge to make a sulfite-free Pinot noir that could hold its own with conventionally made Pinot noirs, and Redford takes justifiable pride in his accomplishment. The Amity philosophy holds that wine is food as well as drink, and should be shared with family and friends. The tasting room is a cozy place where you can enjoy a wide selection of foods and snacks with the wines you sample. Be sure to try the dark chocolates filled with Pinot noir. You will want to linger at Amity to take in the breathtaking views of the Eola Hills and the Coast Range.

18150 SE Amity Vineyards Road, Amity OR
(503) 835-2362 or (888) 264-8966
www.amityvineyards.com

AURORA

Aurora welcomes visitors with a glimpse into the 19th century. Downtown Aurora was Oregon's first National Historic District, with more than 35 structures dating from 1856 to 1900. Most are open to the public as antique stores and restaurants. Aurora has almost a score of antique shops and rightly claims to be the antique capital of Oregon. In 1856, Dr. William Keil of Prussia led colonists down the Oregon Trail to found a religious commune. In those years, such communities were common in the Northeast and Midwest but unheard of in the Oregon Country. The communal life required sacrifice of personal ambition to the common good but did not inhibit creativity. Aurora's colonists manufactured spinning wheels, barrels, furniture, a variety of textiles and other items. Many of these artifacts are on exhibit at the Old Aurora Colony Museum. After the railroad passed through, Aurora became known for its hotel and its delicious German sausage and ham dinners. The surviving hotel register reads like a who's who of Oregon. When Keil died in 1877, the rest of the colonists decided to disband and distribute the communal property. The village of Aurora continued on, however, and even today the community spirit of its residents is notable.

PLACES TO GO

- Aurora Colony National Historic District
  (503) 939-0312

- Old Aurora Colony Museum
  15018 2nd Street NE
  (503) 678-5754

THINGS TO DO

August
- Aurora Colony Days
  (503) 678-1283

October
- Quilt Show
  Old Aurora Colony Museum
  (503) 678-5754

Pacific Hazelnut Candy Factory

FUN FOODS: *Best hazelnut candy*

Opened in 1985, Pacific Hazelnut Candy Factory in Aurora is best known for its chocolate coated hazelnuts, fruits, and hazelnut toffee. Along with his daughter Karen Freedman, Owner Ersel Christopherson runs the candy factory using family recipes first developed and sold from the family farm in 1985 after his wife, Joan (now deceased) began experimenting with toffee and hazelnuts. In addition to their famous hazelnut candies, they also carry milk and dark chocolate, chocolate coated blueberries, razzcherries, cranberries, chocolate coated coffee beans, dry roasted and seasoned hazelnuts, and a line of sugar-free varieties. Their fabulous gift shop also sells linens, teas and popular gift baskets filled with sweet confections. The popularity of their candy is far reaching, both Made In Oregon and Williams & Sonoma carry their products, and their signature hazelnut toffee was featured in *Bon Appetit* magazine. Whether you're a purist and prefer straight milk chocolate or are eager to sample their famous hazelnut candies, Pacific Hazelnut Candy Factory is a great place to visit for viewing, tasting and taking some treats home with you.

14673 Ottaway Avenue, Aurora OR
(503) 678-2755 or (800) 634-7344
www.pacifichazelnut.com

Amish Workbench Furniture Co.

HOME: *Best Amish furniture available in the Northwest*

The founders of Amish Workbench Furniture Co., Jay and Carol Titsworth, came to Oregon from Pennsylvania, where they developed a deep love and respect for the Amish and their ways. When they decided to set up their own business, it was only natural that their thoughts turned to Amish crafts and furniture. Jay and Carol's motto is "Simply the best...Not the most expensive." The inviting nature of their first store in Aurora will impress you the minute you walk inside. It's more than just a showroom for furniture. Jay and Carol sell juried handcrafts, including handmade quilts, many made with traditional and stunningly beautiful 19th-century designs. Any of these quilts would make a perfect complement to the elegant beds available, such as the Spindle Shaker, all of them made in four different sizes. Dining room tables come in different sizes, as well. All of the furniture at Amish Workbench is handcrafted by Amish artisans in Indiana, using only real woods. No particle board, Masonite, or laminate is ever used. Kiln-drying methods, superior to chemical treatments, ensure a more stable grain in the red oak and cherrywoods, and all furniture is coated with a specially formulated varnish that is damage-resistant. The Amish Workbench Furniture store in Aurora was so successful that Jay and Carol have opened two other locations. Their downtown Salem store is inside the historic Reed Opera House, and the Troutdale store is on the Columbia Gorge Scenic Highway.

14936 Third Street NE, Aurora OR
(866) 678-7799
www.amishwbf.com

CARLTON

Modern Carlton is home to more than a dozen vineyards, wineries or cellars, as well as Cuvee, a fine French restaurant. The Yamhill-Carlton District American Viticultural Area (AVA) curves around the town, though many of the best wineries are close to town and outside the limits of the AVA. They are within the limits of the broader Willamette Valley AVA. In 1872, a railroad was built through the area, but the train did not stop. After all, the local area consisted entirely of farm land. The farmers chose one of their number, Wilson Carl, to go to Portland and lobby the railroad for a stop. Carl succeeded, and the resulting town was named Carlton. The city was incorporated in 1899.

PLACES TO GO

- Lower Wennerberg Park
  S River Street

THINGS TO DO

May
- Memorial Day Week-End Open House
  Belle Pente Vineyard and Winery
  (503) 852-9500

June
- Carlton Fun Days
  (503) 852-9504

August
- Carlton's Walk in the Park
  Wennerberg Park
  (503) 852-6572

Anne Amie Vineyards

WINERIES: *A winery of exceptional quality and distinction*

Anne Amie is a new wine label from Oregon's Willamette Valley, producing wines that reflect the passions of Owner Robert Pamplin and winemaker Scott Huffman. Their vision is to produce memorable wines from low-yield vineyards with minimal processing. Dr. Pamplin purchased the Chateau Benoit Winery in 1999, and the Winery was officially renamed in May 2004 after his two daughters. When you visit the Anne Amie winery on a panoramic hilltop in Yamhill County, you will find a European-style tasting room, an open terrace with tables, and a Mediterranean garden, as well as spectacular views and warm hospitality. They offer a complimentary wine tasting daily of several wines, and the Vineyard Designate Pinot noirs are available to taste for a fee. Small lots of other Anne Amie wines are available exclusively here, as well as unique gift and gourmet food items. To capture the quality and distinction of the Vineyard Designate program, winemaker Huffman started with four sites that met specific requirements: Doe Ridge, La Colina, Yamhill Springs, and Laurel, all in Yamhill County. Huffman also oversaw the planting of two Pinot Noir sites west of Newberg. These sites boast breathtaking views of the valley below and Mount Hood to the northeast. Hawk's View is a working study of organic viticulture.

6580 NE Mineral Springs Road, Carlton OR
(503) 864-2991 or (800) 248-4835
www.anneamie.com

Cuneo Cellars

WINERIES: *Distinguished Italian Varietals in the Heart of the Northwest*

Established in 1993 with an exclusive focus on showing how red grapes express themselves in the Pacific Northwest, Cuneo Cellars creates wines that offer a passionate expression of European grape varieties with a uniquely Pacific Northwest sensibility. Under the guidance of Co-owner and winemaker, Gino Cuneo, the winery has pioneered the introduction of Italian varietals to complement its Burgundy, Bordeaux and Rhone-style red wines. They have won praise from authorities such as Northwest Palate magazine, which writes that Cuneo Cellars has the "most distinguished of all Italian varietals tasted from the Northwest." Whether they're trying a Nebbiolo or Brunello, Pinot Noir or Syrah, or even a suave Bordeaux-style blend of Cabernet Sauvignon and Merlot, red wine aficionados will find lots to love at Cuneo Cellars. Conveniently located on Highway 47 in the heart of Oregon Pinot Noir country, Cuneo Cellars offers visitors the opportunity to take part in a variety of activities. You can relax under the spacious skies on the Winery's patio, play a game of bocce ball on the traditional-style courts, and sample the best of Italian condiments and foods as you sip samples of Cuneo Cellar wines. The strategic location of Cuneo Cellars in Carlton, Oregon is situated midway between the warm-climate growing regions of eastern Washington and southern Oregon. To get the best grapes from these regions, the Northwest's best, Cuneo Cellars only works with premier vineyards in order to grow and make great wines of structure and complexity, experienced through their flavor and intensity, balance and length. Wine lovers are sure to appreciate the relaxed atmosphere and varied wines of Cuneo Cellars.

750 W Lincoln Street, Carlton OR
(503) 852-0002
www.cuneocellars.com

PLACES TO GO

- Bald Hill Park
  Oak Creek Drive

- Bryant Park
  801 Bryant Way SW, Albany

- Chip Ross Park
  NW Lester Avenue

- ArtCentric
  700 SW Madison Avenue (541) 754-1551

- Finley National Wildlife Refuge
  26208 Finley Refuge Road (541) 757-7236

- Gill Coliseum (Oregon State basketball)
  SW 26th Street

- Peavy Arboretum
  NW Arboretum Road (541) 737-3562

- Reser Stadium (Oregon State Beavers)
  26th Street and Western Boulevard

- Timber Linn Park
  900 Price Road SE, Albany

- Willamette Park
  SE Goodnight Avenue

THINGS TO DO

May
- Downtown Upstairs Tour (and celebration)
  Albany (541) 928-2469

July
- Red White & Blues Festival
  Downtown (541) 754-6624

- Da Vinci Days
  www.davinci-days.org

- Philomath Frolic & Rodeo
  Philomath www.philomathrodeo.org

- Linn County Fair
  Fairgrounds, Albany (541) 926-4314

August
- Benton County Fair and Rodeo
  Fairgrounds (541) 766-6521

- Willamette River Festival
  Albany (541) 928-0911

- Wah Chang Northwest Art & Air Festival
  Albany (541) 928-0911

September
- *Corvallis Fall Festival
  Central Park (541) 752-9655*

- Shrewsbury Renaissance Faire
  King's Valley www.shrewfaire.com

Oregon Beavers in training
Photo by Greg Keene

CORVALLIS

The name Corvallis is from the Latin cor vallis, heart of the valley. Indeed, Corvallis is the heart of the Willamette Valley. Home to Oregon State University, it is a classic college town. The wide streets, sheltered by ancient trees, red brick and white masonry buildings and its location along the Willamette River make Corvallis a handsome city. The 500 acre Oregon State University campus is the site of the state's oldest institution of higher education and the center of much of the town's activity. There are bookstores, restaurants, boutiques and other shops along the edge of campus. After the University, Hewlett Packard is the town's leading employer. Da Vinci Days is a three day festival held in Corvallis in July, celebrating arts, science and technology. Top-rated for bicycle support, Corvallis has many miles of bike paths, trails and roadside bike lanes. The city's park system is vast, with more than 2,000 acres in all. Corvallis has received a seemingly endless series of accolades. Magazines and books have repeatedly named it one of America's best cities for science, patents and creativity—and one of the nation's best places to live. Corvallis has a twin city in Albany, located a few miles east.

Hilton Garden Inn Corvallis

ACCOMMODATIONS:

Best place for business travelers

On the campus of Oregon State University there is a hotel with one of the most prestigious names in the industry–the Hilton Garden Inn. A full-service hotel with 128 guest rooms (including four suites), it features all of the luxury guests have come to expect from the Hilton name at a price that's surprisingly affordable. The Hilton Garden Inn is the wise business traveler's choice. Rooms feature complimentary high-speed Internet access and secure remote printing facilities, dual-line telephones with voice mail and data ports, work desks with desk level outlets and ergonomic chairs, giving the Garden Inn an unbeatable edge. In town to see the Beavers take on the Ducks? The Inn is located next to Reser Stadium. Comfort goes hand-in-hand with cutting-edge electronic connectivity here. From the in-room hospitality centers with refrigerator, microwave oven and coffee maker to the heated indoor pool, spa and fitness center, the Hilton Garden Inn provides everything you need to take it easy or get down to business. Dine at the Stadium Grill Restaurant or pick up food to go at the Pavilion Pantry. Whatever your needs, you can get it. Planning an event? The Hilton Garden Inn has a 1,000-square-foot University Club Event and Game Room, and an executive boardroom that seats 12. The Business Center has copier, computer and fax service, and is open 24 hours a day. Take advantage of the enhanced accommodations at the Hilton Garden Inn Corvallis.

2500 SW Western Boulevard, Corvallis OR
(877) STAY-HGI (782-9444) or
(541) 752-5000
www.hiltongardeninn.com

OSU Bookstore Beaver Fan Shop

SHOPPING: *Best independent bookseller and Beaver fan shop*

For a large variety of Beaver memorabilia for men, women, children and infants, come to the Oregon State University Bookstore's Beaver Fan Shop in the heart of downtown Portland. Located in the Bank of America Building, this store brings the presence of the OSU campus to Oregon's largest city and makes it easy to keep up the ties to the Corvallis campus for alumni and fans of the OSU Beavers. Open since 1994, the Portland Store is a branch of the OSU bookstore that has been serving Oregon State University students and friends since 1914. Over the years the campus bookstore, now one of the largest bookstores in the area, has changed from a cooperative to a diversified non-profit with more than 140 employees in the OSU Bookstore, Inc. Now offering computer equipment, best sellers, and hosting book signings, the Store serves both OSU students and Corvallis residents. The Beaver Fan Shop has given OSU a presence in the Portland metropolitan area. For students, alumni, friends of the University and Beaver sports fans, the OSU Bookstore in Portland or Corvallis is a wonderful source. For more than 90 years the bookstore has been serving the needs of OSU students, faculty and friends in Corvallis, and it now serves Portland, as well.

121 SW Morrison Street, Portland OR
(503) 525-2678
www.osubookstore.com

Tyee Wine Cellars

WINERIES: *Best area winery*

In the Chinook trading jargon of the early Northwest, Tyee meant *chief* or *the best*, a fitting name for a winery committed to producing varietal wines of the highest quality. The scenic and historic Buchanan Family Century Farm, in the heart of Oregon's Willamette Valley, is home to Tyee Wine Cellars. It was founded in 1985 by two couples, longtime local farmers David and Margy Buchanan, Barney Watson and Nola Mosier. Tyee's labels feature Northwest Indian art and legends, including raven, salmon, Dungeness crab, great horned owl and Canada goose strikingly rendered by Oregon artist James Jordan. Tyee has a special relationship to the Willamette Valley. In 1999, the Buchanans converted 246 acres of their farm into a Wetland Reserve. Their commitment to sustainable agriculture was recognized by the Oregon Wildlife Society, which presented them with a Private Landowner Stewardship award. The vineyard and winery are certified under the Salmon Safe eco label. Tyee specializes in limited releases of Pinot noir, Pinot gris, Pinot blanc, Gewurztraminer and Chardonnay, using grapes from their own Beaver Creek Vineyard, as well as selections from neighboring Willamette Valley growers. Barney Watson, Tyee's winemaker, has an advanced degree in Enology and Viticulture from the University of California at Davis and worked as an enologist at Oregon State University. He received a Lifetime Achievement award from the Oregon Winegrowers Association, citing his "fundamental role in bringing credibility to Oregon wines on the world stage."

26335 Greenberry Road, Corvallis OR
(541) 753-8754
www.tyeewine.com

PLACES TO GO

- Baker Bay Park (Dorena Lake)
  35635 Shoreview Drive
- Bohemia Gold Mining Museum
  724 Main Street
  (541) 942-5658
- Cottage Grove Historical Museum
  147 H Street
  (541) 942-3963
- Lakeside Park
  Cottage Grove Lake
- Schwartz Park (Dorena Lake)
  75819 Shortridge Hill Road
- Shortridge Park
  Cottage Grove Lake

THINGS TO DO

July
- Bohemia Mining Days
  Coiner Park
  (541) 942-2411
- Cottage Grove Rodeo
  State Route 99
  (541) 942-2411

August
- Western Oregon Exposition Family Fair
  (541) 942-2411
- Lorane Valley Wine & Garlic Festival
  Lorane
  (800) 884-4441

September
- Gathering of Gardeners
  Village Green Resort
  (541) 942-2491
- Iris Hill Rhythm & Blues Festival
  Iris Hill Winery, Lorane
  (541) 895-9877

October
- Chili Cook-Off and Harvest Festival
  Main Street (541) 942-2411

Mosby Bridge
Photo by Chris Phan

COTTAGE GROVE

Cottage Grove is a friendly, family-oriented town. It is at the southern, upper end of the Willamette Valley. To the south, I-5 courses through a mountain pass en route to the Umqua Valley. Visitors to Cottage Grove enjoy touring art galleries and antique shops. The shopping district is compact, so the town is a perfect place for browsing from shop to shop. You can picnic at nearby Dorena or Cottage Grove lakes. These lakes also support windsurfing, swimming and camping. They have some of the best fishing around, and you can also fish in the Row River. Rustic covered bridges in the area make Cottage Grove the covered bridge capital of Oregon. The Bohemia Mining District, the site of a mid-19th century gold rush, is featured at a downtown museum. Check with the Ranger Station before you actually visit the district, so that you can avoid trespassing on the mining claims that still exist in the area. Animal House was filmed in Cottage Grove, and on the film's 25th anniversary citizens celebrated with a toga party downtown. (The event has since moved to Eugene.) Cottage Grove is a great place to visit for outdoor activities, touring or just a fun day in town.

Village Green Resort
ACCOMMODATIONS
Best resort for meetings and relaxation

Whether you live in Cottage Grove or are just passing through, the luxuriant gardens of the Village Green Resort make it an enchanting place to visit. The resort has more than a dozen themed gardens on 17 acres. The Bird Habitat contains shrubs, flowers and trees attractive to birds, while the Courtyard, with a gazebo, rose tunnel and fountain, forms a romantic setting for a wedding or reception. The strange and whimsical Widow's Walk, made up of plants with black foliage, flowers or stems, is a hit at Halloween. Hidden in the resort's interior grounds are a rock garden and a winter garden. Guestrooms feature unique paint effects and signature Moonstone beds with luxurious linens and plump, cozy comforters.

Many rooms have a microwave, refrigerator and fireplace. From certain rooms, guests can step out onto a private patio and enjoy views of the gardens from the country-style patio furniture. Guests enjoy the resort's heated outdoor pool and spa in its garden setting. Special weekend retreat packages teach guests about gardens. Other specials focus on Cottage Grove's extensive bicycle trails. Village Green offers multiple indoor and outdoor facilities for meetings, which give business and social functions opportunities to gather in a green, healing atmosphere. The friendly staff members at Village Green Resort invite you to come and experience the difference a green surrounding can make to your overall comfort and pleasure.

725 Row River Road, Cottage Grove OR
(800) 343-7666
www.villagegreenresortandgardens.com

Espresso Bar'n

BAKERIES, COFFEE & TEA: *Best coffee house*

The Espresso Bar'n keeps James and Liz Kline and their seven employees extremely busy serving up some of the best coffee in the county. James spent 14 years in the corporate world before he and Liz, his wife, sat down and decided to start a business of their own. As parents of three young children, their priority was to have more time available to spend with their family. Now, three years on, the Espresso Bar'n offers not only espresso, but an assortment of teas, muffins, cookies and the locally famous Granny's Shortbread. You can also get specialty beans to take home. The Klines are very involved in the community. Each year, the Espresso Bar'n sponsors a golf tournament that benefits local youth athletics. Giving back is second nature to the Klines, and it shows in their work with their employees, high level of commitment to the community and excellent customer service. For a taste of something that will warm your heart as well as please your appetite, visit the Espresso Bar'n.

1551 E Main Street, Cottage Grove OR
(541) 942-2926

Radio Station KNND

BUSINESS: *Best radio station*

AM radio station KNND has been supplying great music to south Lane and north Douglas counties since 1953. Currently owned and managed by Paul Schwartzberg, KNND's major focus is and always has been the community. KNND features some of the best voice talent in the state and is known for its diverse and eclectic programming. Paul jokes that he "had nothing else to do" when he decided to go into radio, but the real reason he chose the business is that it let him put his family first. Radio also gives Paul the opportunity to put the community's priorities firmly front and center. KNND's current format is country and a whole lot more. Paul himself runs the Beeper Show, an 8:30 am hour-long daily talk show with a non-partisan orientation. At 10 am daily, KNND runs Swap 'n' Shop, an area tradition and the station's most popular show. Friday night is for rock and roll from 7 pm until the wee hours. Other weekly shows feature Christian music, polka and horses. For great listening, set the dial to 1400 AM. Let Paul and his team show you why KNND, your heritage station, has been on the air for over 50 years.

321 Main Street, Cottage Grove OR
(541) 942-2468
www.knnd.com

Out of Eden
SHOPPING: *Best arts boutique*

Out of Eden is truly a paradise that showcases everything from quality consignments to local artists' work. Inside this immense warehouse you will find local artists' jewelry, glass-blown items and antiques of exceptional quality. The Weekend Market, commonly referred to as Treasures in the Garden, is an ongoing seasonal event that is regularly attended by people from Seattle to Southern California. When co-owner Beau Wright first came to Oregon to fight fires, he immediately fell in love with the natural beauty of this state. Eventually, he returned with a dream. It was, simply, to live in Oregon. Beau and Roger Marquez have made their passion for the Northwest part of their landmark business. When they created Out of Eden, their goal was to create a place where anyone can come and enjoy themselves for hours. The mini-farm

has goats, chickens and bunnies for kids to pet. Beau states, "There is a fine line here between furnishings and fertilizer." He jokes about what can be found at Out of Eden, but he and Roger are dedicated to creating a comfortable environment that is both friendly and interesting. Beau and Roger can also help you plan a theme party or arrange for a limousine wine tour for you and your friends. If you have an idea, just ask. This creative and community-oriented pair are just waiting for your visit. Once you are in Eden, you'll never want to leave.

125 N Lane Street, Cottage Grove OR
(541) 942-5656

Victoriana Antiques & Costumes
SHOPPING: *Most lively collection of merchandise*

Lesley Neufeld, owner of Victoriana Antiques & Costumes, spent 30 years as a costume designer in the motion picture industry, working on films such as *The Postman*, *Scorpion King* and *Windtalkers*. As a result, her shop in Cottage Grove is rather different from most antique malls. Lesley stocks vintage clothing, rents costumes and will design costumes on request. She has many outfits for Civil War reenactors. Many of her non-clothing items are movie related, such as the film props. You'll also find a large quantity of antique furniture, along with art, toys, dishes and frames. Lesley creates a pleasant, small-town shopping environment with reasonable prices. She is very active in the community and helped organize the response of Main Street merchants to city planning proposals for that street. She is on the board of Bohemia Mining Days, and as the board's secretary, keeps track of the myriad details involved in planning the annual July event. "I really enjoy the costume aspect of the festival," she says. Whenever you are in Cottage Grove, stop in and discover the lively collection of unusual merchandise at Victoriana Antiques & Costumes.

538 E Main Street, Cottage Grove OR
(541) 767-0973

ELMIRA

Elmira was once called Duckworth, which would be a fine name for a town a few miles from the University of Oregon. However, in 1884, one Byron Ellmaker persuaded the government to change the name, because he did not like the old one. Elmira is one of severalcommunities that together make up the district of Fern Ridge—Alvadore, Crow, Elmira, Lorane, Noti, Triangle Lake, Veneta and Walton. The region is centered on the Fern Ridge Reservoir. Driving past the Fern Ridge dam on Clear Lake Road, you get a vivid picture of the power of resources harnessed for a greater community purpose. Likewise, the towns of Fern Ridge work together for the greater good. Six park sites and several remote access points around the lake offer a variety of day use recreation opportunities. A private concession on the peninsula at the south end of the lake has overnight camping sites. The lake has abundant wildlife, notably the snowy white egrets. In July, Veneta hosts the Oregon Country Fair, one of the states' most popular alternative events. The area has a number of fine wineries along the Long Tom River.

PLACES TO GO

• Pioneer Museum
7th and Broadway, Veneta
(541) 935-1836

THINGS TO DO

July
• Oregon Country Fair
Fair site, Veneta
(541) 343-4298

• Zimfest (Zimbabwe festival)
Fair site, Veneta
(541) 607-1000

• The Faerieworlds Festival
Secret House Winery
(541) 687-0945

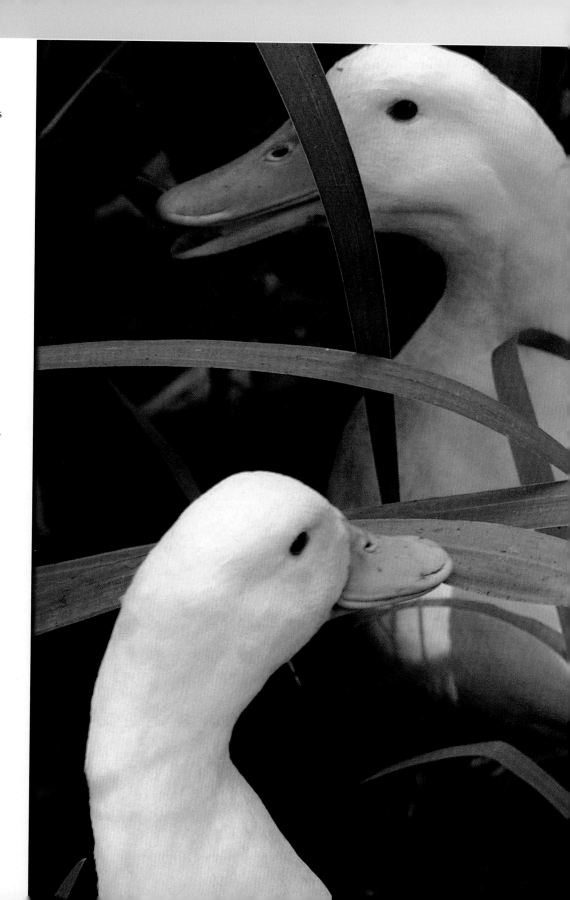

LaVelle Vineyards

WINERIES:

Intimate winery offers big entertainment

The manicured grounds of LaVelle Vineyards are as pleasing to the eye as their high quality wines are to the palate. Located on a secluded hillside 15 miles west of Eugene, this 16-acre estate produces distinctive Pinot Noir, Pinot Gris, Riesling, sparkling wines, and a limited amount of Marechal Foch and Gamay Noir. First planted in 1972, LaVelle Vineyards was originally named Forgeron Winery, and is the oldest winery in the Southern Willamette Valley. Doug LaVelle purchased the Winery in 1994, and the LaVelle Winery and popular tasting room opened in 1996. Every other month they offer a Murder Mystery Dinner Theater. They also have one of the largest wine clubs in the area, with private club parties and wine discounts. During the summer months, visitors are welcome to the vineyards seven days a week. LaVelle Winery presents a Full Moon party in summer. During Labor Day and Memorial Day weekends, live music and wine tasting take place. LaVelle Wine Bar & Bistro was opened in the historic 5th Street Public Market in Eugene to further serve their customers. The tasting room is open daily and serves the same quality wines as those found at the vineyards. On Wednesday, Thursday, Friday and Saturday nights, the lights are lowered as the room is transformed into an upscale wine and piano bar. A mouth-watering fondue buffet with cheese and chocolate is served along with gourmet bistro fare.

Doug invites everyone to visit LaVelle Vineyards to sample their distinctive wines and experience the intimacy of the small winery. LaVelle Vineyards is open daily May through September, and on weekends October through April.

89697 Sheffler Road, Elmira OR
(541) 935-9406
LaVelle Wine Bar and Bistro
296 E 5th Avenue, Eugene OR
(541) 338-9875
www.lavelle-vineyards.com

EUGENE

Eugene enjoys a national reputation as one of the most livable cities in the country, due in part to the University of Oregon. Eugene is more than a college town, however. It has long been considered Oregon's second city, and with Springfield and other neighbors forms a metropolis of about 350,000 people. Eugene has an informed and active citizenry, a thriving and eclectic arts scene, world-class sporting events and unsurpassed natural beauty. Eugene began in 1846 when Eugene Skinner built a cabin by the Willamette River. The university opened in 1876 after a major campaign by local residents. Eugene today has a huge park system with jogging and bicycle paths everywhere. Two large parks, the West Eugene Wetlands and Ridgeline Park, are actually federations of parks. A climb up Spencer Butte in Ridgeline Park offers a lovely view of the city. Eugene's many cultural institutions include the Eugene Symphony, the Eugene Ballet and the Eugene Opera. Performing arts venues include the Hult Center for the Performing Arts, The John G. Shedd Institute for the Arts and Beall Concert Hall on the U of O campus. Eugene is filled with museums and bookstores, and the university boasts the largest library in the state. Eugene is one of the nation's most important centers for track. The U.S. Olympic Track and Field Trials are held at U of O's Hayward Field. The Farmer's Market is among the largest in the state, and Eugene's Saturday Market is the oldest weekly open-air crafts festival in the U.S.

PLACES TO GO

- Cascades Raptor Center
  32275 Fox Hollow Road (541) 485-1320

- Conger Street Clock Museum
  730 Conger Street (541) 344-6359

- Elijah Bristow State Park
  State Route 58

- Jordan Schnitzer Museum of Art (U of O)
  1430 Johnson Lane (541) 346-3027

- Lane County Historical Museum
  740 W 13th Avenue (541) 682-4242

- Maude Kerns Art Museum
  1910 E 15th Avenue (541) 345-1571

- Mount Pisgah Arboretum
  34901 Frank Parrish Road (541) 741-4110
- Museum of Natural and Cultural History
  1680 E 15th Avenue (541) 346-3024
- Oregon Air and Space Museum
  90377 Boeing Drive (503) 461-1101
- Science Factory Children's Museum
  2300 Leo Harris Parkway (541) 682-7888

THINGS TO DO

January
- Oregon Truffle Festival
  (503) 296-5929

February
- Oregon Asian Celebration
  Lane Events Center (541) 687-9600

April
- Chef's Night Out
  Hult Center (541) 343-2822

May
- Eugene Film Festival
  (541) 485-2447
- Willamette Valley Folk Festival
  (541) 346-0635

June
- Sasquatch Brew Fest
  (510) 339-1687

July
- Eugene Pro Rodeo
  Eugene Rodeo Grounds (541) 689-9700

August
- Lane County Fair
  (541) 682-4292
- Oregon Festival of American Music
  (800) 248-1615
- Eugene/Springfield Pride Day
  Alton Baker Park (541) 513-1711
- Springfield Filbert Festival
  Island Park, Springfield (541) 515-2405

September
- Eugene Celebration
  Downtown (541) 681-4108
- Animal House Celebration & Toga Party
  Eugene Hilton (541) 515-2405
- Fiesta Latina
  Island Park, Springfield (541) 344-5070

October
- The Mushroom Festival
  Mount Pisgah (541) 747-1504

The Campbell House
ACCOMMODATIONS: *Best inn*

In 1993, Myra Plant realized her dream when she opened the Campbell House Inn. She transformed the beautiful 1892 Victorian mansion built by gold miner John Cogswell into a 19-room inn of unparalleled elegance. Twelve guest rooms, six suites and a cottage welcome guests seeking comfort and hospitality. Wireless Internet access, spa tubs, and in-room massage are just a few of the amenities available. Within walking distance of downtown Eugene, the Inn's bucolic setting is a welcome oasis in the midst of the bustling city. More than comfort awaits the Campbell House guest. Complimentary full breakfasts have been a feature of the Inn since it opened, and now guests can enjoy dinner there, as well. Wednesdays through Saturdays, the Dining Room serves a Table D'hote style menu. Guests can choose anything from soup and salad to a five-course meal. The menu changes daily and chef Matthew Calzia uses the finest possible local organic ingredients to prepare a superb culinary experience you won't want to miss. The Campbell House is a place for gatherings, offering a perfect space for wedding receptions, family reunions, and holiday parties. Special holiday events include the Victorian Christmas Tea and Mother's Day Tea. Small business meetings are also welcome. Two meeting rooms can accommodate up to 18 people conference-style or 24 theater-style. Off-street parking for up to 19 vehicles is available. What better place could there be for a corporate retreat?

252 Pearl Street, Eugene OR
(541) 343-1119 or (800) 264-2519
www.campbellhouse.com

Hilton Eugene & Conference Center
ACCOMMODATIONS: *Best hotel*

When traveling for either business or pleasure, stay at the Hilton Eugene & Conference Center for the finest accommodations. Located in the heart of downtown Eugene, the Hilton is close to the University of Oregon, Autzen Stadium, the Hult Center for the Performing Arts, and the 5th Street Marketplace. Each of the 272 guest rooms and suites have been redesigned for the utmost in comfort. Choose from standard guest rooms or suites and relax in comfortable surroundings. Standard rooms come with queen or king-size beds and feature such amenities as private mini balconies, premium television channels and wireless Internet access. Rooms are conveniently equipped with irons and ironing boards, complimentary coffee and tea with in-room coffee makers, and free weekday USA Today newspapers. Suites are available, each one featuring a parlor complete with overstuffed furniture, armoire, and an oak table that can accommodate up to eight people. The Hilton also caters to the executive with nightly turndown service and access to the private concierge club room for Continental breakfast or nightly hors d'oeuvres and drinks. The Big River Grille features exemplary Pacific Northwest cuisine. Guests can relax in the Lobby Bar and sip a cocktail or local micro-brew after a long day. Other hotel amenities include a barber shop, beauty salon, indoor pool, Jacuzzi, and fitness center. Complimentary parking and airport shuttle is provided. The Hilton is the premier place to hold a meeting or event in Eugene. This hotel has a well trained banquet and catering staff, and boasts more than 30,000 feet of conference space. Banquet rooms on the top floor feature floor-to-ceiling windows and create a breathtaking backdrop for weddings and other special events.

66 E 6th Avenue, Eugene OR
(541) 342-2000 or (800) 937-6660
www.eugene.hilton.com

Hult Center for the Performing Arts

ATTRACTIONS: *Multi-faceted performing arts center*

Where can you go to experience acrobats and Chopin? Broadway and Brahms? Willie Nelson, jazz, and the Nutcracker Ballet? The answer is the Hult Center for the Performing Arts, and this is just a sample of the wide variety of events in the arts-packed calendar of this Eugene treasure. The Hult Center has been providing symphony, opera, ballet, modern dance, jazz, musical theater, comedy, rock and roll, and live theater for 23 years. With 800 performances per year, this is one of the busiest performing arts centers in North America. Eugene can take justifiable pride in having built a top-notch facility entirely with local funds. Resident companies include the Eugene Symphony, the Willamette Repertory Theatre, Dance Theatre of Oregon, Oregon Festival of American Music, Oregon Mozart Players, Eugene Ballet, Oregon Bach Festival, Eugene Concert Choir and Eugene Opera. Widely acknowledged for its outstanding architecture and acoustical achievement, the Hult Center has been called one of the finest performing arts complexes in the world. National and international performers are happy to come to Eugene to play in the house that Broadway Magician Harry Blackstone junior called a "magical facility for the arts." Visual arts have not been forgotten here either. Art has been integrated into every part of the facility, from the hand-painted tiles in the restrooms to the Jacobs Gallery, which features work by regional artists and hosts the annual Mayor's Art Show. The Hult Center for the Performing Arts is in downtown Eugene, one of the world's great cities for the arts.

One Eugene Center, Eugene OR
(541) 682-5000 or (541) 682-5746
www.hultcenter.org

Oregon Gallery
GALLERIES: *Best gallery*

Oregon Gallery features scenic Pacific Northwest photography by Ron Keebler, as well as wall décor and craft items made in the Pacific Northwest. Opened in 1977, Oregon Gallery is owned and managed by Ron and his wife Laurie. Before opening retail stores, Ron and Laurie sold photographs at arts and crafts fairs throughout the Pacific Northwest. Ron grew up in the Willamette Valley among green rolling hills and farmland, with the snow-topped Cascades to the east and the breathtaking Pacific coastline to the west. From his earliest days, he was fascinated by the exceptional quality of Northwest light. For more than 25 years, Ron has concentrated on creating images that communicate the region's amazing geographic diversity and splendor. Ron's scenic photography can add a sense of natural beauty to any home. His work is found in the offices of major corporations, universities and public agencies. Pricing is very competitive. In addition to the outlet in Eugene, located next to the Steelhead Brewery, Oregon Gallery has locations at RiverPlace in Portland and at Cannon Beach. Come view the beauty of the Pacific Northwest in Ron Keebler's outstanding photographs.

199 E 5th Avenue, Suite 5, Eugene OR (541) 684-0045
315 SW Montgomery Street, Suite 120, Portland OR
(503) 227-8406
233 N Hemlock, Cannon Beach OR (503) 436-0817
www.oregongallery.com

Reed&Cross

Many boutiques under one roof

For a unique shopping experience, don't miss Eugene's elegant Reed&Cross. You'll find something for everyone on your list and special treats for yourself. Touted as one of Oregon's Best Gift Stores by *The Oregonian*, Reed&Cross can be described as many boutiques under one roof. For more than 50 years, Reed&Cross has offered an eclectic mix of merchandise. You can browse for hours for that perfect gift or treat. Of Grape and Grain, the in-store cafe, is a popular spot to sit back, relax and catch up with friends.

Reed&Cross is the largest florist in the area. Their award-winning design team creates every kind of bouquet imaginable including stunning flowers for your wedding or other special event.

In addition to an array of fresh flowers, you'll find indoor and outdoor plants in The Gardens, along with silk and dried flowers, fountains and garden decor. A wonderful selection of women's clothing is available, including Oregon's own Pendleton. Need to accessorize that outfit?

Don't miss their Brighton Shop with many choices in handbags, jewelry, shoes and luggage pieces. The Housewares department is a cook's dream, with gourmet cookware, dinnerware, wine accessories and, of course, all the latest in kitchen gadgets. Gourmet foods and gift baskets round out the selection. From October through the end of the year, the Holiday Trim shop is a magical place that draws crowds from all over the state. When you get tired from all that shopping, unwind at Bello Day Spa and Salon. It's all about pampering yourself. Do as their motto says and, Excite your Senses at Reed&Cross.

**160 Oakway Road,
Eugene OR
(541) 484-1244
or (888) 663-0637**
www.reedcross.com

King Estate Winery

WINERIES:

Best organic wines

The King Estate winery combines breathtakingly beautiful grounds with high quality wines to create an unforgettable experience. The spectacular 1,000-acre mountain estate includes 250 acres of vineyards. This majestic state-of-the-art winery encompasses 110,000 square feet and is one of Oregon's largest. Modeled after a European Chateau, the winery is an impressive sight indeed. Visitors will appreciate both the sight and sweet aroma of the 3,000 lavender plants that adorn the hillsides. The organic garden produces fresh herbs, berries, vegetables and fruits, which the culinary team uses to create masterpieces. The winery has developed two cookbooks and has also sponsored a nationally televised PBS cooking series, *New American Cuisine*. Tours are given daily. The popular tasting room is often full on weekends with a line of people waiting to taste the delicious Pinot Noir, Pinot Gris, and Chardonnay produced by the King Estate Winery. Located southwest of Eugene, the Winery is owned by the King family. Ed King, Jr. and his son, Ed King III began planting the vineyards in 1991. The Winery was built in 1992 and can now produce 400,000 gallons a year. In the fall of 2004, the Kings were recognized by *Wine and Spirits* magazine as two of the 50 Most Influential Winemakers in the World. The King family employs organic growing practices, and in 2002 the farm was certified by the Oregon Tilth Certified Organic Association.

80854 Territorial Road, Eugene OR
(800) 884-4441
www.kingestate.com

GASTON

Gaston is in the Oregon wine country, surrounded by the territory of the Yamhill-Carlton appellation to the south and the proposed Chehalem Mountains appellation to the north. You can buy many area wines at a shop right in Gaston. While it is within urbanized Washington County, Gaston itself is a small, peaceful town with less than a thousand souls. Gaston is named for Joseph Gaston, who came to Oregon from Ohio in 1862 and actively promoted railroads west of Portland. He built a narrow-gauge line from Dayton to Sheridan in 1878 and subsequently wrote and published histories of Portland and of Oregon. The Federal government opened the Gaston Post Office in 1873. Gaston is close to popular recreation areas such as Henry Hagg Lake.

PLACES TO GO

• Bald Peak State Scenic Viewpoint
  SW Bald Peak Road

• Henry Hagg Lake (county park)
  SW Scoggins Valley Road

THINGS TO DO

August
• Wapato Showdown (car show)
  Brown Field
  (509) 985-9548

Elk Cove Vineyards

WINERIES: *Tasteful wine in a captivating setting*

As you approach the Elk Cove Vineyards tasting room, you pass wonderful vineyards surrounded by roses, terraces and scenic views of the North Willamette Valley. As Robert Parker of *The Wine Advocate* wrote: "For the pure beauty of its setting, no winery in Oregon can match the breathtaking views from Elk Cove's splendid wine tasting room." Staffed with friendly and knowledgeable hosts, the Tasting Room is warm and inviting. When Pat and Joe Campbell found their secluded property in 1973, they knew that this was the place to bring their dreams of producing fine wines to fruition. Magnificent Roosevelt Elk roamed the estate and added to the majesty of this wonderful place. The Campbells have been handcrafting wines for more than 30 years. Their son, Adam, grew up on the vineyard, and joined his father in winemaking in 1989. Adam has been the full-time winemaker since 1999. Adam loves the interesting mixture of agriculture and artistry in winemaking. The philosophy at Elk Cove is to allow the grapes to naturally express their best qualities and then to handcraft the wines. All of their Pinot Noirs are aged in the finest quality French oak barrels, and moved from tank to barrel only by gravity or inert gas pressure to protect the inherent qualities of the fruit. Elk Cove is also known for their Pinot Gris and late harvest Rieslings. The winery is a picturesque place for weddings, corporate functions and winemaker dinners. Guided tours are available by appointment.

27751 NW Olson Road, Gaston OR
(877) ELK-COVE (355-2683) or (503) 985-7760
www.elkcove.com

Kramer Vineyards

WINERIES: *Hands-on award-winning family winery*

Visiting family-owned and operated Kramer Vineyards is a welcoming experience for all who venture to this small vineyard just outside the town of Gaston. Keith and Trudy Kramer's dream came true when they planted their vineyard in 1984 and harvested their first batch of wine in 1989. On their 20 acres of land, they now produce high quality Pinot Noir, Pinot Gris, Müller-Thurgau, Dijon Chardonnay, and a special wine, Carmine, otherwise known as Big Red. Although they have won numerous awards and accolades over the years, including a gold medal at the 2003 Oregon State Fair for a Pinot Noir, the Kramers ultimate goal is to produce wines that are enjoyed by their customers and do justice to the fruits. The Vineyard includes a tasting room where at least 10 fine wines are available each day. The deck outside their tasting room boasts an outstanding view of the valley below and is a popular dining spot for visitors who think ahead to a picnic lunch. During the months of July and August, the Kramers host multi-course dinners under the stars. This is a hands-on vineyard, where the owners want guests to understand all aspects of producing hand-crafted wines. Visitors always feel welcome and are invited to experience the harvest by punching down the pinot, (tasting freshly squeezed juice or wine and touring the winery and observing their equipment). The accommodating staff is helpful, the Kramer's Labrador Retriever and big tabby cat casually escort visitors as they tour the Tasting Room and grounds, and the Kramers are always nearby to share information and visit with those who want to learn more about the winemaking process. Kramer Vineyards is an Oregon Treasure you'll want to visit.

26830 NW Olson Road, Gaston OR
(503)662-4545 or 800-61-WINES (619-4637)
www.kramerwine.com

McKenzie Bridge and Leaburg
The McKenzie River Valley

The beautiful McKenzie River Valley is a 60-mile-long corridor stretching east from Springfield past Walterville, Leaburg, Blue River and McKenzie Bridge to Clear Lake. State Route 126 follows the river, providing access to many important sites. Campgrounds and picnic areas are scattered along the river corridor. Covered bridges are common in this area. Among the most scenic are the Goodpasture Covered Bridge and the Belknap Bridge. Famous for fishing, the McKenzie River supports bull trout, spring Chinook, rainbow trout and mountain whitefish. Water fowl along the river corridor include bald eagles, osprey and a variety of ducks. The Leaburg Dam is a good place to watch salmon and steelhead climbing a fish ladder. The town of Leaburg contains the Leaburg Trout Hatchery and the McKenzie Salmon Hatchery. The historical Leaburg Fish Hatchery now houses the McKenzie River Chamber of Commerce Information Center. The McKenzie River is also a favorite place for whitewater rafting. Many outfitters and local guides are available to assist fishermen and rafters. The McKenzie River Valley also boasts golfing, the U.S. Basketball Academy in Blue River and relaxing places to stay. The McKenzie Highway, which begins just past McKenzie Bridge, offers a shortcut over the Cascades to Sisters and Bend. This beautiful drive winds past waterfalls through recent volcanic flows. At McKenzie Pass you can stop at the Dee Wright Observatory, which has breath-taking views of Mount Washington, Mount Jefferson and the Three Sisters. The McKenzie Highway is closed in winter.

McKenzie River
Photo by Carolyn

PLACES TO GO

- Ben & Kay Dorris Park
  State Route 126, Vida

- Deerhorn Landing
  Holden Creek Road, Walterville

- The Dee Wright Observatory
  *McKenzie Pass, McKenzie Highway
  (State Route 242)*

- Jennie B. Harris Wayside
  State Route 126, McKenzie Bridge

- McKenzie Salmon Hatchery
  *43863 Greer Drive, Leaburg
  (541) 896-3513*

- Sahalie Falls and Koosah Falls
  State Route 126, Clear Lake

- Waterboard Park
  State Route 126, Leaburg

THINGS TO DO

June
- Free Fishing Day
  *Leaburg Trout Hatchery, Leaburg
  (541) 896-3294*

July
- McKenzie River Home and Garden Tour
  (888) 942-4547

August
- Leaburg Summer Festival
  *Leaburg Community Center
  (541) 896-3330*

- McKenzie Arts Festival
  *Tokatee Golf Club
  (541) 822-3785*

September
- Walterville Community Fair
  *Walterville
  (541) 746-6674*

Belknap Hot Springs Lodge & Gardens

ACCOMMODATIONS:

Best hot springs on the McKenzie River

Belknap Hotsprings and Gardens in McKenzie Bridge offers 18 spacious lodge rooms, some with relaxing Jacuzzi tubs. The views from the rooms are breathtaking, with a choice of the mighty McKenzie River or the lush Belknap woods. Rooms are available with either one or two king or queen-size beds; some also offer hide-a-beds. For more privacy, stay in one of the seven rustic cabins that come fully furnished and are the perfect spot for a romantic getaway or a family vacation. Pets are welcome in two of the cabins. Those wishing to camp in the beautiful outdoors will be happy to know that Belknap Hot Springs Lodge & Gardens offers 42 RV sites, some with full hook-up, and 18 tent sites. The 45 acres of manicured gardens provide a wonderful spot to relax. The green lawns, beautiful flowers, and soothing sounds of water will still your mind and ease your worries. Take long walks on the spectacular trails or sit under a tree and enjoy a picnic lunch with loved ones. Be on the lookout for osprey, deer, elk and other wildlife. Taking a dip in the hot springs is an unforgettable experience. The source of the hot mineral water ranges from 185 to 195 degrees Fahrenheit. Soaking in the riverside hot springs pools, where the average temperature is 104 degrees Fahrenheit, is a proven way to forget about life's worries and stresses. Norm McDougal and his family, who purchased the Belknap Hot Springs & Gardens in 1995, invite you to visit their paradise and soak your troubles away.

59296 Belknap Springs Road, McKenzie Bridge OR
(541) 822-3512
www.belknaphotsprings.com

Ken Scott River Run Gallery

GALLERIES: *Best metal sculptures*

Ken Scott calls himself an initiator and an innovator, and describes his art as finding ways to make something out of nothing. What gives him the greatest pleasure is "to make-do with what is at hand, to find the gold amongst the rubble." His works have evolved in several directions. He makes wall pieces out of steel, using oxygen/acetylene, thermal-arc cutting torches, welding processes and grinders. He does bronze castings, many of Oregon wildlife, as well as sculptured lighting and garden art. You may have already seen his work, such as the bronze sea lions sculpture at the Sea Lion Caves in Florence. Ken says metal sculpting is not a casual experience. Instead, "it is like working in a metal scrap yard with hard hats and torches, you're dodging sparks, and cooling quenched fingers all day long." To succeed you have to stay with it until both the artist and the project reaches a certain standard, a standard that grows as the artist's experience grows. Ken goes on to say that with metals, the sky is the limit. "And whether the design is geometric or organic, it's all possible." The Ken Scott River Run Gallery is available for wedding celebrations of up to 100 people, with catering offered. Visit his website for a glimpse, but nothing will replace the experience of seeing them in person, as well as enjoying Ken's hospitality and learning about his demanding and rewarding art form.

42837 McKenzie Highway, Leaburg OR
(541) 896-3774
www.kenscottsculptures.com

MCMINNVILLE

McMinnville, the seat of Yamhill County, is often compared to the wine regions of France and Germany. Most of wineries that surround the city have tasting rooms, and a tasting tour is a delightful experience. Many wineries have festivals, musical performances or picnics during the summer. McMinnville is home to Linfield College, one of the oldest liberal arts colleges in the West. The downtown area offers an almost park-like setting, with many restaurants and shops. Copies of a self-guided walking tour of downtown are available from local merchants. The Evergreen Air Venture Museum is home to the famous Spruce Goose and more than 60 historic aircraft and exhibits.

PLACES TO GO

- Aquatic Center
  138 NW Park Drive (503) 434-7309

- Discovery Meadows Community Park
  Cypress Lane

- Erratic Rock State Natural Site
  Oldsville Road

- Evergreen Aviation Museum
  500 NE Captain Michael King Smith Way

THINGS TO DO

March
- McMinnville Wine & Food Classic
  Linfield College (503) 472-4033

May
- UFO Festival
  Hotel Oregon (503) 472-8427

July
- Turkey Rama
  Downtown (503) 472-6196

August
- Yamhill County Fair
  Fairgrounds (503) 434-7524

October
- Art Harvest Studio Tour
  (503) 662-3661

November
- Wine Country Thanksgiving
  (503) 646-2985

Stellar's Jay at the Rotary Nature Preserve at Tice Woods
Photo by Stuart Seeger

Evergreen Aviation Museum

ATTRACTIONS: *Home of the Spruce Goose*

It flew only once, in 1947, but it remains one of the greatest legends in aviation history: Howard Hughes' H-4, famously nicknamed the Spruce Goose, is the largest wooden airplane ever built and the star attraction at the Evergreen Aviation Museum in McMinnville. The Museum was the dream of Captain Michael King Smith, a McMinnville native who served in the U.S. Air Force and the Oregon Air National Guard. He loved flying and envisioned a living museum that would educate the public about aviation and exhibit historic air craft. In 1992, Evergreen acquired the Spruce Goose from the Aero Club of Southern California, and after an epic journey from Long Beach to McMinnville by land and by sea, the legendary flying boat arrived safely at its new home. Sadly, Captain Smith died in an accident shortly afterwards, but his father, Delford Smith, founder of Evergreen International Aviation and co-founder of the Museum, persevered and made sure that the Museum would open, a tribute to his son's vision. Since its opening, the Museum has become one of the most popular attractions in Oregon, fulfilling its mission to inspire and educate, to promote aviation history, and to honor the service and sacrifice of America's veterans. In addition to the Spruce Goose, more than 50 aircraft are on display, ranging from a replica of the Wright Brothers' first successful airplane to the ultra-modern SR-71 Blackbird. Be sure to visit the Museum's Spruce Goose Café, and Rotors Wings and Things store. Admission is free for kids under five and for Evergreen Aviation Museum members.

500 NE Captain Michael King Smith Way, McMinnville OR
(503) 434-4180
www.sprucegoose.org

Oregon Wine Tasting Room & Bellevue Market

MARKETS: *Best wine market*

If you are on your way to the Oregon Coast and need a basket of wine and cheese to make the day memorable, the place to stop is the Oregon Wine Tasting Room & Bellevue Market, which is widely regarded as the number one wine-tasting room in the state. Wine tasting manager Patrick McElligott and market manager Theresa Putman invite you to sample tastings from all five Oregon wine appellations. McElligott is considered one of Oregon's true wine experts. In addition to wine, the market offers gourmet Oregon cheeses, chocolates from a local monastery, locally made bakery goods, fine candies, espresso, ice cream, jellies, sauces, shortbreads, and more. The building, with its high-beam ceilings and concrete floor, has been in existence since the 1920s. It served as a gas station, meat market and general store before being renovated for its present use. The management and staff are happy to put together food, wine, and other essentials for your picnic. The number-one red wine seller at the Oregon Wine Tasting Room & Bellevue Market is Oregon Pinot Noir. Pinot Gris is the number-one selling white wine, with Sparkling Muscat a close second. The fastest-growing grape for white wine is Viognier; Syrah has that distinction among the reds. At any one time, the tasting room features 70 to 80 or more Oregon wines, thereby earning it the recognition as Oregon's number one tasting room.

19690 SW Highway 18, McMinnville OR
(503) 843-3787 or (503) 843-2947
www.winesnw.com/oregonwinetastingroom.htm

RICKREALL

While tiny, bucolic Rickreall has only 57 residents, it does have a significant attraction—the Polk County Fairgrounds. The Polk County Museum is here, as well. Other attractions are located in the neighboring towns of Dallas and Monmouth. In particular, Monmouth is home to Western Oregon University.

PLACES TO GO

- Baskett Slough National Wildlife Refuge
  10995 Highway 22, Dallas

- Delbert Hunter Arboretum
  and Botanic Garden
  SW Park Street, Dallas
  (503) 623-7359

- Jensen Arctic Museum
  590 W Church Street, Monmouth
  (503) 838-8468

- Polk County Museum
  560 S Pacific Highway
  (503) 623-6251

THINGS TO DO

April
- Gem & Mineral Show
  Fairgrounds
  (888) 229-6818

July
- Polk County Fair
  Fairgrounds
  (888) 229-6818

November
- Holiday Fair
  Fairgrounds
  (888) 229-6818

- Craft Fair
  Fairgrounds
  (888) 229-6818

Cherry Hill Winery

WINERIES: *Best local winery*

Nestled in the Eola Hills of Oregon's Willamette Valley, Cherry Hill is an excellent boutique winery. They also provide an unforgettable opportunity to participate in the daily life and work of a Pacific Northwest winery via their viticultural dude ranch. They produce super-premium Pinot Noir, by hand, and you are invited to enjoy the rustic elegance of the unique wine camp that combines first-class wines and marvelous cuisine with a hands-on introduction to the life of a vineyard estate. The winemaker will guide you through tastings, and they'll invite you to "participate in the actual rhythms of the winery year, from tending spring vines to the drama of autumn's first crush." You'll gain a true understanding of winemaking, Oregon-style, from its roots in Willamette Valley soil right to the celebration of corking the finished vintage. Mike and Jan Sweeney have spent many years and much effort seeking outstanding Pinot Noirs in France, California, New Zealand and Oregon. In 1998, they purchased the undeveloped 150-acre vineyard that is now the home of Cherry Hill Winery, Vineyard and guest camp, and currently produce about 5,200 cases of estate-grown Pinot Noir each year. At Cherry Hill they also produce private-label wine for individuals, restaurants, distributors and other organizations, crafted from grapes grown in their vineyard or yours. For more information about private-label wines, refer to the Custom Crush section on their website. It's the best way to have your own wine without having your own winery.

7867 Crowley Road, Rickreall OR
(503) 623-7867
www.cherryhillwinery.com

PLACES TO GO

- A.C. Gilbert's Discovery Village
  116 Marion Street NE (503) 371-3631

- Antique Powerland Museum
  3995 NE Brooklake Road NE, Brooks

- Bush House Museum
  600 Mission Street SE (503) 363-4714

- Historic Deepwood Estate
  1116 Mission Street SE (503) 363-1825

- Martha Springer Botanical Garden
  900 State Street (503) 370-6532

- Minto-Brown Island Park
  River Road S

- Mission Mill Museum
  1313 Mill Street SE (503) 585-7012

- Reed Opera House
  189 Liberty Street NE

- Riverfront Park
  W of Front Street, downtown

- Salem's Riverfront Carousel
  101 Front Street NE (503) 540-0374

- Sarah Helmick State Recreation Site
  Helmick Road, Monmouth

- State Capitol Building
  900 Court Street NE (503) 986-1388

THINGS TO DO

January
- Oregon Wine & Food Festival
  State Fairgrounds (503) 390-7324

April
- Oregon Ag Fest
  State Fairgrounds (800) 874-7012

- Salem Film Festival
  www.salemfilmfestival.com

June
- World Beat Festival
  Riverfront Park (503) 581-2004

July
- The Bite of Salem
  Riverfront Park www.biteofsalem.com

- Salem Art Fair and Festival
  Bush's Pasture Park (503) 581-2228

August-September
- Oregon State Fair
  State Fairgrounds (503) 947-3247

SALEM

The easy pace of Oregon's capital makes Salem a place to come and relax. The variety of things to do makes it a favorite destination for the whole family. The State Capitol Building is a popular destination for visitors. It was built in 1938 mainly of Vermont marble, with a cylindrical tower topped by a burly gold-plated pioneer. Large marble sculptures flank the entrance. Inside the rotunda are paintings, murals and sculptures depicting important events in Oregon's history. Another attraction is the Mission Mill Village. This is a reconstructed woolen mill that has been turned into a living history museum. Guides in period costumes lead tours. Bush Pasture Park downtown is one of Salem's finest. The park contains the Bush House Museum and the Bush Barn Art Center. Downtown you can find the Reed Opera House, a historic structure that now hosts shopping and an art gallery in addition to theater. Salem is home to Willamette University, the first university in the West. Willamette opened the first law school in the Northwest in 1883. The Martha Springer gardens on the campus include an herb garden, alpine rock garden, butterfly garden and gardens dedicated to Oregon native environments.

Oregon Capitol Building
Photo by Chris Phan

Macleay Country Inn

ACCOMMODATIONS:
Best bed and breakfast

Dan and Jerry Miller, the fifth generation to work the Miller Brothers' Ranch, are the hosts of the Macleay Country Inn. The Inn is a great place to stop for lunch or dinner on your way to the Oregon Gardens and Silver Falls State Park. After eating there the first time, you'll likely decide the Inn is worth a trip all by itself. The Millers and general manager Chris Bryant invite you to try a selection from their newspaper-sized menu. For an hors d'oeuvre, try the Shrimp Cocktail, with your choice of cocktail sauce or the Inn's famous garlic sauce. If you're looking for a hamburger, try the Rancher. It's a half-pound of ground beef topped with cheddar cheese served on a French roll. Other signature sandwiches include the Big Reuben, with corned beef, 1,000 Island dressing, sauerkraut and swiss served on rye bread. The Macleay Club has ham, turkey, bacon and cheddar cheese on a sesame seed bun. For dinner, try the Prime Rib, stuffed with garlic and slow-cooked to perfection, or the 20-ounce Porterhouse or 12-ounce ribeye. If steak isn't what you want, try the Chicken Macleay with breaded chicken breast patties covered in Swiss cheese, lean ham and a secret sauce. Or the Spud Fish, cod with a crunchy potato coating. When you're ready for a beverage, the menu lists no fewer than 20 micro and specialty beers among the selections. Call ahead for reservations and avoid the wait.

8362 Macleay Road SE, Salem OR
(503) 362-4225
www.macleayinn.com

Salem Carousel

ATTRACTIONS: *Best carousel*

Who can resist the charm of a carousel, especially one with exquisitely carved and painted wooden horses and old-time organ music? When children see the carousel, they cannot wait to ride. Salem's Riverfront Carousel is located just blocks from the Capitol on the banks of the Willamette River. The carousel is a true community project. Everything about it was created by volunteers, including the fabulously decorated horses, which were carved out of basswood from Linden trees. During four-and-a-half years, 160 volunteer artisans spent more than 80,000 hours carving, sanding, and painting the horses, shields and ornamentation. The carousel, which opened in 2001, is enclosed. In the summer, glass doors slide open to admit the river breezes. In the winter, the building is heated and decorated for the holidays, and you can enjoy hot cocoa or ride with Santa. The carousel is also available for parties and events. In the gift shop, volunteers handcraft ornaments, toys and other wooden treasures. Sales from the gift shop help support the carousel, which is non-profit. The carousel was the dream of Hazel Patton, who discovered a similar community carousel in Missoula, Montana. Helen knew that a project of this type would work in Salem. Today, more than a quarter of a million people ride the carousel every year.

101 Front Street NE, Salem OR
(503) 540-0374
www.salemcarousel.org

Historic Deepwood Estate

ATTRACTIONS:

City of Salem park and living museum

Life goes on at Historic Deepwood Estate. Once a home to three generations of Salem residents, it remains alive as an attraction for guests of all ages. The House at the heart of the estate has been described as a work of art. Built in 1894, the striking Salem landmark is one of Oregon's most ornate examples of Queen Anne architecture. It is a grand design with elaborate stained glass windows by Povey Brothers, golden oak woodwork, and a roof line of multiple gables and peaks. A City of Salem Museum and Park, it is managed by the Friends of Deepwood with the help of a multitude of dedicated volunteers. More artistry pleases the eye in the garden rooms, with a year round wealth of color and greenery. The outdoor rooms include an English tea house garden and an exquisite boxwood garden, connected by hedge-lined corridors that lead under flower covered arches and past ornamental gates and fences. There are 5.5 acres of gardens, nature trails, the original carriage house, conservatory and two gazebos, one from the 1905 Lewis and Clark Centennial Exposition. Deepwood Estate is a gathering place for tours, events, classes and Victorian Teas. The craftsmanship and detail of the House are remarkable, the programs are inviting and fun. A wonderful place to visit, Historic Deepwood Estate could be the perfect place for your catered tea, family celebration or business meeting. The well maintained gardens are a lovely setting for many weddings during the summer. The gardens are open from dawn to dusk, and guided house tours are offered year round.

1116 Mission Street SE, Salem OR
(503) 363-1825
www.deepwood.org

Photos by Ron Cooper

SHERIDAN

Sheridan is named in honor of the Civil War general Philip Henry Sheridan. Sheridan was posted to Yamhill County in the latter half of the 1850s, and was involved in the Yakima and Rogue River wars with Indian tribes. Sheridan is a few miles east of the Grande Ronde Indian Reservation. Native Americans from throughout western Oregon were forced to move here—the Umpqua, Molalla, Rogue River, Kalapuya and Chasta tribes. Fort Yamhill was built to separate them from the European settlers. Today, the Confederated Tribes of Grand Ronde run the most popular casino in Oregon, Spirit Mountain Casino.

PLACES TO GO

- Fort Yamhill State Heritage Area
  State Route 22

- Grand Ronde Natural Resources (hiking and camping)
  47010 SW Hebo Road
  (503) 879-2424

- Spirit Mountain Casino
  27190 SW Salmon River Highway,
  Grand Ronde
  (800) 760-7977

- Veteran's Memorial
  Grand Ronde

THINGS TO DO

June
- Sheridan Days
  (503) 843-7656

August
- Grand Ronde Confederated Tribes' Powwow
  Grand Ronde
  (800) 422-0232

The Lawrence Gallery
GALLERIES: *Best fine arts gallery*

The Lawrence Gallery began 28 years ago in what had been the general store in Sheridan (a spot with a checkered history during Prohibition, when it served as a brothel before becoming a community hall). What began as an artists' enterprise has grown into three exceptional locations. Gary and Signe Lawrence are the owners, and over the years they have expanded the Gallery's offering to include paintings, glass, jewelry and sculpture, including their own artwork. According to *Artisan NW*, the Lawrence Gallery is a "nationally known, highly respected" gallery with a fine service record among collectors around the world. They carry mostly Northwest artists in an inviting mix of works, but also feature world-famous artists such as Picasso, Rembrandt, Chagall and Miro. Their three locations are in Portland's Pearl District, on the Oregon Coast in The Shops at Salishan, and the original gallery in the heart of wine country between McMinnville and Sheridan, which handle more than $8 million worth of art. In addition to the high caliber art work, the Sheridan gallery features an outstanding eatery called the Fresh Palate Cafe, an outstanding atelier eatery, and Jebidiah's Private Reserve, a wine shop and tasting bar located inside Lawrence Gallery. Spend an afternoon dining on enticing cuisine, tasting award-winning wines and viewing an always impressive display of artwork from more than 100 nationally recognized artists. Their website gives a glimpse of the artists and their artwork and features the galleries' new events and shows.

Hwy 18, Sheridan OR
(800) 894-4278
903 NW Davis Street, Portland OR
(503) 228-1776
The Shops at Salishan, Hwy 101,
Gleneden Beach OR
(800) 764-2318
www.lawrencegallery.net

SILVERTON

Silverton is the gateway to Silver Falls State Park, Oregon's largest. The town is also home to the Oregon Garden, an 80-acre botanical park. Silverton is surrounded by flower farms, which together with the Oregon Garden make this locale a horticultural paradise. Each summer, Silvertonians fête their most famous citizen in the Homer Davenport Days celebration and faire. At the end of the 19th century, Davenport was the world's most famous political cartoonist, drawing for the Hearst newspapers. He was a loyal son of Silverton and was also involved in bringing the first Arabian horses to America. Silverton has a notable farmers market where local growers and artisans sell their wares.

PLACES TO GO

- Coolidge & McClaine Park
  300 Coolidge Street

- Mount Angel Abbey
  One Abbey Drive, St. Benedict
  (503) 845-3030

- The Oregon Garden
  879 W Main Street (877) 674-2733

- Silver Falls State Park
  20024 Silver Falls Highway SE

THINGS TO DO

April
- Celebration of Cultures Day
  Community Center (503) 873-0405

- Oregon Craft Brewfest Blooms & Brews
  The Oregon Garden (877) 674-2733

May
- Pet Parade
  (503) 873-5615

July
- Old Stuff on Main Street Antique Fair
  (503) 873-8918

August
- Homer Davenport Days
  (503) 873-5615

- Silverton Fine Arts Festival
  (503) 873-2480

The Oregon Garden
ATTRACTIONS: *Best gardens*

The Oregon Garden in Silverton features 20 specialty gardens and thousands of wonders. You'll find waterfalls, quiet ponds, fountains, and beautiful vistas. Its display of dwarf and miniature conifers is one of the largest collections in the country. Visits every few weeks, or even every few days, can bring wildly varied discoveries. New blooms and emerging plants abound, and birds and frogs provide background music. Migrating birds make each day at The Garden special. Located throughout the Garden, one-of-a-kind works of art blend in with The Garden's living tapestry. You'll want to visit the Signature Oak, an Oregon Heritage Tree more than 400 years old. Then visit the Rediscovery Forest, a working tree farm that demonstrates forest management practices. Learn how the area's treated water is used in an innovative way to create a thriving wetland habitat for a variety of wildlife and plants. While there, tour the Gordon House, designed by legendary architect Frank Lloyd Wright. It is the only Wright-designed home in the Pacific Northwest that is open to the public. You can wander around the grounds on your own or take a tram tour. If you're there in summer, look into the Summer Concert Series. A few of the sites you'll want to experience at The Garden include The Axis Fountain, with a beautiful fountain of Montana stone and a cascading wall of water; Pet Friendly Garden; and the Sensory Garden, a therapeutic garden that features remarkable scents and textures that stretch the imagination. The Sensory Garden includes an in-ground compass, a large wooden trellis of Port Orford cedar, vertical wall gardens and a rain curtain 20 feet long and eight feet high. The Oregon Garden has facilities for meetings, banquets and receptions.

879 W Main Street, Silverton OR (503) 874-8100 or (877) 674-2733 *www.oregongarden.org*

SUBLIMITY

Sublimity, in the foothills of the Cascade Range, is the home of Silver Falls State Park, one of Oregon's most popular. It is a twin city with Stayton, located on the other side of State Route 22. This state highway leads up into the Cascades, to the Santiam State Forest, past Opal Creek and Detroit Lake. As late as 1840, the land on which Sublimity sits was an Indian village and trading post. By the time of the Civil War, the city was one of the largest in the state. It suffered a population collapse after the war, but obtained a rebirth in the 1870 when the area was colonized by German Catholic immigrants. Sublimity became a major center of the Oregon Catholic Church. In 1926, a Sublimity resident discovered the thornless blackberry, today the country's most popular. It was later hybridized into the aromatic and intensely flavorful Marionberry. By the mid-20th century, Sublimity was a center of grass seed production, and also of Christmas trees.

PLACES TO GO

- Silver Falls State Park
  20024 Silver Falls Highway SE

THINGS TO DO

June
- State Parks Day
  (503) 873-8681 ext. 25

July
- Historic Al Faussett Days
  Silver Falls State Park
  (503) 873-8681 ext. 25

September
- Sublimity Harvest Festival
  (503) 769-3579

- Oregon Covered Bridge Festival
  Stayton (541) 752-8269

October
- Harvest Fest
  (503) 873-8681 ext. 25

December
- Holiday Festival
  (503) 873-8681 ext. 25

Silver Falls State Park
ATTRACTIONS: *Best area park*

Would you like to stand behind a 177-foot waterfall and feel the misty, crisp spray? Rent a horse and ride on 22 miles of trails? Watch birds, chipmunks and rabbits beneath Douglas firs? These are a few of the things you can do at Silver Falls State Park. Silver Falls is the largest and most popular state park in Oregon, encompassing more than 13 square miles. The park's most famous feature is the Trail of Ten Falls, a seven-mile hike along the forks of Silver Creek that descends to a forest floor covered with ferns, mosses and wildflowers. Branch trails lead behind four of the falls. Day trippers can hike, picnic or swim in Silver Creek. South Falls Lodge contains displays on the park's history, wildlife and geology. Overnight campers can tent, rent a rustic log cabin or roll in with their RVs. Groups can use sites designed for RVs or tents, or rent either the New or Old Ranch buildings that sleep up to 75. Silver Falls is especially welcoming to horse folk. The Howard Creek Horse Camp provides campsites and corrals that can accommodate 64 people and 32 horses. You can truck your horse in or ride it into the park using a special equestrian entrance. The Silver Falls Conference Center offers two meeting halls, four group lodges and 10 cabins. Much of the park is open all year. The horse camp, group areas and the Old Ranch are closed from November 1 to March 31. Pay a visit Silver Falls State Park, the most diverse of all the Oregon state parks.

20024 Silver Falls Highway SE, Sublimity OR
(503) 873-8681 ext. 23
www.oregonstateparks.org /park_211.php

TURNER

Turner is the good neighbor town. Its population has grown rapidly in recent years, as Salem residents look for a pleasant place to live, but it still has fewer than 2,000 residents. Like so many Western towns, Turner began as a rail stop. As the Oregon & California Railroad built southward it sent a crew to erect a station and warehouse a few miles south of Salem and name it Marion. The crew proceeded to build the station in the wrong place. The town of Marion exists today, 6.5 miles south of where it was supposed to be. The railroad built a second station at the correct location and named it Turner, after Henry and Julia Turner, local landowners and pioneers since 1852. Turner is a town for family fun. Attractions include the Enchanted Forest, a legendary Oregon stop. This 20-acre outdoor theme park, nestled in a forested setting, has been family owned and operated since opening its doors in 1971. It offers kiddy rides and a storybook lane for the youngest, and underground crawls, a haunted house and a Big Timber Log Ride for older kids.

PLACES TO GO

- Enchanted Forest
  8462 Enchanted Way SE
  (503) 363-3060

- Frey's Dahlias
  12054 Brick Rd. SE
  (503) 743-3910

- Thrill-Ville USA
  8372 Enchanted Way SE
  (503) 363-4095

THINGS TO DO

March
- Oregon's Wine, Cheese and Pear Jubilee
  Willamette Valley Vineyards
  (800) 344-9463

Enchanted Forest
ATTRACTIONS: *Best family attraction*

If you're looking for fun and excitement in Oregon, make Enchanted Forest your first stop. From charming storybook scenes to the biggest log flume ride in the Northwest, there's something for everyone in your family. Enchanted Forest began as the dream of Roger Tofte. Roger was raising his young family in the Salem area in the 1960s while working as an artist and draftsman for the Oregon State Highway Department. He became frustrated at the lack of family-oriented attractions in the region and decided to do something about it. He acquired 20 acres of land near Interstate 5 and began building the park in 1964, "one bag of cement at a time." In 1971, the park was finally opened, becoming a hit with local residents and travelers almost immediately. Success allowed the Toftes to expand the park, adding attractions like the Tofteville Western Village, the Comedy Theater, and the Ice Mountain Bobsled Roller Coaster. Expansion continued in the 1990s with the building of the Old Europe Village and the Big Timber Log Ride. New attractions are still being added. Since the park was inspired by Roger's children, it is fitting that several of them now help Roger run it. His daughter Susan is the artistic director, Mary is the chief financial officer, and his son Ken is head of attractions development and ride maintenance. Susan choreographed and composed the music for the dazzling Fantasy Fountains Water-Light Show and Ken designed and built the animatronic figures in the Old Europe Village. Their combined love and dedication makes Enchanted Forest a true family affair.

8462 Enchanted Way SE, Turner OR
(503) 363-3060 or (503) 371-4242
www.enchantedforest.com

Willamette Valley Vineyards
WINERIES: *One of America's great Pinot Noir producers*

Jim Bernau's simple goal for his Willamette Valley Vineyards is to make, "the highest quality Burgundian varietals possible from the Willamette Valley." Jim and his wife, Cathy, purchased the land in 1983 and, after clearing away an old pioneer plum orchard, they planted Pinot Noir (Pommard and Wadenswil clones), Chardonnay (Dijon and Espiguette) and Pinot Gris. Eventually they were able to talk their neighbors into selling the contiguous parcels of land until they had a winery site and 50 acres of vineyard. This is one of the region's leading wineries and has earned the title of One of America's Great Pinot Noir Producers from *Wine Enthusiast* magazine. Architect Saul Zaik designed a uniquely *Oregon* structure to represent this young but promising vineyard. "As native Oregonians, we treasure our environment and use sustainable practices in growing and vinifying our winegrapes," Jim says. Talented artisans, like winemaker Forrest Klaffke, have invested themselves in making the best wine Mother Nature could give them. Their approach is to grow the highest quality fruit using careful canopy management to achieve wines that are truly expressive of the varietal and the place they are grown. Since they ferment and barrel each lot separately (sometimes as little as two barrels), they can save the best barrels for single vineyard bottlings and Signature Cuvée. Visit the Bernaus and celebrate the best of the state at Willamette Valley Vineyards.

8800 Enchanted Way SE, Turner OR
(503) 588-9463 or (800) 344-9463
www.wvv.com

WOODBURN

Surrounded by farmland, Woodburn celebrates the arrival of spring with the annual Tulip Festival. Themes include gardening, kids and Dutch Day. Visitors flock to the Wooden Shoe Bulb Company to view the acres of spectacular color. In 1863, Jesse Holland Settlemier settled here, built a comfortable home and established the Woodburn Nursery Company. The railroad came through in 1871, turning Woodburn into a social and economic center. Modern Woodburn has a rich cultural base with large populations of Anglos, Hispanics and Russians. Woodburn Company Stores is one of Oregon's largest outlet malls and one of the state's most popular destinations. This ultimate outlet mall features many name brand stores.

PLACES TO GO

- Jesse Settlemier House
  355 Settlemier Street (503) 982-1897

- Legion Park
  1365 Park Avenue

- Settlemier Park
  400 S Settlemier Avenue

- Woodburn Dragstrip
  7730 Highway 219 (503) 982-4461

- Woodburn Memorial Aquatic Center
  190 Oak Street

THINGS TO DO

March-April
- Wooden Shoe Tulip Festival
  Wooden Shoe Bulb Company
  (800) 711-2006

July
- Hubbard Hop Festival
  Hubbard (503) 982-5448

August
- Fiesta Mexicana
  (503) 981-6248

September
- Mexican Independence Day
  Settlemeir Park (503) 980-2485

OGA Golf Course Inc.

RECREATION: *Audubon Cooperative Sanctuary and a Top 10 course*

The OGA Golf Course, a project of the Oregon Golf Association (OGA), is one of the most impressive courses in the region. *Golf Digest* awarded the course four and a half stars in 2004 and 2005 editions featuring Best Places to Play. In 1991, when the OGA commissioned a study to determine whether it could build an 18-hole public golf course, the financial conclusions looked grim. In 1992, a private partner stepped in with an astonishing offer. Tukwila Partners Development Corporation offered to donate 179 acres of farmland, located next to its Woodburn real estate development, for a golf course. The partnership between the OGA and Tukwila led to an 18-hole course, a natural grass driving range and a 14,000-square-foot clubhouse. The clubhouse, which opened in 2000, includes a pro shop and the Orchards Grille. This restaurant provides dining and socializing in an atmosphere of subdued elegance. OGA also has its headquarters on these lush grounds. The OGA Golf Course offers play to all golfers with no tee-time restrictions. The facility was named one of the top 10 affordable golf courses in the United States by *Golf Digest* in 1996 and in 2004 was certified as an Audubon Cooperative Sanctuary. If you love golf, you will love the OGA Golf Course.

2850 Hazelnut Drive, Woodburn OR
(503) 981-6105
www.ogagolfcourse.com

YAMHILL

Pinot Noir is king in today's Yamhill, a small town surrounded by the gorgeous Yamhill-Carlton District AVA. Yamhill and Carlton are close neighbors, and share a school district as well as a wine appellation. You can easily tour them together. The name Yamhill, shared with the river and the county, is derived from Che-am-il, an Indian name for the bald hills northeast of the town of Lafayette. In the early years, the place then known as North Yamhill was just a store along the stage road to Tillamook. With the coming of the Southern Pacific Railroad, North Yamhill became the starting point of the Tillamook Trail to the coast. Entrepreneurs built a hotel, a livery barn and other businesses, and the government opened a post office. The oldest house in town, built in 1845 for Mrs. James Burton, still stands. In 1891, area farmers formed a co-operative creamery and the townsfolk incorporated the town. In 1894, the town council passed an ordinance allowing dairy cows to run free in the streets. Other animals were to be confined. The cows lost this freedom in 1907, to the relief of many.

THINGS TO DO

July
- Yamhill Derby Day
  (503) 662-3511

- Yamhill Valley Lavender Festival
  (503) 662-4488

Flying M Ranch
ACCOMMODATIONS: *Best Western adventure*

The site of the Flying M Ranch was once the first Traveler's Home for stagecoach passengers bound for the Oregon Coast and the City of Tillamook. In fact, the road you take to the ranch today is almost the same one the stagecoach took 145 years ago. The Flying M Ranch offers accommodations for a variety of purposes from pure pleasure to productive business meetings in their rustic and charming facilities along the North Yamhill River. Hosts Bryce and Barbara Mitchell foster a comfortable and exciting atmosphere, (or relaxing, if you prefer), for Ranch visitors. This is a family-oriented vacation spot and guests of all ages will feel welcome here. The spectacular log Lodge houses the conference center, dining room and the Sawtooth Lounge. Nestled in the woods, a short distance from the Lodge, are the cabins and a 24-unit bunkhouse motel with Western theme rooms. Each room has two queen beds and a private bath, but there are no telephones or televisions to intrude on the country peace and quiet. Separate from the Lodge, the Motel has a deck that overlooks the Yamhill River on one side and the mountains on the other. The private cabins have intriguing Western-themed names such as Wortman, Wrangler, Honeymoon, Mountain House, Royal, Hunters Hideaway and Rustlers Roost. The Flying M Ranch is off the beaten path, midway between Portland and the Oregon Coast. Your visit will be filled with fun. In the main Lodge, they offer fireside checkers and other activities for the younger visitors. There are outside volleyball nets, tennis courts, horseshoe pits, trails and a swimming pond the size of a city block. The Mitchells invite you to come relax in the sun, participate in the game of your choice or go for a horseback ride.

23029 NW Flying M Rd, Yamhill OR
503) 662-3222 or (503) 662-3611
www.flying-m-ranch.com

WillaKenzie Estate
WINERIES: *Best Gamay Noir*

A successful combination of technology and tradition, the WillaKenzie Estate in Oregon's Willamette Valley is named for the distinctive soil on which the vineyards are planted. Proprietor Bernard Lacroute has a simple goal, to make better wines. Judging from the many favorable reviews in wine publications, his methods work very well. WillaKenzie Estate is renowned for world-class wines from estate grapes grown without synthetic chemicals. *The Oregonian* called the WillaKenzie Gamay Noir "superb," going on to say that it is "comparable to some of the best bottlings in Beaujolais and far superior to the great majority of them." Technology is used selectively here. Herbicides are avoided to preserve native plants that grow between the rows. This practice not only acknowledges that the vineyards are part of a larger ecosystem, but also helps to reduce soil erosion. In line with Lacroute's philosophy, pumps are never used to move either the grapes or the wine through the winery. Using gravity to do the job has been validated by hundreds of years in the vineyards of Burgundy and continues to provide superior results here in Oregon.

19143 NE Laughlin Road, Yamhill OR
(503) 662-3280 or (888) 953-9463
www.willakenzie.com

Umpqua Valley

CANYONVILLE

In the 19th century, travel between California and the Willamette Valley was difficult, to say the least. One important route passed over a series of mountain passes between the Rogue River and Umpqua valleys and was called the Scott-Applegate Trail. On the northern end, the trail dropped 1,235 feet from Canyon Creek Pass to the Umpqua River. Here, settlers established a town to assist travelers. The town was at the mouth of a canyon, and the settlers appropriately named it Canyonville. Today, I-5 follows the line of the Applegate Trail, and tourists can easily see how difficult the trip must have been before modern engineers armed with high explosives and bulldozers carved a passageway for the interstate. Stopping at Canyonville has ceased to be a requirement for exhausted travelers. Today, it is a luxury. In an area of great natural beauty, the Cow Creek Band of Umpqua Indians has erected the Seven Feathers Resort, a casino and convention center that draws visitors from up and down the West Coast. Many of the nation's leading entertainment acts visit Seven Feathers. The resort is named after the seven families of the Cow Creek Band. The fishing is good near Canyonville too. The South Umpqua River is one of the top smallmouth bass streams in the western United States.

PLACES TO GO

- Canyonville County Park
  Pickett Road

- Chief Miwaleta Park
  Galesville Reservoir

- Pioneer-Indian Museum
  I-5, Exit 98 (541) 839-4845

THINGS TO DO

June
- Southern Oregon Regional Chili Cook Off
  Seven Feathers Resort (800) 444-9584

August
- Pioneer Days
  Pioneer Park (800) 444-9584

November-December
- Festival of Trees
  Seven Feathers Resort (800) 444-9584

South Umpqua River
Photo by Donna Lindley

Seven Feathers Hotel & Casino Resort

RECREATION: *Best casino and hotel*

With year round entertainment and Las Vegas-style gaming, Seven Feathers Hotel & Casino Resort is the perfect place to take the entire family. There are fabulous stage shows, professional boxing events, famous performers and plenty of food choices to fit every taste. Seven Feathers houses Kathy's Canyon Café and the Cow Creek Restaurant, which both offer Atkins Diet choices on their menu. You'll find a great sports bar near the gaming area, a modest convention center and the best staff and service anywhere. Seven Feathers has a huge video arcade, an ice cream store, gift shops, 190-plus RV spaces with hook ups, and there's even a smoke-free gaming area. Within a short distance of the Casino there is golfing, excellent fishing areas and many other outdoor activities. Seven Feathers Hotel & Casino Resort is the second largest employer in Douglas County and is active in giving back to the community. Seven Feathers is responsible for creating better health and human services opportunities locally, and they are actively involved in creating more career choices for local youth. Seven Feathers is a place you'll come to spend a weekend and end up staying a week. This destination resort has everything you'd ever need to have a great time.

146 Chief Miwaleta Lane, Canyonville OR
(800) 548-8461
http://sevenfeathers.com

Umpqua River

ROSEBURG

Roseburg is the seat of Douglas County. The Umpqua River forks into the North and South just west of town, and both forks are famous among fishermen. Trout, salmon and bass run in the North Umpqua, which is also one of the world's only rivers with a native run of summer steelhead. The traditional industries in the area have been agriculture and lumber, and Roseburg Forest Products is still Roseburg's largest employer. In the 1990s wine grapes overtook timber as the leading crop. The Oregon wine industry began in the Umpqua Valley, and the region has its own appellation. In the city, Mount Nebo looms over downtown from the west. Stewart Park, on the other side of Mount Nebo, provides a wide range of cultural and sports activities. Downtown Roseburg features two popular micro-breweries along with art galleries, antique shops and other specialty stores. Murals on downtown walls portray Roseburg's history. The city was named for Aaron Rose, who settled here in 1851 and managed a tavern.

PLACES TO GO

- Douglas County Museum of History and Natural History
  I-5, Exit 123 (541) 957-7007

- Douglas County Speedway
  2110 SW Frear Street (541) 957-7010

- John P. Amacher County Park
  I-5, Exit 129

- River Forks Park and Discovery Garden
  River Forks Park Road

- Riverfront Park
  NW Hicks Street

- Stewart Park
  NW Stewart Park Drive

- Winchester Dam Fish Ladder
  I-5, Exit 129

THINGS TO DO

August
- Douglas County Fair
  Fairgrounds (541) 957-7010

September
- Harvest Festival & Grape Stomp
  (541) 672-6080

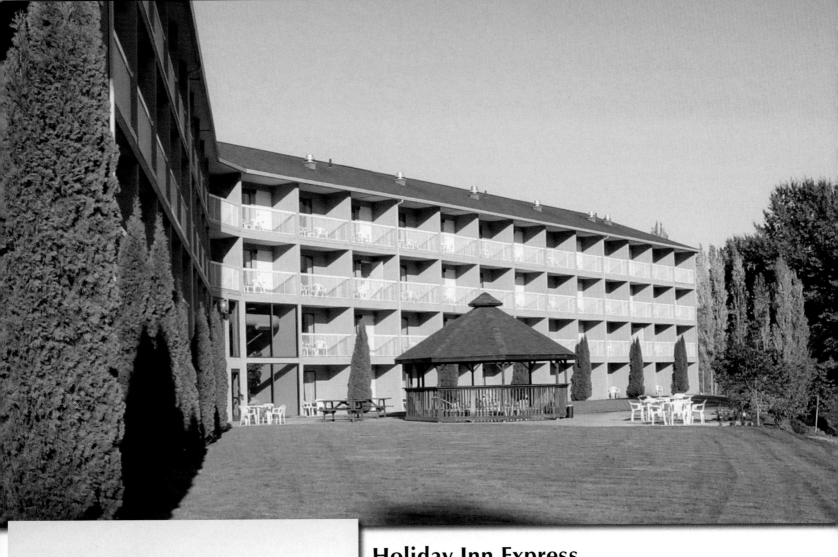

Holiday Inn Express
ACCOMMODATIONS: *Best hotel*

Whether you're in Roseburg to work or play, you won't want to leave the Holiday Inn Express after just one night. Take the time to breathe in the clean air and savor the beauty of the South Umpqua River from your balcony. With its strategic location at the riverside gazebo, the spa is a perfect setting for a romantic evening or to unwind from a busy day. If you're looking for entertainment, Wildlife Safari, golfing and gaming are all within a few minutes of the Holiday Inn Express. There are also countless scenic byways, excellent fishing spots and historic, covered bridges in the surrounding area. If you're in the mood for an afternoon of shopping, you'll enjoy browsing the shops located in an historic church building downtown and lunching at a nearby restaurant. Whatever your reason for stopping in Roseburg, the Holiday Inn Express will fill the bill.

375 W. Harvard Boulevard, Roseburg OR
(541) 673-7517 or (800) 898-7666
www.rogueweb.com/holidayroseburg

Kruse Farms
GARDENS, PLANTS & FLOWERS: *Best produce*

In 1923, Don Kruse's father, Bert Kruse, started with 15 acres of logged-off land. After many years of honest dealings within the community, Kruse Farms became known for growing excellent produce and for being active participants in their community. Your first impression of Don Kruse is that he is a salt-of-the-earth, true Oregonian through and through. His knowledge and skills for farming were passed down the old-fashioned way, by his father. Don and his wife, Sally, live close to the soil. They take great pride in the family's four-generation history of growing the best possible fruits and vegetables. The Kruse family serves Roseburg with their fine produce, and Don's sister is involved, too. She is the head baker for Kruse Farms Bakery. It is there that you can sample some of the most delectable homemade pies. Kruse Farms prepares and ships baskets all over the world. You can select from candies, preserves, syrups, dried fruits, nuts, pastas and mixes for your personalized basket. In the fall, there is a seemingly endless pumpkin patch for the younger members of the community. Don has always found positive ways to be involved in his community, including serving many years on the Roseburg School Board. Don's son, Jeff, followed his example of community service when he was elected to the Oregon Legislature.

532 Melrose Road, Roseburg OR
(541) 672-5697

Gilberto's Mexican Restaurant
RESTAURANTS & CAFÉS:
Best authentic Mexican cuisine

If you love authentic Mexican food, this is it. Owner Gilberto Duarte doesn't just combine exotic and traditional family recipes, he also brings four generations of the Duarte family together to create them for you. You'll probably never see the special copper pots they use to prepare your meal and you won't ever know all of the secret ingredients in Gilberto's great Aunt's mole sauce, but you will probably want to ask for more. The tortillas are always made from scratch and are freshly grilled. The nachos are the best in the western hemisphere and even the rice and refried beans taste superior. Gilberto's extensive lunch and dinner menus include appetizers, low-carb meals, chicken steaks and seafood, all at affordable prices. Even if you're from Mexico City you'll admire the quality, tradition and love that the Duarte family pours into every dish they prepare.

1347 NE Stephens, Roseburg OR
(541) 673-4973

Melrose Vineyards
WINERIES: *Best vineyards*

When planning a wedding, reception, or corporate social event, either indoors or out, consider the spacious, pristine grounds of Melrose Vineyards in Roseburg. Whatever you desire, the catering staff offers some of the best culinary delights to be found anywhere. Pair the great cuisine with their award-winning wines, and the result is an unforgettable event. The vineyard is located on 100 acres of a former river bank terrace of the South Umpqua River, on an early French settlement. The spectacular views are a local favorite, as is the large tasting room housed in a beautifully restored 100-year-old barn, complete with a gift boutique and friendly staff. Be sure to try the Pinot Gris and Pinot Noir, Oregon favorites. The tasting room is only five minutes off I-5 and open daily from 11 am to 5 pm. To find them, take Exit 125 and travel west on Garden Valley Boulevard to Melrose Road. Turn left on Melrose and right on Melqua, by the Melrose Store.

885 Melqua Road, Roseburg OR
(541) 672-6080
www.melrosevineyards.com

WINSTON

In 1972, the Wildlife Safari game preserve opened just outside the Winston city limits. Wildlife Safari is a 600-acre drive-through facility dedicated to public education and the preservation of endangered species. The park, which serves more than 150,000 visitors each year, is the most important institution in the Winston-Dillard area. Recognizing this fact, in 1986 the Winston-Dillard Chamber of Commerce commissioned a statue of a cheetah. It was modeled after Khayam, Wildlife Safari's beloved goodwill ambassador. Junction City sculptor Dennis Jones created the bronze statue, which sits in Winston's downtown triangle. It is realistic enough to have fooled dogs. Up until World War II, the little farming center of Dillard predominated in this district. Winston then came into its own to serve several lumber mills. It incorporated in 1953 as Coos Junction and adopted its current name two years later. The Winstons were a pioneer family who gave their name to an early post office in the area.

PLACES TO GO

- Ben Irving County Park
  1363 Berry Creek Road, Tenmile

- Riverbend Park
  Thompson Boulevard

THINGS TO DO

July
- Robert Trnka Gathering of Artists
  Winston Community Park
  (800) 444-9584

August
- Oregon State Bluegrass Festival
  Riverbend Park
  www.oregonstatebluegrassfestival.com

- Celtic Highland Games
  Riverbend Park (877) 752-2360

September
- Melon Festival
  Riverbend Park

Wildlife Safari

ATTRACTIONS:

Only drive-thru wild animal park in the Northwest

Located on 600 acres in beautiful Southern Oregon, Wildlife Safari is home to animals from around the world. People of all ages can see more than 500 native and exotic animals from the comfort of their vehicle as they drive through Africa, Asia and the Americas. With endless photo opportunities, you will view ostriches, rhinos, lions, giraffes, bears, llamas, wild horses, Tibetan yaks, tigers and camels in three large, naturalistic habitats where the animals co-exist. At the end of your safari, don't miss the signature animal, the cheetah. The park is world renowned for its cheetah breeding program. Amazingly, 143 cheetahs have been born at Wildlife Safari since 1973. After your safari, park your car and tour the Safari Village on foot as you explore the gardens and animal exhibits. The Savannah Snack Shack, daily animal programs, train rides and elephant rides are available on a seasonal basis. Eat lunch and enjoy the spectacular view at the White Rhino Restaurant. Search for the perfect souvenir in the Casbah Gift Shop, featuring gifts from around the world and from local artists. Call or visit their website to learn about the Get Inside events, such as feeding a giraffe or lion, bathing an elephant, walking with cheetahs or spending a half-day with a ranger. Wildlife Safari is a non-profit organization dedicated to the conservation, education and research of endangered animals. The park is open every day of the year except Christmas. The Wildlife Safari park is south of Roseburg off I-5, exit 119.

1790 Safari Road, Winston OR
(541) 679-6761
www.wildlifesafari.org

Southern Oregon

Rogue River in Autumn
Photo by Nancy McClain

APPLEGATE

The Applegate River begins at Applegate Lake high in the Rogue River National Forest, close to the California border. It then tumbles north to Cantrall-Buckley Park and the small town of Ruch. Here, it turns west. The Applegate community consists of the valley from Rauch west to Murphy, along State Route 238. The Applegate Valley is seriously rural, a desirable retreat for Southern Oregonians who enjoy privacy and peace. Among the local agricultural products, wine grapes hold pride of place. In 2001, the Applegate Valley AVA became the sixth official wine appellation in Oregon. Applegate is the home of the Applegate Partnership, a group of local citizens and other stakeholders dedicated to sustainable natural resource management. The upper Applegate, from Ruch up to the lake, is a recreational area of great natural beauty. You can find many hiking trails in the area, one of which leads to the Sasquatch Trap, used until 1970 in a futile attempt to capture the legendary Big Foot. At Applegate Lake, the clear blue waters reflect the forested slopes and often snow-covered peaks of the Siskiyou Mountains.

PLACES TO GO

• Applegate Lake
Upper Applegate Road

• Applegate Valley Wine Trail
(541) 846-9900

• Cantrall-Buckley Park
Hamilton Road

• McKee Bridge Day Use Area
6914 Upper Applegate Road

THINGS TO DO

May
• Buncom Day
www.buncom.org

August
• Applegate Valley Bullfrog Festival
Ruch (541) 899-1113

Applegate River Lodge

ACCOMMODATIONS:

Best accommodations and gourmet food

The Applegate River Lodge is the perfect place for a romantic getaway or family event in Southern Oregon. The Applegate River Lodge consists of seven large rooms, each with its own unique theme, such as the rustic Gold Miner's Cabin and an elegant Honeymoon Suite. All rooms have Jacuzzi tubs big enough for two and private decks overlooking the Applegate River. The lodge has no telephones or televisions, so guests can relax and enjoy the beautiful setting and impeccable service. The focal point of the lodge's Great Room is a beautiful river rock fireplace where guests congregate on cold evenings. The sitting area is a wonderful spot to relax with a great book or play a board game with friends and family. Continental breakfast is served here. The Applegate Restaurant is located next to the Lodge. This casually elegant restaurant offers gourmet dinners that are unforgettable. Guests can sit on the deck during summer and listen to the rushing water of the Applegate River as they sip wine from one of the local wineries. Listen to live music on the deck on Wednesday and Sunday evenings during the summer months and on Wednesdays during winter. The Applegate River Lodge is a popular wedding destination. The beautiful grounds and stunning river backdrop, coupled with delicious food and service, make this an ideal spot to start a new life together. Couples can rent the entire Lodge for their weddings. Owners Joanna and Richard Davis opened the restaurant in 1992. The Lodge was completed in 1997. The Lodge is located between Medford and Grants Pass on Highway 238.

15100 Highway 238, Applegate OR
(541) 846-6690
www.applegateriverlodge.com

PLACES TO GO

- Ashland Food Coop
  237 N 1st Street (541) 482-2237

- Emigrant Lake County Recreation Area
  5505 State Route 66

- Howard Prairie Lake Recreation Area
  Hyatt Prairie Road

- Lake Hyatt
  Hyatt Prairie Road

- Lithia Park
  Winburn Way

- North Mountain Park
  620 N Mountain Avenue

- Oregon Shakespeare Festival
  15 S Pioneer Street (541) 482-4331

- Schneider Museum of Art
  Siskiyou Boulevard and Indiana Street

- ScienceWorks Hands On Museum
  1500 E Main Street (541) 482-6767

- Tub Springs State Wayside
  State Route 66

THINGS TO DO

January
- Rogue Valley Blues Festival
  Ashland Armory (541) 535-3562.

March
- Oregon Chocolate Festival
  Ashland Springs Hotel (541) 488-1700

April
- A Taste of Ashland
  (877) 752-6278

- Ashland Independent Film Festival
  Varsity Theatre (541) 488-3823

July
- 4th of July Parade and Celebration
  (541) 482-3486

- Kids Day
  *Rogue Valley Growers & Crafters Market
  (541) 261-5045*

September
- Labor Day Wine Weekend
  Weisinger's Winery (541) 488-5989

October
- Brews and Boogie
  ScienceWorks (541) 482-6767 ext. 27

ASHLAND

Home of the Oregon Shakespeare Festival, Ashland is one of the most attractive resort and retirement destinations in the entire country. The town stretches along the foothills of the Siskiyou Mountains. Swank residences nestle in the slopes high above Siskiyou Boulevard. Down below, the many tourists are accommodated in motels, by dozens of bed-and-breakfasts or at the incomparable Ashland Springs Hotel, a renovated masterpiece and the tallest building in the Rogue River Valley. Southern Oregon University adds a healthy dose of youth to the population mix. The Shakespeare Festival runs from February to October, and sells more tickets to more performances of more plays than any other theater in the country. In a typical year, the festival sells more than 350,000 tickets and attracts about 100,000 tourists. The three theaters are downtown, right off the Plaza, the heart of Ashland. The Plaza, Main Street and the nearby Railroad District are filled with art galleries, clothing boutiques and trendy restaurants. The galleries sponsor a First Friday art walk. Downtown Ashland is the kind of place where you can buy used books, gorgeous jewelry, fine wine and luscious chocolates, yet it is impossible to find men's BVDs or Styrofoam cups. (Try neighboring Talent.) When you are done shopping or taking in a play, visit Ashland's famous Lithia Park, 100 acres that extend from the Plaza up Ashland Creek to the mountainside. The park includes duck ponds, a Japanese garden and miles of hiking trails. The name Lithia comes from the Ashland's local mineral water, which contains lithium salts.

Oregon Chocolate Festival
EVENTS: *Best event for chocolate lovers*

What could be a more fabulous theme for a festival than chocolate? The landmark Ashland Springs Hotel in Ashland hosts the Oregon Chocolate Festival in March. Chocolate lovers of all ages can spend a weekend reveling in their favorite treat. Events are scheduled throughout Ashland. Naturally, you have ample opportunities for chocolate tasting. Oregon chocolatiers provide bars, truffles and toffees, not to mention fudge and sauce. Other vendors offer chocolate-covered Oregon pears, hazelnuts and berries. Rogue Creamery presents a delightful chocolate infused cheddar cheese and Rogue Ales pours astonishing chocolate stout. Have you ever considered getting your daily ration of antioxidants with a glass of red wine and a piece of dark chocolate? The festival offers chocolate and wine pairing events both in-house and at local wineries. The festival is educational as well as tasty. Seminars at the hotel have covered the health benefits of chocolate, chocolate history, and chocolate varietals. Allyson's of Ashland offers chocolate cooking classes. Local entertainment venues put on chocolate-themed entertainments. The vast local art gallery scene gets into the chocolate spirit, as well. Kids can taste chocolate-covered insects at the Science Works Hands-On Museum. The Oregon Chocolate Festival is a must-see. You will leave the festival with great memories, plus bags full of goodies.

212 E Main Street, Ashland OR (Ashland Springs Hotel)
(888) 795-4545
www.ashlandspringshotel.com/chocolate_festival.php

Albion Inn

ACCOMMODATIONS: *Best Inn*

The Albion Inn is located within the tranquil setting of Ashland's historic Hargadine District. Owner and innkeeper Nancy Morgan and her partner Suzanne Badoux have created an environment that is more than a bed and breakfast. Situated four blocks from the Oregon Shakespeare Festival and one block from downtown Ashland, the Albion Inn puts you within easy walking, biking or hiking distance of all that Ashland offers. The Inn's sweet farmhouse exterior invites you into spacious, book-filled rooms, cozy common areas, and lush gardens. The Inn's organic vegetable and herb beds bestow their riches throughout the summer and fall, and gourmet breakfasts are as bountiful as they are beautiful. Nancy has catered and served as a cooking instructor, and both Nancy and Suzanne are master gardeners. The Inn's five rooms are air conditioned, have private baths, and each one has its own distinctive appeal. The Inn offers wireless remote access, onsite Internet and fax services, and a wealth of written material on Ashland and the surrounding areas. Stay at the Albion Inn and experience one of the ways to visit Ashland.

34 Union Street, Ashland OR
(541) 488-3905 or (866) 933-5688
www.albion-inn.com

Lake of the Woods Mountain Lodge and Resort

ACCOMMODATIONS: *Best lodge*

Rekindling the spirit and tradition of the Great Northwest, Lake of the Woods Mountain Lodge and Resort is a gem set on the shore of one of the most beautiful natural mountain lakes in the Cascades. Situated near lovely Mount McLaughlin, the Lodge and cabins offer visitors a breathtaking view. Built as a 1920s lodge and fishing retreat, the Resort has been restored to its authentic charm. It combines the spirit of the wilderness with casual elegance and comfort. The Resort's 26 distinctive brown clapboard cabins pamper guests with fresh linens and Pendleton blankets, kitchens and some hot tubs. You can also bring your own lodging because full and partial RV hook up sites are available year round. Everyone loves the lake. The fishing is excellent and the sailing, swimming, boating, canoeing and waterskiing make for great times. During the summer you can order a picnic lunch at the Marina Grill, dine at the Lodge Restaurant, or stock up at the General Store and prepare an intimate or family dinner in your own cabin. During the winter the marina transforms into the Nordic center where snowmobiling and cross-country skiing become favorite pastimes. Whether it is adventure, romance or just the desire to step back into a simpler time, Lake of the Woods is a place you can enjoy with your family and friends for four seasons of fun. It is the kind of place you might remember from your childhood, a description in a favorite book or a charming old movie, but it is here for you today. In June 2003 *Sunset Magazine* called it "an irresistible alternative to Crater Lake Lodge," and went on to say, "The lodge and cabins at Lake of the Woods Resort installed a rustic charm surpassing that of the original."

950 Harriman Route, Klamath Falls OR
(866) 201-4194
www.lakeofthewoodsresort.com

McCall House B&B

ACCOMMODATIONS: *Best Ashland bed and breakfast*

Visitors to Ashland can't miss the McCall House. It's an eye-catching Victorian masterwork on Oak Street with elaborately decorated two-story bay windows. The Mansion was originally built in 1883 for Captain John McCall (who founded the Ashland newspaper, library, bank, and the Ashland Woolen Mill). It was converted into a bed and breakfast in 1981 by Shakespearean actress Phyllis Courtney. In 2003 the current owners, the McLaughlins, completed an extensive restoration, making this National Historic Landmark shine. Converting McCall's mansion into a haven for travelers was in keeping with its history. In this lovely home, McCall and his wife, Lizzie, hosted such distinguished guests as General William Tecumseh Sherman, William Jennings Bryan, and President Rutherford B. Hayes. Hayes' visit is commemorated in the President Hayes Guestroom, one of the 10 luxuriously appointed rooms. All rooms feature private baths, antique furnishings, and comfortable beds, and many also have fireplaces. A sumptuous gourmet breakfast is included. If you're in the mood for romance, spend a little extra for the Romantic Getaway Package. With this package, upon your arrival you'll be presented with chilled champagne, chocolates and fruit, roses, and a cozy fire. Superb service is a hallmark of the McCall House. If you're in need of rejuvenation, just let your host know and you'll be scheduled for a relaxing visit to the Blue Giraffe Day Spa, just one block away.

153 Oak Street, Ashland OR
(800) 808-9749
www.mccallhouse.com

Ashland at Sunset
Photo by Nancy McClain

Ashland Springs Hotel
ACCOMMODATIONS: *Best hotel*

The Ashland Springs Hotel harkens back to a simpler time. This beautifully restored landmark hotel is on the National Register of Historic Places. Located in downtown Ashland, just steps from the renowned Oregon Shakespeare Festival. A two-year restoration project transformed this historic beauty into a haven of taste and elegance reminiscent of small European hotels. Today this nine-story boutique hotel offers first-class hospitality to those who are drawn by business, the arts or the area's natural beauty. This lovely hotel offers 70 tastefully appointed, non-smoking guest rooms in an oasis of gentility and charm. Guests are pampered with superb service and luxurious surroundings. Amenities are many, including spa services, high-speed wireless Internet, complimentary light breakfast served on the mezzanine, and free parking. For celebrations, weddings and corporate functions, the Grand Ballroom, with an adjoining Conservatory and adjacent English garden, is an ideal location. The hotel's restaurant marries the magic of Ashland's natural surroundings with food and wines of the Northwest, creating dishes from the freshest local ingredients which are sure to seduce your palate. For more information, photos and a downloadable brochure, visit the Ashland Springs Hotel website.

212 E Main Street, Ashland OR
(541) 488-1700 or (888) 795-4545
www.ashlandspringshotel.com

Cripple Creek Music Company

ARTS & CRAFTS: *Best music store*

Ashland is home to Cripple Creek Music Company, Oregon's unique and unusual music store featuring hundreds of instruments from all over the world. Since 1976, Cripple Creek Music has provided beginner to professional musicians with all their musical needs. There's a dazzling variety of guitars, Celtic harps, mountain and hammered dulcimers, mandolins, violins, saxophones, and exotic instruments such as the sitar. All the staff members from the owner to the repair technicians are musicians. If you are looking to buy a vintage banjo, a new handmade guitar, or get your tuba repaired, this is the place you'll find professional service. Repairs are done in the store and their technicians are available to set up or repair woodwinds, brass and stringed instruments. It's easy to get started musically with Cripple Creek Music's Band and Orchestra Easy Play Rent to Own Program. If you want to play music, the musicians there want to help you. Cripple Creek Music Company also offers a huge variety of print music and musical gifts. From traditional to New Age, whatever your taste in acoustic music; Bluegrass, Folk, Jazz, Latin, World or Ethnic; Cripple Creek Music will start you on the right note. Visit Cripple Creek Music Company, a family business built on the traditions of quality service, knowledge and integrity.

353 E Main Street, Ashland OR
(541) 482-9141
www.cripplecreekmusic.com

The Web•sters

ARTS & CRAFTS:
Best destination for handspinners, weavers and knitters

If you're looking for high quality, one-of-a-kind articles of clothing, look no further than The Web•sters in historic Ashland. Since 1984, owner Dona Zimmerman has been producing and selling her own top quality wool. The progression from raising her own flock of Romney sheep, a breed from the Romney Marshes of England, to opening up The Web•sters was natural for Zimmerman. As a result, her store has become a destination for the most serious knitters, weavers and handspinners. In addition to specializing in natural fiber and handmade clothing, she offers knitting, weaving and spinning workshops. The Web•sters also carries hats, handbags and a wide assortment of knitting, spinning and weaving tools, books and materials. See their website for a list of products and current specials. Visit the experts at The Web•sters. They will help you finish your current project or get you started on your next one.

11 N Main Street, Ashland OR
(541) 482-9801 or (800) 482-9801
www.yarnatwebsters.com

Oregon Cabaret Theatre

ATTRACTIONS: *Best musical theater*

For an unforgettably entertaining experience, don't miss the Oregon Cabaret Theatre, offering the best in musical theater and comedy since 1986. Imaginative West Coast premieres alternate with innovative productions of nationally-acclaimed musical theater in a setting you won't find anywhere else in the world. You will be seated at a table on tiered levels or in the balcony in this elegantly renovated church. Feel free to order anything from a beverage or appetizer to a full gourmet dinner or brunch tailored especially to each production by the master chef. For a special treat, order a delectable dessert to be served during the intermission. Laugh until your sides hurt at a hilarious parody or a raucous English Panto. Enjoy a sparkling revue of song and dance. This cabaret is renowned for presenting top quality productions with talented professional performers and superb production values. You won't find better food, comedy or music anywhere. Shows sell out quickly, so make your reservation, order a season subscription, or call for box office hours or a brochure.

**49 N Main Street,
Ashland OR
(541) 488-2902**
www.oregoncabaret.com

Photo by Tom Lavine

Oregon Shakespeare Festival

ATTRACTIONS:
Winner of the Oregon Governor's Award

What is the location of the oldest existing full-scale Elizabethan stage in the Western Hemisphere? If you didn't guess Ashland, you haven't visited this picturesque town nestled in the mountains along Interstate 5. It's just a dozen or so miles north of the California border. Ashland is so closely associated with its annual Shakespeare Festival that it's a wonder the town isn't named Williamsburg or Avon. Established in 1935, the Oregon Shakespeare Festival (OSF) is among the largest and oldest professional regional repertory theater companies in the U.S. Each year it presents an eight-month season of 11 plays. Three or four are by Shakespeare and seven or eight are by classic and contemporary playwrights. They are performed in rotating repertory in three theaters, one of which is outdoors. OSF employs approximately 450 theater professionals from all over the country, and has a volunteer staff of nearly 750. The awards won by the festival are legion. A rating by *Time* magazine lists the Oregon Shakespeare Festival among the top five regional theaters in the country. Arrive early for evening performances from June to October and you can catch the Green Show, a wonderful dance performance in a romantic outdoor setting. There is no charge for this popular attraction.

15 S Pioneer, Ashland OR
(541) 482-4331
www.osfashland.org

1954
The WINTER'S TALE
The MERRY WIVES
of WINDSOR
HENRY VI,
PART II
HAMLET

1955
TIMON of ATHENS
HENRY VI, PART III
A MIDSUMMER
NIGHT'S DREAM
ALL'S WELL THAT
ENDS WELL
MACBETH

ScienceWorks

ATTRACTIONS:
Best interactive exhibits

ScienceWorks Hands-on Museum in Ashland is an exciting and educational museum dedicated to the exploration of science through fun and interactive exhibits. Founded in 2001, ScienceWorks provides people of all ages with more than 100 themed hands-on exhibits. The exhibits include Art and Science, the Dark Science Tunnel, the Hall of Illusions, the Bubble-ology Room and the Science Playroom. In addition, they are currently in the planning stages for an outdoor interactive Water Exhibit. Serving school children and educators throughout the region with innovative programs, the Museum works to promote science literacy and inspire a love of learning through informal learning environments. Its Discovery Lab, Kirlin Community Lecture Series, Sciencelive! Performances, summer festivals and numerous special events provide visitors to ScienceWorks with a variety of activities. A visit to ScienceWorks will leave you inspired, intellectually stimulated and eager to go back the next time you're in Ashland.

1500 E Main, Ashland OR
(541) 482-6767
www.scienceworksmuseum.org

Nimbus
FASHION: *Best*

Ken Silverman, owner of Nimbus, has collaborated with Carol Brookins to create a fascinating hybrid that's both a craft gallery and an upscale contemporary clothing store. In business since 1971, Nimbus features the best work of contemporary American craftspeople in blown glass, ceramics, handmade jewelry, and woodworking, plus a complete line of men and women's clothing, with an emphasis on the unusual and hard to find. Ken personally selects the items in the men's department and gallery. Carol oversees the women's department and the shoe selection. Gallery selections are continually changing and the clothing selections are updated frequently. This eclectic shop reflects not only Ken and Carol's personal tastes, but also the requests of the many longtime customers who've come to depend on Nimbus for items they can't find anywhere else. Nimbus is a true Ashland staple.

25 E Main Street, Ashland OR
(541) 482-3621

Rocky Mountain Chocolate Factory
FUN FOODS: *Best fine chocolates*

You're driving through the Plaza, minding your own business, when you feel something pulling you, something calling to you. MMMMmmmm, Chocolate. You automatically veer toward the big bear on East Main. Getting out of your car, you float through the door on waves of delectable scents. Swept away by the aroma of mouthwatering confections, you wake to find yourself in the Rocky Mountain Chocolate Factory. A top draw at the annual Taste of Ashland, this family business opened in 1989 and quickly became a community treasure. Owners Jeff Compton and Renee Hallesy invite one and all to come in, have a sample, or just chat. It's great fun to watch the chocolatiers create wonderful treats right before your eyes. The finest gourmet chocolates, handmade fudge, apples dipped in a copper kettle of molten caramel and countless more little goodies vie for your attention. You don't really need a reason, but any special occasion, anniversary, birthday or a sudden craving will be sweeter when blessed with these delicacies. No visit to Ashland is complete without a stop at the Rocky Mountain Chocolate Factory.

33 E Main Street, Ashland OR
(541) 482-6757
http://rmcf.com/OR/Ashland50424

JEGA Gallery and Sculpture Garden
GALLERIES: *Best sculpture gallery*

JEGA Gallery is on the cutting edge of Ashland's thriving gallery scene. Owner and sculptor J. Ellen G. Austin (the gallery takes its name from her initials) has created a space that is both a vibrant working gallery and a sculpture studio. J. Ellen creates sculptures that "combine serious with sensuous, confrontative with humor." JEGA, which recently celebrated its 11th anniversary in Ashland's historic Railroad District, also represents a select group of artists from around the world in a selective variety of media. These artists fit in perfectly with J. Ellen's philosophy and "have the potential to provoke and challenge perspectives of viewing the world." The community looks forward eagerly to JEGA's special events, including Women with Attitude and Men who like Women with Attitude, and an annual summer Jefferson State Sculpture Exhibit. Her mission to combine intellectual social/political challenges with playfulness is reflected in a quadrennial Send in the Clowns show, which runs during presidential election years. J. Ellen's commitment to art in the community led her to help found the Ashland Gallery Association. The Arts Council of Southern Oregon has honored her with the Advocate for the Arts Award, given for her leadership in making Ashland a friendly place for contemporary art with an edge. Her accomplishments have also been recognized by the Baldwin School of Bryn Mawr, Pennsylvania, which honored her with a Lifetime Achievement Award, and the Bradford College of Bradford, Massachusetts, which gave her a Distinguished Alumni Award.

625 A Street, Ashland OR
(541) 488-2474
www.jega4art.com

Gathering Glass Studio
GALLERIES: *Best glass art*

Gathering Glass Studio, located in Ashland's historic Railroad District, is a must see art destination in a town known for Shakespeare. It is owned and operated by glass artists Scott Carlson and Steven Cornett, who have previously worked together as members of Team Chihuly on projects including the Bellagio Hotel's ceiling installation in Las Vegas. They invite you to come and watch as they demonstrate 25 years of combined glassblowing experience. It is free and fun for all ages. Beautiful blown and sculpted art glass creations are on display in the studio gallery and available for purchase. Gathering Glass Studio offers classes for learning the art of glassblowing. Once you have completed the intermediate class, you may rent studio time to perfect your glass blowing skills. Custom orders are welcome. Bring your ideas, drawings or special color scheme and Gathering Glass Studio's artists will create a custom piece of glass art.

322 N Pioneer Street, Ashland OR
(541) 488-4738
www.gatheringglass.com

Blue Giraffe
HEALTH & BEAUTY: *Best destination spa*

A unique retreat awaits you in the heart of Ashland. The Blue Giraffe is a destination spa and salon in a park-like setting. Sounds of the rushing waters of Ashland Creek begin to soothe you the moment you arrive. Choose from the full range of services and deliver yourself into caring hands. You may decide to melt away tensions with a eucalyptus steam bath, relax into any of a variety of massage techniques, then re-energize with an invigorating body polish. The professionals at Blue Giraffe understand that touch heals the body, lifts the spirit, and nourishes the soul, and they employ the finest antioxidant and aromatherapy products to complement your treatments. We recommend any of the combination packages. If only Mom's Expectation could be a regular experience in every pregnancy. The Teen Scene can really get your teen off on the right foot with expert skin, hair and make-up tips. Men appreciate the un-fussy treatments geared specifically to them. In the salon, enjoy a glass of excellent local wine and the beautiful views. The friendly atmosphere invites socializing while you enjoy expert hair cuts and color, manicures, pedicures and cosmetic application. Waxing is available, as well. Make time for yourself when you come to The Blue Giraffe, where they will guide you on your journey to a greater sense of health, centeredness, and well-being.

51 Water Street, Ashland OR
(541) 488-3335
www.bluegiraffespa.com

The Phoenix Day Spa & Salon
HEALTH & BEAUTY: *Best full service day spa*

The Phoenix Day Spa & Salon, opened in July 1996, is the Rogue Valley's premier AVEDA spa and salon. Their mission is to provide a peaceful, relaxing experience for guests from the time they call to reserve services to the time they check out. As winner of Ashland's Business of the Year in 2000, they continue to provide the quality of service that keeps guests returning year after year from such places as Vancouver, Denver, Los Angeles, Las Vegas, New York and Hawaii, while they remain a *locals* spa at heart. The Phoenix is very fortunate to have loyal employees who are dedicated to creating The Phoenix Experience for each and every guest. The dedicated staff provides gentle, healing treatments, including massage, facials, body treatments and hair and nail services. The Phoenix uses Aveda products exclusively for all services, because they are not only great for the skin, hair and body, but also have minimal impact on the environment. Owner Jessica Vineyard invites you to see what The Phoenix Experience is all about. Please call well in advance to reserve time at one of the finest day spas and salons in the state. They look forward to setting the gold standard for all of your spa experiences.

2425 Siskiyou Boulevard, Ashland OR
(541) 488-1281
www.thephoenixspa.com

Mountain Meadows Community

LIFESTYLE DESTINATIONS:
Best active retirement community

Discover the active retirement lifestyle of Mountain Meadows Community in beautiful Ashland. Live independently in a charming Craftsman-style detached home or condominium, knowing that the equity in your investment belongs to you. Nestled on a scenic hillside, this 30-acre campus includes walking paths, a community garden, clubhouse, dining room, library, and fitness center with exercise pool. Just one mile away, explore the exciting theater, restaurants, shopping and university in downtown Ashland. Then come home to watch the sun set behind verdant hills in the comfort of your own living room. Orchestrate any level of service you wish, from care in your own home to residency in assisted living nearby. Mountain Meadows Community has been recognized with numerous awards, including the Best Small Active Retirement Community in America by the National Council on Senior Housing, one of the 100 Best Master Planned Communities in America by *Where to Retire* magazine, and the Gold Nugget Grand Award for Best Senior Housing in the West by the Pacific Coast Builder's Conference. You really can have it all at Mountain Meadows.

857 Mountain Meadows Drive, Ashland OR
(800) 337-1301 or
(541) 482-1300
www.mtmeadows.com

Amuse Restaurant
RESTAURANTS & CAFÉS: *Best Northwest/French cuisine*

At Ashland's Amuse Restaurant, husband-and-wife chef/owners Erik Brown and Jamie North prepare a Northwest/French menu using organic meat and seasonal produce. Amuse serves dinner in an elegant and contemporary atmosphere. The carefully selected wine list focuses on a wide array of excellent Oregon and California wines with smaller wineries included. The wait staff is highly knowledgeable and dedicated to providing professional, warm, unobtrusive service. Erik and Jamie prepare all items on the menu in-house, including their own sausages, breads and desserts. The dining room seats 40, and another 35 can be seated on the patio. On a recent visit to Amuse our

meal choice included a Belgian Endive Salad with Bosc pears, Roquefort, walnuts and date vinaigrette. The main course was Pan Roasted Game Hen with fingerlings, Italian kale and celery root remoulade. We added a cheese called Rogue Creamery "Crater Lake Blue" with quince paste and Lavender Blossom Honey. The dessert was Scharffen Berger Bittersweet Chocolate Truffle Cake with coffee and ice cream. Visit Amuse Restaurant, where Erik and Jamie exhibit an all-consuming love affair with food and each other.

15 N First Street, Ashland OR
(541) 488-9000
www.amuserestaurant.com

Apple Cellar Bistro
RESTAURANTS & CAFÉS: *Best bistro*

Do you feel like a Chocolate Mousse cup or a big slice of German Chocolate cake? How about a fluffy omelet, veggie scramble or French toast for breakfast? Maybe you would rather have a bistro salad or a big signature sandwich on delicious freshly baked bread? Locally owned by Robert Day since 1994, the Apple Cellar Bistro has long been a favorite of Ashland locals. Well known for their sourdough bread and authentic French pastries, the Apple Cellar serves the highest quality Mediterranean delicacies. Robert's family has been in the restaurant business since the 1930s. The Apple Cellar is committed to baking with excellence. They use 100-percent natural ingredients and support sustainable and organic agriculture; they use organics whenever possible. All of the baked goods are made at the bakery fresh daily. All of the soups and sauces are made from scratch. You may eat inside in their charming and casual atmosphere, or find a cozy table in the enclosed garden patio. The Apple Cellar is a great place to stop if you need a delicious meal on the run. Choose from the many selections in their Deli and bakery cases. There are always scrumptious hot main entrées, as well as generously stuffed sandwiches and, of course, all of those delicious temptations in the bakery cases. Try their new Gourmet Dinners for 2 To Go. Who better to cater your special event? Call and ask for catering details. Apple Cellar breads are available at Ashland, Medford and Grants Pass grocery stores. Try them; you'll be back for more.

2255 Highway 66, Ashland OR
(541) 488-8131

Breadboard Restaurant

RESTAURANTS & CAFÉS: *Best breakfasts*

If you like to be greeted like family, receive the best service anywhere, and enjoy a hearty meal, come to the Breadboard Restaurant. Since 1983, Pete and Sarah Foster have made this family-style eatery a community treasure. Serving breakfast and lunch, the Breadboard is a local favorite with a fun and casual atmosphere that appeals to all ages. Start your day off right with something from the amazing breakfast menu. It features Pete's Famous Muffins, homemade granola, multi-grain French Toast, the Ashland Scramble, and the Mountain Man, devised by a couple of regulars of similar description. You'll find perfect buttermilk biscuits and gravy, the best home fries in town, pancakes the way they should be, fluffy omelets, and huevos rancheros that will make you giddy. For lunch, world-famous Rando's Amazing Portobello Gardenburger and the Breadboard's Awesome BLT are two of the great selections. You will have to plan another trip to the Breadboard to experience the Ginger-Chicken Salad. Join the Fosters, kitchen manager extraordinaire Kim Krohr, and the good folk of Ashland for down-home cooking at the Breadboard Restaurant.

744 N Main Street, Ashland OR
(541) 488-0295

Photos by Cindy Tilley Faubion

Chateaulin Restaurant
RESTAURANTS & CAFÉS: *Best French cuisine*

This well-loved restaurant is located next door to the Oregon Shakespeare Festival Theatres in Ashland. Chateaulin Restaurant Français has been highly regarded in the Pacific Northwest since it opened more than 30 years ago. It is reminiscent of a cheerful restaurant in New York or Old World Paris–elegant, yet simple. The mood is relaxed, charming and romantic, with all of the hallmarks of fine dining–white tablecloths, crystal, deep burgundy carpet, lace curtains, and personal touches such as the fin-de-siecle etched glass partitions and polished wood. The small but carefully chosen menu changes frequently and is best described as a blend of contemporary and traditional French cuisine. David Taub is the chef de cuisine and co-owner with Jason Doss. He is a graduate of the Culinary Institute of America. Some of the highlights are the salmon (only wild, line-caught), or the fish flown in weekly from Hawaii. They feature Anderson Ranch Rack of Lamb, and their signature dessert is Chocolate Raspberry Roulade. Visit their website to read their full, mouth-watering menu, and read the glowing critics' reviews. Chateaulin has an award-winning wine list and features an impressive selection of domestic and imported wines, as well as rare boutique wines from Oregon, Washington and California. Your favorite wines from the dinner menu are available for purchase next door at the adjacent Chateaulin Wine and Gourmet Shop, where an array of treats are available.

52 E Main Street, Ashland OR
(541) 488-9463
www.chateaulin.com

Greenleaf Restaurant

RESTAURANTS & CAFÉS:
Best casual eats

Greenleaf Restaurant has been an Ashland favorite since 1985. Owner Daniel Greenblatt is proud to offer a diverse menu of fresh and flavorful selections for the whole family at affordable prices. Touted in *Conde Nast Traveler* and consistently listed in Best of Ashland, Greenleaf provides an upbeat, fun casual dining experience. Breakfast choices include pancakes, waffles, French toast, omelets, scrambles and fritattas. The lunch and dinner menus boast Daniel's special spanakopita along with great deli sandwiches, fresh salads, pasta, pizza, fish n' chips, grilled salmon, and chicken Caesar salad. In addition to the regular menu, Greenleaf offers daily specials and freshly made fresh fruit pies and cakes. For a beverage to go with all of that delicious food, choose from a full line of espresso drinks or make a selection from the beer and wine cooler. Seating is available inside, upstairs and downstairs, and outside on the lovely Greenleaf patio overlooking Lithia Creek. Everything on the menu is also available to take with you, perhaps for a picnic in nearby Lithia Park. Greenleaf's staff is friendly and knowledgeable and will serve you promptly and courteously. Daniel is also proud to offer a catering service for both large and small groups and will tailor a menu to fit any taste and budget. Make a visit to Greenleaf soon. You'll be glad you did.

49 N Main St, Ashland OR
(541) 482-2808
www.greenleafrestaurant.com

Lark's Home Kitchen Cuisine
RESTAURANTS & CAFÉS: *Best Northwest cuisine*

Lark's Home Kitchen Cuisine, located inside the Ashland Springs Hotel, offers a menu that is an ode to Oregon's culinary story. Chef Damon Jones, formerly of Emeril's in New Orleans, uses the area's freshest foods to create his classic dishes. Chef Damon credits his growers right on the menu so you know your meal was created from locally grown crops. This popular eatery was created by area residents Doug and Becky Neuman, who delight in pairing their fresh and flavorful cuisine with Oregon's excellent local wines and artisan chocolate desserts. The open and welcoming restaurant exudes a nostalgic 1940s feel that is heightened by everything from the gorgeous artwork and lamps to the multi-cushioned settees and the waiters' bowties. This ambience is the ideal backdrop for a relaxing dinner over popular favorites like homemade meatloaf or the oft-requested Anderson Ranch osso bucco (veal shins) or maple glazed pork chops. Additional menu favorites include pan-seared Alaskan halibut with summer vegetable relish and the seared duck breast with blue cheese and Bing cherry demi-glàce. Experience the best that Oregon has to offer by dining at Lark's Home Kitchen Cuisine where providing farm-to-table freshness isn't just a saying, it's a way of life.

212 E Main Street, Ashland OR
(541) 488-5558
www.ashlandspringshotel.com

Bloomsbury Books

SHOPPING: *A Southern Oregon institution for 25 years*

For 25 years, Karen Chapman and Sheila Burns have shared their love for reading with visitors to Bloomsbury Books in Ashland. This independent, locally-owned store takes pride in its breadth of selection (including an excellent children's section and periodicals selection) and its friendly customer service. The staff of former (and practicing) writers, artists, actors and teachers are always eager to share their recommendations, from the latest page-turner to a forgotten classic or a just-published provocative political analysis. The large, comfortable store, open until 10 pm, hosts weekly author signings and poetry readings in its lively upstairs coffeehouse. It is a Southern Oregon institution and a community gathering place for readers of all ages.

**290 E Main Street, Ashland OR
(541) 488-0029**

Rare Earth
SHOPPING: *Best round-the-world shopping*

Rare Earth is filled with rare treasures. Found on the Plaza in Ashland, this store is an Aladdin's Cave of the unusual, fun and marvelous. Rare Earth is where you will discover thousands of small treasures, including great imports you won't find anywhere else. Rare Earth offers an eclectic mixture of merchandise, including jewelry, incense, candles and holders, home décor, tapestries and rugs, toys, kitchen equipment, quality bath products, including brands like Terranova Toiletries and Burt's Bees. Rare Earth's selection of clothing for young people is especially notable. This is where you find clothing and shoes when you want something positively unique. But what Rare Earth is most known for is its large selection of goods that are made in other corners of the world. New items arrive continually. They can ship non-breakable items for you and the helpful staff is friendly and welcoming. Come in to see for yourself why this store is a popular favorite with locals and travelers alike.

33 N Main, Ashland OR
(541) 482-9501

Weisinger's of Ashland

WINERIES: *Best Ashland winery*

No trip to Ashland is complete without a visit to Weisinger's, the wonderful family-owned winery just a short drive from downtown. The Weisinger family welcomes you to their tasting room where you can sample superb wines. Stop by the gift shop for wine accessories and gourmet treats and feel free to ask for recommendations for local restaurants or other information about Ashland. The Weisingers know the area better than almost anyone and they are always happy to help. The Winery was founded in 1988 by John Weisinger, a former Presbyterian minister and enthusiastic amateur winemaker since the age of 15, who turned his hobby into a vocation. Today, John and his son, Eric, who is the winemaker, are partners in this family-run business that utilizes locally grown fruit, as well as their Estate vineyard, to produce ultra-premium wine. One of their most famous wines is the Petite Pompadour, an elegant blend of Bordeaux varietals from one of their Estate Vineyards, the Pompadour Vineyard, named after nearby Pompadour Bluff. Among their white wines, the Chardonnay and the Estate-grown dry Gewurztraminer are especially good. The tasting room is located about a mile south of downtown Ashland. Open daily May through September, and Wednesday through Sunday from October through April.

3150 Siskiyou Boulevard, Ashland OR
(541) 488-5989 or (800) 551-WINE (9463)
www.weisingers.com

CAVE JUNCTION

Cave Junction is the gateway to the Oregon Caves National Monument and the commercial, service and cultural center for the Illinois Valley, a rural community of small farms, crafts people and families who like living apart from the crowds. The valley is nestled between the Klamath and Siskiyou mountains. Life is slower in the Illinois Valley, so you need to be patient. Many people here volunteer their time with the schools, local government and civic organizations because it feels good to be part of the community. About 17,000 people live in the Illinois Valley. The valley is fast becoming a favorite year round vacation land. Visitors can enjoy the spectacular beauty of the many rivers, streams and public forest lands available for hiking, fishing and hunting. Cave Junction lies halfway between Grants Pass and Crescent City, making it a natural stop for Oregonians headed for the Pacific Ocean beaches.

PLACES TO GO

- Great Cats World Park
  27919 Redwood Highway
  (541) 592-2957

- Illinois River Forks State Park
  U.S. Highway 199

- Lake Selmac County Park
  500 Reeves Creek Road, Selma

- Oregon Caves National Monument
  19000 Caves Highway

THINGS TO DO

June
- Shining Stars Festival
  Jubilee Park
  (541) 592-2236

July
- Siskiyou Bluegrass Festival
  Lake Selmac
  (541) 592-3326

August
- Illinois Valley Blackberry Festival
  (541) 592-4076

Out 'n' About Treehouse Resort

ACCOMMODATIONS: *Most unusual resort*

Treesort & Treehouse Institute of Arts & Culture in Takilma is a truly unique, exciting and educational vacation destination. Located in the picturesque valley of Takilma, nestled between the Siskiyou Mountains just below the headwaters of the east fork of the Illinois River, Out 'n' About was the dream of owner Michael Garnier and his wife Peggy Malone. After an eight-year battle with Josephine County officials, during which they were ordered to shut down several times, the county at last recognized them as a safe and licensed bed & breakfast. Internationally famous for their tree house guest suites, they offer nine elevated cabins. The cabins include the Swiss Family Complex and the Treezebo, and one ground-level Cabintree for those less inclined to spend the night perched high above in the branches of an oak grove. Their Treehouse Institute, established in the summer of 1996, offers avocational instruction in basic engineering, design and construction methods for building treehouses. In addition, they offer horseback riding, rafting, rope courses, guided tours, and local craft workshops. Out 'n' About is a remarkable and thrilling resort, and it will leave an indelibly fond mark on the memories of all who visit.

300 Page Creek Road, Cave Junction OR
(541) 592-2208
www.treehouses.com

Chateau at the Oregon Caves

ACCOMMODATIONS:
Best lodging near the Oregon Caves

The Chateau at the Oregon Caves National Monument in Cave Junction provides a host of attractions, including a gift gallery featuring works by many Illinois Valley artists, a coffee shop, fine dining, overnight accommodations, area hiking and your ticket to exploring the Oregon Caves. Nestled in the midst of the old growth forest atop the Siskiyou Mountains, the Chateau offers cozy rooms from modestly economical to large, two-room family suites. Their 1930s-style coffee shop and soda fountain serves an appetizing selection of homemade soups, salads and sandwiches. The chefs at the Chateau at the Oregon Caves combine the freshest local ingredients with flavors from the Pacific Northwest and Asia to create delicious dishes you can enjoy in the dining room while overlooking the wooded ravine. Four hiking trail loops spreading out in all directions offer a range of hiking opportunities, and the 90-minute guided tour of the caves is truly remarkable and wondrous. The Chateau at the Oregon Caves is a landmark worth visiting, and will leave you eager to return.

20000 Caves Highway, Cave Junction OR
(541) 592-5020
www.oregoncavesoutfitters.com

Oregon Caves National Monument

ATTRACTIONS: *Best underground tours*

Your family can enjoy a fascinating underground experience at the Oregon Caves National Monument. Bizarre and eerie calcite formations decorate the cave. At the Passageway of the Whale, you squeeze through what appear to be giant ribs. Tiny rimstone dams resemble miniature waves. The drip, drip, drip of water reminds you that this is a living cave that slowly builds new structures. Tours last 90 minutes. Bring your camera. Some areas of the cave are off-limits to flash cameras in deference to sleeping bats, but most areas are open for photography. Small children cannot take the full tour, but the first room of the cave is open to the youngest visitors and to tourists in wheelchairs. During the busy summer season, tours fill quickly. You can avoid long waits by arriving when the caves open or at 5 pm. The cave closes for the winter from late November to mid-March. There is more to the monument than just the caves. You can take a nature walk in one of the most geologically unique and botanically diverse areas in the United States, the Siskiyou Mountains. The remnant old-growth coniferous forest harbors a fantastic array of plants, including the widest-diameter Douglas fir tree in Oregon. Four trails lead you through the forest. Ranger-led programs explain the natural and human history of the monument. You can also visit the Oregon Caves Chateau, a charming lodge with 23 rustic rooms. The gift shop features the work of talented local artists and crafters. Three dining options range from fine cuisine to speedy deli. Be sure to visit Oregon Caves National Monument.

19000 Caves Highway, Cave Junction OR
(541) 592-2100
www.nps.gov/orca

Photos by Nancy McClain

© 2001 Brian Prechtel. All rights reserved image 4885

Photo by Aleš Cerin

Bridgeview Vineyards

WINERIES:

2004 Oregon Winery of the Year

Cave Junction is home to Bridgeview Vineyards, a winery that stands out among the many superb Oregon wineries. Declared Oregon Winery of the Year in 2004 by *Wine Press Northwest*, Bridgeview is dedicated to reasonably-priced wines of extraordinary quality. Bridgeview continually delights wine connoisseurs with its award-winning favorites, such as the Pinot Noir that took Best of Show at the Oregon State Fair in 2002. People thought Bob and Lelo Kerivan were crazy when they first started planting grapes on a 75-acre plot in 1986. The naysayers told them the rows of vines were too close together and too heavily pruned. But ignoring the criticism, the Kerivans proved that they knew exactly what they were doing. They based their techniques on centuries-old practices common in Germany, where Lelo was raised. Now the Kerivans, with Lelo's son, René Eichmann, produce a dazzling selection of reds and whites, highlighted by their signature Blue Moon line. Prices range from $7 to $40. Bob says they have made a $100 bottle of wine, but "we just haven't found anyone silly enough to buy it." Bridgeview's tasting room is a popular stop in Josephine County. It receives 100,000 visitors a year thanks to the nearby proximity of the Oregon Caves and other local attractions. The word about Bridgeview is spreading far and wide. Private tours are available upon request.

4210 Holland Loop Road, Cave Junction OR
(877) 273-4843
www.bridgeviewwine.com

CENTRAL POINT

Mount McLoughlin is emblamatic of Central Point. The snow-capped mountain is visible everywhere in Central Point, but hidden in most other Southern Oregon cities. Central Point got its name because it was where two important wagon roads of the past converged. The city is growing rapidly because local residents consider it a desirable location for new housing. Central Point's biggest draw is the Jackson County Expo Center, home of the Jackson County Fair and also the site of exhibitions, musical events and activities year round. The town hosts the world's oldest and largest hearing dog training facility, Dogs for the Deaf, established in 1977. It is the location of the original Grange Co-op, an agricultural supply cooperative established in 1934. The Rogue Creamery in Central Point is an award-winning, internationally known cheese factory. The nearby Upper and Lower Table Rocks are huge mesas that highlight the surrounding landscape.

PLACES TO GO

- Crater Rock Museum
  2002 Scenic Avenue *(541) 664-6081*

- Rogue Creamery
  311 N Front Street *(541) 665-1155*

- Touvelle State Recreation Site
  8425 Table Rock Road

- Upper Table Rock
  Pumice Lane

THINGS TO DO

July
- Jackson County Fair
  Fairgrounds *(541) 774-8270*

August
- Fiddles 'n Vittles: Music & Food Fair
  Historic Hanley Farm
  (541) 773-6536

September-October
- Harvest Fair & Microbrew Festival
  Fairgrounds
  (541) 774-8270

October-November
- A Taste of the Rogue at Rogue Creamery
  311 N Front Street
  (541) 665-1155

Table Rock
Photo by Nancy McClain

South Valley Construction

BUSINESS: *Best remodelers*

Are you thinking about hiring a contractor? Are you wondering where to start? Mike Hansen, co-owner of South Valley Construction offers this advice, "Do your research. Check out the contractor before you hire anyone. If they do quality work, you'll find out before they even touch your project." South Valley Construction offers the best in residential construction and remodeling. Specializing in custom decks, barn homes, arenas, horse barns, agricultural buildings and equestrian facilities, South Valley Construction is by no means limited to these structures. If you have an idea, if you want to try something "out of the box," give Mike a call. He will be glad to give you a free consultation and a free estimate. South Valley Construction offers a lifetime guarantee on workmanship and defects in their aluminum awnings. Mike started in construction at the age of 15, and 30 years later he is still doing the craft that he learned from his father. He treats each project as if it were for his own family and he treats his clients the way that he would like to be treated. Mike and his co-owner, Pam Hansen, are dedicated, honest local business people who really care about giving their customers exactly what they want. If you have a project, give them a call. Let the best help you realize your dream.

4551 Table Rock Road,
Central Point OR
(541) 665-3310

Photo by Donna K Lindley

Malot Environmental

BUSINESS:

Best remediation services

The Malot Companies have always held firmly to the philosophy of giving back to the community and making the Rogue Valley a better place to work and live. For nearly half a century Tom Malot and his family have been building some of the finest homes and commercial buildings in the area, all of which have been planned and constructed with the betterment of the community in mind. In 2000, founder Tom Malot's son and the current owner of Malot Construction, Tommy Malot, founded Malot Environmental, which specializes in environmental remediation for asbestos, lead and mold abatement projects. The primary goal of the company is to provide exceptional building remediation services, during both demolition and construction. The Malots and their highly trained staff are focused on meeting your immediate goals, as well as helping you refine strategies to ensure environmental compliance in the future. In addition to their other services, the Malot Environmental team can detect and remove the harmful molds that grow exponentially within the first 24 to 72 hours after water damage occurs, be it from a damp basement, flood or poorly ventilated room. When it comes to protecting your family from harmful environmental substances, no job is too big or too small for Malot Environmental, a company dedicated to creating a healthy community today and for future generations.

650 E Pine Street, Central Point OR
(541) 664-1258
www.malotenvironmental.com

Tom Malot Construction/Real Estate

BUSINESS: *Best builders*

During the past 45 years the Malot family has been a significant part of the Rogue Valley's growth. Southern Oregon native Tom Malot returned to the area in 1961 after serving with the U. S. Marine Corps and founded Tom Malot Construction with the help of his wife, Sandra, that same year. Tom completed a carpenter's apprenticeship and journeyman training and then worked in the construction industry prior to opening his own business, which gave him the experience necessary to build one of the community's most prominent organizations. Tom Malot Construction Company, which is now under the ownership of son Tommy Malot, offers a full range of expert building services, including large-scale commercial developments, affordable family housing, custom home design and construction, subdivisions and multifamily dwellings. In the mid 1970s the Malots expanded the business to include Tom Malot Real Estate, where both Tom and Sandra, who are licensed brokers, have helped numerous Rogue Valley families achieve their dreams of home ownership. Tom Malot Construction has built more than 3,000 homes and numerous commercial buildings throughout the valley and continues to be a family-run and family-oriented organization, with Tom serving as president and Sandra at the helm of the real estate company. Tommy Malot's twin sister, Tiffany, works as a broker at the real estate company. When it comes time to buy or build your new home, trust in Tom Malot Construction and Tom Malot Real Estate.

650 E Pine Street, Central Point OR
(541) 664-1258
www.malotrealestate.com

Dorris Construction
HOME: *Best home builder*

Dorris Construction has built a solid reputation for its work on residential and commercial properties in southern Oregon for more than 22 years. Owner and career craftsman Gary Dorris stands by his workmanship with integrity and honesty. He brings excellent communication, high quality, artistic vision and an exemplary team to each and every home he designs. If it's craftsmanship you seek, Dorris Construction can do it. Gary employs a team of master designers, including his wife, Cathy, who offers interior design services. A family-owned and operated business, Dorris Construction has been providing the entire Rogue Valley with quality custom homes. They also place an emphasis on building with energy efficient and recycled materials. Such projects don't just happen overnight or without some trepidation. Gary has weekly meetings with clients and a walk-through at framing, taking the fear out of building. Gary stresses the importance of communication by checking in with his customers to ask each one, "How does it feel when you walk in the door?" He wants the people he builds for to feel comfortable and at peace when they enter their finished home. Let a Dorris Construction custom-built house welcome you.

2209 Old Stage Road, Central Point OR
(541) 821-4199
www.dorrisconstruction.com

Marble Designs
HOME: *Best stone products*

Marble Designs is the oldest and largest manufacturer of cultured marble, onyx and granite products in Oregon and Northern California. The firm manufactures and installs stone surfaces for homes and businesses. Since 1967, owners Marvin and Janine Poulson have built a distinctive reputation for exemplary design and service. Their recipe for success is based on using the right materials and the right processes, having the right attitude and most importantly, doing right by the customers. All of Marble Designs' products are custom made for each job, no matter whether it is large or small, simple or complex. Cultured marble, onyx and granite are low maintenance, cost effective and long-lasting solutions. They add beauty wherever they are installed. Marble Designs stands behind every installation with a one-year unconditional warranty. All creations are certified by the International Association of Plumbing and Mechanical Officials and the American National Standards Institute. You can therefore be confident they meet all federal and local building standards and requirements. You will want to use these affordable and flexible stone finishes in your kitchen and bathroom, but you may find that you can also use them elsewhere in your home or office. Marvin and Janine welcome special orders. Let Marble Designs add a touch of distinction and elegance to your home or business.

**680 S Front Street,
Central Point OR**
(541) 664-1256 or (800) 866-9042

Willie Boats

RECREATION: *Where there's a Willie, there's a way*

With tongue in cheek, Willie Illingworth's life motto speaks to his passion and acumen for his business. "I've always wanted to make my job my life, that way every waking moment is a tax write-off," he says. Tax write-off or not, Willie's drift boats have quietly carved a permanent niche in the minds and adventures of river runners. For more than 30 years, Willie has logged countless hours designing and re-designing drift boats and jet sleds. In 1971, he built the first drift boat out of aluminum and his boats have been in demand ever since. After his success with the aluminum drift boat, he began building jet boats. His jet boats are works of art and considered the barometer of success for jet boats. Once started, he was unable to stop. He introduced the Raptor, which provides extreme stability and shallow water capabilities. Willie says, "the whole idea of aluminum is that there is little or no upkeep and that is why the boats caught on." Are you ready for another of Willie's mottos? "He who dies with the most toys wins." Despite the early loss of one hand, Willie continues to row boats, wield bows, heft rifles and handle fishing rods with expertise. Over time his business has changed due to competition and takeovers, but nearly all of the thousands of metal drift boats on Northwest rivers and across the United States can trace their beginnings to the first aluminum drift boat that Illingworth built in 1971. "Where there's a Willie, there's a way," he says. What do you expect from a living legend? Simply the best, that's all.

1440 Justice Road, Central Point OR
(541) 779-4141
www.willieboats.com

Rostel's

RESTAURANTS & CAFÉS: *Best restaurant in Central Point*

Savor sophisticated cuisine and a casual atmosphere with a visit to Rostel's, a local neighborhood tradition. Housed in the historic Kurth & Miller building, with its exposed brick and gleaming wood, the restaurant specializes in Mediterranean cuisine prepared with a touch of Pacific Coast flair. The popular eatery opened in 2003 under the ownership of lifetime Central Point residents Tom and Tiffany Malot, who shared a dream of creating a gathering place that offered *savoir-faire* and elegance in a relaxed setting. The restaurant's name comes from the building's second owner, C.B. Rostel, who purchased

the 1889 dwelling in 1903 at a sheriff's sale. Before opening, Tom Malot Construction undertook a major renovation of the building, which included the addition of a magnificent 36-foot bar, created from two milled slabs hewn from a single tree. You can expect friendly, efficient service from Michael Bishop, executive chef; Jeremy Overton, chef de cuisine; Micha Willits, bar manager; Kari Hogenson, general manager; and Liz Wan, director of private and special events. Menu favorites include the smoky pear spinach salad topped with Rogue Creamery's Smoky Oregon blue cheese and the blackened chicken fettuccine. The Malots are big believers in local sustainability and use fresh, local goods whenever possible, including produce, cheese and wine. Whether you're planning a quiet dinner for two or a gala event, make your reservations at Rostel's, where you will always be treated like you are part of the family.

311 E Pine Street, Central Point OR
(541) 665-9100
www.rostels.com

CHILOQUIN

On the banks of the Williamson River, Chiloquin is a short distance from Agency and Upper Klamath lakes. This is a land of majestic beauty, with wetlands, woodlands, wildlife and world class fishing. Millions of migrating birds rest and refuel here, and in the winter the area hosts the largest concentration of bald eagles in the lower states. The town of Chiloquin was named after a chief of the Klamath tribe. It was located in the middle of the Klamath Reservation until 1954, when the Federal government terminated its recognition of Klamath tribal sovereignty and sold off the reservation lands. Federal recognition was restored in 1986, but without any restoration of land. Today as in the past, a majority of Chiloquin's residents are Indian. Beginning in 1918, non-Indians purchased allotments to settle at Chiloquin. From then until World War II, Chiloquin was a boom town based on lumber and cattle. In recent years, Chiloquin has been a quiet community. In 1997, however, a degree of bustle returned when the Tribes opened the Kla-Mo-Ya Casino south of town.

PLACES TO GO

- Collier Memorial State Park
  U.S. Highway 97
- Collier Logging Museum
  U.S. Highway 97 (541) 783-2471
- Kla-Mo-Ya Casino
  34333 U.S. Highway 97 N (541) 783-7529
- Train Mountain Railroad Museum
  36941 S Chiloquin Road (541) 783-3030

THINGS TO DO

March
- Return of the C'waam (fish)
  (800) 524-9787 ext. 159

May
- Spring Gas Up
  (541) 545-6510

August
- Klamath Tribes Restoration Celebration
  (800) 524-9787 ext. 147

September
- Logger's Breakfast
  Collier Logging Museum (541) 783-2471

Photo by Wendy Gay

The Klamath Tribes

"gelwipga naalam giisdat"– which means "Come visit our homeland."

The Klamath Basin in Southern Oregon is the original homeland of the Klamath, Modoc and Yahooskin people. As you travel along the east side of Klamath Lake (the largest lake in Oregon), you pass along a steep mountainside, called "nii Laks" (meaning, sunrising place). This is where the Native people come to think and pray. Today, they pray for the protection of endangered fish and the return of salmon to these waters. They also pray and are striving to regain a portion of their former reservation lands. Until the land is restored, the tribes continue to work toward their goal of self-sufficency. With this goal in mind, in 1997 the tribes opened Kla-Mo-Ya Casino, the first tribally owned business in more than 40 years, since the termination of their reservation in 1954. Kla-Mo-Ya Casino is just 20 minutes north of the town of Klamath Falls. It is the second most visited attraction in the county after Crater Lake National Park, another sacred place also located on former tribal lands. South of Klamath Falls is the Lava Beds National Monument, site of the Modoc War of 1872-1873, where 50 Modoc warriors held off 1,000 U.S. troops for more than five months. Following their surrender, the warriors and their families were marched 30 miles to Fort Klamath. Here, four Modoc leaders were hung, two were sentenced to imprisonment at Alcatraz, and the remaining Modocs were exiled to Oklahoma until the early 1900s. The Lava Beds and these locations are sacred and should always be treated with respect. The Klamath Tribes invite you to visit Klamath County, rich in history and natural beauty. The Klamath Basin promises exciting indoor or outdoor adventure. You are welcome to game at Kla-Mo-Ya, attend a rodeo or a tribal powwow. You can enjoy bird watching, fishing, camping and canoeing. The area provides world-class golfing and awesome winter and summer recreation. Come to Klamath County, which has more than 300 days of sunshine each year.

501 Chiloquin Boulevard, Chiloquin OR
(800) 524-9787 (Tribal Administration Headquarters)
(800) 445-6728 (Great Basin Visitor's Center)
www.klamathtribes.org
www.greatbasinvisitor.info

CRATER LAKE

Sublimely beautiful Crater Lake is famous for its intense blue color and spectacular views. Even seasoned travelers gasp at the twenty-mile circle of cliffs fringed with hemlock, fir and pine. The forested slopes reflect off the waters, which are among the purest and clearest in North America. In 1997, scientists observed a record-breaking clarity of 142 feet. The lake is the deepest in the United States and the deepest in the world that is completely above sea level. During summer, visitors to Crater Lake National Park navigate the Rim Drive around the lake, enjoy boat tours on the lake surface, stay in the historic Crater Lake Lodge, camp at Mazama Village or hike the park's trails. In winter, the park receives one of the heaviest snowfalls in the country, averaging 533 inches per year. While the park is mostly closed in this season, cross-country skiing and snowshoe hikes are still possible. Crater Lake was created by the eruption and collapse of 12,000-foot Mount Mazama 7,700 years ago. The Klamath Indians tell a story of how the Creator fought to save the people in a great battle against the spirit chief of the below world. The Creator defeated the chief of the below world, forced him back underground and covered the entrance to the underworld with volcanic debris. Then the Creator brought rain and filled the crater. The Klamaths revered the lake and never spoke of it to white explorers. In the 1850s, however, gold prospectors and the U.S. Geological Survey finally discovered the lake. William Gladstone Steel devoted his life and fortune to establishing Crater Lake as a National Park, and his dream was realized in 1902.

Photo by Jennifer Gifford

Photo by Robert Mutch

EAGLE POINT

Farmers and stock raisers founded Eagle Point after gold was first discovered in Jacksonville in 1852. They liked the untamed natural beauty of the Little Butte Creek area and saw it as a perfect place to settle and raise families. Eagle Point became the bread basket for Jacksonville, and later for Medford. In 1987, the citizens of Eagle Point relocated a Queen Truss covered bridge from Antelope Creek and placed it across Little Butte Creek. This covered bridge now serves as a safe walkway for school children who cross Little Butte Creek to and from school. Eagle Point is experiencing a building explosion due in part to the livability of the area and in part to the construction of the Eagle Point Golf Club, one of the most highly rated courses in the country. Eagle Point is a gateway to the upper Rogue River and Crater Lake for tourists traveling from the south. The town of Shady Cove, to the north, provides direct access to the Rogue.

PLACES TO GO

- Butte Creek Mill (working grain mill)
  402 N Royal Avenue
  (541) 826-3531

- Cole Rivers Hatchery
  200 Cole Rivers Drive
  (541) 878-2235

- Dodge Bridge Park
  Rogue River Drive, Shady Cove

- Eagle Point Museum
  301 N Royal Avenue (541) 826-4166

- Takelma Park
  Cole Rivers Drive

- Upper Rogue Regional Park
  Rogue River Drive, Shady Cove

THINGS TO DO

May
- Memorial Day Services
  Eagle Point National Cemetery

July
- 4th of July Celebration
  (541) 826-2212

August
- SPAM Jam, Parade & Festival
  Shady Cove (541) 878-2948

Larry Walker Cabinet Doors

HOME: *Best cabinet doors*

When you have Larry Walker build your custom cabinet doors, it is Larry's hands on each and every job. The joy of woodworking is what motivated Larry to start in his profession and he has based his continuing business on providing high quality cabinet doors. Paramount to his business success is customer satisfaction. Larry started in a garage nearly 15 years ago and news of his work has spread through word of mouth ever since. Remember, it is doors, and doors only, that he builds; he does not build cabinets. He builds beautiful, handcrafted doors, the kind that only an artist who loves his craft can create. Generally, Larry's business has catered to commercial projects, but Larry is working toward finding a larger location so that he can accommodate more residential building and remodeling projects. If you are thinking of remodeling your kitchen, utility room, or bathroom, and want custom cabinet doors that meet your special desires, Larry Walker is the one to call. Your inquiries are welcome and Larry is happy to provide phone consultations. Arletta Walker, Larry's wife and business partner, and Dave Mitchell, the shop foreman, will be glad to assist you, too. If you have an idea–a vision of a special cabinet door, go to Larry's Cabinet Doors and see what they can do for you.

600 W Dutton, Eagle Point OR
(541) 826-3688

GOLD HILL

In 1941, the U.S. Army constructed Camp White on 67 square miles north of Medford as a training camp for the 91st Infantry. Over the course of four years, 40,000 troops shipped out of Camp White. Little remains of the camp except for a military hospital and military barracks that were deeded to the Veterans Administration and reopened as a veterans' retirement home. The Camp White Museum exhibits uniforms, medals, guns and letters. White City today is best known for manufacturing. White City Industrial Park, west of State Route 62, is southern Oregon's largest factory district. Further west is the Nature Conservancy's Agate Desert Preserve. This area of vernal pools contains what is perhaps the most northerly habitat of fairy shrimp. The two segments of the Denman Wildlife Area, a state-run preserve, lie north and south of the Industrial Park. The southern segment features several small lakes where waterfowl can often be seen. Some hunting is allowed. While TouVelle State Park and Table Rock have Central Point addresses, they are actually closer to White City and provide recreational opportunities to White City citizens. Other recreational possibilities include Jackson County Sports Park, which hosts the Southern Oregon Dragway, the Southern Oregon Speedway and a go-kart track.

PLACES TO GO

- Agate Lake County Park
  E Antelope Road

- Camp White Museum
  (541) 826-2111 ext. 3674

- Jackson County Sports Park
  www.jacksoncountyparks.com

- Southern Oregon Speedway
  6900 Kershaw Road (541) 826-6825

- Willow Lake County Park
  Willow Lake Road

THINGS TO DO

June
Rogue Valley Veterans Powwow
White City Veterans Domiciliary

Rocky Point Bridge
Photo by Nancy McClain

Mildred Tilley

Early Gold Hill

Gold Hill, 1901

Gold Hill Historical Society

ATTRACTIONS:
Best local history

About three miles as the crow flies from the Lucky Bart Gold Mine, you'll find the home of Josiah Beeman. His gold mine was so profitable in its day that in 1901, Josiah built a rambling, two-story home for his wife and young family. A devastating fire gutted part of the meticulously built house, and afterward repairs were never completed. Josiah and descendents of the family lived in the house until 1993, when members of the Gold Hill Historical Society purchased it as a permanent home for their museum. That same group of volunteers lovingly restored the home to its former glory, making it the hub for all things historical in the city of Gold Hill. A warm, comfortable atmosphere is evident the moment you walk through the front door. Volunteers here can give you an interesting tour, help you research information, or even locate photographs of long lost family members. The Gold Hill Historical Society actively provides educational activities for local schools, participates in annual community events and creates the ever-popular Haunted House for Halloween. Its volunteer members give countless hours of their time and share a collective love for things of historical interest. Local families have donated most of the GHHS collection with the confidence that their precious heirlooms will always be cared for with respect and admiration. The society is dedicated to its motto: Recording the Past for the Future. Josiah Beeman would have surely given his nod of approval.

504 First Avenue, Gold Hill OR
(541) 855-1182

PLACES TO GO

- Applegate Interpretive Center
  500 Sunny Valley Loop, Sunny Valley

- Firehouse Gallery
  214 SW 4th Street (541) 956-7241

- Grants Pass Museum of Art
  229 SW G Street (541) 479-3290

- Riverside Park
  E Park Street

- Whitehorse Park
  7613 Lower River Road

- Wiseman Gallery (RCC)
  3345 Redwood Highway (541) 956-7339

- Wolf Creek Inn
  *100 Front Street, Wolf Creek
  (541) 866-2474*

THINGS TO DO

May
- Native American Arts Festival & Mother's Day Pow Wow
  Riverside Park (541) 472-0215

- Boatnik
  Riverside Park (800) 547-5927

June
- Wild Rogue Balloon Festival
  (800) 547-5927

July
- Grants Pass Motorcycle Show
  Riverside Park (541) 660-8730

August
- Josephine County Fair
  Fairgrounds (541) 476-3215

September
- Asian Cultural Festival
  Riverside Park (541) 660-7247

- Oktoberfest
  Wolf Creek (541) 866-2602

- Take a Walk on the Rogue
  Reinhardt Volunteer Park (541) 474-6360

- Art among the Vines
  (541) 846-6372

October
- Art along the Rogue
  Downtown (800) 547-5927

November-December
- Festival of Trees
  (541) 890-5472

GRANTS PASS

Grants Pass is a year 'round playground for outdoor enthusiasts of every age. It is the most popular spot for accessing the legendary Rogue River, one of the best places in the West for whitewater adventures, fly-fishing and scenic hikes. Salmon and steelhead are the best catches. Thousands of tourists see the wild river by taking a Hellgate Jetboat excursion. The Rogue River is a designated National Wild and Scenic River, which means the wilderness is largely unspoiled. The growth of Grants Pass was catalyzed in 1851 by the discovery of gold along the Illinois River near modern Cave Junction, causing a major migration to the area. In 1865, workers improving the road north of town received news that Ulysses S. Grant had captured Vicksburg. They celebrated by naming the area Grants Pass. Downtown Grants Pass, a National Historic District, is filled with antique shops, ice cream parlors and sidewalk espresso stands. Riverside Park, downtown on the Rogue River, is the home of the world famous Boatnik festival in May. The main event is a thrilling hydro boat race. The nearby Oregon Caves National Monument gave rise to an unusual booster club in 1922—the Oregon Cavemen. For many years, this group of local businesspeople donned shaggy animal skins to welcome such visiting dignitaries as Shirley Temple, John F. Kennedy and Ronald Reagan.

Grants Pass Miner
Photo by Nancy McClain

Weasku Inn

ACCOMMODATIONS:
One of the country's Top 25 greatest inns

Since 1924, the Weasku Inn in Grants Pass has been providing a comfortable and relaxing environment for its guests, including notables such as President Herbert Hoover, Zane Grey, Walt Disney, Clark Gable and Carole Lombard. Since being purchased in 1993 by Country House Inns, the Inn has added 12 cabins, a new meeting room, and freestanding boardroom. This historic lodge, hailed by *Travel & Leisure* as "one of the country's top 25 greatest inns," is situated on 10 forested acres resting along the scenic Rogue River. Its log exterior blends perfectly with its uniquely decorated Pacific Northwest interior and the vaulted ceilings and exposed beams add a rustic touch. Enjoy a complimentary Continental breakfast or an evening of wine and cheese while viewing the spectacular waterfall and pond from the outdoor deck. With accommodations including 12 river cabins and five lodge rooms, and a peaceful setting that only Southern Oregon can provide, your stay at the Weasku Inn will be memorable.

5560 Rogue River Highway, Grants Pass OR
(541) 471-8000
www.weasku.com

Pacific Aviation Northwest

ATTRACTIONS: *Only place for single and multi-engine flight training*

Turn your dream of flying into reality at Pacific Aviation Northwest. Pacific Aviation is a full-service airport business providing ground school, flight training, aircraft rental, pilot supplies, aircraft fuel and aircraft maintenance services. Rent a plane for your pleasure, your business or maybe for a friend and add an aerial photography package for recreational and commercial use. Ride along with them, or tell them what you need. With introductory flight lessons for reasonable price, you can fly the plane yourself, with an FAA-certified flight instructor at your side. See the Rogue Valley from a birds-eye view and find out how to get a pilot license. Pacific Aviation uses the very popular Cessna 152 and Cessna 172, also known as the Sparrowhawk and Skyhawk. Other aircraft in the fleet include the classic Champ and the multi-engine Piper Apache. Pacific Aviation can give instruction for a variety of licenses and endorsements, including sport, recreational, private, commercial, multi-engine, complex, high performance and flight instructor. The flight staff includes commercial pilots and seasoned instructors who are well-versed in all of the requirements of general aviation. If you already own a plane, this is the place for maintenance and repair. The mechanics bring years of experience, as well as modern knowledge and expertise, and will help you maintain your aircraft in an efficient and professional atmosphere. If you're thinking of buying a plane, let Pacific do a pre-purchase inspection. Owners David and Brad Traeger are Rogue Valley natives living the dream. You can too at Pacific Aviation Northwest.

2244 Carton Way, Grants Pass OR
(541) 479-2230
www.pacificaviationnw.com

Orange Torpedo Trips

ATTRACTIONS:

Best inflatable kayak outfitter

Orange Torpedo Trips is the world's foremost inflatable kayaking outfitter, running trips on six different rivers in four states throughout the west. In 1969, local Grants Pass banker Jerry Bentley recognized the commercial potential of guided adventures by an inflatable kayak company after buying a couple of Sevylor Tahiti inflatable kayaks and running the lower Rogue River Canyon. The Rogue features many Class III rapids and two challenging class IV rapids. Maintaining a guest to guide ratio of three or four to one, Jerry and the successive owners have been able to safely provide first-time paddlers with a safe, scenic and educational river experience. Expanding their repertoire to include many multi-day adventures, Orange Torpedo Trips now offers trips in Idaho, Oregon, California and Arizona. With more than 60 employees during the summer, they take approximately 3,000 people down the rivers annually. For an amazing, spectacular and unforgettable adventure, take a trip with Orange Torpedo Trips. It will be the trip of a lifetime.

PO Box 1111, Grants Pass OR
(800) 635-2925
www.OrangeTorpedo.com

Pacific Aviation Northwest

BUSINESS: *Only place for single and multi-engine flight training*

Turn your dream of flying into reality at Pacific Aviation Northwest. Pacific Aviation is a full-service airport business providing ground school, flight training, aircraft rental, pilot supplies, aircraft fuel and aircraft maintenance services. Rent a plane for your pleasure, your business or maybe for a friend and add an aerial photography package for recreational and commercial use. Ride along with them, or tell them what you need. With introductory flight lessons for reasonable price, you can fly the plane yourself, with an FAA-certified flight instructor at your side. See the Rogue Valley from a birds-eye view and find out how to get a pilot license. Pacific Aviation uses the very popular Cessna 152 and Cessna 172, also known as the Sparrowhawk and Skyhawk. Other aircraft in the fleet include the classic Champ and the multi-engine Piper Apache. Pacific Aviation can give instruction for a variety of licenses and endorsements, including sport, recreational, private, commercial, multi-engine, complex, high performance and flight instructor. The flight staff includes commercial pilots and seasoned instructors who are well-versed in all of the requirements of general aviation. If you already own a plane, this is the place for maintenance and repair. The mechanics bring years of experience, as well as modern knowledge and expertise, and will help you maintain your aircraft in an efficient and professional atmosphere. If you're thinking of buying a plane, let Pacific do a pre-purchase inspection. Owners David and Brad Traeger are Rogue Valley natives living the dream. You can too at Pacific Aviation Northwest.

2244 Carton Way, Grants Pass OR
(541) 479-2230 *www.pacificaviationnw.com*

Mountain View Landscaping

GARDENS, PLANTS & FLOWERS:
Best landscapers

Over the last 20 years, Mountain View Landscaping has proven itself time and again to be one of the premier landscaping firms in Southern Oregon. The company employs more than a dozen people and provides complete landscape design, installation and maintenance services. Owners René and Robin Paré constantly strive to provide excellent service and quality work. In addition to residential and commercial work, they have undertaken major projects for the cities of Ashland, Medford and Grants Pass. René, a native of Grants Pass, earned a Bachelor of Science degree in horticulture, with an emphasis in landscape design, construction, irrigation and maintenance from Oregon State University in 1986. René gives back to the community through participation in organizations such as the Kiwanis Club, the Grants Pass Chamber of Commerce and the Oregon Landscape Contractors Association (OLCA). In addition to owning and operating Mountain View Landscaping, René and Robin also own Penniesworth Acres Nursery. This enterprise features beautiful, robust plants and specializes in rare or hard-to-get varieties. Both René and Robin are ardent believers in keeping up with the advances and rapid changes within the landscape industry. It has paid off for them—their company has received many area business-of-the-year awards and has won the OLCA State Landscape Competition five times. Call or visit Mountain View Landscaping and you will meet people who are ready, willing and able to provide any landscaping service you need.

**PO Box 404, Grants Pass OR
(Mountain View Landscaping)
(541) 474-0224
7016 New Hope Road, Grants Pass OR
(Penniesworth Acres Nursery)
(541) 761-1908**
www.mountainviewlandscaping.com

La Bella Faccia
HEALTH & BEAUTY: *Best facials*

High-end professional skin care is in demand, and La Bella Faccia of Grants Pass serves this demand in Southern Oregon. Owner Robbie Buckley offers a wide variety of spa services, but it is the corrective work, such as treatments for anti-aging, sun damage and acne, that draws the most people. Voted the best place to get a facial in the Rogue Valley in 2005, La Bella Faccia is results-oriented. The staff takes your lifestyle into consideration when suggesting treatments. Robbie and her staff are highly trained skin-care specialists who believe in providing superior services and educating clients on how to care for their skin. For exquisite relaxation as well as beauty, La Bella Faccia offers facial and full-body treatments complemented by aromatherapy. They invite people of all ages, genders and interests to try their cutting-edge services. A secondary aspect of the business is the Oregon Dermal Academy, considered one of the most intensive training programs for skin-care specialists in the country. Whether you seek a private spa day with champagne and a gourmet lunch or a chance to repose in an elegant and comfortable atmosphere, La Bella Faccia is the place to visit in Southern Oregon when you want to nurture your skin and your spirit.

1034 NW 6th Street, Grants Pass OR
(541) 471-4405

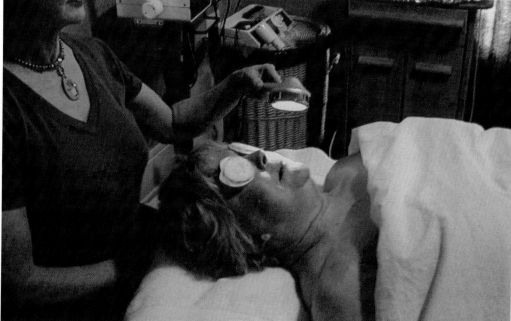

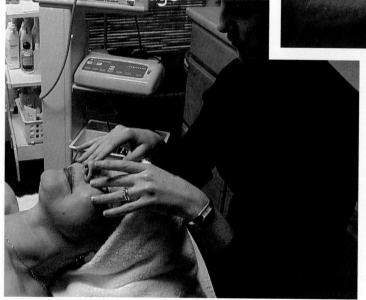

Mountain View Landscaping

HOME: *Best landscapers*

Over the last 20 years, Mountain View Landscaping has proven itself time and again to be one of the premier landscaping firms in Southern Oregon. The company employs more than a dozen people and provides complete landscape design, installation and maintenance services. Owners René and Robin Paré constantly strive to provide excellent service and quality work. In addition to residential and commercial work, they have undertaken major projects for the cities of Ashland, Medford and Grants Pass. René, a native of Grants Pass, earned a Bachelor of Science degree in horticulture, with an emphasis in landscape design, construction, irrigation and maintenance from Oregon State University in 1986. René gives back to the community through participation in organizations such as the Kiwanis Club, the Grants Pass Chamber of Commerce and the Oregon Landscape Contractors Association (OLCA). In addition to owning and operating Mountain View Landscaping, René and Robin also own Penniesworth Acres Nursery. This enterprise features beautiful, robust plants and specializes in rare or hard-to-get varieties. Both René and Robin are ardent believers in keeping up with the advances and rapid changes within the landscape industry. It has paid off for them—their company has received many area business-of-the-year awards and has won the OLCA State Landscape Competition five times. Call or visit Mountain View Landscaping and you will meet people who are ready, willing and able to provide any landscaping service you need.

**PO Box 404, Grants Pass OR
(Mountain View Landscaping)
(541) 474-0224
7016 New Hope Road, Grants Pass OR
(Penniesworth Acres Nursery)
(541) 761-1908**
www.mountainviewlandscaping.com

Troon Vineyard

WINERIES: *One of Southern Oregon's oldest wineries*

Located just outside of Grants Pass, Troon Vineyard is a boutique winery in the heart of the Applegate Valley. Founder, Dick Troon first planted the vineyard in 1972, and 20 years later produced roughly 1,500 cases of his first wine. When Mr. Troon decided to retire, current owners, the Martin family jumped at the chance to buy the Vineyard. Since purchasing it in August of 2003, Vintner Chris Martin and Winemaker Herb Quady have worked to expand both its size and production. The 11,000-square-foot expansion project was completed in the summer of 2005 and included adding an architecturally stunning new winery and tasting room, as well as the planting of 16 additional acres. One of the oldest vineyards in Southern Oregon, Troon produces world-class wines, including Alice's Rose, Jeanie in the Bottle (blush wine), Chardonnay, Cabernet Sauvignon, Zinfandel, River Guide Red and Druid's Fluid (their most popular blend). You can also enjoy the delicious pairings of food and wine their visiting chefs offer up. Soak up the grandeur of Troon Vineyard's 100-acre estate and their magnificent tasting room and winery.

1475 Kubli Road, Grants Pass OR
(541) 846-9900
www.troonvineyard.com

Woolridge Creek Vineyard
WINERIES: *Wines that will inspire your palate*

At Wooldridge Creek Vineyard and Winery in Grants Pass, owners Ted and Mary Warrick and winemakers Kara Olmo and Greg Paneitz invite you to stop in and experience an intimate family vineyard and winery. Wooldridge Creek is located in the heart of the Applegate River Valley. The winery and vineyards are situated on a beautiful rolling hillside that overlooks the majestic valley. The vineyards were first planted in the 1970s. Woolridge Creek now produces 12 varietals, including Cabernet Sauvignon, Merlot and Voignier. Wooldridge Creek's goal is to offer boutique wines that are approachable, just like the people you will meet during your visit here. Expect to learn about the history of the vineyards, about food that pairs well with the wines, and hear colorful local tales (be sure to ask about the local bears).

818 Slagle Creek Road, Grants Pass OR
(541) 846-6364
www.wcwinery.com

JACKSONVILLE

Jacksonville is one of the best-preserved historic sites in the western United States. More than 100 individual buildings are on the National Register of Historic Places. In 1966, the entire town of Jacksonville was designated a National Historic landmark. Jacksonville is filled with specialty shops, cozy inns and some of the Rogue Valley's best restaurants, all in the original brick and wood. Jacksonville hosts the Britt Festivals, a series of outdoor summer concerts. The Britt Gardens, home of the festival, were once an elaborate Victorian estate belonging to the early Oregon photographer Peter Britt, the first person to capture Crater Lake on film. In 1851, prospectors discovered gold nearby. Miners flocked to the Rogue Valley to seek their fortune. The bustling mining camp was transformed into a city with saloons, gambling halls, supply shops and a bank. It was home to the first Chinatown in Oregon. Jacksonville became the hub of Southern Oregon and the Jackson County seat. In 1884, however, the railroad bypassed Jacksonville for the new town of Medford. For the next 50 years, Jacksonville remained relatively unchanged, and the stasis preserved the town as an architectural monument.

PLACES TO GO

- Britt Gardens
  350 S 1st Street (541) 776-7001

- C.C. Beekman House
  Laurelwood and California Streets

- Jacksonville Children's Museum
  206 N 5th Street (541) 773-6536

- Jacksonville Woodland Natural Park
  Jacksonville Highway (State Route 238)

THINGS TO DO

January-February
- Chinese New Year Parade and Celebration
  (541) 899-8118

June
- Jacksonville Block Party
  (541) 899-8118

July
- Children's Festival
  Britt Gardens (541) 774-8678

The Jacksonville Inn
ACCOMMODATIONS: *Best accommodations*

In rustic Jacksonville, the Jacksonville Inn stands as a National Historic Landmark known throughout the West for its elegance and superb service. Housed in one of Jacksonville's early permanent buildings, the Inn, built in 1861, perpetuates the nostalgic romances of the gold-rush era. The walls of the dining area and lounge are built of locally quarried sandstone where specks of gold are still visible in the mortar. Hosts Jerry and Linda Evans and Mike and Jennifer Higgins offer you eight beautifully decorated hotel rooms plus four luxurious honeymoon cottages. One of the hotel rooms has a whirlpool tub, another offers a steam shower. The beds are queen-sized and some are canopied. All rooms are equipped with laptop computer connections. One of the cottages is now known as the Presidential Cottage, following an overnight stay by President George W. and Laura Bush. The Inn's wine and gift shop offers more than 2,000 wines, making it the largest retail wine collection in the area. The *Wine Spectator* bestowed its Award of Excellence on the Inn for its comprehensive wine list. Connoisseurs can look for special hard-to-find vintages dating back to 1811, or shop for everyday bargains. Redmen's Hall, the Inn's banquet facility, provides a charming atmosphere that enhances private meetings, weddings and receptions.

175 E California Street, Jacksonville OR
(541) 899-1900 or
(800) 321-9344
www.jacksonvilleinn.com

The Magnolia Inn

ACCOMMODATIONS:
Most romantic place to stay

Jacksonville is renowned for comfortable, luxurious lodgings, but even here the excellence of the Magnolia Inn distinguishes it as a cut above. The newest and most spacious bed and breakfast in this historic, perennially popular village, the Magnolia Inn combines the most appealing elements of a country inn with the amenities found in the most fashionable boutique hotels. In the three years since it opened, the Magnolia Inn has attracted clientele from as far away as Sweden and the Philippines, as well as having a strong local following. The Inn has earned AAA's prestigious Triple Diamond rating, and was featured in the December 2004 issue of *Sunset* magazine. Nine beautiful rooms, all with private baths, invite you to rest and relax. A refreshing night's sleep leads to the inviting smell of freshly brewed gourmet coffee and tempting pastries from local bakeries. During the day you can take a leisurely stroll through Jacksonville's downtown. Once there, you can take in the fascinating history of this former gold rush boom town or go shopping in one of the many delightful specialty stores that line the main street. But you don't need to go out; you can read a book, sip wine on Magnolia Inn's spacious outdoor veranda, or just watch the sights unfold. In the evening, dinner awaits you in any one of a number of award-winning restaurants. All are within easy walking distance. From herbal wraps to dinner reservations to a surprise in-room bouquet, the Magnolia Inn's owners, Frank and Cheryl Behnke, make sure that guests feel pampered.

245 N Fifth Street, Jacksonville OR
(866) 899-0255
www.magnolia-inn.com

Britt Festivals
ATTRACTIONS:
Southern Oregon's premier summer music festival

In 1963 the Northwest's first outdoor music festival was launched on an acoustically resonant hillside estate that once belonged to pioneer photographer Peter Britt. Since then, Britt Festivals has become the premier outdoor summer music festival in the region. Located in the historic 1850s gold rush town of Jacksonville, Britt presents a summer-long series of concerts featuring world-renowned artists in jazz, country, dance, folk, pop, world, blues, musical theater and classical music. Past performers include Willie Nelson, Bill Cosby, Ringo Starr, Crosby Stills & Nash, Wynton Marsalis, Vince Gill, Jean Pierre Rampal, Smokey Robinson, Peter Paul & Mary, and the Danish Royal Ballet, to name a few. With a capacity of 2,200, the natural amphitheater is a venue of unparalleled beauty overlooking the Rogue River Valley. Each summer about 75,000 patrons travel from all over to enjoy Britt's world-class performances, spectacular scenery and relaxing atmosphere.

(800) 882-7488
www.brittfest.org

Anita's Alterations
FASHION: *Best wedding designs and alterations*

Think of the next important occasion you'll be attending. Now think about how good you'll feel when you walk into the room and all heads turn to admire your clothing. Making people feel confident and creating gowns for weddings or special occasions has been Anita Ritchey's passion for more than 40 years. Anita is a direct descendant of 1880s Rogue Valley pioneers and the longevity of her career is testament to the way she treats her customers. What originally began as a hobby eventually became a lifelong profession when Anita searched to find work she could do while raising her three children. Her attention to detail and her love of creativity combine to make Anita's Alterations one of the very best alterations businesses in the country. Anita especially enjoys sewing for weddings. In fact, she creates custom designs for entire wedding parties. Anita artfully fits everyone from the flower girl to the father of the bride. She once made a wedding gown for a young bride and then, a generation later, she made a wedding dress for the same woman's daughter. Anita's work has been in numerous southern Oregon pageants and celebrations. She has created costumes for a Ms. Oregon contestant and competition clothing for Miss Teen Oregon. Her work has been on national television. She has created designs for movie stars. But her skill was proven when she created two green velvet dresses for a wedding in Ireland. Both dresses were made from measurements only, with no trial fittings. The dresses fit perfectly. At Anita's Alterations, you'll be in superb hands.

555 N 5th Street, Jacksonville OR
(541) 324-9721 or (541) 899-7536

Pico's Worldwide
FASHION: *Best eco-friendly clothing*

Walk through the doors of Pico's Worldwide in historic downtown Jacksonville and you will be greeted by Pico the bearded collie, store proprietor and mascot. He is just one of the many fantastic finds you will be pleased to discover at this unique shop, established in 2004 by Bethany Mulholland and Michael Richardson. Pico's is your southern Oregon source for hemp, organic cotton, recycled cotton and other eco-friendly clothing, as well as a large selection of other environmentally and socially responsible products, both imported and domestic. Shop Pico's for a full complement of home accents and personal accessories such as jewelry, handbags, scarves, genuine Panama hats, soap, soy candles, weavings, lamps, wall decorations, world music and a wide variety of other fun and functional products. When you're in Jacksonville, remember to leave plenty of time to visit Pico's Worldwide. You will need it to explore all of the interesting items that'll tickle your fancy.

160 E California Street, Jacksonville OR
(541) 899-4400

Jacksonville Inn Restaurant
RESTAURANTS & CAFÉS: *Most romantic restaurant*

To appreciate the Jacksonville Inn Restaurant, you may want to start with the critical acclaim they've received. First there is the fact that *Medford Mail-Tribune* readers voted it the Best Restaurant and Most Romantic Spot in the Rogue Valley. Then consider that the Mobil and AAA tour guides rate it at three stars, and the *Star Academy Award* of the Restaurant Industry gives it five stars. Frequently featured on CNN and The Learning Channel, *Pacific Northwest Magazine* and the *Oregon Magazine* have recognized it as one of Oregon's best restaurants. The *Wine Spectator* bestowed an award on the restaurant for its comprehensive wine list. Are you getting hungry? Then try the superb international cuisine prepared by the Jacksonville Inn Restaurant's master chefs. You can select Fresh Oregon Salmon or Razor Clams, Stuffed Hazelnut Chicken, Northern Velvet Venison, and Healthy for your Heart choices. Fresh herbs and spices, many of which are organically grown in the garden at the Inn, are used. End your meal with a choice from the tempting array of sumptuous desserts from the onsite bakery. You can enjoy it all in the formal dining room with its five-course *Table d'Hote*, or have a more casual experience in the bistro or lovely patio garden.

175 E California Street, Jacksonville OR
(541) 899-1900 or (800) 321-9344
www.jacksonvilleinn.com

Gogi's Restaurant
RESTAURANTS & CAFÉS:
First-class cuisine at the foot of Britt Gardens

Tucked away at the foot of Britt Gardens in historic Jacksonville, you'll find Gogi's Restaurant featuring first class cuisine exquisitely prepared by renowned Chef/Owner William Prahl. Chef Bill and his wife, Joyce, have brought the fine-dining experience of quality, selection and service known in the finest restaurants in San Francisco, New York and Paris to the quaint, romantic town of Jacksonville. Bill's passion for using the freshest ingredients while preparing each meal will excite your senses and keep you coming back. His intensely flavorful and creative cooking has earned him a reputation of being one of Oregon's most influential chefs. First tease your palate with an enticing appetizer followed by the signature Grilled Romaine Salad, a highly recommended creation of Bill's. The menu changes seasonally, although you can always find favorites such as the Pan Roasted Rack of Lamb, Mushroom Crusted Ahi Tuna, or the delicious duck breast. There is a good selection of wines to complement your meal, as well as a full bar. Whether you're dreaming about a romantic dinner for two or a casual place to dine, locals have deemed Gogi's a favorite you'll want to visit.

235 W Main Street, Jacksonville OR
(541) 899-8699
www.gogis.net

The Bella Union Restaurant & Saloon

RESTAURANTS & CAFÉS:
Award-winning food in historic Jacksonville

The Bella Union Restaurant & Saloon in historic Jacksonville has garnered a multitude of awards. The Bella Union remains a first choice for an intimate lunch, dinner or savory Sunday brunch. Once you taste their delicious fare, you'll become a Bella regular, too. Enjoy fresh, flavorful cuisine creatively prepared by executive chef Tom Bates. Savor the delicious pizza or the authentic pasta made fresh daily along with delectable homemade desserts and breads. Choose from more than a dozen lunch and dinner specials created daily, and enjoy an extraordinary selection of wines served by the glass or bottle. Select from four unique indoor dining areas or be seated on the outdoor deck in the shade of the 600-square-foot canopy of wisteria. Owner Jerry Hayes and his attentive staff will pamper you as you experience the great food and informal atmosphere. Stop by and experience for yourself all the delights of the Bella Union Restaurant & Saloon. Food to die for at a price that won't kill you. Open seven days a week for lunch and dinner.

170 W California Street, Jacksonville OR
(541) 899-1770
www.bellau.com

Scheffel's Toys Inc.
SHOPPING: *Best toy store*

Scheffel's Toys is a specialty toy store oriented toward one-on-one customer service. As befits a store that welcomes families, Scheffel's is family-owned and operated by Bill and Linda Graham, who have dedicated themselves to furnishing customers with the highest quality toys and collectibles available, at very affordable prices, for the young and young at heart. Found in historic Jacksonville, its whimsical window displays make the store seem like a vision of the small-town toy stores of yesteryear. Linda's parents, Jim and Judie Scheffel, opened the store in 1983. Originally the focus was on antiques, but Jim and Judie began to focus on toys out of frustration at being unable to find high-quality toys for their grandchildren. After visiting the original FAO Schwartz store in Manhattan, they were spurred to re-create that experience in their own store. In 1986, they decided to dedicate the store entirely to toys, and in 1992 Bill and Linda took over the store and have been running it happily ever since. The couple's vast product knowledge ensures that customers can find what they're seeking. There are toys for toddlers, books, games, dolls and science and craft kits. Scheffel's offers international shipping and free gift wrapping. Its no small wonder that some of Bill and Linda's customers have told them that the store represents what a toy store should be. For high quality toys at a competitive price, take your family to Scheffel's Toys.

180 W California Street, Jacksonville OR
(541) 899-7421
www.scheffels.com

Valley View Winery
WINERIES: *Best winery*

Valley View Winery offers a spectacular setting to enjoy an array of premium wines. Visitors will be struck by the breathtaking scenery. The winery specializes in delicious Cabernet Sauvignon, Merlot, Viognier, Syrah and Chardonnay wines. Valley View offers two labels of wines. The Anna Maria label represents the finest wines in the best vintages. The wines are available at many fine-dining restaurants and wine shops in Oregon. Valley View is also able to ship its wines to nearly all 50 states. The tasting room at Valley View Winery is beautiful and elegant. Large windows take advantage of the gorgeous view and allow natural light to stream in. Visitors will enjoy relaxing in the comfortable seating and sipping a selection of delicious wines. During the warmer months, visitors can bring a picnic lunch. Valley View Winery was established in 1972 by Anna Maria Wisnovsky and her husband, Frank. After Frank's death in 1980, Anna Maria and her children continued Frank's legacy. Sons Mark and Michael now run the winery. The Wisnovsky family invites you to visit their beautiful winery and tasting room.

1000 Upper Applegate Road,
Jacksonville OR
(541) 899-8468 or (800) 781-9463
www.valleyviewwinery.com

PLACES TO GO

- Baldwin Hotel Museum
  31 Main Street (541) 883-4207
- Bill Scholtes Sportsmans Park
  State Route 66, Keno (541) 882-1098
- Favell Museum of Western Art Artifacts
  125 W Main Street (541) 882-9996
- Klamath Art Association Gallery
  120 Riverside Drive (541) 883-1833
- Klamath County Museum
  1451 Main Street (541) 883-4208
- Lava Beds National Monument
  1 Indian Wells, Tuelake CA
- Lower Klamath National Wildlife Refuge
  State Line Road (California Route 161)
- Tulelake Museum of Local History
  800 S Main Street, Tulelake CA
- Upper Klamath National Wildlife Refuge
  West Side Road (530) 667-2231

THINGS TO DO

February
- Winter Wings Festival
  (541) 882-1219

May
- Great Northwestern Pro Rodeo
  Fairgrounds (541) 891-7547
- A Taste of Klamath
  (541) 884-LIVE (5483) ext 14
- Spirit of Captain Jack Memorial Pow Wow
  Fairgrounds (541) 891-8073

August
- Klamath County Fair
  Fairgrounds (541) 883-3796

September
- Tulelake-Butte Valley Fair
  Tulelake CA (530) 667-5312

October
- Rocky Point Fall Festival
  (541) 356-2550
- Klamath Basin Potato Festival
  Merrill (541) 883-6458
- Autumn Festival of Arts
  Fairgrounds (541) 883-2009

December
- Snowflake Festival
  (541) 883-5351

KLAMATH FALLS

Klamath Falls sits on the southern shore of Upper Klamath Lake on the eastern slopes of the Cascade Mountains. At an altitude of 4,100 feet, the basin is considered high desert and enjoys nearly constant sunshine. The area is home to the Oregon Institute of Technology and many historical, cultural and recreational attractions. Upper Klamath Lake, the largest lake in Oregon, hosts the greatest concentration of fall waterfowl on the West Coast and the largest wintering concentration of Bald Eagles in the lower 48 states. In February, nature enthusiasts from around the world celebrate this phenomenon at the Winter Wings Festival. Near town, the OCE&E Woods Line State Trail, a 100-mile rails-to-trails conversion, is paved from Klamath Falls to the small rural community of Olene and leads past scenic ranch lands, rivers and forested buttes. Across the California state line to the south is the Lava Beds National Monument, a rugged landscape punctuated by cinder cones, lava flows, spatter cones, underground lava tube caves and pit craters. In Klamath Falls you can find four historical museums, the landmark Ross Ragland Theater of performing and visual arts center and the Linkville Playhouse. Just outside of town are five golf courses.

Rocky Point Resort

ACCOMMODATIONS:
Best lodge resort

Sunsets and sunrises are gorgeous at Rocky Point Resort, but for a truly special treat plan dinner at the lodge during the full moon. The sight of the moon shining across Upper Klamath Lake will prove as memorable as your meal. The resort's restaurant provides a spectacular view of the lake with opportunities for viewing ducks, geese and other waterfowl. Set among ponderosa pines and Douglas firs on the northern shore of the lake, Rocky Point Resort is an excellent spot for fishing, canoeing and bird watching. Opportunities for observing wildlife abound with frequent spottings of bald eagles, beaver and white pelicans. Huge rainbow trout prowl Upper Klamath Lake. The unofficial record trout weighed more than 26 pounds. You can rent canoes, kayaks or motorboats, or berth your own vessel at the dock. The Upper Klamath Canoe Trail meanders nine and a half miles through marsh and lake. Hikers are only a few minutes away from the Sky Lakes Wilderness and the Pacific Crest Trail. Guests can rest easy in one of five guest rooms or four cabins equipped with kitchens. If you roll in prepared to camp, you can use one of the 29 RV hookups or four lakeside tent sites. RV and tent guests enjoy immaculate restrooms, showers and laundry facilities. The resort features a special romantic getaway package that provides dinner and breakfast for two, iced champagne in the room and a canoe rental for viewing wildlife. Visit Rocky Point Resort from April through October and be sure to bring your camera.

28121 Rocky Point Road, Klamath Falls OR
(541) 356-2287
www.rockypointoregon.com

2ND LT. DAVID R. KINGSLEY

Kingsley Field Mural, Klamath Falls
Photos by Nancy McClain

Kingsley Field, Oregon Air National Guard

ATTRACTIONS:

Serving the nation in war and peace

On a 4th of July in Southern Oregon, a military jet swoops low down the length of Main Street. The roar of the jet stirs every parade-goer. That plane almost certainly came from Kingsley Field and was flown by a member of the 173rd Fighter Wing (FW) of the Oregon Air National Guard. The 173rd FW sponsors a community open house, a popular local event, as part of the Century Eagle large force exercise. About 50 aircraft of varying types visit Kingsley Field during Century Eagle, which takes place in the second week of August in every odd-numbered year. While supporting community events is perhaps the most visible mission of the Air National Guard, the primary mission of the 173rd FW is to train pilots. The Kingsley Field unit provides basic flight instruction on the F-15 aircraft. It also trains new pilots and pilot instructors on air-to-air combat tactics, including nighttime lights-out exercises. The 173rd FW serves at home and abroad; members of the Oregon Air National Guard have been mobilized for service in Afghanistan and Iraq. The 173rd FW regularly flies flight surgeons and other medical specialists, giving these personnel a firsthand understanding of the physical pressures that pilots experience. Physicians who experience these flights can better evaluate the physical condition of the pilots back on the ground. Kingsley Field is the home of a world-class training center that serves the community, the state of Oregon and the nation.

211 Arnold Street, Suite 11, Klamath Falls OR
(541) 885-6198
www.orklam.ang.af.mil

The Scrapper's Corner

ARTS & CRAFTS: *Best scrapbook supplies*

Kristen Knoll, owner of the Scrapper's Corner, is passionate about scrapbooking. Her shop is a resource for preserving your most precious memories and can supply you with ideas for future projects. The Scrapper's Corner offers the newest scrapbooking products for cardmaking, rubber stamping and paper crafting. If you are short of ideas or want to add metal, ribbon, lettering or watercolor effects to your scrapbooks and cards, the friendly staff at the Scrapper's Corner can help. The Scrapper's Corner offers inspiring classes for people at all experience levels. Fees for classes are low, and a private introductory class is free. Receiving the undivided attention of a staff member gets new scrappers off to a good start. Special classes for kids or moms and kids together are always popular. You can learn to make holiday cards, study stamping techniques or layouts. The Scrapper's Corner recently became an EK Elite Store. This means that along with the EK Success product line, the shop offers SDU (Scrapbook Design University) classes. This exceptional educational program teaches beginning through advanced scrapbookers essential scrapbook theories and principles of design. Customers enjoy the crop room, which is free and available during store hours. Bring your lunch and bring your friends; bring your gear or use the store's. For hours of fun and satisfaction, visit the Scrapper's Corner.

2650 Washburn Way, Suite 102, Klamath Falls OR
(541) 273-6125
www.thescrapperscorner.com

Howard's Meat Center
MARKETS: *Best homemade sausage*

Klamath Falls is a great town for meat lovers, and Howard's Meat Center is one of the reasons. Founded by Dick Howard in 1964, this family business is now run by Michael, Dick's son. Howard's has a complete line of meat products, but for many customers, beef is what's for dinner. Howard's offers USDA Choice beef, including natural beef from Prather Ranch. Michael is proud of Howard's wide variety of homemade sausages. These include British bangers, spicy sweet Italian and Howard's own little chicken apple links. Of course, you can also pick up smoked bratwurst or dinner franks. Howard's has five flavors of pepperoni. Freezer owners can buy half a beef or half a hog, cut and wrapped. The shop stocks elk and buffalo pepperoni, salami and jerky, and from time to time buffalo and elk cuts are available. Whatever meat you prefer, Howard's can dress it up. Michael prepares Howard's special marinades, for example Pop's Secret Sauce and Howard's own teriyaki sauce. You can shop for cuts prepared in the store, such as the marinated tri-tips, or buy the sauces to take home. Howard's has many local products to complement the meat. You can sample wild plum syrup or preserves, huckleberry products and local honey. Howard's is a full-service meat counter that gives personal service to every customer. For a variety of meats that will keep you running back, come to Howard's Meat Center.

5717 S 6th Street, Klamath Falls OR
(541) 884-8430

Diamond S Meat Co.
MARKETS: *Best jerky and snack sticks*

Whether you need a star attraction for your holiday table or snacks on the run, Diamond S Meat Co. has something for you. This company's award-winning custom and specialty meat shop offers tasty wares that range from marinated tri-tips and bacon-stuffed prime rib to jerky and beef snack sticks. You can pick up smoked turkey or maple-cured ham. Diamond S prepares delightful gift baskets with salami, summer sausage and much else that you can give during the holidays. Other sausages include bratwurst, Andouille and smoked Kielbasa. The Northwest Meat Processors Association has awarded Diamond S a wall's worth of awards for its products. The beef jerky, snack sticks and breakfast pork sausage have won multiple prizes. The ham, bacon and summer sausage have also received awards. In addition to meats, the shop carries items such as specialty barbecue sauces and spices. Co-owner Steve Robnett entered the meat business 20 years ago with a custom mobile processing service. Since then, Steve has traveled the Klamath Basin in his custom truck, processing livestock for small producers. In 1997, Steve and Dayle Robnett, his wife, opened the specialty meat shop that Dayle now manages. The specialty shop and the mobile processing service are the two halves of the family business. If you run a few head of cattle, Steve is your man. Everyone can enjoy the mouth-watering merchandise that Dayle sells at the Diamond S Meat Co. retail shop.

7400 Kings Way, Klamath Falls OR
(541) 884-8767

New Northwest Broadcasters

MEDIA: *Best broadcasting company*

New Northwest Broadcasters (NNB) provides top quality radio on its 37 stations, five of which are in Klamath Falls. Because of Klamath's unique location, citizens rely greatly on radio for community information. NNB's KAGO AM supplements up-to-the-minute local and regional news with personalities such as Rush Limbaugh, Sean Hannity and Laura Ingraham. KAGO FM, The Rock, plays straight-up rock-and-roll with plenty of attitude. Led Zeppelin, the Beatles and ZZ Top are just a few of the masters of rock you'll hear, along with the newest rock from bands such as Def Leppard, Metallica and the Red Hot Chili Peppers. KKJX gives the area's many Hispanic residents a station they can call their own. Its *La Maquina Musical* format is immensely popular. KLAD is the most listened to radio station in the region. It is a modern country station with Southern Oregon's most powerful signal, award-winning programming and total commitment to community. KLAD's sound is built around artists such as Reba McEntyre, Garth Brooks and Shania Twain. Along with Nashville's best, KLAD provides local news, weather and community information. KYSF is Klamath's hit music station for today's young adult listener. It features today's best-selling artists such as Kelly Clarkson, the Black Eyed Peas and Mariah Carey, and programs such as Rick Dee's Weekly Top 40. Whether you want great listening, news or a fruitful place to advertise, the NNB stations have a format for you.

4509 S 6th Street, Suite 201, Klamath Falls OR
(541) 882-8833
www.nnbradio.com/stations/klamathfalls.html

Klamath Lake
Photo by Nancy McClain

The Epicenter Bowling Complex

RECREATION:

Best wholesome entertainment in Klamath Falls

Bowling is among the most social of sports, an excellent way for friends and family to meet and mix. The brainchild of Dennis and Reba VanAcker in 1999, the Epicenter Bowling Complex offers 32 PBA-approved lanes with the latest in scoring, lighting and equipment. With automated bumpers for the kids, state-of-the-art audio and video systems, there is never a dull moment for any age at the Epicenter. For serious bowlers, there is Wile E's Corner, a pro shop brought to you by three-time PBA Champion Joe Salvemini. If you need coaching, there are three USBA-certified coaches on staff to help polish up your game. The Epicenter is host to numerous leagues throughout the year, as well as state and national tournaments, including a regular stop for the Senior PBA Tour, the Epicenter Senior PBA Classic. The complex also hosts a 2,700-square-foot, state-of-the-art arcade, called Faultline, where the latest in arcade games and redemption prizes can be won. After Shock Sports Bar & Grill is the center's 4,000-square-foot sports bar, featuring four 110-inch high-definition projection systems, along with 16 other televisions for everyone's sports viewing pleasure. In addition, do not forget the great food. After Shock offers a meal for any taste. After hours, it's the Nightclub @ The After Shock, where the best DJs and music combine to provide the best party in the Basin. So come visit The Epicenter Bowling Complex, where everyone can have an earth-shaking good time.

**3901 Brooke Drive
(across from Wal-Mart),
Klamath Falls OR
(541) 273-0700**
www.epicenterbowl.com
www.aftershockclub.com

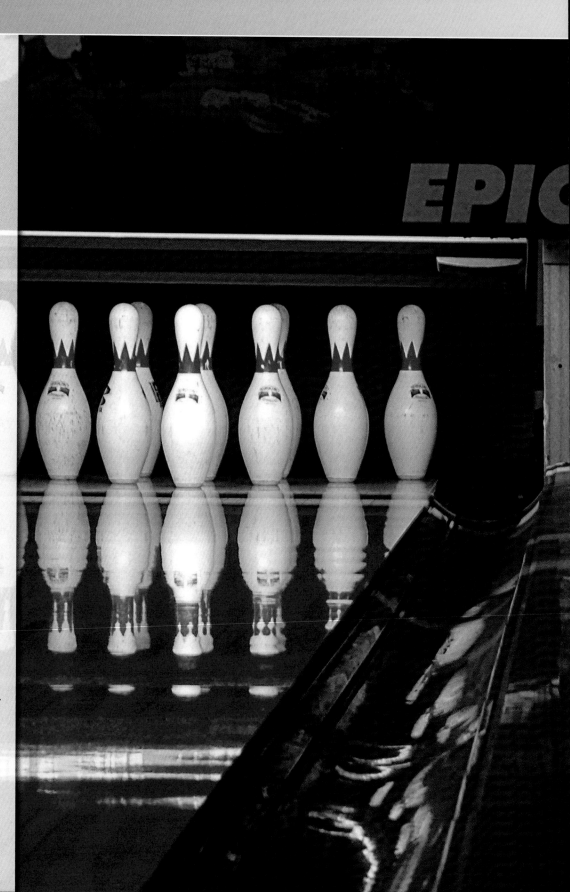

Photo by Nancy McClain

PLACES TO GO

- Bear Creek Park
  Siskiyou Boulevard

- Fichtner-Mainwaring Park
  334 Holmes Avenue

- Harry and David's Country Village (store and tours)
  1314 Center Drive, Suite A
  (877) 322-8000

- Hawthorne Park and Pool
  Hawthorne Avenue

- Prescott Park (Roxy Ann Peak)
  Roxy Ann Road

- Railroad Park (scale model train rides)
  Berrydale Avenue

- Rogue Gallery & Art Center
  40 S Bartlett Street
  (541) 772-8118

THINGS TO DO

April
- Pear Blossom Parade & Street Fair
  541-734-PEAR (7327)

- Roxy Ann Gem & Mineral Show
  Medford Armory
  (541) 878-1445

May
- Art in Bloom
  Downtown
  (541) 608-8524

June
- A Taste of History
  Vogel Plaza
  (541) 779-1435

- Medford Cruise
  (541) 608-8516

July
- Rogue Valley Balloon Rally
  Airport
  (541) 664-2171

September
- Multicultural Fair
  Alba Park
  (541) 292-2169

October
- Medford Jazz Jubilee
  (541) 770-6972 ext. 313

MEDFORD

Medford, an all-American city, lies in the Bear Creek Valley on flat land rimmed by mountains. The rich farmland that surrounds Medford has made it the pear capital of the world. Medford's largest employer is Harry & David's, the mail-order company world-famous for its Royal Riviera Pears. Increasingly, however, wine grapes are replacing pears. The region has its own wine appellation, the Rogue Valley AVA, and dozens of wineries offer tours and tastings. Llamas are another area farm attraction—children love to pet these friendly beasts. The Oregon & California Railroad created Medford in 1884 by running its line through here. The town was initially called Middle Ford, because it was on the middle ford of Bear Creek, but a railroad engineer from Medford, Massachusetts soon shortened the name. Medford has several landmark sights that include Roxy Ann Peak, an undeveloped park east of town that offers hikers fabulous views. Another landmark is the two buildings of the Rogue Valley Manor, perched on a high hill overlooking the southern approaches to town. It says something about Medford's family values that the city's tallest structures are retirement centers rather than office buildings. Medford is a major health care and shopping center. North Californians flock to the Rogue Valley Mall, the Medford Center, Crater Lake Plaza and other shopping districts because Oregon has no sales tax. Cultural attractions include the Craterion Ginger Rogers Theater, an important venue for national and local performers. The sports-minded can visit Lava Lanes, an impressive, nationally ranked bowling facility.

Rogue Regency Inn

ACCOMMODATIONS: *Finest full service hotel*

The Rogue Regency Inn is the place to stay in Medford. Whether you're just visiting or are here on business, this full-service hotel has everything to make your stay comfortable and enjoyable. The beautiful two-story lobby reflects Rogue Regency's reputation for service and hospitality. Fully remodeled in 2005, you can expect the best room service or you can enjoy a meal at Chadwicks, the Regency's own Pub and state-of-the-art Sports Bar. Check the website for more information about Comedy Night at Chadwicks. If you choose to stay for the night, you may want to reserve a suite with a hot tub so you can truly relax and unwind, or you can sleep in one of the 203 beautiful rooms. Conveniently located in the heart of the Rogue Valley, the Rogue Regency Inn is just off Interstate 5 near the Jackson County Airport, giving you perfect access to rivers, mountains, forests and all of the recreational and cultural attractions found nearby.

2300 Biddle Road, Medford OR
(541) 770-1234 or (800) 535-5805
www.rogueregency.com

Wild Birds Unlimited

ANIMALS & PETS: *Best place for backyard birders*

For more than a decade, Medford's Wild Birds Unlimited has been successfully feeding the curiosity of bird watchers and nature lovers in a store that captures the tranquil beauty of the outdoors. Wild Birds Unlimited is the first and largest retail store franchise to cater to the backyard birdwatcher. Established in 1981, there are now more than 300 stores in North America. Their mission is to bring people and nature together, and to do so with excellence. They accomplish this goal by offering knowledgeable sales and service, including educating patrons about backyard and wilderness bird watching. When you do your nature shopping at Wild Birds Unlimited in Medford, you'll find that owner Katy Reed and assistant store manager Jeanne Rapet will introduce you to a fascinating array of nature gift items. Bird houses and feeders are in stock, as well as field guide books and other accessories to help you with your bird watching experience. They carry the best in bird feed products, as well as regionally formulated seed blends. Garden enhancements, such as wind chimes, mobiles and ornaments, are also available. Some of Wild Birds Unlimited's revenue goes to support Pathways to Nature, which promotes the creation and maintenance of trails, boardwalks, wildlife-viewing platforms and nature center exhibits. Come discover the world of bird watching at Wild Birds Unlimited.

712 Crater Lake Avenue, Medford OR
(541) 770-1104
www.wbu.com/medford

Rogue Automotive

AUTO: *Best automotive service in the Rogue Valley*

Owners Buddy and Amie Pickard of Rogue Automotive have been providing outstanding automotive service for Southern Oregon and Northern California for years. Loyal customers will tell you that at Rogue Automotive you'll get immediate, fast, professional service. They are proud of their consistent attention to detail and all of their services are provided with honesty and courtesy. Rogue Automotive is a family-owned, friendly, total-service facility that is focused on satisfied customers and repeat business. All of Rogue Automotive's staff are fully trained and highly experienced. One of their missions is to provide a unique automotive experience. Customers come from many miles away because of their past successful dealings and because of Rogue's reputation. In addition to their regular fine service, Amie and Buddy provide free air-conditioning check-ups year round. Bring your automobile to Rogue Automotive and you will both leave satisfied.

940 N Central Avenue, #B, Medford OR
(541) 245-1740 *www.rogueautomotive.com*

Les Schwab

AUTO: *If they can't guarantee it, they won't sell it*

The birth of the Les Schwab Tire Company occurred in January of 1952, when Les Schwab purchased a small OK Rubber Welders tire store in Prineville. With a $3,500 investment and a strong desire to own his own business, Les increased the sales of his store from $32,000 to $150,000 in the first year. Les had a strong determination to provide a business opportunity for people who could not afford to go into business for themselves. As the company continued to grow, Les came up with what is known as the supermarket tire store concept. His goal was to have his warehouse in his showroom so that customers could walk through the racks of tires and pick out the actual tires that would go on their vehicle. He also stocked more than one brand of tire in each size to give customers a choice. Today, the Les Schwab Tire Company is one of the largest independent tire companies in the United States. Les is the first to say the success of the Les Schwab Tire Company has been made possible by wonderful customers who are the most important people in the business. Nothing happens in the Les Schwab Tire Company until a customer leads the way by choosing new tires, a wheel alignment or any of the other services they offer. Les Schwab is proud to feature neat clean stores, supermarket selection, convenient credit, sudden service, and a written warranty you don't pay extra for. Les's slogan is, "If we can't guarantee it, we won't sell it!" Come into one of the 385 Les Schwab stores today.

www.lesschwab.com

Tires LES SCHWAB

Mellelo Coffee Roasters

BAKERIES, COFFEE & TEA:
Best coffee roasters

In Medford, Sal and Tami Mellelo know very well that coffee sales are based on quality, not price. Their response is to offer a fine Italian coffee that pleases an ever-growing cadre of coffee lovers who find Mellelo distinguished for its quality. Say Sal and Tami, "We roast to order in small batches and hand blend each origin one at a time. This process takes one-third longer, but we don't mind, as this is what sets us apart from commercial roasters.

Our process of roasting combines Old World quality and artistry with today's technology. It produces a smooth, rich, aromatic espresso and a full-bodied cup of coffee." Not only do customers agree, so does the Specialty Coffee Association of America, which recently awarded Mellelo its Tops Award, one of the most coveted awards a coffee roaster/retailer can receive. Sal started with a six-foot expresso cart on a downtown Medford street corner, and as of this writing has four locations in Medford. He supplies many fine restaurants, performing arts centers and hotels. He also supplies drive-through locations all over the U.S. Every batch is roasted to order, using gas-fired German roasters, from a company that has been in business for more than 160 years, and is considered the finest of its type. Try a cup of Colombian Supremo, Costa Rican Terrazu, Panama Lerida Estate, Celebes Kalossi, or their other roasts. The friendly and efficient staff at Mellelo Coffee Roasters are waiting to help you to take that first perfect sip.

3651 Lear Way, Medford OR
229 W Main Street, Medford OR
100 E 6th Street, Medford OR
205 S Central,
(Jackson County Library Building)
(541) 779-9884
www.mellelo.com

View from Hillcrest Drive, Medford
Photo by Wendy Gay

Scarab Media
BUSINESS: *Best web design*

Scarab Media provides the latest tools to make interaction with websites simple and easy. Known for quality website development and redesign, graphics and logo creation, print media, business cards and e-commerce solutions, Scarab Media has more than a decade of experience. Lead developer and president Andy Spliethof says his business is "the best you can get, whatever your price range." Andy focuses on making Scarab Media's work professional, artistic, reasonably priced and prompt. With these goals in mind, Andy and his staff create award-winning websites. Some of Scarab Media's clients include Adventure White Water, Heritage Motors and the Willows Bed and Breakfast. The level of site design can range from basic, affordable web pages to more advanced database solutions for your company's e-commerce needs. Scarab Media is officially authorized by UPS for e-commerce. Staff members are dedicated to providing exceptional service to all their patrons. They have reliable servers for hosting, work with both small and large businesses and offer websites that are well designed, functional and visually appealing. They are also, in effect, an artistic wing for ad agencies. Scarab Media can give your business a professional edge online, so visit their website or call them today.

835 E Main Street, Suite A, Medford OR
(541) 734-7308 or (888) 755-7308
www.scarabmedia.com

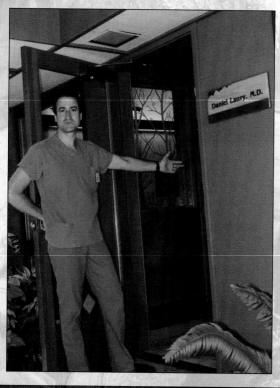

Dr. Daniel Laury

HEALTH & BEAUTY:

Dr. Laury started the TV Show "The Doctor is Listening"

Dr. Daniel Laury's philosophy is, "The better informed a woman is concerning her health options, the better decisions she will be able to make." A graduate of Albert Einstein College of Medicine in New York, Dr. Laury is committed to this belief and is continuously researching the best choices available for his patients. He enjoys keeping up with changes and being able to offer state-of-the-art procedures. For example, in the last few years new techniques have been developed that may replace invasive surgeries such as hysterectomies. Being able to offer an outpatient procedure in place of an overnight hospital stay and weeks of recovery is exciting. Dr. Laury started the Rogue Valley TV program *The Doctor is Listening* to help inform women of their options. Women e-mail their questions to the doctor for discussion on the program. To reach more people, he gives educational talks, seminars and writes articles for various journals. His concern with keeping track of the latest health advancements led him to be on the advisory board of the Life Extension Foundation. Dr. Laury is a photography enthusiast and his lovely waiting room and office reflect this hobby. "Women tell me they want to have our waiting room in their home. We want them to feel comfortable and relaxed." He also enjoys scuba diving and hiking during his free time, and is fascinated by the organic propagation of exotic plants, such as Pomegranate and Medlar. If you're concerned about your health, visit Dr. Laury's for a checkup.

786 State Street, Medford OR
(541) 773-5500
www.drlaury.yourmd.com/drlaury

Dermatology & Laser Associates
HEALTH & BEAUTY: *Most advanced dermatological care*

The most advanced dermatological care is now available in Medford at Dermatology & Laser Associates, located in a new 8,500-square-foot facility. You will appreciate the comfortable waiting and exam rooms and the friendly and professional staff. The caring doctors are all board certified in dermatology. Dr. Douglas Naverson took over the practice from the founder, Dr. Lee Harlow, in 1982. He is certified in dermatopathology and is a published writer on the subject of dermatology. He is also considered a regional laser expert. Dr. Dwight Tribelhorn has special expertise in skin cancer surgery and reconstruction, including advanced training in microscopically controlled surgery. Dr. David Igelman was an Air Force flight surgeon before joining the practice, and has done volunteer work at clinics in Korea and Thailand. He also donates his time to teaching southern Oregon school children about skin care and protection. Dr. Jen Mendelson, the newest team member, was a field wildlife biologist before she entered the medical profession, bringing a unique perspective to general dermatology. A full range of services are provided, from cosmetic procedures and treatments for acne and other skin diseases to surgery for even the most aggressive skin cancers. For the best skin care anywhere, come to Dermatology & Laser Associates of Medford, LLP.

2959 Siskiyou Boulevard, Suite B, Medford OR
(541) 773-3636
www.dermlaser.org

Laser Derm
HEALTH & BEAUTY: *Best laser treatments*

Enhancing the health and beauty of your skin is the focus of Laser Derm, Inc. Elliott Meyerding, M.D., has been a Rogue Valley physician and surgeon since 1984. During the complimentary MD consultation, each patient participates in an assessment of their skin, a discussion of environmental factors affecting the skin, and the development of their customized treatment plan. Treatment for facial and leg veins, 3-D skin rejuvenation (for skin laxity, sun spots and skin texture), and permanent hair reduction are accomplished for both men and women with a laser that is safe for all skin colors. At Laser Derm, located near Rogue Valley Medical Center, you can investigate alternatives to plastic surgery and discover how the most advanced technology and latest skin care products can be combined with your knowledge to permanently improve your skin's texture, health and beauty.

2931 Doctors Park Drive, Medford OR
(541) 773-7219

Fireside Masonry

HOME:
Best natural stone work

Tom Cavanaugh has been building natural stone fireplaces, arches, flower planters, brick and paver pathways, retaining walls, and porches for Rogue Valley residents since he was 17 years old. Tom's grandfather taught Tom's father and uncle the masonry trade and then Tom apprenticed with his uncle. Now, 20 years later, the strong tradition of excellence set by the Cavanaugh family thrives at Fireside Masonry. When you speak with Tom, you can tell he loves his work and has great passion and justifiable pride in the service he provides. His crew is devoted to the trade and goes out of their way to provide customer satisfaction in everything they do. As for special project requests, Tom says they "do it all." Not sure about what you want? Tom has a solution for nearly every situation. Tom will do "whatever it takes to get the job done right." His motto is, "If you ever say, 'that's good enough' then it's time for you not to do it anymore." He has completed a long list of Rogue Valley projects and will gladly share them with you during your free consultation. Although his daughter, Hailey, is only five years old, Tom hopes that someday she will take an interest in the family profession and become the fourth generation Cavanaugh dedicated to the field of masonry. The next time you plan to beautify or improve your home's appearance, call Fireside Masonry and discover what Tom can do for you.

7696 Gladstone, White City OR
(541) 890-8294

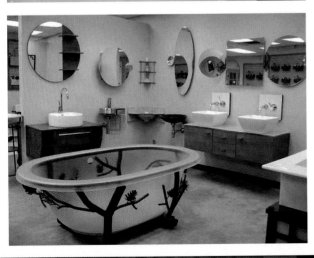

Budge-McHugh Supply

HOME: *Best plumbing fixtures and hardware*

With a sales staff that has a combined 224 years of experience in the plumbing and hardware industry, a visit to Budge-McHugh Supply ensures that you will receive honest and accurate information to guide you in your purchasing decisions. Budge-McHugh is a second generation, family-owned and managed business. Founded in 1959 by Boyd Budge and Ken McHugh, the company has operated continuously from their historic location. Every aspect of the customer's order is processed, tracked and delivered from this same location. It is the mission of Budge-McHugh to "provide a luxury experience by offering only the best designed and engineered products, made with the highest quality materials, and manufactured to exacting standards by leading companies in the world of decorative plumbing and hardware." Managed by Jim Cheshire, Budge-McHugh's extensive showrooms will provide you with the opportunity to see high quality products that are both beautiful and functional. It is Budge-McHugh's aim to ensure that their customers are provided with a lifetime of trouble-free use and that their purchases are an investment that offers the highest value possible. If you have ever thought that choosing bathroom plumbing and accessories would be lacking in excitement, think again. Give Budge-McHugh Supply a visit and see plumbing fixtures that are works of art.

125 W 4th Street, Medford OR
(541) 779-6180

Interiors at the Livery Stable
HOME: *Best interior design*

Have you ever been in a beautifully decorated home that didn't reflect the owner's personality? Marlys Weinman, owner of Interiors at the Livery Stable, believes a professional designer should listen to a client and create a home that mirrors their lifestyle. A successfully designed space should reflect the client's lifestyle rather than the designer's. Marlys helps her clients achieve their goals by spending time with them and getting to know them. She then works directly with clients and their contractors to ensure that they attain a masterful design with maximum lifestyle compatibility. Interiors at the Livery Stable has been a full service design studio since 1972 and offers a complete selection of fabrics, wallpapers, accessories and furnishings. They can provide qualified tradesmen, such as upholsterers, fabricators, and installers. The staff at Interiors at the Livery Stable handle all phases of interior design, from initial concept to placing orders and overseeing installation. Let Marlys and her staff at Interiors at the Livery Stable incorporate your ideas into a home that makes you look forward to coming home.

29 S Grape Street, Medford OR
(503) 772-3333

Lotus Imports
HOME: *Best Asian-inspired imports*

Ray and Ronnie Konopasek, owners of Lotus Imports, are creating a buzz with their extraordinary, Asian-inspired indoor and outdoor furnishings and gifts. The owners select each piece with care. Lotus Imports offers a continually updated inventory with new merchandise always in stock. The furniture includes popular pieces, such as rattan chairs or loungers, fountains, a variety of water features and teak benches. Lotus Imports buys directly from suppliers, allowing lower pricing and savings to be passed on to customers. In many cases, the suppliers are also the craftspeople who make the products, so custom orders are possible through Lotus Imports. The shop is serene and beautifully arranged. Mellow, uplifting music plays in the background while Ronnie's exquisite orchids grace the room settings. Offering new and interesting imported furniture and gifts at reasonable prices, Lotus Imports is a hot spot for home and garden decor.

4778 Crater Lake Avenue, Medford OR
(541) 772-1730

Two Sisters Teak
HOME: *Best handcrafted teak*

For solid, luxurious indoor and outdoor teak furnishings, Two Sisters Teak is the place to shop. Owners Phil T. and Deborah Burke provide a wide variety of solid teak. Phil encourages people to come in and smell the teak, because many people really like the fresh, clean scent of this hardwood. The teak originates on the tropical island of Java, Indonesia where the trees take 40 to 60 years to grow and are sustainably forested. Teak is a beautiful hardwood that lasts a lifetime. Water doesn't penetrate it and it is naturally insect-resistant. At Two Sisters Teak, all the furniture is teak through and through. There are no veneers or mixes with other woods, and all of the work is handmade and hand sanded. Quality furniture draws a lot of attention, so browsers are more than welcome. Phil designs some of his own furniture, which is available in the store. In addition, he is willing to take on custom work. Customer satisfaction equal to the superlative beauty of teak is the top priority at Two Sisters Teak. Visit their shop and experience the aesthetics and aroma of this exotic wood for yourself.

4934 Crater Lake Avenue, Medford OR
(541) 770-6790
www.twosistersteak.com

D & D Plumbing & Repair
HOME: *Best plumbers*

Don Slater and his sons have been able to do something few fathers and sons have the opportunity to do: build strong personal relationships with each other at the same time they build a strong and respected business. Don started D & D Plumbing & Repair in Medford almost 30 years ago and gave his sons Cory and Daniel the opportunity to learn precious skills, make some money and spend some working hours with their dad from an early age. Cory has been able to build a similar relationship with his son Randy. D & D customers are highly satisfied with the family's high standards and strong work ethic. If you have a particularly difficult project, these are the men to call. They will squeeze into narrow crawl spaces, snake pipes in places few dare to go and repair broken pipe in scorching or freezing temperatures. You could say plumbing is in their blood; after all they come from a family of plumbers, going back to Don's great-great-grandfather John James Slater, a Washington plumber who apprenticed in Chicago. Don's great-grandfather Charles learned the trade as a 13-year-old apprentice in Austin, Texas and went on to become an Oregon state plumbing inspector. For many generations of accumulated plumbing know-how, fair prices and thoroughness, call D & D Plumbing & Repair. The Slaters will keep the water in your life running smoothly and efficiently.

1207 Sage Road, Medford OR
(541) 772-2111

Northridge Center

LIFESTYLE DESTINATIONS:
Best assisted living

Northridge Center is a licensed assisted living facility owned and operated by the Connell family for 30 years. Aging poses challenges in varying degrees and the services offered by Northridge are designed to give support where it is needed. Five levels of care, tailored to each resident, range from minor assistance to total care in all activities of daily living. A registered nurse coordinates all medical issues, including medication management, also offering individual consultations whenever necessary. The highly trained and dedicated staff carries on the tradition of uncompromising care. Independence, dignity, and privacy are the watchwords at Northridge, and every resident is treated with the utmost respect. Studio and one-bedroom apartments are available in the state-of-the-art building and residents are encouraged to decorate with their own treasured possessions. Residences and mail boxes are privately locked for independence and security. Maintenance and housekeeping are included and beautiful grounds, extensive common areas, and restaurant-style dining are available to all residents. While many enjoyable activities are offered, residents may be as social or as solitary as they choose and families are always welcome. For yourself or a loved one, Northridge is an excellent choice for living all of life to the fullest.

3737 S Pacific Highway, Medford OR
(541) 535-5497
www.northridgecenter.net

by Nancy McClain

Horton Plaza

LIFESTYLE DESTINATIONS:
Best resort-style retirement community

Since 1995, Horton Plaza has been Southern Oregon's premier retirement community. Located in Medford, Horton Plaza's residents are able to enjoy Southern Oregon's pristine surroundings, mild climate and strong community values. Owners Ann and Larry Horton proudly offer seniors the extraordinary lifestyle that comes with living in a full-service senior community living facility. Spacious studios, one-bedroom and two-bedroom apartments are available, all featuring abundant storage, well equipped kitchenettes and bay windows. Horton Plaza will delight residents with all of its first-class amenities.

Indulge yourself in their elegant, full-service dining room, where three delicious restaurant-style meals are served daily. A private dining room is available for entertaining family or for other special occasions. Curl up with a book in the library, receive a little pampering at the beauty salon, enjoy a gourmet cooking class in the community kitchen, participate in an invigorating exercise class or take a leisurely stroll through the lush Oriental courtyard. Whatever your pleasure, Horton Plaza provides the very best in resort-style living for the active senior, in the heart of the Pacific Northwest.

1122 Spring Street, Medford OR
(541) 770-1122 or (800) 844-4058
www.hortonplza.com

Porters Dining at the Depot
RESTAURANTS & CAFÉS: *Best prime rib*

In the heart of Medford stands a wonderfully restored 1910 Historic Landmark Train Station with a soaring tile roof, massive beams and hand-cut brick and stone exterior. Step inside and feel the warm, comfortable and authentic Craftsman-era detailing of Porters Dining at the Depot. Renowned for slow roasting of the Rogue Valley's finest prime rib, Porters is also the place to find superb fresh seafood, chops, aged beef steaks and creative seasonal and local specials. The Chef's flavors, ranging from Asian to Mediterranean to Pacific Northwest, are perfectly complemented by the offerings from Porters' popular bar. Choose from more than 60 classic and regional wines, ice-cold draft beers that rotate once a month, a stellar selection of scotches, bourbons and vodkas or the legendary martini menu. Add to this the friendly, knowledgeable service and you will understand why AAA rewarded Porters with Medford's only 3 Diamond Rating, a level usually reserved for more formal and expensive restaurants. Warm weather brings *al fresco* dining on the vine shaded patio, once used as the passenger landing for the old train station. A close look will reveal writings on the bricks taking you back to the Golden Era of railroads.

147 N Front Street, Medford OR
(541) 857-1910
www.PortersTrainStation.com

Zinnia Café
RESTAURANTS & CAFÉS: *Best soups and sandwiches*

Simplicity and freshness are the bywords at Zinnia Café. Owner Lisa Lawrence and her staff consider minutes and hours the measure of freshness in their offerings. Breads are baked at Zinnia Café and used the same day. Also prepared daily are all of the sandwich ingredients, and their homemade soups. Speaking of soup, Monday's special is called Cook's Inspiration. Other daily specials are portobello tortellini, broccoli cheddar, French onion or tomato bisque. East coast style sandwiches include the Italian grinder, chili chicken, pastrami on rye and grilled portobello on foccacia. Scrumptious wraps are available in combinations that will appeal to anyone. Delicious salads are presented in whole and half sizes. Try the Zinnia Chef Salad or the other tasty combinations made especially to tempt your taste buds. Want to do your own thing? Build your own sandwich from Zinnia Café's long and enticing list of ingredients. One thing is for sure, if you go to Zinnia Café once, it's guaranteed that you will be back. Zinnia Café's loyal customers boast that whatever their choice was for that day, it was the best food they've ever had.

820 Crater Lake Avenue, Cedar Mall, Medford OR
(541) 773-8114

Main Antique Mall
SHOPPING: *Best antiques*

The Main Antique Mall in Medford is a 30,000-square-foot treasure trove of ever-changing antiques. Doris and Ken Cearley have owned and operated the Main Antique Mall for more than 15 years. Two hundred-plus dealers rent booths where they show and sell their special interests and collections to the public. Fascinating in itself are the different personalities expressed in the individual booths. Local dealers mix with dealers from Seattle, southern California, Idaho, and as far away as Florida. You'll find everything from china, glass, crystal, needlework, quilts and linens, to military, Western, sports and fishing collectibles. Treasures include furniture, costume jewelry, silver, pottery, crocks, toys, political memorabilia and nostalgia items. Main Antique Mall prides itself on providing high-quality products from reputable dealers. February and October are sale months when you'll find discounts throughout the store. Browsing at the Main Antique Mall can become a hobby in itself. The inventory changes frequently and you might miss something, so stop in often.

30 N Riverside, Medford OR
(541) 779-9490

Photo by Donna K. Lindley

Pacific Wine Club
WINERIES: *Best wine club*

Victoria and Ken Green love everything about fine wines. These two aren't just mere wine connoisseurs, they love all the myriad details that go into the making of a great wine, from where the grapes grow to the philosophies of winemaking that different vintners espouse. They've explored this passionate hobby since the 1970s, and finally turned it into a business in 2004—the Pacific Wine Club. Victoria and Ken decided to open the Pacific Wine Club in the Rogue Valley because of its proximity to Oregon, California and Washington wineries. They travel this tri-state area visiting small, family-owned vineyards to select what they believe are the best wines these exclusive boutique wineries have to offer. What's exciting is that they often find wines that are unavailable in stores, as well as wines of exceptional value, from only $10 a bottle to $40 library wines suitable for aging. Victoria and Ken love introducing people to wine, and have a public tasting room where they hold wine tastings every week complete with descriptive educational notes. Every six weeks or so they hold a wine and food pairing, which offers a good time to all participants. They organize vineyard tours and have special membership options where you can receive distinguished wines on a monthly basis. If you love good wine, good company and people who really know how to enjoy it, then the Pacific Wine Club is the perfect way to share it.

3588 Heathrow Way, Medford OR
(541) 245-3334 or (800) 792-6410
www.pacificwineclub.com

Eden Valley Orchards & EdenVale Winery

WINERIES:
A Rogue Valley tradition

Eden Valley Orchards in Medford was established in 1885 by early fruit grower Joseph H. Stewart, and expanded between 1899 and 1932 by Colonel Gordon Voorhies. This time period marked the first planting of a commercial pear orchard, and its subsequent expansion into a leading industry for the area. After revitalizing the lands once used for pear planting, current owners Tim and Anne Root continue its unique tradition as a destination facility for wine lovers, promoting sustainable agriculture, historical preservation and agricultural education in the heart of Southern Oregon's wine country. Tour the Voorhies Mansion and gardens, a hallmark of the area's hospitality and an ideal place for meetings, wine tastings and weddings. Visit the Rogue Valley Wine Center's Wine Tasting Room & Market to sample their award-winning EdenVale wines, as well as other boutique Southern Oregon wines. Finally, take a tour of the EdenVale Winery and experience the tremendous amount of effort that goes into producing a top-quality wine. Eden Valley Orchards will delight you with its history, exquisite wines and gorgeous location with spectacular views. Make sure to visit the next time you're in Southern Oregon.

2310 Voorhies Road, Medford OR
(866) 512-2955
www.edenvalleyorchards.com

RoxyAnn Winery

WINERIES: *Handcrafted bold and exciting wines*

In just a few short years, RoxyAnn Winery has become the most exciting story in the burgeoning field of Rogue Valley winemaking. The story started in 1908 when Reginald Parsons started growing pears on the southwest slopes of Roxy Ann Butte (named for Roxy Ann Bowen, one of the first settlers). An innovator, Parsons was among the first fruit growers to sell gift packs. Today, his descendants continue to innovate, converting 32 acres of pear orchards into prime vineyard. The limestone-clay soil and southern exposure of the vineyard, combined with the Rogue Valley's moderate climate, produce an ideal environment for growing red varietals such as Cabernet Sauvignon, Merlot, Cabernet Franc, Malbec, Grenache and Syrah. Orchard and vineyard manager Jon Meadors is committed to sustainable growth, using time-tested natural methods to ensure that the soil remains healthy and to preserve the surrounding ecosystem. Though it takes a while for some of these stocks to reach full maturity, RoxyAnn's veteran winemaker, Gus Janeway, has already created a superb blend of Merlot, Cabernet Sauvignon and Cabernet Franc called Claret. Working with other local grape producers, Gus, currently serving his third year as president of the local Oregon Winegrowers Association, has also demonstrated his skills by producing a 2003 Pinot Gris that won numerous awards and has already sold out. Pears are still grown at RoxyAnn and sold along with wines inside the original and historic Hillcrest Barn. In fact, all of the buildings on the property are listed on the National Historic Register. At RoxyAnn Winery you can enjoy the best of the present day in the midst of rich history.

3285 Hillcrest Road, Medford OR
(541) 776-2315
www.roxyann.com

Hellgate Canyon
Photo by Nancy McClain

MERLIN

The little hamlet of Merlin northwest of Grants Pass is a home base for outfitters and fishing guides. Merlin is a gateway to the wild and scenic Rogue River. One of the most scenic spots is the 250-foot-deep Hellgate Canyon, where the river rushes through a narrow rock cleft. You can see it from an overlook on the Merlin-Galice Road or pass through it on a Jetboat excursion or raft. Another way to experience the Rogue is to hike the Rogue River Trail. The trail, 40 miles one-way, follows the river several hundred feet above the water, giving the hiker spectacular views. The best time to hike the trail is in the later spring months, when wildflowers and water are abundant. For an easier seven-mile round-trip hike, take the trail from Graves Creek to Whiskey Creek and back. Drivers who want a scenic route to Gold Beach on the Oregon Coast can take Forest Service roads west of Merlin, the Galice and Agness roads. Like the hiking trails, these passageways are blocked by snow in winter and early spring.

PLACES TO GO

- Almeda Park
  14800 Merlin Galice Road

- Hellgate Canyon Overlook
  Merlin Galice Road

- Indian Mary Park
  7100 Merlin Galice Road

THINGS TO DO

May
- Magical Merlin Parade
  (541) 476-8047

- Mother's Day at Wildlife Images
  www.wildlifeimages.org

June
- Antique Tractor Show & Fair
  (800) 547-5927

September
- Pottsville Pow Wow
  (541) 471-1892

October
- Quilt & Craft Fair
  Hugo (541) 479-9452

Morrison's Rogue River Lodge

ACCOMMODATIONS:
Best lodge for outdoor enthusiasts

Morrison's Rogue River Lodge is an authentic log lodge half hidden by groves of evergreens, maple and oak. The Lodge is 16 miles downstream from Grants Pass, along the banks of its namesake river. The Lodge and its individual cottages attract all kinds of outdoor enthusiasts, including fishermen who come for the legendary steelhead and salmon fishery, whitewater rafters tackling one of the first commercially-rafted rivers in the country, as well as hikers, birdwatchers, families, romantics, and all who enjoy being immersed in the sights and sounds of the wilderness. River guide and lumber mill worker Lloyd Morrison built the lodge in 1945 as a fishing lodge. B.A. and Elaine Hanten bought the property in 1964. Their first year was greeted with disaster in the form of the 1964 flood. The cottages were swept away by the rampaging river. The main building survived, and the Hantens were able to rebuild. Despite this early setback, the Hantens created a thriving business. In 1967, B.A. pioneered guided whitewater raft trips down the wild section of the Rogue River. These journeys were the beginning of his rafting company, Rogue River Raft Trips, Inc. Today you can take three-day rafting adventures with overnight stays at remote lodges along the way. Morrison's became an Orvis Endorsed Fly Fishing Lodge in the late 1980s and remains one of the best destinations for Steelhead and Salmon fishing on the West Coast. As chef, Elaine created a reputation for providing outstanding gourmet cuisine that continues today. It is still a family business, with second-generation family member Michelle managing operations. Lodge amenities include a heated swimming pool, two tennis courts, putting green, volleyball, horseshoes and all manner of lawn games. Additional services are available to accommodate small business meetings, family reunions and weddings.

8500 Galice Road, Merlin OR
(800) 826-1963
www.morrisonslodge.com

Bear Creek
Photo by David Smigelski

PHOENIX

Phoenix was one of the earliest pioneer settlements in Southern Oregon. Many vestiges of its rich past are still visible today. The impressive Samuel Colver House, on Highway 99 at the south end of town, was built in 1855 by one of the first settlers. Colver took up a square-mile land claim where Phoenix now stands. In the early years, Phoenix was the hub of the Rogue Valley. The completion of the Oregon & California Railroad in 1887 changed travel and trade in the region forever. Agricultural products could now reach markets across the country and the world. Fruit orchards, particularly pears, grew to become one of the leading local industries. You can enjoy Phoenix products today at Rising Sun Farms, which sponsors a retail store and tasting room overlooking the Siskiyou Mountains. Rising Sun Farms features international and national award-winning tortas, pestos and marinades. Also available are artisan cheeses, jams, mustards and chocolate. To compliment the food, sample the beautifully crafted wines of the Pacific Northwest. Phoenix currently has 4,400 residents. The city is growing and is on the brink of even more explosive growth. During the next 20 years, the Southeast Medford Plan will create new homes for more than 10,000 people in the area directly north of Phoenix, east of North Phoenix Road.

PLACES TO GO

• Rising Sun Farms
  5126 S Pacific Highway
  (541)-535-8331 ext. 201

Leave Your Mark!

BUSINESS: *Best providers of memorial pavers*

For more than 13 years, Leave Your Mark! has been leaving its mark locally and nationally. Owners Pete and Deborah Cislo have a strong sense of community. Their pavers are the ideal tool for home and garden enhancement or memorials, as well as fundraisers or to generate revenue for a non-profit organization. The Leave Your Mark! paver is a concrete brick that is designed to hold an engraved plaque with a personalized message. The personalized plaques invite community spirit and create a sense of history. Their staff of installers is highly trained and they can provide technical assistance to ensure proper self installation. Pete Cislo founded his business with the belief that you treat customers like you would want to be treated. A former assistant principal, he keeps his customers' best interests at heart. Leave Your Mark! supports the community on a regular basis, such as by selling Oregon manufactured products. In addition to pavers, they have an extensive selection of do-it-yourself landscape supplies. For personalized garden enhancement or community fundraising projects, Pete and Deborah invite you to visit Leave Your Mark!

4631 S Pacific Highway, Phoenix OR
(541) 535-3445 or (800) 569-9869
www.leaveyourmark.com

Bug in a Rug

HOME: *Best selection of area rugs*

A well made rug can completely change the look and feel of a room by adding new interest, life and color. At Bug in a Rug in Phoenix you can easily find exquisite decorator rugs that will add interest to every room in your home. Owners D.J. and Shirleen Bransom began operating Bug in a Rug in 2005 and quickly became Southern Oregon and Northern California's destination store for beautiful, masterfully made area rugs of all sizes. Bug in a Rug offers an extensive selection of both machine made and handmade rugs, displayed on easy-to-see racks that line their 2,700-square-foot facility. Here, shoppers can find everything from 2-by-3-foot entry rugs for as little as $10 to giant 8-by-11-foot pieces that can range from $3,000 to $4,000. The rugs displayed at Bug in a Rug come from Egypt, India and Belgium, as well as China and the United States; however, Bransom likes to minimize discussion on a rug's origin and help his customers focus on the look and style that they ultimately want for their home. Bug in a Rug has a generous check-out policy that allows customers to take a rug home to see how it will look in their space before making the investment. This policy goes a long way toward ensuring complete customer satisfaction, which is the Bransoms' goal. Choose the rugs that will help make your house a home at Bug in a Rug.

205 Fern Valley Road, Phoenix OR
(541) 535-3024
www.buginaruginc.com

Toys for the Home
HOME: *Best home recreation store*

Toys for the Home is an indoor/outdoor recreation store. Owners Patricia and Tom Gillin call Toys for the Home "a big want store." They have a huge selection of one-of-a-kind, high quality products for people who want to have a fun lifestyle in their home. They carry items such as tropical decor, outdoor kitchens, patio and casual furniture, as well as billiards and game room supplies. Tom and Patricia have also been in the spa industry for over 11 years. Their experience includes running a national showteam for major spa manufactures, as well as training, special event purchasing and coordination. After their success on the road, they decided to bring their knowledge back home and open a retail store. This enabled them to remain at home with their school aged children. Now, Tom and Patricia keep Toys for the Home a family-run business by employing their sons Sean and Travis. At Toys for the Home, their products are replaceable, but their customer care not. They believe in exemplary customer service and helping patrons find exactly what they desire. Toys for the Home promotes relaxation in the company of family and friends. When you are seeking extraordinary furnishings and products to enhance home entertainment, come to Toys for the Home and discover what fun is possible.

205 Fern Valley Road, Suite O, Phoenix OR
(541) 535-3800
www.toysforthehome.com

Rising Sun Farms
MARKETS: *Best farm store*

Since opening in 1984, the response to Rising Sun Farms artisan food has been overwhelmingly positive. They grow and provide foods made with fresh, healthful and savory ingredients. Visit their store and tasting room with a view, which is set on the herb farm's 28-acre backdrop off Old Highway 99 between Phoenix and Talent. The store features international, award-winning tortas, pesto, dressings, marinades and fine food products that Rising Sun Farms has been creating for years. Alongside the Rising Sun Farms line is a selection of artisan cheeses, jams, mustards, chocolates and other epicurean delights from around the United States. As a complement to the food selection, the Tasting Room features wines from the Pacific Northwest, including their first offerings from Rising Sun Farms' beautifully crafted Merlots, Pinot Noirs, Chardonnays and blends. Come and relax with a glass of wine and some cheese on the patio while gazing at the scenic views, or stop by on Saturdays for the Growers Market featuring produce from local farmers.

5126 S Pacific Highway, Phoenix OR
(800) 888-0795
www.risingsunfarms.com

Annie's Café

RESTAURANTS & CAFES: *Best eggs Benedict in the Rogue Valley*

When you get that craving for a good home-cooked meal, Annie's Café knows how to satisfy it. Annie's is known for homemade corned beef hash, delicious omelets and the best eggs Benedict in the Rogue Valley. Located near picturesque Ashland and Mt. Ashland Ski Resort, the café is known for big, deli-style sandwiches and a variety of lip-smacking, juicy burgers. Annie and Allan King, the proud owners, use only the freshest ingredients to provide their customers with flavorful American fare. The café has a comfortable family atmosphere with friendly service. Annie's Café serves breakfast all day, so whether you are in the mood for a chiliburger or large fluffy pancakes, Annie's can satisfy you. Other menu selections bound to please are a French toast sandwich, a meat lovers omelet and a great steak sandwich. Annie's Café is ready to welcome you any day of the week, so come in soon and experience home cooking without going home.

723 Main Street, Phoenix OR
(541) 535-3666

ROGUE RIVER

The Rogue River's headwaters start near Crater Lake and twist and roar for 215 miles before spilling into the Pacific. Many small towns dot its journey west, notably the City of Rogue River, which takes its name from the river. Early settler Davis "Coyote" Evans operated a ferry at this spot. The Rogue River's native trout, salmon and steelhead are justifiably famous among anglers. Gracious river homes line the banks where lucky residents live amidst the natural splendor. The city, just off Interstate 5, is nestled along the banks of the river. The Cascades, the Siskiyous, and the Coast Range meet around the Rogue Valley to create an enviable climate. Warm, dry summers with cool evenings and moderate winters provide an opportunity to enjoy country living at its best. City of Rogue River attractions include Valley of the Rogue State Park, Palmerton Arboretum, which features a fine collection of specimen trees and access to Evans Creek, and the Woodville Museum, which displays pioneer artifacts. Rogue River's next-door neighbor, Gold Hill, has attractions that include the spooky Oregon Vortex.

PLACES TO GO

- Gold Hill Museum
  504 1st Avenue, Gold Hill (541) 855-1182

- House of Mystery at the Oregon Vortex
  *4303 Sardine Creek L Fork Road, Gold Hill
  (541) 855-1543*

- Palmerton Arboretum
  W Evans Creek Road (541) 776-7001

- Valley of the Rogue State Park
  Rogue River Highway (State Route 99)

- Woodville Museum
  1st and Oak Streets (541) 582-3088

THINGS TO DO

June
- Rooster Crow and Car Show (festival)
  (541) 582-0242

September
- World of Wine Festival
  Del Rio Vinyards (541) 855-2062

Rogue River Rooster
Photo by Nancy McClain

Baci's Pizza & Pasta
RESTAURANTS & CAFES: Best *hand-tossed pizza*

The word Baci, roughly translated, is the Italian word for kiss. At Baci's Pizza & Pasta they feel their pizzas and pastas are reminiscent of kisses, so good you can never get enough of them. Fresh pizza dough is made daily, along with their special blend of pizza sauces. Only the freshest and finest ingredients are used, including 100-percent real cheese and Italian sausage. Mediterranean pizzas, turkey BLTs, homemade meatball sandwiches and cheesy lasagnas are local favorites. Customers can choose from nine selections of domestic and microbrews on tap, many of which are made in Oregon. Owner Oren Ben-Dayan gives credit for his success to his mentor Stan Miller, who founded Bruno's Pizza & Pasta in Medford. Stan was Oren's role model for developing a superior work ethic, attention to detail and learning how to give exemplary customer service. Oren is known throughout the valley for his community involvement. In fact, he regularly donates to so many different fundraisers even he can no longer keep track of all of them. The Ben-Dayan family continues to support programs such as the local fire department, the Wimer Covered Bridge project, the SMART reading program, and numerous sports programs. For this community-minded family, giving back is a way of life. Baci's is open for lunch and dinner seven days a week. The next time you are in the Rogue Valley, come give Baci's Pizza & Pasta a try.

510 East Main, Rogue River OR
(541) 582-0508

Fly Fishing on the Rogue River
Photo by Cindy Tilley Faubion

TALENT

In 1852, the first recorded settler, Jacob Wagner, arrived in the Talent area. Naturally, Jacob named his settlement Wagner. In 1854, the military set up a fort on Jacob's property called Fort Wagner, which in time became a community center. In 1889, however, one Aaron P. Talent platted a town site and named it after himself. Talent became known for fruit orchards along Bear and Wagner Creeks fed by an extensive irrigation system that developed into today's Talent Irrigation District. Talent's neighbor to the south, Ashland, has a limited-growth policy that prices many would-be residents out of the market. One result is boom times for Talent. A Talent feature is the Bear Creek Greenway, a corridor of public land that follows lush Bear Creek. When complete, the Greenway will be a continuous 21-mile path from Ashland to Central Point. The Greenway currently connects Talent to Ashland and Medford to Central Point. Work on the Talent-to-Medford section is nearly complete. The Greenway is paved and suitable for walkers and bicyclists. Cars and motorcycles are prohibited. Another Talent attraction is the Camelot Theatre, which offers an intimate performance area. Camelot creates high-quality theater from classic and new works that reflect the diversity of American culture.

PLACES TO GO

• Ignition Gallery of Car and Motorcycle Art
324 Talent Avenue (541) 535-7209

• Talent Skate Park
Main Street

THINGS TO DO

September
• Talent Harvest Festival
(541) 535-1566

Wagner Creek
Photo by Nancy McClain

Paschal Winery & Vineyard

WINERIES:
Best Talent winery

A few minutes from Ashland, the hilltop Paschal Winery and Vineyard overlooks world-famous pear orchards and the Cascade-Siskiyou mountain ranges. Here in the Eastern Rogue Valley Appellation, owners Roy and Jill Paschal and award-winning winemaker Joe Dobbes ply their craft to create the elegant aromas, balance and complexity that are the signature of Paschal wines. There is a wide selection available. White wines include Pinot Gris, Chardonnay, Pinot Blanc and Viognier. Reds include Syrah, Merlot, Cabernet Sauvignon and Pinot Noir. Additionally, Paschal is starting to produce Italian-style wines, including Tempranillo, Dolcetto and Sangiovese. While at the Tasting Room, enjoy the lovely views of the vineyard and surrounding area. Let the extremely knowledgeable tasting room staff keep you informed as you sample the wines along with a selection of local cheeses and tortas. If you visit and can't stand the thought of leaving, ask about the vacation villa available for lease.

1122 Suncrest Road, Talent OR
(800) 446-6050
www.paschalwinery.com

WHITE CITY

In 1941, the U.S. Army constructed Camp White on 67 square miles north of Medford as a training camp for the 91st Infantry. Over the course of four years, 40,000 troops shipped out of Camp White. Little remains of the camp except for a military hospital and military barracks that were deeded to the Veterans Administration and reopened as a veterans' retirement home. The Camp White Museum exhibits uniforms, medals, guns and letters. White City today is best known for manufacturing. White City Industrial Park, west of State Route 62, is southern Oregon's largest factory district. Further west is the Nature Conservancy's Agate Desert Preserve. This area of vernal pools contains what is perhaps the most northerly habitat of fairy shrimp. The two segments of the Denman Wildlife Area, a state-run preserve, lie north and south of the Industrial Park. The southern segment features several small lakes where waterfowl can often be seen. Some hunting is allowed. While TouVelle State Park and Table Rock have Central Point addresses, they are actually closer to White City and provide recreational opportunities to White City citizens. Other recreational possibilities include Jackson County Sports Park, which hosts the Southern Oregon Dragway, the Southern Oregon Speedway and a go-kart track.

PLACES TO GO

- Agate Lake County Park
  E Antelope Road

- Camp White Museum
  (541) 826-2111 ext. 3674

- Jackson County Sports Park
  www.jacksoncountyparks.com

- Southern Oregon Speedway
  6900 Kershaw Road (541) 826-6825

- Willow Lake County Park
  Willow Lake Road

THINGS TO DO

June
Rogue Valley Veterans Powwow
White City Veterans Domiciliary

Photo by Donna K. Lindley

Fireside Masonry

HOME:
Best natural stone work

Tom Cavanaugh has been building natural stone fireplaces, arches, flower planters, brick and paver pathways, retaining walls, and porches for Rogue Valley residents since he was 17 years old. Tom's grandfather taught Tom's father and uncle the masonry trade and then Tom apprenticed with his uncle. Now, 20 years later, the strong tradition of excellence set by the Cavanaugh family thrives at Fireside Masonry. When you speak with Tom, you can tell he loves his work and has great passion and justifiable pride in the service he provides. His crew is devoted to the trade and goes out of their way to provide customer satisfaction in everything they do. As for special project requests, Tom says they "do it all." Not sure about what you want? Tom has a solution for nearly every situation. Tom will do "whatever it takes to get the job done right." His motto is, "If you ever say, 'that's good enough' then it's time for you not to do it anymore." He has completed a long list of Rogue Valley projects and will gladly share them with you during your free consultation. Although his daughter, Hailey, is only five years old, Tom hopes that someday she will take an interest in the family profession and become the fourth generation Cavanaugh dedicated to the field of masonry. The next time you plan to beautify or improve your home's appearance, call Fireside Masonry and discover what Tom can do for you.

7696 Gladstone, White City OR
(541) 890-8294

Columbia Gorge
Mt. Hood

BOARDMAN

You can visit Boardman for hunting, fishing, water sports, and great views of the Columbia River. Boardman Marina Park, downtown on the river, offers 63 RV sites and additional tenting sites, free showers and boat slips, and three miles of paved trails along the river's edge. The river at this point is also called Lake Umatilla, because it is a reservoir behind the John Day Dam. This portion of the river is famous for the fighting walleye. Samuel Herbert Boardman homesteaded in the area in 1903. From 1929 to 1950, he served as the first superintendent of the Oregon State Parks System. Boardman began planting trees to make small roadside parks where travelers could stop and rest in the shade along the Columbia River Highway. These were the state's first rest stops. A project is underway to place the very first rest stop building in a Boardman mini-park just off I-5. Boardman is surrounded by military installations that are closed to the public, such as the Boardman Bombing Range and the Umatilla Army Depot. Interesting facilities that you can visit are the Umatilla National Wildlife Refuge and the Irrigon Hatchery, both east of town.

PLACES TO GO

- Irrigon Hatchery
  74135 Riverview Lane, Irrigon
  (541) 922-5732

- Marina Park
  Marine Drive NW

- Umatilla National Wildlife Refuge
  72650 Riverview Lane
  (509) 545-8670

THINGS TO DO

May
- Cinco de Mayo Celebration
  (541) 481-9252

July
- 4th of July Celebration & Fireworks Show
  (541) 481-3014

Sunset on the upper Columbia River near Boardman

River Lodge and Grill

ACCOMMODATIONS:
Best lodge

The River Lodge and Grill is the only hotel in Oregon east of Hood River with Columbia River frontage. Built in 2001, the lodge is reminiscent of the great lodges of the West. The building's exterior features a log cabin-style façade and the grounds are beautifully landscaped. Guests are sure to enjoy the lobby with its two-story stone fireplace, vaulted ceilings and extensively glassed walls. Massive pine log supports and a log railing run along the second floor balcony. The River Lodge offers many first-class amenities, including a sauna, an outdoor pool and a spa. Two meeting rooms, along with a 24-hour fitness room and an outdoor bike and walking path meet a variety of needs. The restaurant and lounge feature panoramic views of the Columbia River and the state of Washington. Enjoy a sunset or simply watch the river traffic go by while you feast on superior cuisine. The restaurant provides room service and catering for its conference facilities and banquet hall. Build your tan, play volleyball or relax on their private beach. Pleasure boating on the Columbia River is an option, and Washington wineries offer tours. Visit River Lodge and Grill, where sunsets, activities and restful rooms and suites await.

6 Marine Drive, Boardman OR
(541) 481-6800 or (888) 988-2009
www.riverlodgeandgrill.com

BRIDAL VEIL

Eastern Multnomah County, past Troutdale and the Portland urban growth boundary, boasts the densest collection of state parks in Oregon. These include Multnomah Falls, one of the most-visited sites in the state. Vista House at Crown Point, built in 1916 as a place of refreshment along the new Columbia River Highway, is a stunning octagonal building with a copper dome. Bridal Veil Falls is an elegant and graceful lady that can be fully appreciated from the deck of a viewing platform rebuilt in 1996. The 140-foot-high falls cascade down a cliff in giant steps. The falls were named when a lady traveling the Columbia River on the sternwheeler Bailey Gatzert saw the waterfall and said it looked like a "delicate, misty bride's veil." The town of Bridal Veil, next to the falls, lends its postal address to many of the surrounding parks, including Multnomah Falls. The Bridal Veil Post Office is one of the smallest in the country, at only 10 feet by 14 feet. More than 200,000 wedding invitations yearly are hand-stamped here. Bridal Veil was once a lumber mill town. Loggers here pioneered several logging techniques. A flume down Bridal Veil Creek transported rough-sawn lumber from the mill at Palmer a mile and a half down the canyon to the finishing plant in Bridal Veil.

PLACES TO GO

- Ainsworth State Park
  I-84 exit 35

- Benson State Recreation Area
  I-84 exit 30 or 31

- Bridal Veil Falls State Park
  I-84 exit 28

- Multnomah Falls
  I-84 exit 31 (503) 695-2372

- Portland Women's Forum Scenic Viewpoint
  Columbia River Highway

- Rooster Rock State Park
  I-84 exit 25

- Vista House at Crown Point
  Columbia River Highway

Photo by Larry Osborne

Multnomah Falls Lodge

ACCOMMODATIONS: *Best lodge*

Multnomah Falls spills into the Columbia River Gorge from its origins on Larch Mountain. At the base of the 620-foot falls is Multnomah Falls Lodge, an impressive stone lodge built in 1925. The Lodge offers everything a visitor needs to make the most out of a visit to this natural wonder, the second highest falls in the nation. This day lodge houses a U.S. Forest Service Interpretive Center, a gift store, dining room and a lounge with a bar. You'll also find a snack bar and an espresso cart. The lodge is the jumping off spot for a hike to the top of the falls. A meal at the lodge is certain to be a memorable occasion, whether you choose from a light meal at the lounge or something more substantial from the restaurant, where you'll have a panoramic view of the falls from your table. Breakfast, lunch and dinner showcase regional offerings. Look for exciting salads and meals featuring salmon, trout, grilled flatiron steak and tasty burgers. The lounge is a great place for onion soup, grilled oysters or steamer clams. Before leaving this special destination, stop by the gift shop for a memento of your stay. You'll find all kinds of tasteful souvenirs, including the Multnomah Falls Lodge Cookbook. An experience of the Columbia River Gorge is not complete until you experience Multnomah Falls and the rustic Multnomah Falls Lodge, just 20 minutes east of Troutdale on the beautiful Columbia Gorge Historic Highway.

50000 Historic Columbia River Highway, Bridal Veil OR
(503) 695-2376
www.multnomahfallslodge.com

Multnomah Falls

ATTRACTIONS:
Region's top tourist draw

At 620 feet, Multnomah Falls is one of the highest year round waterfalls in the nation. Nearly two million visitors a year come to see the falls. The flow over the falls varies, and is usually highest during winter and spring. Unusually cold weather can turn the falls into a spectacular frozen icicle, with a few drops of water dripping off the ice. The falls are a great place to study geology. Five flows of Yakima basalt are visible in the falls' cliff face. Benson Bridge, crafted by Italian stone masons, allows visitors to cross the falls between the lower and upper cataracts. The bridge was erected in 1914 by Simon Benson, a prominent businessman who owned the falls at the time. Benson later donated the falls to the City of Portland. In 1943, the USDA Forest Service took ownership of the falls and the associated lodge. The lodge was built in 1925 by A.E. Doyle, and contains every kind of stone found in the gorge. It hosts a gift shop and a Forest Service Information Center where you can find trail maps. In the restaurant, you can dine on Northwest cuisine while taking in unbeatable views of the falls. According to American Indian lore, Multnomah Falls was created to win the heart of a young princess who wanted a hidden place to bathe. Multnomah Falls rewards your visit in any season of the year.

I-84 exit 31
(503) 695-2372
www.fs.fed.us/r6/columbia/
millennium2

CASCADE LOCKS

Cascade Locks lies within the Columbia River Gorge National Scenic Area. In town, Cascade Locks Marine Park boasts historic lock tenders' homes, the first steam engine operated in the West, a museum, access to fishing on the Columbia River and a marina. The park is also home to the Columbia Gorge Sternwheeler. Lewis and Clark's discovery corps portaged around the rapids of the Cascades here in 1805. The small settlement that grew up on the banks of the Cascades helped early travelers get around the rapids, first by foot and then by mule-drawn rail cars. With the completion of a navigational canal and locks in 1896, modern Cascade Locks was born. Indian stories say the Great Spirit built a bridge of stone across the Columbia River at this spot that was a great gift. Scientists say that about 1,000 years ago a mountain caved off, blocking the river. The natural dam created a great inland sea covering prairies as far away as Idaho. Natural erosion weakened the dam and finally washed it out. The waters of the inland sea tore a great tunnel under the mountain range, leaving a natural bridge over the water. Today's man-made Bridge of the Gods was built in 1926.

PLACES TO GO

- Bonneville Dam Visitor Center
  I-84 exit 40 (541) 374-8820

- Cascade Locks Marine Park
  I-84 exit 44

- Columbia Gorge Interpretive Center
  990 SW Rock Creek Drive, Stevenson WA

- Sternwheeler Columbia Gorge (excursions)
  (800) 224-3901

THINGS TO DO

July
- Sternwheeler/Portage Days Festival
  Marine Park
  (503) 380-7676

September
- Festival of Nations
  Marine Park (541) 374-8427

Sternwheeler Columbia Gorge

ATTRACTIONS: *Most romantic adventure in the Northwest*

Step aboard the Sternwheeler Columbia Gorge and experience history, legend and riverboat hospitality along the Columbia River Gorge on an authentic triple-deck paddle wheeler. The historical narration of Lewis and Clark's adventures, the Oregon Trail, Bridge of the Gods, and riverboats accentuate the relaxing river cruise and stunning sights. Starting from Marine Park at Cascade Locks, in the heart of the Columbia River Gorge National Scenic Area, you may enjoy watching Native American tribes fish from their legendary platforms as they have done for centuries. You will take in many stunning and fascinating sights during the two-hour cruise. For something extra special consider one of the Sunset Dinner Cruises for a fine meal and romantic experience, or try the Sunday Brunch Cruise. You may also seek out the Cascade Locks Museum, located in the Marine Park, where you'll find more information on waterways, transportation, fishwheels and indigenous history. Don't miss the adjacent Thunder Island and its scenic beauty. Owned and operated by the Port of Cascade Locks, the 23-acre park and private three-acre island can be your solution to planning your next event. Sailing competitions sponsored by the Columbia Gorge Racing Association occur March through September and windsurfing occurs year round. To visit the Sternwheeler Columbia Gorge, take I-84 E to exit #44 about 45 minutes east of Portland.

Marine Park, Cascade Locks OR
(503) 224-3900 or (800) 224-3901
www.sternwheeler.com

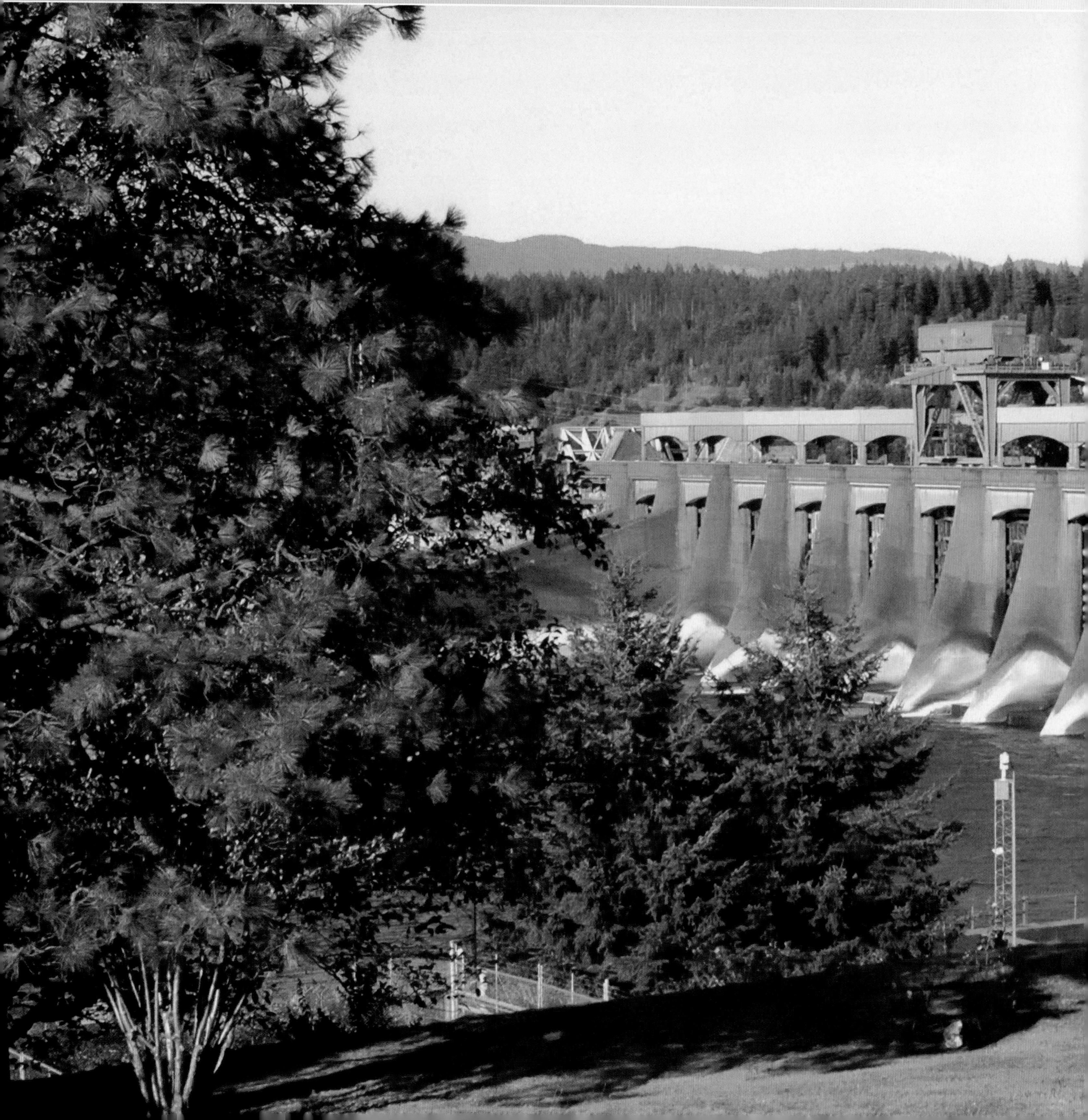

Bonneville Lock and Dam

ATTRACTIONS:

Best place to see migrating salmon

The Visitor Centers at Bonneville Lock and Dam are located at Bradford Island for the Oregon side and at Washington Shore for the Washington side. Visitors on the Oregon side will find a five-level facility with an observation deck, interior exhibits, a large theater and panoramic views of the Columbia River Gorge, drawing hundreds of thousands of visitors a year. Just a walk away is the viewing area inside the first Powerhouse. Visitors can watch the navigation lock in operation on the Oregon shore. On the Washington side, visitors will enjoy one of the world's most accessible views of a powerhouse. Inside the powerhouse, visitors will see generators from 85 feet above the powerhouse floor, get close-up views of a generator and can examine a rotating turbine shaft through special viewing windows. Visitors can also enjoy fish ladder viewing from this location. Learn about alternative transportation modes, why river transport is an important ecological choice and how power is managed. Learn to identify the local fish types, which are endangered, and what is the best time of year to view each type. Educational centers provide films and displays about hydropower, river navigation and the history of this significant area. The Visitors Centers at Bonneville Lock and Dam can be reached by taking Interstate 84 to exit 40 or Washington State Highway 14 to milepost 40. The Bridge of the Gods, located about two miles upstream from the Dam, links Oregon and Washington.

(541) 374-8820
www.nwp.usace.army.mil/op/b/

GOVERNMENT CAMP

Government Camp, elevation 3,888 feet, is the business district for Mount Hood, the best-loved recreation district in Oregon. Mountain biking and skiing, both downhill and cross-country, are the town's biggest sports. Government Camp is on the south side of the mountain on the Mount Hood Scenic Byway, U.S. Highway 26, near the Barlow Pass summit. It is a gateway to ski resorts such as Timberline Lodge, the Mount Hood Ski Bowl and the Summit Ski Area. Settlers traveling the Barlow Road gave Government Camp its name when they discovered several wagons abandoned by the Regiment of Mounted Riflemen.

PLACES TO GO

- Mount Hood Museum
  88900 E Highway 26 (503) 272-3301

- Mount Hood Ski Bowl
  87000 E Highway 26 (503) 222-BOWL

- Timberline Lodge

- Trillium Lake
  Off Forest Road 2656

THINGS TO DO

March
- Winter Games of Oregon
  Mount Hood Ski Bowl (503) 272-3503

- Ski Glade Trail Day
  Mount Hood Museum (503) 272-3301

July
- The Fish Crew Mount Hood Adventure
  Mount Hood Ski Bowl (503) 786-0600

August
- Smokey Bear's Birthday Party
  Timberline Lodge (503) 622-7979

- Hood to Coast Relay
  www.hoodtocoast.com

September
- Family Feast & Fun
  Mount Hood Ski Bowl (503) 622-3017

- Mount Hood Heritage Day
  Mount Hood Museum (503) 272-3301

December
- New Year's Eve Firework Extravaganza
  Mount Hood Ski Bowl (800) 754-2695

Mt. Hood Reflected in Trillium Lake

Mount Hood

At 11,245 feet, Mount Hood is the tallest mountain in Oregon. When the weather is clear, the snow-capped summit is easily visible from Portland. As a result, Mount Hood is a major emblem of the state. Mount Hood is one of the major volcanoes of the Cascade Range, and has erupted repeatedly for hundreds of thousands of years. The last major episode ended shortly before the arrival of Lewis and Clark in 1805. Northwest Indian legends tell of hot rocks hurtling from gaping holes, streams of liquid fire and the loss of formerly high summits. According to legend, the brothers Wy'east (Mount Hood) and Pahto (Mount Adams) battled for the hand of the maiden La-wa-la-clough (Mount St. Helens). The eruptions were the battles. Mount Hood is one of the most-climbed mountains in the world, in part because of its proximity to Portland. While the south slope is not considered difficult, the sheer number of climbers means that the mountain has claimed many lives. Climbers must register at the famous Timberline Lodge on the volcano's south flank. Twelve glaciers and named snowfields cover about 80 percent of the cone. Nestled in the volcano's crater is Crater Rock. A volcanic lava dome only 200 years old, Crater Rock stands about 300 feet above the sloping crater floor. Warm fumaroles along its base emit sulfur gases and plumes of steam. The mountain is surrounded by the Mount Hood National Forest, which extends south from the strikingly beautiful Columbia River Gorge across more than 60 miles of forested mountains, lakes and streams.

www.mthood.org
http://vulcan.wr.usgs.gov/Volcanoes/Hood

The Mt. Hood Cultural Center and Museum

ATTRACTIONS:

Best source for Mt. Hood info

The Mt. Hood Cultural Center and Museum opened its doors in 1991 with a mission of strengthening the community while protecting, stabilizing and showcasing all aspects of the area's diverse history. Curator Lloyd Musser and his knowledgeable staff offer interpretive exhibits, educational programs, and a study of the arts in order to promote understanding about the community's history and the challenges the future brings. Cultural programs at the center include arts-and-crafts classes, lectures, participatory living-history events, and guided interpretive hikes. The Mt. Hood Cultural Center and Museum offers numerous engaging exhibits that display various aspects of the area's background, such as the history of winter sports and watercolors by area artists. The non-profit facility houses many one-of-a-kind Mt. Hood National Forest history exhibits that include early exploration settlement pieces and a series on the natural history of Mt. Hood. Viewing includes a satellite exhibit for Timberline Lodge, donated by the Friends of Timberline, and the Hal Lidell Collection of famous Mt. Hood photographs taken by Hugh Akroyd and Ray Atkeson. The museum is available for meetings, receptions and other private social events by special arrangement. Mt. Hood Cultural Center and Museum represents several skiing, hiking and outdoors clubs. Learn about Mt. Hood's vivid past while viewing stunning photographs and majestic artwork at the Mt. Hood Cultural Center and Museum.

**88090 East Highway 26,
Government Camp OR**
(503) 272-3301
www.mthoodmuseum.org

Timberline Lodge

ATTRACTIONS: *Authentic jewel of the Northwest*

Timberline Lodge is located at 6,000 feet on Mt. Hood, 60 miles east of Portland. This beautiful piece of history is owned by the National Forest Service, so everyone is welcome to come up, relax by the fire and take pleasure in the outstanding views and unique architecture. Timberline is a ski resort, a first-class restaurant, a superb hotel, but most of all it is a public building of extraordinary historical and artistic interest. Created at the height of the Depression, Timberline was built entirely by hand, inside and out, by unemployed craftspeople hired by the Federal Works Projects Administration between 1936 and 1937. Artwork abounds throughout the Lodge in paintings, wood carvings, mosaics, wrought iron and stonework. The guest rooms are furnished with such items as original watercolors, hand appliquéd draperies and bedspreads, hand-hooked rugs, handcarved furniture and hand-forged lamps. As a ski resort, Timberline has the longest season in North America, with skiing and snowboarding every month of the year when weather permits. Due to its unique location, there is also summer skiing on the Palmer Snowfield. Non-skiers can take the Magic Mile Sky Ride year round (weather permitting) up to 7,000 feet. Gaze through a telescope or explore the Silcox Hut, then ride or hike back down to the Lodge if the snow has cleared on the trails. Other amenities include an outdoor heated pool and whirlpool, several restaurants, and the magnificent fireplace lobby. Come visit this authentic jewel and icon of the Northwest. Timberline Lodge is absolutely a one-of-a-kind.

Timberline Lodge OR
(503) 622-7979
www.timberlinelodge.com

Hood River

At the panoramic crossroads of the Columbia River Gorge and the Cascades, Hood River County offers a huge variety of recreational activities year round. Discover a world of scenic pleasures, historic landmarks, and friendly people—all in the shadow of Mount Hood and the footsteps of Lewis and Clark. The 21,000 people of Hood River County welcome more than 650,000 visitors every year. Though it is one of Oregon's smallest counties in square miles, Hood River County offers an enormous range of geological and climatic features. Cascade Locks, on the western edge of the county, sits at just 60 feet above sea level, while the county's southwestern border runs past the 11,245 foot summit of Mount Hood. The city of Hood River sits in the middle of the transition zone from the moist rainforest climate of Cascade Locks to the arid desert climate of The Dalles. The steep walls of the Columbia River Gorge, coupled with this abrupt change in climates, force strong winds to blow year round through Hood River, giving it a claim to being the windsurfing capital of the world. Hood River also boasts world-class skiing, snowboarding and snowshoeing. You can enjoy mountain biking, hiking, whitewater kayaking and fishing within 40 miles of downtown Hood River. An astounding number of publications have named Hood River as one of the nation's best spots, including *Outside*, *Progressive Farmer* and *Skiing Magazine*. Come to Hood River County and see what the buzz is about.

405 Portway Avenue, Hood River OR
(Chamber of Commerce)
(541) 386-2000 or (800) 366-3530
www.hoodriver.org

Photos courtesy of Hood River Chamer of Commerce

Downtown Hood River

PLACES TO GO

• Chamber of Commerce Visitor's Center
405 Portway Avenue
(800) 366-3530
www.hoodriver.org

• Hood River County Historical Museum
300 E Port Marina Drive
(541) 386-6772

• Hutson Museum
Baseline & Clear Creek Roads, Parkdale
(541) 352-6808

• International Museum of Carousel Art
304 Oak Street
(541) 387-4622

• Koberg Beach State Recreation Site
Old Columbia River Drive

• Mount Hood Railroad (excursions)
110 Railroad Avenue
(800) 872-4661

• Viento State Park
I-84 exit 56

THINGS TO DO

April
• Hood River Valley Blossom Festival
Fairgrounds, Odell
(541) 354-2865

July
• Hood River County Fair
Fairgrounds, Odell
(541) 354-2865

October
• Hood River Valley Harvest Fest
Hood River Expo Center
(800) 366-3530

• Gorge Fruit and Craft Fair
Fairgrounds, Odell
(541) 354-2865

• Hops Fest
Downtown
(541) 490-0022

Columbia Gorge Hotel

ACCOMMODATIONS: *Most majestic hotel in Hood River*

When Lewis and Clark were documenting their travels through Hood River, they couldn't have foreseen the luxurious simplicity that would come in the form of the Columbia Gorge Hotel. The hotel is situated in a perfect setting for grand hospitality. Overlooking the Columbia River, the grounds boast acres of manicured gardens, as well as a stunning 208-foot waterfall. The hotel hosts events throughout the year including the annual Hood River Blossom Festival. Eight thousand lights are displayed every holiday season that are unveiled during a gala event in November, featuring a gourmet dinner and caroling. Every Sunday from Blossom Festival to New Year, the hotel provides a traditional high tea in the dining room. They will also arrange it any time for parties of eight or more with advance notice. The selection of homemade scones, delicious tea sandwiches, and tempting sweets makes a lovely treat for special occasions, or an everyday touch of elegance. Owner Boyd Graves insists on giving visitors comfort and warmth in this opulent setting. He strives to continue to "bring glamour back" to the hotel experience without pretense or stuffiness. The hotel offers a hearty world-famous farm breakfast. The spectacular views from the rooms are unparalleled. The immense stone fireplace in the lounge burns with real logs, providing a perfect place to relax in solitude or gather with friends. Come visit the Columbia Gorge Hotel and feel like royalty without the pomp.

4000 Westcliff Drive, Hood River OR
(541) 386-5566
www.coulmbiagorgehotel.com

Oak Street Hotel

ACCOMMODATIONS:

Historic charm and modern amenities

While the Colombia River Gorge may be known for its natural beauty, one of its nicer features is made by man. The Oak Street Hotel is a historic nine-room building built in 1909. It belies its age thanks to a recent renovation by owner Denise McCravey. To keep up with modern necessities, she equipped each room with DSL and wireless capabilities, televisions and refrigerators. To make the boutique hotel unique, she went back to basics. Continental breakfasts feature locally roasted coffee and McCravey's own farm-fresh eggs. A gas fireplace in the lobby invites tired feet to rejuvenate in a living room setting. The porch is used during better weather months for educational forums that guests are free to join. Handcrafted furniture sprinkled throughout the rooms add to the charm. In the private baths, exclusive toiletries made from all-natural products and essential oils are provided and are available for sale. The artwork is rotated every two months to keep the look fresh. The entire hotel can be rented for weddings, and vacation rentals are available nearby to accommodate larger parties. Whether you're hitting the slopes, tackling the terrain or browsing the local shops, you are welcome to rest your weary bones by the fire at the Oak Street Hotel.

610 Oak Street Hotel, Hood River OR
(541) 386-3845 or (866) 386-3845
www.oakstreethotel.com

Inn at the Gorge
ACCOMMODATIONS: *Best inn*

Within minutes of Mt. Hood, Inn at the Gorge offers both indoor and outdoor opportunities for fun and rejuvenation. Built in 1908, the Queen Ann-style home has operated as a bed and breakfast since 1987. Inn at the Gorge has five rooms with private baths decorated and furnished with beautiful antiques and premium beds. All the rooms feature amenities such as televisions, DVD players and refrigerators. High-speed wireless Internet is available. Each room has a special highlight that sets it apart from the others. The Rose Suite catches the morning sun and the Garden Suite is on the quiet backside of the house overlooking the rose gardens. A wrap-around porch and a shaded background terrace provide additional opportunities for relaxing with friends or simply being on your own with a book. Owners Marilyn Fox and Jon Johnson are your hosts at this grand yet cozy bed and breakfast. "We want people to feel like this is home," they say. Marilyn and Jon are avid sports enthusiasts who can help you plan activities during your stay at the Inn. World-class wind surfing, mountain biking, and year round skiing at Mt. Hood are all just minutes away and storage facilities are available for your sports equipment. Guests are treated to a delicious three-course gourmet breakfast and Marilyn and Jon will cater to special diets. Inn at the Gorge hosts small weddings and family reunions. Recognized as one of the Best Places to Kiss, Inn at the Gorge is perfect for a romantic escape.

1113 Eugene Street, Hood River OR
(541) 386-4429 or (877) 852-2385 *www.innatthegorge.com*

Flightline Services
ATTRACTIONS: *Best scenic flights*

Narrated scenic flights over the Columbia River Gorge and the Cascade Mountain volcanoes and glaciers are a wonderful opportunity to view the grandeur and geology of the area in a way that you simply can't from the ground. Flightline Services offers this spectacular opportunity in 30 to 90-minute flight tours for up to three passengers at a time. If you prefer, you can design your own tour and pay just the hourly rate for the plane. Owners Anne Yannotti and Denny Kindig are justifiably proud of their perfect safety record during 10 years of business. They hire only highly qualified and experienced pilots who are committed to flying and safety in the air. If you think you might like to learn to fly yourself, take the special 30-minute introductory flight with an instructor who will show you basic flight maneuvers and spectacular scenery. If you decide to pursue it, Flightline Services can provide you with all the instruction you need to achieve your goal. Anne and Denny are devoted to sharing their love of flying with others and they have developed a high school outreach program to work with young people who are interested in aviation as a career. For your convenience, Flightline Services operates out of both the Hood River Airport and The Dalles Airport. Give them a call soon and experience the beauty of northern Oregon and southern Washington in a way you will never forget.

3608 Airport Road, Hood River OR
(541) 386-1133 *www.flythegorge.com*

Frame Gallery
GALLERIES: *Best custom framing*

Since 1991, Rupert Webb has been working single-handedly to accomplish his goal to "enhance art to the next level" at his popular Hood River custom frame shop and gallery. Webb has been nationally certified as a picture framer by the Professional Picture Framer Association and sees framing as an art form in and of itself. Through his business, Frame Gallery, Webb specializes in master craftsmanship framing and in offering unsurpassed customer service. With a focus on assuring that every customer has an excellent experience, Webb uses only superior quality products when designing his custom pieces. His loyal following of clientele is far better than any award, and because Webb works alone without any employees, customers are certain of getting his undivided attention and expertise on every project. Frame Gallery also houses and exhibits the work of local artists in a small, intimate salon inside the elegant shop. Take your cherished art to the next level and give it the care, attention and quality framing it deserves by taking it to Frame Gallery.

402 Oak Street, Hood River OR
(541) 386-1844

Hood River Lavender Farms
GARDENS, PLANTS & FLOWERS: *Best organic lavender*

Diane and Joel Orcutt have a fondness for lavender that led to their evolution into lavender specialists. Hood River Lavender Farms is a two-and-a-half acre wholesale organic lavender farm nestled in the lush Hood River Valley. It is nurtured by rich volcanic soil with excellent drainage, clean air and glacial water, and is located close to the majestic mountains. The Orcutts grow 46 varieties of lavender, using the flowers for fragrant crafts, cooking and essential oil production. The English lavender is the hardiest and most fragrant of the lavender species. The farm's lavender oil is of the highest quality and is often in demand by the aromatherapy and perfume industries. Joel and Diane opened a second farm in the upper valley of the Hood River. This you-pick farm is open for public drop-in tours and lavender products are available for purchase. The Orcutts have a firm commitment to quality that ensures they will not cut corners to bring prices down. Their love for lavender is evident in the vigor of their plants, the smoothness of their essential oil and the beauty of their crafts and products. Enjoy the spectacular views of the Hood River Valley as you pick your own lavender. Take the opportunity to relax, sip some lavender tea and savor the Orcutts fine products at Hood River Lavender Farms.

3801 Straight Hill Road, Hood River OR
(888) Lav-Farm (528-3276)
www.lavenderfarms.net

The Fruit Company, Inc.
MARKETS: *Best fruit gifts*

The Fruit Company, located in the fertile Hood River Valley, is passionate about delivering the best tasting fruit in the world right to your doorstep. Brothers and best friends Scott and Addison Webster expanded the business that their grandfather Roy Webster began in 1942 by adding an extensive gift-pack business. Roy and his son Wayne managed the operation, which grew to include approximately 600 acres of orchard, along with a packing facility that shipped fruit across the nation and across the globe. Today, the Webster brothers welcome visitors to The Fruit Company, where they can tour the orchards and the original fruit packing facility. Visitors learn about the future home of the Fruit Heritage Museum and get a close-up look at the company's gift packing operation. The Fruit Company can be reached by automobile or with select stops on the Mount Hood Railroad, which travels through the breathtaking Hood River Valley. In the Outlet Store, visitors can choose from the orchard's 18 fruit varieties, along with a vast assortment of gourmet goodies like chocolate covered Bing cherries or piquant, garlic cheddar cheese. Additional favorites from The Fruit Company include wild Pacific Northwest smoked salmon, flavorful preserves and vanilla pear cider, all of which can be displayed in an artful handwoven basket or packaged in elegant Watercolor Art boxes. Experience the joys of giving with a gift of Oregon's best from The Fruit Company.

2900 Van Horn Drive, Hood River OR
(541) 387-4100 or (800) 387-3100
www.TheFruitCompany.com

Indian Creek Golf Course

RECREATION: *Best golf course*

Indian Creek Golf Course in Hood River is the only *Golf Digest* Four-Star course in the Columbia Gorge area. With unrivaled views of Mt. Adams and Mt. Hood, Indian Creek has been challenging golfers since 1989. The impeccably maintained grounds include some of the best kept greens in the region. Vast improvements have been made over the years, including a new clubhouse which features a full service pro shop and Divots Restaurant—a popular place for locals and out-of-town guests alike. The course features picturesque views, meandering streams, doglegged fairways and varied terrain which combine for a tremendous golf experience. If you enjoy great golf and great food, Indian Creek Golf Course should be on your trip list.

3605 Brookside Drive, Hood River OR
(541) 386-7700 *www.indiancreekgolf.com*

The Sixth Street Bistro & Loft
RESTAURANTS & CAFÉS: *Best bistro*

If you're looking for delicious, perfectly prepared cuisine served in a casual atmosphere, visit The Sixth Street Bistro & Loft on your next trip to Hood River. Located on Cascade Avenue, this classic bistro was opened in 1992 by Maui Meyer. His goal was to create a place where locals and visitors alike could come to relax and enjoy a great meal. Meyer was joined in 1995 by a chef and managing partner, Ben Stenn, who was an attendee of the famed La Varenne, Ecole de Cuisine in the Burgundy region of France. The third member of this dynamic triumvirate is Jacqueline Carey, who joined the team full time in 1996 and became a full partner in 1999. Jacqueline is now the front house manager, having worked her way up through the ranks beginning as a hostess. The Sixth Street Bistro & Loft is committed to maintaining a healthy and sustainable future, and to this end they have been certified as being a Green Smart business. They recycle or reuse all appropriate products and compost their vegetable waste and coffee grounds. Additionally, the bistro prides itself on using only naturally raised and organic products when available. Everything they use is purchased locally. The restaurant is open seven days per week for lunch and dinner. It features a menu filled with globally inspired dishes, such as Cider Braised Carlton Farms Pork Tenderloin, Coconut Red Curry and Phad-Thai. The bar offers 13 local microbrews on tap along with several regional wines. Make the fresh choice with The Sixth Street Bistro & Loft.

509 Cascade Avenue, Hood River OR
(541) 386-5737
www.sixthstreetbistro.com

Celilo Restaurant
RESTAURANTS & CAFÉS: *Best Northwest cuisine*

Celilo Restaurant in Hood River offers a spectacular menu that abounds with the flavors of the Northwest. Simple dishes, each prepared with a gourmet touch, are created by chef and managing partner Ben Stenn, who received his training in France. Popular menu favorites include black cod, served over butternut squash risotto and finished with butter and grana cheese, and cassoulet, a traditional white bean stew with sausage, duck, lamb, pork, and vegetables. In the bar, patrons can choose from a wide selection of sprits, including several local draft beers on tap and a variety of regional wines. After dinner, pass the time with a glass of brandy, fortified wine, or 18-year-old scotch. If you prefer chocolate, be sure to try the Wy'east Chocolate Volcano Cake, a decadent chocolate cake filled with luscious Valrhona Chocolate. Stenn, along with his partners Jacquelin Carey and Maui Meyer, purchase only locally grown, farm fresh, and organic ingredients for their kitchen. Additionally, the triad has dedicated themselves to reducing waste, recycling and composting whatever possible. Celilo Restaurant is available for private parties and can provide catering for your special event. The welcoming atmosphere and elegant interior design offers a relaxing, intimate dining experience. Celilo Restaurant features high ceilings, tall, stately windows and walls that are lined with beautiful artwork created by local artisans. Take the time to relax and taste the difference at Celilo Restaurant.

16 Oak Street, Hood River OR
(541) 386-5710
www.celilorestaurant.com

Pacifica Candle & Soap Outlet

SHOPPING: *Best aromatic products*

Step inside the Pacifica Candle & Soap Outlet Store in Hood River and your senses swirl through the aromatic hints of herb gardens and global farmers' markets. Breathe in the subtle splendor of Thai Lemongrass or take a tranquil trip to Africa with the Tunisian Jasmine candle. Owner Maureen Donald is proud to show you how her gorgeous array of toxin-free handmade soy candles can provide hours of ambrosial pleasure. She enjoys helping newcomers discover unique creations such as the flowery bouquet of the Bergamot Amber Rose candle or Pacifica's variations on popular standards featuring vanilla, champaca or sandalwood. In keeping with the all-natural theme, Maureen offers vegetable glycerin soaps that are free of dyes. She also stocks a skin care line that uses only pure essential oils with fragrances tailored to please both genders that are biodegradable and never tested on animals. "People feel they're doing the healthy thing buying any of these products," Maureen says. Even those with hypersensitivity will find this a safe place to shop. Visit the Pacifica Candle & Soap Outlet, and while your eyes feast on the vibrant colors, your olfactory nerves will get a much appreciated break from the norm.

410 Oak Street, Hood River OR
(541) 490-1957

Cathedral Ridge Winery

WINERIES: *Award-winning wines created by Michael Sebastiani*

Cathedral Ridge Winery is located in the viticultural region of Hood River in the Columbia River Gorge. As providers of a full selection of fine wines they take great pride in sharing their award-winning creations. The Tasting Room is open every day from 11 am to 5 pm. If you are familiar with the selection at Cathedral Ridge Winery, or would simply like to have your wine delivered regularly, try the Cathedral Ridge Wine and Food Club. There isn't any membership fee, just fill out a simple form with your selection of wine and gourmet foods. With the Wine and Food Club you will be guaranteed to receive all of the Cathedral Ridge wines when they are first released and you can choose a package to be delivered to you once a month or seven times a year. Regular selections include Halbtrocken, a very rare blend of several different wines, a toasty vanilla Chardonnay, a full bodied Pinot gris, crisp and clean white Riesling, a rare Riesling blush, a Pinot noir, Merlot and a few Cabernets. Banked by views of Mt. Adams and Mt. Hood, the winery's seven acres of sweeping vineyards and lush garden landscapes are perfect for special events, receptions and weddings. Let them know what you would like to do and they will help you plan it.

4200 Post Canyon Drive, Hood River OR (800) 516-8710 *www.cathedralridgewinery.com*

A view of Mt. Hood as seen from Parkdale

MOUNT HOOD PARKDALE

The community of Mount Hood-Parkdale lies in the Hood River Valley on the northern approaches to Mount Hood, Oregon's great mountain recreation district. As the name suggests, Mount Hood-Parkdale is actually two communities, Parkdale and the smaller hamlet of Mount Hood. When the smaller community applied for a post office, it requested the name Mount Hood because the mountain was the most important object in the landscape. Parkdale, the name of the larger community, is in fact an accurate description of the area, which is indeed pleasant park-like valley land, albeit overshadowed by a considerable mountain. You can enjoy the valley and the view of Mount Hood at Toll Bridge Park. In 1976, the Postal Service merged the post offices of the two towns, and after much public discussion, the unified post office was named Mount Hood, though it is actually located in Parkdale. The post office serves the ski resorts on the east side of the mountain.

PLACES TO GO

- Elliot Glacier Public House
  4945 Baseline Road (541) 352-1022

- Mount Hood Artisans Market
  4933 Baseline Road (541) 352-3582

- Routson County Park
  State Route 35

- Toll Bridge County Park
  State Route 35

THINGS TO DO

January
- College Daze Celebration
  Mt. Hood Meadows
  (800) SKI-HOOD (754-4663)

March
- Kids Carnival
  Mt. Hood Meadows
  (800) 754-4663

April
- Vegetate (festival)
  Mt. Hood Meadows
  (800) 754-4663

Cooper Spur Mountain Resort

ACCOMMODATIONS:
Best retreat for year round recreation

For half a century, the Cooper Spur Mountain Resort has been welcoming guests to the north face of Mt. Hood. The staff is committed to providing a warm and welcoming experience and sharing this special place. The Resort is a mountain lodge and meeting center, featuring log cabins, lodge condo suites, hotel rooms, a log home, restaurant, lounge, tennis court, outdoor deck, and three therapeutic hot tubs. The property is located on 775 acres of private forest land surrounded by Mt. Hood National Forest, providing access to recreation year round. In winter, the resort offers a Nordic Center with cross country and snowshoe trails, and an Alpine ski area for skiing, snowboarding and tubing. Winter guests receive discounted lift tickets to nearby Mt. Hood Meadows Ski Resort. The Resort is ideal for catered group functions both large and small, ranging from corporate sessions to family reunions. The combination of privacy and accessibility allows groups to reserve the property for special occasions. The lodge condos, cabins, and lodge rooms offer flexibility for sleeping arrangements.

17055 Cooper Spur Road, Mt. Hood OR
(541) 352-6692 (lodging)
(541) 352-7803 (snow report)
www.cooperspur.com

Mt. Hood Meadows Ski Resort

ATTRACTIONS:
Most versatile full-service resort

Looking for the most spectacular and varied terrain in the Northwest? You can find it at the Mt. Hood Meadows Ski Resort. Mt. Hood Meadows is a full-service winter resort providing everything you need for a refreshing and memorable day on the mountain. Main base facilities are housed in the North and South lodges (which offer easy access to five lifts), but there is also a satellite base lodge and Skier Services Center at Hood River Meadows. You can purchase daily lift tickets and EpiCenter Snow Sports Learning Center sessions in the lift ticket building just off the South Lodge deck. There are always special packages for skiers of all types, including deeply discounted lift tickets when staying at Hood River Lodging Properties. Hood River was named among the Top 10 Ski Towns in America by *SKIING* magazine. The EpiCenter is a snow sports learning center that offers innovative programs including: The Optimizer, Sunday Ladies Day Clinics, Front Line Guide Services, Snow Monsters, Snow Rangers, High Cascade Snowboard Camp, and the NW School of Survival Adventures. Fifteen percent of the terrain at Mt. Hood Meadows is suitable for beginners, 50 percent for intermediate skiers, 20 percent for advanced, and 15 percent for expert skiers. There are 240 acres available for night skiing. The longest run at the Resort is three miles.

10755 Cooper Spur Road, Mt. Hood OR
(503) 337-2222 or (800) SKI-HOOD (754-4663)

PLACES TO GO

- Columbia Gorge Discovery Center/Wasco County Historical Museum
  5000 Discovery Center Drive
  (541) 296-8600

- Colombia Hills State Park
  Milepost 85, State Route 14,
  Dallesport WA

- Dalles Dam Visitor's Center
  Seufert Park, I-84 exit 87
  (541) 298-7650

- Deschutes River State Recreation Area
  State Route 206

- Fort Dalles Museum
  500 W 15th Street
  (541) 296-4547

- Mayer State Park
  I 84 exit 76

- Memaloose State Park
  I-84 at the Memaloose Park exit

- Old St. Peter's Landmark (historic church)
  405 Lincoln Street
  (541) 296-5686

- Sorosis Park
  E Scenic Drive

THINGS TO DO

April
- Northwest Cherry Festival
  (541) 296-2231

July
- Ft. Dalles Days Pro Rodeo
  (541) 296-2231 ext 21

September
- Historic The Dalles Days
  (541) 296-2231

Columbia River by the Dalles

THE DALLES

Visitors to The Dalles enjoy windsurfing, fishing and camping. The Dalles is an excellent place to learn windsurfing. Celio Park, nine miles east of town, is a favorite windsurfing spot. Anglers can try for walleye and sturgeon in the Columbia River. On the Washington side of the river, Columbia Hills State Park is the site of some of the most famous Indian pictographs anywhere. French-Canadian fur traders gave the name The Dalles to the narrows of the Columbia River, above the present city. The French word dalle means flagstone, and the basalt rocks along the narrows looked like paving to the traders. Fort Dalles was a military post during various disputes between settlers and Indians from 1850 to 1866. In 1955, the government ordered the Warm Spring, Wascoe and Paiute tribes to move from the Columbia Gorge to the high desert. Visitors to The Dalles can see the many murals on downtown buildings sponsored by The Dalles Mural Society. These works depict scenes from local history. Completion of Dalles Dam in 1957 gave the area vast amounts of low-cost electricity, and aluminum smelters were built to take advantage of the power. The smelters closed by 2000, but a new heavy power consumer has came to town—Google, which has built one of its largest computer centers here.

The Dalles Ranch

ACCOMMODATIONS:
Best place for retreats

Two hours from Portland, The Dalles Ranch is the perfect low-key destination for retreats, weddings or family getaways. Owners Eugene and Lorraine Gravel welcome you to experience the rustic Western lifestyle combined with a touch of elegance in the perfect wilderness location. The Dalles Ranch features a panoramic view of Mt. Hood, as well as hiking, fishing, hunting, cross-country skiing, and many other outdoor activities. Accommodations for up to 21 guests make it possible to include your entire family. The gourmet kitchen is open at all times so guests are free to prepare their own meals. Amenities such as a hot tub, a Finnish spa, a solid copper cowboy soaking tub, and a wine cellar are all available. A huge deck encircling the home allows you to enjoy the spectacular view. Lodging is even available for your horses. Weddings can be held at The Dalles Ranch amidst spectacular views with a backdrop of Ponderosa pines, ponds and Mt. Hood, on 100 feet of cedar decking with ledge-stone walls and green lawns. Visit The Dalles Ranch for an ideal experience.

**6289 Upper 5 Mile Road,
The Dalles OR**
(360) 892-7352 or (541) 298-9942
www.thedallesranch.com

Columbia Gorge Discovery Center

ATTRACTIONS: *Most inspirational, educational and interactive museum*

The Columbia Gorge is one of the last best places, an unspoiled treasure with a spectacular river canyon cutting the one and only sea-level route through the Cascade Mountain Range. From the Columbia Gorge Discovery Center you can see the mouth of the gorge, terraced canyons and scablands crafted by nature from the ancient lava flows and massive Ice Age floodwaters of Lake Missoula. For 10,000 years, The Dalles area has been continuously occupied by the ancestors of the Wasco, Wishram and Klickitat people and has served as North America's largest trade center. The Dalles was a stopping point for Lewis and Clark, Hudson Bay Company, Oregon Trail emigrants and Columbia River steamboats. These themes and much more are brought to life through exhibits, films, living history and public programs offered at the federally designated interpretive center. Innovative distance education programs, using web-based and video-conference interfaces bring cutting-edge, NASA-Discovery Center Lewis and Clark research to students across the country. Surrounded by recreational trails and ponds, the Center rests on 54 acres with scenic vistas of the Columbia River and rolling Klickitat Hills. The grounds offer native vegetation, including 90 blooming species for the enjoyment of visitors. The Discovery Center is not just an educational delight, but a treat for all ages. Their café features home-cooked soups, sandwiches and pastries, and the museum store includes an extensive book selection, educational toys, jewelry and artwork by local artisans. Wool products are offered, originating from the Imperial Stock Ranch. The exhibits, research library, café and museum store are open daily except Thanksgiving, Christmas and New Years Day. Enjoy the view and the lessons learned at Columbia Gorge Discovery Center.

5000 Discovery Drive, The Dalles OR
(541) 296-8600
www.gorgediscovery.org

The Dalles Art Center

GALLERIES: *Best community art gallery*

Discover the limitless talent to be found in the Columbia Gorge region at The Dalles Art Center. Whether you are interested in purchasing art, collecting art or just spending the day admiring the works of the many gifted participants, you will find inspiration. The Dalles Art Center is owned, operated and maintained by The Dalles Art Association, a community-supported non-profit organization. Director Carolyn Wright provides supervision and guidance in the showcasing of multi-media art by local and regional artists. You'll find pastels, watercolors, oils, acrylics, blown, stained and fused glass, ceramics, basketry, sculpture, jewelry, fiber art and more. One portion of the gallery is dedicated to guest artist exhibits, which change monthly. Shows are scheduled to represent a variety of media with a diversity of styles, featuring exceptional artists of the area. The focus of the Center is to provide support, and to stimulate knowledge and a love for the arts. An interesting assortment of classes is offered, so feel free to ask for a schedule. Each January and February brings an opportunity for school students to display their talents by participating in competitions designed especially for them. Juried competitions are offered in the spring and summer for all artists to enter. Located in one of 2,509 original libraries funded by the Carnegie Foundation, the center hosts monthly public receptions to honor the featured artists. Come and join the festivities and enjoy the never-ending creativity at The Dalles Art Center. The gallery is open to all and there is no admission charge. Donations are appreciated.

220 E 4th Street, The Dalles OR
(541) 296-4759

Nichols Art Glass

GALLERIES: *Best art glass*

Artist Andy Nichols' first experience with glass was in 1980 at the Kilbuckcreek Glass Studio in Rockford, Illinois. After a time spent working with stained glass, Andy fell in love with hot glass and the possibilities of three-dimensional creation. Glasswork has been his passion ever since, and you can see the results at Nichols Art Glass in The Dalles. In addition to the items on display at Andy's gallery, his work can be found in galleries and private collections throughout the Northwest. Among Andy's most famous creations in glass are his salmon and trout, which are remarkably realistic. The fish average about a foot in length, and each is unique in character and color. Andy is also known for his large handblown glass flowers, which can enhance a yard or patio. Other three-dimensional objects include chandeliers, vases and floats. One of his largest and most gorgeous chandeliers consists of more than 200 sea life forms and hangs at the Ocean Lodge in Cannon Beach. The Ocean Lodge is a major outlet for Andy's works, along with the Real Mother Goose in Portland. In addition to creating his glass art, Andy gives lessons in glass blowing, both at Nichols Art Glass and at other galleries across the country. A visit to Nichols Art Glass will open your eyes to the creative potential of glass.

912 W 6th Street, The Dalles OR
(541) 993-4022
www.nicholsartglass.com

Wheatacres Irrigation

GARDENS, PLANTS & FLOWERS:
Best watering supplies

Superior customer service, top quality products and exceptional expertise are a few examples of why Wheatacres Irrigation has become so successful. Owners Larry and Cameron Kaseberg are known not only for the irrigation, garden and pond supplies they sell, but also for their commitment to being customer and service oriented. The family-run business, started in 1970, sells to both commercial and residential customers. By conducting classes throughout the year on various topics they help their customers become smarter buyers. Some of the other services they offer are help with custom irrigation projects and innovative design work. They sell products ranging from drip and micro irrigation systems to products for your own decorative water garden or farm pond. Their showroom is filled with gifts, garden art and water fountains of all sizes. Larry and Cameron invite you to stop by and see their wide array of products and services at Wheatacres Irrigation.

3012 E Second Street, The Dalles OR
(541) 298-5331 or (800) 788-5331
www.wheatacres.com

Fly Shop of the Dalles

RECREATION: *Best fly shop*

To be a true success, find your passion and make it your business. At Fly Shop of The Dalles, Jeff Cottrell, experienced guide and devoted fisherman, and Jan Sage, former Santa Fe graphic artist and interior designer, have combined their loves and talents to create a thriving and popular business. Here you will find all the fly fishing and tying supplies you will ever need. The shop is a full-service facility with rods, reels, flies and fishing apparel, as well as other fishing equipment. Jeff, world traveler and outdoor guide for 27 years, provides lessons, trip planning and international booking services. Spend time in the store and you are likely to become part of Jeff's "daily forums." In other words, come in and talk about fishing. The studio and gallery, hosted by Jan, feature the works of David Hall, internationally known watercolorist. Prints, paintings, sculptures and jewelry, as well as other types of art related to fishing, water and conservationist themes, are available to add to your home or business. Jeff and Jan have beautifully restored the historic Gates House where their business is located. Situated in the heart of the city's historical district, the house is on the National Historical Register. Whether you visit the Fly Shop for fly-fishing demonstrations, workshops, art classes or an opportunity to see the restorations made to the Gates House, you will enjoy your time.

511 Union Street, The Dalles OR
(541) 296-3005 *www.flyshopofthedalles.com*

Casa El Mirador

RESTAURANTS & CAFÉS:
Best Mexican food

Casa El Mirador is dedicated to serving spectacular fresh food. In business for 12 years, they have been serving the largest selection of Mexican food in the Columbia Gorge area. They are known for their sizzling fajitas with tantalizing fillings including chicken, beef or shrimp. Casa El Mirador offers more than 15 delectable seafood specialty dishes. Their popular Mexican favorite, flan, allows you to finish off a fabulous meal with a traditional dessert. Casa El Mirador prides itself on its friendly service-oriented staff. They believe in the philosophy of always treating the customer right. Casa El Mirador offers dine-in or takeout service, as well as catering and banquet facilities for up to 50 people. Visit Casa El Mirador for their wide variety of Mexican food, savvy service and popular desserts.

1424 W 2nd Street, The Dalles OR
(541) 298-7388

Romul's

RESTAURANTS & CAFÉS: *Best gourmet European cuisine*

Owner Romul Grivov and his staff are known for their gourmet European cuisine, familial European atmosphere and warm hospitality. Romul has been in the restaurant business for 15 years, waiting tables at several area restaurants before opening his own establishment. Offering the highest quality food at reasonable prices, Romul brings his Bulgarian flair to The Dalles with European-inspired dishes like Tuscany Scampi and Pork Schnitzel. On the weekends, live music from an accordion player or guitarist contributes to the carefree atmosphere. If you get the impression that this mix of casualness and fine dining is a unique approach to running a restaurant, it's no accident. Romul says, "Everyone was waiting for something different. We brought something different." You can easily get lost here. Shrug off the cares of the outside world and enjoy the company of friends and family, partaking of savory dishes and something from Romul's exquisite wine list. Stay and linger for their fabulous Gelato, homemade in house. Romul invites you to come and spend a long evening.

312 Court Street, The Dalles OR
(541) 296-9771 *www.romuls.com*

Maryhill Winery

WINERIES: *Best winery*

Maryhill Winery began as a partnership between four wine enthusiasts: Craig and Vicki Leuthold, Donald Leuthold and Cherie Brooks. In 2000, the four broke ground on a site with a sweeping view of the Columbia River Gorge and Mt. Hood. Maryhill Winery focuses on producing premium red wines, with special attention to Zinfandel and Sangiovese. The vineyards include the largest planting of Zinfandel in Washington State, as well as Viognier, Cabernet, Sauvignon and Merlot. John Haw, a 25-year industry veteran, is Maryhill Winery's winemaker. John produces many complex blends and wines that are ready to drink upon bottling. In competitions, the wines have won too many gold, silver and bronze medals to mention. Visitors to the winery find their attention split between the stunning views and the massive carved wood tasting bar. Samplers can take a glass onto the deck or grounds. Maryhill Winery also has a 4,000-seat outdoor amphitheater, which is a major concert venue. The 2005 season included Bob Dylan, B. B. King and ZZ Top. The audience has panoramic views of the stage, the river and Mount Hood. Guests can bring blankets or chairs for the grass-terraced general admission area or purchase reserved seats. The 2006 season was suspended due to construction, but a full schedule returns in 2007. Open daily, Maryhill Winery offers an experience you will want to repeat.

9774 Highway 14, Goldendale WA
(877) 627-9445
www.maryhillwinery.com

Sunset at Maryhill

WELCHES

Welches is a part of the Villages of Mount Hood on the Mount Hood Scenic Byway, U.S. Highway 26. The Villages are a federation of local communities that joined together as an official Clackamas County village to coordinate services. In addition to Welches, the 3,500 people of the Villages live in the communities of Brightwood, Wemme, Zigzag and Rhododendron. A variety of classic resorts are located in this area, notably the Resort at the Mountain in Welches. A beautiful RV park in Welches is named Mt. Hood Village Resort. For a gorgeous hike that is easy for children and older citizens, consider the Old Salmon River Trail near Welches.

THINGS TO DO

June
• Fly Fishing Festival and
  A Taste of the Mountain
  (800) 266-3971

July
• Fiesta Days
  Mt. Hood Village Resort
  (503) 622-4011

August
• Huckleberry Festival
  Mt. Hood Village Resort
  (503) 622-4011

September
• Festival of the Forest
  Wildwood Park
  (503) 622-5560

October
• Mount Hood Salmon
  & Mushroom Festival
  Brightwood
  (503) 622-4798

November
Wine and Art Festival
  Resort at the Mountain
  (800) 669-7666

Salmon River Trail Near Welches

Resort at the Mountain

ACCOMMODATIONS:

Best golf, ski and meeting resort

The luxuriously appointed Resort at The Mountain is nestled in the western highlands of Mt. Hood, just an hour east of Portland. Here you will find a wealth of gorgeous rooms and stunning views. Located within a few minutes of the Mount Hood National Forest, The Resort offers a multitude of outdoor activities, including downhill and cross-country skiing, wildlife viewing, hiking, mountain biking and fly fishing. Within The Resort you will enjoy some of the finest golfing Oregon has to offer. Understanding that golf was created in Scotland, the Resort has worked hard to present tastes of Scotland in everything they do, from Scottish-style bunkers and Scottie dog tees to the Tartans Pub and Steakhouse and Highlands Restaurant. Further outdoor offerings include a heated pool and Jacuzzi, four tennis courts, two full-sized croquet courts and lawn bowling greens. The Resort provides equipment rentals for tennis, biking, volleyball, badminton, croquet and lawn bowling. They can help organize group recreational activities or help you find local excursions. Each year The Resort at The Mountain presents several events, including the Wild About Game Cook-Off and the Wine and Art Festival. With so much to do and see, it is a great getaway for families and companies. The Resort at The Mountain is located at the western base of Mt. Hood, one-half mile off Highway 26 in Welches.

68010 E Fairway Avenue, Welches OR
(503) 622-3101 or (800) 669-7666
www.theresort.com

Central Oregon

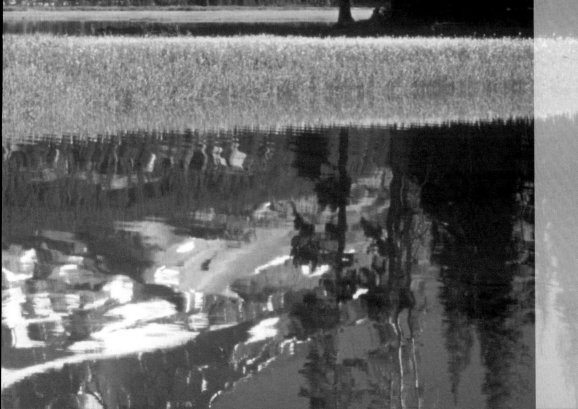

South Sister above Sparks Lake

PLACES TO GO

- Deschutes Brewery (tours and tastings)
  901 SW Simpson Avenue (541) 385-8606

- Deschutes County Historical Museum
  129 NW Idaho Avenue (541) 389-1813

- Drake Park/Mirror Pond
  901 NW Riverside Boulevard

- High Desert Museum
  59800 S Highway 97 (541) 382-4754

- High Desert Museum Praegitzer Gallery
  916 NW Wall Street (541) 323-2000

- La Pine State Park
  La Pine State Recreation Road

- Lava Lands Visitor Center and Lava Butte
  Off U.S. Highway 97 (541) 593-2421

- Lava River Cave
  Off U.S. Highway 97 (541) 383-5300

- Mount Bachelor Ski Resort
  13000 SW Century Drive (800) 829-2442

- Newberry Caldera
  Forest Service Road 21 (541) 383-5300

- Pilot Butte State Park
  NE Pilot Butte Summit Drive

- Pine Mountain Observatory
  Burns Star Road (541) 382-8331

- Sunriver Nature Center & Observatory
  57245 River Road, Sunriver
  (541) 593-4394

- Tumalo Falls
  Tumalo Falls Road off Skyliner Road

- Working Wonders Children's Museum
  520 SW Powerhouse Drive #624
  (541) 389-4500

THINGS TO DO

January
- Atta Boy 300 IFSS World Cup Sled Dog Championship
  www.ultimateiditarod.com/attaboy.htm

February
- Bach 'n' Brew
  Sunriver Resort (541) 593-9310

- Bend Winterfest
  www.bendwinterfest.org

April
- Earth Day Parade
  Riverfront Plaza (541) 385-6908

BEND

Bend is the urban heart of Central Oregon and the center of one of the fastest-growing metropolitan areas in the United States. Originally a logging town, Bend has become a jump-off point for outdoor sports such as mountain biking, fishing, hiking, camping, rock climbing, skiing and golf. Central Oregon, a major retirement destination, is a land of contrasts: desert and forest, lava and snow, volcanoes and plains. Bend is on the eastern edge of a ponderosa pine forest as it transitions into high desert junipers and sagebrush. The city is a mix of snowboarders and professionals, locals and visitors. Downtown Bend is filled with high-end shops and art galleries, which you can tour during the First Friday art walk. Mirror Pond in Drake Park, the jewel of downtown, contains ducks, geese, and a pair of swans from Queen Elizabeth's royal swannery in England. The Old Mill District features upscale shopping, trendy restaurants and an outdoor amphitheater for summer concerts. For a panoramic view of Bend and the volcanic peaks around it, take a walk or a drive to the top of Pilot Butte. An even finer view can be found at the Newberry National Volcanic Monument south of town. This monument includes lava formations, obsidian fields, waterfalls, hotsprings and caves. It is hard to fathom as you drive through the summit area that you are within the 17-square-mile caldera of a 500-square-mile volcano that is still active.

Magnificent Mt. Bachelor rises behind Lava Lake

May
- Riverfest
  Bend, Sisters and Sunriver (541) 420-0452

June
- Sunriver Sunfest
  Sunriver Village (541) 593-8149

- Balloons Over Bend
  Summit High School www.
  balloonsoverbend.com

- Bite of Bend
  The Shops at the Old Mill (541) 312-0131

July
- La Pine Frontier Days
  (541) 536-9771

- La Pine Rodeo
  Rodeo Grounds (541) 536-9202

- Bend Summer Festival
  www.bendsummerfestival.com

- Cascade Cycling Classic
  Downtown (541) 280-0777

- Blues, Brews & BBQs
  Sunriver Village (541) 593-8149

August
- Bend Brewfest
  Les Schwab Amphitheater (541) 312-8510

September
- Dixieland Party Band & Friends
  La Pine (541) 548-0679

- Sunriver's Fall Festival
  Sunriver Village (541) 593-8149

- Wine by the River
  www.winebytheriver.com

- Bend Oktoberfest
  (541) 385-6570

September-October
- Pacific Amateur Golf Classic
  www.pacamgolf.com

October
- BendFilm Festival
  (541) 388-FEST (3378)

- Bend Fall Festival
  www.bendfallfestival.com

- Original Central Oregon Pumpkin Festival
  Tillicum Ranch (541) 389-7275

November
- The Nature of Words (literary festival)
  www.thenatureofwords.org

Juniper Acres Bed & Breakfast
ACCOMMODATIONS: *Best bed and breakfast*

The awe-inspiring view from Juniper Acres Bed & Breakfast takes in seven majestic mountains. Vern and Della Bjerk built this lovely lodge-style B&B seven miles from Bend on 10 acres of lushly wooded land. Juniper Acres sits in the middle of recreation heaven. White water rafting, canoeing, and fishing on the Metolius and Deschutes Rivers are nearby, as are more than 20 golf courses. If you would rather relax during your stay at Juniper Acres, you'll enjoy the large sun-filled decks. Each of the bedrooms has a private bath, sitting area, television and air conditioning. Hospitality comes naturally to Vern and Della. Through the bed and breakfast they have created an opportunity to do what they love most: care for and serve others. Creative gourmet breakfasts are their specialty, and they will do their best to accommodate special dietary needs. The little extra touches make Juniper Acres a memorable place to stay. You'll remember the homemade cookies in your room, the readily available tea by the cozy fire in the woodstove, and the bottomless fruit bowl that is always available. The Bjerks will provide you with maps of the area, and for your entertainment there are books, games, videos and puzzles. Juniper Acres is open year round, so pay the Bjerks a visit. You'll be glad you did.

65220 Smokey Ridge Road, Bend OR
(541) 389-2193
www.juniperacres.com

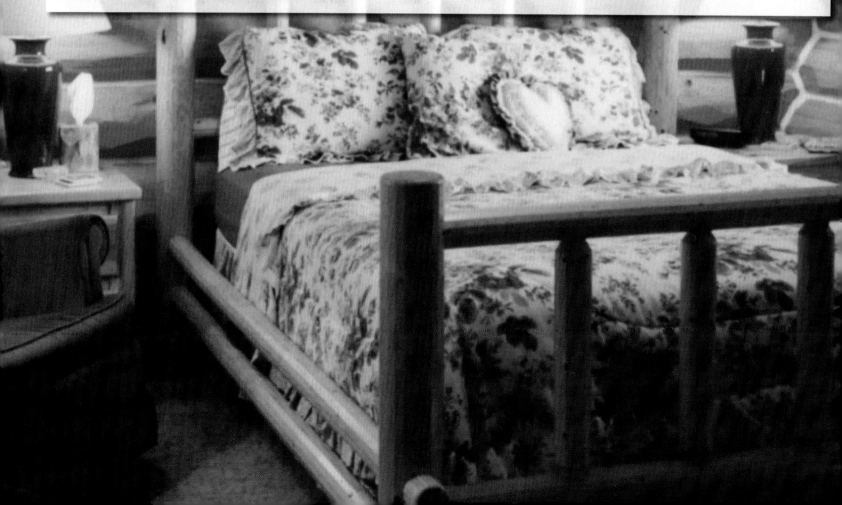

Mt Bachelor
Photo by Don Osborn

Phoenix Inn Suites

ACCOMMODATIONS:
Best premium hotel

Providing prized customer service, beautiful clean suites, luxurious amenities and an excellent location, Phoenix Inn Suites is a premium hotel in a scenic locale. A multitude of nearby attractions include golfing, hiking, fishing and skiing. There are many fun cultural activities in the area, such as concerts, theaters and established film festivals. No matter what first attracts you to Bend, a stay at the Phoenix Inn will make this a favorite destination for future visits. Every suite is complete with refrigerator, microwave, iron with ironing board and coffee maker. They also offer complimentary wireless Internet. Want a break from it all? Treat yourself or someone special to a spa suite. The Phoenix Inn Suites has a year round swimming pool and hot tub, in addition to a fitness facility and guest laundry. Wake up and enjoy a delicious start to your morning with Belgian waffles and a buffet-style continental breakfast before starting your day. Visit them every time you come to Bend, whether to ski or snowboard, see a concert or shop. You could even visit just to relax and enjoy this beautiful area. You'll be surrounded by elegance and welcomed with the same cheerful courtesy every time you stay at the Phoenix Inn Suites.

300 NW Franklin Avenue, Bend OR
(541) 317-9292 or (888) 291-4764
www.phoenixinnsuites.com

Rock Springs Guest Ranch

ACCOMMODATIONS:
Best ranch accommodations

Begin the day with an invigorating breath of fresh mountain air, sit down to a savory breakfast ready and waiting for you, and luxuriate in open invitation to spend the rest of the day any way you choose. Managers John and Eva Gill are carrying on a family tradition that began with their aunt Donna Gill's 1969 founding of Rock Springs. Horseback riding is the heart of the ranch. 65 special horses, each with a personality and level of performance that the wranglers know well, are individually matched to suit the guest rider. Beginning riders enjoy the terrain at a pace that progresses daily. More experienced riders take to the trails at a faster clip and explore in their own group. Many of the guests return year after year for the second-to-none horseback riding program. Others return to play tennis, swim or to go fishing. There is a relaxing spa and lots of games, everything from ping-pong to basketball or billiards. Twenty-six golf courses, fly fishing and whitewater rafting are all available nearby. Rock Springs guests can take advantage of the all-inclusive American Plan, a single package that incorporates lodging, meals, horseback riding and all ranch activities. The excellence of their breakfast, lunch, hors d'oeuvres and dinner reveal the ranch's commitment to quality. Guests with special dietary preferences will be accommodated. Capacity is limited to 50, so your service is personal and access to Ranch facilities is unlimited. A special children's activity program makes everyone feel welcome. You can be assured that the Rock Springs management and staff will do more than their part to make your stay an unforgettable experience.

64201 Tyler Road, Bend OR
(800) 225-3833
www.rocksprings.com

Seventh Mountain Resort

ACCOMMODATIONS: *Best resort*

Seventh Mountain Resort is located near Mt. Bachelor on the sunny side of The Cascades. Seventh Mountain Resort has long been a destination for families, groups and those looking for adventure. Gold Crown rated and open year round, the resort offers enough activities to last a lifetime. In the summer, nearby Deschutes River is one of Oregon's premier whitewater rivers. During ski and snowboarding season, the resort provides shuttles to Mt. Bachelor. You don't have to ski to take in the view from the spectacular chairlift ride. At the resort you'll find an ice skating rink, horseback riding, tennis and volleyball courts, swimming pools, hot tubs, saunas and a fully equipped Fitness Center. If you still have energy, you can venture out into the gorgeous countryside on well maintained hiking trails. Want to ride a mountain bike instead? The resort can make that happen too. Golfers can take in a round on the challenging Widgi Creek course, adjacent to the resort. When you've had your fill of activity, you might want to relax and enjoy a superb dining experience at Seasons Restaurant, set in the Deschutes National Forest. Seasons Restaurant presents delicious Pacific Northwest-style cuisine. Enjoy authentic regional flavors with fresh, locally grown ingredients. The resort condominiums come with fireplaces and decks providing outstanding accommodations for any occasion. Ask about special package offers. Encircled by peaks, lakes and meadows, whatever you choose to do at Seventh Mountain Resort will be indelibly etched in your memory.

18575 SW Century Drive, Bend OR
(541) 382-8711
www.seventhmountain.com

Tumalo Falls

Bend Equine Medical Center

ANIMALS & PETS:
Best medical facility for horses

Bend Equine Medical Center is an exceptional, first-class medical facility dedicated entirely to the care of horses. Dr. Wayne Schmotzer and Dr. Daniel Harrison opened this state-of-the-art large animal clinic in 1998, after incorporating the best features from top veterinary institutions across the country into their design. The construction phase lasted 14 months and resulted in this 7,000-square-foot climate-controlled equine hospital with a clinical laboratory, large equine treatment area and surgery suite. Pre- and post-surgery induction and recovery rooms are heavily padded for the safety and comfort of the horses. The Center has the most advanced diagnostic and therapeutic equipment available and can offer first-class support that includes radiology, surgery, dentistry and reproductive services. The Center's extraordinary team of doctors and staff encompasses complementary areas of expertise to ensure the most comprehensive care available for your horse. Students of veterinary medicine from all over the world come to observe and learn, while interns and residents are mentored by this concerned group of medical experts every year. The doctors and staff of the Bend Equine Medical Center are committed to community outreach and client education, believing that people who are well informed will be able to make the best decisions for the health and welfare of their horse. For horses and the people who love them, Bend Equine Medical Center is the place to come.

19121 Couch Market Road, Bend OR
(541) 388-4006
www.bendequine.com

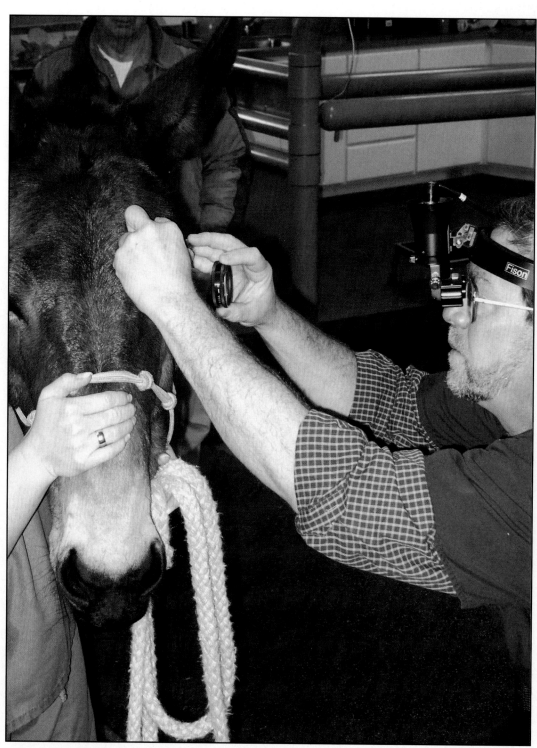

VCA Cascade Animal Hospital
ANIMALS & PETS: *Best animal hospital*

New clients are always welcome at VCA Cascade Animal Hospital. Doctors Janette Wells, Rex Ulrich and the rest of the staff are dedicated to top-notch care for your dog, cat or exotic pet. They will provide compassionate treatment and the best possible care to your furry or feathered friend. Dr. Janette, medical director of the hospital, is one of the first doctors in Oregon to be certified in the PennHIP X-ray technique. This method permits early detection and a better chance to successfully fight hip dysplasia, the most common inherited joint problem of large-breed dogs. Dr. Rex has more than 30 years of practice in small animal surgery. He has special knowledge and experience in soft tissue surgeries and orthopedic surgeries. Part of the VCA network of more than 375 animal hospitals, VCA Cascade offers preventive medicine, microchip implants (to permanently identify your pet) and ultrasound services. Pet boarding is another valuable service. Pets are part of your family. Pet wellness is as important as your own personal wellness. VCA Cascade Animal Hospital invites you to bring in your pet and become a part of their family.

61535 S Highway 97 #3, Bend OR
(541) 389-6612 *www.vcacascade.com*

Cascades Theatrical Company
ATTRACTIONS: *Best theater company*

Providing quality productions for more than 25 years, the Cascades Theatrical Company (CTC) is Central Oregon's premier community theater. The group practices the Three E's: Enrichment, Entertainment and Education. In addition to providing Central Oregonians with six main stage productions a year, CTC is the parent company to the Bend Theatre for Young People and The Children's Music Theatre Group. CTC utilizes local talent onstage and backstage, so everyone gets the opportunity to participate, gaining valuable experience. Productions at the CTC far exceed the standard expectations for community theater. You never know when the theater bug might bite, so remember that opportunities for participation in productions are available. Catch a show at Cascades Theatrical Company and see what they can do.

148 NW Greenwood Avenue, Bend OR
(541) 389-0803
www.cascadestheatrical.org

High Desert Museum

ATTRACTIONS:

Best info on the high desert

Have you ever had a morning meeting with a bobcat or felt a hawk swoop over your head? Would you like to chat with a stagecoach driver or buckaroo? You can do all of this and more at the High Desert Museum, where every day is wild. At daily shows and demonstrations, experts will help you experience the wildlife and historical characters of the High Desert. Find out what it's like inside a tipi. Ask yourself whether you would have survived the Oregon Trail or would have made it as a fur trader. The High Desert Museum offers unique experiences that have earned it national acclaim for promoting understanding of the high desert's wildlife, people, culture, art and natural resources. It is on 135 pristine acres just 10 minutes from the Old Mill District in Bend. *The New York Times* described the Museum as an architectural jewel "nestled into the spare basalt of Central Oregon as if it grew there." The Museum's 53,000-square-foot main building anchors a quarter-mile trail that winds along a tranquil stream through aspen and ponderosa pine. Guests may walk the trail to reach 32,000 square feet of exhibits and animal habitats, including a real working steam-powered sawmill. Indoors, detailed dioramas let you experience the lives of travelers on the Oregon Trail and of Plateau Native Americans. Live a wild life. Come to the museum and experience the high desert as you never have before.

59800 S Highway 97, Bend OR
(541) 382-4754
www.highdesertmuseum.org

Todd Lake, with Broken Top standing majestically in the background

Central Oregon High Cascades

ATTRACTIONS:
Biggest draw in the region

Five large Cascade volcanoes climb to the sky west of Bend in Central Oregon. These are the Three Sisters, Broken Top, and Mount Bachelor. The Sisters were named Faith, Hope and Charity by early settlers. The North Sister is oldest, with towering rock pinnacles and glaciers. It has not erupted since the late Pleistocene. It is the most dangerous climb of the Three Sisters, due to its level of erosion, which promotes rock fall. The Middle Sister is the smallest and is the middle in age. The South Sister is the youngest and tallest of the trio. It last erupted about 1,600 years ago. It has a well developed crater that holds a glaciated lake. The climb is long, steep and non-technical. It can be completed in a day by fit hikers. In September 2005, scientists discovered that a 100-square-mile area southwest of South Sister is rising at 1.4 inches per year, probably due to a newly formed lake of magma. Broken Top rises southeast of South Sister. As its name indicates, Broken Top is highly eroded by Ice Age glaciers. Mount Bachelor, the southernmost of the five peaks, took its name because it stands apart from the Three Sisters. Mount Bachelor is the youngest major volcano in the area, and last erupted between 8,000 and 10,000 years ago. The entire cone of Mount Bachelor is now a ski area with lifts reaching all the way to the glacier at the summit. The resort is one of the largest in the Pacific Northwest, with a skiable area of 3,683 acres.

http://vulcan.wr.usgs.gov/Volcanoes/ Oregon/HighCascades

Di Lusso Bakery Café
BAKERIES, COFFEE & TEA: *Best coffee*

Once upon a time, laptop users seeking bandwidth wandered far and wide to locate a network connection. These mobile computer users adopted an inventive practice of drawing chalk symbols near the hotspots they found. These symbols were a sort of nouveau-technological hobo language. Thankfully these days, *guerrilla chalking* is hardly necessary. Many businesses now offer wi-fi as a complimentary service to their customers. Di Lusso Bakery Cafe in Bend is a great example of a provider of this service, but only one of the many reasons that this cafe is a vital part of the Bend community. Lisa and Bob Golden have made Di Lusso a desirable place to visit. They serve delicious, artisan, handmade bread and pastries so it is a perfect place to enjoy a freshly made breakfast and a pleasing array of lunch items. Everything is made in-house and from scratch daily. Di Lusso is also the largest and oldest coffee roaster in the area. Not only does Di Lusso strive to provide customers with the best local products and services in Bend, but they also are a quality wholesaler that provides various local businesses and restaurants with handcrafted bakery goods and coffees. After eight years in operation, they now have two bustling locations in Bend and one in Redmond at the airport. Make your way to Di Lusso to try some of their wonderfully rich roasted coffee or delicious food. Don't forget to visit the Di Lusso website.

744 NW Bond, Bend OR (541) 312-4036
1135 NW Galveston, Bend OR (541) 383-8155
Redmond Airport Concession, Roberts Field (541) 504-4481
www.dilusso.com

Photo by Joseph Eastburn

Photo by Wendy L. Gay

Balay

BAKERIES, COFFEE & TEA: *Balay is like visiting good friends*

Located in a house that was built in 1905 in the heart of Bend, Balay coffeehouse and tea room overlooks Mirror Pond on the Deschutes River. *Balay* is the Philippine name for "my house." It is a fitting name because visiting Balay is like visiting good friends in a warm and friendly atmosphere. Owners Chris and Merrideth Padre are always present to welcome you and want you to feel free to linger and relax. The specialty of the house is delicious iced Bubble Tea, a green tea-based smoothie with fruit and tapioca pearls. The coffee beverages are made with kosher coffee and touted as *Cafe D'Arte*. To add to your enjoyment, choose from among their delectable pastries and light lunch selections. In the evening, snuggle by the wood-burning fireplace in the main room and enjoy Balay's evening dessert café. Dogs are welcome to accompany guests out on the lawn seating area. Available for private event rental, Balay is the perfect spot for special occasions. Chris and Merrideth welcome all ages at Balay, though they describe their oasis as a "young ma and pa" place. Visit Balay next time you're in Central Oregon. It's one of the places that makes Bend so special.

961 NW Brooks Street, Bend OR
(541) 389-6464

RE/MAX Equity Group of Bend

BUSINESS:

Best start on the good life

People who discover Bend feel they are truly in their element. The good life means finding your place anywhere from the fairways to the slopes. When Bob Wienk discovered the Bend secret, he felt immediately at home with the community and the active lifestyle. Bob Wienk's previous executive career caused him and his family to move often. So much moving means that Bob and his wife, Judi, have friends wherever they travel, but it also means they appreciate the good life here in Bend. Bob and Judi worked as a real estate team before moving to Bend and now Bob puts that professional expertise to work in a place where he feels he is in his element. Not only does Bob's affinity for and knowledge of the area make him a successful real estate professional, his ability to key into the needs of his clients makes him uniquely qualified. It is no secret that whether you are looking to relocate to Bend or you already live here, you can turn to Bob Wienk to make the most of your move. As Bob's clients know, "For the Good Life, Just Wienk!"

210 SW Wilson Avenue, Bend OR
(541) 322-9960
www.bobwienk.com

Karen Bandy Design Jeweler

FASHION: *Best jewelry designs*

In downtown Bend, Karen Bandy is the owner, president and designer of the elegant Karen Bandy Design Jeweler. Her shop is cozy and quaint. The exposed brick walls and original paintings provide a perfect backdrop for her custom made jewelry cases. Designed to make viewing easy, the cases present Karen's artistic creations in settings arranged to spotlight their unique beauty. Karen considers the lifestyle of her clients as she creates wearable, comfortable jewelry. The stones are set in bezels, rather than prongs, to make them more appropriate for active lifestyles. Karen is known for colored stone work, as well as her diamond and precious gem jewelry. She enthusiastically creates for bridal occasions using colored diamonds as well as white diamonds. In addition to her own work, Karen carries the works of other talented Northwest and nationally known jewelers. Karen has won many awards, including first place in the prestigious International/National Spectrum Awards for a ring she designed. Take your design ideas to Karen and see what she can create just for you.

126 NW Minnesota, Bend OR
(541) 388-0155 or (800) 245-0155

Photo by Wendy L. Gay

Goody's Ice Cream Candy
FUN FOODS: *Best ice cream*

If you try Goody's once, you will be back for more. As owners Brett and Marion Palmateer say, "Only too much is enough." People come from all over the West Coast to get the old-fashioned sodas, malts and milkshakes made at Goody's authentic old-fashioned soda fountains. When you walk in the door at Goody's, that special aroma takes you right back to your childhood. Great memories of some of your favorite times come bubbling up to the surface of your consciousness. The sweet sugary smell of ice cream and handmade cones is blissful. Goody's is one of the most well known and trusted names in the industry. Their products are made daily in small batches using natural ingredients to ensure the ultimate in freshness and natural taste. You won't find preservatives in the ice cream or wax in the chocolates. Whipped cream, nuts and cherries, all the favorites are here, along with hot fudge sundaes, banana splits, turtle sundaes, and black forest sundaes. How about a root beer float? For East Coast traditionalists, Goody's will make you an egg cream to rival the best in New York City. Goody's Ice Cream & Candies has a great espresso and coffee bar and they make incredible chocolates that are a fantastic choice for gift giving. Go ahead and indulge.

330 SE Bridgeford Road, Bend OR
(541) 385-7085

Blue Spruce Gallery & Pottery Studio

GALLERIES: *Best pottery studio*

In 1993, Bob Sant bought a Bend pottery studio that was named by its former owners after a blue spruce that flourished in their yard in 1976, the year they began their pottery business. Under Bob's stewardship, Blue Spruce Gallery & Pottery Studio gained a far-flung reputation for great clay art. Bob worked at Pottery Northwest in Seattle and at O'Hare Stoneware in Bend before purchasing Blue Spruce. He is the descendent of 19th century English potter Henry William Sant, whose work is still collected. After building the Blue Spruce into the Northwest's largest clay art gallery, in 2002 Bob decided to continue his own stoneware line and redefine the gallery with an online store and a new location on Industrial Way. His high-end custom work includes big architectural features like columns and fireplaces. He also works directly with designers to craft sinks, tiles, lamps, murals and dinnerware. His gallery represents the work of a select group of Oregon's best potters and his online catalog contains everything from baking dishes to personalized awards. Bob's popular Empty Bowls project is an annual charity luncheon, where participants take home a pottery bowl and proceeds feed the homeless. Bob has chaired the Pottery Showcase, a formal event held by the Northwest's professional clay artists, and was inspirational in the beginnings of Art Central and the Mirror Pond Gallery, projects that support the arts and offer places to work, teach and display art. Next time you want pottery, turn to Blue Spruce Gallery & Pottery Studio.

550 SW Industrial Way, #45, Bend OR
(541) 389-7745
www.thebluesprucegallery.com

Lava Gallery
GALLERIES: *Best glass gallery*

From the shimmering depths of molten glass, husband-and-wife team Jeffrey and Heather Thompson create imaginative glass art sculptures sure to tickle your fancy. The Thompsons, owners and operators of Lava Gallery in Bend, began blowing glass together in 2000. In 2001, Jeff built their hot-shop and furnace, which is able to hold 350 pounds of glass at a liquid temperature. Over the past several years, Jeff and Heather have mastered the intricate choreography involved in balancing what the glass wants to do and what they want the glass to do. Heather was raised in Florida, where she cultivated an affinity for the ocean, and has studied art her entire life, which led her to become a gifted seamstress and weaver with a cultured eye for design. Jeff grew up in Bend and graduated from Bend Senior High School with both academic and art honors. He went on to study glass working while pursuing undergraduate studies at the University of Oregon. He has since studied the field intensively and has learned everything from Old World Italian techniques to cutting-edge, vacuum-encased sculpture. Heather's work ranges from the whimsical to the classic, while Jeff's work is strongly influenced by his native Pacific Northwest environment. Lava Gallery provides both residential and commercial work as well as custom architectural pieces. Find out more about this stunning art form and see the Thompsons' newest creations at Lava Gallery.

62807 NE Snowcap Court, Bend OR
(541) 990-8624
www.lavagallery.com

Donner Flower Shop
GARDENS, PLANTS & FLOWERS: *Best florist*

The Donner Flower Shop is tantamount to stepping into an enchanting live and fragrant garden. Owners Doris Dilday and Eileen Chandler have created a visual and aromatic paradise with a large selection of high quality seasonal fresh flowers. Healthy live house plants fill spaces with vibrant energy. Exquisite gifts round out the possibility of finding just what you want. Lovely Lampe Berger home fragrance lamps from France and elegant Nambe metalware from New Mexico are among your varied choices. More whimsical gifts include many sizes of their very popular decorative ceramic chickens. If fresh flowers are not practical for your decorating or gift giving needs, Doris and Eileen will be happy to fashion a beautiful silk flower arrangement just for you. These talented owners purchased the shop in 1999. They have more than 40 years of floral experience between them. Sharing their love of flowers is the essence of their business, and they are clearly passionate about their work. Doris and Eileen are proud to have their motto quoted: "We're the best!" Enjoy superior customer service and be transported by the fragrance and beauty at the Donner Flower Shop.

909 NW Wall Street, Bend OR
(541) 383-3791 or (800) 433-4588
www.donnerflower.com

Alpine Acupuncture
HEALTH & BEAUTY: *Best acupuncture clinic*

Gentle, effective health care is the promise of Steven A. Foster-Wexler, LAc, a licensed acupuncturist and certified Qigong instructor. His goal at Alpine Acupuncture is to work with you to achieve optimum health. Oriental medicine, which includes Acupuncture, Chinese herbs, Tuina (Chinese therapeutic massage), Qigong (exercise therapy), and Chinese dietary counseling, offers an approach that may be different from, but is very complementary to, other forms of medicine. Alpine Acupuncture refers to and works closely with other health care specialists. Because each patient is unique, Alpine Acupuncture will tailor treatments to address each individual's needs. Some of the issues addressed include chronic pain, infertility, allergies, addictions, insomnia and stress. By getting to the root of the problem, people often find long-term health gain rather than temporary symptom relief. There are very few side effects with acupuncture, making it ideal for people of all ages and health care needs. Steven is certified by the National Acupuncture Detoxification Association to treat chemically dependent drug and alcohol clients. In addition to maintaining his practice in Bend, Steven sees Hospice patients in Redmond and Sisters, teaches in the massage program at Central Oregon Community College, and provides AcuDetox to addiction clients. Steven strongly believes in each person's ability to discover their full health potential. Everyone deserves optimal health, and a visit to Alpine Acupuncture can get you on your way to a better you.

628 NW York Drive, Suite 104, Bend OR
(541) 330-8283
www.bendacupuncture.com

Bend Memorial Clinic

HEALTH & BEAUTY:
Most comprehensive healthcare

Bend Memorial Clinic was established in 1946. Dr D.J. Rademacher and several colleagues formed the clinic to provide patients, and each other, the convenience of a group practice. Specialization in the medical field had become necessary and the practice could provide more equipment and services to patients than a single practice could. By 1957, the practice had grown to include seven physicians and two surgeons, requiring the clinic to relocate. By 1976 the clinic moved once more. This time, the clinic allowed for growth and today Bend Memorial Clinic has more than 30 service specialties and 80 physicians. Family Practice satellite offices were started in La Pine in 1987 and in Sisters in 1991. The La Pine clinic has become a rural health clinic in order to provide more economical care for that community. The Sisters clinic offers a family practice physician as well as complete lab and x-ray services. In 1994, a satellite Ophthalmology office with a small optical dispensary was opened in Redmond. A variety of other specialties are offered at the Redmond clinic, including pulmonology and cardiology. BMC opened the first freestanding outpatient surgery center in Central Oregon in 1996. The Bend Surgery Center allows BMC physicians and other community physicians to perform outpatient surgeries conveniently and less expensively than in the hospital. As it has from the very beginning, Bend Memorial Clinic provides high quality, comprehensive, convenient health care for patients.

1501 NE Medical Center Drive, Bend OR
(541) 382-2811 or
(866) 670-2811
www.bendmemorialclinic.com

Deschutes Dental Center

HEALTH & BEAUTY: *Best dental care*

The treatment suites at Deschutes Dental Center provide tranquil views of the Deschutes River rapids. For five years, it has been the preferred dental center for discerning Bend patrons. Dr. Phillippe Freeman has received the Fellowship Award from the Academy of General Dentistry, and is an active member of the Academy of Osseointegration, a international group of specialists who focus on dental implant treatment and research. He is also a member of the American Academy of Cosmetic Dentistry and the Academy of Operative Dentistry. Dr. Freeman is a magician in the processes of cosmetic gum surgeries, bonded porcelain restorations, and corrective treatments for occlusion and dysfunction. By using the latest state-of-the-art equipment he has eliminated 90 percent of radiation, and 100 percent of the chemicals used to take traditional x-rays. Digital x-ray and intra-oral cameras take the place of the bulky x-ray apparatus of the past. Patients rest in plush dental chairs supplied with blankets and head pillows, with no fear of the drill. Drill-less technologies also have no need of anesthetic. The center is an ultra modern facility that provides adult-oriented restorative dentistry, rehabilitative and implant options. Deschutes Dental Center is a confident dental center that warranties its cosmetic and restorative services.

159 SW Shevlin-Hixon Road, Bend OR
(541) 317-1300

Healing Bridge Physical Therapy
HEALTH & BEAUTY: *Best physical therapy*

Founded in 1997, Healing Bridge Physical Therapy offers the most comprehensive selection of physical therapy care in Central Oregon, treating everything from sports injuries to auto and on-the-job injuries. Founder Allison Suran and her team have developed expertise in their fields of interest, which run the gamut from pediatrics to geriatrics, women's health and orthopedics. In addition, holistic treatments like Feldenkrais®, cranial-sacral, and biofeedback are available. Having access to this variety of skills offers an integrative model, and each patient, while working with a primary therapist, is actually tapping into the knowledge of the whole team to create an ideal healing program. "We take time to weigh the myriad aspects of each patient's health concerns to come up with really effective solutions, including post-therapy exercises to further improve health and wellness," Allison says. "Our statistics show our average patient gets better in nine visits or less. This success is due to our focus on patient education and empowerment, while working together as a team to create the best results." The building design, the lovely landscaping, the soothing colors, everything at Healing Bridge is designed for comfort, balance and to encourage healing and health. Along with private treatment rooms, there's a gym and a warm water rehabilitation pool. Visit Healing Bridge Physical Therapy for all your physical therapy needs. Create better health and wellness for yourself and your loved ones.

404 NE Penn, Bend OR
(541) 318-7041
www.healingbridge.com

Shelby Chiropractic
HEALTH & BEAUTY: *Best chiropractic*

Dr. Tyge Shelby was born and raised in Oregon. When selecting a location to build his practice, he was attracted to Bend, because of its strong community and extensive recreational opportunities. Shelby Chiropractic offers a natural approach to healthcare with a focus on spinal rehabilitation and posture correction using the biophysics technique. Chiropractic Biophysics (CBP) is a spinal structural rehabilitation technique with a basis in biomechanical engineering. During the last 10 years, CBP has developed into the most researched chiropractic technique in the world. It is a very exciting technique, as it demonstrates actual visual changes in the spine. The premise of CBP is that abnormal posture and spinal curves affect the normal biological functions of the body. These abnormalities lead to early degeneration of the discs and joints of the spine, as well as interference with the overall nervous system. CBP uses exercise, adjustments and specialized traction equipment to restore healthy spinal curvature and achieve optimal function. Patients who come to Shelby Chiropractic want to fix their spinal problem or get to as near normal as possible. Dr. Shelby uses before and after x-rays to show how much your spine has changed with treatment; in this way, you never have to wonder if you are improving, and you will definitely know when you are done with care. Shelby Chiropractic offers affordable care in a comfortable and relaxing environment.

561 NE Bellevue Drive, Suite 102, Bend OR
(541) 330-7080

Athletic Club of Bend
HEALTH & BEAUTY: *Best athletic, dining and social club*

If health, fitness and fun are priorities in your life, then the Athletic Club of Bend is the place for you. Located on 13 pine-filled acres on the road to Mt. Bachelor, the Athletic Club of Bend represents one of the finest and most diverse athletic, dining and social clubs in the Northwest. Members and guests may enjoy a variety of activities, including tennis, aerobics, yoga, stretch classes, indoor track, racquetball and swimming in the indoor or outdoor pools. Personal trainers will share their expertise and develop an ongoing program for you. For the outdoor types, a three-minute walk from the club takes you to River Trail, adjacent to the Deschutes River. The gym can be used for shooting hoops, an organized game of basketball game, or badminton. Test your skills on the Climbing Wall. When you're finished with exercise and recreation, you may want to enjoy a quick bite or refreshing post-workout drink at the Courtyard Café. For a more elaborate meal, make reservations at Scanlon's, one of Central Oregon's top fine-dining establishments. While you are working out or dining, you can take advantage of the excellent child care programs for children six weeks old to age 12. Social and special events include the Club's popular outdoor summer concert series, holiday brunches, kids' triathlons and senior fitness days. On a daily basis, the Club runs numerous programs for all ages and fitness levels. Call the Athletic Club of Bend for information on joining and current membership fees. Give a gift of health, caring and fun to your family.

61615 Athletic Club Drive, Bend OR
(541) 385-3062
www.athleticclubofbend.com

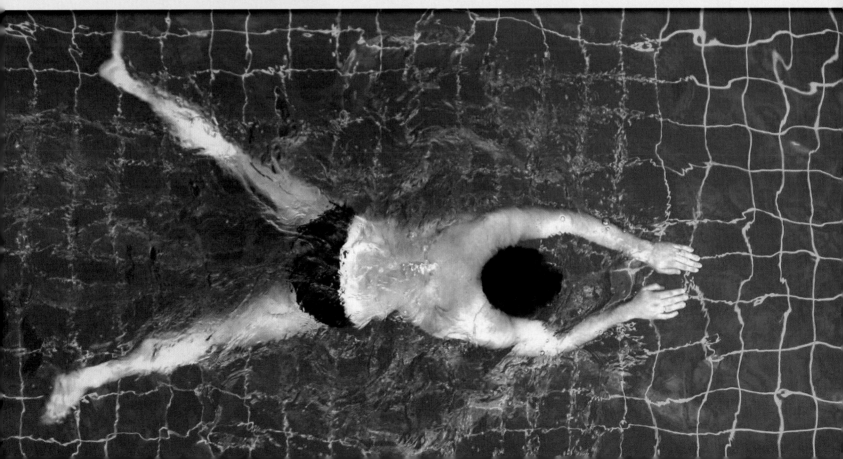

Environmental Building Supplies
HOME: *Best building products*

In 1992, Environmental Building Supplies opened with a pioneering vision of homes that are healthy for people and our world. The Portland store, housed in a 14,000-square-foot former factory, stands at the epicenter of today's sustainable building movement. A 5,000-square-foot satellite store operates in Bend, Oregon's fastest-growing city. The top-selling product is Marmoleum, a flooring made from natural linseed oil that comes in a full spectrum of colors. Unlike petroleum-based vinyl flooring, the color and pattern go all the way through, so it wears for up to 30 years and biodegrades harmlessly. Environmental Building Supplies performs extensive research before bringing a product into the showroom, always mindful of the different and even conflicting values consumers balance when deciding what to use in their home. The result is a carefully curated, beautifully presented selection of local products, such as Madrone flooring sourced from cooperatively managed forests, efficient products, like RAIS wood-burning stoves, and innovative natural products that are easier to use, such as itch-free insulation made from recycled blue jeans. Environmental Building Supplies stocks FSC-certified lumber and plywood, in addition to several lines of low toxic, no-VOC paints, American Clay Plaster, and a broad selection of books on topics ranging from straw bale construction to color theory. The store installs wool carpet, flooring, countertops and photovoltaic systems that generate free electricity from the sun. The knowledgeable staff is committed to helping you find the best product for your values. Stop by and see what's new in Portland or Bend.

819 SE Taylor Street, Portland OR
(503) 222-3881
50 SW Bond Street, Suite 4, Bend OR
www.ecohaus.com

Devil's Lake is one of the many lakes nestled among the trees along the Cascade Lakes Scenic Byway

Furniture Outlet
HOME: *Best furniture store*

Imagine an empty house. It doesn't feel like home, does it? Now, imagine a house filled with high quality furniture purchased at a low price. When you shop at the Furniture Outlet, your vision of your home will be complete. Furniture Outlet owners David and Debra Guzman have been providing central Oregonians with well priced and well made home furnishings for more than 14 years. Their most recent location is twice as big as their original space, allowing them to more than double the amount of product they offer. Because they buy in bulk, David and Debra are able to pass their savings on to you. There isn't any sales pressure at the Outlet either, because none of the salespeople are commissioned. The warm, friendly atmosphere is created by the staff working as a team, with the goal being to help as many customers as possible make their house a home. Besides, the staff says they want to sleep well at night and that is only possible if you are satisfied and have received good quality for a good price. Come to the Furniture Outlet and see for yourself what your home could be.

1735 NE Highway 20, Bend OR
(541) 385-0373

Ivy Rose Manor

HOME:

Best home décor selection

Ivy Rose Manor may be packed with treasures, but it is not cluttered. Instead, it sparkles with the inventory that owner, Kathleen Drgastin has thoughtfully chosen. Imagine an atmosphere of femininity, warmth and romance. Kathleen has customers who come in on their lunch break just to relax. Drgastin was a corporate interior designer for years and now she provides customers with the benefits of her experience, connections and talent at Ivy Rose Manor. While European cottage style is the focus of the shop, merchandise includes items appropriate for shabby chic and eclectic combinations, as well. French and English antiques that can be mixed with any style are present in abundance. Fine English bone china sits side by side with French and Tuscan linens. Mary Kay Crowley's giclee prints of relaxing and comfortable interior and exterior settings, chairs and quaint objects bring a fanciful ambience to any home. Distinctly original and beautiful floral prints by Christie Repasy represent Kathleen's love of flowers and vintage items, and add charm and romance to your surroundings. Cards, stationery, napkins and plates are available, and Venetian glass vases make the perfect containers for your creative garden arrangements or personal renditions of Repasy bouquets. Specially chosen seasonal and holiday items will be sure to draw your admiration. Kathleen invites you to come and explore all the nooks and crannies of her shop. You won't want to leave Ivy Rose Manor empty-handed and a wide variety of prices allow everyone to find something special.

120 NW Minnesota, Bend OR
(541) 388-6872

Cultus Lake is one of the many beautiful lakes found on the Cascade Lakes Scenic Byway

The Mattress Factory
HOME: *Family-owned and operated Since 1976*

Are your feet hanging over the end of your bed? Do you feel like you're sleeping on the edge of a cliff? Do you sleep on the deck of your boat because you can't fit a mattress through the galley? Have you always wanted a heart-shaped bed? You want the Mattress Factory. Jerry Seed, president, and Brian Seed, vice-president, have been manufacturing beds for more than 14 years. They have been in business in Bend, in one capacity or another, for more than 29 years. The Mattress Factory has been family-owned and operated since 1976. The Mattress Factory produces a full range of high quality mattresses. They are especially skilled and accommodating when it comes to custom shapes and sizes. Creation of the best mattress for your RV or boat is a happy challenge for Jerry, Brian and the crew. They especially enjoy making quality mattresses in extended sizes for professional athletes. The Mattress Factory carries a full selection of bedroom furniture, including Made in Oregon collections. Visit the Mattress Factory. You'll enjoy a good night's rest.

**571 #A NE Azure Drive, Bend OR
(541) 382-9091**

Photo by Wendy L. Gay

Mountain Comfort Furnishings and Designs
HOME: *Best designs*

There is a reason the word "comfort" is used in this company's name. Every aspect of Mountain Comfort Furnishings and Design is designed for your comfort. The showroom is locally owned and managed, located in a picturesque mountain setting. Complimentary design counseling services are available to help you to either embellish your existing décor, or create an entirely new room setting. Their knowledgeable counselors breathe life into your design concepts by helping to establish basic color and pattern combinations, then finding the right assortment of furnishings and accessories. With so many styles to choose from, whether it be lodge, transitional, rustic or eclectic, the possibilities are endless. Mountain Comfort provides quality furniture and attractive accessories to enhance virtually every room in your house. Each piece is hand selected from the most reputable brands around the world with an eye for fine craftsmanship in mind. Most items are in stock or available for quick dependable delivery. Dee Dee Keith and her staff want to ensure your complete satisfaction with every aspect of your custom-tailored Mountain Home experience. Visit Mountain Comfort's fascinating website and see how beauty, comfort and value can strike a perfect balance.

1036 NW Wall Street, Bend OR
(541) 388-4347
www.mountaincomfortbend.org

SolAire Homes
HOME: *Best custom builder*

No one is able to control the sun, but with the help of SolAire Homes you can manage it. They can design for summer cooling or for winter warmth. Solaire puts Central Oregon's abundant sunshine to work by capturing light and using its power to heat your home, provide hot water, and generate electricity. Many homeowners envision solar homes as not only unappealing in appearance but also expensive. SolAire designs custom homes that are aesthetically pleasing inside and out, affordable, and built to stringent energy efficiency standards. Investments in active solar components can provide lasting energy savings. SolAire works hand in hand with subcontractors to ensure that homes qualify for energy incentives and tax credits for their customers. All of SolAire's homes incorporate passive solar and high quality insulation into an economical and traditional home design. They are proud to be the first Earth Advantage certified builder in Oregon. With energy costs rising, SolAire offers a long-term solution to a growing problem. Whether your interest is a custom solar home, superior insulation, high efficiency windows, or healthy indoor air, Mike and Cindi O'Neil, owners of SolAire, guarantee your project will utilize the sun's energy at an affordable price. Their goal is complete customer satisfaction in the realm of maximizing solar gain, minimizing building waste and environmental impact, and reducing maintenance for years to come.

593 NW York Drive, Bend OR
(541) 389-3085
www.solairehomes.com

Aspen Ridge Retirement Community

LIFESTYLE DESTINATIONS:
Best retirement community

Life-enhancing amenities are among the many benefits of living in Aspen Ridge Retirement Community. Aspen Ridge offers four distinct living arrangements to meet your lifestyle preference: Independent Cottages, Retirement Living, Assisted Living and Memory Care. The Cottages allow for independence with the comforts of home. Residents can entertain family and friends in their own private dwelling. The cottages feature an attached garage, gas fireplaces and emergency call stations throughout. The Independent apartments offer spacious private studios, and one or two bedroom apartments which you furnish with your own treasured belongings. The Assisted Living apartments are staffed by a 24-hour dedicated staff, as is the Memory Care building. The Memory Care staff embraces the Best Friends Approach philosophy of care for residents with varying degrees of dementia, including Alzheimer's. All four choices, albeit distinct, offer similar luxuries, such as three meals daily, access to the beauty/barber shop, exercise programs and outings. The entire community at Aspen Ridge is barrier free. Residents have the opportunity for maintaining an active lifestyle, such as walking and biking amidst the landscaped campus or in nearby Pilot Butte State Park. The professional staff is dedicated to maintaining a family-like atmosphere, including pets. Aspen Ridge is located near shopping, St. Charles Medical Center, doctor's offices and excellent restaurants. Experience the family feeling at Aspen Ridge Retirement Community.

1010 NE Purcell Boulevard, Bend OR
(541) 385-8500
www.frontiermgmt.com

Tumalo Farms
MARKETS: *Best goat cheeses*

After 20 successful years in the corporate world, Flavio and Margie DeCastilhos took a vacation that landed them in Brazil's wine country, in the midst of its local cheese industry. Fascinated by the wonderful tastes and textures of the artisan cheeses they discovered, a dream was born, and a few short years later Tumalo Farms, Inc. was a reality. Tumalo Farms produces specially aged goat cheeses of exceptional character, flavor and quality. Flavio and Margie spent two years researching all there is to know about cheeses, farms and goats, then started completely from scratch, which means that Tumalo Farms is a state-of-the-art cheese-making operation. Tumalo Farms has a technologically and environmentally advanced processing plant and aging cellar. An innovative goat farm ensures their supply of the best and freshest milk. Their herd of almost 300 Alpine and Saanen goats are carefully and lovingly tended on 84 lush acres, because a happy goat produces fabulous milk, and fabulous milk produces fabulous cheese. Flavio focuses on traditional Dutch and Italian cheeses as a base for new recipes with a touch of Oregon flavor. Tumalo Farms has perfected its own chèvre cheeses, including gouda and feta, and continually cultivates its own signature recipes using unusual scents and flavors like fenugreek, sage, lavender and hazelnut. At Tumalo Farms, cheese-making is both an art and a science, mixed together with love. Come by and enjoy this wonderful combination.

2633-2 High Lakes Loop, Bend OR
(541) 350-3718
www.tumalofarms.com

Newport Avenue Market
MARKETS: *Best selection of specialty and imported foods*

When you're looking for a delectable treat to make your meal fantastic, and you're concerned about the quality of the food you feed your family, shop at the Newport Avenue Market. Owners Rudy and Debbie Dory are committed to their community and to providing specialty foods that are healthful. This market is the logical destination for customers looking for hard-to-find items. If you can't find what you're looking for, tell Rudy and Debbie. They'll be happy to research your request. Browse their abundant selection of quality wines and enjoy the bounty from their tempting deli. Newport Avenue Market carries Country Natural Beef. This is the only beef association whose sustainable agricultural practices are documented through third-party certification from the Food Alliance for environmentally friendly and socially responsible ranching practices. Because natural beef has become so popular, some companies routinely purchase live cattle through video auction markets to fill the need. Country Natural Beef does not buy outside cattle in this, or any other manner, to supplement their supply. You can be assured of wholesome quality and a refreshingly different selection when you visit the Newport Avenue Market. Whether you are buying something you've never had before, or are seeking a tried-and-true favorite, the Newport Avenue Market is a great place to shop.

1121 NW Newport Avenue, Bend OR
(541) 382-3940
www.newportavemarket.com

The top of Mt. Bachelor provides a sweeping view of the valley

Mountain Supply
RECREATION:
Most informative outdoor professionals

When Owner Erin McClaskey refers to her specialty outdoor store, Mountain Supply of Oregon, as a "one stop shop from street to summit," she means business. Whether your passion is mountaineering, rock or ice climbing, backpacking, cross country or backcountry skiing, Mountain Supply has items for you. They can accommodate the Everest adventurer, the yoga master and even the après ski partier. After 25 years of business, the family at this immaculate, well stocked establishment still takes pride in being one of the few remaining Mom & Pop shops in the Bend area. Their well trained and knowledgeable staff is on-site every day, making sure the store is the mandatory place to go for all of your outdoor adventure clothing and gear. Mountain Supply carries an extensive collection of durable, high-quality brand names at reasonable prices. Erin's distinctive clothing selections include the latest in high-tech synthetics and performance-based natural fibers such as Merino wool. There is a wide variety of footwear, including names like Montrail, Merrell, Garmont, Chaco, The North Face and Keen. To find just the right piece of equipment for any of your outdoor adventures, visit Erin and the friendly, informative team at Mountain Supply.

834 NW Colorado Avenue, Bend OR
(541) 388-0688 or (800) 794-0688

Snowy peak of Mt.Bachelor
Photo by Don Osborn

Powder House Ski and Patio

RESCREATION: *Best ski shop*

For more than 25 years, Powder House has been Central Oregon's premier ski and snow sports store. Voted the number one ski shop in Bend, Powder House is one of the original ski shops and has been owned by the same family for 20 years. Whether you are looking for technical clothing for the mountain or fashionable winter wear for around town, Powder House has the style and selection to fit you perfectly. The friendly and knowledgeable staff is dedicated to providing skiers with award-winning customer service. It is their goal to help you make your buying decisions and to increase your enjoyment on the snow. Powder House has the largest demo and rental center in Bend and offers a full service repair shop. Their professional, certified technicians are dedicated to providing the highest quality service for tuning and maintaining your skis and snowboards. Through their unique leasing program, the whole family can lease ski equipment for the entire year. After the snow has melted, Powder House transforms into Central Oregon's largest patio furniture showroom. Displaying premier designs and collections of outdoor furniture, Powder House has patio furniture to complement every home. Experience outdoor living at its finest at the Powder House.

**311 SW Century, Bend OR
(541) 389-6234**

Di Lusso Bakery Café
RESTAURANTS & CAFÉS: *Best wi-fi hotspot*

Once upon a time, laptop users seeking bandwidth wandered far and wide to locate a network connection. These mobile computer users adopted an inventive practice of drawing chalk symbols near the hotspots they found. These symbols were a sort of nouveau-technological hobo language. Thankfully these days, guerrilla chalking is hardly necessary. Many businesses now offer wi-fi as a complimentary service to their customers. Di Lusso Bakery Cafe in Bend is a great example of a provider of this service, but only one of the many reasons that this cafe is a vital part of the Bend community. Lisa and Bob Golden have made Di Lusso a desirable place to visit. They serve delicious, artisan, handmade bread and pastries so it is a perfect place to enjoy a freshly made breakfast and a pleasing array of lunch items. Everything is made in-house and from scratch daily. Di Lusso is also the largest and oldest coffee roaster in the area. Not only does Di Lusso strive to provide customers with the best local products and services in Bend, but they also are a quality wholesaler that provides various local businesses and restaurants with handcrafted bakery goods and coffees. After eight years in operation, they now have two bustling locations in Bend and one in Redmond at the airport. Make your way to Di Lusso to try some of their wonderfully rich roasted coffee or delicious food. Don't forget to visit the Di Lusso website.

744 NW Bond, Bend OR (541) 312-4036
1135 NW Galveston, Bend OR (541) 383-8155
Redmond Airport Concession, Roberts Field (541) 504-4481
www.dilusso.com

Photo by Joseph Eastburn

Photo by Wendy L. Gay

Sun Mountain Fun Center
RECREATION: *Best family fun center*

If you are looking for a great place for a birthday party, fun with your whole family, or a chance to get your best friend soaking wet, go to Sun Mountain Fun Center. Located behind Shopko off Highway 97 North, you will discover this 5.5-acre center that specializes in having fun. At Sun Mountain, you can ride the go-karts, play miniature golf, go bowling, perfect your swing in the batting cages, or beat your buddies playing billiards on regular or tournament size tables. Check out the largest arcade in Central Oregon, the full snack bar (including beer and wine for the big kids), and for a really wild time have a water war and soak someone with the water balloon launching system. Sun Mountain Fun Center focuses on providing the best family entertainment in town. If you need to schedule a birthday party, they offer a full range of birthday party activities. Just give them a call and they will help you celebrate the special day. There is no minimum or maximum number of guests required. Sun Mountain is the perfect host for summer parties, reunions, fundraisers, bridal showers, bachelor parties and other group functions. Sun Mountain Fun Center wants to put fun in your special occasions or your everyday adventures. Bring your family and be ready for a fantastic experience.

300 NE River Mall Avenue, Bend OR
(541) 382-6161
www.sunmountainfun.com

Baldy's Barbeque
RESTAURANTS & CAFÉS: *Best barbeque*

Since the discovery of fire by that first humble caveman, families have been gathering for meals built around meat cooked over an open flame. Barbeque has come a long way since then. Today 31 percent of all Americans grill food at least once a week. Pork ribs have been prime, succulent barbeque fare since barbeque was invented, probably somewhere in the West Indies and possibly drawing on African roots. Although the origins of barbeque are unknown, in the United States it developed as a Southern tradition that prospered during the Civil War. Geography hasn't hindered Baldy's at all. They proudly represent the Northwest nationwide, consistently defeating competition from all over the country. For award-winning baby back ribs, sauce and homemade side dishes, Baldy's Barbeque is the place to be. They are famous for their pulled pork and beef brisket. They have won more than 50 national barbeque competitions. To find your way to Baldy's, follow your nose to the smell of deliciously aromatic ribs. On the way to Mt. Bachelor from downtown, Baldy's is on the west side of Century Drive just before the Simpson Roundabout. Mention the website when you come in and receive half off the price of an order of onion rings with the purchase of an entrée.

235 SW Century Drive, Bend OR
(541) 385-RIBS (7427)
www.baldysbbq.com

Merenda Restaurant and Wine Bar

RESTAURANTS & CAFÉS:
Hippest downtown Bend restaurant

Merenda Restaurant and Wine Bar is a lively urban gathering place in the heart of downtown Bend. Owner and chef Jody Denton and his staff have integrated a bit of France and Italy into Central Oregon. She renovated their turn-of-the-century red brick building, transforming it into a striking contemporary dining space. A warm palette of rich mahogany, honey, olive and jewel tones, an open row of wood-burning rotisserie, grill and oven, 20-foot ceilings and 85-year-old hardwood floors create a delightful ambience. Michael Denton, Merenda's general manager and wine director, ensures the award-winning restaurant has the most extensive by-the-glass wine list in the State of Oregon. They also feature an impressive selection of spirits. With a reputation as the hippest downtown Bend restaurant, Merenda offers country French and Italian cuisine. Fresh ingredients, combined with traditional Old World methods of cooking, bring distinctive flavor to the ever-evolving menu. Accustomed to handling events and budgets of all sizes, Jody and his staff will customize their menu to suit your needs. Visit their website, mention that you did, and you will receive a free appetizer. Stop by Merenda's Restaurant and Wine Bar.

900 NW Wall Street, Bend OR
(541) 330-2304
www.merendarestaurant.com

Bon Bien
RESTAURANTS & CAFÉS: *Best New Orleans-style dining*

Bon Bien in Bend is an homage to New Orleans' French Quarter. From the moment you step inside this lavishly decorated restaurant, the spicy flair of Creole and Cajun cooking and ambience is evident. Though Mardi Gras beads hang in the marble foyer, this is no novelty strewn restaurant. Fine linen-covered tables and a luxurious raised hardwood bar await you inside. Crystal lighting and wrought-iron balconies look perfectly placed indoors, although they are reminiscent of the exterior of the oldest Big Easy buildings. Owners Christine and Terry Malpass strive to create an atmosphere of great service and great food, sharing New Orleans-style French cuisine with their loyal patrons. Bon Bien opened in 2005 under the expertise of chef Terry, who has 20 years of restaurant experience. He grew up working in family-owned restaurants in the Willamette Valley, then left to study under Paul Prudhomme in New Orleans. There he adopted what would become his signature, French Creole-style dishes. This allowed him to create a previously untouched niche when he returned to Bend. Terry's dishes also integrate African and Canadian French trapper influences. All of Bon Bien's stocks, sauces and baked goods are made from scratch, in-house. They are open for lunch and dinner every day, and from 6 pm to 9 pm they provide Dixieland-inspired jazz on the piano. Indulge in the music and enjoy a slice of their decadent pecan-chocolate pie when you experience a taste of New Orleans at Bon Bien.

62070 NE 27th Street, Bend OR
(541) 382-3152

Giuseppes
RESTAURANTS & CAFÉS: *Best Italian food*

Photo by Wendy L. Gay

When you ask local residents where to find the best Italian food in Bend, the answer is always the same. If you ask for the location of the most romantic place to dine locally, invariably the answer will remain the same: Giuseppes. A 20-year landmark restaurant, Giuseppes has been added to the Oregon Historical Walk. The restaurant's building once housed a thriving feed store called Aune's Feed & Grain that serviced Central Oregon ranchers throughout the late 1800s and early 1900s. The matriarch of this fine establishment is Peggy Falcaro. A true Italian transplant from Long Island, New York, she has crafted Giuseppes into a local dining haven. Falcaro has procured the elite of local chefs over the years to keep her food up to date with fresh ideas. Current chef Joe Morgan has traveled the United States mastering techniques and preparations not commonly found in the Northwest. This translates to an unforgettable dining experience. Giuseppes offers not only regional Italian dishes, but also a wide array of International and American cuisine. The emphasis is on seasonal produce and the use of the best quality ingredients. With a menu that changes monthly, there is always something new and exiting to try. Say no to cookie-cutter Italian restaurants, and say yes to a culinary experience at Giuseppe's.

932 NW Bond, Bend OR
(541) 389-8899

Photo by Wendy L. Gay

Ranchero Mexican Restaurant

RESTAURANTS & CAFÉS:
Best Mexican food

If you can't quite muster the cash for a trip to Mexico, a meal at Ranchero's Mexican Restaurant isn't the next best thing, it's the best thing. José Balcazar and Joel Carillo have brought the best of authentic Mexican cuisine to Central Oregon. Joel and José opened the first Ranchero Mexican Restaurant in Prineville in 1994, and it was such an immediate runaway success that Bend was lucky enough to coax them into opening a second restaurant. Not content with their reputation for the finest Mexican food this far north of the border, the entire crew at Ranchero's were determined to give their guests the feel and experience of old Mexico, as well. In the past year this terrifically popular restaurant has transformed itself, with Jose traveling to Mexico many times to bring back gorgeous Mexican art, artifacts and hand-made furniture. Colorful Mexican murals grace the walls, and you'll hear strains of mariachi-like music wafting through from the kitchen. Sample their famous top-shelf Ranchero Margarita while you watch fresh guacamole made right at your table. If you order the Combinaciones Mexicanos, you'll be able to combine your own amazing assortment of tacos, enchiladas or tostadas. Both restaurants maintain the kind of old-fashioned family-oriented business that builds a following of loyal customers and employees. Joel and José believe in taking excellent care of their staff, and their staff will take excellent care of their customers. Come in to Ranchero's Mexican Restaurant and enjoy the taste and feel of Mexico.

150 Bend River Plaza, Bend OR
(541) 330-0685
www.rancerogrill.com

Café Rosemary
RESTAURANTS & CAFÉS: *Best romantic dining*

Café Rosemary is the ideal getaway for those in search of a romantic dinner for two or an intimate gathering place where friends can enjoy a relaxed meal together. This popular Bend eatery is owned and operated by chef Robert Braun, who offers an extraordinary dining experience highlighted by a welcoming atmosphere and a fabulous wine list. Chef Braun's focus is to provide his customers with a gastronomic feast that is expertly served by a professional and friendly waitstaff, and he has met this goal beautifully. Café Rosemary is housed inside an elegantly converted, cottage-style home that offers separate dining rooms and a luxurious ambience filled with crisp white linens, a cheerful fireplace and a wealth of lovely candles that add sparkling warmth to the room. Chef Braun utilizes his culinary expertise to create an exciting, Continentally-inspired cuisine that is both delicious and satisfying, including his wildly popular Wild Game Sampler and his fabulously decadent desserts. Café Rosemary also features occasional wine dinners where patrons are treated to a five or six-course meal with a personally selected wine served at every course. During these dinners, a wine expert from one of the area's local wineries is on hand to answer questions about the vintage and share wine tips and secrets. Take your fine dining experience to the next level with reservations at Café Rosemary.

550 SW Industrial Way, Suite 21, Bend OR
(541) 317-0276

Photo by Wendy L. Gay

Cibelli's New York Pizza
RESTAURANTS & CAFÉS:
Best New York-style pizza

Bend is an awfully long way from Manhattan's Little Italy, where Gennaro Lombardi opened America's first pizzeria in 1905. That said, you can still get a real New York pizza in two Bend locations. Cibelli's New York Pizza is just what the name says. The signature pie here is not New York *style* pizza. It is the real thing. In New York City, pizza is sold in oversized, thin and flexible slices. It is traditionally hand-tossed and light on sauce. The slices, typically one-eighth of an 18-inch pizza, are sometimes folded in half, because the size and flexibility of the slices may otherwise make them unwieldy. This type of pie is closer to the original Neapolitan style than any of the other American regional varieties, though New York pizza is much larger than anything sold in Naples. At Cibelli's, you can order a huge slice or a whole huge pie. In addition to New York pizza, the shop has other dishes that also taste great. Try the stromboli. The white pie is fantastic. The crust is wonderful, as with all the pies, but the garlic sauce and the five cheeses make it heaven on pizza dough. You might add onion and sausage, but it is good with just about anything. Whatever you order, get lots of napkins. There is no indoor seating, so you must sit outside or take it with you. For pizza that's out of this world, come to Cibelli's New York Pizza.

2095 NE Highway 20, Bend OR
(541) 330-8646
64670 Strickler Avenue #101B, Bend OR
(541) 385-8646

Photo by Joseph Eastburn

Kanpai Sushi & Sake Bar
RESTAURANTS & CAFÉS: *Best sushi*

According to *The Source Weekly*, Kanpai Sushi and Sake Bar is "Fresh as fresh can be this far from the ocean, the seafood is perfectly prepared and everything tastes great." Proprietor Justin Cook has created a rarity among sushi bars, a casual, yet high-end dining atmosphere. He has fresh fish delivered daily, so that from the maguro tuna that virtually melts in your mouth to the best salmon the Northwest has to offer, Kanpai is the gold standard for nigiri and sashimi. Kanpai also offers a stunning selection of hand rolls, maki, appetizers, and hot dishes with a Pan-Asian flair and a slight French influence. As if this wasn't enough to whet your appetite and ignite your epicurean curiosity, Kanpai also offers a great variety of wines and sake. *Gusto* magazine says, "Kanpai Sushi and Sake Bar is Central Oregon's antidote for big city cuisine." Be sure to visit Kanpai's website. It is filled with comprehensive information about the menu, prices, hours, location, and photographs of their exquisite creations. If you mention the website when you visit the restaurant, you will receive a free cup of soothing hot green tea. Visit Kanpai Sushi & Sake Bar for the best sushi and wine combinations in Central oregon.

990 NW Newport Avenue, Bend OR
(541) 388-4636
www.kanpai-bend.com

Olde Towne Pizza Company
RESTAURANTS & CAFÉS: *Best pizza selection*

Instead of slices brought by the delivery boy and hastily served in front of the TV, or a loud pizza joint where the kids will spend their time distracted by video games, pizza lovers can unite at Olde Towne Pizza Company. This clean and friendly restaurant on Greenwood Avenue is the ideal place for friends and family to have a nice chat over a wonderful meal. Owner Terry Parker has been creating the pleasant and cheerful dining environment here for the last five years. No gimmicks, just delicious pizza in offered in enough different styles to please any pizza aficionado. *The Source Weekly* notes that, "If you want choice, then Olde Towne Pizza is your kind of place." Choose from New York, Sicilian, or Chicago-style pies, all on delicious wheat crusts in your choice of four thickness levels. Customize your pie with white or red sauce or optional soy cheese. Add your choice of toppings, fresh garlic, and other seasonings and you have your perfect pizza pie. Fresh salads are also available to either make a complete meal or as an alternative to pizza, if you like. Make your way to Olde Towne Pizza Company soon and treat yourself to truly great pizza in a comfortable social environment.

118 NW Greenwood Avenue, Bend OR
(541) 318-9018
www.oldetownepizza.com

Demetri's Greek American Cusina

RESTAURANTS & CAFÉS:
Best Greek cuisine

Photo by Wendy L. Guy

Demetri's Greek American Cusina brings the authentic taste of Greece directly from Mt. Olympus to you. Are you familiar with the gyro, salad and gyro meat in pita bread? If you are, you will find that Demetri's does a fabulous gyro. If you have never had one, prepare yourself. The pork or chicken souvlaki is mouthwatering. Check out what can be done with feta or grape leaves. Demetri's cooks to order using old-country recipes that date back 100 years. For less adventurous guests, Demetri's serves broasted chicken and hamburgers. Only a little adventurous? Try the Greek burger. For dessert, you must have one of the handcrafted Greek pastries, such as the baklava. Wine is available by the glass or bottle, and beers include microbrews. The atmosphere at Demetri's is casual and festive with music and great views. The restaurant is great for a romantic evening, or you can bring the whole family—the staff prides itself on being kid-friendly. Catering and takeout are available. Demetri's family emigrated from Greece in the late 1950s and brought along authentic Greek recipes. Stop by Demetri's Greek American Cusina and see the results for yourself.

425 NE Windy Knolls Drive, Suite 1, Bend OR
(541) 318-0111

Tumalo Feed Company Steak House & Saloon

RESTAURANTS & CAFÉS: *Best steak house*

Close to the Deschutes River and Mt. Bachelor is Central Oregon's favorite steakhouse, the Tumalo Feed Company Steak House & Saloon. Walk through the doors and you are back in the Old West. The décor is strictly Old West with a working ranch theme, complete with charming checkered tablecloths and mismatched wooden chairs. John Bushnell and Robert Holley opened the Tumalo Feed Company on Valentine's Day in 1991. It has been a runaway success since that first night. The house specializes in great steaks and hand-cut beef, served family-style with big bowls of beans and potatoes. Every entrée begins with a piping hot platter of homemade onion rings and salsa and ends with sherbet, a root beer float or an after-dinner liqueur. Pat Thomas plays Country Western music on his guitar Thursday through Saturday nights. A separate lounge sports a full bar, and during Bend's beautiful warm weather you can enjoy the large outdoor patio that overlooks a field of aspen and pine. Bend's local folk have voted the steaks at the Tumalo Feed Company number one in town five years in a row and *Sunset Magazine* has featured Tumalo Feed Company as one of the top Western houses. Bring the family for a good time and a great steak at the Tumalo Feed Company Steak House & Saloon.

64619 W Highway 20, Bend OR
(541) 382-2202
www.tumalofeedcompany.com

Seasons at Seventh Mountain Resort

RESTAURANTS & CAFÉS: *Freshest seasonal menu*

How does ice skating followed by gourmet hot chocolate with peppermint schnapps sound? How about fresh juniper sorbet, served as an intermezzo, made from juniper berries hand-picked from the very property where you are staying? Now add stunning views, meals made with local organic produce, and a summer season filled with its own seasonal menu. You can only be talking about Seasons at Seventh Mountain Resort. This restaurant aims to utilize the Northwest's bountiful resources in creating a distinctive dining experience. In their support of local and regional organic produce and free-range meals, the chefs create menus that change and evolve around the four different seasons in central Oregon. An example from seasons past would be the all-natural Snake River Kobe beef tri-tip with toasted sesame, topped with Oregon forest mushrooms. Another recipe, echoing the sun-soaked taste of summer, includes local peaches and sweet Walla Walla onions, slowly simmered in their signature rich barbeque sauce and generously brushed over a roasted local, free-range half chicken. A different presentation of Angus Ribeye each night and other nightly specials guarantee a unique epicurean encounter with each visit. Visit the new and stylish River Rock Bar, located near Seasons, and enjoy their one-of-a-kind menu pairing appetizers and spirits. Come to Seasons at Seventh Mountain for a taste of seventh heaven.

18575 SW Century Drive, Bend OR
(541) 693-9143
www.seventhmountain.com

Jake's Diner
RESTAURANTS & CAFÉS:
Best breakfast

The owners of Jake's Diner boast that they serve the largest portions in Central Oregon. Winner of numerous awards for having the Biggest Breakfast in Town, the meals at the diner live up to the reputation. You will need two plates for their most popular breakfast–chicken fried steak with eggs, hash browns and toast. Pancakes are bigger than the plate. Small omelets are made with four eggs. Top off a gargantuan breakfast with a mug of Farmer's Bros. coffee. Jake's focus is on giving the best value and best service around. When it first opened as a truck stop in 1976, Jake's was located on Highway 97. Lyle Hicks had served as the manager for almost 20 years when he learned that Jake's was being sold and the restaurant would likely close. When this opportunity knocked, Lyle and his wife, Judy, answered. They were able to buy the name and the equipment and moved the restaurant across town to Bend's eastside. Devotees of the Biggest, Baddest, Beefiest Burger in Bend could relax because the new owners kept the legendary diner's traditions intact. All 35 employees followed Lyle across town, so even the helpful, friendly service is the same. Lyle recommends that customers use two hands for the Big Bad Jake. Jake's signature burger is one pound of ground beef with an additional four ounces of ham, bacon or chili, plus Swiss and jack cheese. Stop in at Jake's today and enjoy a meal of massive flavor and proportions.

2210 NE Highway 20, Bend OR
(541) 382-0118

Pilot Butte Drive-In

RESTAURANTS & CAFÉS:
Best burgers

"We're not fast food and you can taste the difference," say Jack and Dee Mangin, Steve Mangin and his wife Melanie, co-owners of the Pilot Butte Drive-in. Home of the 18-ounce Burger, the drive-in located at the base of Pilot Butte was established in 1983 by Jack and Dee Mangin. In March 1987 all the Mangins joined forces to form an outstanding partnership that has greatly impacted business and has profoundly strengthened the family. The Pilot Butte Drive-In now employs 20 people and is open for breakfast and lunch seven days a week. The Mangins are hands-on owners who work side-by-side with their staff. Each of the family members is active in the daily operation of the restaurant, as well as in the social and business community of Central Oregon. All of the meals are cooked to order. Their sandwiches are unforgettable, made with the finest fresh ingredients. When you're extra hungry, add an additional six-ounce patty to your burger. If you are craving something sweet to quench your thirst, try a milkshake, float, freeze, malt or ice cream soda from their fountain. If you want lighter fare, check out the salad menu. You'll find Taco, Cobb and Garden salads. All are guaranteed to satisfy your taste buds. Children under 12 can choose from the Sibling's Menu; it's full of suggestions and smaller portions for the younger palate. The Mangin family guarantees you won't leave Pilot Butte Drive-In hungry.

917 NE Greenwood Avenue, Bend OR
(541) 382-2972
www.pilotbutte.com

Drake Park
Photo by Wendy L. Gay

Toomie's Thai Cuisine

RESTAURANTS & CAFÉS:
Best Thai food

Photo by Wendy L. Gay

If you desire an artful dining experience, Toomie's Thai Cuisine offers Southeast Asian food in a relaxed atmosphere with an air of elegance. The warm and comfortable ambience and extensive menu are just a couple of reasons why Toomie's earned the award for Best Thai Food in Central Oregon eight years in a row. Toomie Staver's culinary experience began in Thailand where an uncle guided her in her endeavors. Later, she opened her first restaurant in Corvallis before moving to the high desert in 1995. Toomie's native Thai chefs have a combined 80 years of experience. Their creations include catfish in a rich, spicy sauce with crispy basil, and Pa-Nang, a blend of kaffir leaves and bell peppers in a thick, red curry sauce mixed with coconut milk. You might also choose Thai iced tea or a selection from the impressive list of imported and domestic wines to complement your meal. Known for fine quality and service for 10 years, Toomie's has become a favorite among locals and tourists alike, with each menu specially hand-crafted to satisfy the most discriminating customer. No wonder Toomie's has been featured in *L.A. Magazine*, *The New York Times* and *Food and Wine Magazine*, as well as being honored by *Best Restaurants in America*.

119 NW Minnesota Avenue, Bend OR
(541) 388-5596

Bend Book Barn

SHOPPING: *Best bookstore*

The Bend Book Barn first opened its doors in 1973. Throughout a succession of owners and additions to the physical space, it has more than quadrupled in size since then. Present owner Linda Torres and her staff love books and that is what Bend Book Barn is all about. The Book Barn is the only independent book store in Bend. It stocks all the most recent best sellers and popular titles. If you have difficulty finding a book, they will be happy to do a book search for you. They specialize in finding out-of-print and hard-to-find titles. Visit the website for the schedule of book events, an opportunity to meet authors in person, have your book autographed, and learn the stories behind the writing of the books. You will also find the titles and descriptions of the staff's current favorites on the website. The children's department at the Bend Book Barn is second to none, so you will be sure to find the perfect book for the small people in your life. Book Sense Gift Certificates are available in amounts from $10 to $100 and are good at any of the thousands of independent book sellers across the country. Shipping is available to any destination. Affectionately calling all book worms, the Bend Book Barn is the place for you.

135 NW Minnesota Avenue, Bend OR
(541) 389-4589
www.bendbookbarn.com

Stereo Planet

SHOPPING: *Best for sound*

For well over 25 years, Stereo Planet has been designing and installing state-of-the-art home entertainment systems throughout Central Oregon. Located in downtown Bend, they have a full staff of helpful and experienced specialists to guide you through the entire process of putting your home entertainment system together: Anything from a small system, with just a pair of speakers, to a custom-designed home theater system with music in every room. The Stereo Planet can design and install it to match your home's interior while exceeding your performance expectations.

1008 NW Bond Street, Bend OR
(541) 382-9062
www.stereoplanet.com

The Curiosity Shoppe

SHOPPING: *Best for gifts and metaphysical supplies*

The people of Bend describe The Curiosity Shoppe as a comforting, warm and welcoming place. Owner Joyce Scott has created a beautifully healing environment and provided the tools to develop personal and spiritual awareness. The inventory is packed with metaphysical items and gifts for the curious explorer. Scott has been offering these services for more than 20 years. The jewelry selection here is not mass produced. Much of it is made by local artists and chosen for inclusion in the store on the basis of its beauty and meaning. Obsidian wind chimes are regularly kept in stock. Everything needed for aromatherapy, including scents, lotions, essential oils and candles, can be found here. Other items on hand to entertain and expand the mind include books, tapes, CDs and gifts. The Curiosity Shoppe is a wonderful resource in the community for networking and connecting with others. Joyce also promotes Fair Trade in her shop, paying special attention to the credibility and ethics of the vendors supplying her shelves. Come by and soak up the positive energy in The Curiosity Shoppe.

550 SW Industrial Way, #45, Bend OR
(541) 382-3408
www.curiosityshoppe-bend.com

Leapin' Lizards Toy Co.

SHOPPING: *Best toy store*

Imagine a hands-on toy store that engages even the youngest customers with a Thomas the Tank play table, Rokenbok vehicle system, puppet theater, dress-up area, plus a large science and nature section and game department. You don't have to imagine it any longer. Come to Leapin' Lizards Toy Co. and you will discover a whole new definition of toy store. Leapin' Lizards carries creative, imaginative, specialty toys for children of all ages. Owners Donna Dobkin and Linda Harp employ a great staff that is well trained to give helpful suggestions. Leapin' Lizards provides quality hand-picked toys for all stages of development. It is a fun, friendly and delightful place to visit. The shop is artfully designed with toys organized by developmental stages and areas of interests. There is a special section of the store for children to shop with their own money. Every Tuesday is Grandparents Day, where grandparents get a 15-percent discount if they bring in a picture of their grandchild or bring their grandchild with them. The best part about Leapin' Lizards Toy Co. is that it is designed for your kids to play as well as shop. The staff loves to interact with parents and children alike. They also offer a free gift wrapping service. Take your kids or grandkids to Leapin' Lizards Toy Co., but prepare to have fun, because that's what this toy store is all about.

953 NW Wall Street, Bend OR
(541) 382-8326
www.leapinlizardstoys.com

My Baby and Me

SHOPPING: *Best recycled goods for moms and babies*

Babies grow from children to teens in the blink of an eye. To cherish this time, it helps if you do not have to sweat the small stuff. That is why My Baby and Me is a great find with its ever-changing inventory of quality baby and maternity clothing, furniture, strollers, books and toys, all at up to 75 percent off retail. They say, "Why buy new when you can buy gently used?" As quickly as most children grow, many items endure

very little use before they make their way to My Baby and Me. Not only does the shop provide a great place to get everything you need for children from infancy to school age, it is also a great place to recycle items when you are finished with them. You can trade your gently used baby and children's clothing, toys and furniture for cash or store credit equivalent to 40 percent of the estimated sale price. As an alternative, you may consign your items and receive 50 percent of the final selling price. The staff will display and mark down your items as needed in order to provide the best and fastest selling price for both you and the store. Owner Cheryl Hafter looks forward to helping you with all your pregnancy and baby needs. My Baby and Me is closed Sundays and Mondays, but stop by the corner of 4th and Seward any other day of the week.

405 NE Seward Avenue, Bend OR
(541) 330-9115

CAMP SHERMAN

Camp Sherman, on the upper reaches of the Metolius River, is the headquarters of the Metolius Recreation Area. A national Wild and Scenic River, the Metolius flows north and then east to Lake Billy Chinook. Fly fishing, hiking and wildlife viewing are favored pastimes. The clear, cold water is home to several types of trout and kokanee salmon. Camp Sherman itself is a quiet and peaceful place, but there's still a lot going on. Hiking is a favorite activity. If you'd like a guide, the Deschutes Basin Land Trust offers tours of its Metolius Preserve on scheduled days throughout the summer. Friends of the Metolius also sponsors a series of summer forest walks. Part of the Oregon Cascades Birding Trail is located in this area. Visitors can search for the elusive white headed woodpecker and many other species. The legendary Camp Sherman Store holiday barbecues run on each Saturday of the major holiday weekends. The picturesque store serves great food hot off the grill, accompanied by lively music from local bands. Further up the Metolius you can tour the Wizard Falls Fish Hatchery, which raises trout, kokanee and Atlantic salmon.

PLACES TO GO

- Hoodoo Mountain Resort (skiing)
  Santiam Pass, U.S. Highway 20
- Suttle Lake
  U.S. Highway 20
- Wizard Falls Fish Hatchery
  7500 Forest Service Road 14

THINGS TO DO

Summer
- Metolius Preserve hikes
  (541) 330-0017
- Metolius River walks
  Friends of the Metolius
  (541) 595-2269

July
- Metolius Bamboo Rod and Flyfishing Fair
  (541) 595-6711

Lake Creek Lodge

ACCOMMODATIONS:
Most scenic lodge in the Deschutes

People have been coming to Lake Creek Lodge for family vacations, reunions and meetings since 1935. Towering Ponderosa pines and the sound of Lake Creek running outside the cabin door provide a lush setting for waterfowl, mule deer and guests. With 18 cabins to choose from, you are sure to find the perfect spot whether you are having a family vacation, reunion, wedding, or large group function. Lake Creek Lodge is located in the Metolius River Recreation Area. The quiet surroundings and warm hospitality make this a perfect location for a business meeting or retreat. Electronic equipment is available for rental in nearby Bend. All cabins have fully equipped kitchens, some with wood stoves or fireplaces. Wireless Internet access is available on the property. Just outside your door you'll find hiking, mountain biking, fly fishing, and snow sports. You can shoot hoops on the basketball court, play ping pong or pool. The tennis courts and large heated swimming pool are great places to enjoy the beautiful summer days. Comfy couches and soft green grass are just waiting for you and your good book or afternoon nap. A family-style dinner on the deck has been a tradition during the summer months. During cooler weather, or for special events, meals are served in the lodge dining room. Breakfast is available during the summer season. Once you visit this pine-covered paradise, you will want to make regular treks to Lake Creek Lodge.

13375 SW Forest Service Road 1419, Camp Sherman OR
(800) 797-6331
www.lakecreeklodge.com

Metolius River Lodges
ACCOMMODATIONS: *Best lodge*

Thoreau said, "I went to the woods because I wished to live deliberately... and not, when I came to die, discover that I had not lived." From the moment you arrive at Metolius River Lodges, 15 miles northwest of Sisters, you can feel the weight of the world melting away. Without the distraction of modern conveniences to interfere with the beauty of nature, this respite on the river offers an effortless and immediate reconnection with all that is basic and pure. This collection of rustic cabins sits under majestic Ponderosa Pines on the banks of the Metolius River. There are no phones or televisions here, although there is a phone conveniently placed outside of the office for the use of guests. This pristine location in Camp Sherman makes a perfect base camp for numerous activities, including fly-fishing, hiking and biking. Lakes and cross-country ski trails are just minutes away. Metolius River Lodges offer family-oriented accommodations with homespun beauty evident in the large stone fireplaces and knotty pine interiors. Each cabin is named after a fishing fly and beautifully furnished with fully functioning kitchens and comfortable furniture. Owners Vickie and John Hornbeck invite you to leave the outside world behind and revel in the serenity at Metolius River Lodges.

Highway 20-126, Camp Sherman OR
(541) 595-6290 or (800) 595-6290
www.metoliusriverlodges.com

Metolius River Resort

ACCOMMODATIONS: *Best rustic resort*

Metolius River Resort offers clean air, sunny days, crisp cool nights and miles and miles of picturesque river front. Stream-side and forest trails invite bird watching, hiking, biking, picnicking, snow shoeing and cross country skiing. Would it sound too good to be true if water sports, golf, horseback riding, downhill skiing and shopping were all available within a short distance? No, you aren't dreaming. You can have all this and more by making your reservation at Metolius River Resort. Each of the privately-owned, architecturally designed non-smoking cabins is available to rent. Each cabin has a full kitchen and is distinctly decorated to reflect the Northwest cabin experience. The cabins come fully equipped with just about everything necessary for a relaxing, restful stay. If you decide that you would like to eat out, the Kokanee Café features creative Northwest cuisine on-site. The property size is just right for the number of cabins and a maximum occupancy has been established for reasons of safety, health, liability and noise level. Nancy Morris is the resident manager. The Resort is unable to accommodate visitors on the grounds or in the cabins and they do not allow groups of any kind, resulting in an exclusive, peaceful stay for the guests. Seize the opportunity to revel in nature's bounty at Metolius River Resort. The flowing sound of the river will leave you relaxed and refreshed.

25551 SW Forest Service Road #1419, Camp Sherman OR
(800) 81-TROUT (818-7688)
www.metoliusriverresort.com

MADRAS

Madras has Central Oregon's most culturally diverse population. Hispanic Americans make up 36 percent of the city's residents, and American Indians make up eight percent. The area's population is growing rapidly, a trend expected to continue. Nearby Lake Billy Chinook is the most popular weekend spot in Jefferson County. Surrounded by Cove Palisades State Park, this beautiful lake is the gathering point for the Deschutes, Metolius and Crooked rivers. People flock to the park for fishing, house boating, water skiing, jet skiing and picnicking. Cove Palisades Park offers one of the most popular hiking trails in the high desert, the seven-mile Tam-a-lau Trail. Madras was incorporated in 1911 as an agricultural and railroad center. The Madras Airport today boasts the longest non-commercial airport runway in Central Oregon, and has become an industrial center. Jefferson County produces four-fifths of the nation's carrot seed.

PLACES TO GO

- The Cove Palisades State Park
  7300 SW Jordon Road, Culver

- Jefferson County Museum
  34 SE D Street (541) 475-3808

- Round Butte Overlook Park
  SW Round Butte Drive

THINGS TO DO

February
- Eagle Watch (festival)
  Cove Palisades Park
  (541) 923-7551

May
- Wings over Central Oregon
  Migratory Bird Celebration
  (541) 383-5300

- Collage of Culture in Madras
  (541) 475-2350

June-July
- Jefferson County All Rockhound Pow Wow
  Fairgrounds (541) 325-5050

July
- Jefferson County Fair & Rodeo
  Fairgrounds
  (541) 325-5050

The Cove Palisades State Park
Photo by Stuart Seeger

Raining Fresh Daisies

ARTS & CRAFTS: *Best scrapbooking store*

Scrapbooking isn't just a quaint, old-fashioned hobby anymore, it's a new and very personal 21st century art form, and Raining Fresh Daisies in Madras is the place to discover it. "Scrapbooking is the fastest growing craft in America," Peggy Boyle says, and she should know. Peggy and daughter Jennifer Oppenlander are the mother-daughter team that started Raining Fresh Daisies in 2004 as a way to share their passion for scrapping. The two of them took a fading Victorian home and turned it into a fabulously fun showplace for all things scrappable. Walk in the door of this beautifully restored home and you'll feel the joyful energy these two generate with their warm enthusiasm. Their lovely shop is alive with vibrant colors and textures and a dizzying array of beautifully displayed scrapbooking paraphernalia. Peggy and Jennifer love to teach, advise and help their customers with their ideas and encourage their creativity. They have a workroom upstairs where they hold classes on special scrapbooking techniques with projects of all kinds for both adults and children. Raining Fresh Daisies has everything you could possibly need, whether it's beautiful papers or special glue or wonderful embellishments. Let Jennifer and Peggy help you have as much fun preserving your most cherished memories as you had making them, because they're a team you'll never forget.

123 SW 'H' Street, Madras OR
(541) 475-1000
www.rainingfreshdaisies.com

Raining
Fresh Daisies
A Scrapbook Store

Opal Day Spa

HEALTH & BEAUTY: *Best day spa*

Escape the pressures of everyday life with a visit to Opal Day Spa in Madras, a place brimming with personal services and small town charm. Sarah Gannon's upscale and modern establishment features professional staff and cutting-edge equipment. Spend the day indulging in a full slate of spa and salon services, while highly trained professionals see to your every need. Among the many therapeutic massages is the ODS Signature Massage. Complimentary use of the relaxing steam bath and dry sauna is included with any massage service. Make-up applications use the natural mineral make-up line Youngblood. Consultations for weddings, glamour and everyday are always popular, as are hair coloring, weaves and perms. Redken hair stylists provide recommendations for hair care and style maintenance. European-style facials use France Laure products from Paris. Customized body treatments utilize France Laure's Aqua Laure line and feature the amazing Violet Clay wrap that decongests skin and soothes muscles while offering a fragrant invitation to relaxation. Nail care services are supported by Creative nail design products and are applied in a comfortable, semi-private setting. Consider a citrus manicure for a smooth, supple treatment for your hands. Waxing is a popular and effective way to remove unwanted hair and promote silky skin. Sarah researches all products used at Opal Day Spa and promises to deliver results you can see and feel. This premier Central Oregon day spa operates from a remodeled historic building in downtown Madras. The business is active in its community and proudly offers services that earned it the prestigious Madras Chamber of Commerce Business of the Year Award for 2003. The day spa draws its name from the local water source, Opal Springs, and the native opals found in the area. You will truly treasure your time at Opal Day Spa.

162 SW 5th Street, Madras OR
(541) 475-4677
www.opaldayspa.com

POWELL BUTTE

Have you ever dreamed about living on a few acres where you could keep some horses, a few head of cattle or maybe just grow alfalfa? A lot of people have had such dreams. Powell Butte is a place where they can live them out. Nestled at the foot of the Powell Buttes with magnificent views of the Three Sisters and her companions, the community of Powell Butte has traditionally been devoted to ranching and farming. Springtime in the high desert brings the fresh smell of rain on grass and beautiful blooming wildflowers. About 2,000 people now live in the Powell Butte area, and there is a great sense of community. Powell Butte Elementary School is excellent. The Powell Buttes were named for members of the Jacob Powell family of Linn County. Several of the Powells crossed the Cascade Range into central Oregon to run stock.

PLACES TO GO

- Sierra Luna Pottery
  6645 SW Steffey Lane
  (541) 416-0292

THINGS TO DO

November
- Lord's Acre Day (festival)
  Powell Butte Christian Church
  (541) 548-3066

Brasada Ranch

ACCOMMODATIONS:
Best master-planned community

The 1,800-acre Brasada Ranch is a great place to enjoy life in Central Oregon from a different perspective. *Brasada*, the Spanish word for desert land, is a magnificent panorama distinguished by long stretches of wide open spaces interrupted by twisted Juniper trees and fragrant Sagebrush. It is a land of contrasts, with towering mountains covered with snow in the distance, coupled with the intimate urban charm of Bend and Redmond. Developed jointly by Jeld-Wen and Eagle Crest, Brasada includes the spectacular Peter Jacobsen-designed Brasada Canyons Golf Course and the Brasada Activity Center, which includes a spa, wellness program, swimming pools and workout area. An extensive trail system will provide plenty of opportunity for hiking, mountain biking and horseback riding. Easily accessible for water buffs are fly fishing, kayaking and canoeing. In season, snow skiing and snowshoeing are available for the snow bunnies. Brasada Riding Stables, tennis courts and restaurant will complete the picture for perfect high-desert luxury living. One of the themes for this project is "walking softly on the land." All of the homes will be built to Earth Advantage green standards. Water for the golf course will be recycled. Authentically designed Western ranch cabins are available to rent. These elegant residences come complete with the furniture, linens and table settings. Imagine yourself as a resident in this spectacular community where the sun shines nearly 300 days a year.

**16986 SW Brasada Ranch Road,
Powell Butte OR**
(541) 504-3203
www.brasada.com

PRINEVILLE

Prineville is in the high desert, surrounded by golf courses, fishing spots and forests. Bike trails, parks and greenways make Prineville an outdoors city. Hunters, boaters and rock hounds visit the area. You can dig for agates, jasper and thunder eggs on more than 1,000 acres provided by the Chamber of Commerce. The nearby Ochoco National Forest is an oasis of lush vegetation. Prineville was the major city in Central Oregon in the 19th century. In 1911, railroad tycoons bypassed Prineville and ran their line through Bend. In 1917, Prineville residents voted to build their own railway and connect to the main line north of Redmond. The municipal railroad prospered for decades by transporting timber. Today, Prineville benefits as home of the Les Schwab tire store chain, the number two private tire retailer in the United States.

PLACES TO GO

- Bowman Museum
  246 N Main Street (541) 447-3715

- Crooked River Park
  1037 S Main Street

- Wildland Fire Fighter's Monument
  450 NE Elm Street

- Prineville Reservoir State Park
  19020 SE Parkland Drive

THINGS TO DO

March
- Star Party (astronomy)
  Prineville Reservoir (541) 923-7551

May
- Street Rod Association Car Show
  Pioneer Park (541) 447-6304

June
- Crooked River Roundup (rodeo)
  Fairgrounds (800) 428-5574

- Rockhound Pow Wow
  Fairgrounds (541) 447-6304

July
- Central Oregon Spirit of the West (festival)
  (541) 788-4415

August
- Oregon Star Party (astronomy, camping)
  www.oregonstarparty.org

Ochoco National Forest Near Prineville
Photo by Matt Kern

Les Schwab

AUTO: *If they can't guarantee it, they won't sell it*

The birth of the Les Schwab Tire Company occurred in January of 1952, when Les Schwab purchased a small OK Rubber Welders tire store in Prineville. With a $3,500 investment and a strong desire to own his own business, Les increased the sales of his store from $32,000 to $150,000 in the first year. Les had a strong determination to provide a business opportunity for people who could not afford to go into business for themselves. As the company continued to grow, Les came up with what is known as the supermarket tire store concept. His goal was to have his warehouse in his showroom so that customers could walk through the racks of tires and pick out the actual tires that would go on their vehicle. He also stocked more than one brand of tire in each size to give customers a choice. Today, the Les Schwab Tire Company is one of the largest independent tire companies in the United States. Les is the first to say the success of the Les Schwab Tire Company has been made possible by wonderful customers who are the most important people in the business. Nothing happens in the Les Schwab Tire Company until a customer leads the way by choosing new tires, a wheel alignment or any of the other services they offer. Les Schwab is proud to feature neat clean stores, supermarket selection, convenient credit, sudden service, and a written warranty you don't pay extra for. Les's slogan is, "If we can't guarantee it, we won't sell it!" Come into one of the 385 Les Schwab stores today.

www.lesschwab.com

Tires LES SCHWAB

Body & Soul on 7th

HEALTH & BEAUTY: *Best full service spa*

Located in a former church building, Body & Soul on 7th is a full service spa facility and a rare sanctuary with restful modern treatments that restore you body and soul. Body & Soul owners Jayne Heyne & Rachel Carnahan believe their spa should be a service to the community, so they offer services not otherwise available here. When you walk in the front doors, you are met with elegant décor and a comforting atmosphere. Body & Soul offers a full range of hair services, all performed by highly trained hair designers. Nail treatments are available, as well, and for pedicures they have installed pedicure thrones where you can enjoy massage and heat while your feet relax in a Jacuzzi tub. Cutting-edge facial and body treatments are here also, all provided by highly trained professionals. A large retail area offers high-quality body, hair, nail and massage products. Also available is infra-red sauna treatment, well known for its deep healing benefits. Body & Soul features comfortable and very private massage rooms and state-of-the-art equipment, bringing to Prineville the very best. Come to Body & Soul on 7th for a truly relaxing experience and let Jayne, Rachel and their excellent staff pamper you.

310 NE 7th Street, Prineville OR
(541) 416-1893 *www.bodyandsoulon7th.com*

Nature's Bounty

HEALTH & BEAUTY: *Best health food store*

Located in a cheery yellow building in the busy community of Prineville, Nature's Bounty is the place to go for all of your health food and nutritional needs. Nature's Bounty carries a large selection of name brand supplements, bulk spices, dried fruits and nuts. They carry a variety of canned and prepared foods and Burt's Bees products. A large selection of nutritional books is kept in stock and the shop carries all-natural body care products. Owner Jamie Walker has always had an interest in health and in helping people. Her staff at Nature's Bounty is helpful and knowledgeable about the products and can help guide you to what you need. Jamie's desire is "to help people and be of service to the community." The shop has a gazebo out front that is covered with flowers and hanging baskets in warm weather, making it a charming place to visit. While you are here you can visit the Ochoco Viewpoint, Meadow Lakes Golf Course, and farms and ranches that stretch for miles. On your next drive through Prineville, enjoy the scenery and stop by Nature's Bounty. Meet Jamie and her great staff and find all of your natural foods and nutritional needs.

143 NW 3rd Street, Prineville OR
(541) 447-2247

Prineville Athletic Club
HEALTH & BEAUTY: *Best health club*

Prineville Athletic Club is a fully equipped athletic facility. The large roomy club offers classes ranging from yoga and kick-boxing to spinning and nutrition. Owners Sharon McPhetridge, a personal trainer, and Lori Goodman are community minded and dedicated to helping their members improve all aspects of their health. Lori and Sharon bring a definite personal touch to their business, perhaps because they grew up together in Prineville. These two entrepreneurs remain the best of friends as well as successful business partners. Prineville Athletic Club received the Business of the Year award and has been the subject of stories in several magazines. Prineville Athletic Club offers cardio

machines, weights, and the other equipment typical of a large gym. Lori and Sharon have been in the personal fitness business for 17 years and have the experience to help you improve your health. As evidence of their community dedication, they started the annual Hotshot Memorial Run to honor firefighters who have died in the line of service, and to raise money for their families. They invite you to visit Prineville Athletic Club and experience the benefits they can offer you and your family.

211 N Main Street, Prineville OR
(541) 447-4878

Northwest Desert Home Furnishings
HOME: *Best store for the home*

In Northwest Desert Home Furnishing's shop on Third Street an incredible 4,200 square feet of furniture await you, and all without a hint of big box impersonality. Northwest Desert Home Furnishings brings the best in home furnishings to Prineville. Virtually everything you need to furnish your home is here, including furniture, lamps, rugs, and the special accessories to provide personalized finishing touches. Featuring contemporary brands such as Intermountain Furniture and Zocalo USA, they have something to suit any design sensibility. Whatever you can imagine, owner Darcie Davis will find it and order it just for you. Nearly all of the furniture is made in the US, and accent pieces and paintings come from regional and national artists throughout the country. Northwest Desert Home Furnishings offers free delivery in the Prineville area. Darcie encourages you to visit, enjoy some chocolate and, of course, have a seat in your next new chair.

127 NW 3rd Street, Suite A, Prineville OR
(541) 447-7015

Meadow Lakes Golf Course

RECREATION: *Best golf course*

The word is out and golfers from all over the Pacific Northwest are flocking to Meadow Lakes Golf Course, set in the beautiful desert highlands of sunny Central Oregon. Designed by Canada's premier golf course architect, Bill Robinson, this quality course offers challenging championship golf year round, and has proudly played host to two Oregon Amateur State Championships. Ten man-made ponds lay scattered among the large, bent grass greens and generous blue grass fairways of this player friendly course. Meadow Lakes features its own beautiful clubhouse with upscale facilities and a full service restaurant and lounge. There's a terrific friendly staff on hand, eager to take care of your every need. PGA professionals manage the Golf Shop. They are dedicated to providing you with the best in golf equipment and apparel. A full line of products and services are available, including lessons for every level of player and a range that features target, putting and chipping greens. Meadow Lakes was built in 1993 to handle Prineville's affluent population. The environmental experiment has been an unqualified success, resulting in lush green meadows and water features that host abundant wildlife. Meadow Lakes was given the first-ever *Golf Digest* National Environmental Leaders Award. It has been featured in many national publications since. In fact, it has become the model for other golf courses due to the astonishing quality and ecologically sound design. Pack your clubs and enjoy a magnificent round of golf under sparkling blue skies.

300 SW Meadow Lakes Drive, Prineville OR
(541) 447-7113
www.meadowlakesgc.com

Photo by Wendy L. Gay

Ranchero Mexican Restaurant

RESTAURANTS & CAFÉS:
Best Mexican food

If you can't quite muster the cash for a trip to Mexico, a meal at Ranchero's Mexican Restaurant isn't the next best thing. It's the best thing. José Balcazar and Joel Carillo have brought the best of authentic Mexican cuisine to Central Oregon. Joel and José opened the first Ranchero Mexican Restaurant in Prineville in 1994, and it was such an immediate runaway success that Bend was lucky enough to coax them into opening a second restaurant. Not content with their reputation for the finest Mexican food this far north of the border, the entire crew at Ranchero's were determined to give their guests the feel and experience of old Mexico, as well. In the past year this terrifically popular restaurant has transformed itself, with Jose traveling to Mexico many times to bring back gorgeous Mexican art, artifacts and hand-made furniture. Colorful Mexican murals grace the walls, and you'll hear strains of mariachi-like music wafting through from the kitchen. Sample their famous top-shelf Ranchero Margarita while you watch fresh guacamole made right at your table. If you order the Combinaciones Mexicanos, you'll be able to combine your own amazing assortment of tacos, enchiladas or tostadas. Both restaurants maintain the kind of old-fashioned family-oriented business that builds a following of loyal customers and employees. Joel and José believe in taking excellent care of their staff, and their staff will take excellent care of you. Come to Ranchero's Mexican Restaurant for the taste and feel of Mexico.

150 Bend River Plaza, Bend OR
(541) 330-0685
www.rancerogrill.com

The Vineyard
RESTAURANTS & CAFÉS:
An Oregon mainstay

Terri and John Hite opened The Vineyard in 2004, enticing their community with wine lists, olive oil and lovely hand-painted murals of the Italian countryside. Prineville's first Italian eatery, this alluring addition to the local dining scene is a wonderful alternative to the burger booths that once reigned supreme. Terri's great grandfather was one of the first three original vintners in Oregon, and the Vineyard's Italian theme and warm hospitality honor his memory. Locals and visitors alike are surprised and delighted by the consistently delicious Italian food, fine service and respectable wine list The Vineyard offers. Prices are reasonable, and Terri and John have assembled and trained a fine staff of friendly servers, all of them knowledgeable and helpful in selecting wines to accompany any entree. Well known Italian favorites are wonderfully executed here, including Eggplant Parmesan, Chicken Marsala and Pork Osso Bucco. With tasty antipasti, other superb appetizers and a dessert menu that is irresistibly dangerous, you're guaranteed an evening of satiety. Because of its location, The Vineyard is a great venue for birthdays, anniversaries and fun business meetings. Prineville is growing rapidly, and the Vineyard is part of the exciting new changes taking place, so come in and savor what the Vineyard has to offer.

386 N Main Street, Prineville OR (541) 447-1980

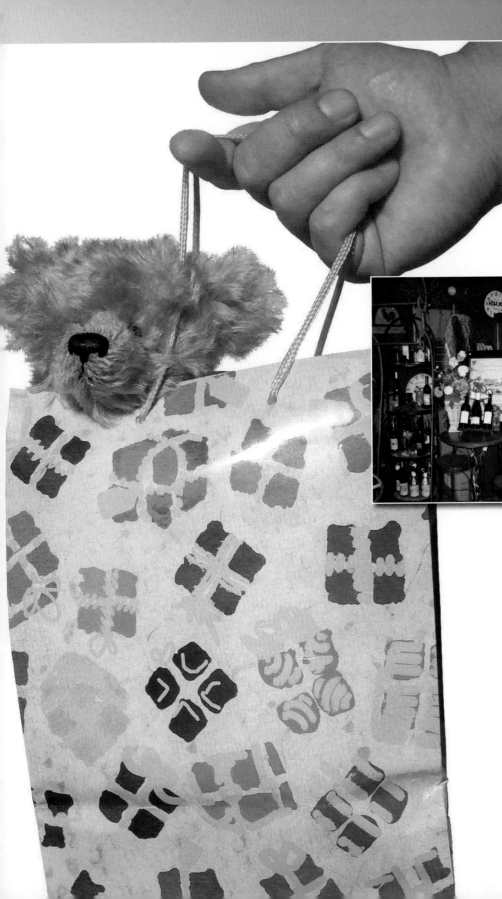

Bayberry Lane

SHOPPING: *Best gift shop*

Casie Allen and Julie Vaughn saw the need for a quality gift store in Prineville and decided to fill the niche themselves. Welcome to Bayberry Lane. Mellow background music creates a soothing atmosphere as you enter the warm and welcoming shop. Scented candles, beautiful décor and the relaxing sound of a water fountain beckon. A marvelous eclectic mix of merchandise draws you forward where you discover fascinating treasures. The family-run business specializes in antique furniture, collectibles and pottery. Light up your home with Yankee candles, set your table with several lines of dinnerware, and fill the plates with their supply of gourmet foods. For your walls and garden, they stock framed artwork, along with garden and home décor. An assortment of interesting merchandise includes beautiful cards, scrapbooking supplies and the ever-popular collectible Beanie Babies. Bayberry Lane is a premium supplier of fine Oregon and Washington wines and gifts. They feature jewelry, lotions, bath and body soaps, "Jelly bath" and many specialty items. The merchandise changes often and new products are constantly being introduced. Prices are very reasonable for the quality offered. If you need an energy lift to continue shopping, or if you just like a great cup of coffee or espresso, visit Bayberry Lane's Espresso Bar. The coffee is brewed "just right" and their handmade scones are the perfect accompaniment. Bayberry Lane is a dream fulfilled for Casie and Julie, and they would love to share it with you.

395 N Main, Prineville OR
(541) 447-6569 or (920) 206-9202
www.bayberrylanehome.com

REDMOND

Redmond is in heart of Central Oregon, within easy access to all the area's towns and recreational opportunities. Incorporated in 1916, Redmond is one of the fastest growing communities in Oregon. Redmond operates the region's only commercial airport, Roberts Field. The Redmond Air Center at the airport is a major local institution. Here, the Forest Service trains fire fighters in smoke-jumping and other wild fire techniques. The metropolis of Bend is only a short drive away, so many Redmondites work in Bend and return home to Redmond's comfortable pace and reasonable housing prices.

PLACES TO GO

- Cline Falls State Scenic Viewpoint
  State Route 126

- The Crooked River Dinner Train
  O'Neil Road (541) 548-8630

- Juniper Grove Farm (goat cheese)
  2024 SW 58th Street (541) 923-8353

- Operation Santa Claus Reindeer Ranch
  4355 W Highway 126 (541) 548-8910

- Petersen Rock Gardens & Museum
  7930 SW 77th Street (541) 382-5574

THINGS TO DO

March
- Wine Event at Eagle Crest Resort
  (800) 845-8491

June
- Rockhound Gem and Mineral Show
  Fairgrounds (541) 548-2711

July
- 4th of July Battle of the Bulls
  Fairgrounds (866) 800-EXPO (3976)

August
- Deschutes County Fair
  Fairgrounds (866) 800-EXPO (3976)

- Celtic Festival & Scottish Highland Games
  Cline Falls Ranch (541) 389-6228

September
- Rotary Club of Bend's Kobe Q (barbecue)
  Fairgrounds (541) 317-1527

Crooked River Gorge
Photo by Kris Arnold

Eagle Crest Resort

ACCOMMODATIONS:

Best resort

When choosing a destination spot for a family vacation, it is often a tug of war between choosing a scenic, relaxing resort or a fun-filled action-packed amusement park. Eagle Crest Resort solves that problem. With something for everyone, Eagle Crest provides an experience that bridges generations. With a luxurious spa and pool, and casual elegant dining, Eagle Crest Resort satisfies the visitor who is longing for peace and serenity. The excitement seekers will love the opportunities for whitewater rafting, rock climbing and other adventurous activities that abound in this area. Eagle Crest offers three outdoor pools, an indoor pool for adults, another for children, and an outdoor pool and outdoor spray park for children; and those are just the swimming facilities. Three sports centers and three golf courses offer a great chance for families to relax and play together. Eagle Crest Resort focuses on family-oriented vacations packaged for value. From comfortable rooms and suites at the inn to their unique and fully furnished chalets, Eagle Crest has the perfect accommodations to fit your taste and budget.

1522 Cline Falls Road, Redmond OR
(541) 923-0807
www.eagle-crest.com

Crooked River Dinner Train
ATTRACTIONS: *Best murder mystery train ride*

The Crooked River Dinner Train is more than a glimpse into the Wild West of yesteryear. It is a way to experience it for yourself. If you enjoy solving mysteries during dinner and a show, Crooked River Dinner Train can provide the entertainment you crave. Based on the adventures of Jesse James' gang of outlaws, you will enjoy a murder mystery dinner and a three-hour train ride. You can find the Crooked River Dinner Train just 15 minutes north of Bend. While aboard the 1800s Western Theme Dinner Train, the staff will take you back 100 years to the time when trains were robbed and murder was the way disputes were settled. On the journey, watch out for hawks, coyotes, deer, cattle and cowboys as you ride through the Crooked River Valley and see the beautiful scenery of jagged rim-rock, lush fields, and 19 miles of high desert. For dinner you can choose Jesse James pot roast, Ochoco mountain chicken & dumplings, or vegetarian lasagna. All entrees are served with appetizers, dinner salad and rolls, vegetables, dessert and coffee or tea. This city-owned attraction is managed by Teri Hisaw who focuses on providing interactive entertainment to all guests. Hitch a ride on the Crooked River Dinner Train for a night of murder, mystery and comic relief.

495 NE O'Neil Way, Redmond OR
(541) 548-8630
www.crookedriverrailroad.com

Mocha Moose
BAKERIES, COFFEE & TEA: *Best coffee spot*

Mocha Moose co-owners Susan Bruggeman and Patricia Hackbart have created such a warm, friendly atmosphere that visitors are encouraged to stop awhile, take a deep breath and just relax at the hospitable coffee cottage and café in Central Oregon. Tastefully decorated with wicker furniture and glass-topped bistro tables, Mocha Moose is situated in a charming, refurbished house near central downtown Redmond. Abundant flowers draw you to the lovely outdoor deck and patio. Mellelo's fine coffee, roasted the Italian way, is Mocha Moose's featured specialty. Sample it hot, or try a delicious freeze made from scratch with vanilla low-fat yogurt. As an alternative to coffee, tea drinkers will also find a wide selection of specialty loose leaf herbal teas. A full menu includes lunch offerings of freshly made soups, sandwiches and salads, and for breakfast you'll find homemade scones, bagels, light omelets and breakfast sandwiches, as well as waffles, griddlecakes and French toast. For a finishing touch to your meal, choose from irresistible homemade cookies or scrumptious homemade pie. Pat and Susan will be glad to cater for small parties and invite you to inquire about special events held a couple of times a month. Take a breather from a busy day and visit Mocha Moose.

427 SW 8th Street, Redmond OR
(541)923-8870
www.mochamoose.biz

Falcon Crest Art Gallery

GALLERIES: *Best regional art gallery*

Visitors to Eagle Crest resort have incredible access to two championship golf courses and limitless outdoor recreational amenities. The Falcon Crest Art Gallery is the icing on the cake. Gallery director Linda Chase fills the gallery with works that amaze and capture the interest of visitors. Chase's close connection with local artists has provided an introduction to more than 27 premium creators who are eager to show their works in the gallery. The eclectic mix includes original oil paintings, watercolors, pastels, sculptures, raku pottery, stained glass and textiles. Visitors to Eagle Crest are treated to an engaging sample of regional art. The 1,800-square-foot gallery provides an exceptional viewing experience. High ceilings create a feeling of spaciousness and light. The tall double glass doors of the elegant gallery look out onto a small lake that is surrounded by beautiful high-desert landscaping. The lake provides the perfect backdrop for the champagne receptions, media events, and concerts that are all a part of the gallery's artistic scene. Despite its elegance, the atmosphere in the gallery is relaxed. Large, over-stuffed chairs provide comfortable places to gaze at the art or simply to appreciate your surroundings. Excellent customer service encourages a loyal returning clientele, and interior design service is available for guests inspired to change their own surroundings. You may enter as a stranger, but you will leave as a friend.

7535 Falcon Crest, Suite 200, Redmond OR
(541) 280-7181

Bend Memorial Clinic

HEALTH & BEAUTY:
Most comprehensive healthcare

Bend Memorial Clinic was established in 1946. Dr D.J. Rademacher and several colleagues formed the clinic to provide patients, and each other, the convenience of a group practice. Specialization in the medical field had become necessary and the practice could provide more equipment and services to patients than a single practice could. By 1957, the practice had grown to include seven physicians and two surgeons, requiring the clinic to relocate. By 1976 the clinic moved once more. This time, the clinic allowed for growth and today Bend Memorial Clinic has more than 30 service specialties and 80 physicians. Family Practice satellite offices were started in La Pine in 1987 and in Sisters in 1991. The La Pine clinic has become a rural health clinic in order to provide more economical care for that community. The Sisters clinic offers a family practice physician as well as complete lab and x-ray services. In 1994, a satellite Ophthalmology office with a small optical dispensary was opened in Redmond. A variety of other specialties are offered at the Redmond clinic, including pulmonology and cardiology. BMC opened the first freestanding outpatient surgery center in Central Oregon in 1996. The Bend Surgery Center allows BMC physicians and other community physicians to perform outpatient surgeries conveniently and less expensively than in the hospital. As it has from the very beginning, Bend Memorial Clinic provides high quality, comprehensive, convenient health care for patients.

1501 NE Medical Center Drive, Bend OR
(541) 382-2811 or
(866) 670-2811
www.bendmemorialclinic.com

Deschutes Dental Center
HEALTH & BEAUTY: *Best dental care*

The treatment suites at Deschutes Dental Center provide tranquil views of the Deschutes River rapids. For five years, it has been the preferred dental center for discerning Bend patrons. Dr. Phillippe Freeman has received the Fellowship Award from the Academy of General Dentistry, and is an active member of the Academy of Osseointegration, a international group of specialists who focus on dental implant treatment and research. He is also a member of the American Academy of Cosmetic Dentistry and the Academy of Operative Dentistry. Dr. Freeman is a magician in the processes of cosmetic gum surgeries, bonded porcelain restorations, and corrective treatments for occlusion and dysfunction. By using the latest state-of-the-art equipment he has eliminated 90 percent of radiation, and 100 percent of the chemicals used to take traditional x-rays. Digital x-ray and intra-oral cameras take the place of the bulky x-ray apparatus of the past. Patients rest in plush dental chairs supplied with blankets and head pillows, with no fear of the drill. Drill-less technologies also have no need of anesthetic. The center is an ultra modern facility that provides adult-oriented restorative dentistry, rehabilitative and implant options. Deschutes Dental Center is a confident dental center that warranties its cosmetic and restorative services.

159 SW Shevlin-Hixon Road, Bend OR
(541) 317-1300

Blue Buffalo

HOME: *Best home and garden store*

For an exquisite shopping experience, visit Blue Buffalo where you will find distinctive home and garden décor in a boutique-style setting. Blue Buffalo is a treasure trove of fine items and gifts for all of your informal and special occasions. Blue Buffalo features an exciting array and abundance of merchandise, such as fresh flowers, European soaps, slipcovers and other extraordinary and eclectic items. The shop is elegant and beautifully arranged, and the comfortable atmosphere is warm and inviting. Owner Beth Wark believes in treating her customers well. She is a personable, talented decorator who is eager to assist her customers in making the very best selections to suit their tastes, needs and lifestyles. Her staff at Blue Buffalo is as helpful as she is and they are all friendly and service-oriented. Stop in to Blue Buffalo and shop the exclusive collection of distinctive items and gifts.

249 NW 6th Street, Redmond OR
(541) 923-8855

Niblick & Greene's

RESTAURANTS & CAFÉS: *Best area eatery*

Wherever you are in Central Oregon it is just a short drive to enjoy Niblick & Greene's, one of the best restaurants the area has to offer. A restaurant perfect for the first-class Eagle Crest Resort, Niblick & Greene's is focused on making sure they offer something for everyone, from steak and lobster to beer and burgers. Already partners in a legendary local restaurant, Robert Holley and John Bushnell opened Niblick & Greene's on Valentine's Day 10 years ago, and it covers all the bases when it comes to great food and great times. Eagle Crest offers a huge array of amenities and activities for its many guests, so Niblick & Greene's cheerfully set out to serve the diverse needs of the resort, whether fine dining with live music, a catered wedding, or a place to just hang out after a good round of golf. The extensive menu is consistently terrific, offering fine Northwest American Cuisine and a great beer and wine selection. You can enjoy quiet elegance and classic sophistication in the dining room, a pub complete with a 36-foot bar and beer on tap, or outside seating on the lovely stone patio overlooking a waterfall and golf course on a warm summer afternoon. Stop in and experience Niblick & Greene's flawless food, fabulously friendly service and fantastic golf.

7525 Falcon Crest #1, Redmond OR
(541) 548-4220
www.niblickandgreenes.com

My Country Touch
SHOPPING: *Best antiques*

Involved in the antiques business for 14 years, Leila Irwin, owner of My Country Touch, really knows her stuff. Her store, boasting an ever-changing inventory of antiques, collectibles, country décor and gift items, is exceptionally well organized, sparkling clean and offers creative displays throughout. Here you will find items in a wide price range to fit almost any pocketbook, including antiques from the 1800s, the retro period and some European and Oriental pieces. Leila focuses her energy on the well-being of her customers in order to make a "happy place to come into and feel comfortable browsing." When you enter the shop, you are greeted by beautiful music, a cinnamon candle aroma and no fewer than two water fountains. Leila states that her business is God-driven, and she feels there is a strong sense of spirit in her store. My Country Touch is Redmond's only authorized dealer of the collectible Willow Tree angels. Leila is involved in the community and supports local artists as much as possible. Visiting the shop is a perfect reason to explore the beautiful city of Redmond. At the western edge of Oregon's high desert, this community is just four miles from the Deschutes River, a half hour from the Cascade Mountains and within minutes of several lakes. At My Country Touch, the beautiful displays will add to your enjoyment of the shopping experience.

422 SW 6th Street, Redmond OR
(541) 923-0164

SISTERS

Sisters takes its name from the three Cascade peaks that grace the southwestern skyline: Faith, Hope and Charity, the Three Sisters. Sisters thrives as a vacation and retirement destination. The town hosts many lively festivals. The Sisters Outdoor Quilt Show is the nation's largest outdoor quilt show. Sisters also puts on a series of art strolls featuring music, art and wine tasting throughout the downtown area. Come meet wonderful Sisters artists and hear local musicians perform.

PLACES TO GO

- The Dee Wright Observatory
  McKenzie Pass State Route 242

- St. Winefride's Garden
  123 Trinity Way (541) 549-9391

- Three Creek Lake
  Forest Service Road 16

THINGS TO DO

May
- Riverfest
  Sisters, Bend and Sunriver (541) 420-0452

June
- Sisters Rodeo
  (541) 549-0121

July
- Sisters Outdoor Quilt Show
  www.stitchinpost.com

July & August
- Sisters Summer Faire
  Village Green Park
  (541) 549-0251

August
- Country Fair & Juried Art Show
  (541) 504-9358

- Sisters Antique Faire
  Village Green Park
  (541) 549-0251

September
- Western and Native American Arts Festival
  Creekside Park (541) 549-0251

- Sisters Folk Festival
  www.sistersfolkfestival.org

October
- Sisters Harvest Faire
  Downtown (541) 549-0251

Aerial view of the Three Sisters
Photo by Marie Richie

Black Butte Ranch
ACCOMMODATIONS:
Best luxury resort

Outdoor recreation and excitement are not hard to find in Oregon. Each river, mountain and trail offers new and wonderful things to explore. The Black Butte Ranch, located just eight miles west of Sisters on highway 20, has everything your family needs to enjoy the splendor of this lovely state. Black Butte features two championship golf courses and scenic views of seven of the peaks of the Cascade Mountains. Black Butte Ranch is a serene luxury resort offering myriad ways to enjoy nature, including hiking, biking, fishing, rafting, canoeing, tennis, trail rides and more. Black Butte Ranch offers dining at The Lodge, the Big Meadow Clubhouse, or Lakes de Bistro. No matter which you choose, the cuisine will be as magnificent as the views. The Ranch offers a Recreation Center that includes a playground, rock wall, video arcade, sports equipment and games. During summer, the Ranch Days Kids Camp is open Monday through Friday. Guests of the Ranch have several accommodation options available ranging from smaller hotel-style rooms to full vacation homes. The Black Butte Ranch has several packages available, such as golf packages and holiday getaways. Head to either of the Ranch's two sport shops for equipment or great souvenirs. You can even make reservations for a facial or massage. Black Butte has more than 30 years of experience in welcoming people and helping them make the most of their Oregon vacation. Treat yourself and your family to the trip of a lifetime at the Black Butte Ranch.

Highway 20,
8 Miles west of Sisters OR
(541) 595-1536
www.blackbutteranch.com

Blue Spruce B&B
ACCOMMODATIONS:
Best bed and breakfast

The Blue Spruce Bed & Breakfast is a beautiful home built in 1999 specifically as a B&B. Its décor has all the ambience of Sisters with theme rooms representing hunting (the Lodge), fishing (the Metolius), logging (the Cascade) and Western living (the Ponderosa). Each of the guest rooms offers a king-size bed, gas log fireplace, television with VCR, private bath with jetted tub, towel warmer and mini-fridge. Innkeeper Sandy Affonso offers warm hospitality and comfort while respecting your privacy. Her goal is to provide you with a peaceful and restorative visit that feels like coming home. The Blue Spruce can facilitate your corporate training or retreat and offers multi-media accessibility. One of the joys of the bed and breakfast is, of course, the breakfast. Your meal begins with a choice of juices and a fruit plate. The main course features delicious entrees such as lemon soufflé pancakes, orange pecan stuffed French toast or hash brown quiche. Special diets, such as Atkins or South Beach, can be accommodated. The Blue Spruce's central location makes it the perfect staging area for the numerous festivals and recreational opportunities of Sisters. Complimentary bicycles are provided for guests to explore the beauty of the area. Shoppers are within an easy stroll to the downtown boutiques. When you come back to your room and need a snack, the cookie jar is always full. Give yourself a treat. Stay at the Blue Spruce Bed & Breakfast.

**444 S Spruce Street,
Sisters OR
(541) 549-9644 or
(888) 328-9644**
www.blue-spruce.biz

Cascade House LLC

ACCOMMODATIONS: *Historic vacation home*

When friends and family come to visit, local residents give Suzi Sheward a call to reserve the Cascade House, an historic vacation home set in the heart of downtown Sisters. Built in 1945 by Sisters' first schoolteacher, Cascade House is a charming and beautifully decorated cottage-like home that exudes small town warmth and comfort. This immaculate home has everything any guest could desire. Up to eight people can enjoy the three lovely bedrooms and two full baths, furnished with the finest linens. The upstairs bedroom has the bonus of an adorable sitting room with cable television. The pleasant living area downstairs features cozy seating in front of a gas fireplace, ideal for relaxing after a day of exploring all the great shops, galleries and restaurants Sisters offers. If terrific cycling, hiking and skiing are your cup of tea, bikes and skis are available for rent a few blocks from the house. There's a large, fully equipped kitchen where you can prepare anything from toast and coffee to a full Thanksgiving dinner. Well behaved pets are welcome, and the house is surrounded by a lovely yard and rose-filled garden in the back complete with deck and barbecue for summertime festivities. The top priority is the guests, and Suzi will go to great lengths to make sure you feel at home in this Sisters retreat. The next time you pass through Sisters, try Cascade House, and give yourself the gift of a gracious getaway.

490 E Cascade Avenue, Sisters OR
(541) 504-9000 or (866) 294-8400
www.cascadehouse.com

The Lodge at Suttle Lake Resort

ACCOMMODATIONS:
Best boutique hotel

The Lodge at Suttle Lake was built on sacred Wasco Native American land. The property was blessed in an elaborate ceremony by tribal members prior to construction of the lodge. After such a perfect start, it's no surprise that this charming boutique hotel books some of its suites and cabins a full year in advance. Owners Gary and Ronda Sneva recommend reservations for your choice of their three historic cabins, five waterfront cabins, six rustic cabins, and 11 lodge suites. The entire lodge is decorated in elegant Northwest mountain style. Rooms filled with soft leather, tapestry upholstery and log furniture, fireplaces and fluffy down comforters surround every guest with comfort. The oldest cabin on the property was built in 1925. It is a riverfront cabin on one side and faces the lake on the other. Beautifully restored while retaining its original charm, it was treated with exceptional attention to detail, just like the rest of this fine facility. The lodge is situated amid soaring pines, with gorgeous views of the lake and river, accentuated by the beauty of the lodge itself. Enjoy an enchanted escape at the Lodge at Suttle Lake Resort.

13300 Hwy 20, Sisters OR
(541) 595-2628
www.thelodgeatsuttlelake.com

Long Hollow Ranch
ACCOMMODATIONS:
Best ranch-style B&B

At the Long Hollow Ranch you can book a cowboy vacation, an Oregon horseback riding vacation, a fly fishing vacation, and others besides, along with comfortable bed and breakfast accommodations. Owners Richard and Shirley Bloomfeldt recently remodeled the 100-year-old ranch house, formerly known as the headquarters building. They welcome you to Historic Central Oregon to partake in the ranch's 600 acres of beauty and wildlife. The cozy ranch-style guestrooms are furnished with your comfort in mind. Their home-cooked, delicious farm breakfasts are more than satisfying. Additional outdoor activities around the ranch include riding lessons, hiking, horseshoes and basking in the outdoor hot tub. Expert, caring wranglers give riding lessons and guide horseback rides. The Ranch caters to all levels of riders and they will match you with a horse that suits your abilities. Long Hollow Ranch is a working cattle ranch, so you can work with ranch hands on ranch activities. Leave your television-watching life behind and get reacquainted with nature. Wildlife abounds on the ranch. Elk, deer, eagles and hawks have all made the town of Sisters their playground. If you decide you need a little more civilization, Long Hollow Ranch is located in the heart of the Northwest's most scenic recreation areas. Championship golf courses and whitewater rafting are available nearby. Roam the antique and quilt stores in Sisters, then return to relax in your peaceful room at the ranch. Long Hollow attracts guests from all over the world. While there is plenty of opportunity for adventure and great recreation, the ranch also provides an atmosphere of rest and relaxation, meaning that you won't have to spend the week following your Long Hollow Ranch trip recovering from your vacation.

71105 Holmes Road, Sisters OR
(541) 923-1901
www.lhranch.com

Sisters Motor Lodge
ACCOMMODATIONS: *Best motor lodge*

Sisters Motor Lodge is far more than a place to overnight on your way somewhere else. It is a serene, comfortable, friendly destination point in and of itself with year round recreation nearby. Country Inn-style décor graces the immaculate, fully appointed rooms. Antiques, collectibles, fresh flowers, original artwork and handmade quilts add to the ambience and give you the feeling you are staying in a friend's home. Owners Mary and Ted Fowler take pride in providing one of the best romantic bargains in Central Oregon. All rooms are non-smoking and are equipped with coffee pots, cable television and DVDs. You may choose from a two-bedroom suite, a room with a fully stocked kitchenette, a studio with spectacular views of the Three Sisters or a suite that is reminiscent of a visit to grandmother's cottage. The owners invite you to choose a room and create a memory. If you want to venture outside the comfort of your room, you may relax on the large outdoor patio. Enjoy a secluded park-like setting, the sound of water flowing from the fountain and the peacefulness of the lovely pond. Mary has a reputation as the best concierge in Sisters because she has the ability to make people feel especially welcome. Let her welcome you soon.

511 W Cascade, Sisters OR
(541) 549-2551
www.sistersmotorlodge.com

Eagle Bear Ranch
ACCOMMODATIONS: *Best horse lodge*

After a day of horseback riding on trails in the Deschutes National Forest, you may want to part company with your beloved horse to enjoy shopping, great food and a stay in one of Sisters' motels. To make sure your horse is as comfortable as you are, turn to the experts at Eagle Bear Ranch, central Oregon's finest horse lodge. The horse lodge is only minutes from downtown Sisters with the Deschutes National Forest at its back gate. T.K. Schnell, a horse expert and member of the local Search and Rescue horse team, opened the lodge in 2004 to provide first-class lodging for horses. Tuck your horse into one of 12 clean, safe stalls with spacious outside runs. Your horse will receive quality hay twice daily, grooming with warm water, use of the Hot Walker exerciser and an outdoor riding arena. You can count on meticulous cleaning and sanitation at Eagle Bear Ranch, where your peace of mind and the health and comfort of your horse are always priorities. The horse lodge has ample parking, a secure tack room, a store with supplies, books and tack, plus access to veterinarian services. Specialized farrier services are available upon request. Eagle Bear Ranch is open year round and is always willing to meet your horse's special boarding and feeding needs. A reservation for your horse at Eagle Bear Ranch will enable you to rest easy, knowing your horse is having a vacation as pleasant as your own.

69437 Crooked Horseshoe Road, Sisters OR
(541) 504-1234

Out West Designs
ARTS & CRAFTS:
Best beading and jewelry

Out West Designs is not just another bead store, in large part due to the inventory and the ambience created by the owners. Gary and Nancy Tripp are committed to supplying their clients with unusual treasures and infusing the shop with a sense of fun. You'll find an extensive array of jewelry supplies that have been chosen to help you fashion your own unique creations. A vast selection of beads, stones and silver spark the imagination. Locally mined stones, semi-precious beads and beads from around the world brighten the shop with a riot of colors. The entire inventory is hand selected by Gary and Nancy. They never buy bulk product. The Tripps bring to their store a love for their business and a clear commitment to quality and service. Artfully arranged supplies are well organized, either by being openly displayed, or stored in easily accessible, natural wood cabinets with clearly labeled drawers. The Tripps enjoy sharing their business and the creativity that it inspires by holding classes. Their goal is to make people happy and able to have frustration-free fun with their beading. One of the owners, if not both, is always present. They are cheerful, welcoming and enthusiastic about teaching or helping in any way they can. They are sensitive to those who like to browse on their own. If you like beading or bead products, a visit to Out West Designs will be a treat.

**103 B Hood Street,
Sisters OR
(541) 549-1140**

The Stitchin' Post
ARTS & CRAFTS: *Best quilting supplies*

A quilt shop nestled in the small town of Sisters has become a Mecca for quilters and knitters alike: The Stitchin' Post, rated in the Top 10 best quilt stores in America, draws customers from all over the world. Owners Jean and Valori Wells work hard to provide their customers with inspiration and innovative ideas. For more than 30 years, Jean has been teaching students to quilt, and motivating them to explore color and design. Jean Wells founded the Sisters Outdoor Quilt Show™ in 1975. Today the show is world-renowned and displays more than 1,000 quilts on the storefronts of this picturesque Western town. The show is always held on the second Saturday of July. Her daughter Valori joined her in the business in 1999, bringing a young and modern approach to the shop and industry. Valori designs fabric for Free Spirit of New York, as well as her own collection of patterns for the store. Both Jean and Valori have authored several books combining the beauty of nature and quilting (autographed copies are available). Classes, workshops, and weekend retreats are available, allowing customers to immerse themselves in their favorite project. The Stitchin' Post offers an extensive and exquisite selection of artfully displayed, top quality fabrics, quilt kits, fabric bundles and yarns. Events at the store include the Fall schoolhouse session, which offers a variety of classes exploring new techniques, the Spring Tea Party, Wednesday Demos, and the Pajama Sale. Access The Stitchin' Post's user friendly website for up-coming events, presentations, and easy ordering.

311 W Cascade, Sisters OR
(541) 549-6061
www.stitchinpost.com

Sisters Coffee Company
BAKERIES, COFFEE & TEA: *Best coffee house*

For 18 years, Sisters Coffee Company has provided a beautiful neighborhood coffeehouse for its patrons. Joyce and Winfield Durham have worked together to build a sense of community and friendship in their café. They do on-site roasting daily, creating an impressive list of rich, dark, roasted coffee blends. They offer homemade pies, coffee cakes and homemade soups. If you have a personal choice of coffee, Sisters Coffee Company will make custom blends of coffees and beans. The Durhams have succeeded in creating an ambience that makes it easy for strangers to talk to each other. Sisters Coffee Company has been thoughtfully arranged so that people can sit down and have a relaxing chat. A large, real-wood fireplace made from river rock is the centerpiece of one wall. There is hardwood flooring throughout, giving everything a cozy lodge feeling. Inviting leather sofas are situated in front of the fireplace, or you can lounge on the open balcony. Joyce strives to create a warm, meaningful and homey feeling in people's hearts. Sisters Coffee Company is a beautiful place to meet friends or relax with someone close to you. Visit their coffeehouse and enjoy a warm, rich cup of joe.

273 W Hood, Sisters OR
(541) 549-0527

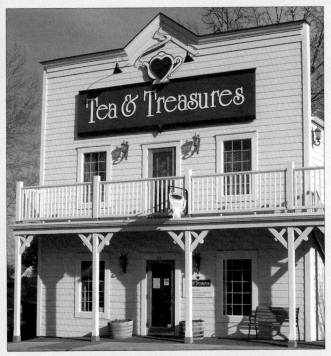

Tea & Treasures

BAKERIES, COFFEE & TEA: *Best tea house*

For Central Oregon's largest selection of tea and tea-related gifts, visit Tea & Treasures. The shop is located in the heart of Sisters, in a beautiful two-story Victorian building on the corner of Cascade and Oak Streets, next to Doc Holliday's Western Emporium. Designed and constructed by owners Barb and Steve Wilson, it was created to be a tea lover's paradise. Barb's intention in the design of her shop is to welcome all visitors into a tranquil place. She wants your shoulders to drop as you enjoy relaxing music, delightful scents and quality merchandise. The first floor is filled with exquisite gifts with a Victorian flair. You will find everything for the tea drinker, from infusers to books on tea parties. Tea & Treasures has become known throughout the state for their large selection of imported fine English china. The crowning visual focal point is their wall of more than 100 varieties of teas displayed in beautiful silver canisters. Barb's tea buyers search the world for the best premium loose leaf teas available. Upstairs is their Victorian-era tearoom, which provides a trip back in time. Every detail has been selected to create a visually appealing and tranquil place to relax with friends. The tantalizing smell of homemade scones and delicious soups permeates the air. Make time to enjoy Tea & Treasure's tea lunch, because it's a treat you will remember for years to come.

114 N Oak Street, Sisters OR
(541) 549-TEAS (8327)
www.teaandtreasures.com

Swiss Mountain Log Homes

BUSINESS: *Best log homes*

Warm colors, unique shapes, the fresh wood aroma, the tactile surfaces, and even the solid knocking sound are all part of the appealing quality of a log home. Custom-built, handcrafted, authentic log homes are the specialty and pride of Phil and Kris Rerat, owners of Swiss Mountain Log Homes, Inc. The operative word for the company is quality. It is most important to choose an experienced log builder who refuses to compromise on materials or workmanship. Every Swiss Mountain Log Home is built to International Log Builders Association construction standards, which meet or exceed all local building codes throughout the United States and Canada. The primary focus is on building custom Scandinavian full-scribe log homes, meaning that each log is scribed and notched by hand along is entire length so that it fits exactly on top on the one beneath it. This creates a weather tight, chinkless fit. No filler is needed. Their love and passion for Scandinavian full-scribe logwork is reflected in the precision and quality of every Swiss Mountain Log Home. They provide complete log home restoration, remodel and specialty services. They will be happy to answer your log-related questions and, if necessary, direct you to appropriate resources. Building handcrafted log homes is an art form. Swiss Mountain Log Homes provides experienced and talented logsmiths who delight in helping bring their customers' dream homes to life.

P.O. 2012, Sisters OR
(541) 385-6006
www.swissmtloghomes.com

Sisters Chamber of Commerce

BUSINESS: *Hardest working civic organization*

There's a treasure nestled on the east side of the Cascade Mountains in Central Oregon. With its western flair and huge array of recreational choices, Sisters is a gem of a town that packs a lot of punch in a small package. The Sisters Area Chamber of Commerce website is the best place to start when planning your Sisters adventure. With the 1.6 million-acre Deschutes National Forest a step away, the opportunities for immersion in the wilderness are limitless. Locally, Aspen Lakes and Black Butte Ranch offer outstanding golf experiences, and 18 more golf courses are within easy driving distance. Skiing and snowboarding are available at Hoodoo and Mt. Bachelor Ski Areas, and the Deschutes and Metolius Rivers offer incredible fly fishing. You don't have to leave the town of Sisters for entertainment. The town offers an eclectic schedule of events throughout the year. One of the more popular offerings is the annual Sisters Rodeo, a Professional Rodeo Cowboys Association-sanctioned rodeo now in its 66th year. For a week in July, Sisters becomes a quilters Mecca. Area businesses display quilts by artists from all over the world and there are quilting classes and lectures, demonstrations and exhibits. The week culminates in the largest outdoor quilt show in the country, an absolute feast for the eyes. The Sisters Folk Festival and the Sisters Jazz Festival in September provide two music filled weekends of enjoyment. With a variety of excellent lodgings and restaurants to choose from, and unique shops and businesses to provide for your every need, Sisters is the perfect vacation destination. Come and play in Sisters.

P.O. Box 430, Sisters OR
541-549-0251
www.sisterschamber.com

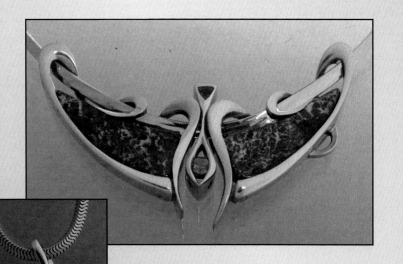

The Jewel

FASHION:

Best jewelry destination

The Jewel is one of the largest and longest established jewelry galleries on the West Coast. Far from a conventional jewelry store, it's a natural history gallery featuring spectacular museum quality minerals and fossils, from gorgeous crystalline geodes, an ancient turtle or crab frozen in stone, to Oregon's rare scenic-agates and fiery Sunstones. Owner Jan Daggett's background is as diverse as her gallery. For 10 years she operated her own mine, wholesaling collections to the Smithsonian and other museums. As a talented sculptor she taught herself goldsmithing, selling her first line of silver and agate jewelry on Rodeo Drive in Beverly Hills at the age of 17. For 30 years she has continued to seek and find her own unique way of transforming the Earth's valuable elements into jewelry. Her subtle blending of colors and materials and the ability to cut and shape her own stones gives her work distinctive depth and style. Although often featuring single gems, she also is known for combining humble and exotic stones such as a luminescent agate side-by-side with diamonds or a Fine Burma Ruby flanked by colorful dinosaur bone. A lifelong connoisseur, Jan has built an unsurpassed collection of fine gem materials from which she creates pieces for the gallery and for individual clients. There is a complete workshop on the premises and as many as 200 pieces of her jewelry. In addition, the gallery is full of outstanding designs by independent jewelry artists with many unique collections in sterling and mixed metals. Open since 1991, The Jewel is truly a landmark and a repeat destination for many Central Oregon visitors.

221 W Cascade Avenue, Sisters OR
(541) 549-9388

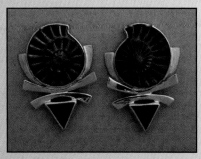

Leavitt's

FASHION: *Best Western styles*

John Leavitt is the genuine article. In 1977, he took his ranch and rodeo background, seasoned it with business schooling in Reno, and opened Leavitt's, a high-end Western store in Sisters. Leavitt's can supply you with everything you need to take you from the tall grass to a night on the town. The store offers many exclusive items that are available nowhere else. Leavitt's is an outlet for name brand products from vendors such as Imperial Ranch and Pendleton Woolen Mills. As John moves through Leavitt's answering questions and assisting customers, there is no doubt that he spent his life in the saddle. Even today, John continues his riding and roping in the rodeo circuit, including the Sisters Rodeo, also known as the Biggest Little Show in the World. John and his wife, Kathryn, enjoy helping the diverse customers who come through their store, visitors from England, Australia, and more exotic locales such as Mongolia. For a Western experience that takes you from wool and leather to rhinestones and silver, mosey on down to Leavitt's.

100 E Cascade, Sisters OR
(541) 549-6451
www.leavitts.net

Clearwater Gallery
GALLERIES: *Best gallery*

Gallery owners Dan Rickards and his wife, Julia, would be the first to tell you to relax and enjoy the retreat experience of being in their gallery. Dan is the gallery's featured artist. His American Dream series showcases his ability to create a view for a windowless wall, or anywhere a client wants to capture a landscape the way it once was. His work helps to maintain a memory of where we have been, or at least give hope to the possibilities of where we might like to go. As a child, Dan evidenced an interest in drawing, but painting did not become his primary occupation until 1991. The springboard to his career was the watercolor titled Autumn Rise. He shifted to acrylics to create his second piece, Bare Camp. He describes his technique as painting "loose, with a small brush." While his natural talent has been important, he attributes much of his success to the support of his wife and parents. Dan paints landscapes and wildlife and, on request, will customize artwork to create a one-of-a kind painting with personal and individual details. His work reflects a strong sense of place and character. His use of color and light allows you to feel as though you are present in the place he has portrayed. Dan has received many awards and sees a future filled with creative possibilities. Believing that a balance between business and artistry is essential to success as an artist, the Rickards look forward to building relationships and enriching the lives of their customers with both Dan's artwork and the ambience of Clearwater Gallery. Visit the gallery, relax, enjoy.

391 W Cascade Avenue, Sisters OR
(541) 549-4994 or (800) 348-9453
www.clearwaterstudio.com

Bend Memorial Clinic

HEALTH & BEAUTY:
Most comprehensive healthcare

Bend Memorial Clinic was established in 1946. Dr D.J. Rademacher and several colleagues formed the clinic to provide patients, and each other, the convenience of a group practice. Specialization in the medical field had become necessary and the practice could provide more equipment and services to patients than a single practice could. By 1957, the practice had grown to include seven physicians and two surgeons, requiring the clinic to relocate. By 1976 the clinic moved once more. This time, the clinic allowed for growth and today Bend Memorial Clinic has more than 30 service specialties and 80 physicians. Family Practice satellite offices were started in La Pine in 1987 and in Sisters in 1991. The La Pine clinic has become a rural health clinic in order to provide more economical care for that community. The Sisters clinic offers a family practice physician as well as complete lab and x-ray services. In 1994, a satellite Ophthalmology office with a small optical dispensary was opened in Redmond. A variety of other specialties are offered at the Redmond clinic, including pulmonology and cardiology. BMC opened the first freestanding outpatient surgery center in Central Oregon in 1996. The Bend Surgery Center allows BMC physicians and other community physicians to perform outpatient surgeries conveniently and less expensively than in the hospital. As it has from the very beginning, Bend Memorial Clinic provides high quality, comprehensive, convenient health care for patients.

1501 NE Medical Center Drive,
Bend OR
(541) 382-2811 or
(866) 670-2811
www.bendmemorialclinic.com

EquusEmbrace
HEALTH & BEAUTY: *Harnessing the healing power of horses*

Transport yourself to a world of love and acceptance with a visit to EquusEmbrace. Here you will find one of nature's most intuitive and authentic beings—the horse. Founder Claudia Lamphere, through her blend of passion and natural talent, has developed a program that harnesses the powerful insight of these magnificent creatures to help people with personal healing and self-discovery. Born of the instinct that keeps them safe from predators is the horse's natural tendency to read the emotions and moods of a person. Through knowledge, training and experience, Claudia interprets the horse's message and helps the client understand what they are feeling and projecting. Once this self-awareness is established, clients can move toward a new sense of self, deliberately choosing their path and living life with a more positive intention. The results are compelling. Clients often remark that they accomplish in a few sessions or a weekend that which has eluded them for years. With programs for individuals, women, adolescent girls and families, the goal of EquusEmbrace is to bring clarity of purpose and self-empowerment to as many people as possible. EquusEmbrace is a nonprofit organization funded by individual donations, as well as grants and corporate gifts, and has scholarships to help those who cannot pay full tuition. Take some much deserved quality time for the things in life that are the most important. These extraordinary horses will help reaquaint and reconnect you to your true self. An unforgettable and life-changing experience awaits you at EquusEmbrace.

18349 Fadjur Lane, Sisters OR
(541) 548-6331
www.equusembrace.com

Ponderosa Forge & Ironworks, Inc.

HOME: *Best look at blacksmithing*

Jeff Wester, owner of Ponderosa Forge & Ironworks, Inc., will tell you that if the functional beauty of hand-forged iron sparks your soul, he can provide the right accents and fixtures to transform your home. Jeff's creations are works of art.

Blacksmithing at Ponderosa Forge is done the way it has been done for hundreds of years. Some of the shop machinery is more than a century old and is still in perfect working condition. Ponderosa Forge opened its doors in 1988 and has grown to be the largest blacksmith shop in Oregon. Traditionally crafted functional art is a specialty. Whether you're building a new home or remodeling an existing fireplace, these blacksmiths can customize beautiful fireplace doors, tools and andirons. Handsome products include wine racks, nutcrackers, candle holders, door knockers, handles and pulls, coat and hat hooks, shelf brackets, and towel bars. Each creation is a unique expression of the blacksmith's art. New designs are always in process and keep the inventory interesting. Because every piece is sold directly through the showroom in Sisters, you won't pay boutique prices. You can buy personally from the artisans who create the work, and you will gain a fascinating glimpse into the world of blacksmithing.

207 W Sisters Park Drive, Sisters OR
(541) 549-9280
www.ponderosaforge.com

Village Interiors
HOME: *Best interior design*

Let your home decorating dreams come true. Village Interiors motto is Details Make the Difference. Owner and interior designer Patricia Molesworth and her competent and creative staff are committed to providing their clients with the best in customer service. They work closely with homeowners and customize service to complement individual lifestyles and interests. Pat emphasizes from the first meeting that they are there to listen and then guide you to a solution. Village Interiors is a treasure-house of expertise for complicated issues such as color, coordination of furniture and accessories within specific settings, and the right surroundings to make your home a beautiful and comfortable expression of your life. The shop carries everything for the home interior: furniture, home décor, all flooring products, countertops, Hunter Douglas blinds, custom fabric and fabrications, and wallpaper. If you can't find it in the store or through their usual resources they will help you do the research for that hard-to-find item. Pat and staff work extensively and closely with home builders, keeping them on top of the latest trends and apprised of availability. Word of mouth has been Village Interiors' best merchandising tool. Call Village Interiors to make your vision a reality or visit their website.

382 Hood Avenue E, Sisters OR
(541) 549-3431
www.villagedesigncenter.com

Cork Cellars
and Oregon Vineyard Selection

MARKETS: *Best wine and wine accessories*

Your wine is good to you. Be good to your wine. That is the advice of Mark and Emily Pelletier, owners of Cork Cellars and Oregon Vineyard Selection, a joint venture in wine retail and custom wine cellars. Emily, owner of Cork Cellars, a fine wine and tasting room in downtown Sisters, has an impressive wine selection varying from everyday drinking wines to wine cellar selections. Great care is taken in the selection of all wines sold at Cork Cellars, which focuses primarily on boutique, classic, and hard-to-find wines of the Northwest. Cork Cellars also carries exceptional wine accessories and gifts, and provides delivery, wine classes and cellar stocking services. Wines sold by Cork Cellars are housed in custom racks built by Oregon Vineyard Selection, which is Mark's passion and forte. Oregon Vineyard Selection operates throughout the state of Oregon and specializes in designing and installing custom wine cellars in residential and commercial properties. Cork Cellars is evolving into an inviting showroom for Mark's work. Between the services and talents of Mark and Emily, you can be sure you will be purchasing the best in fine wine and gifts, as well as receiving superior service and quality products for all of your wine cellar needs.

167 Elm Street, Sisters OR
(541) 549-2675
www.corkcellars.com
www.oregonvineyardselection.com

Sisters Olive and Nut Company

MARKETS: *Exotic Tastes in Comfortable Surroundings*

Local olive lovers know that the place to go for quality olives and nuts is Sisters Olive and Nut Company. Kevin and Susan King had the idea for the business after a trip to the Olive Pit in California. They have enthusiastically embraced the concept and created a comfortably elegant store where everyone feels at home. The family-oriented atmosphere welcomes children and encourages all visitors to touch, experience and taste the products. More than 90 varieties of olives from as far away as Spain, Italy and France, and as near as California are waiting to be tasted. In addition to the colorful array of olives, there is a generous sampling of nuts to explore, including Oregon's state nut, the hazelnut. The most popular nut, however, is the good old, delicious, can't-be-beat, roasted, salted, unshelled peanut. Kevin and Susan carry a small representation of wines from select Willamette Valley wineries. Specialty meats, cheeses, sausages and candies are available, too. Sister's Olive and Nut Company will happily design a gift basket for you, or you can make your own. For your convenience, they deliver anywhere in the country. The aisles in the store were built extra wide so they are wheelchair accessible. Stop by soon for a taste treat you will not soon forget, or check out the website for lists of available olives and nuts.

101 E Cascade Avenue, Sisters OR
(541) 549-8047
www.sistersolive.com

Aspen Lakes Golf Course

RECREATION: *Best golf course*

The community of Sisters offers visitors a wealth of recreational opportunities and is fast becoming a destination city of Central Oregon. Just three miles east of Sisters on highway 126, visitors will find the Aspen Lakes Golf Course, offering scenic views and 18 holes of exciting golf. The Cyrus Family has owned and operated this popular course since 1997. Their commitment to natural resource sustainability has led them to practice water and energy conservation. In addition, they are members of the Audubon International Signature Sanctuary Program and a Certified Signature Sanctuary. This public golf course was designed by William Overdorf. It features red sand bunkers, bent grass fairways and multiple tees for all skill levels. This lovely course is both breathtaking and challenging. Aspen Lakes offers a full-service clubhouse, pro-shop and beverage cart along with a friendly and knowledgeable staff who are always on hand to help maximize your enjoyment of the game and the stunning grounds. Private lessons, coaching and classes are available to guests at reasonable fees. In 2001, Aspen Lakes Golf Course was named eighth in the nation on *Golf Digest's* list of Best New Affordable Public Courses. Enjoy the majestic beauty of Oregon while playing the sport of Kings at the Aspen Lakes Golf Course.

**16900 Aspen Lakes Drive, Sisters OR
(541) 549-4653**
www.aspenlakes.com

The Fly Fisher's Place
RECREATION: *Best fly shop*

In 1969, Arnold Gringrich, founder of *Esquire* magazine, stated that "fly-fishing is the most fun you can have standing up," and generations of fly-fishers profoundly agree. At the Fly Fisher's Place in Sisters, you too can discover this majestic sport that pits man against fish. Known as Oregon's number one place to gain information on the Metolius River, a wild and scenic waterway that offers blue ribbon fly-fishing, the Fly Fisher's Place can provide professional guides for the Deschutes, Crooked and Fall Rivers, and many of the region's sylvan lakes. In addition to offering professional guides, the Fly Fisher's Place books exciting fly fishing excursions around the world, including destinations like Chili and the Caribbean. Owner and proprietor Jeff Perin, who purchased the shop 15 years ago, is dedicated to educating people on the art of fly fishing. He offers classes where beginners can get started and intermediate fishermen can get better. In conjunction with guided tours, excursions and instructional classes, the Fly Fisher's Place provides a full-service pro shop, where you can find everything from specialty rods, fly reels and hip-boots to wading jackets, gear bags and apparel. Discover for yourself the serenity and joy that come from practicing this graceful art that began in the Middle Ages and remains a popular, and fairly unchanged, sport by visiting the Fly Fisher's Place in beautiful downtown Sisters.

151 W Main Street, Sisters OR
(541) 549-3474
www.flyfishersplace.com

El Rancho Grande

RESTAURANTS & CAFÉS:

Best Mexican food

The special ingredient at El Rancho Grande in Sisters is family pride. Owned and managed by the Robles and Rodriguez families, the restaurant has gained scores of loyal customers with its authentic, high-quality Mexican food. The homemade salsa served with chips at the beginning of every meal is an old family recipe. The signature dishes are family favorites, too. Try the *cochinita pibil*, which is shredded pork seasoned with achiote, a Mexican spice, and red onions. The *camarones chiapanecos* are another crowd pleaser. This zesty dish features prawns sauteed in lime juice with onions and jalapenos, and pairs beautifully with a fresh fruit margarita. The eye-catching deck out back beckons for al fresco dining in nice weather, while inside the environment is friendly and attractive. The authentic Mexican decor includes a colorful handpainted mural. The lounge is smoke-free. You will find the same excellent food and cheerful atmosphere at two new locations in Redmond and Bend. Family members are always on hand at El Rancho Grande. They will welcome you, as if into their own home.

150 E Cascade, Sisters OR
(541) 549-3594
www.elranchograndesisters.com

The Candle House
SHOPPING: *Best selection of candles*

Gifts that bring light can be magical, personal expressions of appreciation. Visit the Candle House in the heart of downtown Sisters for the widest selection of candles in the Northwest. Established in 1994 by Verna and Gordon Bowman, the shop is exquisitely decorated and warmly inviting. Step through the door into elegance, glowing energy and the peacefulness of Verna's signature music, soft melodies by Aeoliah. The shop is filled with specialty products and gifts made from crystal, pewter, brass and bronze. The essence of scented candles will guide you to your favorite choices. The Candle House features candles, oil candles, lamps and all the accessories. Well known, high-quality brands such as Eternal Flame, Catskill Mountain Crystal and Calla Lily Oil candles are available for you to browse. If you have a request that is not in stock, they will gladly order it for you. In addition to candles, Verna and manager Robin have chosen tapestries, wall sconces, music boxes and a large selection of imported items to add to the charm of the store. Gift wrapping is free and world-wide shipping is available. Verna's Candle House is a labor of love that enfolds you with warmth as you visit the shop.

331 W Cascade, Sisters OR
(541) 549-0744
www.thecandlehouseinc.com

Coyote Creek Café & Lounge
RESTAURANTS & CAFÉS:
Best down-home dining

Imagine fabulous food that combines the best of the Old West with a gourmet flair, and what you have is the Coyote Creek Café & Lounge. Eric and Jane Metzel have dazzled Sisters visitors and locals alike for 14 years serving downright great American food. Coyote Creek is open seven days a week, and on their menu, you'll find something for absolutely everyone. You can enjoy an excellent, hearty breakfast of eggs Benedict or biscuits and gravy. Choose a big juicy burger or a carb-friendly wrap for lunch. And whatever mood you are in for dinner, whether pizza or prime rib, this is the place to find it. You can savor a delectable dinner in a comfortable and casual setting with live music on the weekends, or kick back and tuck into a mouthwatering meal while you watch your favorite game via satellite in the sports bar. If you are there for the beautiful Sisters summer season, you can enjoy views of the mountains and the lushly manicured grounds as you savor your meal on the outdoor patio. Coyote Creek's staff offers comfort, warmth, and a friendly welcome, so make sure you circle this stop on your travel plan. Coyote Creek Café & Lounge is the place for upscale, down-home dining at its best.

497 Highway 20 W, Sisters OR
(541) 549-9541

Bedouin

SHOPPING: *Best boutique*

Travelers passing through Sisters are surprised and delighted when they stumble on the gem of a boutique that is Bedouin. This colorful emporium is filled with eclectic high-quality goods for women with discriminating tastes. Bedouin has a sumptuous selection of contemporary, artisan, and world market clothing in soft natural fibers that will attract appreciative attention. You will also find fascinating jewelry, hats, and handbags to complement the beautiful apparel. Add to the mix a mingling of gifts and home décor and children's items and you are guaranteed something for everyone. Janit Brockway started Bedouin 15 years ago, and it has been such a favorite with Sisters' residents that she has had to move and expand three times since then. An artist and sculptor, Janit's taste and sense of style are everywhere, from her merchandise to her beautiful displays and the ambience of this unique shop. Janit is committed to the community and Bedouin reflects that dedication. Adjoining Janit's shop, her husband, Jim, serves organic coffee at his coffee bar called Navigator News. He also offers a wide variety of magazines and ceramic gifts. According to one long-time Sisters resident, "The Bedouin is where we come when we are looking for something very special." If Bedouin is where the locals go, you know you will not go wrong by paying them a visit when you pass through Sisters.

**143 E Hood, Sisters OR
(541) 549-3079**

Eurosports

SHOPPING: *Best sporting goods*

If you are an avid outdoor enthusiast, cyclist, hiker or skier, then the breathtaking beauty of the country surrounding Sisters is the place for you. Sisters has become a magnet for outdoor sports, and Eurosports is where you'll find the gear to do it all. For more than 16 years, Brad Boyd's wonderful cycling and winter sports store has been the community resource for those who want to get out there and experience the natural wonders of Sisters' wild countryside. In the winter, this magnificent area boasts some of Oregon's finest trails for cross-country skiing and snowshoeing, with the Hoodoo Ski Area offering fabulous downhill skiing and snowboarding. In the summer you can blast down more than 50 miles of tree-lined mountain trails or cycle more sedately over flat farmland and winding mountains roads. Brad carries a wide range of quality equipment, clothing and supplies and provides rentals, as well. Brad practices what he preaches and is a first-class bicyclist, skier and hiker himself, so he is well versed in the area and the variety of opportunities you will find. Brad leads group bike rides in the summer and cycling classes year round. He enjoys sharing his knowledge and helping people enjoy and learn about the outdoors. His many regular customers testify to his expertise in his field. His motto is Get out and do it, and he's the perfect person help you do it.

182 E Hood Avenue, Sisters OR
(541) 549-2471

Beacham's Clock Co.

SHOPPING: *Best handcrafted clocks*

At Beacham's Clock Co., the music of clock chimes fills the air hourly as the sun shines through the windows on dozens of old clocks, new clocks and clocks handcrafted by Ed Beacham, the complete master clockmaker. Ed is one of the few masters who can design and craft a complete product from start to finish. This work requires a mastery of computer design, metal machining and woodworking skills. Ed and his wife, Kathi, moved to Sisters in 1978. Together they own and operate this wonderful shop located in a beautifully styled Victorian building. A fascinating aspect of visiting the shop is that you can actually observe Ed's clockmaking talents in action. He makes the entire clock, starting with his own gear train design, and proceeds through all the steps of movement and case making to the spectacular finished product. He has made more than 600 clocks, all weight driven, predominately wall clocks. Ed Beacham averages about 50 new clocks per year, usually in batches of 12, with most of them spoken for before they are made. He has received numerous awards, including the prestigious Dana Blackwell Award for Excellence in Clockmaking. All of Ed's clocks are numbered and signed. His clocks can be found in fine collections and elegant homes around the world and come with a lifetime warranty. Beacham's Clock Co. store not only stocks beautiful clocks that have been made by some of the finest clockmakers in the world, but also provides a full repair service for all clock owners. Stop by Beacham's Clock Co. to view approximately 1,000 clocks, and experience the rare opportunity to observe a master clockmaker working at his craft.

300 W Hood Street, Sisters OR
(541) 549-9971
www.beachamsclockco.com

Paulina Springs Books

SHOPPING: *Best bookstore*

Paulina Springs Books is your source for handpicked quality books. Owned by Brad Smith, this bookstore offers personal service in an attractive, browser friendly store. The books are shelved in a unique face-out display, letting you scan quickly through the books without the hassle of pulling books out one at a time to see the cover. The store is located in the Western town of Sisters, named for the three prominent peaks that grace the southwestern skyline, Faith, Hope and Charity, collectively known as the Three Sisters. Paulina Springs Books has a good reputation for carrying

a wide range of books and is noted for its strong outdoor book selection. The focus of Brad's business is providing better written books, and he possesses a keen sense of what his clients like and want. In the store you will find many award-winning books and a high percentage of non-fiction books. Paulina Springs Books provides a diverse cultural experience to the Sisters community. Throughout the summer the bookstore hosts author presentations twice a week. Paulina Springs Books is an exceptional bookstore in a beautiful town. Come in today, browse their selections and pick out your favorite book.

252 W Hood Avenue, Sisters OR
(541) 549-0866

Sisters Cascade Gifts
SHOPPING: *Best gifts*

The three beautiful Cascade mountain peaks surrounding the charming town of Sisters are called Faith, Hope and Charity. Legend has it that they were named The Three Sisters by a Methodist missionary in the 1840s. Sisters has been the home of Barbara Turner's delightful gift shop, Sisters Cascade of Gifts, for more than 25 years. Sisters Cascade of Gifts is known for its eclectic selection of gifts and collectibles, many imported from all over the world. She carries fine, high-end home décor accessories, such as Armani porcelain and Swarovski crystal. If you happen to be a Red Hatter, you'll find a fine selection of beautiful red hats to choose from for that next society function. If the everchanging selection of wonderful gifts doesn't tempt you, you still won't be able to get out the door without indulging in some of Barbara's irresistible homemade fudge. She has an astounding array of delectable flavors. Be sure to try her cream and butter fudge. Barbara treats every person who comes through her door as a guest and a friend. Her passion is keying in to the likes and interest of her customers, and since some of them are third generation by now, she does it very well indeed. Stop in and see Barbara's lovely shop in Sisters.

150 W Cascade, Sisters OR
(541) 549-8591

The Wild Hare
SHOPPING: *Best home and garden accessories*

The Wild Hare is guaranteed to tempt you with its focus on high quality home and garden accessories. Whether your passion is custom woodwork, luxuriant bath and body products, tools for the garden or unique accents for the home, this shop offers something for everyone. The Wild Hare adjoins The Stitchin' Post and is the creation of Jean and Valori Wells. This mother-daughter team combines their passion to create an atmosphere of inspiration for their customers. The store offers the famed Burt's Bees products, Caldera home cleaning essentials, and pure shea butter soaps by Mistral. DANI bath and body care line is just one example of the outstanding products offered in the shop. DANI, a locally made product, has become a favorite. With fragrances such as passion fruit, grapefruit ginger, lemongrass lavender and plum flower, it is sure to tickle your senses. The Wild Hare continually offers new selections of tableware, such as specialty serving pieces and hand-painted imported linens, perfect to dress up any occasion. Fresh vibrant plants for the indoors help bring the outdoors inside. For the true gardener the shop has an ample supply of specialty garden tools, seeds, books, gloves and fascinating garden sculptures. Celebrate living and giving by spending an afternoon at the Wild Hare.

321 W Cascade, Sisters OR
(541) 549-6061

TERREBONNE

Terrebonne, a small town just north of Redmond, is the home of one of Central Oregon's favorite state parks. Smith Rock State Park is specially noted for world class-rock climbing. Its sheer cliffs of tuff and basalt are ideal for beginners and experts alike. Many climbers consider Smith Rock to be the birthplace of modern American sport climbing. Many of its climbing routes are cutting-edge even by today's standards. You can pick up climbing supplies right in Terrebonne. Miles of hiking trails also make Smith Rock a popular retreat for hikers. Trails offer views of the meandering Crooked River and the Cascade peaks. Crooked River Ranch, a major planned development, spans more than 18 square miles northwest of Terrebonne.

PLACES TO GO

- Peter Skene Ogden State Scenic Viewpoint
  U.S. Highway 97

- Smith Rock State Park
  9241 NE Crooked River Drive

THINGS TO DO

June
- Dixieland Jazz in the Canyon
  Crooked River Ranch
  (541) 548-0679

July
- Buffalo Roast
  MacPherson Park
  (541) 548-0679

September-October
- Corn Maze and Pumpkin Patch
  Central Oregon Pumpkin Company
  (541) 504-1414

Smith Rock State Park

Crescent Moon Ranch

ANIMALS & PETS: *Best alpaca ranch*

After 35 years in the busy restaurant industry, Joe and Diane Nelson were ready for a change. They decided to raise alpacas, expecting a quiet, leisurely path to retirement. What they got in Crescent Moon Ranch was an exciting and involved second shared career. They started their farm on San Juan Island with Jerry Dunne. In 2002, they moved the herd to Terrebonne. Today, Debbie Miller and Scott Miller manage the Crescent Moon Ranch for the Nelsons and Jerry, who remain involved in some aspects of the farm. With 400 Huacaya alpacas on 137 acres, Crescent Moon is the largest of the 17 alpaca breeders in Central Oregon. The precise science of breeding is used to produce amazing animals for sale and also for the prized fleece of the alpaca. The fleece has a texture that is similar to that of cashmere and is a favorite of hand-knitters. The business of breeding is very competitive and breeders are constantly working to improve the fleece. Crescent Moon Ranch, however, is more than just a perfect place to acquire a prize alpaca, it is also a joy to visit. With an enchanting view of the Cascades, rolling emerald green pastureland and a one-acre pond, it is a breathtaking sight to see. The owners and staff at Crescent Moon Ranch invite you to come walk on the moon with them and to check out their retail store loaded with premium alpaca wool products.

70397 Buckhorn Road, Terrebonne OR
(541) 923-2285
www.crescentmoonranch.com

WARM SPRINGS

The Warm Springs Indian Reservation, home of the Warm Springs, Wasco and Paiute tribes, stretches from the snowcapped summits of the Cascades to the cliffs of the Deschutes River in Central Oregon. The Warm Springs tribes are among the most welcoming Native American nations and offer many forms of recreation to their guests. You can immerse yourself in traditional culture at the Museum at Warm Springs or attend one of the many cultural events held throughout the year. These include salmon bakes, dancing, drumming and storytelling. You can enjoy the exhilaration of kayaking or horseback riding, or the peace of hiking and fishing. The reservation boasts a championship golf course and the Kah-Nee-Ta High Desert Resort & Casino. This gaming facility features one of the friendliest staff in the casino industry. *Shape Magazine* has rated Spa Wanapine, in the village at Kah-Nee-Ta, as one of the top five spas in the country. The soothing spring waters flow directly from the source and surface at 140 degrees Fahrenheit. In addition to the spa, the spring waters warm the Olympic-sized swimming pool at the resort.

PLACES TO GO

- Kah-Nee-Ta High Desert Resort & Casino
  6823 Highway 8 (800) 554-4SUN (4786)

- Museum at Warm Springs
  2189 U.S. Highway 26 (541) 553-3331

- Pelton Park
  NW Pelton Dam Road

THINGS TO DO

February
- Lincoln's Pow Wow and Celery Feast
  Simnasho Longhouse (541) 553-3243

April
- Root Feast
  (541) 553-3257

June
- Pi-Ume-Sha Treaty Days Powwow
  (541) 553-3257

August
- Huckleberry Feast
  (541) 553-3331

Warm Springs Landscape
Photo by Larry Osborne

The Museum at Warm Springs

ATTRACTIONS:

Traditions of the Warm Springs, Wasco and Piute Peoples

The Museum at Warm Springs has found a beautiful way to preserve, share, and propagate knowledge of the rich culture of the Confederated Tribes of Warm Springs. The Museum is arranged to resemble a traditional encampment among the cottonwoods along Shitike Creek in the Deschutes River Canyon. It is a place that exists in harmony with the natural environment and includes an arboretum that serves as an outdoor classroom and a small amphitheatre for outdoor performances, demonstrations and public programs. The use of native stone, heavy timbers, and brick demonstrates the integration of art into everyday life. Visitors begin their experience beside a quiet pool and follow a stream to a circular stone drum which serves as the Museum's entrance. The water symbolically turns into a gray polished slate, carving a stream-like pattern into the earth-toned tile floor and gradually leads visitors to the entrance of the permanent exhibition. Tribal histories and traditions of the Warm Springs, Wasco and Piute peoples are told in interactive permanent displays. The tribal leaders and the Warm Springs community undertook an aggressive acquisition program and now the Museum has one of the best and most complete collections of artifacts, photographs, family heirlooms, clothing, jewelry, tools, baskets, tribal documents and trade items owned by an Indian tribe. All of this combines to make the Museum a gesture of welcome to the general public and a conservatory for ancient and revered traditions.

2189 Highway 26, Warm Springs OR (541) 553-3331

Land Yachting, Alvord Desert, Southeast Oregon
Photo by Robert Mutch, www.robmutch.com

Eastern Oregon

ADAMS

Adams, 13 miles northeast of Pendleton on Wildhorse Creek, was named for John F. Adams, part of whose homestead is now included in the town. Adams, along with neighboring Weston and Athena, is a jumping-off point and supply center for a number of attractions. The Spout Springs Ski Resort is located northeast of Adams in the heart of the Blue Mountains on State Route 204. Spout Springs is one of the most family-friendly resorts in Oregon and the majority of the runs cater to beginner or intermediate skiers. Spout Springs also has terrific cross country skiing and has been an Olympic training park. The staff is helpful, especially when teaching children how to ski. There are plenty of lights for night skiing. Snowboarders can enjoy a snow park and a pipe. Another great family vacation getaway is east of Adams—the Bar M Ranch, just off County Road 900 near the hamlet of Bingham Springs along the Umatilla River. The historic ranch house was built in 1864 as a stagecoach stop. It offers horseback riding in the Blue Mountains, a hot springs swimming pool and amazing massages at Stagecoach Spa.

PLACES TO GO

- The Frazier Farmstead Museum
  1403 Chestnut Street, Milton-Freewater
  (541) 938-4636

- Spout Springs Ski Resort
  State Route 204, Weston
  (541) 566-0327

THINGS TO DO

June
- Frazier Farmstead Wine & Food
  Tasting Festival
  Milton-Freewater (541) 938-4636

- Pioneer Days
  Weston (541) 566-3916

July
- Caledonian Days
  Athena (800) 547-8911

August
- Muddy Frogwater Country Classic
  Festival & Corn Roast
  Milton-Freewater (541) 938-5563

Western Fence Lizard
Photo by Robert Mutch, www.robmutch.com

Bar M Ranch

ACCOMMODATIONS:

Best ranch accommodations

Create new traditions while reveling in the beauty of Oregon's Blue Mountains at the Bar M Ranch, a memorable vacation destination that takes you back to the Old West. The three-story, hand-hewn log building that serves as the Bar M's ranch house was built in 1864 as a stagecoach stop for the California Stage Company. Howard and Bonnie Baker purchased the property in 1938 and opened it as the Bar M dude ranch in the early 1940s. Three generations of the Baker family offered hospitality to travelers, a tradition that Kent and Shannon Madison have continued since buying the popular site in 2002. Nestled in the foothills 31 miles from Pendleton, the Bar M Ranch offers guests a full range of exciting outdoor adventures, including horseback riding, fishing and swimming in the natural hot springs pool. The ranch further offers a recreational barn, where guests can practice archery, play basketball and gather for other activities. Guests at the Bar M keep flexible schedules, so they can be as active or relaxed as they like while enjoying the ranch's scenic views and casual atmosphere. Mouthwatering barbecue, freshly baked bread and the Bar M's famous raspberry jam are just a few of the delicious treats in store for guests at three daily ranch-style meals. Experience Western living at its finest with a stay at the sensational Bar M Ranch.

58840 Bar M Lane, Adams OR
(541) 566-3381 or (888) 824-3381
www.barmranch.com

Wallowa Mountains

ENTERPRISE

Enterprise is located in one of the most beautiful settings on the planet. Wide-open grassy meadows surround the town. Pine forests stretch to the north, and the stunning Wallowa Mountains line the southern horizon. The Wallowa River, which runs along State Route 82 north of town, is a popular fishing and wildlife viewing area. It is clear and cold, and is popular with fly fishing enthusiasts because it can be waded in many spots. Steelhead fishing is good during the spring and fall. The canyon above the river rises steeply on both sides of the road and is frequented by deer, elk and bear. Wallowa County is home to the deepest gorge in the United States: Hells Canyon along the Idaho Border. The area also boasts a wealth of history, including that of the Nez Perce people.

PLACES TO GO

- Hells Canyon National Recreation Area
  Wallowa Mountains Visitor Center
  88401 Highway 82 (541) 426-5546

- Minam State Recreation Area
  Wallowa Lake Highway (State Route 82)

THINGS TO DO

March
- Old Time Fiddlers Show
  Cloverleaf Hall (541) 886-7885

April
- Wallowa Valley Auto & RV Show
  (541) 426-4574

June
- Enterprise Summerfest
  (541) 426-9026

July
- TamKaLiks Celebration
  Wallowa (541) 886-3101

August
- Wallowa County Fair
  Fairgrounds (541) 426-4097

September
- Hells Canyon Mule Days
  Fairgrounds (541) 426-3271

December
- Enterprise Winterfest
  (541) 426-9026

Parks Bronze
GALLERIES: *Best Bronze Art*

Since 1986, Parks Bronze in Enterprise has completed more than 20,000 bronze castings, many of them monumental in size. The foundry takes pride in the high quality of its craft and on the fantastic patinas on the bronze statues. Under owners Steve and Cindy Parks, the business has grown to employ 29 people. The foundry casts the work of some of the top artists in the United States. Pieces from Parks Bronze have made it into the hands of United States presidents and other top national and state officials. In addition to his work for artists, Steve does his own sculpting, specializing in wildlife and marine animals. Much of his work is commissioned by clients. Visitors can tour the foundry and see how a bronze is made from start to finish. Call ahead for times and availability. Visit Parks Bronze for an inspirational tour of fine sculpture and an education in the foundry arts.

**331 Golf Course Road, Enterprise OR
(541) 426-4595**

FOSSIL

Decades back, Fossil townspeople digging into a hillside to build a football field exposed an ancient lakebed rich with fossils. Today, that field is a public fossil dig behind the high school—the only public fossil field in the country. Anyone can pay three dollars and hunt through the shale and dirt, with a good chance of finding something 32 million years old. Incorporated in 1891, Fossil is the Wheeler County seat. Its name was chosen by the first postmaster, Thomas Hoover, who had found some fossil remains on his ranch. Fossil is small but has loads of community spirit. One out of every four residents is a member of Friends of the Fossil Library, which in October stages a murder-mystery weekend to raise money for the library. Fossil supports a six-hole golf course, the Kinzua Hills Golf Club. *The Oregonian* observed, "Once golfers figure that three times around is 18 holes and learn to dodge the balls on the fifth fairway, they're home free."

PLACES TO GO

- Fossil City Museum
  Historic Schoolhouse and Courthouse
  (541) 763-2698

- John Day Fossil Beds—Clarno
  State Route 218 (541) 763-2203

- John Day Fossil Beds—Painted Hills
  Bridge Creek Road, N of U.S. Highway 26
  (541) 462-3961

- John Day Fossil Beds—Sheep Rock
  State Route 19, N of U.S. Highway 26
  (541) 987-2333

THINGS TO DO

September
- Fossil Quilt Show
  (541) 763-4617

- Painted Hills Festival
  Mitchell (541) 462-3585

- Wheeler County Mule Days
  (541) 763-4560

John Day Fossil Beds

ATTRACTIONS:

Best place to find dinosaur bones

Fifty million years ago, dry eastern Oregon was near-tropical. Volcanoes towered over forests fed by 100 inches of rain per year. Tiny four-toed horses and huge rhino-like brontotheres roamed the land. The John Day Fossil Beds National Monument preserves the remains of these creatures. The three units that make up the monument span more than 50 miles near the towns of Mitchell and Kimberly. All units offer hiking trails, exhibits and picnic areas. The Palisades Cliffs at the Clarno Unit were formed 44 million years ago by volcanic mudflows called lahars. They preserve a great diversity of fossils. The first horses evolved here 50 million years ago, and scientists have found more than a dozen species. The sublime golds, blacks and reds of the Painted Hills Unit come from layers of eroded volcanic ash. Trails, some with boardwalks, allow close examination of the hills. Colors may change from one visit to another. The Painted Hills are best seen in the late afternoon. Wildflowers, which peak in late April to early May, are spectacular. To see the monument's fossils, visit the Thomas Condon Paleontology Center at the Sheep Rock Unit. The Paleontology Center features exhibits, interpretive programs, and films on fossils, geology and the science of paleontology. You can also visit the historic Cant Ranch house and Cant Ranch Museum, which depict the settlement of the John Day Valley. You'll remember your visit to the John Day Fossil Beds forever.

State Route 218 between Shaniko and Fossil OR
(541) 763-2203 (Clarno)
Bridge Creek Road aka Burnt Ranch Road, N of
U.S. Highway 26, W of Mitchell OR
(541) 462-3961 (Painted Hills)
State Route 19, N of U.S. Highway 26
(541) 987-2333 (Sheep Rock)
www.nps.gov/joda

Wallowa Mountains

JOSEPH

Joseph is the home of many artists, some recognized nationally and others waiting to be discovered. It is easy to understand why they live here: the natural beauty of the area is beyond words. The local art includes seven permanent bronze pieces on display downtown. Joseph offers outdoor activities that include fishing, hiking and backpacking. The town is a gateway to the Hells Canyon National Recreation Area and the Eagle Cap Wilderness. One mile south of town is Wallowa Lake, a perfect morainal lake (a lake formed by a glacier). A state park provides full hook ups and tent camping. At the lake you can rent a boat, swim or water ski. There are opportunities for parasailing, horseback riding and miniature golf. Go karts and paddle boats are available. A trail head takes you deep into the Eagle Cap Wilderness Area. Back in town, you can pick up the Eagle Cap Excursion Train, Oregon's newest ride through some of Oregon's most beautiful scenery.

PLACES TO GO

- Hells Canyon National Recreation Area
  Little Sheep Creek Highway

- Wallowa County Museum
  110 S Main Street (541) 432-6095

- Wallowa Lake State Park
  72214 Marina Lane

THINGS TO DO

January
- Eagle Cap Dog Sled Races
  (541) 432-3125

June
- Wallowa Valley Festival of Arts
  Community Center (541) 426-4620

July
- Chief Joseph Days Rodeo
  (800) 585-4121

August
- Wallowa Lake Bluegrass
  Wallowa Lake State Park (503) 829-8481

September
- Alpenfest
  Wallowa Lake (541) 432-4704

White Mariposa lily , on an overlook on Hell's Canyon
Photo by Noah Elhardt

Hells Canyon

ATTRACTIONS: *Deepest river gorge in North America*

Hells Canyon, North America's deepest river gorge, encompasses a vast and remote region. The Snake River flows more than a mile below the west rim of the canyon, and 8,000 feet below snowcapped He Devil Peak to the east. When the surrounding peaks are visible from the river, the sense of depth is tremendous. The Hells Canyon National Recreation Area holds 652,488 acres, 215,233 of which are wilderness. Almost 900 miles of trails are available for hiking, horseback riding, mountain biking and other uses. Odds are good that you'll see bighorn sheep, ospreys and eagles on your trip. For camping and day use, you can stop at any of 36 developed sites. Fishing for the legendary Hells Canyon white sturgeon, which grows up to 15 feet, is catch-and-release. Whitewater rafting is popular on the upper Snake. In the old days, Hells Canyon was known as Snake River Canyon or Box Canyon. According to the Nez Perce, Coyote dug the canyon in a day to protect the people on the west side from the Seven Devils, evil spirits living in the mountains to the east. Scientists say that until a million years ago, the Owyhee Mountains acted as a dam between the Snake and Columbia rivers, creating a vast lake in Idaho. When the mountains were finally breached, the Snake roared northward, cutting a giant chasm through volcanic rock. The resulting canyon is roughly 10 miles across. The southern part of the area is accessible from Joseph by the Imnaha Highway (State Route 350) and the Wallowa Mountain Loop (forest road 39).

88401 Highway 82, Enterprise OR (visitor's center)
(541) 426-5546
www.fs.fed.us/hellscanyon

Valley Bronze of Oregon
GALLERIES: *Best gallery and metal arts foundry*

Excellence is the essence of Valley Bronze of Oregon. From its modest headquarters in Joseph in the heart of Northeast Oregon's isolated Wallowa Valley, Valley Bronze has established itself as one of the nation's best fine art and ornamental foundries and specialized metal fabrication services. The 24-year-old company achieved wide acclaim and recognition for its high-quality work and performance on projects such as the National World War II Memorial in Washington, D.C., for which it received a Star Award for excellence in 2005, and for casting and fabricating bas relief bronze cathedral doors for Our Lady of the Lourdes in Spokane, Washington. Highly visible monuments, such as the longhorn bulls that adorn Houston's Reliant Stadium, the Freedom Horses that grace the George Bush presidential library and remnants of the Berlin Wall in Germany were all cast, assembled and installed by Valley Bronze artisans. In 2006, the foundry cast, fabricated and installed bronze frames and metal and protective glass display cases for the original Declaration of Independence, Bill of Rights and U.S. Constitution in the National Archives Building. The foundry works in all metals, including stainless and silver. They accept a full range of casting projects, including small editions, monuments, ornamental metal, and investment cast parts for antique airplane and marine hardware. The company expanded its ornamental metal fabrication services following its work on the cathedral doors and the National World War II Memorial, and has increased its capacity for specialized metal fabrication. For fine art enthusiasts, Valley Bronze's elegant showrooms in Joseph and Astoria feature sculptures by a variety of artists, many of whose works are cast at the foundry, and paintings and prints by nationally and internationally known artists.

18 S Main Street, Joseph OR (Gallery) (541) 432-7445
307 W Alder Street, Joseph OR (foundry) (541) 432-7551
1198 Commercial Street, Astoria OR (Gallery)
(503) 325-3076 or (800) 559-2118
www.valleybronze.com

Mountain Air Café
RESTAURANTS & CAFÉS: *Best cafe in town*

A visit to the Mountain Air Café is an opportunity to enjoy home-style cooking, local wildlife and extraordinary fudge. The café's bread is baked at the café, and so are its delicious cinnamon rolls, Mountain Berry cobbler and pies. Soups are also homemade. The baked goods make popular take-out items. Mountain Air offers some specialties that must be tried, such as the Holy Moly Pancakes and Bob's Everything Omelet. The omelet is named after Bob Van Winkle, who owns the restaurant with his wife, Shellea. Shellea's sister, Lezlea Means, is the manager. You can enjoy breakfast all day long at the café, where a kid's menu and daily specials offer variety. Two banquet rooms are available for private parties. While you are at the café, be sure to stroll through the Natural Wildlife Museum, which features more than 40 preserved animals in naturalistic settings. Most of the animals are native to Wallowa County and all are beautifully displayed thanks to a local artisan. Prepare yourself for the rattler that's curled up and ready to strike. A third family business, Fudge by All Means, sells exceptional homemade fudge either through the restaurant or online. The Means sisters, Shellea and Lezlea, make the fudge in 26 flavors, ranging from Espresso and Peanut Butter to Mountain Berry Walnut. Fudge by All Means packages the fudge for freshness up to six months. Visit the Mountain Air Café with its mountain-inspired atmosphere for breakfast or lunch year round.

4 S Main Street, Joseph OR
(541) 432-0233
www.eoni.com/~mtnair
www.fudgebyallmeans.com

PLACES TO GO

- Children's Museum of Eastern Oregon
  400 S Main Street
  (541) 276-1066

- Emigrant Springs State Heritage Area
  I-84 exit 234

- Pendleton Center for the Arts
  214 N Main Street
  (541) 278-9201

- Pendleton Underground Tours
  37 SW Emigrant Avenue
  (800) 226-6398

- Pendleton Blanket Mill (tours)
  1307 SE Court Place
  (541) 276-6911

- Tamastslikt Cultural Institute
  72789 Highway 331
  (541) 966-9748

- Heritage Station Museum
  108 SW Frazer Avenue
  (541) 276-0012

- Wildhorse Gaming Resort
  72777 Highway 331
  (800) 654-WILD

THINGS TO DO

July
- Wildhorse Pow Wow
  Wildhorse Gaming Resort
  (800) 654-9453

August
- Umatilla County Fair
  Hermiston
  (800) 700-3274

- Salmon Walk and Art Show
  Tamastslikt Cultural Institute
  (541) 966-1977

September
- Pendleton Roundup
  and Happy Canyon Pagent
  (800) 45-RODEO (457-6336)

October
- Hot Air Balloon Bash
  Wildhorse Gaming Resort
  (800) 654-9453

PENDLETON

Pendleton, the Real West, is the home of the Pendleton Woolen Mills and the world-famous Pendleton Round-Up, one of the best rodeos in America. Pendleton is the Umatilla County seat. The Umatilla Indian Reservation, immediately east of Pendleton, dates to 1855, and is home to the Umatilla, Walla Walla and Cayuse tribes. The gold rush of 1862 brought miners and stock raisers to the mountains and grasslands of Umatilla County. Another economic stimulus was the arrival of the railroad in 1881, which opened the area for dry land wheat farming. Today, irrigation allows areas such as Hermiston in the northwest part of the county to grow watermelons and other thirsty crops. From 2004, EZ Wireless of Hermiston has been one of the largest Wi-Fi wide-area networks in the United States, covering parts of Umatilla County, Morrow County and Benton County, Washington. An unusual attraction in Pendleton is Pendleton Underground Tours, which leads visitors through the tunnels below Pendleton, dug by Chinese laborers. The tour was once controversial because it focuses on the old red light district, bordellos and opium dens. The tour has become Eastern Oregon's number-one year-round tourist attraction.

Pendleton Roundup
ATTRACTIONS: *Best rodeo*

Let'er Buck! That's the rallying call for the Pendleton Round-Up, one of the oldest and most prestigious rodeos in the world. Pendleton's population of 16,500 swells to 50,000 during this event, held in the second full week of September. The celebration dates to July 4, 1909, when Indians and settlers feasted, watched war dances, raced horses and tried to capture greased pigs. This was such a success that community leaders decided on an annual event. The rest is history. Fueled by the unbridled energy of hundreds of volunteers, the Round-Up displays how community spirit can be funneled into an outstanding international event. Round-Up week begins with the Westward Ho parade featuring mules, oxen-drawn covered wagons, marching bands and Indians dressed in their tribal regalia. At the rodeo, the world's best cowboy athletes ride broncs and bulls, rope calves and wrestle steers. The fest includes cowboy breakfasts, a country music concert and dances. You can see wild cow milking, stagecoach races and tribal dancing. A historical pageant, Happy Canyon, traces the development of the West, including the battles between white settlers and Native Americans. The Roundup is held simultaneously with the Happy Canyon Pageant, the largest pow wow of the Confederated Tribes of the Umatilla. Indians from across the West meet to display and sell their crafts, which include quality quill and beadwork, silver jewelry, woven rugs and clay pottery.

1205 SW Court, Pendleton OR
(541) 276-2553
or (800) 45-RODEO (457-6336)
www.pendletonroundup.com

Tamástslikt Cultural Institute

ATTRACTIONS:
Traditions of the Cayuse, Umatilla and Walla Walla peoples

Three Plateau Tribes invite you to experience Tamástslikt Cultural Institute. Within this place, exhibits span centuries, a world of rare shopping exists and great appetites are satisfied. The Cayuse, Umatilla and Walla Walla Tribes offer a unique perspective on the history and vision of their homelands. With state-of-the-art exhibits and interactive displays, local history is interpreted through the voices, collective memories and objects of their culture, and through their lifeways. Enjoy demonstrations by elders, guided tours through the multi-media exhibits, storytelling, lectures and performances. The newly constructed Living Culture Village, which showcases the evolution of tribal life and the dramatic Coyote Theater, add even greater value to your visit. While you are here, be sure to dine at the Kinship Café, featuring native-inspired dishes and delightful huckleberry juleps. Savor your meal while admiring a spectacular view of the Blue Mountains through the floor-to-ceiling windows or from the covered terrace. Also, take time to discover the Native books and music, handcrafted Tribal art pieces and exclusive Pendleton blanket designs in the Museum Store. Plan a visit to Tamástslikt Cultural Institute. Adjacent to Wildhorse Resort and Casino, this important attraction might prove to be the journey of a lifetime.

I-84 Exit 216, 72789 Hwy 331,
Pendleton, OR
(541) 966-9748
www.tamastslikt.org

Oxford Suites Pendleton

ACCOMMODATIONS: *Best suites*

Traveling families have learned that staying at a suite hotel is one of the best ways to combine comfort with reasonable cost. The Oxford Suites Pendleton Hotel is an ideal example. It's a great choice for business travelers, too. The suites are tastefully appointed and have every convenience. Seven floor plans are available. The spacious Executive Suite is a fine room for the business traveler. It has pocket doors to separate the living area from the bedroom, a king bed and a sofa sleeper. The Studio Two suite is a perfect room for the family with two queen beds and a sofa sleeper, while the Honeymoon Suite sports a large in-room soak tub. The hotel reaches out to guests with varying interest by providing special packages. A Taste of the Real West comes with dinner at Stetson's House of Prime. The Country Golf package offers 18 holes of golf for two at the Pendleton Country Club. The Family Fun Night provides free movies or a board game, plus popcorn and soda. Several other packages offer further options. Guests can enjoy an evening reception with drinks and full buffet breakfast. The hotel has a complete business center and conference rooms that can accommodate sizable groups. It is pet-friendly and offers a pool and exercise facility. For a relaxing stay in an attractive, roomy setting, visit the Oxford Suites Pendleton Hotel.

2400 SW Court Place, Pendleton OR
(541) 276-6000 or (877) 545-7848
www.oxfordsuitespendleton.com

The Pendleton Coffee Bean

BAKERIES, COFFEE & TEA:
Best coffee house

You can thank the meticulous efforts of owner Paula Dirks and her staff for the consistently great coffee and espresso at The Pendleton Coffee Bean. Known for their coffee drinks, The Bean, as it is known around town, roasts their own coffee right in the shop. But it doesn't stop at coffee. An extensive lunch menu is also offered. Developed by California chef Chad De Young and finely executed by The Bean's chef, Cody Nash, the menu offers a wide variety of sandwiches, salads, soups and innovative daily specials. Try a tiger shrimp, avocado and pistachio salad, a slice of the daily made quiche or The Pendleton Coffee Bean's famous BLAT—a gourmet BLT with avocado on freshly baked ciabatta bread. The shop also offers a wide selection of beer and wine to accompany your meal, and sells an even greater selection of wine by the bottle, which makes a great hostess gift. Be sure to check out its newly renovated and cozy interior, including the old black-and-white photos of Pendleton in its early days. The patio tables out front provide the perfect place for enjoying the activity on Main Street, especially the Friday evening Farmers' Market.

428 S Main Street, Pendleton OR
(541) 276-2242

Hamley & Company

SHOPPING: *Best tack and Western gear*

The American cowboy has been counting on Hamley & Company for quality saddles and leather goods for almost 125 years. Brothers John and Henry Hamley opened their first harness and saddle shop in the Dakota territory in the mid 1880s. The craftsmen worked their way across the West, and in 1905 John and his son Lester established Hamley & Company in Pendleton. They branched out into just about anything a rancher might need, including chaps, spurs, bridles and bits. The store continues to carry saddles and leather accessories, along with hats, boots and scarves. The Hamley's label stands for quality and durability and has earned the trust of cowboys in the new West as it did in the Old West. Pendleton started a rodeo known as the Round-Up in 1910 and Hamley provided the trophy saddles. Today, the company has awarded nearly 80 such saddles, featuring quality leather, elaborate tooling and silver accents. A Hamley saddle or a silver belt buckle, all made by Pendleton craftsmen, will last through many generations and increase in value. The shop also carries beautifully made leather wallets, handbags and briefcases, along with thoughtful gift items bearing the Hamley label. Hamley & Company celebrated its 100-year anniversary with the introduction of several limited edition products and an extensive renovation that pays tribute to the store's early days. Let the smell of leather take you back to the pioneer West with a visit to the legendary Hamley & Company, where quality comes first.

30 SE Court Street, Pendleton OR
(541) 278-1100
www.hamley.com

Index by Business

Index by City